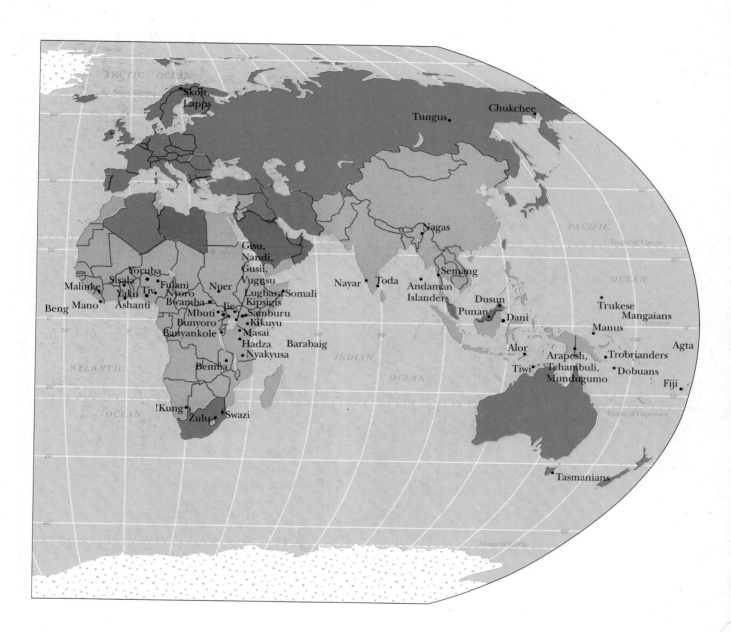

CULTURAL ANTHROPOLOGY

An Applied Perspective

Second Edition

CULTURAL ANTHROPOLOGY

An Applied Perspective

Second Edition

Gary Ferraro
The University of
North Carolina
at Charlotte

West Publishing Company

Minneapolis/St. Paul • New York • Los Angeles • San Francisco

Production Credits

Copyedit	Pat Lewis
Composition	G&S Typesetters, Inc.
Design	Nancy Shehorn Norall
Index	E. Virginia Hobbs
Cover Image	Loren McIntry
Front Map	Adapted by permission from pages 12-13 of *World Regional Geography: A Global Approach* by George F. Hepner and Jesse O. McKee. Copyright c 1992 by West Publishing Company. All rights reserved.
Photos	Individual credits follow index.

West's Commitment to the Environment
In 1906, West Publishing Company began recycling materials left over from the production of books. This began a tradition of efficient and responsible use of resources. Today, up to 95 percent of our legal books and 70 percent of our college and school texts are printed on recycled, acid-free stock. West also recycles nearly 22 million pounds of scrap paper annually—the equivalent of 181,717 trees. Since the 1960s, West has devised ways to capture and recycle waste inks, solvents, oils, and vapors created in the printing process. We also recycle plastics of all kinds, wood, glass, corrugated cardboard, and batteries, and have eliminated the use of Styrofoam book packaging. We at West are proud of the longevity and the scope of our commitment to the environment.

Production, Prepress, Printing and Binding by West Publishing Company.

British Library Cataloguing-in-Publication Data. A catalogue record for this book is available from the British Library.

Copyright ©1992 By West Publishing Company
Copyright ©1995 By West Publishing Company
610 Opperman Drive
P.O. Box 64526
St. Paul, MN 55164-0526

Printed in the United States of America

02 01 00 99 98 97 96 95   8 7 6 5 4 3 2 1 0

Library of Congress Cataloging-in-Publication Data

Ferraro, Gary P.
Cultural anthropology: an applied perspective / Gary Ferraro. — 2nd ed.
p.   cm.

Includes bibliographical references and index.
ISBN 0-314-04425-6 (soft : alk. paper)
1. Ethnology.   2. Applied anthropology.   I. Title.
GN316.F46   1995
306—dc20
                                                                94-28333
                                                                CIP

CONTENTS

CHAPTER FIFTEEN

 CHAPTER SIXTEEN

 CHAPTER SEVENTEEN

PREFACE

When the average American hears the term "cultural anthropologist," several images usually come to mind. One image is the cultural anthropologist as an irrelevant academic, who wears Birkenstocks and native shirts to class, dispenses curious facts about such exotic peoples as the Yanomamo, the Giriama, and the Dani, and contributes little more than making university undergraduates slightly more interesting cocktail party conversationalists. This popular image of cultural anthropology, however, is a grossly misleading stereotype that obscures both the nature of the discipline and its relevance to the world. As this text attempts to demonstrate, cultural anthropology is far more relevant to our everyday lives than most of us imagine.

Pointing out that cultural anthropology has utility to our everyday lives is not to suggest that cultural anthropology's worth as a scientific and humanistic discipline depends upon its capacity to solve specific and immediate societal problems. That cultural anthropology is, by its very nature, enlightening is certainly sufficient to justify its place in a liberal arts curriculum. If, like the early Greeks, we believe that to be educated involves "knowing thyself," then what better way of acquiring that self-knowledge than through the comparative study of culture? In other words, before you can understand yourself, you must first understand your own culture. And, of course, the only way to understand your own culture is to study other cultures.

As with the earlier edition, this text has two essential objectives. First, the book is designed as an introduction to the field of cultural anthropology for university undergraduates. With its cross-cultural approach to the study of human societies, this text provides a comprehensive overview of the discipline. And second, with its applied focus, this text demonstrates how an understanding of other cultures can contribute to the solution of societal problems. Since the great majority of students enrolled in introductory courses in cultural anthropology will never take another course in anthropology, it is important to make the relevance of the discipline explicit at the introductory level rather than expecting students to take additional courses in more applied forms of anthropology.

The applied perspective—this text's most distinctive characteristic—is apparent in two features found throughout the text. The most extensive treatment of the applications of cultural anthropology appears in the "Applied Perspectives" found at the end of Chapters 2 through 16. Each of these chapters has two case studies that illustrate how the data and concepts presented in the chapter have been used to help solve specific societal problems. For example, one of the case studies in Chapter 3 demonstrates how the anthropological study of women's attitudes and behavior in Ecuador resulted in practical recommendations for improving the delivery of medical services at a family planning/maternity clinic in that country; and one of the case studies in Chapter 5 discusses the contributions cultural anthropologists are making to the ongoing search for a solution to the AIDS epidemic.

The second applied feature of this text consists of the boxed sections entitled "Cross-Cultural Miscues." Appearing twice in each chapter, these short scenarios illustrate the potential negative results of failing to understand cultural differences. To illustrate, a Cross-Cultural Miscue in Chapter 14 (Religion) describes an incident in which a representatives of a U.S. corporation lost a major business contract in Qatar because he brought two miniature bottles of brandy in his briefcase to celebrate the completion of the deal. Not only was he deported immediately when the liquor was discovered, but his firm both lost the contract and was barred from doing future business in that country for flouting a religious belief prohibiting the use of alcohol.

This text's applied focus was very well received in its initial edition. Over the past several years, a gratifyingly large number of cultural anthropologists have agreed that an introductory cultural anthropology textbook with an applied bent was long overdue. The first edition of this text has been adopted at a wide variety of schools ranging from small schools to large ones, both public and private. As pleased as we were with the reception of the first edition, there is always room for improvement. Responding to many helpful suggestions from both solicited and unsolicited reviewers, a number of substantive changes have been made in this second edition. To illustrate, a completely new chapter (Chapter 11) on gender and gender roles has been written for the second edition. All of the original chapters have received substantial revisions, and some have received major additions, such as Chapter 4 (Theory), which has new sections on cultural materialism and interpretive anthropology, and Chapter 13 (Stratification), which now includes new sections on race and ethnicity. References and the suggested readings have been updated throughout the book. More material on the culture of the United States has been integrated into the new edition, particularly in the applied case studies at the end of each chapter. Approximately one-third of the Applied Perspectives are new as are more than 60 percent of the Cross-Cultural Miscues.

In addition to these substantive changes, several features in the second edition have been redesigned to make the book's applied focus even stronger. First, the Applied Perspectives now appear before, rather than after, the end matter of the chapter (chapter summaries, key terms, and suggested readings). Second, the text is more closely tied to the applied case studies by a series of in-text references alerting the reader to the case studies at the end of the chapter. And finally, each case study in the Applied Perspectives is followed by a series of questions designed to stimulate further thinking about the application.

Acknowledgments

I want to thank a number of people who have contributed to the second edition of *Cultural Anthropology: An Applied Perspective*. I am particularly indebted to those scholars and colleagues whose comments on the first edition of the text were so helpful in the revision process. West Publishing Company had the first edition and the manuscript for this edition reviewed by the following cultural anthropologists, some users and some nonusers:

- Lee Cronk, Texas A&M University
- Daniel Grossman, Cuyahoga Community College
- Jeanne Humble, Lexington Community College
- A. K. M. Aminul Islam, Wright State University
- Susan Johnston, University of Rhode Island
- Kenneth Keller, Metropolitan State College
- R. Jon McGee, Southwest Texas State University
- Ronald McIrvin, University of North Carolina at Greensboro
- Jeanne Simonelli, SUNY at Oneonta
- Thomas Stevenson, Ohio University at Zanesville

The comments from all of these reviewers were thorough, insightful, and very useful. I also want to thank a number of other scholars in the field who sent their unsolicited, yet most helpful, comments over the course of the past several years. I trust that all of these reviewers will see that many of their suggestions have been acted upon and incorporated into this second edition.

Again, as with the first edition, it has been a pleasure working with the very professional staff at West Publishing Company. I am grateful to my executive editor, Pete Marshall, for originally encouraging me to write an introductory cultural anthropology text with an applied focus and for his continued support and involvement. Production editors at West are responsible for attending to the myriad of details that it takes to turn a final manuscript into a book, a process that has always appeared to me to be both overwhelming and mysterious. The production editor for the second edition (as well as the first edition) has been Christine Hurney, an extraordinarily talented editor who has taken on this assignment with her usual high energy, thoroughness, and personal concern. I also want to thank Jane Bass at West for her attention to a number of administrative details connected with the production of this second edition.

And finally, I am most grateful to a number of people at my home institution, the University of North Carolina at Charlotte, for their help in making the second edition of this text a reality. First, I want to thank all of my departmental colleagues who supported and encouraged my writing efforts over the past academic year while I served as Interim Department Chairperson. I also want to thank my two graduate research assistants, Alex Calves and Shannon Ellis for their help in locating materials and proofreading various drafts of the manuscript. And last, I want to thank my many students over the last several decades who have helped me shape and refine the ideas and interpretations in this book.

WHAT IS ANTHROPOLOGY?

CHAPTER ONE

A young girl from Guatemala peers from behind the door of her home to see what is going on in the world around her, an activity in which students of cultural anthropology also engage.

- How does anthropology differ from other social and behavioral sciences?
- What is the four-field approach to the discipline of anthropology?
- What contributions can anthropology make to the solution of social problems?

When most North Americans hear the word "anthropologist," a number of images come to mind. They picture, for example,

- Dian Fossey devoting years of her life to making systematic observations of mountain gorillas in their natural environment in Rwanda
- a field anthropologist wearing natural-fibered clothing and Birkenstocks, interviewing an exotic tribesman about the nature of his kinship system
- the excavation of a jawbone that will be used to demonstrate the evolutionary link between early and modern humans
- a linguist meticulously recording the sounds of various words from a native informant who speaks a language that has never before been written down
- a team of archaeologists in pith helmets unearthing an ancient temple from a rain forest in Guatemala

Each of these impressions—to one degree or another—accurately represents the concerns of scientists who call themselves anthropologists. Anthropologists do in fact travel to the far corners of the world to study little-known cultures (cultural anthropologists) and languages (anthropological linguists). There are also anthropologists who unearth fossil remains (physical anthropologists) and various artifacts (archaeologists) of people who lived thousands and, in some cases, millions of years ago. Even though these anthropological subspecialties engage in substantially different types of activities and generate different types of data, they are all directed toward a single purpose, that is, the scientific study of humans, both biologically and culturally, in whatever form, time period, or region of the world they might be found.

Anthropology—derived from the Greek words *anthropos* for "human" and *logos* for "study"—is, if we take it literally, the study of humans. In one sense this is an accurate description to the extent that it raises a wide variety of questions about the human condition. And yet this literal definition is not particularly illuminating, since a number of other academic disciplines—including sociology, biology, psychology, political science, economics, philosophy, and history—also study human beings. What gives the discipline of anthropology the right to refer to itself as the study of humans? What is it that distinguishes anthropology from all of these other disciplines?

Anthropology is the study of people—their origins, their development, and contemporary variations, wherever and whenever they have been found on the face of the earth. Of all the disciplines that study humans, anthropology is by far the broadest in scope. The subject matter of anthropology includes fossilized skeletal remains of early humans, artifacts and other material remains from archaeological sites, and all of the contemporary and historical cultures of the world. The task that anthropology has set for itself is an enormous one. Anthropologists strive for an understanding of the biological and cultural origins and evolutionary development of the species. They are concerned with all humans, both past and present, as well as humans' behavior patterns, thought systems, and material possessions. In short, anthropology aims to describe, in the broadest sense, what it means to be human (see Peacock 1986).

In their search to understand the human condition, anthropologists—drawing on a wide variety of data and methods—have created a diverse field of study. Many specialists within the field of anthropology frequently engage in research that is directly relevant to other fields. It has been suggested (Wolf 1964:13) that anthropology spans the gap between the humanities, the social sciences, and the natural sciences. To illustrate, anthropological investigations of native art, folklore, values, and supernatural belief systems are primarily humanistic in nature; studies of social stratification, comparative political systems, and means of distribution have a good deal in common with the social science investigations of sociology, political science, and economics, respectively; and studies of comparative anatomy and radio-carbon dating are central to the natural sciences of biology and chemistry.

The breadth of anthropology becomes apparent when looking at the considerable range of topics discussed in papers published in the *American Anthropologist* (one of the primary professional journals in the field). For example, the following are just a few of the topics that have been discussed in the *American Anthropologist* during the 1990s:

- recovery of American Indian populations following smallpox epidemics
- the origins of agriculture in the Near East
- the migration, education, and status of women in southern Nigeria
- an explanation of differences in overseas experiences among employees of the General Motors Corporation
- sexual behavior among bonobos (pygmy chimpanzees)
- status and power in classical Mayan society
- men's and women's speech patterns among the Creek Indians of Oklahoma
- theories of modern human origins
- a comparison of social interaction among old women and old female Japanese monkeys
- the role of maize in bringing about political changes in Peru between A.D. 500 and 1500.

The global scope of anthropological studies has actually increased in recent years. In the early 1900s, anthropologists concentrated on the non-Western, preliterate, and technologically simple societies of the world, and were content to leave the study of industrial societies to other disciplines. Within the past several decades, however, anthropologists have been studying cultural and subcultural groups in the industrialized areas while continuing their studies of more exotic peoples of the world. It is not at all uncommon today for anthropologists to apply their field methods to the study of hardcore unemployed men in our nation's cities, rural communes in California, or urban street gangs. Only when the whole range of human cultural variation is examined will we be in a position to test the accuracy of theories about human behavior.

Traditionally, anthropology as practiced in the United States during the present century is divided into four distinct branches or subfields: (1) physical anthropology, which deals with humans as biological organisms; (2) archaeology, which attempts to reconstruct the cultures of the past, most of which have left no written records; (3) anthropological linguistics, which focuses on the study of language in historical, structural, and social contexts; and (4) cultural anthropology, which examines similarities and differences between contemporary cultures of the world (see Table 1–1). While this last branch—cultural anthropology—is the central focus of this text, it is important to discuss the other three branches as well to provide an adequate description of the whole discipline.

Despite this four-field division of anthropology and the considerable specialization among the practitioners, the discipline has had a long-standing tradition of

TABLE 1-1			
Branches of Anthropology			
Physical	Archaeology	Linguistics	Cultural Anthropology
Paleontology	Historical Archaeology	Historical Linguistics	Economic Anthropology
Primatology	Prehistoric Archaeology	Descriptive Linguistics	Psychological Anthropology
Human Variation	Contract Archaeology	Ethnolinguistics	Educational Anthropology
Forensic Anthropology		Sociolinguistics	Medical Anthropology
			Urban Anthropology
			Political Anthropology

emphasizing the interrelations among these four sub-fields. Moreover, in recent years there has been considerable blurring of the boundaries among the four branches. For example, the relatively new area of specialization known as medical anthropology draws heavily from both physical and cultural anthropology; educational anthropology addresses issues that bridge the gap between cultural anthropology and linguistics; and sociobiology looks at the interaction between culture and biology.

Physical Anthropology

Physical anthropology is the study of the human condition from a biological perspective. Essentially, physical anthropologists are concerned with two broad areas of investigation. First, they are interested in reconstructing the evolutionary record of the human species; that is, they ask questions about the emergence of humans and how humans have evolved up to the present time. This area of physical anthropology is known as **human paleontology** or **paleoanthropology.** The second area of concern to physical anthropologists deals with how and why the physical traits of contemporary human populations vary across the world. This area of investigation is referred to as human variation. Physical anthropologists differ from comparative biologists in that they study how culture and environment have influenced these two areas of biological evolution and contemporary variations.

Evolutionary Record of Humans

In their attempts to reconstruct human evolution, paleoanthropologists have drawn heavily upon fossil remains (hardened organic matter such as bones and teeth) of humans, protohumans, and other primates. Once these fossil remains have been unearthed, the difficult job of comparison, analysis, and interpretation begins. To which species do the remains belong? Are the remains human or those of our prehuman ancestors? If not human, how do the remains relate to our own species? When did these primates live? How did they adapt to their environment? To answer these questions, paleoanthropologists use the techniques of comparative anatomy. They compare such physical features as cranial capacity, teeth, hands, and the shape of the head of the fossil remains with those of humans or other non-

human primates. In addition to comparing physical features, paleoanthropologists look for signs of culture (such as tools) to help determine the humanity of the fossil remains. If, for example, fossil remains are found in association with tools, and if it can be determined that the tools were in fact made by these creatures, it is likely that the remains will be considered to be human.

The work of paleoanthropologists is frequently tedious and must be conducted with meticulous attention to detail. Even though the quantity of fossilized materials is growing each year, the paleoanthropologist has relatively little data to analyze. Much of the evolutionary record remains under the ground. Of the fossils that have been found, many are partial or fragmentary, and more frequently than not they are not found in association with tools or other cultural artifacts. Consequently, to fill in the human evolutionary record, physical anthropologists need to draw upon the work of a number of other specialists: paleontologists (who specialize in prehistoric plant and animal life), archaeologists (who study prehistoric material culture), and geol-

A paleontologist unearths a prehistoric burial.

ogists (who provide data on local physical and climatic conditions).

Since the 1950s, physical anthropologists have developed an area of specialization of their own that helps shed light on human evolution and adaptation over time and space. This is the relatively new field of study known as **primatology**—the study of our nearest living relatives (apes, monkeys, and prosimians) in their natural habitat. Primatologists study the social behavior of such nonhuman primate species as gorillas, baboons, and chimpanzees in an effort to gain clues about our own evolution as a species. Since physical anthropologists do not have the luxury of observing the behavior of our human ancestors several million years ago, we can learn how early humans responded to certain environmental conditions and changes in their developmental past by studying contemporary nonhuman primates in similar environments. For example, the simple, yet very real division of labor among baboon troops can shed light on role specialization and social stratification in early human societies.

Physical Variations among Humans

Although all humans are members of the same species and therefore are capable of interbreeding, considerable biological variations exist among human populations. Some of these differences are based on visible physical traits, such as the shape of the nose, the thickness of the lips, and the color of the skin. Other variations are based on less visible biochemical factors, such as blood type or susceptibility to diseases.

For decades, physical anthropologists attempted to document the human physical variations throughout the world by dividing the world's populations into various racial categories. (A **race** refers to a group of people who share a greater statistical frequency of genes and physical traits with one another than they do with people outside the group.) Today the physical anthropologist's attention is focused more on trying to explain *why* the variations exist by asking such questions as, Are Eskimos better endowed physically to survive in colder climates? Why do some populations have darker skin than others? Why are most Chinese adults unable to digest milk? Why is the blood type B nonexistent among Australian aborigines? How have certain human populations adapted biologically to their local environments? To help answer these and other questions involving human biological variation, physical anthropologists draw upon the work of three allied disciplines: (1) **genetics** (the study of inherited physical traits), (2) **popu-**

Primatologists study such nonhuman primates as this mountain gorilla of Rwanda.

lation biology (the study of the interrelationship between population characteristics and environment), and (3) **epidemiology** (the study of differential effects of disease on populations).

Archaeology

Archaeology is the study of the lifeways of people from the past through excavating and analyzing the things these people leave behind, including, in some cases, written records. The purpose of archaeology is not to fill up museums by collecting exotic relics from prehistoric societies. Rather, it is to reconstruct the cultures of people who are no longer living. Since archaeology concentrates on societies of the past, archaeologists are limited to working with only one of the three basic components of culture—material culture—because the other two components—ideas and behavior patterns—

An excavation of a prehistoric culture at Twin Ditch in Eldred, Illinois.

are not preserved in the absence of people for thousands, and in some cases millions, of years.

The data that archaeologists have at their disposal are very selective. Not only are archaeologists limited to material remains, but also the overwhelming majority of material possessions that may have been part of a culture do not survive thousands of years under the ground. As a result, archaeologists search for those fragments of material evidence that will enable them to piece together as much of the culture as possible—such items as arrowheads, hearths, beads, post holes, and burial stones. A prehistoric garbage dump is particularly revealing, for the archaeologist can learn a great deal about how people lived from what they threw away. These material remains are then used to make inferences about the nonmaterial aspects of the culture being studied. For example, the finding that all women and children are buried with their heads pointing in one direction while the heads of adult males point in a

different direction could lead to the possible explanation that the society practiced matrilineal kinship (that is, children followed their mother's line rather than their father's).

Once the archaeologist has collected the physical evidence, the difficult work of analysis and interpretation begins. By studying the bits and pieces of material culture left behind (within the context of both environmental data and anatomical remains), the archaeologist seeks to determine how the people supported themselves, whether or not they had a notion of an afterlife, how roles were allocated between men and women, if some people were more prominent than others, and whether the people engaged in trade with neighboring peoples.

Present-day archaeologists work with both historic and prehistoric cultures. Historic archaeologists help to reconstruct the cultures of people who used writing and about whom historical documents have been written. For example, historical archaeologists have contributed significantly to our understanding of colonial American cultures by analyzing material remains that can supplement such historical documents as books, letters, graffiti, and government reports.

Prehistoric archaeology, on the other hand, deals with that vast segment of the human record prior to writing. In the several million years of human existence, writing is a very recent development, first appearing about 5,500 years ago. Prehistoric archaeologists attempt, then, to reconstruct those cultures that existed before the development of writing. Archaeology thus remains the one scientific enterprise that systematically focuses on prehistoric cultures, and consequently, it has provided us with a much fuller time frame for understanding the record of human development.

Anthropological Linguistics

Anthropological linguistics is that branch of the discipline that studies human speech and language. Although humans are not the only species that have systems of symbolic communication, they have by far the most complex form. In fact, some would argue that language is the most distinctive feature of being human, for without language we could not acquire and transmit our culture from one generation to the next.

Linguistic anthropology, which studies contemporary human languages as well as those of the past, is divided into four distinct branches: historical linguistics, descriptive linguistics, ethnolinguistics, and sociolinguistics.

Historical linguistics deals with the emergence of language in general and how specific languages have diverged over time. Some of the earliest anthropological interest in language was focused on the historical connections between languages. For example, nineteenth-century linguists working with European languages demonstrated similarities in the sound systems between a particular language and an earlier parent language from which the language was derived. In other words, by comparing contemporary languages, linguists have been able to identify certain language families. More recently, through the technique known as glottochronology, linguists can now determine when two related languages began to diverge from each other.

Descriptive linguistics is the study of sound systems, grammatical systems, and the meanings attached to words in specific languages. Every culture has a distinctive language with its own logical structure and set of rules for putting words and sounds together for the purpose of communicating. In its simplest form, the task of the descriptive linguist is to compile dictionaries and grammars for previously unwritten languages.

Ethnolinguistics is that branch of anthropological linguistics that examines the relationship between language and culture. In any culture, aspects that are emphasized (such as types of snow among the Eskimos,

For the sociocultural linguist, the graffiti on this New York City subway car are an important source of information on language and culture.

cows among the pastoral Masai, or automobiles in our own culture) are reflected in the vocabulary of that culture's language. Moreover, ethnolinguists explore how different linguistic categories can affect how people categorize their experiences, how they think, and how they perceive the world around them.

The fourth branch of anthropological linguistics, known as **sociolinguistics,** examines the relationship between language and social relations. For example, sociolinguists are interested in investigating how social class influences the particular dialect a person speaks. They also study the situational use of language—that is, how people use different forms of a language depending on the social situation they may find themselves in at any given time. To illustrate, the words, and even grammatical structures, a U.S. college student would choose when conversing with a roommate would be significantly different from the linguistic style used when talking to a grandparent, a priest, or the personnel director during a job interview.

Cultural Anthropology

Cultural anthropology is that branch of the discipline that deals with (1) the study of specific contemporary cultures (**ethnography**) and (2) those more general underlying patterns of human culture derived through cultural comparisons (**ethnology**). Before cultural anthropologists can examine cultural differences and similarities throughout the world, they must first describe the features of specific cultures in as much detail as possible. These detailed descriptions (ethnographies) are the result of extensive field studies (usually a year or two in duration) in which the anthropologist observes, talks to, and lives with the people he or she is studying. The writing of relatively large numbers of ethnographies over the course of the present century has provided an empirical basis for the comparative study of cultures. In the process of developing these descriptive accounts, cultural anthropologists may provide insights into such questions as, How are the marriage customs of a group of people related to the group's economy? What effect does urban migration have on the kinship system? In what ways have supernatural beliefs helped a group of people adapt more effectively to their environment? Thus, while describing the essential features of a culture, the cultural anthropologist may also ex-

plain why certain cultural patterns exist and how they may be related to one another.

Ethnology refers to the comparative study of contemporary cultures wherever they may be found. Ethnologists seek to understand both why people today and in the recent past differ in terms of ideas and behavior patterns and what all cultures in the world have in common with one another. The primary objective of ethnology is to uncover general cultural principles, those "rules" that govern human behavior. Since all humans have culture and live in collectivities called societies, there are no populations in the world today that are not viable subjects for the ethnologist. The lifeways of Eskimos living in the Arctic tundra, Greek peasants, !Kung hunters of the Kalahari Desert, and the residents of a retirement home in southern California have all been studied by cultural anthropologists. See Exhibit 1–1 for an illustration of the ethnic diversity in the United States.

Ethnographers and ethnologists face a task of great magnitude as they attempt to describe and compare the many peoples of the world during the twentieth century. The relatively small number of cultural anthropologists must deal with enormous cultural diversity (thousands of distinct cultures that speak mutually unintelligible languages), numerous features of culture that could be compared, and a wide range of theoretical frameworks for comparing them. To describe even the least complex cultures requires many months of interviewing people and observing their behavior. Even with this large expenditure of time, rarely do contemporary ethnographers describe total cultures. Instead, they usually describe only the more outstanding features of a culture and then investigate a particular aspect or problem in greater depth.

Areas of Specialization

Since the description of a total culture is usually beyond the scope of a single ethnographer, in recent decades cultural anthropologists have tended to specialize, frequently identifying themselves with one or more of the following areas of specialization:

1. Psychological anthropology. Concerned with studying the individual within a cultural context, psychological anthropology examines such topics as emotional functioning, motivation, personal well-being, mental models, comparative human development, the acquisition of culture, and the relationship between culture and personality.

EXHIBIT 1-1

Ethnicity in the United States

Despite our reputation as the great "melting pot," there is still considerable ethnic diversity in the United States.

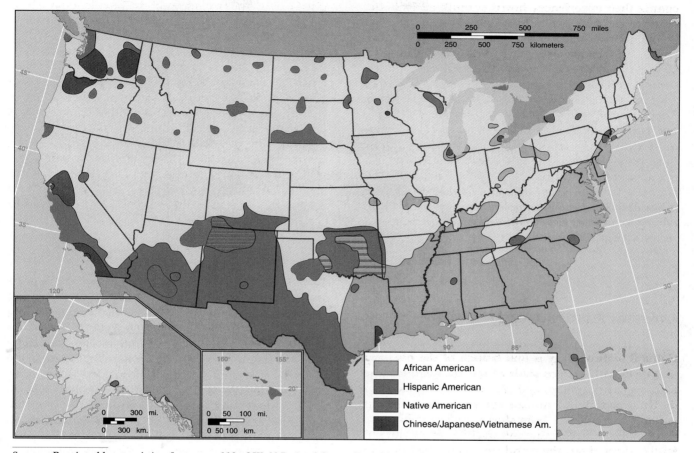

African American
Hispanic American
Native American
Chinese/Japanese/Vietnamese Am.

2. Economic anthropology. Dealing with how goods and services are produced, distributed, and consumed cross-culturally, this area of specialization focuses on such topics as division of labor, patterns of work, systems of exchange, and control of property.

3. Urban anthropology. By concentrating on how such demographic factors as size, density, and heterogeneity affect customary ways of behaving, urban anthropologists examine a number of important issues including urban poverty and homelessness, the role of women in cities, problems of labor migration, and modern urban subcultures such as street gangs, truck drivers, prostitutes, cocktail waitresses, and drug addicts.

4. Educational anthropology. This specialized branch of cultural anthropology explores the relationship between anthropological theories, methods, and insights on the one hand and educational practices, problems, and institutions on the other. Among the concerns of the educational anthropologist are bilingual education, comparative forms of education, and the ethnography of the classroom.

5. Medical anthropology. Practitioners of this specialized area study the biological and cultural factors that affect health, disease, and sickness. By incorporating cultural, biological, historical, and linguistic data within its domain, medical anthropology has contacts with a

Cultural anthropologists gather information about the contemporary peoples of the world by conducting direct field studies. Here cultural anthropologist Marjorie Shostak interviews a !Kung informant.

number of other disciplines and draws upon a wide variety of approaches.

   6. Applied anthropology. Cutting across most of the other five areas, this specialized branch conducts research aimed at the solution of specific societal problems. See Chapter 3 for a discussion of this branch of anthropology.

   These six areas are only a partial listing of the specializations within cultural anthropology. Other specialties include agricultural anthropology, legal anthropology, ecological anthropology, political anthropology, the anthropology of work, and nutritional anthropology, among others.

Holism

A distinguishing feature of the discipline of anthropology is its **holistic** approach to the study of human groups. The study of anthropology is comprehensive in a number of important respects. First, the anthropological approach involves both biological and sociocultural aspects of humanity. That is, anthropologists are interested in people's genetic endowment as well as what people acquire from their sociocultural environment after birth. Second, anthropology has the deepest possible time frame, starting with the earliest beginnings of humans several million years ago right up to the present. Anthropology is holistic to the extent that it studies all varieties of people wherever they may be found. That is, anthropology's global perspective considers the lifeways of East African pastoralists, Polynesian fishermen, and Japanese businesspeople all to be equally legitimate subjects of study. And finally, anthropology studies many different aspects of human experience. To illustrate, a cultural anthropologist who is conducting direct, participant-observation fieldwork may be collecting data on a wide variety of topics, including family structure, marital regulations, house construction, methods of conflict resolution, means of livelihood, religious beliefs, language, space usage, and art.

   In the past, cultural anthropologists have made every effort to be holistic by covering as many aspects of a culture as possible. In more recent decades, however, the accumulated information from all over the world has become so vast that most anthropologists have needed to become more specialized or focused. To illustrate, one anthropologist may concentrate on marital patterns while another may focus on farming and land-use patterns. Despite the recent trend toward specialization, anthropologists continue to analyze their findings within their proper cultural context. Moreover, when all of the various specialties within the discipline are viewed together, they represent a very comprehensive or holistic view of the human condition.

Contributions of Anthropology

One of the major contributions of anthropology to the understanding of the human condition stems from the very broad task that it has set for itself. Whereas such disciplines as economics, political science, and psychology are considerably more narrow in scope, anthropology has carved out for itself the task of examining *all* aspects of humanity for *all* periods of time and for *all* parts of the globe. Owing to the magnitude of the task, anthropologists must draw upon theories and data from a number of other disciplines in the humanities, the social sciences, and the physical sciences. As a result, anthropology has been in a good position to integrate the various disciplines dealing with human physiology and culture.

Enhancing Understanding

Because of its holistic approach, the data and theories of anthropology have served as a powerful corrective to deterministic thinking. That is, this broad, comparative perspective serves as a check against oversimplified explanations concerning all of humanity based on evidence obtained from the Western world. A case in point is the revision of the notion of what a city is. Based largely on the study of American and European cities in the first several decades of the twentieth century, Western social scientists defined a city as a social system in which kinship ties were less elaborate than in rural communities. Though this was an accurate picture of cities in the industrialized areas of Europe and the United States, it was hardly accurate as a universal definition of urbanism. Since the 1950s, urban anthropologists studying cities in the non-Western world have called into question this "universal" characteristic of the city. For example, Horace Miner (1953) found substantial kinship interaction—which took the form of joint activities, mutual assistance, and friendship ties—in the West African city of Timbuktoo; Oscar Lewis (1952), in an article aptly entitled "Urbanization without Breakdown," found that extended kinship networks

were every bit as real in Mexico City as they were in rural Tepoztlan; and more recent studies (Moock 1978–79; Keefe 1988) have found equally significant kinship ties in urban areas. Thus, urban anthropology, with its broad cross-cultural approach, has served to revise our thinking about the theory of urbanism.

Cultural anthropology examines cultural differences and similarities among the contemporary peoples of the world. Although some people view cultural anthropology as devoted to documenting the exotic customs of people in far-off places, it is only by learning about cultural variations and similarities that we will be able to avoid generalizing about "human nature" solely on the basis of observations from our own culture. It is not unusual for people to believe that their beliefs and behaviors are natural, reasonable, and therefore human while believing that those who think and act differently are somewhat less than human.

This strong comparative tradition in cultural anthropology helps to reduce the possibility that our theories about human nature will be culture bound. For example, studies in cultural anthropology have revealed that great works of art are found in all parts of the world; that social order can be maintained without having centralized, bureaucratic governments; that reason, logic, and rationality did not originate solely in ancient Greece; and that all morality does not stem from Judeo-Christian ethics. Cultural anthropology, in other words, prevents us from taking our own cultural perspective too seriously. As Clifford Geertz (1984:275) reminds us, one of the tasks of cultural anthropology is to ". . . keep the world off balance; pulling out rugs, upsetting tea tables, setting off fire crackers. It has been the office of others to reassure; ours to unsettle."

Still another contribution of anthropology is that it helps us better understand ourselves. The early Greeks claimed that the educated person was the person with self-knowledge ("know thyself"). One of the best ways to gain self-knowledge is to know as much as possible about one's own culture, that is, to understand the forces that shape our own thinking, values, and behaviors (see, for example, De Vita and Armstrong 1993). And the very best way of learning about our culture is to learn something about other cultures. The anthropological perspective, with its emphasis on the comparative study of cultures, should lead us to the conclusion that *our* culture is just one way of life among many found in the world and that it represents one way (from among many) to adapt to a particular set of environmental conditions. Through the process of contrasting and comparing, we gain a fuller understanding of both other cultures and our own.

Applications

Anthropology, with its holistic, cross-cultural perspective, has thus contributed in a number of important ways to the scientific understanding of humanity. Moreover, the study of anthropology is important because it enables the individual to better comprehend and appreciate his or her own culture. But, it may be asked, does anthropology have any practical relevance to our everyday lives? Students of biochemistry can apply their skills to the discovery of new wonder drugs; creative arts students can produce lasting works of art; and students of architecture can design buildings that are both beautiful and functional. According to popular perceptions, however, the study of anthropology has little to offer other than a chance to dabble in exotic cultures of the world. But, as we hope to demonstrate in this text, nothing could be further from the truth. Anthropology *can*

have relevance for all of our lives, both personally and professionally. Since anthropology is primarily concerned with the scientific study of culture, and since our lives and our jobs are conducted within a cultural context, anthropologists do indeed have some practical things to say.

Anthropology, like other social science disciplines, engages in both basic and applied research. Basic research in anthropology is directed at gaining scientific understanding for its own sake rather than for any practical ends. Applied research in anthropology, on the other hand, seeks to gain scientific knowledge for the sake of solving particular social problems. For much of the twentieth century, anthropologists have devoted most of their energy to basic research—that is, testing hypotheses concerning such theoretical issues as the rise of civilization, the functions of religious institutions, and the variations in systems of social stratification.

Anthropologists from all four subdisciplines have also applied many of the methods, theories, and insights gained from basic research to the solution of

This group of snake-handling fundamentalists would be a possible subject of study for present-day cultural anthropologists.

societal problems. For example, specialists in forensic anthropology, an applied branch of physical anthropology, work closely with medical examiners and coroners by using their expertise with bones to help identify human skeletal remains for legal purposes (Stewart 1979). Archaeologists in recent decades have applied their unique skills to the area of cultural resource management, which evaluates and helps preserve our nation's cultural heritage (Hill and Dickens 1978). Anthropological linguistics has been applied in a wide range of settings, including the improvement of language instruction (Cowan 1979), the development of intercultural training programs (Samovar and Porter 1994), and public decision making for language use in specific language communities (Eastman 1983). Cultural anthropologists have applied their trade to the evaluation of various social programs both here and abroad, market research, classroom management, and the improvement of health delivery systems, to mention but a few.

Even though all four subfields of anthropology have well-developed applied components, this text focuses on applied cultural anthropology. As discussed in greater depth in Chapter 3, interest in applying cultural anthropology has increased over the past decade. Graduate and undergraduate courses in applied anthropology, as well as doctoral dissertations on applied topics, have been on the rise in recent years. Moreover, there has been a noticeable increase in the number of anthropologists working outside universities and museums in such capacities as administrators, evaluators, planners, and research analysts. In fact, within the last several years, there has been a movement within the American Anthropological Association to recognize applied anthropology as the fifth major subdivision of anthropology. Acknowledging this increasing interest in making anthropology practical, this text has developed a particular focus toward applying cultural anthropology. To demonstrate how widely cultural anthropology has been applied to the solution of practical societal problems, each chapter in the rest of the book concludes with applied case studies. Each case study has been selected to show how the information from the particular chapter has been applied to the understanding and solution of practical problems.

The study of anthropology looks at the human condition in both an evolutionary and a contemporary perspective. It examines how humans have changed physically and culturally over the course of the past several million years, and it studies the various similarities and differences among the thousands of linguistic and cultural groups that inhabit today's world. And while this remains the core of anthropology, it is important to bear in mind that anthropology is not an esoteric subject that serves little purpose other than making university students slightly more interesting cocktail conversationalists. Rather—and this is the major thrust of this text—the study of anthropology does impact our personal and professional lives in very significant ways.

 ## Summary

1. The academic discipline of anthropology involves the study of both the biological and cultural origins of humans. The subject matter of anthropology is wide-ranging, including fossil remains, nonhuman primate behavior, artifacts from past cultures, past and present languages, and all of the prehistoric, historic, and contemporary cultures of the world.

2. As practiced in the United States, the discipline of anthropology follows an integrated four-field approach comprising (a) physical anthropology, (b) archaeology, (c) anthropological linguistics, and (d) cultural anthropology.

3. The subdiscipline of physical anthropology focuses on three primary concerns: (a) paleoanthropology (constructing the biological record of human evolution through the study of fossil remains), (b) primatology (the study of nonhuman primate behavior for the purpose of gaining insights into human adaptation to the environment), and (c) studies in human physical variation (race) among the contemporary peoples of the world.

4. The subfield of archaeology has as its primary objective the reconstruction of past cultures, both historic and prehistoric, from the material objects the cultures leave behind.

5. Anthropological linguistics, which studies both present and past languages, is divided into four major subdivisions: historical linguistics (the study of the emergence and divergence of languages over time); descriptive linguistics (the structural analysis of phonetic and grammar systems in contemporary languages); ethnolinguistics (the explanation of the relationship between language and culture); and sociolinguistics (how social relations affect language).

6. Cultural anthropology has as its aim the study of contemporary cultures wherever they may be found in the world. One part of the task of cultural anthropology involves describing particular cultures (ethnography),

while the other part involves comparing two or more cultures (ethnology).

7. A long-standing tradition in anthropology is the holistic approach. The discipline is holistic (or comprehensive) in four important respects: it looks at both the biological and the cultural aspects of human behavior; it has the broadest possible time frame by looking at contemporary, historic, and prehistoric societies; it is global in that it examines human cultures in every part of the world; and it studies many different aspects of human cultures.

8. The study of anthropology is valuable from a number of different viewpoints. From the perspective of the social and behavioral sciences, cultural anthropology is particularly valuable for testing theories about human behavior within the widest possible cross-cultural context. For the individual, the study of different cultures provides a much better understanding of one's own culture. From a societal point of view, the understanding of different cultures can contribute to the solution of pressing societal problems.

Key Terms

anthropological
  linguistics
archaeology
cultural anthropology
descriptive linguistics
epidemiology
ethnography
ethnolinguistics
ethnology
genetics

historical linguistics
holism
human paleontology
  (paleoanthropology)
physical anthropology
population biology
primatology
race
sociolinguistics

Suggested Readings

Angeloni, Elvio ed. *Anthropology 1994–95*. Guilford, Conn.: Dushkin, 1994. Each year this annual edition of readings put out by Dushkin contains a new selection of articles that covers the field of social and cultural anthropology. As a useful supplement to the "broad brush" approach taken by most textbooks, this collection of readings provides the student with forty in-depth articles by anthropologists writing on their own research.

Barrett, Richard. *Culture and Conduct: An Excursion in Anthropology*. 2d ed. Belmont, Calif.: Wadsworth, 1991. By examining some of the questions, ideas, and issues facing modern anthropology, Barrett provides an interesting introduction into how cultural anthropologists investigate unfamiliar cultures.

Campbell, Bernard G. *Humankind Emerging*. 5th ed. Boston: Little, Brown, 1988. Up-to-date, encyclopedic, and handsomely illustrated, this is perhaps the best single introduction to the field of human biological evolution.

Fagan, Brian M. *People of the Earth*. 6th ed. Glenview, Ill.: Scott, Foresman, 1989. A readable and straightforward presentation of the human record from the origins of humankind up to the rise of civilization.

Fromkin, Victoria, and Robert Rodman. *An Introduction to Language*. 4th ed. New York: CBS College Publishing, 1993. A spritely written introduction to the field of anthropological linguistics.

Kluckhohn, Clyde. *Mirror for Man: Anthropology and Modern Life*. New York: McGraw-Hill, 1949. Although written in 1949, this classic study remains one of the best introductions to the discipline because it demonstrates in a number of concrete ways how the study of different cultures—both past and present—can contribute to the solution of contemporary world problems.

Liebow, Elliot. *Tally's Corner*. Boston: Little, Brown, 1967. This ethnographic study of hardcore unemployed street-corner men in Washington, D.C., serves as a reminder that anthropologists, despite their emphasis on non-Western societies, use participant observation as a method of study in their own society.

Peacock, James L. *The Anthropological Lens*. Cambridge: Cambridge University Press, 1986. A very readable book that discusses the philosophical underpinnings of the discipline of anthropology, with special emphasis on cultural anthropology. The work is divided into three sections that deal with anthropology's substance, methods, and significance.

THE CONCEPT OF CULTURE

CHAPTER TWO

A !Kung woman of the Kalahari region in southwestern Africa.

- What do anthropologists mean by the term *culture?*
- How do we acquire our culture?
- Despite the enormous variation in different cultures, are some common features found in all cultures of the world?
- What is "cultural relativism" and how can it help us better understand other cultures?

Although the term "culture" is used today as a scientific concept by most of the social sciences, over the years it has received its most precise and thorough definition from the discipline of anthropology. Whereas sociology has concentrated on the notion of society, economics on the concepts of production and distribution, and political science on the concept of power, anthropology has focused on the culture concept. From anthropology's nineteenth-century beginnings, culture has been central to both ethnology and archaeology and has been an important, if not major, concern of physical anthropology. Anthropology, through its constant examining of different lifeways throughout space and time, has done more than any other scientific discipline to refine our understanding of the concept of culture.

Culture Defined

In its ordinary, nonscientific usage, the term *culture* refers to such personal refinements as classical music, the fine arts, world philosophy, and gourmet cuisine. For example, according to this popular use of the term, the "cultured person" listens to Bach rather than the Beatles, orders escargot rather than barbecued ribs when dining out, can distinguish between the artistic styles of Monet and Toulouse-Lautrec, prefers Grand Marnier to Kool-Aid, and attends the ballet instead of a hockey game. The anthropologist, however, uses the term in a much broader sense to include far more than just the "finer things in life." The anthropologist does not distinguish between "cultured" people and "uncultured" people. All people have culture, according to

the anthropological definition. The Australian aborigines, living as they do with a bare minimum of technology, are as much cultural animals as Pavarotti and Barishnikov. Thus, for the anthropologist, arrowheads, creation myths, and grass huts are as legitimate items of culture as a Beethoven symphony, a Warhol painting, and a Sondheim musical.

Over the past century, anthropologists have formulated a number of definitions of the concept of culture. In fact, in the often-cited work by Kroeber and Kluckhohn (1952), over 160 different definitions of culture were identified. This proliferation of definitions should not, however, lead to the impression that anthropology is a chaotic battleground where no consensus exists among practicing anthropologists. In actual fact, many of these definitions say essentially the same thing. One early definition, which has been widely quoted up to the present time, was suggested by the nineteenth-century British anthropologist Edward Tylor. According to Tylor, culture refers to "that complex whole which includes knowledge, belief, art, morals, law, custom, and any other capabilities and habits acquired by man as a member of society" (1871:1). More recently, culture has been defined as "a mental map which guides us in our relations to our surroundings and to other people" (Downs 1971:35), and perhaps most succinctly as "the way of life of a people" (Hatch 1985:178).

Adding to the already sizable number of definitions, for our purposes we will define the concept of culture as *everything that people have, think, and do as members of a society.* This definition can be instructive because the three verbs correspond to the three major components of culture. That is, everything that people *have* refers to material possessions; everything that people *think* refers to those things they carry around in their heads, such as ideas, values, and attitudes; and everything that people

According to the anthropological perspective, this African hunter has as much culture as this classical violinist.

do refers to behavior patterns. Thus, all cultures comprise (1) material objects, (2) ideas, values, and attitudes, and (3) patterned ways of behaving (see Exhibit 2-1).

Culture Is Shared

The last phrase in our working definition—"as members of a society"—should remind us that culture is a shared phenomenon. For a thing, idea, or behavior pat-

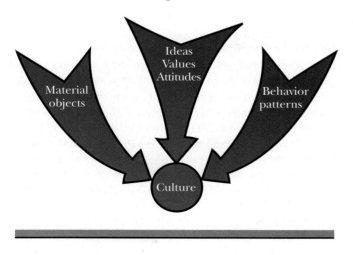

EXHIBIT 2-1

The Three Components of Culture

Material objects — Ideas Values Attitudes — Behavior patterns → Culture

tern to qualify as being "cultural," it must have a meaning shared by at least two people within a society. It is this shared nature of culture that makes our lives relatively uncomplicated. Since people *share* a common culture, they are able to predict, within limits, how others will think and behave. For example, when meeting someone for the first time in the United States, it is customary to shake the person's hand. If both people are from the United States, neither party will have to wonder what is meant by an outstretched hand. They will know, with near absolute certainty, that the extended hand is a nonverbal gesture signifying friendship rather than a sexual advance, a hostile attack, or an attempt to go for one's wallet. It is when we step outside our familiar cultural setting—where meanings are not shared with other people—that misunderstandings and breakdowns in communication occur.

People from the same culture are able to predict one another's behavior because they have been exposed to similar cultural conditioning. Yet a word of caution is necessary. To say that culture *conditions* our thoughts, values, and behaviors is hardly to imply that culture *determines* them. People are influenced by their cultures, but we should not think of them as unthinking robots who live out their lives exactly according to cultural dictates. If this were the case, we would expect total conformity to the cultural norms in all societies. But the study of anthropology informs us that although most of the people conform to most of the cultural norms most of the time, there will always be some segment of the culture's population that, for a number of reasons, deviates from those norms. For example, some people may deviate from expected norms for purely biological

Large, complex societies such as the United States are comprised of a number of distinct subcultural groups such as these Harley-Davidson bikers from Sunnyvale, California.

reasons such as hormonal imbalances, hyperactivity, or physiologically based mental disorders. Or an individual's personal history can lead to a culturally unorthodox way of thinking or acting (such as the person who was traumatized by a hurricane as a child and still expresses unreasonable reactions to inclement weather). Another explanation is that even in the most small-scale, homogeneous societies one can expect to find a certain amount of differentiation based on either class or ethnicity. For example, the son of a wealthy physician in Athens will likely have a different set of values and behavioral expectations than the son of a rural Greek peasant farmer. And, finally, societal rules are never adhered to strictly. Although culture exerts a powerful influence, people continue to exert their "free will" by either reinterpreting the rules, downplaying their consequences, or disregarding them altogether (such as the Catholic who practices birth control or the conscientious objector who flees to Canada rather than serve in a war).

Culture Is Learned

Culture is not transmitted genetically. Rather, it is acquired through the process of learning or interacting with one's environment. This process of acquiring culture after we are born is called **enculturation.** We acquire our culture (ideas, values, behavior patterns) by growing up in it. When an infant is born, he or she enters a cultural environment in which many solutions al-

ready exist to the universal problems facing all human populations. The child merely needs to learn or internalize those solutions in order to make a reasonable adjustment to his or her surroundings. A male child who is born in Kansas will probably watch a good deal of TV, attend schools with books, desks, and teachers, eventually learn to drive a car, and marry one wife at a time. On the other hand, a male child who is born among the Jie of Uganda is likely to grow up playing with cows, learn most of what he knows from peers and elders rather than teachers, undergo an initiation ceremony into adulthood that involves being anointed with the undigested stomach contents of an ox slaughtered for the occasion, and look forward to having at least three or four wives at one time. Even though these children were born into radically different cultures, they share one important thing in common—that is, both children were born into an already existing culture, and they have only to *learn* the ways of thinking and acting set down by their culture.

If we stop to think about it, a great deal of what we do during our waking hours is learned. Brushing our teeth, eating three meals a day, sweeping the floor, attending school, wearing a wristwatch, knowing to stop at a red light, sleeping on a mattress, and waving goodbye are all learned responses to our cultural environment. To be certain, some aspects of our behavior are not learned but are genetically based or instinctive. For example, a newborn infant does not need to attend a workshop on the "Art of Sucking"; or if someone throws a brick at your head, you do not have to have been taught to duck or throw your hands up in front of your face. Nevertheless, the overwhelming majority of our behavioral responses are the result of complex learning processes.

Learning Versus Instincts

During the first half of the twentieth century, psychologists and other social scientists tended to explain human behavior in terms of various instincts or genetically based propensities. Gypsies traveled about because they were thought to have wanderlust in their blood; black people were musical because they were believed to have natural rhythm; and some people, owing to their genetic makeup, were supposedly born criminals. Today this instinctive interpretation of human behavior is no longer held. Instead, while acknowledging the role of biology, most social scientists would come closer to agreeing with the notion of the **tabula rasa,** whereby humans are born with relatively little predetermined behavior. If humans are to survive, they must learn most of their coping skills from others in their culture. This usually takes a number of years. As early as 1917, anthropologist A. L. Kroeber recognized the importance of learning for human adaptation to the environment:

> Take a couple of ant eggs of the right sex—unhatched eggs, freshly laid. Blot out every individual and every other egg of the species. Give the pair a little attention as regards warmth, moisture, protection and food. The whole of ant "society," every one of the abilities, powers, accomplishments, and activities of the species . . . will be reproduced, and reproduced without diminution, in one generation. But place on a desert island . . . two or three hundred human infants of the best stock from the highest class of the most civilized nation; furnish them the necessary incubation and nourishment; leave them in total isolation from their kind; and what shall we have? . . . only a pair or a troop of mutes, without arts, knowledge, fire, without order or religion. Civilization would be blotted out within these confines—not disintegrated, not cut to the quick, but obliterated in one sweep. (1917:177–78)

Learning Styles

Even though there is an enormous range of variation in cultural behavior throughout the world, all people acquire their culture by the same process. People frequently assume erroneously that if a Hadza tribesman of Tanzania does not know how to solve an algebraic equation, he must be less intelligent than we are. Yet there is no evidence to suggest that some cultures are fast learners while others are slow learners. The study of comparative cultures has taught us that people in different cultures learn different cultural content (attitudes, values, ideas, and behavioral patterns), and that

Although these children growing up outside Bombay, India learn different cultural content than do U.S. children, the process of acquiring culture through learning is common to all cultures.

they accomplish this with similar efficiency. The Hadza tribesman has not learned algebra because such knowledge would not particularly enhance his adaptation to life in the East African grasslands. He would know, however, how to track a wounded bush buck that he has not seen for three days, where to find groundwater, and how to build a house out of locally available materials. In short, people learn (with relatively equal efficiency) what it is they need to know to best adapt to their environment.

Some degree of learning is nearly universal among all animals. But no other animal has a greater capacity for learning than do humans or relies as heavily on learning for its very survival. This is an extraordinarily important notion, particularly for those people who are directly involved in the solution of human problems. If human behavior were largely instinctive (genetic), there would be little reason for developing programs aimed at changing people's behavior, such as programs in agricultural development, family planning, or community health.

How Culture Influences Biological Processes

All animals, including humans, have certain biologically determined needs that must be met if they are to stay alive and well. We all need to ingest a minimal number of calories of food each day, protect ourselves from the elements, sleep, and eliminate wastes from the body, to mention but a few. It is vital for us to distinguish between these needs and the ways by which we satisfy them. To illustrate, even though all people need to eliminate wastes from the body through defecation, how often, where, in what physical position, and under what social circumstances we defecate are all questions that are answered by our individual culture.

A dramatic example of how culture can influence or channel our biological processes was provided by anthropologist Clyde Kluckhohn (1949:19), who spent much of his career in the American Southwest studying the Navajo culture. Kluckhohn tells of a non-Navajo woman he knew in Arizona who took a somewhat perverse pleasure in causing a cultural response to food. At luncheon parties she frequently served sandwiches filled with a light meat that resembled tuna or chicken but had a slightly distinctive taste. Only after everyone had finished lunch would the hostess inform her guests

that what they had just eaten was neither tuna salad nor chicken salad but rather rattlesnake meat salad. Invariably, someone would vomit upon learning what she had eaten. Here, then, is an excellent example of how the biological process of digestion was influenced by a cultural idea. Not only was the process influenced, it was reversed! That is, the culturally based idea that rattlesnake meat is a despicable thing to eat triggered a violent reversal of the normal digestive process.

Our Bodies and Culture

The nonmaterial aspects of our culture, such as ideas, values, and attitudes, can have an appreciable effect on the human body. Culturally defined attitudes concerning male and female attractiveness, for example, have resulted in some dramatic effects on the body. Burmese

This tattooed woman from the United States illustrates the principle that cultural ideas of beauty can affect our physical bodies.

The Western ideal of equating physical attractiveness with thinness is not shared by all cultures of the world.

women stretch out their necks with large numbers of neck rings; Chinese women traditionally would bind their feet; men in New Guinea put bones through their noses; scarification and tattooing are all practiced in various parts of the world for the very same reasons that women and men in the United States pierce their ear lobes (that is, because their cultures tell them that it looks good). People intolerant of such different cultural practices frequently fail to realize that had they been raised in one of those other cultures, they would be practicing those allegedly disgusting or irrational customs.

Even our body stature is related to a large extent to our cultural ideas. In the Western world, people go to considerable lengths to become as slender as possible. They spend millions of dollars each year on running shoes, diet plans, appetite suppressants, and health spa memberships to help them take off those "ugly pounds." However, our Western notion of equating slimness with physical beauty is hardly universally accepted. In large parts of Africa, for example, Western women are perceived as emaciated and considered to be singularly unattractive. This point was made painfully obvious to me when conducting fieldwork in Kenya during the 1970s. After months of living in Kenya, I learned that many of my male Kikuyu friends pitied me for having such an unattractive wife (5 feet 5 inches tall and 114 pounds). Not infrequently Kikuyu friends would come by my house with a bowl of food or a chicken and discreetly whisper, "This is for your wife."

Even though I considered my wife to be beautifully proportioned, my African friends thought she needed to be fattened up in order to be beautiful.

Culture Changes

Thus far, culture has been presented as a body of things, ideas, and behavior patterns transmitted from generation to generation through the process of learning. Such a view of culture, focusing as it does on continuity between the generations, tends to emphasize its static rather than its dynamic aspects. And yet a fundamental principle underlying all cultures is that there is nothing as constant as change. Some cultures, particularly those small-scale, non-Western societies that are so often the object of anthropological study, change quite slowly, while for others, change occurs more rapidly. Despite the wide variation in the speed by which cultures change, one thing is certain: no cultures remain completely static year after year.

The Processes of Change

Cultures change according to two basic processes: internal changes (innovations) and external changes (cultural diffusion). **Innovations**—the ultimate source of all culture change—can be spread to other cultures. Those same innovations can also occur at different times and in different cultures independently. But it is important to bear in mind that not all innovations lead to culture change. An individual can come up with a wonderfully novel thing or idea, but unless it is accepted and used by the wider society, it will not lead to a change in the culture.

 looking ahead

To see how an innovation did not lead to a culture change, see Applied Perspective 1.

Some internal changes involve only slight variations in already existing cultural patterns. In other cases, the changes involve the fairly complex combination of a number of existing cultural features to form a totally new cultural feature. To be certain, internal culture changes involve creativity, ingenuity, and in some cases genius. To a large extent, however, the internal changes possible in any given culture are usually limited to what already exists in a culture. The automobile was invented in the United States because it was part of a cultural tradition that included many previous innovations, such as the internal combustion engine, the horseless carriage, and the wheel, to mention but three. Since innovations depend on the recombination of already existing elements in a culture, innovations are most likely to occur in those societies with the greatest number of cultural elements. This is another way of saying that internal culture change occurs more frequently in technologically complex societies than it does in less-developed ones.

The other source of culture change, which comes from outside the culture, is known as **cultural diffusion**—the spreading of a cultural element from one culture to another. As important as innovations are to the process of culture change, cultural diffusion is actually responsible for the greatest amount of change that occurs in any society. In fact, it has been estimated that the overwhelming majority of cultural elements found in any society at any time got there through the process of cultural diffusion rather than innovation. The reason for this is that it is easier to borrow a thing, an idea, or a behavior pattern than it is to invent it. This is not to suggest that people are essentially uninventive, but only that cultural items can be acquired with much less effort by borrowing than by inventing them.

Causes of Cultural Change

Most anthropologists acknowledge that cultures change by means of both internal and external mechanisms, but there is no such agreement on the primary causes of culture change. Do cultures change in response to changing technologies and economies, or do these changes originate in values and ideologies? Some people argue that the "prime mover" of change is technology. They cite, for example, the invention of the automobile and its many effects on all aspects of the American way of life. Others assert that ideas and values lead to culture change to the extent that they can motivate people to explore new ways of interacting with the environment, thereby inventing new items of technology. Still others suggest that cultures change in response to changes in the physical and social environment. For example, U.S. attitudes concerning mothers working outside the home have changed because of changing economic conditions and the need for two salaries. The discipline of anthropology has not been able to make definitive statements about the actual causes of culture change; no doubt the truth is a combination of these views. The forces of culture change are so complex, particularly in more technologically advanced societies, that it is difficult, if not impossible, to identify any single factor as most important. The most reasonable way of viewing culture change, then, is as a phenomenon brought about by the interaction of a number of different factors, such as ecology, technology, ideology, and social relationships. The topic of culture change will be discussed in greater depth in Chapter 16.

✶Evaluating Cultural Differences

While waiting to cross the street in Bombay, India, an American tourist stood next to a local resident who proceeded to blow his nose in the street. The tourist's reaction was instantaneous and unequivocal: "How disgusting!" he thought to himself. He responded to this cross-cultural encounter by evaluating the Indian man's behavior on the basis of standards of etiquette established by his own culture. According to those standards, it would be considered proper to use a handkerchief in such a situation. But if the man from Bombay were to see the American tourist blowing his nose into a handkerchief, he would be equally repulsed, thinking it strange indeed for the man to blow his nose into a handkerchief and then put the handkerchief back into his pocket and carry it around for the rest of the day.

Ethnocentrism

Both the American and the Indian would be evaluating each other's behavior based on the standards of their own cultural assumptions and practices. This way of responding to culturally different behavior is known as **ethnocentrism**—the belief that one's own culture is most desirable and superior to all others. In other words, it means viewing the rest of the world through the narrow lens of one's own culture.

Incidents of ethnocentrism are extensive. For example, we can see ethnocentrism operating in the historical accounts of the American Revolutionary War by both British and American historians. According to U.S. historians, George Washington was a folk hero of gargantuan proportions. He led his underdog Continental Army successfully against the larger, better equipped redcoats, he threw a coin across the Potomac River, and he was so incredibly honest that he turned himself in for chopping down a cherry tree. What a guy! But according to many British historians, George Washington was a thug and a hooligan. Many of Washington's troops were the descendants of debtors and prisoners who couldn't make it in England. Moreover, Washington didn't fight fairly. Whereas the British were most gentlemanly about warfare (for example, standing out in open fields in their bright red coats shooting at the enemy), Washington went sneaking around ambushing the British. Not a few British military historians have described Washington in much the same way that recent American historians have described the leaders of the Viet Cong during the Vietnam conflict. Even though the U.S. and British historians were describing the same set of historical events, their own biased cultural perspectives led to two radically different interpretations.

No society has a monopoly on ethnocentrism, for it is a deeply ingrained attitude found in all known societies. It should be quite obvious why ethnocentrism is so pervasive throughout the world. Since most people are raised in a single culture and never leave that culture during their lifetime, it is only logical that their own way of life—their values, attitudes, ideas, and ways of behaving—would appear to them to be the most natural. Even though ethnocentrism to some degree is present in all peoples and all cultures, it nevertheless serves as a major obstacle to the understanding of other cul-

Although most people in the United States consider their bathing habits to be very hygienic, most Japanese would disagree. The Japanese—who clean themselves before soaking in a tub with clean water—feel that North Americans can't be really clean if they step out of a bath filled with dirty soapy water.

tures, which is, after all, the major objective of cultural anthropology. Even people who think of themselves as open-minded will have difficulty controlling the impulse to evaluate the ideas or actions of culturally different people. And when individuals do make a valuative judgment, it will in all likelihood be based on their own cultural standards. Because it is so difficult to suppress our ethnocentrism, we frequently find ourselves expressing surprise, horror, outrage, disgust, disapproval, or amusement when encountering a lifestyle different from our own. Although we cannot eliminate ethnocentrism totally, by becoming aware of our own ethnocentrism, we will be able to temporarily set aside our own value judgments long enough to learn about how other cultures operate.

Nineteenth-century anthropology was plagued with ethnocentrism. Some of the early contributors to the discipline of anthropology (which was masquerading as science) described culturally different peoples in the most bigoted of terms. To illustrate, William McGee, the first president of the American Anthropological Association, was frequently guilty of the most obnoxious forms of ethnocentrism. Here, for example, McGee manages to debase the non-Western societies of his

CROSS-CULTURAL MISCUE

Such nonverbal forms of communication as hand gestures have different meanings in different cultures. For example, in the United States when referring to oneself (without using words), it is customary to point to one's chest with the index finger. In Japan, however, a person would convey the same nonverbal message by pointing to his or her nose. On the first day of a Japanese language class at a U.S. university, the Japanese instructor told his students in Japanese "I am your teacher" while pointing to his nose. The students thought he was saying, "This is my nose."

time by confusing the concepts of race, language, and culture:

> Possibly the Anglo-Saxon blood is more potent than that of other races; but it is to be remembered that the Anglo-Saxon language is the simplest, the most perfectly and simply symbolic that the world has ever seen; and that by means of it the Anglo-Saxon saves his vitality for conquest instead of wasting it under the Juggernaut of a cumbrous mechanism for conveyance of thought. (McGee 1895:281)

Cultural Relativism

Since the turn of the century, the discipline of anthropology has led a vigorous reaction against the perils of ethnocentrism. As cultural anthropologists began to conduct empirical fieldwork among the different cultures of the world, they recognized a need to achieve dispassionate and objective descriptions of the people they were studying. Following the lead of Franz Boas in the United States and Bronislaw Malinowski in Britain, twentieth-century anthropologists have been part of a tradition that calls upon the fieldworker to strive to prevent his or her own cultural values from coloring the descriptive accounts of the people under study.

According to Franz Boas, the father of modern anthropology in the United States, the way anthropologists are to strive for that level of detachment is through the practice of **cultural relativism.** This is the notion that any part of a culture (such as an idea, a thing, or a

behavior pattern) must be viewed from within its proper cultural context rather than from the viewpoint of the observer's culture. The cultural relativist asks, "How does a cultural item fit into the rest of the cultural system of which it is a part?" rather than "How does it fit into my own culture?" First formulated by Franz Boas at the turn of the century and later developed by one of Boas's students, Melville Herskovits (1972), cultural relativism rejects the notion that any culture, including our own, possesses a set of absolute standards by which all other cultures can be judged. Cultural relativity is a cognitive tool that helps us understand why people think and act the way they do.

Perhaps a specific example of cultural relativity will help to clarify the concept. Anthropologists over the years have described a number of cultural practices from around the world that would appear to be morally reprehensible to most Westerners. For example, the Dani of western New Guinea customarily cut off a finger from the hand of any close female relative of a man that dies; the Kikuyu of Kenya routinely remove part of the genitalia of teenage girls for the sake of suppressing their maleness; and the Dodoth of Uganda extract the lower front teeth of young girls in an attempt to make them more attractive. Some Eskimo groups practice a custom that would strike the typical Westerner as inhumane at best. When aging parents become too old to contribute their share of the workload, they are left out in the cold to die. If we view such a practice by the standards of our own Western culture (that is, ethnocentrically), we would have to conclude that it is cruel and heartless, hardly a way to treat those who brought you into the world. But the cultural relativist would look at this form of homicide within the context of the total culture of which it is a part. Friedl and Pfeiffer (1977:331) provide a culturally relativistic explanation of this Eskimo custom:

> It is important to know . . . that this . . . (custom is not practiced) against the will of the old person. It is also necessary to recognize that this is an accepted practice for which people are adequately prepared throughout their lives, and not some kind of treachery sprung upon an individual as a result of a criminal conspiracy. Finally, it should be considered in light of the ecological situation in which the Eskimos live. Making a living in the Arctic is difficult at best, and the necessity of feeding an extra mouth, especially when there is little hope that the individual will again become productive in the food-procurement process, would mean that the whole group would suffer. It is not a question of Eskimos not liking old people, but rather a question

of what is best for the entire group. We would not expect—and indeed we do not find—this practice to exist where there was adequate food to support those who were not able to contribute to the hunting effort.

For Boas, cultural relativism was an ethical mandate as well as a strategic methodology for understanding other cultures. In his attempt to counter the methodological abuses of people like McGee and set anthropology on a more scientific footing, Boas perhaps overemphasized the importance of cultural relativism. If cultural relativism is taken to its logical extreme, we arrive at two indefensible positions. First, from a methodological perspective, if every society is a unique entity that can be evaluated only in terms of its own standards, then any type of cross-cultural comparison would be virtually impossible. Clearly, however, if cultural anthropology is to accomplish its major objective—that is, scientifically describing and comparing the world's cultures—it needs some basis for comparison.

When trying to understand the behavior of culturally different people (such as the Inuits of Alaska), it is important to view their behavior within their own cultural and environmental contexts.

A second difficulty with taking the notion of cultural relativism too literally is that, from an ethical standpoint, we would have to conclude that absolutely no behavior found in the world would be immoral provided the people who practice it concur that it is morally acceptable or that it performs a function for the well-being of the society. Practicing cultural relativity, however, does not require that we view all cultures as morally equivalent. That is, not all cultural practices are equally worthy of tolerance and respect. To be certain, some cultural practices (such as the genocide perpetrated by Stalin, Hitler, or the Serbs in Bosnia) are morally indefensible within any cultural context. And, as Bagash (1981) reminds us, if we refuse to acknowledge our own values and compare, evaluate, and judge other cultures, we may be paralyzed in coping with the everyday world. Yet, if our goal is to *understand* human behavior in its myriad forms, then cultural relativism can help us identify the inherent logic behind certain ideas and customs. Sometimes cultural anthropologists have been criticized for being overly nonjudgmental about the customs they study, but as Barrett (1991:8) has suggested,

> . . . the occasional tendency for anthropologists to treat other cultures with excessive approbation to the extent that they sometimes idealize them, is less cause for concern than the possibility that they will misrepresent other societies by viewing them through the prism of their own culture.

looking ahead

To better understand the notion of cultural relativity, see Applied Perspective 2.

✱ Cultural Universals

A major contribution of cultural anthropology during the twentieth century has been its descriptive documentation of the thousands of cultures that inhabit the face of the earth. Again, following the Boasian tradition of empirical descriptive ethnography, hundreds of cultural anthropologists have set out since the turn of the century to describe the wide variety of cultures found in the contemporary world. As a result, the discipline of anthropology has been far more effective at documenting cultural differences than at showing similarities among cultures. This preoccupation with different forms of behavior and different ways of meeting human needs was the result, at least in part, of wanting to move away from the premature generalizing about "human nature" that was so prevalent around the turn of the century.

This vast documentation of culturally different ways of behaving has been extraordinarily important for our understanding of the human condition. The significant number of cultural differences illustrates how flexible and adaptable humans are compared to other animals because each culture has developed a different set of solutions to the universal human problems facing all societies. For example, every society, if it is to survive as an entity, needs a system of communication enabling its members to send and receive messages. That there are thousands of mutually unintelligible languages in the world today certainly attests to human flexibility. Yet, when viewed from a somewhat higher level of abstraction, all of these different linguistic communities have an important common denominator; that is, they all have developed some form of language. Thus, it is important to bear in mind that despite the many differences, all cultures of the world share a number of common features (**cultural universals**), because they have all worked out solutions to a whole series of problems facing all human societies. We can perhaps gain a clearer picture of cultural universals by looking in greater detail at the universal societal problems or needs that give rise to them.

Basic Needs

One of the most fundamental requirements of all societies is to see that the basic physiological needs of its people are met. Clearly, people cannot live unless they receive a minimum amount of food, water, and protection from the elements. Since a society will not last without living people, every society needs to work out systematic ways of producing (or procuring from the environment) those absolutely essential commodities and then distributing what it regards as necessary to its members. In the United States, goods and services are distributed according to the capitalistic principle of "each according to his or her capacity to pay." In such socialist countries as Cuba and China, distribution takes place according to the principle of "each according to his or her need." The Hadza of Tanzania distribute meat according to how an individual is related to the person who killed the animal. The Pygmies of Central Africa engage in a system of distribution called silent barter, whereby they avoid having face-to-face interaction with their trading partners. Many societies distribute valuable commodities as part of the marriage sys-

Although this U.S. school and this Koranic school in Africa differ in many respects, both schools represent a response to the universal need shared by all societies to pass along their cultures to the younger generation.

tem, sending considerable quantities of livestock from the family of the groom to the family of the bride. Even though the details of each of these systems of distribution vary greatly, every society has worked out a patterned way of ensuring that people get what they need for survival. As a result, we can say that every society has an *economic system.*

All societies face other universal needs besides the necessity to produce and distribute vital commodities to their members. For example, all societies need to make provisions for orderly mating and child rearing that give rise to patterned *systems of marriage and family.* If a society is to endure, it will need to develop a systematic way of passing on its culture from one generation to the next. This universal societal need for cultural transmission leads to some form of *educational system* in all societies. A prerequisite for the longevity of any society is the maintenance of social order. That is, most of the people must obey most of the rules most of the time. This universal societal need to avoid destruction through anarchy leads to a set of mechanisms that coerce people to obey the social norms that we refer to as a *social control system.* Since people in all societies are faced with life occurrences that defy explanation or prediction, all societies have developed systems for explaining the unexplainable, most of which rely on some form of supernatural beliefs such as religion, witchcraft, magic, or sorcery. Thus, all societies have developed a *system of supernatural beliefs* that serve to explain otherwise inexplicable phenomena. And since all societies, if they are to function, need for their members to be able to send and receive messages with relative efficiency, they all have developed *systems of communication,* both verbal and nonverbal.

Despite what may appear to be an overwhelming amount of cultural variety found in the world today, all cultures, owing to the fact that they must meet certain universal needs, share a number of traits in common. Those just mentioned represent some of the more obvious cultural universals, but many more could be cited. Anthropologist George Peter Murdock (1945:124) compiled a list of cultural universals that can provide us with a look at what our species has in common (see Table 2-1).

For much of the present century, cultural anthropologists have been focusing their efforts on explaining

cultural differences. In an attempt to reestablish the discipline's focus that petered out with Murdock's list of cultural universals in the 1940s, Donald Brown (1991:130–40) has explored in considerable detail what is common to all cultures and societies. Of particular interest is Brown's description of "The Universal People," a composite culture of all peoples known to anthropologists. While drawing heavily from Murdock's (1945) listing, as well as from Tiger and Fox (1971) and Hockett (1973), Brown makes a convincing case that cultural universals exist, are numerous, and are theoretically significant for carrying out the work of anthropology.

Culture Is Adaptive

Culture represents the major way by which human populations adapt or relate to their environments so that they can continue to reproduce and survive. Most living organisms other than humans adapt to their environments by developing physiological features that equip them to maximize their chances for survival. For ex-

TABLE 2-1			
Murdock's Cultural Universals			
Are there any additional universals you would add to the following list?			
age grading	etiquette	joking	postnatal care
athletics	faith healing	kin groups	pregnancy usages
bodily adornment	family	kin terminology	property rights
calendar	feasting	language	propitiation of
cleanliness training	fire making	law	supernatural beings
community organization	folklore	luck superstitions	puberty customs
cooking	food taboos	magic	religious ritual
cooperative labor	funeral rites	marriage	residence rules
cosmology	games	mealtimes	sexual restrictions
courtship	gestures	medicine	soul concepts
dancing	gift giving	modesty	status differentiation
decorative art	government	mourning	surgery
divination	greetings	music	tool making
division of labor	hair styles	mythology	trade
dream interpretation	hospitality	numerals	visiting
education	housing	obstetrics	weaning
eschatology	hygiene	penal sanctions	weather control
ethics	incest taboos	personal names	
ethnobotany	inheritance rules	population policy	

Source: George Peter Murdock, "The Common Denominator of Cultures," in Ralph Linton, ed., *The Science of Man in the World Crisis.* New York: Columbia University Press, 1945, p. 124.

CROSS-CULTURAL MISCUE

Sometimes our best intentions can lead to breakdowns in cross-cultural communication. Among middle-class North American men, it is customary to shake hands as a gesture of friendship. When wanting to communicate extra friendliness, a male in the United States may, while shaking hands, grasp with his left hand his friend's right arm. However, if a North American businessman should attempt to emphasize the sincerity of his friendship in this manner to his Saudi Arabian business partner, he would be sending an extremely offensive message, since in Saudi Arabia, and generally throughout the Muslim world where the right hand is sacred and the left hand is profane, touching someone with the left hand is considered highly offensive.

ample, certain species of predators such as wolves, lions, and leopards have developed powerful jaws and canine teeth used for killing animals and ripping the flesh of the animal. Humans, on the other hand, have relied more on cultural than biological features for adapting to their environments. Through the invention and use of such cultural tools as spears, arrows, guns, and knives, humans are able to kill and butcher animals even more efficiently than an animal could with its massive jaws and teeth. The discovery of such chemical substances as penicillin, quinine, and the polio vaccine has provided the human species a measure of protection against disease and death. The proliferation of agricultural technology over the past century has dramatically increased humans' capacity to feed themselves. Since humans rely much more heavily upon cultural adaptation than biological adaptation, they are enormously flexible in their ability to both survive and thrive in a wide variety of natural environments. Because of the **adaptive nature of culture,** people are now able to live in many previously uninhabitable places, such as the Kalahari Desert, the Arctic region, under the sea, and even in outer space.

The notion that culture is adaptive should not lead us to the conclusion that every aspect of a culture is adaptive. It is possible for some features to be adaptively neutral; that is, neither enhancing nor diminishing the capacity of a people to survive. Moreover, it is even possible for some features of a culture to be maladaptive or dysfunctional. To illustrate, the large-scale use of automobiles coupled with industrial pollutants is currently destroying the quality of the air in our environment. If this set of cultural behaviors continues much longer, it will destroy our environment to such an extent that it will be unfit for human habitation. Thus, it is not likely that such a maladaptive practice will persist indefinitely. Either the practice will disappear when the people become extinct, or the culture will change so that the people will survive. Whichever occurs, the maladaptive cultural feature will eventually disappear.

An understanding of the adaptive nature of culture is further complicated by its relativity. What is adaptive in one culture may be maladaptive or adaptively neutral in another culture. For example, the mastery of such skills as algebra, word analogies, and reading comprehension is necessary for a successful adaptation to life in the United States, for these skills all contribute to academic success, landing a "good" job, and living in material comfort. Such skills, however, are of little value in helping the Nuer herdsman adapt to his environment in the Sudan. Furthermore, the adaptability of a cultural item will vary over time within any particular culture. To illustrate, the survival capacity of traditional Eskimo hunters living on the Alaskan tundra would, no doubt, be enhanced appreciably by the introduction of guns and snowmobiles. Initially, such innovations would be adaptive because they would enable the Eskimo hunters to obtain caribou more easily, thereby enabling people to eat better, be more resistant to disease, and generally live longer. After several generations, however, the use of guns and snowmobiles would, in all likelihood, become maladaptive, for the newly acquired capacity to kill caribou more efficiently would eventually lead to the destruction of a primary food supply.

Cultures Are Integrated

To suggest that all cultures share a certain number of universal characteristics is not to imply that cultures comprise a laundry list of norms, values, and material objects. Instead, cultures should be thought of as integrated wholes, the parts of which, to some degree, are interconnected with one another. When we view cultures as integrated systems, we can begin to see how particular culture traits fit into the whole system and, consequently, how they tend to make sense within that context. Equipped with such a perspective, we can begin to better understand those "strange" customs found throughout the world.

One way of describing this integrated nature of cultures is by using the **organic analogy** made popular by some of the early functionalist anthropologists. This approach makes the analogy between a culture and a living organism such as the human body. The physical human body comprises a number of systems, all functioning to maintain the overall health of the organism; these systems include, among others, the respiratory, digestive, skeletal, excretory, reproductive, muscular, circulatory, endocrine, and lymphatic systems. Any anatomist or surgeon worth her or his salt will know (1) where these systems are located in the body, (2) what function each plays, and (3) how the various parts of the body are interconnected. Surely no sane person would choose a surgeon to remove a malignant lung unless that surgeon knew how that organ was related to the rest of the body.

Cultural Interconnections

In the same way that human organisms comprise various parts that are both functional and interrelated, so too do cultures. When conducting empirical field research, the task of the cultural anthropologist is to describe the various parts of the culture, show how they function, and show how they are interconnected. When describing cultures, anthropologists frequently identify such parts or "systems" as the economic, kinship, social control, marriage, military, religious, aesthetic, technological, and linguistic systems, among others. These various parts of a culture are more than a random assortment of customs. Even though more often than not anthropologists fail to clearly spell out the nature and dimensions of these relationships, it is believed that most of the parts of a culture are to some degree interconnected. Thus, we can speak of cultures as being logical and coherent systems.

The notion of the interconnectedness of the parts of a culture can be illustrated from any culture. The Samburu of East Africa are seminomadic pastoralists who keep relatively large numbers of cows. An anthropologist studying the Samburu and their herds would no doubt describe the cow as part of the economic system. The cow's blood and milk are routinely consumed as a source of food; skins are used to make clothing, shoes, and jewelry; the cow's urine is used as an antiseptic; and cow dung is both a principal material for house construction and a fuel for cooking. Even though cows are an integral part of the economic system of the Samburu, they play an important role in (or are related to) other systems as well. To illustrate, since an exchange of cattle is necessary for a legal marriage to take place, cows are part of the marriage system; since cows are exchanged by men to establish obligations and bonds of friendship, cattle play an important role in social relationships; and since cows are frequently the subject of such artistic expressions as songs, poems, epics, and folktales, they are an integral part of the aesthetic system. Thus, to the extent that cattle function as part of a number of distinct components in the Samburu culture, we can see how the culture tends to be integrated.

"Primitive" Cultures

A fundamental feature of the discipline of cultural anthropology is that it is comparative in approach. Whether studying religions, economic systems, ways of resolving conflicts, or art forms, cultural anthropologists look at these aspects of human behavior in the widest possible context, ranging from the most technologically simple foraging societies at one end of the continuum to the most highly industrialized societies at the other. Those societies with simple technologies, once

For this East African pastoralist, cattle are more than just an economic commodity. Since cattle also play roles in legitimizing marriages, allocating social status, and making religious sacrifices, we say that the various parts of a culture tend to be interconnected.

referred to as "primitive," are described by contemporary cultural anthropologists by other terms such as "preliterate," "small-scale," "egalitarian," or "technologically simple." Owing to the misleading implication that something "primitive" is both inferior and earlier in a chronological sense, the term *primitive* will not be used in this text. Instead we will use the term "small-scale" society, which refers to societies that (1) have relatively small populations, (2) are technologically simple, (3) are usually preliterate (that is, not having a written form of language), (4) have little labor specialization, and (5) are unstratified. Making such a distinction between small-scale and more complex societies should not be taken to imply that all societies can be pigeonholed into one or the other category. Rather, it would be more fruitful to view all of the societies of the world along a continuum from most small-scale to most complex.

Culture and the Individual

Throughout this chapter we have used the term *culture* to refer to everything that people have, think, and do as members of a society. Whether we are talking about the Chinese, Yanamamo, or Samoans, all peoples have a shared set of meanings that serve as a collective guide to their behavior. Since people from the same culture learn essentially the same set of values, rules, norms, and expected behaviors, their lives are made somewhat less complicated because they know, within broad limits, what to expect from one another. To illustrate, when walking down a crowded hallway in the United States, there is a general understanding that people will keep to their right. Since most people share that

free will

common cultural understanding, the traffic in a crowded hallway will usually flows without serious interruption. Should someone walk down the left-hand side of the hallway, it is likely that traffic will slow down because many people will be unsure of how to cope with the oncoming person. Such an incident is disruptive and anxiety producing for the simple reason that normal, expected, and predictable behavior has not occurred.

This chapter dealing with the concept of culture has shown in a number of different ways how individuals are constrained, or at least influenced, by their cultures—those sets of material objects, ideas, and behavior patterns that they internalize from birth. And, in fact, how effectively people fit into their own group will depend largely on the extent to which they adhere to those cultural expectations. To be certain, our cultures exert a powerful influence on our conduct, often without our even being aware of it. However, to assert that culture influences our behavior is hardly the same as asserting that it determines our behavior.

Deviance from the cultural norms is found in all societies. Since individual members of any society maintain (to varying degrees) a free will, they have the freedom to say "no" to cultural expectations. Unlike the honey-bee, which behaves totally according to its genetic programming, humans have a range of behavioral choices they can make. Choosing an alternative may, of course, result in unpleasant consequences, but all people have the option of doing things differently from what their culture would expect. People sometimes choose to go against cultural conventions for a number of reasons. In some cases where adherence to a social norm involves a hardship, people may justify their noncompliance by stretching the meaning of the norm. Or sometimes people flaunt a social norm or custom because doing so enables them to make a social statement. To illustrate, in the United States it is generally considered rude to be more than 15 or 20 minutes late to a dinner party at someone's home without an excuse. If the host had insulted you in public several days earlier, however, you could return the insult by showing up at the dinner party two hours late, thereby demonstrating contempt for both the host and his party. Whatever the reason one has for deviating from the norms, the fact remains that social norms rarely, if ever, receive total compliance. For this reason, cultural anthropologists distinguish between "ideal" behavior (what people are expected to do) and "real" behavior (what people actually do).

applied PERSPECTIVE

Culture

Culture is a powerful force on the life of the individual. Within broad limits, our culture influences our values, beliefs, behaviors, perceptions, and view of the world. The degree to which this is true becomes particularly apparent to us when we step outside our own culture or when we interact with people from different cultural backgrounds. Our own culture tends to shape our thinking to such a degree that we often fail to realize that people from other cultures don't share our assumptions or perceptions of reality.

Anthropological understanding of the local food production system in rural Mexico is applied to the area of new-product marketing.

During the 1960s, anthropologist Hendrick Serrie was hired by the Rockefeller Foundation to field-test a newly developed solar cooking stove in a Mexican village in Oaxaca. Foundation-supported researchers wanted to introduce the new stove (which was capable of producing the same heat as conventional wood fires) to Mexican villagers as a more energy-efficient alternative to burning wood. As a way of introducing the cooker to the local people, a prototype was made on a limited scale using local materials, labor, and technology. The Rockefeller Foundation wanted to "test market" the solar cooker before going into mass production. Serrie conducted a field study of the local food production system and found that despite initial interest among the local people, several important cultural factors strongly suggested that the cooker might not be widely used by the local population.

applied PERSPECTIVE *continued*

One cultural factor that militated against the adoption of the solar cooker was the existing cooking routine of local women. According to Serrie's findings, local women did most of their cooking early in the morning or in the early evening, the times of day when solar energy is at its lowest. As a general rule, women did no cooking during the middle of the day when the sun is strongest, preferring instead to eat a cold lunch in the fields.

A second cultural problem involved the major type of food normally prepared in that part of the world—that is, the *tortilla*. Although a solar cooker works well for boiling beans or making a stew, it is quite inadequate for baking these cornmeal pancakes. The focal point of heat coming from the cooker's four-foot-wide parabolic reflector is so concentrated that it tends to burn a hole in one part of the *tortilla* while leaving the rest uncooked.

Finally, Serrie found that the solar cooker was incompatible with the "complex of behaviors associated with cooking" (1986:xvii). Women in this part of Mexico are accustomed to cooking while sitting on their kitchen floors for relatively long periods of time. From a sitting position, a woman is able to tend her fire, knead the dough, cook the tortillas, and serve members of the family, all without having to move around the kitchen.

Thus, having to stand up and cook while leaning over a solar cooker in the hot sun might be a difficult adjustment for women who are used to doing all of the cooking from a seated position in their kitchens. Moreover, the parabolic reflector must be adjusted every fifteen minutes to compensate for the movement of the sun.

Owing to these cultural realities—which were revealed by direct participant-observation of an applied anthropologist—the decision was made not to mass-produce these solar cookers for local use, thereby avoiding a costly mistake. In all likelihood, the traditional patterns of food preparation were so well entrenched that local women would not have been willing to change them in exchange for a cooker that operated on a less expensive source of energy. Thus, in this situation the applied anthropologist played an important role as a marketing consultant.

THOUGHT QUESTIONS

1. How would you describe the major anthropological contribution in this case study?

2. Why was the solar cooker not appropriate for local use in Oaxaca?

3. Can you think of how the introduction of some other Western item of technology would be inappropriate in another culture (for example, the introduction of the product "Hamburger Helper" in India)?

Cultural anthropologists can assist in the design of appropriate housing for culturally different people.

When designing buildings, architects need a thorough understanding of both the laws of physics and the nature of building materials if the

structure is not to fall down. Architecture, however, involves more than bricks and mortar. Since buildings are used by people to serve certain functions, the architect must also pay particular attention to the culture or subculture of the people who will eventually use the building. Because people have different values, attitudes, and behavior patterns, it is likely that they will use their physical space differently. In other words, low-income housing in Djakarta, Indonesia, that is designed with the users in mind will look substantially different from low-income housing in Philadelphia.

In recent years, architects have increasingly collaborated with cultural anthropologists to ensure that buildings are designed in culturally appropriate ways. One such effort was the Payson Project, a U.S. government project aimed at building a community of homes for a group of Apaches in central Arizona during the late 1970s. Much to the credit of the project, anthropologist George Esber was invited to be part of the planning team and to serve as a cultural adviser. His role involved conducting anthropological research on the space needs of the local Apache people and translating these needs into appropriate design features for the architects.

Esber's research (1977, 1987) was an interesting mixture of using traditional methods along with a creative technique designed specially to elicit data relevant for this housing project. The initial data gathering involved ethnographic mapping of the location of houses in the existing community and the interior use of space in these houses. Interviewing was also used to determine the social networks of relationships that existed in the community. Esber gave each family a model house kit with movable wall segments and pieces of furniture so that they could design their own housing preference. He then photographed and analyzed the families' model plans before sharing the information with the architects.

This anthropological research revealed some important features of contemporary Apache life that had important design implications for the housing project. In terms of the internal house design, most Apaches preferred a layout that divided the space into sleeping areas and a large living area. Esber found that his informants preferred an open design very much in keeping with traditional Apache houses, with a minimum of partitions in the general living space. Such a floor plan (combining cooking, eating, and general living in a single room) is very much in keeping with the Apaches' patterns of social interaction. Through participant observation, Esber learned that Apaches enter social situations in a slow, gradual manner. This step-by-step approach permits the somewhat reticent Apaches to determine if they want to continue the interaction after having assessed the social situation.

This is just one example of how anthropological insights about the cultural needs of the Apaches were accommodated through architectural design. The anthropological contribution involved an understanding of patterns of social interaction and space usage among the Apaches. Unlike houses built for other Apache communities without anthropological input, the houses designed for the Payson Project met with a high degree of satisfaction. Many Apaches on other reservations were unwilling to move into new homes built on an Anglo model that were not designed in collaboration with anthropologists. When they did, they found the new houses unsatisfying, and many moved back into their old homes.

THOUGHT QUESTIONS

1. How can the patterns of social interaction between members of a culture influence how they use space?

2. How would ideal housing interiors be different for contemporary Apaches and low-income families in Atlanta, Georgia?

3. If an anthropologist were to make recommendations for building the dream house for your family, what cultural/social factors would you want the anthropologist to consider?

4. Were the methods used for obtaining data on Apache housing appropriate? Why or why not?

applied PERSPECTIVE *continued*

Summary

1. For purposes of this book, we have defined the term *culture* as "everything that people have, think, and do as members of a society."

2. Culture is something that is shared by members of the same society. This shared nature of culture enables people to predict—within broad limits—the behavior of others in the society. Conversely, people become disoriented when attempting to interact in a culturally different society because they don't share that culture with members of that society.

3. Culture is acquired not genetically but through a process of learning, which anthropologists refer to as enculturation. People in different cultures learn different things, but there is no evidence to suggest that people in some cultures learn more efficiently than people in other cultures.

4. Certain aspects of culture—such as ideas, beliefs, and values—can affect our physical bodies and our biological processes. More specifically, certain culturally produced ideas concerning physical beauty can influence the ways by which people alter their bodies.

5. Cultures—and their three basic components of things, ideas, and behavior patterns—are constantly experiencing change. Though the pace of culture change varies from society to society, no cultures are totally static. Cultures change internally (innovation) and by borrowing from other cultures (diffusion).

6. There are essentially two ways of responding to unfamiliar cultures. One way is ethnocentrically—that is, from one's own cultural perspective. The other way is from the perspective of a cultural relativist—that

is, from within the context of the other culture. Cultural anthropologists strongly recommend the second mode.

7. Although cultures found throughout the world vary considerably, certain common features (cultural universals) are found in all cultures. Cultural anthropology—the scientific study of cultures—looks at both similarities and differences in human cultures wherever they may be found.

8. Cultures function to help people adapt to their environments and consequently increase their chances for survival.

9. A culture is more than the sum of its parts. Rather, a culture should be seen as an integrated system with its parts interrelated to some degree. This cultural integration has important implications for the process of culture change, since a change in one part of the system is likely to bring about changes in other parts.

Key Terms

adaptive nature of culture
cultural diffusion
cultural relativism
cultural universals
enculturation

ethnocentrism
innovation
organic analogy
tabula rasa

Suggested Readings

Brown, Donald E. *Human Universals*. New York: McGraw-Hill, 1991. Drawing upon the works of earlier theorists, this recent work argues convincingly that cultural universals (those aspects of culture shared by all cultures) are numerous and theoretically significant.

DeVita, Philip R., and James D. Armstrong. *Distant Mirrors: America as a Foreign Culture*. Belmont, Calif.: Wadsworth, 1993. A readable collection of fourteen articles on American culture as seen through the eyes of foreign scholars who had conducted field research in the United States. This slim volume, written from the critical perspective of foreign observers, should give American readers a different view of their own culture.

Freilich, Morris, Douglas Raybeck, and Joel Savishinsky, eds. *Deviance: Anthropological Perspectives*. South Hadley, Mass.: Bergin and Garvey, 1990. This collection of essays looks at the relationship between culture and deviance (or noncompliance with cultural prescriptions) in a wide range of societies throughout the world.

Gamst, Frederick C., and Edward Norbeck, eds. *Ideas of Culture: Sources and Uses*. New York: Holt, Rinehart and Winston, 1976. This is a collection of writings over the past hundred years on the notion of culture, the concept that is central to the discipline of anthropology.

Hall, Edward T. *The Hidden Dimension*. Garden City, N.Y.: Doubleday, 1969. Hall introduces the science of proxemics to show how a very subtle aspect of culture—how people use space—can have a powerful impact on international business relations, cross-cultural encounters, and the fields of architecture and urban planning.

Linton, Ralph. *The Study of Man*. New York: Appleton-Century, 1936. Written more than half a century ago to provide beginners with the basics of anthropology, Linton's classic work remains one of the best introductions to the field of cultural anthropology.

White, Leslie A., with Beth Dillingham. *The Concept of Culture*. Minneapolis: Burgess, 1973. The written version of a series of lectures White gave on the concept of culture in which he defines culture essentially as a symbolic system.

APPLIED ANTHROPOLOGY

CHAPTER THREE

A mother and her baby from India.

- How have cultural anthropologists applied their theories, methods, and insights to the solution of practical problems during the course of this century?

- What special contributions can cultural anthropology make as an applied science?

- What ethical dilemmas do applied anthropologists face when conducting fieldwork?

A distinguishing feature of cultural anthropology is its direct, experiential approach to research through the technique known as participant-observation. Although they have been working increasingly in recent years in industrialized societies, cultural anthropologists for the most part have conducted field research in those parts of the world experiencing serious societal problems, such as poor health, inadequate food production, high infant mortality, and rampant population growth, to mention but a few. The very nature of anthropological research—involving, as it does, living with people, sharing their lives, and frequently befriending them—makes it difficult for cultural anthropologists to ignore the enormity of the problems these societies face on an everyday basis. It should therefore come as no surprise that many cultural anthropologists feel a sense of responsibility for helping to solve—or at least alleviate—some of these pressing social problems.

Even though anthropologists to one degree or another have always applied their findings, theories, and methods to the solution of human problems, an increasing number of anthropologists at various times during the past half century have become involved in research aimed very explicitly at practical applications. These practitioners represent a relatively new and growing subdiscipline known as applied anthropology, which is characterized by problem-oriented research among the world's contemporary populations. Pragmatic anthropologists attempt to apply anthropological data, concepts, and strategies to the solution of social, economic, and technological problems, both at home and abroad. Over the past decades a number of terms have been given to these many attempts to use anthropological research for the improvement of human conditions. They include *action anthropology, development*

anthropology, practical anthropology, and *advocacy anthropology.* For purposes of this chapter, however, we will use the more widely accepted and generic term, *applied anthropology.*

Applied versus Pure Anthropology

For much of this century, many anthropologists have distinguished applied anthropology from "pure" or "academic" anthropology. So-called pure anthropology was seen as being concerned only with the advancement of the discipline in terms of refining its methods and theories and providing increasingly more valid and reliable anthropological data. Applied anthropology, on the other hand, was characterized as being primarily aimed at changing human behavior in order to ameliorate contemporary problems. The two types of anthropology are hardly mutually exclusive enterprises, however. Applied anthropology, if it is to be done effectively, needs to take into account all of the theories, methods, and data that have been developed by the discipline as a whole. The more academically or theoretically oriented anthropologists are indebted to applied anthropologists for stimulating their interests in new areas of research. Applied anthropology has contributed significantly to scholarly and research activities. As Goldschmidt (1979:5) reminds us, "the more a field is engaged in practical affairs, the greater the intellectual ferment; for programmatic activities raise issues and often new approaches which would otherwise escape the attention of the discipline." In actual fact, the distinction between pure and applied anthropology is a false

Applied cultural anthropologists study a wide variety of social settings including such inner city neighborhoods as this one in Washington, D.C.

dichotomy, for the two have experienced a parallel development and have been mutually supportive.

Applied Anthropology's Image

To claim that applied and academic anthropology grew up together is not to suggest that they have enjoyed equal status within the profession. For much of this century, applied anthropology has had a relatively negative image, in large part because of its early association with colonialism. Most colonial powers—the British in particular—employed anthropologists to help facilitate the administration of local populations. The findings from their anthropological studies were used to meet the needs of the colonial administrators, which were not always the same as the needs of the people themselves. Because of this association with colonial administrations, applied anthropology was stigmatized as an enterprise with a dubious set of ethical standards. In a more general sense, some anthropologists have rejected applied anthropology because they feel it would require them to compromise their cultural relativity. How can one be a cultural relativist, they would argue, when making suggestions on how people should change their cultures? Until quite recently, many anthropologists regarded applied anthropology as something less than fully legitimate. As one commentator (Angrosino 1976:3) has put it, "like an aristocratic family going into trade to keep up payments, applied anthropologists were felt to be simplifying the complex wisdom of their craft and getting their hands dirty in service."

Organizations Supporting Applied Anthropology

Much of the applied anthropology carried out in recent decades has been supported by large public and private organizations seeking to better understand the cultural dimension of their sponsored programs. These organizations include such international agencies as the U.S. Agency for International Development (USAID), the World Bank, the World Health Organization (WHO), the Ford Foundation, and the Population Council; certain national organizations such as the National Institute of Health (NIH), the Bureau of Indian Affairs, and the U.S. Department of Agriculture; and on a more local level, various hospitals, private corporations, school systems, urban planning departments, substance abuse programs, facilities for the aged, and family planning clinics.

Recent Literature

Perhaps the best way to illustrate how anthropological data have been applied to the solution of human problems is by briefly listing a selection of case studies that have appeared in the recent literature. Although the range of applied anthropology is far wider than can be surveyed here, the following case studies should serve to illustrate the diversity of uses to which anthropological data have been put:

- The use of cultural data concerning African pastoralists to develop a more workable livestock development program (Horowitz 1986).
- An analysis of the housing policy implications of anthropological data gathered in a soup kitchen in a Connecticut town (Glasser 1989).
- The application of ethnographic data on Apache Indians to a clinical nursing program on the San Carlos Apache Indian Reservation in San Carlos, Arizona (Gronseth 1988).
- The introduction of an anthropological approach to the training of U.S. Peace Corps Volunteers (Nolan 1986).
- The analysis of cultural differences between Japanese and U.S. businesspersons involved in a joint venture contract (Hamada 1988).
- The assessment of the social feasibility of a settlement project in northern Cameroon (Hoben 1986).
- The study of local communities whose environments are affected by contaminated groundwater by an anthropologist who served on an interdisciplinary groundwater research project (Fitchen 1988).

The Anthropologist's Involvement in Applied Projects

The extent to which an applied anthropologist becomes involved in any given project can vary considerably. At the least interventionist extreme are those applied anthropologists who provide information for planners and decision makers. This information can range from very concrete observational data, through low- and intermediate-level concepts and propositions, to the most abstract level of general theory. At another level, applied anthropologists, either working alone or as members of an interdisciplinary team, may use the collected data to construct a plan for bringing about a desired change in a particular population. And finally, at the most interventionist extreme, applied anthropologists

become involved in actual implementation and evaluation of particular change projects. Although relatively rare, these "action anthropologists" feel a professional responsibility not only to make their research findings available but also to propose, advocate, and carry out policy positions.

Specialized Roles of Applied Anthropologists

Applied anthropologists also play a number of specialized roles, which are more thoroughly described by Van Willigen (1993:3–6):

Policy Researcher. This role, perhaps the most common role for applied anthropologists, involves providing cultural data to policymakers so they can make the most informed policy decisions.

Evaluator. This role is also quite common; evaluators use their research skills to determine how well a program or policy has succeeded in its objectives.

Impact Assessor. This role entails measuring or assessing the effect that a particular project, program, or policy has on local peoples. For example, the anthropologist serving in the role of impact assessor may determine the consequences, both intended and unintended, that a federal highway construction project might have on the community through which the highway runs.

Planner. In this fairly common role, applied anthropologists actively participate in the design of various programs, policies, and projects.

Research Analyst. In this role, the applied anthropologist interprets research findings so that policymakers, planners, and administrators can make more culturally sensitive decisions.

Needs Assessor. This role involves the conduct of a fairly specialized type of research designed to determine ahead of time the need for a proposed program or project.

Trainer. This is essentially a teaching role, whereby the applied anthropologist imparts cultural knowledge about certain populations to different groups that are expected to work in cross-cultural situations (e.g., training a group of U.S. engineers to be better aware of the cultural environment of Saudi Arabia where they will work for two years building a U.S. embassy).

Advocate. This relatively rare role involves becoming an active supporter of a particular group of people. Usually involving at least some political action, this role is most frequently combined with other roles.

Expert Witness. This role, usually played on a short-term basis, involves the presentation of culturally rele-

Applied anthropologists can serve as consultants, or "cultural brokers," to help businesspersons better understand the cultures of their international business partners.

vant research findings as part of judicial proceedings through legal briefs, depositions, or direct testimony.

Administrator/Manager. An applied anthropologist who assumes direct administrative responsibility for a particular project is working in this specialized role.

Cultural Broker. This role involves serving as a liaison between the program planner and administrators on the one hand and local ethnic communities on the other.

looking ahead

To see how anthropologists serve as cultural brokers, see Applied Perspective 1 at the end of this chapter.

These specialized roles are not mutually exclusive. In many cases, applied anthropologists will play two or more of these roles as part of the same job. For example, an applied anthropologist who is working as a policy researcher may also conduct research as a needs assessor before a program is initiated and as an impact assessor and evaluator after the program has concluded.

Special Features of Anthropology

What does the discipline of anthropology have to offer as an applied science? The answer to this question lies largely in the unique approach to the study of humans that anthropology has taken from its earliest begin-nings. Among some of the special features of anthropology that contribute to its potential as a policy science are the following: (1) **participant-observation,** (2) the **holistic perspective,** (3) the development of a **regional expertise,** (4) the **emic view,** and (5) the basic value orientation of **cultural relativism.**

Participant-Observation. Direct field observation, a hallmark of twentieth-century anthropology, can lead to a fuller understanding of the sociocultural realities than might be possible by relying on secondary sources of information. Also, the rapport developed while conducting participant-observation research can be drawn upon in the implementation stage of the applied project.

The Holistic Perspective. This distinctive feature of anthropology forces us to look at multiple variables and see human problems in their historical, economic, and cultural contexts. This conceptual orientation reminds us that the various parts of a sociocultural system are interconnected so that a change in one part of the system is likely to cause changes in other parts. The holistic approach also encourages us to look at the problems in terms of both the short run and the long run.

Regional Expertise. Many anthropologists, despite recent trends toward specialization, continue to function as "culture area specialists" (e.g., Africanists, Micronesianists). The cultural anthropologist who has conducted doctoral research in Zambia, for example, will frequently return to that country for subsequent field studies. Thus, long-term association with a cultural region provides a depth of geographic coverage that most policymakers lack.

looking ahead

To better understand how anthropologists bring their regional cultural expertise to bear on a specific problem in Latin America, see Applied Perspective 2 at the end of this chapter.

The Emic View. A major insight of anthropology in general—and applied anthropology specifically—is that linguistic and cultural differences invariably exist between project bureaucrats and the local client populations. Whatever the setting of a particular project—be it an agricultural development scheme in Zimbabwe, an inner-city hospital in Detroit, or a classroom in rural Peru—the applied anthropologist brings to the project the perspective of the local people, what anthropologists call the emic view. By describing the emic view (using the mental categories and assumptions of the local people rather than their own), anthropologists can provide program planners/administrators with strategic information that can seriously affect the outcome of programs of planned change.

Cultural Relativism. The basic principle of cultural relativism (refer to Chapter 2)—a vital part of every cultural anthropologist's training—tends to foster tolerance, which can be particularly relevant for applied anthropologists working in complex organizations. For example, tolerance stemming from the perspective of cultural relativism can help anthropologists cross class lines and relate to a wide range of people in the complex organization (e.g., hospital, school system) in which they are working.

These five features of anthropology can very definitely enhance the discipline's effectiveness as a policy science. Nevertheless, when compared to other disciplines, anthropology has some drawbacks that limit its effectiveness in solving societal problems. First, anthropologists have not, by and large, developed any time-effective research methods; the premier anthropological data-gathering technique of participant observation, which usually requires up to a year or more, is not particularly well suited to the accelerated time schedules of applied programs of change. Second, in an attempt to protect "their people," anthropologists frequently assume an "underdog bias," that prevents them from balancing the interests of the local people with those of the project administrators. And, finally, with their strong tradition of qualitative research methods, anthropologists have been relatively unsophisticated in their use of quantitative data, although recently a number of anthropologists have begun to use more quantitative approaches.

The Rise of Applied Anthropology

Although it is possible to trace the roots of applied anthropology back to Herodotus in the fifth century B.C. (Van Willigen 1993:18), World War II marked a significant acceleration of interest in applying the insights of anthropology to the solution of contemporary societal problems. To be certain, the decade of the 1930s before the war witnessed an appreciable increase in the number of anthropologists being hired in nonacademic settings. As previously mentioned, anthropologists outside the United States were hired by colonial governments to conduct research on native populations for the purpose of administering these dependent peoples more effectively. Closer to home, anthropologist John

John Collier, an applied anthropologist, became the Commissioner of Indian Affairs during Franklin Roosevelt's administration.

CROSS-CULTURAL MISCUE

When trying to operate in a cross-cultural situation, we frequently face a myriad of potential communication hazards. Not only do different cultures speak unintelligible languages, but their body languages are often mutually incomprehensible as well. A simple gesture, such as scratching one's earlobe, can have a number of unanticipated consequences when dealing with people from other cultures. As Desmond Morris (1988:5) reminds us, an innocent tug on one's earlobe has five different meanings in five different Mediterranean cultures. To a Spaniard, the gesture means "You rotten sponger"; to a Greek, "You better watch it, mate"; to a Maltese, "You're a sneaky little so-and-so"; and to an Italian, "Get lost, you pansy." Only a Portuguese, to whom the earlobe pull signifies something wonderful, would not interpret such a gesture as an insult.

Collier, Franklin Roosevelt's Commissioner of Indian Affairs, created the Applied Anthropology Unit of Indian Affairs in the early 1930s for the purpose of studying the prospects of certain Indian groups developing self-governing organizations as required by the 1934 Indian Reorganization Act; anthropologists hired by the U.S. Department of Agriculture conducted research on economic development at certain Indian reservations; and such anthropologists as W. Lloyd Warner and Burleigh Gardner, working as part of the interdisciplinary Committee on Human Relations in Industry at the University of Chicago, engaged in applied anthropological research on issues related to industrial management, working conditions, and productivity.

Applied Anthropology During World War II

Even though applied anthropologists were becoming increasingly active during the years of the Great Depression, the real stimulus came in the 1940s. According to Partridge and Eddy (1978:27), ". . . the crisis of war provided unprecedented opportunities for anthropologists to participate in efforts related to war activities."

Anthropologists made a wide range of practical contributions during the war years. After years of working among contemporary "primitive" cultures, a sizable number of U.S. anthropologists returned to the United States to apply their skills to their own society. The war generated so much interest in the practical uses of anthropology that in 1941 the Society for Applied Anthropology was founded at Harvard University, along with the new scholarly journal called *Applied Anthropology* (which was subsequently renamed *Human Organization*.) In fact, the entire profession of anthropologists in the United States was so committed to the war effort that the American Anthropological Association passed a resolution in 1941 pledging the skills and knowledge of its membership to the successful completion of the war. Although anthropologists' activities during the war years were too extensive to describe completely, the following were among some of the more notable contributions:

1. In 1939 the National Research Council established the Committee for National Morale to consider how insights from anthropology and psychology could be applied to improve national morale during wartime.
2. The National Research Council in 1940 set up the Committee on Food Habits to provide scientific research on nutritional levels and food preferences.

The findings from this research effort were instrumental in establishing the government's policy on wartime food rationing.

3. After the United States officially entered the war in late 1941, an appreciable number of distinguished anthropologists joined the war effort by providing cultural data for the Office of War Information. The national character studies conducted by Geoffrey Gorer, Margaret Mead, Ruth Benedict, and others were used to help the federal government make important decisions on the conduct of relations with our allies as well as our adversaries—the Germans, the Italians, and the Japanese.

4. Perhaps the best-known (and most controversial) activities of anthropologists during the war years involved their work with the relocation of Japanese-American interns on the West Coast. Such anthropologists as Conrad Arensberg, Alexander Leighton, and Edward Spicer both conducted research in the intern camps and served as liaisons between the Japanese-American interns and the government administrators. Even though the professional ethics of the anthropologists involved came under question (some colleagues believed they were supporting an illegal, immoral, and inhumane process), the anthropologists themselves viewed their participation as helping to alleviate a potentially more inhumane process.

Applied Anthropology During the 1950s and 1960s

In the decades after World War II, applied anthropology continued its development but in a different fashion and without much of the fervor of the war years. Whereas most of the leading U.S. anthropologists contributed their skills to government service during the war, during the 1950s and 1960s a chasm began to develop between applied and academic anthropology. This was to a large extent the result of the unprecedented growth of higher education in the years immediately following the war. The personnel shortages in academia caused by this sudden growth in higher education led many new Ph.D.'s to take teaching/research positions in departments of anthropology. In addition to the postwar availability of academic positions, the general exodus from government employment was further accelerated by an increasing disenchantment with national policy due to the politics of McCarthyism, the cold war, and the Vietnam conflict. The upshot of this, of course, was that many anthropologists turned their

attention once again to more theoretical, rather than applied, problems.

This accelerated growth of academic anthropology during the 1950s and 1960s by no means put an end to applied anthropology. Nevertheless, the way applied anthropology was practiced did undergo several significant changes. First, the relatively limited role of researcher/consultant that applied anthropologists played during the 1930s and 1940s was expanded considerably to include more implementation and intervention. According to Van Willigen (1993:28), "instead of merely providing information and an occasional recommendation, anthropologists began to take responsibility for problem solution."

A second change, closely related to the first, involved the way applied anthropologists dealt with their own values. Prior to the 1950s, most anthropologists adhered to a **value-free philosophy,** whereby they studiously tried to avoid interjecting any of their own values into their work. The earlier applied anthropologists, in an attempt to maintain their scientific objectivity, avoided making recommendations as to what policy they thought *should* be followed. During the postwar

After World War II, many anthropologists left government service and returned to positions in colleges and universities. This trend, which continued through the 1950s and 1960s, witnessed a return to more theoretical concerns.

The understandings that emerge from applied anthropological studies of peasant farming communities can be helpful in agricultural development programs.

years, however, some applied anthropologists argued that since separating personal values from one's own work was, in fact, impossible, applied anthropologists should feel free to set goals and objectives for their clients, provided they made explicit their own value positions.

This greatly expanded role of applied anthropologists during the 1950s was perhaps best illustrated by two projects, one involving a Native American group in Iowa and the other involving Peruvian peasants. In the first, under the direction of Sol Tax, six graduate students from the University of Chicago participated in the **Fox Project,** a program involving both research and intervention in the culture of the Fox Indians. Viewing many of the problems faced by the Fox Indians as stemming from their relationship to the wider community, the project participants introduced several innovations, such as adult education programs, crafts projects, and scholarships, designed to instill self-confidence and enable these people to take greater control over their lives. (For a good description of some of the consequences of this early attempt at "action anthropology," see Gearing, Netting, and Peattie 1960).

The other example of anthropological intervention during the 1950s was the **Vicos Project,** headed by Allan Holmberg and his colleagues at Cornell University (Holmberg 1971). This experimental five-year project, administered jointly with the Peruvian Institute of Indigenous Affairs, focused on transforming a nonproductive and dependent hacienda (a large farm worked by serflike peasants) into an economically productive and self-governing community. Under the careful supervision of both anthropologists and technicians, a number of innovations were introduced, including new farming technology (seeds, fertilizers, insecticides, and the like), educational programs, a hot school-lunch program, and sewing lessons for women.

Traditional suspicions among peasant farmers gradually decreased to the point where the farmers became so empowered that they began to seek communal solutions

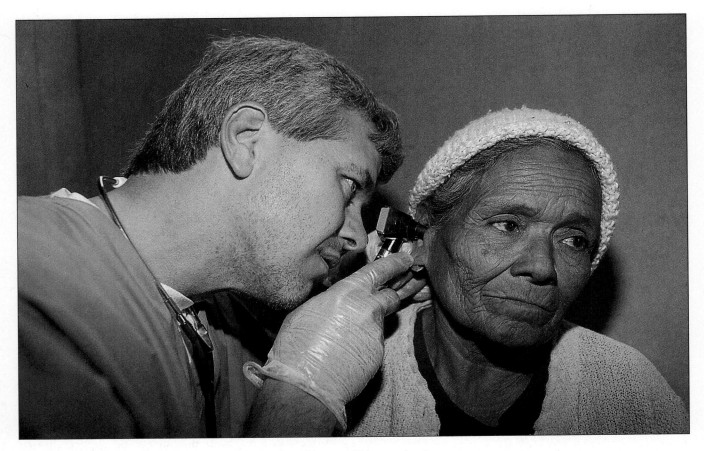

Applied anthropological research helps medical personnel provide more efficient services to peoples in developing countries. Here a Western doctor provides medical assistance in rural Honduras.

to their problems. By the end of the project, levels of family income, health standards, and education showed significant improvement. Perhaps the most dramatic consequence of the Vicos Project was that the families living on the hacienda now owned the land themselves rather than working on it as sharecroppers. The Vicos Project, then, serves as a model development project whereby planned social and economic changes are brought about by cooperative efforts between applied anthropologists, local administrators, and the indigenous people.

Applied Anthropology During the 1970s, 1980s, and Early 1990s

The 1970s, 1980s, and early 1990s have witnessed what Angrosino (1976) refers to as the **new applied anthro-** **pology,** characterized by contract work for public service agencies done away from academic campuses. Whereas many of the applied anthropologists of the 1950s and 1960s were essentially academics who were engaged in short-term applied projects, many of the new applied anthropologists are not academics but rather full-time employees of the hiring agencies. This developmental stage is largely the result of two important trends essentially external to the discipline of anthropology. First, over the past two and a half decades, the market for academic jobs has declined dramatically. The abundance of jobs that marked the 1950s and 1960s turned into a shortage of jobs during the 1970s, 1980s, and into the nineties. A second factor contributing to the new applied anthropology has been the increase in federal legislation mandating policy research that can be accomplished effectively by cultural anthropologists. For example, the National Historic Preservation Act (1966), the National Environmental Policy Act (1969), the Foreign Assistance Act (1973), and the Community Development Act (1974) all provide for policy research of a cultural nature.

As a consequence of these two factors (fewer academic jobs coupled with greater research opportunities), more anthropology Ph.D.'s are finding permanent employment outside academia. This trend has been marked by the development of various M.A. programs in applied anthropology as well as by the rise in professional organizations of applied or practicing anthropologists such as the Washington Area Association of Professional Anthropologists (WAPA), and a proliferation of state and regional organizations.

The Ethics of Applied Anthropology

All field anthropologists—both applied and theoretical—find themselves in social situations that are both varied and complex because they work with people in a number of different role relationships. They are involved with and have responsibilities to their subjects, their discipline, their colleagues both in and outside anthropology, their host governments, their own governments, and their sponsoring agencies.

Applied anthropologists must operate in an even more complex situation, for their work frequently is aimed at facilitating some type of change in the culture or social structure of the local population. Under such socially complex conditions, it is likely that the anthropologist, having to choose between conflicting values, will be faced with a number of ethical dilemmas. For example, how do you make your findings public without jeopardizing the anonymity of your informants? Can you ever be certain that the data your informants gave you will not eventually be used to harm them? How can you be certain that the project you are working on will in fact be beneficial for the target population? To what extent should you become personally involved in the lives of the people you are studying? Should you intervene to stop illegal activity? These are just a few of the ethical questions that arise when doing anthropological research. (For case materials on a wider range of ethical issues, see Appell 1978.) While recognizing that anthropologists continually face such ethical decisions, the profession has made it clear that each member of the profession ultimately is responsible for his or her own ethical conduct. According to the Statement on Ethics of the American Anthropological Association (as amended through 1976):

> It is a prime responsibility of anthropologists to anticipate these (ethical dilemmas) and to plan to resolve them in such a way as to do damage neither to those whom they study nor, insofar as possible, to their scholarly community. Where these conditions cannot be met, the anthropologist would be well advised not to pursue the particular piece of research.

A concern for professional ethics is hardly a recent phenomenon among anthropologists. As early as 1919, Franz Boas, the guru of the first generation of anthropologists in the United States, spoke out vociferously against the practice of anthropologists engaging in spying activities while allegedly conducting scientific research. Writing in the *Nation,* Boas (1919:797) commented, "A person who uses science as a cover for political spying . . . prostitutes science in an unpardonable way and forfeits the right to be classed as a scientist." While anthropologists have been aware of the ethical dilemmas they face since the beginning, the profession did not adopt a comprehensive code of behavioral standards until the 1970s. In 1971 the American Anthropological Association adopted its "Principles of Professional Responsibility" and established its Committee on Ethics, while the Society for Applied Anthropology published its Statement on Professional and Ethical Responsibilities in 1975.

Project Camelot

The publication of these professional codes of ethics in the 1970s was, to a large degree, precipitated by a controversial event that occurred in the preceding decade—**Project Camelot,** a $6 million research project funded by the U.S. Army to study the causes of civil violence in a number of countries in Asia, Latin America, Africa, and Europe. More specifically, Project Camelot was designed to gather data on counterinsurgency that would enable the U.S. Army to cope more effectively with internal revolutions in foreign countries.

The research project, which had hired the services of a number of prominent anthropologists and social scientists, was scheduled to begin its work in Latin America and later in other parts of the world. Six months after the project director was hired, however, Project Camelot was canceled by the secretary of defense. Word

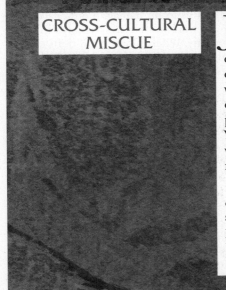

CROSS-CULTURAL MISCUE

Just as it is necessary to understand other languages, it is necessary to understand the meanings attached to various nonverbal messages or cues. A particular hand gesture, touch, glance, or body position can carry very different messages from one culture to another. And unless we are familiar with the way other cultures communicate nonverbally, we can send messages that we do not intend to send, and we can misinterpret the messages being sent by culturally different people. Condon and Yousef (1975:122) describe the case of a British professor of poetry who, while lecturing to a class at an Egyptian university, unintentionally sent a nonverbal message that had disastrous consequences:

So carried away was he in explicating a poem that he leaned back in his chair and so revealed the sole of his foot to an astonished class. To make such a gesture in Moslem society is the worst kind of insult. The Cairo newspapers the next day carried banner headlines about the student demonstration which resulted, and they denounced British arrogance and demanded that the professor be sent home.

about this clandestine operation in Chile was brought to the attention of the Chilean senate, which reacted with outrage over the apparent U.S. interference in its internal affairs.

Although the project never really got under way, it had enormous repercussions on the social sciences in general and the discipline of anthropology in particular. The heated debate among anthropologists that followed revolved around two important questions. First, was Project Camelot a legitimately objective attempt to gather social science data, or was it a cover for the U.S. Army to intervene in the internal political affairs of a sovereign nation? And second, were the participating anthropologists misled into thinking that scientific research was the project's sole objective while in fact they were really (and perhaps unwittingly) serving as undercover spies?

One of the very practical and immediate consequences of the Project Camelot controversy was the cloud of suspicion that fell over all legitimate anthropological research. For years afterwards, many U.S. anthropologists experienced difficulties trying to prove that they were not engaged in secret research sponsored by the CIA or the Department of Defense. On a personal note, five years after the demise of Project Camelot in Chile, this author was questioned on several occasions by his Kikuyu informants in Kenya (who were aware of Project Camelot) about his possible links with the United States government.

The discipline of anthropology learned an important—albeit costly—lesson from the Project Camelot affair. That is, anthropologists have a responsibility to their subjects, their profession, their colleagues, and themselves to become much more aware of the motives, objectives, and assumptions of the organizations sponsoring their research. In other words, all anthropologists have an ethical responsibility to avoid employment or the receipt of funds from any organization that would use their research findings to support policies that are inhumane, potentially harmful to the research subjects, or in any way morally questionable. Given the nature of applied anthropology, such ethical questions are particularly relevant for the simple reason that they are more likely to present themselves.

Anthropologists' Major Areas of Responsibility

The codes of professional ethics adopted by the American Anthropological Association (AAA) and later by the Society for Applied Anthropology are not appreciably different. Both codes cover the major areas of responsibilities for practicing anthropologists, including:

Responsibility to the People Studied. According to the AAA, the anthropologists' paramount responsibility is to the people they study. Every effort must be made to protect the physical, psychological, and social well-being of the people under study. The aims and anticipated consequences of the research must be clearly communicated to the research subjects so they can be in the best position to decide for themselves whether or not they wish to participate in the research. Participation is to be voluntary and should be based on the principle of informed consent. Informants should in no way be exploited, and their rights to remain anonymous must be protected.

Responsibility to the Public. Anthropologists have a fundamental responsibility to respect the dignity, integrity, and worth of the communities that will be directly affected by the research findings. In a more general sense, anthropologists have a responsibility to the general public to disseminate their findings truthfully and openly. They are also expected to make their findings available to the public for use in policy formation.

Responsibility to the Discipline. Anthropologists bear responsibility for maintaining the reputation of the discipline and their colleagues. They must avoid engaging in any research the results or sponsorship of which cannot be freely and openly reported. Anthropologists must refrain from any behavior that will jeopardize future research for other members of the profession.

Responsibility to Students. Anthropologists should be fair, candid, and nonexploitive when dealing with their students. They should alert students to the ethical problems of research and should acknowledge in print the contributions that students make to anthropologists' professional activities, including both research and publications.

Responsibility to Sponsors. Anthropologists have a professional responsibility to be honest about their qualifications, capabilities, and purposes. Before accepting employment or research funding, an anthropologist is obligated to reflect sincerely upon the purposes of the sponsoring organizations and the potential uses to which the findings will be put. Anthropologists must retain the right to make all ethical decisions in their research while at the same time reporting the research findings accurately, openly, and completely.

Responsibility to One's Own and the Host Governments. Anthropologists should be honest and candid in their relationships with both their own and the host governments. They should demand assurances that they will not be asked to compromise their professional standards or ethics as a precondition for research clearance. They should not conduct clandestine research, write secret reports, or engage in any debriefings.

Since programs designed to reduce rapid population growth must be sensitive to local cultural patterns, applied anthropology is playing an increasingly important role in family planning efforts throughout the world. Here nurses provide contraceptive information to local people at a family planning clinic in Papua New Guinea.

Some Detailed Examples

Cultural anthropologists have applied their theories, methods, and insights to a wide range of practical social problems throughout much of the present century. They have played a number of different roles as they have brought their unique anthropological skills to bear on the solution of social problems. Here we examine in some depth two specific instances of how cultural anthropology can be useful in our everyday lives. These cases show how applied anthropologists have (1) served as cultural mediators in a dispute between local Trukese villagers and the government and (2) suggested practical measures for improving a family planning clinic in Ecuador.

Applied anthropologists serve as mediators in a dispute between Trukese villagers and the local government over a government-sponsored construction project.

Whenever central governments institute programs of planned change—be it in the field of agriculture, medicine, family planning, or education— more likely than not problems will emerge with the local target population. This is because, in large measure, governments and local populations frequently have different cultural values and interests and start from a different set of cultural assumptions. In some situations, the policies and plans of the central government are so much at odds with the needs of the local population that an impasse develops. Demonstrations, petitions, and other forms of popular protest may arise in opposition to the government's plans; hostilities and mistrust may be generated in both camps; and, in some serious cases, the progress of the proposed project may come to a virtual standstill. In such situations, cultural anthropologists have been recruited to serve as intercultural mediators between the government and the local people whose lives are being affected by the government programs. In the words of Richard Salisbury (1976:255), anthropologists serve in the role of "societal ombudsmen."

In the late 1970s, the government of the Trust Territories for the Island of Truk (administered by the United States) made plans to expand the airport. The plans were drawn up, and the environmental impact study (required by U.S. law) was completed without any consultation with the local villagers. The airport expansion as proposed would have created a number of problems for the local people. For example, proposed dredging operations would destroy certain local fishing areas; the expanded runway would prevent the villagers from mooring their boats near their homes; construction would destroy several cultural/historical landmarks; and during construction, the project would generate high levels of noise and dust. The people naturally objected. Protest demonstrations and the threat of a legal injunction to stop construction convinced the government that it had a serious problem.

In an attempt to address some of the complaints of the local people, the government appointed Thomas King, an archaeological consultant in historic preservation, to mediate officially between the government and the local villagers on all matters pertaining to construction impact. While having no official status in the mediation process, King's wife, Patricia Parker, a cultural anthropologist who was conducting ethnographic research on Trukese land law, played an important role by translating the villagers' concerns into language the government officials could understand (see Parker and King 1987).

The first order of business facing this wife-husband negotiating team was to work with the villagers to develop a list of specific grievances that could serve as the basis for negotiations. Meetings were held in the various villages to allow the local people themselves to reach some consensus on the nature of their complaints against the proposed airport expansion. Parker, the cultural anthropologist fluent in the local language, attended these meetings and provided detailed outlines of the villagers' concerns to King, who in turn brought the concerns up with the responsible government officials. This wife-husband team of "cultural negotiators" worked very successfully, for they supplemented one another's strengths.

Parker and King were thus able to serve as cultural mediators or cultural brokers between the government and the local Trukese villagers. Since they came to understand the constraints and interests of both sides of the controversy, they were able to mediate from a fairly strong knowledge base, thereby avoiding a hardening of positions on either side. As a result of the efforts of these anthropological intermediaries, the following modifications were made. First, dredging operations were changed so that local fishing areas were only minimally affected; and where they were affected, the villagers received block grant compensation for the potential loss of food. Second, the government agreed to construct a new anchorage for local fishing boats. And, third, construction plans were altered so that the cultural/historic landmarks were not destroyed. In the final analysis, the use of two anthropologists to mediate between the interests of the government and those of the local Trukese villagers worked out satisfactorily for all parties concerned. The villagers were pleased with most of the modifications made in the original plans and the compensation they received. The government now has an expanded airport; although the cost of the airport was increased, its building was not delayed by litigation.

THOUGHT QUESTIONS

1. While mediating between the government and the villagers, are anthropologists responsible to the government, the Trukese villagers, or both?

2. What specialized role or roles (discussed in the chapter) did these applied anthropologists play?

3. What ethical concerns do you think the applied anthropologists faced in their work in Truk?

Anthropological study of women's attitudes and behaviors in Ecuador results in practical recommendations for maximizing the use of family planning clinics.

For the past several decades, many development experts have identified high birthrates as the major obstacle to economic development among the less-developed nations of the world. No matter how successful programs in health, education, and agriculture may be, any gains will be offset if the society is experiencing high annual population growth. Consequently, many international development organizations have given top priority to programs designed to slow population growth through family planning. Since any attempt to reduce rapid population growth must be particularly

sensitive to local cultural patterns, applied anthropologists have played an increasingly significant role in family planning programs throughout the world.

A common method of evaluating the success of family planning programs is by measuring the extent to which people actually participate in them. A family planning clinic, for example, is only as successful as the number of people who use its services. A number of significant factors may affect whether women initially attend (or return to) family planning clinics, including the women's attitudes toward contraception, the quality of the interaction with staff members, and the length of time they must wait to see a doctor. Susan Scrimshaw (1976), an applied anthropologist studying family planning clinics in Ecuador, identified another significant factor—women's modesty—that had important implications for how women felt about attending family planning clinics.

Using traditional anthropological methods, Scrimshaw collected data on sixty-five families living in Guayaquil, Ecuador, a tropical port city of approximately one million people. Scrimshaw found that small girls in Guayaquil—as in South America generally—are taught the virtues of modesty at a very early age. Even though boys are frequently seen without pants up until the age of four or five, little girls always have their genitals covered. Since girls usually reach puberty without any prior knowledge of menstruation, their first menstruation is both frightening and embarrassing. In general, then, Scrimshaw found that girls and women in Guayaquil do not have very positive attitudes about their bodies, their sexuality, or such natural bodily processes as menstruation, all of which are associated with the word *verguenza* (literally shame or embarrassment). Given this strong sense of modesty about their bodies, their sexuality, and reproduction, it is not surprising that these Ecuadorian women would feel uncomfortable even talking about contraceptives, let alone submitting to gynecological examinations.

Scrimshaw also conducted a survey on the use of family planning clinics among 2,936 women. She found that even though 74 percent of the women questioned wanted more information on birth control methods, only 20 percent of them had actually ever taken the initiative to obtain the information, and less than 5 percent of the women surveyed had ever been to a family planning clinic. When those women who had attended were asked why they never returned, nearly half (48 percent) had been influenced by *verguenza*.

Information gained through participant observation at a number of these family planning clinics helped explain why women were so reluctant to return to the clinics. Screening questions were asked by an intake worker usually within earshot of other patients. Doctors gave patients very little explanatory information while requesting a large amount of information from them, much of which was never used. The clinics provided no place for women to undress in private and did not supply the women with gowns, nor were the women properly draped during their physical exams. Even for women in the United States who were usually afforded these courtesies, gynecological exams are often uncomfortable and embarrassing. Submitting to a physical examination under conditions of minimal privacy, however, would be even more difficult for these Ecuadorian women owing to their strong cultural emphasis on feminine modesty.

On the basis of these findings on women's modesty, Scrimshaw (1976:177–78) made the following practical recommendations for maximizing the utility of family planning clinics in Guayaquil:

1. Discreetness. Interviews with women in clinics should not be within the hearing of anyone but the parties directly involved. Questions should be kept to a minimum.

2. Privacy. Wherever possible, a woman should be given privacy to undress (even a screen or curtain will help). The examining room should ensure security and privacy.

3. Awareness of modesty. A drape should be provided for a woman's legs.

4. Talk during the examination. Talking during the examination both between the doctor and other staff and the doctor and the patient should be confined to the examination. Trivial talk should be avoided.

5. Frequency of visits to the clinic and examination. Many clinics require monthly visits for examinations and supplies. In most cases, such frequent examinations are unnecessary, and supplies can be picked up every three months.

6. Male versus female physicians. All women questioned said they preferred female physicians. At this time in Latin America, this is simply not possible. Women need to be actively recruited and employed wherever possible.

These, then, are the types of recommendations that can be useful to those in charge of administering family planning clinics in Ecuador. While none of these proposed changes by themselves will make or break a family planning program, this case study does point up the need for the clinical staff to understand and acknowledge the feelings of modesty of Ecuadorian women and the role that cultural anthropologists can play in bringing this important social value to the attention of the clinical staff.

THOUGHT QUESTIONS

1. In what ways can applied anthropologists contribute to family planning programs in developing nations that are attempting to lower the birthrate and reduce population growth?

2. How does female modesty (*verguenza*) in Guayaquil shape attitudes about birth control clinics and gynecological examinations?

3. Do you think that the sex of the researcher studying family planning clinics affects the type of information gathered?

● Summary

1. Traditionally, many anthropologists have distinguished between pure anthropology (aimed at refining the discipline's theory, methods, and data) and applied anthropology (focusing on using anthropological insights toward the solution of practical social problems). For much of this century, applied anthropology has occupied a lower status within the discipline, although in recent years it has gained increasing respectability within the profession.

2. Applied anthropologists work in a wide range of settings, both at home and abroad. Moreover, they play a number of specialized roles including policy researcher, impact assessor, expert witness, trainer, planner, and cultural broker.

3. When compared to other social sciences, cultural anthropology can make a number of unique contributions as a policy science. For example, anthropologists bring to a research setting their skills as participant-observers, the capacity to view sociocultural phenomena from a holistic perspective, their regional expertise, a willingness to see the world from the perspective of the local people (emic view), and the value orientation of cultural relativism.

4. Applied anthropology was growing in activity during the 1930s, and at the beginning of the following decade, World War II provided vast opportunities for anthropologists to turn their efforts to applied projects relating to the war. The postwar boom in higher education lured many anthropologists back into academic positions during the 1950s and 1960s, but the subsequent decline in academic positions for anthropologists during the 1970s, 1980s, and early 1990s has resulted in an increase in applied types of employment outside colleges and museums.

5. Cultural anthropologists in general—but particularly applied anthropologists—face a number of ethical problems when conducting their research. One very important ethical issue to which applied anthropologists must be sensitive is whether or not the people being studied will benefit from the proposed changes. Both the American Anthropological Association and the Society for Applied Anthropology have identified areas of ethical responsibility for practicing anthropologists, including responsibilities to the people under study, the local communities, the host governments as well as their own government, other members of the scholarly community, organizations that sponsor research, and their own students.

 **Key Terms**

cultural relativism   participant-observation
emic view   Project Camelot
Fox Project   regional expertise
holistic perspective   value-free philosophy
new applied anthropology   Vicos Project

Suggested Readings

Appell, G. N. *Ethical Dilemmas in Anthropological Inquiry: A Case Book.* Waltham, Mass.: Crossroads Press, 1978. This case book presents scenarios dealing with a broad range of ethical situations faced by cultural anthropologists in the field. Over ninety different cases are presented explaining the relations of the anthropologist to informants, the host community, the host government, funding agencies, and other scholars.

Bodley, John H. *Anthropology and Contemporary Human Problems.* Palo Alto, Calif.: Mayfield Publishing, 1984. Bodley argues that many of the problems facing the world today—overconsumption, resource depletion, hunger and starvation, overpopulation, violence, and war—are inherent in the basic cultural patterns of modern industrial civilization.

Chambers, Erve. *Applied Anthropology: A Practical Guide.* Englewood Cliffs, N.J.: Prentice-Hall, 1985. A synthesis of the field of applied anthropology focusing on how the profession has responded to changing career opportunities during the present century, types of applied anthropology being conducted, and the ethical issues involved in applied anthropology.

Eddy, Elizabeth, and W. Partridge, eds. *Applied Anthropology in America* 2d ed. New York: Columbia University Press, 1987. A collection of essays by noted applied anthropologists on various aspects of applying anthropology to American society. The introductory essay by the editors provides a particularly good discussion of the development of applied anthropology in the United States.

Podolefsky, Aaron, and Peter J. Brown, eds. *Applying Anthropology: An Introductory Reader.* Mountain View, Calif.: Mayfield, 1989. A collection of essays designed to help students better understand how anthropological insights and methods can contribute to the solution of human problems. While the majority of the volume is devoted to applied cultural anthropology, eighteen segments deal with applied biological anthropology and applied archaeology.

Van Willigen, John. *Applied Anthropology: An Introduction* 2d ed. South Hadley, Mass.: Bergin and Garvey, 1993. Along with Chambers (1985), an excellent introduction to the growing field of applied anthropology for students contemplating a nonacademic career in anthropology. Topics covered include the history of applied anthropology, various intervention strategies, ethical issues, and the role of applied anthropologists in evaluation research.

Van Willigen, John, Barbara Rylko-Bauer, and Ann McElroy, eds. *Making Our Research Useful.* Boulder, Colo.: Westview Press, 1989. A recent collection of firsthand reports by applied anthropologists that tends to focus on strategies for increasing the use of anthropological research findings by policy makers.

Wulff, Robert, and Shirley Fiske, eds. *Anthropological Praxis: Translating Knowledge into Action.* Boulder, Colo.: Westview Press, 1987. A collection of writings by applied anthropologists especially for this volume on how they applied their trade to the solution of specific societal problems. Dealing with cases from both home and abroad, all of the case studies, written in the same format, discuss client and problem, process and players, results and evaluation, and the anthropological difference.

THE GROWTH OF ANTHROPOLOGICAL THEORY

CHAPTER FOUR

Men in ceremonial dress from the Ivory Coast in West Africa.

- Who have been the important theorists in cultural anthropology since the mid-nineteenth century?
- What theories have been used by anthropologists to explain cultural differences and similarities among the people of the world?
- How can anthropological data be used to make large-scale comparisons between cultures?

Differences in the way people look, speak, think, and behave have been recognized throughout the course of human history. Even in the absence of any written records we can assume that early humans recognized differences in what we now refer to as the "culture" of foreign peoples. It is possible, for example, to trace the roots of anthropological thinking back to such early classical philosophers as Herodotus, Tacitus, and Strabo, all of whom had considerable curiosity about the different customs of those with whom they came into contact.

Our understanding of foreign populations took a quantum leap forward from the fifteenth century onward as a result of the worldwide explorations set into motion by Prince Henry the Navigator of Portugal. By the early nineteenth century, the Western scholarly community had accumulated sufficient "ethnographic" data to realize that there was enormous diversity in the world's populations.

As we accumulated more and more data on the uniqueness of lifestyles of the world's population, a need arose to explain the cultural differences and similarities. This desire to account for the vast cultural variations found in the world gave rise to anthropological theories. A theory is a statement that suggests a relationship between phenomena. Theories enable us to reduce reality into an abstract set of principles, and these principles should then enable us to make sense out of a variety of ethnographic information from different parts of the world. A good theory is one that can both explain and predict. In other words, theories as models of reality enable us to bring some measure of order to a complex world.

Even when theories remain unproven, they are useful for research, for they can generate hypotheses to be tested in an empirical research investigation. In testing a hypothesis, it is possible to determine how close the

actual findings are to the expected findings. If what is found is consistent with what was expected, the theory will be strengthened; if not, the theory will likely be revised or abandoned. Anthropological theory changes constantly in response to the scientific need to develop new theories in light of the new data being brought forth continuously.

Anthropological theories attempt to answer such questions as Why do people behave as they do? and How do we account for human diversity? These questions guided the early nineteenth-century attempts to theorize and continue to be relevant today. This chapter explores—in roughly chronological order—the major theoretical schools of cultural anthropology that have developed since the mid-nineteenth century. Some of the earlier theoretical orientations (e.g., **diffusionism**) no longer attract much attention; others (e.g., **evolutionism**) have been refined and reworked into something new, while still others (e.g., **functionalism**) continue to command some popularity. It is easy, of course, to be a Monday morning quarterback by demonstrating the inherent flaws in some of the early theoretical orientations. We should keep in mind, however, that contemporary anthropological theories that may appear plausible today were in fact built on what we learned from those older theories. Table 4-1 is a summary of the theories discussed in this chapter. Table 4-2 is a time line that lists significant world events that occurred during various stages of anthropological development.

looking ahead

To see how one anthropological theory—the learned nature of culture—has been applied to a cross-cultural training program, see Applied Perspective 2 at the end of this chapter.

TABLE 4-1
Some Anthropological Theories and Their Proponents

School	Major Assumption	Principal Advocates
Evolutionism	All societies pass through a series of stages.	Tylor, Morgan
Diffusionism	All societies change as a result of cultural borrowing from one another.	Smith, Perry, Graebner, Schmidt
American historicism	The collection of ethnographic facts through direct fieldwork must precede the development of cultural theories.	Boas, Kroeber
Functionalism	Through direct field research, early twentieth-century functionalists sought to understand how parts of contemporary cultures functioned for the well-being of the individual.	Malinowski
Structural functionalism	Disregarding the search for origins, the task for the anthropologist is to determine how cultural elements function for the well-being of the society.	Radcliffe-Brown
Psychological anthropology	The central task of the anthropologist is to show the relationship between psychological and cultural variables.	Benedict, Sapir, Mead
Neoevolutionism	Cultures evolve in direct proportion to their capacity to harness energy.	White
French structuralism	Human cultures are shaped by certain preprogrammed codes of the human mind.	Levi-Strauss
Ethnoscience	The ethnographer must describe a culture in terms of native categories (emic view) rather than in terms of his/her own categories.	Sturtevant, Goodenough
Cultural materialism	Material conditions determine human consciousness and behavior.	Harris
Interpretive anthropology	Human behavior stems from the way people perceive and classify the world around them.	Geertz

Evolutionism

Trying to account for the vast diversity in human cultures, the first group of early anthropologists, writing during the mid-nineteenth century, suggested the theory of cultural evolution. The basic premise of these early anthropological theorists was that all societies pass through a series of distinct, sharply bounded evolutionary stages. We find differences in contemporary cultures because they are at different evolutionary stages of development. According to this theory, developed by **Edward Tylor** in England and **Lewis Henry Morgan** in the United States, European culture was at the top of the evolutionary ladder, while "less-developed" cultures

occupied the lower stages. The evolutionary process was thought to progress from simpler (lower) forms to increasingly more complex (higher) forms of culture. Thus, those "primitive" societies occupying the lower echelons of the evolutionary ladder need only wait an indeterminable length of time before eventually (and inevitably) rising to the top. It was assumed that all cultures pass through the same set of preordained evolutionary stages. Although both Tylor and Morgan were familiar with the writings of Darwin, they were more heavily influenced by the notions of progress set forth by such social evolutionists as Comte and Spencer.

Edward B. Tylor

Edward B. Tylor (1832–1917) was an Englishman who took issue with earlier theories that contemporary

TABLE 4-2
Social Theory in Historical Context

Milestone Works in Anthropology	What Else Was Going On in the World?
Lewis Henry Morgan, *Ancient Society* (1877) (example of 19th-century evolutionism)	• Rutherford B. Hayes elected U.S. president • Edison invents phonograph • Publication of Tolstoy's *Anna Karenina* • First Wimbledon tennis championship • Queen Victoria (England) proclaimed Empress of India
Fritz Graebner, "Kulturkreise und Kulturschichten in Ozeanien" (1903) (example of diffusionist school)	• First Tour de France bicycle race • Ford Motor Company founded • Alaskan frontier settled • First powered aircraft flown by Wright brothers • Oscar Hammerstein builds Manhattan Opera House
Franz Boas, *The Mind of Primitive Man* (1911) (example of American historicism)	• Sun Yat-sen elected president of China • Marie Curie wins Nobel Prize for chemistry • Ronald Reagan born • Roald Amundsen reaches the South Pole • Irving Berlin writes "Alexander's Ragtime Band" • Golfing great Bobby Jones wins first tourney at age nine
B. Malinowski, *Argonauts of the Western Pacific* (1922) (example of British functionalism)	• Insulin first administered to diabetic patients • Mussolini forms Fascist government in Italy • King Tut's tomb discovered at Luxor • Publication of James Joyce's *Ulysses* • Gandhi sentenced to six years imprisonment • Prohibition against alcohol in effect in United States
Margaret Mead, *Coming of Age in Samoa* (1928) (example of psychological anthropology)	• Amelia Earhart flies across Atlantic Ocean • Herbert Hoover elected U.S. president • First Mickey Mouse animated cartoon released • First scheduled TV broadcast in Schenectedy, New York • Chiang Kai-shek elected president of China • First color motion picture exhibited in Rochester, New York, by George Eastman
Leslie White, *The Evolution of Culture* (1959) (example of neo-evolutionism)	• Charles de Gaulle becomes president of France • Hawaii becomes fiftieth state in the Union • Richard Rodgers writes *The Sound of Music* • Zinjanthropus skull discovered at Olduvai Gorge • Pope John XXIII calls first Ecumenical Council since 1870 • Fidel Castro comes to power in Cuba • "The Twilight Zone" premieres on TV
Claude Levi-Strauss, *Structural Anthropology* (1963) (example of French structuralism)	• Assassination of John F. Kennedy • Release of film *Tom Jones* • Sonny Liston retains heavyweight boxing crown • Jack Nicklaus wins his first Masters tournament

(continued)

preliterate societies were examples of cultural degeneration. He posited that all cultures evolve from simple to more complex forms, passing through three basic stages (**savagery, barbarism,** and **civilization**). Even though this threefold evolutionary scheme appears terribly ethnocentric by today's standards, we must remember that it replaced the prevailing theory that explained the existence of small-scale, preliterate societies by claiming that they were people whose ancestors had fallen from grace. Hunters and gatherers, it had been argued previously, possessed simple levels of technology because their degeneration had made them

Milestone Works in Anthropology	What Else Was Going On in the World?

TABLE 4-2 (*continued*)
Social Theory in Historical Context

Milestone Works in Anthropology	What Else Was Going On in the World?
W. Sturtevant, "Studies in Ethnoscience" (1964) (example of ethnoscience)	• U.S. Post Office introduces zip codes • Kenya wins independence from Britain • Joan Baez and Bob Dylan are most popular folk singers • USSR puts first woman in space • Marilyn Monroe dies of drug overdose • Publication of Betty Friedan's *The Feminine Mystique* • James Hoffa found guilty of jury tampering • Poll tax abolished by Twenty-Fourth Amendment • U.S. Surgeon General declares cigarette smoking hazardous to health • Nelson Mandela sentenced to life imprisonment • Martin Luther King wins Nobel Peace Prize • Popular song: "I Want to Hold Your Hand" (Beatles) • Jomo Kenyatta becomes president of Kenya • China explodes its first atomic bomb • North Americans dance the Watusi at discos • Elizabeth Taylor divorces Eddie Fisher and marries Richard Burton ten days later • 796 arrested at Berkeley free speech movement protest
Marvin Harris, *Cultural Materialism* (1979)	• U.S. President Jimmy Carter, Israeli Premier Menachem Begin and Egyptian President Anwar Sadat agree on Camp David peace treaty • Pope John Paul II becomes the first pope to visit a communist country (Poland) • Soviets sign SALT II agreement with United States • John McEnroe wins his first U.S. Open tennis tourney • *Kramer vs. Kramer* (Dustin Hoffman and Meryl Streep) wins Academy Award for best picture • Sony Walkman, portable tape player with headphones, is introduced • "Knots Landing" starts a 10-year run on prime-time TV
Derek Freeman, *Margaret Mead and Samoa* (1983) (stirred a controversy over the validity of ethnographic data) Clifford Geertz, *Local Knowledge: Further Essays in Interpretive Anthropology* (1983)	• United States invades Grenada • Sally Ride becomes first U.S. woman in space • *Cats* is the biggest show on Broadway • Korean airliner shot down after straying into Soviet airspace • Michael Jackson's *Thriller* becomes best-selling album of all time (more than $12 million in sales) • Drought in Ethiopia brings famine to millions • Bombing of U.S. embassy in Beirut, Lebanon • The first person to receive an artificial heart, Barney Clark, dies 112 days after its implantation • The TV series "M*A*S*H" ends after 251 episodes • Baltimore Orioles defeat Philadelphia Phillies to win World Series

intellectually inferior to those peoples with more technological sophistication.

To counter this theological/biological interpretation of human differences, Tylor suggested the notion of progressing through a series of different cultural stages. Yet despite his insistence upon the primacy of evolution, Tylor never discounted the notion of diffusion. For example, he was particularly struck by the incredible similarities between the Aztec game of *patolli* and the game of pachisi, which originated in Asia and later became popular in Europe and the United States. Since he felt that a game so complicated could not be invented at two different times, he concluded that it must have been diffused.

Lewis Henry Morgan

While Tylor was writing in England, Lewis Henry Morgan (1818–1881) was founding the evolutionary "school" in the United States. A lawyer in Rochester, New York, Morgan was hired to represent the neighboring Iroquois Indians in a land grant dispute. After the lawsuit was resolved, Morgan conducted an ethnographic study of the Seneca Indians (one of the Iroquois group). Fascinated by the Senecas' matrilineal kinship system, Morgan circulated questionnaires and traveled fairly extensively around the United States gathering information about kinship systems found among North American Indians and elsewhere in the world. This kinship research—which some have suggested may be Morgan's most enduring contribution to the comparative study of culture—was published in *Systems of Consanguinity and Affinity* in 1871.

Morgan's most famous book was *Ancient Society*, published in 1877. In it, in keeping with the general evolutionary tenor of the times, he developed a system of classifying cultures to determine their evolutionary niche. Morgan, like Tylor, used the categories of savagery, barbarism, and civilization but was more specific in defining them according to the presence or absence of certain technological features. Moreover, Morgan subdivided the stages of savagery and barbarism into three distinct subcategories—lower, middle, and upper. Morgan defined these seven evolutionary stages—through which all societies allegedly passed—in the following way:

1. *Lower savagery*. From the earliest forms of humanity subsisting on fruits and nuts.
2. *Middle savagery*. Began with the discovery of fishing technology and the use of fire.
3. *Upper savagery*. Began with the invention of the bow and arrow.
4. *Lower barbarism*. Began with the art of pottery making.
5. *Middle barbarism*. Began with the domestication of plants and animals in the Old World and irrigation cultivation in the New World.
6. *Upper barbarism*. Began with the smelting of iron and use of iron tools.
7. *Civilization*. Began with the invention of the phonetic alphabet and writing. (1877:12)

Defense of Early Theories

The theories of the early evolutionists Tylor and Morgan have been criticized by succeeding generations of anthropologists. The nineteenth-century evolutionists have been charged with being ethnocentric, for they concluded that Western societies represented the highest levels of human achievement. They have also been criticized for being armchair speculators, putting forth grand schemes to explain cultural diversity based on fragmentary data at best. While there is considerable substance to these criticisms, we must evaluate the nineteenth-century evolutionists with an eye toward the times in which they were writing. As Kaplan and Manners (1986:39–43) remind us, Tylor and Morgan may have overstated their case somewhat because they were trying to establish what Tylor referred to as "the science of culture"—whereby human behavior was explained in terms of a secular evolutionary process rather than supernatural causes. Moreover, to fault Tylor and Morgan for not relying more heavily on empirical data overlooks two important points: (1) very little data existed in nineteenth-century libraries, and (2) both men made considerable efforts to obtain empirical data from fieldwork (at least in the case of Morgan), extensive travel, and correspondence with other scholars. Kaplan and Manners also point out:

> Faced with this shortage of data, they attempted to bridge the gaps in their evolutionary schema with logical and frequently imaginative reconstructions, i.e., by engaging in "armchair speculation." Of course, this kind of speculation is perfectly acceptable scientific procedure. The mistake the speculators often made was to assume that the empirical world was under some obligation to conform to their logical reconstructions. (1986:40)

Despite these very real methodological and theoretical shortcomings, the contributions of these early evolutionists should not be overlooked. For example, they firmly established the notion—upon which modern cultural anthropology now rests—that differences in human lifestyles are the result of certain identifiable cultural processes rather than biological processes or divine intervention. Moreover, Morgan's use of techno-economic factors to distinguish between fundamentally different types of cultures remains a viable concept. As Leacock reminds us:

> In spite of the disfavor into which Morgan's work fell, his general sequence of stages has been written into our understanding of prehistory and interpretation of archeological remains, as a glance at any introductory anthropology text will indicate. (1963:xi)

 looking ahead

For a discussion of how an understanding of evolutionary theory helped solve a problem of agriforestry in Haiti, see Applied Perspective 1 at the end of the chapter.

Diffusionism

During the late nineteenth and early twentieth centuries, the diffusionists, like the evolutionists, addressed the question of cultural differences in the world. They came up with a radically different answer to that question. The evolutionists may have overestimated human inventiveness by claiming that cultural features have arisen in different parts of the world independently of one another, due in large measure to the **psychic unity** of humankind. At the other extreme, the diffusionists held that humans were essentially uninventive. According to the diffusionists, certain cultural features were invented originally in one or several parts of the world and then spread, through the process of diffusion, to other cultures.

The diffusionists were divided essentially into two different groups—one from England and the other from Germany/Austria. The British group included, by all accounts, the most extreme proponents of the notion of diffusionism. The main proponents of this position, Sir **Grafton Elliot Smith** (1871–1937) and **W. J. Perry** (1887–1949), held that people were so incredibly uninventive that virtually all culture traits found anywhere in the world were first invented in Egypt and subsequently spread to other parts of the world. To Smith and Perry, the parallel evolution of a particular culture trait in two different parts of the world was most unlikely, if not impossible. We must bear in mind that neither Smith nor Perry was a professional anthropologist. What Smith (an Australian anatomist and surgeon) and Perry (a

Two different cultural traditions meet in Calgary, Canada. The diffusionist school of anthropology was based on the notion that borrowing things, ideas, and behavior patterns will occur when two cultures come into contact with each other.

school headmaster) had in common was that they both were uncritically enamored with early Egyptian civilization. According to their oversimplified (and inaccurate) scheme, the people of Egypt first developed agriculture and then shortly thereafter invented an elaborate complex of cultural features, which then diffused to other parts of the world. Although it was supported by no acceptable body of data, Smith and Perry's brand of diffusionism found a popular audience. This extreme diffusionist position was never widely accepted in anthropology, its limited credibility was very short-lived, and today it has been totally rejected.

Fritz Graebner (1877–1934) and Father **Wilhelm Schmidt** (1868–1954), the driving forces behind the German-Austrian group, took a far more scholarly approach to the subject of diffusion than Smith and Perry. The German-Austrians differed from their British counterparts in several important respects. First, whereas the British were concerned with the spread of individual culture traits, the German-Austrians concentrated on the diffusion of entire complexes of cultures. And second, unlike the British, who assumed that all culture traits were invented in one place (Egypt), Graebner and Schmidt suggested that a small number of different cultural complexes called culture circles (kulturkreise), had served as sources of cultural diffusion. This kulturkreise group devoted its energies to reconstructing these culture circles and demonstrating how they were responsible for worldwide patterns of cultural diffusion.

The diffusionists eventually ran their course after the first several decades of this century. To be certain, they started off with a particularly sound anthropological concept—that is, cultural diffusion—and either took it to its illogical extreme or left too many questions unanswered. Few cultural anthropologists today would deny the central role that diffusion plays in the process of culture change, but some of the early diffusionists, particularly Smith and Perry, took this essentially valid concept *ad absurdum* by suggesting that everything found in the world could ultimately be traced back to the early Egyptians. Moreover, even though they collected considerable quantities of historical data, the diffusionists were not able to prove primary centers of invention. Nor were the diffusionists able to answer a number of important questions concerning the process of cultural diffusion. For example, when cultures come into contact with one another, what accounts for the diffusion of some cultural items but not others? What are the conditions required to bring about diffusion of a cultural item? What determines the rate at which a cultural item spreads throughout a geographic region? Further-

more, diffusionists failed to even raise some questions, such as why certain traits arise in the first place. In spite of these limitations, however, the diffusionists did make a major contribution to the study of comparative cultures—that is, they were the first to point out the need to develop theories dealing with contact and interaction between cultures.

As we have seen, the nineteenth-century evolutionists and the diffusionists tried to explain why the world was inhabited by large numbers of highly diverse cultures. The evolutionists invoked the principle of evolution as the major explanatory variable. Thus, according to Tylor and Morgan, the world's cultural diversity resulted from different cultures being at different stages of evolutionary development. The diffusionists proposed a different causal variable to explain the diversity, namely, differential levels of cultural borrowing between societies. Even though these nineteenth-century "schools" offered different explanations for the diversity, they both took a deductive approach to the discipline (reasoning from the general to the specific). They started off with a general principle (either evolution or diffusion) and then proceeded to use that principle to explain specific cases. The evolutionists and diffusionists based their theories on inadequate data at best. They seemed to be more interested in universal history than in discovering how different people of the world actually lived their lives. This type of genteel armchair speculation was poignantly illustrated by the evolutionist Sir James Frazer, who, when asked if he had ever seen any of the people about whom he had written, replied, "God forbid!" (Beattie 1964:7).

American Historicism

Around the turn of the century, a reaction to this deductive approach began, led primarily by **Franz Boas** (1858–1942). Coming from an academic background in physics and geography, Boas was appalled by what he saw as speculative theorizing masquerading as science. To Boas's way of thinking, anthropology was altogether on the wrong path. Rather than dreaming up large, all-encompassing theories to explain why particular societies are the way they are, Boas wanted to turn the discipline around 180 degrees by putting it on a sound inductive footing. At that time, the discipline of anthropology simply did not have very much information about the various cultures of the world. According to

Boas, any attempt to theorize on such a small and unreliable database was absolutely premature. Instead, the discipline needed to shift its attention away from theorizing to the careful collection of empirical data on as many specific cultures as possible. The development of theories must proceed from a strong empirical database. In other words, Boas argued that anthropology as a discipline must become more inductive by proceeding from large numbers of specific (empirically based) cases to increasingly higher levels of theories and generalizations.

Boas, who was born and educated in Germany, received a doctorate in physical geography from the University of Kiel. Following his own advice to collect precise and accurate ethnographic facts, Boas conducted extensive fieldwork among the Central Eskimos during the 1880s. Interested in exploring the effects of environment on Eskimo culture, among other topics, Boas concluded that environment does not completely determine the shape a culture will take but only sets broad limits on it. In contrast to the geographic determinism that was popular at the time, Boas took the position that cultures are shaped by a number of determinants, some historical, some environmental, and some resulting from the interaction with other cultures.

These early fieldwork experiences sensitized Boas to the complexities of human cultures. Boas felt that this enormous complexity of factors influencing the development of specific cultures rendered any type of sweeping generalization, such as those proposed by the evolutionists and diffusionists, totally inappropriate. Thus, Boas and his followers insisted upon the collection of detailed ethnographic information and at the same time called for a moratorium on theorizing. Boas devoted a considerable amount of his professional energy to uncovering specific cases that would refute the generalizations being set forth by the early evolutionists. As one anthropologist put it, the strategy of Boas

> . . . required an almost total suspension of the normal dialectic between fact and theory. The causal processes, the trends, the long range parallels were buried by an avalanche of negative cases. (Harris 1968:251)

Indeed, some of Boas's more vociferous critics claimed that this antitheoretical stance was responsible for retarding the discipline of anthropology as a science. Yet, in retrospect, most commentators would agree that his experience in the areas of physics and mathematics enabled Boas to bring to the young discipline of anthropology both methodological rigor and a

Franz Boas, the teacher of the first generation of cultural anthropologists in the United States, put the discipline on a firm empirical basis.

sense of how to define problems in scientific terms. Even though Boas himself did little theorizing, he did leave the discipline on a sound empirical footing. Ruth Benedict perhaps said it best when she wrote:

> Boas found anthropology a collection of wild guesses and a happy hunting ground for the romantic lover of primitive things; he left it a discipline in which theories could be tested. (1943:61)

In addition to his insistence upon a rigorous type of empiricism, Boas also made significant contributions to the field of anthropological linguistics and took a strong stance against racism and genetic determinism.

The impact that Boas had on the discipline is perhaps most eloquently demonstrated by the long list of anthropologists that he trained. As the first anthropological "guru" in the United States, Boas trained virtually the entire first generation of American anthropologists. The list of Boas's students reads like a *Who's Who in Twentieth-Century U.S. Anthropology:* Margaret Mead, Robert Lowie, Alfred Kroeber, Edward Sapir, Melville J. Herskovits, Ruth Benedict, Paul Radin, Jules Henry, E. Adamson Hoebel, and Ruth Bunzel.

In recruiting graduate students to study anthropology with him at Columbia University, Boas from the beginning was very purposeful about attracting women into the discipline. Recognizing that male fieldworkers would be excluded from observing certain aspects of a culture by virtue of their gender, Boas felt that the discipline needed both male and female ethnographers if all of a culture was to be described. Today, compared to other academic disciplines, the discipline of anthropology has a relatively high number of women professionals, a legacy that can be traced back to Boas's methodological concerns when the discipline was in its formative period.

Functionalism

While Franz Boas was putting anthropology on a more empirical footing in the United States, **Bronislav Malinowski** (1884–1942) was proceeding inductively by establishing a tradition of firsthand data collection in the United Kingdom. After completing a doctorate in physics and mathematics in his native Poland, Malinowski read a copy of Frazer's *The Golden Bough* and became so fascinated with comparative cultures that he went to London in 1910 for postgraduate study in anthropology. When World War I broke out in 1914, Malinowski was traveling in the Pacific. When Britain went to war with Poland, Malinowski was regarded as an enemy national and was interned for the duration of the war, which he spent doing fieldwork on the Trobriand Islands in the Pacific. During what was to become one of the longest uninterrupted fieldwork experiences on record, Malinowski not only set standards for the conduct of participant-observation research but also developed an important new way of looking at cultures, known as functionalism.

Like Boas, Malinowski was a strong advocate of fieldwork. Both men learned the local language and attempted to understand a culture from the perspective of the native. They differed, however, in that Malinowski had no interest in asking how a cultural item got to be the way it is. Believing that little could be learned about the origins of small-scale societies, Malinowski

concentrated on how contemporary cultures operated, or functioned. This theoretical orientation assumed that cultures provided various means for satisfying both societal and individual needs. According to Malinowski, no matter how bizarre a cultural item might at first appear, it had a meaning and performed some useful function for the individual or the society. The job of the fieldworker is to become sufficiently immersed in the culture and language to be able to identify these functions. Malinowski's major disagreement with the early evolutionists revolved around Tylor's concept of survivals—those traits that have lost their functions. For Malinowski there were no functionless traits.

Not only do all aspects of a culture have a function, but, according to Malinowski, they are also interrelated to one another. This functionalist tenet is no better illustrated than in Malinowski's own description of the kula ring found among the Trobriand Islanders. The kula not only performs the function of distributing goods within the society, but is related to many other areas of Trobriand culture, including, among others, political structure, magic, technology, kinship, social status, myth, and social control. To illustrate, the kula involves the exchange of both ceremonial necklaces and bracelets and everyday commodities between trading partners on a large number of islands. Even though the exchanges are based on the principle of reciprocity, usually long periods of time elapse between repayments between trading partners. Gouldner (1960:174) has suggested that during these periods debtors are morally obligated to maintain peaceful relationships with their benefactors. If this is, in fact, the case, we can see how the kula ring maintains peace and thereby functions as a mechanism of social control as well as a mechanism of material exchange. Thus, by examining a cultural feature (like the kula ring) in greater depth, the ethnographer, according to this functionalist perspective, will begin to see how it is related to many other aspects of the culture and what it contributes to both individuals and society as a whole.

Malinowski's theory of culture rested on three types of individual human needs: basic needs, such as food, protection, and sexual outlets; instrumental needs, such as the need for education, law, and social control; and integrative needs, such as the need for psychological security, social harmony, and a common worldview. It is important to emphasize that Malinowski saw these as individual, not group, needs. Nevertheless, Malinowski held that every aspect of a culture functions in terms of one of these three types of needs. For Malinowski, then, culture was the instrument by which these basic human needs were met.

CROSS-CULTURAL MISCUE

Chris, a U.S. college student from Boston, was spending his junior year in Japan. During his first month as a foreign exchange student, Chris was talking to Makoto, one of his Japanese classmates, after class about their mutual interest in bicycling. Since he wanted to make new friends and learn more about cycling in Japan, Chris was pleased Makoto invited him to go cycling the following weekend. But when they met that Saturday morning for a day-long ride, Makoto had brought along six of his friends to join them. Chris was somewhat disappointed because much of Makoto's attention during the trip was taken up by his Japanese friends. Thus, Chris didn't have much of an opportunity to get to know Makoto or talk about cycling. Makoto was aware of Chris's disappointment, but could not understand it since, after all, he had gone to the trouble of organizing the trip and inviting Chris to come along. Chris was never invited on another bike outing for the rest of the year he spent in Japan.

Chris could have spared himself the hurt feelings and, no doubt, been successful at developing his friendship with Makoto if he had understood that the Japanese—who are much more group oriented than North Americans—prefer social activities that involve a group of people rather than a single pair. Even dating among Japanese college students tends to be done in groups. Rarely do people pair up into couples; instead, they go out to the movies or to dinner in larger groups.

Structural Functionalism

Another form of functionalism was developed by the British theoretician, **Alfred Reginald Radcliffe-Brown** (1881–1955). Like Malinowski, Radcliffe-Brown posited that the various aspects of a society should be studied in terms of the functions they perform. However, while Malinowski viewed functions mostly as meeting the needs of the individual, Radcliffe-Brown saw them in terms of how they contributed to the well-being of the society. Because of this emphasis on social functions rather than individual functions, Radcliffe-Brown's theory has taken the name of **structural functionalism.**

After studying anthropology at Cambridge University under W. H. R. Rivers, Radcliffe-Brown conducted fieldwork among the Andaman Islanders (a group of islands south of Burma) from 1906 to 1908 and again in Australia from 1910 to 1912. Nevertheless, with his some-what reserved and aloof temperament, he was not particularly well suited to being a fieldworker. Even though he expected extensive fieldwork from his students, he will not be remembered for his accomplishments as a brilliant participant-observer. Instead, his major contributions were as a theorist and a teacher. During much of his career, he was an "itinerant scholar," teaching at universities in Chicago, Sydney, Cape Town, and Oxford.

Malinowski and Radcliffe-Brown were similar in some basic respects. For example, both men were strong advocates of direct fieldwork as the only legitimate way of obtaining ethnographic data. Moreover, both took a synchronic approach to the discipline, that is, looking at contemporary societies in terms of the relationship between customs and institutions rather than looking for historical origins. But the theoretical constructs they used also involved some fundamental differences. Malinowski drew heavily upon the concept of *culture,* a broadly defined abstraction used in much the same way as we defined it in Chapter 2. On the other hand, Radcliffe-Brown used a unit of analysis, which he called social structure, that was more limited in scope than the concept of culture. Although not always precisely defined, social structure for Radcliffe-Brown referred to the network of social relations found among a group of people. More specifically, as one social theorist put it (Garbarino 1977:58), social structure involves the "underlying principles of organization among persons and groups in society or the set of actual roles and relationships that could be observed." Since Radcliffe-Brown called for the comparative study of contemporary social structures, he viewed the discipline of anthropology largely as comparative sociology.

Radcliffe-Brown's analysis of **mother-in-law avoidance** serves as an excellent example of his structural-functional approach. Found in a number of different parts of the world, mother-in-law avoidance refers to a custom whereby the social interaction between a man and his wife's mother is either limited in some specific way or prohibited altogether. The nature of the avoidance takes a number of different forms: prohibitions against a man having face-to-face interaction with his mother-in-law, mentioning her name in public, or eating her food. Radcliffe-Brown saw his task as one of explaining why this type of avoidance exists rather than seeking its historical origins. In other words, Radcliffe-Brown wanted to reveal what function the custom performs for the well-being of the social system.

If we were to view mother-in-law avoidance from the perspective of our own culture, we might conclude that it represents a form of hostility, for we tend to avoid people we dislike. However, based on research that he conducted among the Australian aborigines who practice an extreme form of mother-in-law avoidance, Radcliffe-Brown found that a man avoids contact with his wife's mother for exactly the opposite reason; that is, he has great respect and admiration for his mother-in-law because she was responsible for giving him his wife. The best way to ensure that nothing happens to jeopardize that relationship is to avoid, or seriously restrict, the amount of interaction that takes place. By minimizing potential conflict between family members, the custom of mother-in-law avoidance functions to ensure harmony and thus helps to maintain the social structure.

Functional Analysis

The language of functional analysis can be very confusing. The term *function* is used in a number of different ways in the English language. For example, it is sometimes used to refer to a social gathering, such as a party or a wedding ("Wasn't it a lovely social *function*?"); economists use the term synonymously with *occupation;* political scientists speak of "political functionaries"; and mathematicians use the term to mean a relationship as in the statement "X is a function of Y." Anthropologists have still another definition. For them, the function of any cultural item (i.e., thing, idea, or behavior pattern) is the *part it plays* either in satisfying individual needs or in contributing to the cohesion and perpetuation of the society. To further complicate matters, cultural anthropologists sometimes use the term *function* synonymously with use, motive, purpose, aim, utility, and intention.

The functionalist approach, most closely associated with Malinowski and Radcliffe-Brown, is based on two fundamental principles. First, the notion of **universal functions** holds that every part of a culture has a function. For example, the function of a hammer is to drive nails into wood; the function of a belief in an omnipotent god is to control people's behavior; and the function of shaking hands in the United States is to communicate nonverbally one's intentions to be friendly. The second principle, known as **functional unity,** states that a culture is an integrated whole comprising a number of interrelated parts. As a corollary to this second principle, it follows that if the parts of a culture are interconnected to one another, then a change in one part of the culture is likely to result in changes in other parts.

During the early twentieth century, when Malinowski and Radcliffe-Brown were first proposing their functionalist approach, they no doubt overstated the case for these two principles. They claimed, essentially, that *every* part of a culture had some function; there were, in other words, no functionless survivals. Moreover, in terms of the principle of functional unity, they claimed that *every* part of a culture was interconnected to every other part. Much of this exaggeration can be attributed to the exuberance of youth. Both Malinowski and Radcliffe-Brown insisted upon these two principles because they were engaged in an ideological reaction against the deductive speculations of the evolutionists and the diffusionists that had dominated the anthropological imagination up until that time.

Merton's View of Functionalism

Once functionalism was accepted into the discipline of anthropology, it appears that the functionalist anthropologists were distracted from reevaluating and revising their theory by the overwhelming demands of ethno-

As Robert Merton would suggest, the manifest function of the rain dance was to cause rain, while the latent function was to promote social cohesion.

graphic field research. Even though anthropologists such as Malinowski and Radcliffe-Brown fought vigorously for the acceptance of the functionalist approach, the most effective revisions of functionalist theory have come from sociologists, most notably Robert Merton. For example, in his influential book *Social Theory and Social Structure* (1957), Merton suggests that although every cultural item *may* have a function, it is premature to assume that every item *must* have a function. As a result, Merton proposed the notion of **dysfunction,** which tends to cause stress or imbalance within a cultural system. According to Merton, whether a cultural trait is functional or dysfunctional can be resolved only by empirical research.

In addition, Merton took issue with Malinowski and Radcliffe-Brown's notion of functional unity. While fully recognizing that all societies have some degree of functional integration, he could not accept the very high degree of interconnectedness suggested by the early British functionalists. Merton's more moderate views on the issue of functional unity are, at least in part, the result of his being a sociologist. Merton warns against applying these extreme functionalist assumptions (which may be more valid for small-scale, undifferentiated societies that anthropologists tend to study) to the large, complex societies that are most often studied by sociologists.

A fundamental weakness of the early functionalist approach was its inability to distinguish between *functions* (the part something plays as perceived by the scientific observer) and *motives* (the actual intentions of members of the group). To suggest, for example, that a rain dance functions to build social cohesion among group members does not prove that this was in fact the intention of the people themselves. It may well be that the people themselves were conducting a rain dance for the rather straightforward purpose of causing rain. At the same time, it may also be true that one of the objective consequences of the rain dance is that it does in fact promote social cohesion. Again, Merton provides some needed clarification on this point with his distinction between *manifest* and *latent* functions. Manifest functions are those objective consequences that are intended and recognized by members of the society (i.e., the function of the rain dance is to produce rain). Latent functions, on the other hand, are considerably less obvious because they are neither intended nor recognized (i.e., the function of the rain dance is to promote social cohesion among group members).

Psychological Anthropology

As early as the 1920s and 1930s, some American anthropologists became interested in the relationship between culture and the individual. Radcliffe-Brown, warning against what he called psychological reductionism, looked almost exclusively to social structure for his

Psychological anthropologists would be interested in such questions as how the television-watching habits of U.S. children affect the children's personality structures and how these personality structures, in turn, affect other parts of the culture.

explanations of human behavior. A number of Boas's students, however, were asking some theoretically powerful questions: What part do personality variables play in human behavior? Should personality be viewed as a part of the cultural system? If personality variables are part of culture, how are they causally related to the rest of the system? Wanting to relate some of the insights of Gestalt and Freudian psychology to the study of culture, the early **psychological anthropologists** looked at child-rearing practices and personality from a cross-cultural perspective. They held that child-rearing practices (which are an integral part of a culture) help shape the personality structure of the individual, which in turn influences the culture. Thus, they saw an interactive relationship between child-rearing practices, personality structure, and culture.

Edward Sapir

Although best known for his linguistic research, **Edward Sapir** (1884–1934) was very interested in the area of culture and personality. Individuals learned their cultural patterns unconsciously, Sapir suggested, in much the same way that they learn their language. Rejecting the notion that culture existed above the individual, Sapir believed that the true locus of culture was in the interaction of individuals. Even though Sapir did no di-

rect fieldwork himself in this area of culture and personality, his writings and lectures piqued the interest of others, most notably Ruth Benedict and Margaret Mead. Psychological anthropologists, who look at the relationship between culture and personality, would be interested in the question, How do the TV-watching habits of U.S. children affect children's personality structure, and how do these personality structures, in turn, affect other parts of the culture?

Ruth Benedict

One of the first to pick up on Sapir's notions was **Ruth Benedict** (1887–1948) who held that every society produces its own unique personality structure. At birth every individual is taught a limited number of traits (from a vast number of alternative traits) that the society deems important. By using a series of positive and negative sanctions, the society gradually molds the child into a certain personality type. Since all people in the society are coerced into conforming to the same set of limited traits, a group personality emerges. Thus, cultures are really individual personalities generalized to the whole culture.

Benedict presented her theory in 1934 in her widely read book *Patterns of Culture,* in which she attempted to describe cultures in terms of several major psychologi-

THE GROWTH OF ANTHROPOLOGICAL THEORY ● CHAPTER FOUR 69

cal traits. Drawing upon data from three different cultures, Benedict characterized the Kwakiutl as violent, warlike, aggressive, highly competitive, and excessive; the Zuni as restrained, unemotional, peaceful, serene, and moderate; and the Dobuans as paranoid, suspicious, and fearful. According to Benedict, these characterizations were more than mere stereotyping but rather were patterned and integrated configurations that emerged after an in-depth study of the institutions and values of these three cultural groups. In another work, *Chrysanthemum and the Sword* (1946), Benedict again characterized cultural configurations in psychological terms by suggesting that the dual traits of aesthetic preoccupation and militarism dominated Japanese culture during the 1940s.

Despite its initial popularity, *Patterns of Culture* has been widely criticized. First, Benedict was more interested in artful description than in explanation, for she never offered a reason why each society selected a limited number of traits from a vast number of possibilities. Moreover, Benedict has been accused of being somewhat overzealous in her attempt to fit the ethnographic facts into her conceptual scheme. The beautiful symmetry of Benedict's descriptions, according to Marvin Harris (1968:405), rested upon "the omission or selective de-emphasis of nonconforming data."

Margaret Mead

Margaret Mead (1901–1978), a student of both Benedict and Boas, was one of the earliest and most prolific writers in the field of culture and personality. After completing her graduate training under Boas at Columbia University, Mead became fascinated with the general topic of the emotional disruption that seemed to accompany adolescence in the United States. Certain scholars at the time (such as psychologist Stanley Hall) maintained that the stress and emotional problems found among American adolescents were a biological fact of life and occur at puberty in all societies. But Mead wanted to know if this emotional turbulence was the result of being an adolescent or being an adolescent in the United States. In 1925 she left for Samoa to try to determine if the strains of adolescence were universal (i.e., biologically based) or if they varied from one culture to another. In her first book, *Coming of Age in Samoa* (1928), Mead reported that the permissive family structure and relaxed sexual patterns among Samoans were responsible for a relatively calm adolescence. Thus, she concluded that the emotional turbu-

lence found among adolescents in the United States was culturally rather than biologically based.

Some fifty years after her original study, Mead's *Coming of Age in Samoa* was challenged on both methodological and factual grounds by Derek Freeman (1983), initiating a controversy of unprecedented proportions within the discipline (see, for example, Brady 1983). Freeman strongly took issue with Mead on both the idyllic portrait she painted of Samoan adolescence and the theory of cultural relativity on which the description

Margaret Mead devoted the early years of her long and distinguished career in anthropology to the study of cultural patterns in Samoa and New Guinea.

CROSS-CULTURAL MISCUE

Cross-cultural illiteracy has had some embarrassing consequences for North Americans engaging in international marketing. U.S. chicken entrepreneur, Frank Purdue, decided to translate one of his very successful advertising slogans into Spanish. Unfortunately, the new slogan didn't produce the desired results. The slogan "It takes a tough man to make a tender chicken" was translated into Spanish as "It takes a virile man to make a chicken affectionate."

was based. Contrary to Mead's description, Freeman's research, conducted over a forty-year period, showed a good deal of tension, aggression, and hostility in Samoan society. Freeman also argued that Samoans are not relaxed, playful, and natural about their sexuality, as Mead had contended, but are prudish and even sexually aggressive. Moreover, Freeman presented his own findings, which challenged Mead's description of Samoan families as being informal and permissive and having weak emotional bonds between parents and children, all traits that Mead claimed lead to a stress-free adolescence.

The Mead-Freeman controversy has not been resolved in any definitive way. While neither has emerged a clear winner or loser, the discipline of cultural anthropology has been forced to do some soul-searching by reexamining a number of important issues, including the importance of ethnographic restudies, the effects of one's political or social ideology on the investigation, and the very nature of scientific anthropological inquiry.

From the turbulence of adolescence, Mead next turned to the question of male and female sex roles. Based on her research among the Arapesh, Tchambuli, and Mundugumor of New Guinea, she attempted to demonstrate that there were no universal temperaments that were exclusively masculine or feminine. More specifically, Mead reported that among the Arapesh, both men and women had what Westerners would consider "feminine" temperaments (i.e., nur-

turing, cooperative, nonaggressive, maternal); both Mundugumor men and women displayed exactly the opposite traits (i.e., ruthless, aggressive, violent demeanors), while among the Tchambuli there was a complete reversal of the male-female temperaments found in our own culture. Based on these findings, Mead concluded in her *Sex and Temperament in Three Primitive Societies* (1935) that our own Western conception of "masculine" and "feminine" are not sex-linked but rather are culturally determined.

Mead's formulations, like Benedict's, were criticized on the basis of both accuracy and methodology. Being more impressionistic art than objective social science, Mead's research paid little attention to issues of sampling, controls, or experimental design. Despite these and other criticisms leveled against her, Mead's major contribution to anthropological theory was her demonstration of the importance of cultural rather than biological conditioning.

Neoevolution

As we have seen, Franz Boas and others were extremely critical of the nineteenth-century evolutionists, in part because they were accustomed to making sweeping generalizations based on little or inadequate data. Despite all of the criticisms, however, no one, including Boas himself, was able to demonstrate that cultures do not develop or evolve in certain ways over time.

Leslie White

As early as the 1930s, **Leslie White** (1900–1975), a cultural anthropologist trained in the Boasian tradition, resurrected the theories of the nineteenth-century evolutionists. It was White's position that Tylor and Morgan had developed a useful theory. Their major shortcoming was only that they lacked the data to demonstrate it.

Like Tylor and Morgan, White believed that cultures evolve from simple to increasingly more complex forms and that cultural evolution is as real as biological evolution. White's unique contribution was to suggest the cause (or driving force) of evolution, which he called his Basic Law of Evolution.

According to White,

> . . . culture evolves as the amount of energy harnessed per capita per year increases or as the efficiency of the means of putting energy to work is increased. (1959:368–69)

According to this theory, culture evolves when people are able to increase the amount of energy under their control. For most of human prehistory, while people were hunters and gatherers, the major source of energy was human power. But with the invention of agriculture, animal domestication, the steam engine, the internal combustion engine, and nuclear power, humans have used technology to dramatically increase the levels of energy at their disposal. To illustrate, the daily average energy output for a healthy man is a small fraction of a horsepower per day; the amount of energy produced from a kilo of uranium in a nuclear reactor is approximately thirty-three billion horsepower! For White, the significant equation was $C = E \times T$, where C is culture, E is energy, and T is technology. Cultural evolution, in other words, is caused by advancing levels of technology and a culture's increasing capacity to "capture energy."

Julian Steward

Another ethnologist who rejected the particularist orientation of Franz Boas in the mid-twentieth century was Julian Steward. Like White, Steward was interested in the relationship between cultural evolution and adaptation to the environment. But White's approach—which focused on the whole of human culture—was far too general for Steward. Even though Steward rejected Boasian particularism, he was equally unaccepting of approaches that were overly abstract. The main problem with White's orientation is that it cannot explain why some cultures evolve by "capturing energy" while others do not. One way of characterizing the difference between these two prominent **neoevolutionists** is that White was interested in the broad concept of culture while Steward was more interested in developing propositions about specific cultures or groups of cultures.

Steward distinguished between three different types of evolutionary thought. First, there were **unilinear evolutionists** (Tylor and Morgan), who attempted to place particular cultures into certain evolutionary stages. Second, Steward referred to White's approach as **universal evolution,** since it is concerned with developing laws that apply to culture as a whole. In contrast to these two earlier forms of evolutionism, Steward referred to his own form as **multilinear evolution,** which focuses on the evolution of specific cultures without assuming that all cultures follow the same evolutionary process.

Steward held that by examining sequences of change in different parts of the world, it would be possible to identify paths of development and some limited causal principles that would hold true for a number of societies. To test out his formulation, Steward selected areas of the world that had produced complex societies (civilizations), such as Egypt and the Middle East in the Old World and Mexico and Peru in the New World. In all of these cases, Steward tried to show certain recurring developmental sequences from earliest agriculture up through large, complex urbanized social systems. For example, in all of these instances, people were faced with relatively dry environments that required them to develop some methods of irrigation to obtain water for their fields.

Steward's approach was based on analysis of the interaction between culture and environment. That is, he argued that people who face similar environmental challenges (such as arid or semiarid conditions) are likely to develop similar technological solutions, which, in turn, lead to the parallel development of social and political institutions. Even though environment was a key variable in Steward's theory, he was not an environmental determinist, for he recognized the variety of human responses to similar environmental conditions. By focusing on the relationship between people, environment, and culture, Steward was the first and leading proponent of the study of cultural ecology.

According to Steward's theory of multilineal evolution, these irrigation systems in present-day Arizona resulted from the same set of developmental sequences experienced by ancient civilizations that created irrigation systems.

French Structuralism

No single theoretical orientation is as closely associated with a single person as **French structuralism** is associated with **Claude Levi-Strauss** (1908–). Although both Radcliffe-Brown and Levi-Strauss are called structuralists, their approaches to cultural analysis are vastly different. Whereas Radcliffe-Brown focused on identifying how the parts of a society function as a systematic whole, Levi-Strauss concentrates on identifying those mental structures that undergird social behavior. For Levi-Strauss, ethnology tends to be more psychological or cognitive than sociological.

The approach taken by Levi-Strauss draws heavily upon the science of linguistics. After assuming for decades that language is purely a learned response, many linguists in recent years have hypothesized that basic grammatical structures are preprogrammed in the human mind. Likewise, Levi-Strauss argues that certain codes programmed into the human mind are responsible for shaping cultures. Cultural differences occur, according to Levi-Strauss, because these inherent mental codes are altered by environment and history. Yet, while recognizing these surface differences, Levi-Strauss suggests that in the final analysis the mental structure of all humans is essentially the same. Although the *content* of a cultural element may vary from one society to another, the *structure* of these elements is limited by the very nature of the human mind. In essence, Levi-Strauss has reintroduced his own version of the psychic unity of humankind.

One of the basic tenets of the human mind for Levi-Strauss is that it is programmed to think in binary oppositions—or opposites. All people have a tendency to think in terms of such opposites as male-female, hot-cold, old-young, night-day, right-left, and us-them. It is these dichotomies that give shape to culture. Consider, for example, Levi-Strauss's interpretation of totemism—a belief system found in many parts of the world that states a relationship between social groupings (such as clans or lineages) and aspects of the natural world (such as plants or animals). Levi-Strauss suggests that totemic beliefs are complex mental devices that enable people to classify the units of their culture and relate them to the natural world. How totemism serves as a dual system of classification for Levi-Strauss is described by Kaplan and Manners:

> . . . when a native says he is a member of the Raccoon clan and his neighbor is a member of the Wild Cat clan, and that each of these clans is separately descended from these animals, his statement is not to be taken literally, as a biological theory of paternity. Rather he is employing a metaphor to characterize the differences and relationships between the two clans, to emphasize that these differences and relationships are similar to those that obtain in nature between the species. Totemism, then, is a kind of primitive science, an imaginative and aesthetic ordering of the world in terms of the perceived, sensible aspects of things. (1986:175)

Levi-Strauss's structuralism has been criticized for being overly abstract. Since his theories—while often brilliantly creative—are not susceptible to empirical testing, many anthropologists have rejected them. Even though French structuralism does not appeal to the more empirically oriented anthropologists, Levi-Strauss has made a major contribution by directing our attention to the relationship between culture and cognition. In all likelihood, Levi-Strauss will be remembered not for developing theories that will help explain the real world but rather for prodding other researchers to generate more imaginative hypotheses, which can then be tested through empirical research.

Ethnoscience

The theoretical approach of Levi-Strauss is similar in several significant respects to that of the **ethnoscientists,** a small but vocal group of American cultural anthropologists who gained considerable recognition during the 1950s and 1960s. For example, both approaches (1) draw on a linguistic model, (2) seek explanations in the human mind, and (3) view human behavior from a logical or rational perspective. The methods, however, are radically different. Whereas the French structuralists would infer mental structures or codes from cultural traits, the ethnoscientists (whose approach is also referred to as ethnosemantics, componential analysis, or the new ethnography) attempt to understand a culture from the point of view of the people themselves. Proponents of ethnoscience include Ward Goodenough (1956) and William Sturtevant (1964).

Aimed at making ethnographic description more accurate and replicable than in the past, ethnoscientists try to describe a culture in terms of how it is perceived, ordered, and categorized by the members of that culture rather than by imposing the categories of the ethnographer. To illustrate, traditionally Western ethnographers used categories from their own cultures for describing another culture. Whereas most middle-class North Americans would divide all of the items in the fresh produce department of a supermarket into either fruits or vegetables, people from some other cultures would not. While English speakers have different words for turquoise, aqua, and green, other cultures might include them all under a single color term, while still others would have thirty or more different words for various shades of blues and greens. Whereas some cultures have different linguistic categories for mother's brother's daughter and mother's sister's daughter, in the United States these two family members are lumped together under the single kinship category of *cousin.* Thus, the primary aim of ethnoscience is to identify the implicit rules, principles, and codes that people use to classify the things and events in their world. The ethnoscientific approach assumes that if we can describe another culture by using native categories rather than our own, we will be able to both minimize investigator bias and get a more accurate picture of reality.

By using a linguistic model, the ethnoscientists treat cultures in much the same way that linguists treat language. That is, they assume that rules, principles, and codes can be derived for cultures just as linguists derive grammatical rules and codes for languages. In developing their theoretical positions, ethnoscientists have distinguished between the **emic** and the **etic** approaches to methodology. The emic approach—which they strongly advocate—attempts to understand a culture from the native's point of view. The etic approach, on the other hand, describes a culture in terms of the categories of the ethnographer.

Despite their somewhat idealistic claims for objectivity, the ethnoscientists have been criticized on several fronts. First, while admitting that it may be desirable to get the natives' viewpoint, some anthropologists feel that one's own conditioning and preconceptions make it impossible to get into the mind of someone from another culture. In other words, since they too have cultures, all ethnographers are conceptually musclebound well before they ever get into fieldwork. Second, even if it is possible to understand another culture from the natives' point of view (that is, by using native concepts and categories), how does one communicate one's findings to others in one's own linguistic/cultural group? Third, if every ethnographer describes specific cultures using native categories, there would be little or no basis for comparing different societies. And fourth, ethnoscience is extremely time-consuming. To date, ethnoscientific studies have been completed on very specific domains of culture, such as kinship terms or color categories. The completion of an ethnoscientific study of a total culture would, no doubt, be beyond the time capabilities of a single ethnographer. Yet, while admitting the impracticality of the ethnoscientific approach, it has served as a useful reminder of a fundamentally sound anthropological principle: that people from different cultural and linguistic backgrounds organize and categorize their world in essentially different ways.

Cultural Materialism

Cultural materialism, which is most closely associated with the name of **Marvin Harris** (1968, 1979), is the theoretical position based on the concept that material conditions determine human consciousness and behavior. According to this strategy, the primary task of anthropology is to provide causal explanations for the similarities and differences in thought and behavior found among human groups. Cultural materialists do this by studying material constraints that arise from the universal needs of producing food, technology, tools, and shelter. These material constraints are distinguished from mental constraints, which include such human factors as values, ideas, religion, and aesthetics. Harris and the cultural materialists see the material constraints as the primary causal factors accounting for cultural variations.

Harris has been criticized for devaluing the importance of ideas and political activities as sources of cultural change. But rather than ignoring these nonmaterial factors, Harris suggests that they have a secondary, or less important, role in causing cultural changes/variations. Ideas and political ideologies can either accelerate or retard the process of change, but are not themselves factors of change. In other words, if the material constraints are not in place, change will not take place through the existence of ideas or ideologies alone. To illustrate this point, Harris cites the United States during the 1960s. Despite the abundance of alternative ideologies proposed by the antiestablishment countercultures in the 1960s, no significant or lasting changes took place in U.S. society because our capitalistic economic institutions were strong and consequently conditions were not ripe for change.

The cultural materialists rely heavily upon an etic research methodology—that is, one that assumes the viewpoint of the anthropologist rather than the native informant. This research strategy relies heavily on the scientific method, logical analysis, the testing of hypotheses, measurement, and quantification. Using these scientific methods, cultural materialists attempt to explain the similarities and differences between the sociocultural structures by focusing on the material/economic factors.

Although cultural materialism has much in common with the ideas of Karl Marx (in particular, a materialist interpretation), the two schools should not be equated. The cultural materialists reject the Marxist notion of dialectic materialism, which calls for destroying capitalism and empowering the working class. Cultural materialism, which doesn't have a particular political agenda, is committed to the scientific study of culture. Harris has been critical of the dialectical materialists for their ideological stance, which he suggests distorts the way they view sociocultural phenomena. Harris (1979:151) speaks of dialectical materialism as being a form of "political mysticism" that is at war with an objective science of society.

At the same time, Harris is equally critical of the cultural idealists, those anthropologists who rely on an emic approach (native's point of view) and use ideas, values, and ideologies as the major explanatory factors. As Harris (1979:285) has argued, codes and rules (a la the ethnoscientists) are not at all helpful in explaining such phenomena as poverty, underdevelopment, imperialism, population explosions, minorities, ethnic and class conflict, exploitation, taxation, private property, pollution, the military-industrial complex, political repression, crime, urban blight, unemployment, and war.

While Harris is quite willing to show the theoretical limitations of every other theoretical "school," his cultural materialist position has generated a great deal of debate in anthropology. As Applebaum (1987:297) has suggested:

> [Cultural materialism] is a theoretical orientation that vigorously asserts the need to found anthropology on a sound empirical and scientific basis. It offers a general theory, a grand theory, if you will, which is rare in a field that continues to fissure and specialize. Its originator, Marvin Harris, is steeped in a knowledge of anthropological literature and continues to offer the field new and challenging works of anthropological theory.

Interpretive Anthropology

At the opposite end of the theoretical spectrum from Marvin Harris and the cultural materialists are the **interpretive anthropologists.** The materialists emphasize the objective conditions under which people live whereas the interpretive anthropologists contend that the way people perceive (and classify) those objective material conditions are the most significant factors in human behavior. Materialists see the prime factors as the satisfaction of basic human material needs such as food, water, shelter, and wealth. The interpretive anthropologists, on the other hand, focus on such non-

The cultural materialists believe that the prime factors in determining behavior are such material phenomena as the means of food production. They would hold that certain features of Amish culture in Pennsylvania are influenced by their farming technology.

material factors as ideas, values, worldviews, and satisfying social relationships. Whereas the cultural materialists assume a scientific posture in which they are searching for generalizations about cultures, the interpretive anthropologists are more interests in describing and interpreting particular cultures. The interpretive anthropologists see cultural anthropology more as a humanistic enterprise than as a scientific one and believe it has more in common with art and literature than with biology or psychology. The major spokesperson for this interpretive school is **Clifford Geertz.**

Rather than searching for general propositions about human behavior, Geertz (1973, 1983) and the interpretive anthropologists take a more idiographic approach—that is, they seek to explain a single culture by examining how the people themselves interpret their own values and behaviors. According to the interpretive approach, cultures can best be understood by listening and recording the ways that the natives explain their own customary behavior. Thus, like the ethnoscientists, the interpretive anthropologists are strongly wedded to

the emic, rather than the etic, approach to the discipline. According to Geertz, the job of the anthropologist is not to generate laws or models that will predict human behavior, for they tend to ignore the complexity and living qualities of human cultures. Rather Geertz would have anthropology concentrate on cultural description, literature, folklore, myths, and symbols.

The interpretive orientation is admittedly relativistic and is designed to sensitize anthropologists to their own views and values as well as those of the informant. In fact, Geertz advocates combining self-knowledge with knowledge of the people under study so that the anthropologists learn something about themselves at the same time they are learning about the culture of the informant. The recent writings of Cuban-American anthropologist Ruth Behar of the University of Michigan represent an excellent example of what Geertz had in mind for interpretive anthropology. In her book *Translated Woman: Crossing the Border with Esperanza's Story* (1993), Behar tells how she started her research by listening to the life story of Esperanza, a Mexican woman she had befriended. But before long Behar found that Esperanza's life history was causing her to reflect on her own life. Anthropologist Behar began to question aspects of her own life and work, including the role of the ethnographer, the validity of comparing her life with Esperanza's, and her achievements as a relatively affluent and successful academic. The book, written from an interpretive perspective, turned out to be two life stories rather than one: Esperanza's and anthropologist Behar's. According to Behar (1993):

> Esperanza challenged me continually to articulate the connections between who she is as a visibly invisible Indian street peddler and who I am as an academic woman with a certain measure of power and privilege. Inevitably, if you sit facing another woman at the table long enough, you start to feel like mirrors for one another.

Behar has certainly captured the interpretive or humanistic approach that Geertz advocates, for by telling Esperanza's story (and her own), she was able to retain the complexity and individuality of human behavior.

Statistical Cross-Cultural Comparisons

During the first half of the twentieth century, anthropologists, following the lead of Boas in the United States and Malinowski in Britain, amassed considerable descriptive data on a wide variety of cultures throughout the world. Because of the many firsthand ethnographic field studies conducted by the students of Boas and Malinowski, by the end of World War II sufficient data existed to begin testing hypotheses and building theory inductively.

The emergence of statistical, cross-cultural comparative studies was made possible in the 1940s by **George Peter Murdock** and his colleagues at Yale University who developed a coded data retrieval system known as the **Human Relations Area Files (HRAF)**. The largest anthropological data bank in the world, HRAF has vast amounts of information organized according to over 300 different cultures and over 700 different cultural subject headings. The use of the simple coding system enables the cross-cultural researcher to access large quantities of data within minutes for the purpose of testing hypotheses and drawing statistical correlations.

The creation of HRAF has opened up the possibility for making statistical comparisons between large num-

This student is using the world's largest anthropological data bank, the Human Relations Area Files (HRAF), in its microfiche format. HRAF is now available in a CD ROM format as well.

bers of cultures. Murdock himself used HRAF as the basis for his ground-breaking book, *Social Structure* (1949), in which he compiled correlations and generalizations on family and kinship organization. In the area of culture and personality, Whiting and Child (1953) used HRAF as the database for their cross-cultural study of the relationship between child-rearing practices and adult attitudes toward illness. More recently a host of studies using HRAF data have appeared in the literature, including studies on the adoption of agriculture (Pryor 1986), sexual division of labor (White et al 1981), female political participation (Ross 1986), reproduction rituals (Paige and Paige 1981), and magico-religious practitioners (Winkelman 1987). Such cross-cultural studies are significant, for they allow us to test the universality of anthropological theories by using large numbers of ethnographic cases.

The HRAF data bank must be used carefully and in full recognition of some potential methodological pitfalls. For example, critics have noted the following:

1. Much of the data contained in HRAF varies considerably in quality.
2. The coverage is uneven, with a greater amount of material coming from non-Western cultures.
3. Since the data describe a wide range of types of social systems (such as tribes, clans, nations, ethnic groups), one can question if the units of analysis are in fact comparable.
4. There is a problem determining the independence of individual cases, for if a cultural institution that is found in ten different societies is traceable to a single source, should they all be considered independent units?
5. There is a problem of functional unity—that is, if, as the functionalists remind us, all parts of a culture are to some degree interconnected, how legitimate is it to pull a cultural trait from its original context and compare it to other cultural traits that have been similarly ripped from their contexts?

In the past several decades, however, largely through the efforts of Murdock and Raoul Naroll, most of these criticisms and objections to using HRAF for cross-cultural research have been adequately answered. Since many of these methodological shortcomings can now be overcome by thoughtful researchers, HRAF remains a powerful tool for testing universal theories and identifying causal relationships between cultural phenomena.

Some Concluding Thoughts on Anthropological Theory

This chapter has been written with distinct subheadings dividing the field of anthropological theory into neat, discrete schools. These divisions can serve as a useful device to help track, in general terms, the various emphases that anthropologists have taken since the mid-nineteenth century. However, these "schools" of anthropology are not particularly relevant categories for distinguishing between the different approaches used by contemporary anthropologists. Few anthropologists today would tie themselves to a single school or theoretical orientation such as neoevolutionist, structuralist, or functionalist. Contemporary anthropologists tend to be more eclectic and problem oriented, focusing on explaining cultural phenomena while drawing upon a wide variety of research methods and sources of data. Today it is generally recognized that many of these theoretical schools are not mutually exclusive. It is, no doubt, a sign that anthropology as a discipline is becoming mature when its practitioners reject hard-drawn lines between themselves and thereby can enrich one another's thinking.

Applied anthropology, which is thought of as being immanently practical, has traditionally been contrasted with "pure" or "theoretical" anthropology, which, by implication, has often been characterized as not being practical. It is generally thought that anthropological theories, while serving to help us make sense of the vast array of ethnographic data, contribute little to the solution of everyday human problems. But as Van Willigen (1993:17) has pointed out, theoretical anthropology and applied anthropology developed together and are intimately interrelated. It should, therefore, come as no surprise that anthropological theories can make direct contributions to solving specific societal problems. This section examines several specific case studies that used anthropological theory in some very practical ways.

Anthropological Theory

Evolution theory helps an applied anthropologist solve the problem of deforestation in Haiti.

The Agroforestry Outreach Project (AOP), a reforestation program in Haiti, is an excellent example of the role that anthropological *theory* can play in the design of a multimillion-dollar development project (see

Murray 1984, 1986, 1987). In recent decades, extreme population growth coupled with rapid urbanization has created high market demands in Haiti for both construction wood and charcoal. The cash-poor Haitian peasants have willingly attempted to meet this demand by cutting down large numbers of trees (estimated at approximately fifty million trees per year). The effect of this deforestation on the long-term health of the nation's economy can, of course, be devastating, for it not only denudes the country of trees but also significantly lowers agricultural productivity through soil erosion.

Faced with this rapid demise of trees in Haiti, the U.S. Agency for International Development (USAID) hired Gerald Murray, an anthropologist who had conducted research on land tenure and population growth in Haiti, to study the factors that would contribute to the success or failure of potential reforestation projects in Haiti. Based on his previous research, Murray outlined a set of determinants that would need to be designed into any reforestation project in Haiti if it was to be successful.

One design feature suggested by Murray seemed to fly in the face of most other government attempts at reforestation. Previous reforestation projects in Haiti (and in other parts of the world as well) took a conservationist approach, whereby peasants were rewarded for planting trees and penalized in certain ways for cutting them down. Moreover, whatever trees were planted were defined as belonging to the government or, at least, the general public. The peasants, in other words, had no particular ownership of the trees. Murray suggested, however, that peasant farmers should be given seedlings to plant on a cash-crop basis. Wood trees, in other words, were meant to be harvested and sold in much the same way as corn or beans. Murray based this radical (some might say heretical) assumption on the ethnographic reality that Haitian farmers are aggressive cashcroppers. Murray wanted to capitalize on this strong tradition of crop marketing by making wood trees just one more crop to be sold or traded.

Much to Murray's surprise, USAID not only accepted his recommendations but actually hired him to direct a $4 million reforestation project that came to be known as the Agroforestry Outreach Project (AOP). To enlist the active participation of local farmers, three barriers had to be overcome. First, farmers had to be convinced that the new seedlings could in fact reach maturity in four years. This barrier was eliminated with relative ease by showing skeptical peasants existing four-year stands of the types of tree under consideration. Second, the project had to persuade farmers that it was feasible to plant trees *along with* their food crops. By demonstrating border and row planting techniques, the AOP was able to show local farmers that they could plant 500 seedlings on only a small fraction of their land in a way that would not interfere with their other crops. And, finally, the peasant farmers needed reassurance that whatever trees they planted on their own land did in fact belong to them (rather than to the government or the project) and that they had total rights to harvest the trees. The AOP gladly relinquished all tree rights to the farmers.

The AOP, funded by USAID from 1981 through 1985, met with enormous success. The project had set for itself the goal of having 6,000 peasants plant three million trees. When the project ended, some 20 million trees had been planted by 75,000 peasant farmers! This reforestation project in Haiti was significant in that it not only drew heavily on anthropological insights but also was implemented and directed by an anthropologist. To be certain, anthropological data played an important role in the success of the project. To illustrate, an understanding of the highly individualistic land tenure system of Haitian farmers led to the decision to design a program based on a more free-enterprise (cash-cropping) basis.

The project design was also directly affected by anthropological *theory*. Murray admits that his ideas about tree planting were heavily influenced by cultural evolutionary theories. Cultural evolutionists remind us that for the overwhelming majority of prehistory, humans, who were hunters and gatherers, faced food shortages. If hunters and gatherers became too efficient in exploiting these environments, they would eventually destroy their sources of food (i.e., wild plants and animals). The cultural evolutionists also remind us that this age-old problem of food shortages was not solved eventually by a conservationist's approach to the problem but rather by domesticating plants and animals. In other words, a quantum leap in the world's food supplies occurred when people began to *produce* food (around 10,000 years ago) rather than rely on what nature had to offer.

Murray saw the connections between tree planting in Haiti and the evolutionary theory of the origins of agriculture. He rejected the conservationist approach, which would have called for raising the consciousness of peasant farmers about the ecological need for conserving trees. Instead, he reasoned that trees will reemerge in Haiti when people start planting them as a harvestable crop, in much the same way that food supplies were dramatically increased when people started planting and harvesting food crops. Thus, the theory of plant domestication—arising from the anthropological study of the beginnings of agriculture—held the key to the solution of Haiti's tree problem.

THOUGHT QUESTIONS

1. How did an anthropologist contribute to the huge success of the reforestation project in Haiti?

2. What difficulties would the project have encountered if it had used a conservationist approach?

3. Did the researcher use an ethnoscientific approach to the problem of reforestation in Haiti?

Some cultural anthropologists apply their insights to developing training programs for businesspeople preparing for international assignments.

It has become commonplace to say that the world is shrinking. To be certain, rapid technological developments in communications and transportation have brought the peoples of the world closer together in a physical sense. Yet, as we have greater contact with one another, there is an increasing need for better understandings of cultural differences. Nowhere is this

more true than in international business. Unlike in the past when U.S. businesses could stay at home and wait for their international customers to come to them, today's highly competitive world markets require Western businesspersons to conduct their business abroad, frequently in different cultures where the rules of conduct are often unfamiliar.

Recognizing the pressing need for businesspersons to familiarize themselves with the cultures of their international business partners, some cultural anthropologists have become cross-cultural trainers/consultants working for the private sector. The author of this textbook, for example, has conducted predeparture training programs for corporation officials who are about to assume international assignments. These training sessions are based on a fairly straightforward assumption: that is, the more businesspeople know about foreign business cultures, the more likely they will be to meet their professional objectives, whether they are marketing, managing, or negotiating. Although anthropologists follow a variety of formats in conducting this type of predeparture training, this author (Ferraro 1994) used a fourfold approach: (1) mastering information about a particular culture; (2) developing an understanding of the communication system (both linguistic and nonverbal) of the culture being studied; (3) gaining an awareness of one's own culture, a prerequisite for learning about other cultures; and (4) understanding certain anthropological concepts (theories) that can be applied to any cross-cultural situation.

The fourth component—the application of basic concepts to a foreign business setting—can serve as an example. This part of the training program assumes that it is impossible for anyone to master all of the facts about all of the thousands of different cultures in the world. Instead, a more conceptual approach is used, whereby the program presents useful concepts or generalizations that can be applied to any cross-cultural situation. In Chapter 2 we have discussed a number of generalizations about the concept of culture that hold true for all cultures of the world. One such generalization—*that culture is acquired through learning rather than through the genes*—has some important implications for the conduct of international business. First, it reminds the international businessperson that no cultures are "dumber" than others. To be certain, different cultures learn different things, but no cultural groups are inherently slow learners. Thus, the general understanding that people from one culture learn every bit as effectively as people from other cultures can lead to greater tolerance for cultural differences, a prerequisite for effective intercultural communication in the business arena. Second, the concept of the learned nature of culture can lead to the understanding that since we have mastered (learned) our own culture, it is possible for us to learn to function in other cultures as well. And finally, the notion that culture is learned leads to the inescapable conclusion that foreign workforces, although perhaps lacking certain job-related skills today, are perfectly capable of learning those skills in the future, provided they are exposed to culturally relevant training programs.

This, then, is the type of general concept that cultural anthropologists can apply to the world of international business. When such general concepts are combined with other specific cultural information—such as language, customs, beliefs, values, and nonverbal forms of communication—cultural anthropologists are able to develop very effective cross-cultural training programs for international businesspeople.

THOUGHT QUESTIONS

1. Why is it so important for international businesspersons to be familiar with the cultural features of those with whom they are conducting business?

2. In addition to the notion that culture is learned, what other general concepts about culture can be helpful to those engaged in international business?

3. What other professions besides international business could benefit from cross-cultural training programs?

4. What are the implications for businesspeople of the anthropological principle that culture is learned, not passed on through the genes?

Summary

1. Anthropological theory—which arose from the desire to explain the great cultural diversity in the world—enables us to reduce reality to an abstract yet manageable set of principles.

2. The first group of anthropologists used the notion of evolution to account for the vast diversity in human cultures. Such nineteenth-century evolutionists as Tylor and Morgan suggested that all societies pass through a series of distinct evolutionary stages. Though criticized by their successors for being overly speculative and ethnocentric in their formulations, these early evolutionists fought and won the battle to establish that human behavior was the result of certain cultural processes rather than biological or supernatural processes.

3. The diffusionists explained cultural differences and similarities in terms of the extent of contact cultures had with one another. The British diffusionists, represented by Smith and Perry, held that all cultural features, wherever they may be found, had their origins in Egypt. The German-Austrian diffusionists, most notably Graebner and Schmidt, took a more methodologically sound approach by examining the diffusion of entire complexes of culture.

4. In contrast to the evolutionists and diffusionists, Franz Boas took a more inductive approach to cultural anthropology, insisting on the collection of firsthand empirical data on a wide range of cultures before developing anthropological theories. Though criticized for not engaging in much theorizing himself, the meticulous attention Boas gave to the methodology put the young discipline of cultural anthropology on a solid scientific footing.

5. The British functionalists Malinowski and Radcliffe-Brown, who, like Boas, were strong advocates of fieldwork, concentrated on how contemporary cultures functioned to both meet the needs of the individual and perpetuate the society. Not only do all parts of a culture serve a function (universal functions), but they are interconnected to one another as well (functional unity) so that a change in one part of the culture is likely to bring about changes in other parts.

6. The early psychological anthropologists, most notably Ruth Benedict and Margaret Mead, were interested in exploring the relationships between culture and the individual. By examining the configuration of traits, Ruth Benedict described whole cultures in terms of individual personality characteristics. Margaret Mead's early research efforts brought her to Samoa to study the emotional problems associated with adolescence and later to New Guinea to study male and female sex roles.

7. The theory of evolution was brought back into fashion during the twentieth century by Leslie White and Julian Steward. White, like Tylor and Morgan before him, held that cultures evolve from simple to complex forms, but for White, the process of evolution was driven by his "basic law of evolution" ($C = E \times T$). Steward's major contribution was to introduce the concept of multilinear evolution, a form of evolution of specific cultures that did not assume that all cultures passed through the same stages.

8. Drawing heavily upon the models of linguistics and cognitive psychology, Claude Levi-Strauss maintains that certain codes or mental structures preprogrammed in the human mind are responsible for culture and social behavior. A fundamental tenet of Levi-Strauss's theory

is that the human mind thinks in binary oppositions—opposites that enable people to classify the units of their culture and relate them to the world around them.

9. Like the French structuralism of Levi-Strauss, the theoretical approach known as ethnoscience is cognitive in that it seeks explanations in the human mind. By distinguishing between the emic and the etic approaches to research, the ethnoscientists attempt to describe a culture in terms of how it is perceived, ordered, and categorized by members of that culture rather than by the codes/categories of the ethnographer's culture.

10. Led by Marvin Harris, the cultural materialists believe that tools, technology, and material well-being are the most critical aspects of cultural systems. Diametrically opposed to the cultural materialists is the school of interpretive anthropology, which tends to emphasize more subjective factors such as values, ideas, and worldviews. A leading debate in anthropological theory today involves the cultural materialists and the interpretive anthropologists.

11. Largely through the efforts of George Peter Murdock and his colleagues at Yale, the Human Relations Area Files (HRAF)—the world's largest anthropological data retrieval system—was developed for the purpose of testing hypotheses and building theory. The files include easily retrievable ethnographic data on over 300 different cultures organized according to more than 700 different subject headings.

Key Terms

barbarism	Human Relations
Benedict, Ruth	Area Files (HRAF)
Boas, Franz	interpretive
civilization	anthropology
cultural materialism	kulturkreise
diffusionism	Levi-Strauss, Claude
dysfunction	Malinowski, Bronislaw
emic approach	Mead, Margaret
etic approach	Morgan, Lewis Henry
ethnoscientists	mother-in-law avoidance
evolutionism	multilinear evolution
French structuralism	Murdock, George Peter
functional unity	neoevolution
functionalism	Perry, W. J.
Geertz, Clifford	psychic unity
Graebner, Fritz	psychological anthropology
Harris, Marvin	Radcliffe-Brown, A. R.

Sapir, Edward	Tylor, Edward
savagery	unilinear evolutionists
Schmidt, Wilhelm	universal evolution
Smith, Grafton Elliot	universal functions
structural functionalism	White, Leslie

 Suggested Readings

Applebaum, Herbert, ed. *Perspectives in Cultural Anthropology* Albany: State University of New York Press, 1987. An anthology of articles organized around the general theme of different nineteenth- and twentieth-century schools of anthropology including evolutionism, structural functionalism, psychological anthropology, cultural ecology, cultural materialism, sociobiology, and symbolic anthropology. Substantial introductions precede each of the twelve major sections of this reader.

Bohannan, Paul, and Mark Glazer, eds. *High Points in Anthropology*. 2nd ed. New York: Alfred A. Knopf, 1988. A collection of writings dating back to Spencer, Morgan, and Tylor tracing the history and development of cultural anthropological thought up to the present time. Each selection is prefaced by editorial background notes on the theorists and their works.

Garbarino, Merwyn S. *Sociocultural Theory in Anthropology: A Short History*. New York: Holt, Rinehart and Winston, 1977. An overview of anthropological theory in historical perspective written for beginning undergraduates.

Harris, Marvin. *The Rise of Anthropological Theory: A History of Theories of Culture*. New York: Thomas Y. Crowell, 1968. A comprehensive and critical review of the history of anthropological theory over the course of the past 200 years. Writing from his own cultural materialist perspective, Harris is quite willing to point up the theoretical and methodological shortcomings of all theoretical orientations other than his own. Despite its very opinionated stance, or perhaps because of it, this spritely written book remains the best single history of anthropological theory.

Kaplan, David, and Robert A. Manners. *Culture Theory*. Prospect Heights, Ill.: Waveland Press, 1986. Discusses the major theoretical orientations of cultural anthropology and some of the major theoretical/methodological issues facing contemporary ethnologists. In terms of depth of coverage, this volume is a nice compromise between the very brief overview of Garbarino and the more encyclopedic work of Harris.

Kardiner, Abram, and Edward Preble. *They Studied Man*. New York: Mentor Books, 1961. The authors analyze the works of ten major scientists—Darwin, Spencer, Durkheim, Freud, Kroeber, Tylor, Boas, Frazer, Benedict, and Malinowski—and their contributions to our understanding of human behavior.

METHODS IN CULTURAL ANTHROPOLOGY

Ethnographer Margaret Kieffer collects information from a Mayan Indian of Santiago Atitlan in Guatemala.

- How do cultural anthropologists conduct fieldwork?
- What types of data-gathering techniques do cultural anthropologists use?
- What are some of the very real problems faced by cultural anthropologists that make fieldwork somewhat less than romantic?

A distinctive feature of twentieth-century cultural anthropology is the reliance on **fieldwork** as the primary context in which research is conducted. To be certain, cultural anthropologists carry out their research in other contexts as well—such as libraries and museums—but they rely most heavily upon experiential fieldwork. Like professionals from any other discipline, anthropologists want to describe the basic subject matter of their discipline. They are interested in documenting the enormous variety of lifeways found among the contemporary peoples of the world. How do people feed themselves? What do they believe? How do they legitimize marriages? In addition to learning the what and the how of different cultures, cultural anthropologists are interested in explaining why people in different parts of the world behave and think the way they do. To answer these questions of both description and explanation, cultural anthropologists collect their data and test their hypotheses by means of fieldwork.

As a research strategy, fieldwork is eminently experiential. That is, cultural anthropologists collect their primary data by literally throwing themselves into the cultures they are studying. This involves living with the people they study, asking them questions, surveying their environments and material possessions, and spending long periods of time observing their everyday behaviors and interactions in their natural setting. Doing firsthand fieldwork has become a necessary rite of passage for becoming a professional anthropologist. In fact, it is very unusual to receive a Ph.D. in cultural anthropology in the United States without first having conducted fieldwork in some cultural milieu other than one's own.

The strong insistence on direct fieldwork has not always been an integral part of the discipline. As we saw in the previous chapter, most of the deductive theorizing of the nineteenth century was based on secondhand data at best and, frequently, on superficial and impressionistic writings of untrained observers. Morgan's classic work *Ancient Society* (1877), for example, was based largely on data collected by ships' captains, missionaries, explorers, and others who inadvertently came across cultures in some of the more exotic parts of the world. It wasn't until the turn of this century that fieldwork became the normative mode of collecting cultural data. As we saw, this new emphasis on fieldwork came largely at the insistence of Franz Boas.

Even though cultural anthropologists have been routinely conducting fieldwork for most of the twentieth century, they have not been particularly explicit about discussing their field techniques until quite recently. Before the 1960s, it was usual for an anthropologist to produce a book on "his" or "her" people several years after returning from a fieldwork experience. Nowhere in these books, however, was much written about field methods or the fieldwork experience itself. The reader had no way of knowing, for instance, how long the investigator stayed in the field, how many people were interviewed and observed, how samples were selected, what data-gathering techniques were used, what problems were encountered, or how the data were analyzed. Since the credibility of any ethnographic study depends, at least in part, on its methodology, cultural anthropologists since the 1960s have been producing some excellent accounts of their own fieldwork experiences. Perhaps even more significantly, a number of books and articles have appeared in recent decades that explore the methodological issues involved in designing a fieldwork study, collecting the data, and analyzing the results.

Any general discussion of how to do fieldwork is difficult for the simple reason that no two fieldwork situations are ever the same. The problems encountered while studying the reindeer herding Chukchee of Si-

THE FAR SIDE   By GARY LARSON

"Anthropologists! Anthropologists!"

beria would be quite different from those faced when studying hardcore unemployed street people in Philadelphia or rural peasant farmers in southern Greece. Even studies of the same village by the same cultural anthropologist at two different times will involve different experiences, since in the period between the two studies, both the anthropologist and the people under analysis will have changed. Despite these differences, all fieldworkers have a number of concerns, problems, and issues in common. For example, everyone entering fieldwork must make many preparations before leaving home, gain acceptance into the community, select the most appropriate data-gathering techniques, understand how to operate within the local political structure, take precautions against investigator bias, choose knowledgeable **informants,** cope with **culture shock,** learn a new language, and be willing to reevaluate his or her findings in the light of new evidence. This chapter explores these and other common concerns of the fieldworker, fully recognizing that every fieldwork situation has its own unique set of concerns, problems, and issues.

Preparing for Fieldwork

The popular image of the cultural anthropologist in the field tends to be overly romanticized. Field anthropologists are frequently envisioned going about their data collection in an idyllic setting, reclining in their hammocks while being served noncarcinogenic foods by beautiful native people. In reality, conducting anthropological fieldwork is not a carefree vacation. Like any scientific enterprise, it makes serious demands on one's time, patience, and sense of humor and requires a lot of hard work and thoughtful preparation. Although luck is a factor, the success of a fieldwork experience is usually directly proportional to the thoroughness of one's preparations.

Any fieldwork project lasting more than a few months may well require a minimum of a year's lead time. If a fieldwork project of a year or two is to be a realistic possibility, the anthropologist must attend to a number of essential matters during this preparatory period. First, since doing fieldwork is expensive, unless the would-be fieldworker is independently wealthy, it is necessary to obtain funding from a source that supports anthropological research, such as the Social Science Research Council, the National Science Foundation, or the Wenner-Gren Foundation. Financial support (covering living expenses, transportation to and from the field, and various research-related costs) is awarded on a highly competitive basis to those proposals that have the greatest scientific merit. Even though a proposal may require months of preparation, there is no guarantee that it will result in funding.

Second, prefieldwork preparation involves taking the proper health precautions. Before leaving home, it is imperative to obtain all relevant shots. A fieldworker traveling to a malaria-infested area must take malarial suppressants before leaving home. It is also prudent to obtain information about available health facilities ahead of time in case the anthropologist or a dependent becomes ill while in the field.

Third, if the field research is to be conducted in a foreign country (as most is), permission or clearance must be obtained from the host government. Since field projects usually last a year or longer, no foreign government will allow a cultural anthropologist to conduct research without prior approval. Some parts of the world are simply off-limits to U.S. citizens because of travel restrictions established by either U.S. officials or the

No two anthropological field studies are ever the same. The study of contemporary Japanese culture presents different problems and challenges to the field anthropologist than does the study of village life in the Cameroons.

governments of the particular countries. Even those countries that are hospitable to Westerners will require that the researcher spell out the nature of his or her research in considerable detail. The host governmental officials frequently want to make sure that the research will not be embarrassing or politically sensitive, that the findings will be useful, and that the researcher's presence in the host country will not jeopardize the safety, privacy, or jobs of any local citizens. Moreover, host governments often require cultural anthropologists to affiliate with local scholarly institutions to share their research experiences with local scholars and students. Sometimes, particularly in developing countries, the approval process can be painstakingly slow.

A fourth concern that must be addressed before leaving for the field is proficiency in the local language. An important part of the tradition of anthropological fieldwork is that it must be conducted using the native language. If the fieldworker is not fluent in the language of the culture to be studied, it is advisable that she or he learn the language before leaving home. That may not always be possible, however, depending on the language. Dictionaries and grammar books may not even exist for some of the more esoteric languages, and finding a native speaker to serve as a tutor while still at home may not be possible. In such cases, the ethnographer will have to learn the language after arriving in the field.

Finally, the soon-to-be fieldworker must take care of a host of personal details before leaving home. Arrangements must be made for personal possessions such as houses, cars, and pets while out of the country; decisions have to be made about what to ship and what to purchase abroad; if families are involved, arrangements need to be made for children's education; equipment such as cameras and tape recorders needs to be purchased, insured, and protected against adverse environmental conditions; up-to-date passports need to be obtained; and a schedule for transferring money needs to be worked out between one's bank at home and a convenient bank in the host country. These and other pre-departure details should put an end to the illusion that fieldwork is a romantic holiday.

Stages of Field Research

Even though no two fieldwork experiences are ever the same, every study should progress through the same basic stages:

1. Selecting a research problem
2. Formulating a **research design**   *& describe*
3. **Collecting** the **data**
4. **Analyzing** the **data**
5. **Interpreting** the **data**

Rather than describing these five stages in abstract terms, it will perhaps be more meaningful to discuss them within the framework of an actual fieldwork project (the Kenya Kinship Study, a comparative analysis of rural and urban kinship interaction in Kenya) conducted by the author during the 1970s.

Stage 1: Selecting a Research Problem

In the early part of this century, the major aim of fieldwork was to describe a culture in as much ethnographic detail as possible. In recent decades, however, fieldworkers have moved away from general ethnographies to research that is focused, more specific, and more problem oriented. That is, rather than study all of the parts of a culture equally, contemporary cultural anthropologists are more likely to examine more limited theoretical issues dealing with the relationship between various phenomena, such as the relationship between matrilineal kinship and high levels of divorce or the relationship between nutrition and food-getting strategies. This shift to a more problem-oriented approach has resulted in the formulation of hypotheses (stating the predicted relationship between two or more variables) that are then tested in a fieldwork setting.

The theoretical issue that gave rise to the Kenya Kinship Study (KKS) was the relationship between family interaction and urbanization. What happens to family patterns in the face of rapid urbanization? Throughout most of Western social thought, there has been general agreement concerning the effects of urbanization on the family. The general proposition—which has been stated in one form or another since the mid-nineteenth century—sees a "nuclearization" of the family when confronted with urbanization. This relationship is perhaps best stated by Goode, who holds that urbanization brings with it ". . . fewer kinship ties with distant relatives and a greater emphasis on the 'nuclear' family unit of couple and children" (1963:1). The purpose of the KKS was to see if this alleged relationship between family interaction and urbanization held up in Kenya, a country that has been experiencing rapid urbanization since independence in the early 1960s. The general research problem thus generated the following hypothesis: As Kenya becomes more urbanized, extended-family interaction will be replaced by more nuclear-family interaction.

Stage 2: Research Design

In this stage, the would-be fieldworker must decide how to measure the two major variables in the hypothesis: urbanization and family interaction. In this hypothesis, urbanization is the **independent variable** (that is, the variable that is capable of affecting change in the other variable), while family interaction is the **dependent variable** (that is, the variable whose value is dependent on the other variable). In our research design, the dependent variable (family interaction) is the variable we wish to explain, while the independent variable (urbanization) is the hypothesized explanation.

Both the dependent and the independent variable in our hypothesis need to be made less abstract and more concrete and measurable so as to test the validity of the relationship. One way to do this with regard to the concept of urbanization is to design the study in a comparative fashion. This involves selecting two different populations in Kenya—one rural and one urban. The urban sample selected was from Nairobi, by far the largest city in Kenya and indeed in all of East Africa; the rural sample was selected from a small village very isolated from Nairobi and having none of the major features of a city, such as large populations, industrialization, or labor specialization. If we find that rural people interact with extended-family members to a greater extent than urban people, the hypothesis is supported. If we find no appreciable differences in patterns of family interaction between rural and urban populations, the hypothesis will be rejected.

The dependent variable in our hypothesis (family interaction) also needs to be defined more specifically so that it can be measured quantitatively. The task, in other words, is to identify certain concrete measures of family interaction. The KKS identified several such measures:

1. Residence patterns (Who lives with whom in the same house or compound? How close do people live to various types of family members?)
2. Visitation patterns (How frequently do people have face-to-face interaction with various types of family members?)
3. Mutual assistance (How frequently and to what extent do people exchange gifts or money with various types of family members?)
4. Formal family gatherings (How frequently and to what extent do people get together for formal family meetings or ceremonies?)

Whenever designing a research project, it is important to control for any extraneous factors that might interfere with the testing of the hypothesis. If we are examining differences in kinship interaction between rural and urban residents, it is important that we eliminate any variable (other than degree of urbanism) that

CROSS-CULTURAL MISCUE

During the 1960s, a group of recent Cuban-American immigrants in New York City applied for and received a permit to conduct a peaceful demonstration in front of the United Nations building. On the day of the demonstration, one of the leaders approached a New York City policeman to ask which areas the demonstrators could use. As the two men talked, the police officer became increasingly uncomfortable because the demonstrator kept getting too close to him. The officer told the demonstrator to "get out of my face," but owing to language differences, the demonstrator didn't understand what the policeman wanted. The Cuban-American just continued talking to the policeman while standing closer to the officer than the officer felt was appropriate. Within minutes, the Cuban-American was arrested for threatening the safety of a law enforcement officer.

This scenario, which ended unhappily, illustrates a cross-cultural misunderstanding of a very subtle aspect of culture. According to Edward T. Hall (1966), people adhere to predictable spatial distances when communicating. In other words, how close an individual will get to another while talking is, to a large extent, dictated by one's culture. To illustrate, Hall has found that most middle-class North Americans choose a normal conversational distance of no closer than twenty-two inches from each other's mouth. For certain South American and Caribbean cultures (such as Cubans), however, the distance is approximately fifteen inches, while other cultures (in the Middle East) maintain a distance of nine to ten inches. These culturally produced spatial patterns are extremely important when communicating, or trying to communicate, with culturally different people because they are so subtle and, thus, so frequently overlooked.

The problem that occurred between the Cuban-American and the New York City policeman was that their respective cultures had different ideas about spatial distancing. The Cuban-American was attempting to establish what for him was a comfortable conversational distance of approximately fifteen inches. Unfortunately, the policeman felt threatened because his personal space, as defined by his culture, was being violated. Had either the patrolman or the Cuban-American demonstrator understood this aspect of cultural behavior, the breakdown in communication—and the arrest—could have been avoided.

might explain the differences. For example, if we select the rural sample from among the Kikuyu and the urban sample from a neighborhood comprising Luo and Nandi, the differences in family interaction may be the result of tribal affiliation (ethnicity) rather than degree of urbanization. Consequently, to control for this ethnic variable, only one ethnic group (the Kikuyu) was used for both rural and urban samples.

Stage 3: Collecting the Data

Once the hypothesis has been made concrete, the next step involves selecting the appropriate data-gathering techniques for measuring the variables. The KKS used three principal data-gathering techniques: (1) participant-observation; (2) structured interviews; and (3) day histories, a highly specific type of biographical interview that focuses on what a person did and with whom he or she interacted during a twenty-four-hour period.

Participant-observation and interviewing—two primary field techniques used by cultural anthropologists—are discussed in the next section of this chapter. Since the day history technique was developed (or at least modified) especially for this study, it is described here in some detail. Day histories were designed to answer such questions as Whom were you with? What relationship is this person to you? How much time did you spend with this person? How long have you known this person? How often do you see this person? What did you do while you were together?

Day histories were collected from fifty-three informants from the rural sample and eighty-six from the urban sample. Although there are obvious limitations to the usefulness of this technique, in the KKS, day histories generated specific and quantitative data on family interaction. Moreover, the day histories proved beneficial as an initial device for gathering general sociocultural data that were later helpful in the construction of the questionnaire used in the structured interviews.

Stage 4: Analyzing the Data

Once the day histories had been collected, their content was analyzed and the various time segments categorized into one of nine types of social interaction (e.g., interaction with nonrelatives, interaction with nuclear-family members, interaction with extended-family members). Since every hour of the twenty-four-hour period was accounted for, it was a relatively straight-

Cultural anthropologists gather information by having direct contact with the people being studied. Here anthropologist Ed Tronick makes direct observations of Efe children.

forward matter to code the various time segments according to one of the nine categories. The next step in the analysis involved simply counting the number of minutes per twenty-four-hour period that each interviewee spent in nuclear-family interaction and the number of minutes spent in extended-family interaction. From there, it was a routine mathematical exercise to determine the mean number of minutes spent in each type of family interaction for both rural and urban samples.

When all of the data were coded and analyzed, no significant differences in family interaction emerged between urban and rural samples. In fact, part of the urban sample (those having resided in Nairobi for five years or longer) showed greater involvement with extended-family members than did those in the rural sample. These data generated from the day histories

CROSS-CULTURAL MISCUE

Just as languages differ from culture to culture, so too do various forms of nonverbal communication such as hand gestures. According to Roger Axtell (1991:7):

An American teenager was hitch-hiking in Nigeria. A carload of locals passed him. The car screeched to a halt. The locals jumped out and promptly roughed up the visitor. Why? Because in Nigeria, the gesture commonly used in America for hitch-hiking (thumb extended upward) is considered a very rude signal.

were supported by data collected from 298 structured interviews and thirteen months of participant-observation. The KKS concluded that living and working within the highly differentiated, industrial urban complex of Nairobi does not in itself lead to the truncation of extended kinship ties.

Stage 5: Interpreting the Data

Like any science, the discipline of anthropology does more than simply describe cultures as the anthropologists sees them in the field. The next step—and by far the most difficult to accomplish—involves explaining or interpreting the findings. Has the original hypothesis been confirmed or rejected? What factors can be identified that will help explain the findings? How do these findings compare with the findings of other similar studies? How generalizable are the findings to wider populations? Have these findings raised methodological or theoretical issues that have bearing on the discipline? These are the types of questions that the anthropologist must wrestle with, usually after returning home from the fieldwork experience.

The significant lack of fit between the data and the so-called nuclearization hypothesis in the KKS requires an explanation. The key to understanding these data lies in the general socioeconomic status of the people under study. Kenya, like most other African nations in the 1970s, was a nation with a dual economy comprising two quite distinct categories of people. On the one

hand was a small elite with secure, well-paying jobs and potential for further upward mobility; on the other hand was everyone else, with either poor-paying jobs or no jobs at all and little or no economic mobility. The critical dimension, then, is between the haves and the have-nots, and with but a few exceptions, all of the people in both rural and urban samples clearly qualify for have-not status.

The wide range of family interaction found among both rural and urban populations in Kenya can be understood largely in terms of lack of both money and economic security. For example, in the absence of a public welfare program protecting workers against accidents, illness, old age, and unemployment, it is reasonable to expect that welfare will continue to take place along already established lines of kinship. Moreover, family ties between rural and urban areas remain high in Kenya because of two important economic facts of life: (1) the instability of employment in Kenya and (2) the Kikuyu land tenure system whereby most land remains in the hands of the lineage (extended family). Urban migrants who neglect their rural kinship obligations are, in effect, relinquishing their rights to a portion of their lineage land, which for most impoverished migrants remains their sole retreat from the insecurities of urban employment. Thus, given the national economy within which all Kikuyu are operating, the maintenance of strong kinship ties for both rural and urban residents is the most rational choice they can make.

Data-Gathering Techniques

A central problem facing any anthropological field-worker is determining the most appropriate methods for collecting data. Data collection methods that might work in one culture may be totally inappropriate for a neighboring culture. Given the wide variety of cultures in the world, it is important that anthropologists have a number of options so that they can match the appropriate set of data-gathering techniques to each fieldwork situation. There is a need to be flexible, however, for the techniques originally planned in the **research proposal** may prove to be inappropriate when actually used in the field. Whatever techniques are finally chosen, a variety of methods is needed so that the findings from one technique can be used to check the findings from others.

looking ahead

To get a clearer picture of how anthropological data-gathering techniques have been used in agricultural research in Ecuador, see Applied Perspective 1 at the end of this chapter.

Participant-Observation

It seems only fitting to start a discussion of data-gathering techniques with **participant-observation** because anthropologists use this technique more than any other single technique and more extensively than any other social science discipline (see Jorgensen 1989). Participant-observation, as the name implies, involves participating in the culture under study while making systematic observations of what is going on. When fieldworkers participate, they become as immersed in the culture as the local people permit. They share activities, attend ceremonies, eat together, and generally become part of the rhythm of everyday life. Bernard captured the complexity of participant-observation when he said:

It involves establishing rapport in a new community; learning to act so that people go about their business as usual when you show up; and removing yourself every day from cultural immersion so you can intellectualize what you've learned, put it into perspective, and write about it convincingly. If you are a successful participant observer you will know when to laugh at

what your informant thinks is funny; and when informants laugh at what you say, it will be because you *meant* it to be a joke. (1988:148)

From the very first day of fieldwork, gaining entry into the community presents a major problem for the participant-observer. Cultural anthropologists in the field can hardly expect to be accepted as soon as they walk into the local community. Under the best of circumstances, the fieldworker, as an outsider, will be an object of curiosity. More frequently, however, the beginning fieldworker encounters a wide variety of fears, suspicions, and hostilities on the part of the local people that must be overcome. There is no reason whatsoever for traditional Samoan fishermen or Pygmy hunters to understand who the fieldworker is or what he or she is doing in their midst. In his classic study of the Nuer of the Sudan, Evans-Pritchard stated that the Nuer were so suspicious and reluctant to cooperate with him that after just several weeks of fieldwork ". . . one displays, if the pun be allowed, the most evident symptoms of Nuerosis" (1940:13).

Guidelines for Participant-Observation Fieldwork. By and large, the anthropologist conducting participant-observation fieldwork for the first time has probably received little instruction in how to cope with these initial problems of resistance. For most of the twentieth century, cultural anthropology has been notorious for its sink-or-swim approach to preparing doctoral candidates for fieldwork. In a sense, it is not really possible to prepare the first-time fieldworker for every eventuality for the obvious reason that no two fieldwork situations, cultures, or ethnographers are ever the same. Nevertheless, it is possible to identify some general guidelines applicable to most fieldwork situations (see, for example, Fetterman [1989] and Jorgensen [1989]).

First, since the participant-observer is interested in studying people at the grass-roots level, it is always advisable to work one's way down the political hierarchy. Before entering a country on a long-term visa, the fieldworker must obtain **research clearance** from a high level of the national government. In the case of the KKS, research clearance came in the form of a brief letter from the office of the president of the country. Starting with this letter from the top of the political pyramid, courtesy calls were made on each descending rung of the administrative ladder (from the provincial commissioner, through the district commissioner, location chief, sub-location chief, and finally to the local headman in the area where the study was to be conducted). Since the study had the approval of the president, it was not likely that any of the administrators down the line would oppose it.

Second, when introducing oneself, it is important to select one role and use it consistently. There are any number of ways that a field anthropologist could answer the question, Who are you? (a question, incidentally, that will be asked frequently and requires an honest and straightforward answer). In my own case when conducting the KKS, I could have said, with total honesty, that I was a student (I was finishing my Ph.D.), an anthropologist (my research was funded by NIMH), Pam's husband, a visiting research associate at the University of Nairobi, Kathryn's father, a teacher, a former basketball player, Charles's son, a Catholic, and a member of the Democratic Party. Yet, many of these roles, while accurate, were not particularly understandable to the people asking the question. Even though the reason for my being there was that I was an anthropologist, that particular role has little meaning to people with little or no education. So I selected a role that was comprehensible—the role of teacher, a role that was both well-known and, much to my advantage, well-respected. Even though I wasn't teaching at the time, I had taught professionally prior to doing fieldwork, and I had planned on a career in college teaching upon returning to the States. So, when asked who I was and what was I doing there, I *always* said that I was a teacher collecting information about Kikuyu culture so that I could teach my students about it. Had I not standardized my introductions, but instead told one person that I was an anthropologist, another that I was a student, and still another that I was a teacher, the local people would have thought that either I was lying or, perhaps equally as bad, that I didn't know who I was.

A third general piece of advice for most fieldworkers is to proceed slowly. Coming from a society that places such a high value on time, most U.S. anthropologists do not take kindly to the suggestion to slow down. After all, since they will be in the field for a limited amount of time, most Western anthropologists feel that they must make the best use of that time by collecting as much data as possible. The natural tendency for most Westerners is to want to "hit the ground running." There seems to be so much to learn and so little time.

Compelling reasons exist for not rushing into asking specific questions. First, since most fieldworkers have such an imperfect understanding of the culture during the initial weeks and months, they frequently do not know enough to even ask the right types of questions. And, second, the very quality of one's data will vary directly with the amount of social groundwork the fieldworker has been able to lay. In other words, ethnographers must invest a considerable amount of time and energy establishing their credibility by allowing the local people to get to know them. For example, in the KKS, I spent the first three months engaging in a number of activities that didn't seem particularly scientific, including helping people with their tax forms, showing teenage boys how to shoot a fifteen-foot jump shot, taking people for rides in my car, sharing large quantities of food, and talking about life in the United States. None of these activities involved the gathering of cultural data about the Kikuyu, but they did help to demonstrate that I was interested in them as people rather than merely as sources of information. Once the local people got to know and trust me, they were far more willing to give me the type of cultural information that I was looking for.

Advantages of Participant-Observation. The use of participant-observation has certain methodological advantages for enhancing the quality of the data obtained. For example, people in most cultures appreciate any attempt on the part of the anthropologist to live according to the rules of their culture. No matter how ridiculous one might appear at first, the very fact that the fieldworker is sufficiently interested in the local culture to struggle with it is likely to enhance rapport. And as trust levels increase, so too do the quantity and quality of the data.

Another major advantage of participant-observation is that it enables the fieldworker to distinguish between normative and real behavior—that is, between what people *should* do and what people *actually* do. When conducting an interview, there is no way to know for certain if people behave as they say they do. The participant-observer, however, has the advantage of seeing actual behavior rather than relying on hearsay. To illustrate, as part of the KKS, urban informants were asked how frequently they traveled to their rural homelands to visit family. A number of male informants who lived up to ninety-five miles away said that they went home every weekend to visit family. Through participant-observation, however, it became apparent that many of the men remained in the city for a number of consecutive weekends. When confronted with this discrepancy between what they said they did and what they actually did, the men claimed that their families wanted them to

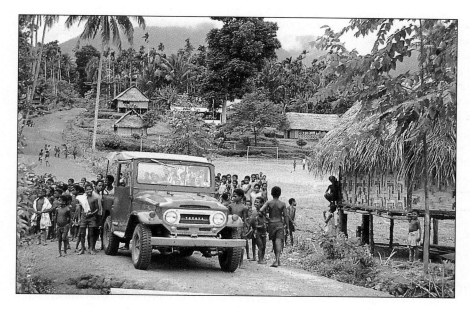

One disadvantage of participant-observation research is that the presence of the cultural anthropologist affects the very thing that is under study—people's normal way of life. Here the arrival of the anthropologist at a small village causes a stir.

come home every weekend, but it was usually too costly and time-consuming. In actual fact, they traveled home on an average of about once a month. The difference between once a week and once a month constitutes a 400 percent error in the data. Thus, the participant-observer gains a more accurate picture by seeing both actual and expected behavior.

Disadvantages of Participant-Observation. On the other hand, participant-observation poses certain methodological problems that can diminish the quality of the data. For example, the very nature of participant-observation precludes a large sample size. Because participant-observation studies are both in-depth and time-consuming, fewer people are actually studied than in studies using questionnaires or surveys. A second problem with participant-observation is that the data are often hard to code or categorize, which makes synthesizing and comparing the data difficult. Third, participant-observers face special problems when recording their observations, since it may be difficult, if not impossible, to record notes while attending a circumcision ceremony, participating in a feast, or chasing through the forest after a wild pig. The more time that passes between the event and its recording, the more details that are forgotten. And, finally, a major methodological shortcoming of participant-observation is that it has an obtrusive effect on the very thing that is being studied. Inhibited by the anthropologist's presence,

many people are likely to behave in a way they would not behave if the anthropologist was not there.

Table 5-1 reviews the advantages and disadvantages of participant-observation.

Interviewing

In addition to using participant-observation, cultural anthropologists in the field rely heavily upon ethnographic interviewing. This particular technique is used for obtaining information on what people think or feel

TABLE 5-1	
Methodological Advantages and Disadvantages of Participant-Observation	
Methodological Advantages	Methodological Disadvantages
Generally enhances rapport	Small sample size
Enables fieldworkers to distinguish actual from expected behavior	Difficult to obtain standardized comparable data
Permits observation of nonverbal behavior	Problems of recording
	Obtrusive effect on subject matter

(attitudinal data) as well as on what they do (behavioral data). Even though interviewing is used widely by a number of different disciplines to gather data (sociologists, economists, political scientists, psychologists, among others), the ethnographic interview is unique in several important respects. First, in the ethnographic interview, the interviewer and the subject almost always speak different first languages. Second, the ethnographic interview is frequently much broader in scope because it elicits information on the entire culture. Third, the ethnographic interview cannot be used alone but must be used in conjunction with other data-gathering techniques.

looking ahead

Ethnographic interviewing has been used to collect data on Skid Row men in Washington, D.C., as described in Applied Perspective 2 at the end of this chapter.

Structured and Unstructured Interviews.   Ethnographic interviews can be unstructured or structured, depending on the level of control retained by the interviewer. In **unstructured interviews,** which involve a minimum of control, the interviewer asks open-ended questions on a general topic and allows interviewees to respond at their own pace using their own words. At the other extreme, in **structured interviews,** the interviewer asks all informants exactly the same set of questions, in the same sequence, and preferably under the same set of conditions. If we can draw an analogy between interviews and school examinations, structured interviews would be comparable to short-answer questions, while unstructured interviews would be more like open-ended essay questions.

Structured and unstructured interviews have advantages that tend to complement each other. Unstructured interviews, which are usually used early in the data-gathering process, have the advantage of allowing informants to decide what is important to include in their information. In an unstructured interview, for example, an informant might be asked to describe all of the steps necessary for getting married in her or his culture. Structured interviews, on the other hand, have the advantage of producing relatively large quantities of data that are comparable and thus lend themselves well to statistical descriptions. Since structured interviews ask questions based on highly specific cultural information, they are used most commonly late in the field-

work—only after the anthropologist knows enough about the culture to ask highly specific questions.

Guidelines for Conducting Interviews.   In the past, some field anthropologists to one degree or another have made use of certain field guides that identify various aspects of culture about which questions can be asked. The two most widely used field guides are *Notes and Queries on Anthropology,* published around the turn of the century by the Royal Anthropological Institute of Great Britain and Ireland, and the more recent *Outline of Cultural Materials,* published by George Peter Murdock as part of the Human Relations Area Files. The use of such field guides can be helpful in eliciting certain aspects of culture expected but not yet observed or aspects of culture that are not particularly obvious in people's behavior (such as values, attitudes, and beliefs). The danger in relying too heavily on such field guides for structuring ethnographic interviews is, of course, that they can force one's thinking into Western categories that have no relevance for the culture being studied.

Whenever using interviewing as a data-gathering technique, the fieldworker must take certain precautions to minimize distortions in the data. For example, it has been found that respondents are more likely to answer a question negatively when it is worded negatively. The fieldworker is less likely to bias the response by phrasing a question positively (e.g., Do you smoke cigarettes?) rather than negatively (You don't smoke, do you?). Moreover, questions asked as part of a structured interview should be pretested—that is, given to a small number of people so as to eliminate ambiguous or misleading questions.

It is also important to be aware of the social situation in which the interview takes place. In other words, what effect does the presence of other people have on the validity of the data? In his field study of the Dusun, Williams explains how sex, age, or status influenced the way that his informants answered questions in front of others:

> Women would not talk about childbirth before nonrelated males, adolescent boys did not want to talk about their games before young men for fear of being held childish, and most informants did not wish to appear to be questioning the status of a senior man or woman among the onlookers. (1967:27)

Validity of the Data Collected.   The cultural anthropologist in the field must devise ways of checking the va-

Ethnographers in the field are interested in studying all segments of a population. They would include both these Bali girls in traditional dress performing a dance and their parents.

lidity of interview data. One way of accomplishing this is to ask a number of different people the same question: if all people independent of one another answer the question in essentially the same way, it is safe to assume that the data are valid. Another method of checking the validity of interview data is to ask a person the same question over a certain period of time. If the person answers the question differently, there is reason to believe that one of the responses might not be truthful. A third way of determining validity is to compare the responses with people's actual behavior. As we saw in the discussion on participant-observation, what people *do* is not always the same as what they *say they do.* And finally, since all people rationalize, project, or sublimate their fears and desires, the field anthropologist can learn something about the motives for distortions by studying the ego defense mechanisms of the informants.

looking ahead

For a discussion of the use of anthropological data gathering in the area of AIDS research, see Applied Perspective 3 at the end of this chapter.

Some Additional Data-Gathering Techniques

Even though participant-observation and interviewing are the mainstays of anthropological fieldwork, cultural anthropologists use other techniques for the collection of cultural data at various stages of the field study. These techniques include **census taking,** mapping, **document analysis, genealogizing,** and photography, although this list is hardly exhaustive.

Census Taking. Usually, early on in the fieldwork, anthropologists will conduct a census of the area under investigation. Since this involves the collection of basic demographic data—such as age, occupation, marital status, and household composition—it is relatively non-threatening to the local people. It is important for the fieldworker to update the census data continuously as he or she learns more about the people and their culture.

Mapping. Another data-gathering tool used in the early stages of fieldwork is **ethnographic mapping**—the attempt to locate people, material culture, and environmental features in space. To illustrate, anthropologists are interested in mapping where people live, where they pasture their livestock, where various public and private buildings are located, how people divide up their land, and how the people position themselves in relation to such environmental features as rivers, mountains, or oceans. While not advocating the notion of environmental determinism, we can learn a good deal about a culture by examining how people interact with their physical environment. Aerial and panoramic photography are particularly useful techniques for mapping a community's ecology.

Document Analysis. Sometimes cultural anthropologists use documentary data to supplement the information collected through interviewing and observation. Some examples of the types of documents used by anthropologists in certain circumstances are personal diaries, colonial administrative records, newspapers, marriage registration data, census information, and various aspects of popular culture, such as song lyrics, television programs, and children's nursery rhymes. As an illustration of how anthropologists can use already existing documents, consider how tax records in Swaziland from the 1920s and 1930s can shed light on the changing practice of polygyny (a man having more than one wife at a time). For example, an anthropologist might be interested in determining how the incidence of polygyny has changed over time. The present practice of polygyny can be assessed by using such direct methods as interviewing and participant-observation. To compare the present practice of polygyny with the practice in the 1930s, one needs only to consult the tax rolls, because during the decade of colonial rule (the 1930s), men were taxed according to the number of wives they had. A man with three wives paid three times as much tax as a man with one wife. The advantages of using this type of historical tax data are ob-

Anthropologist Richard Lee uses participant-observation to collect cultural data about the !Kung of Southwestern Africa.

vious: it provides large quantities of data, it is relatively inexpensive, and it is totally nonreactive or unobtrusive.

Collecting Genealogies. Another technique used to collect cultural data is the genealogical method, which involves writing down all of the relatives of a particular informant. Collecting this type of information is especially important in the small-scale, preliterate societies that anthropologists frequently study because kinship relationships tend to be the primary ones in those societies. Whereas in Western societies much of our lives are played out with nonfamily members such as teachers, employers, coworkers, and friends, in small-scale societies, people tend to interact primarily with their family. When using the genealogical method, each informant is asked to state the name and relationship of all family members and how they are referred to, addressed, and treated. From this information the anthropologist can deduce how family members interact with one another and what behavioral expectations exist between different categories of kin.

Photography. A particularly important aid to the fieldworker's collection of data is photography, both motion pictures and still photography. Recent decades have witnessed a proliferation of ethnographic films portraying a wide variety of cultures from all parts of the globe. To be certain, ethnographic films are valuable for introducing anthropology students to different cultures, but filmmaking can also have more specific uses for anthropological research. For example, motion pictures can be extremely helpful in **proxemic analysis** (i.e., how people in different cultures distance themselves from one another in normal interaction) or **event analysis** (i.e., documenting such events as circumcision ceremonies, marriages, or funerals). Owing to technological advances in recent years, video cameras (which are less expensive, more versatile, and easier to use) have largely replaced motion picture photography.

Still photography has become such an important part of anthropological research that it is hard to imagine an anthropologist in the field without a 35mm camera. As a research tool, the camera can be put to many uses. First, as mentioned above, the camera can produce a lasting record of land-use patterns and the general ecological arrangements in the community under study. Second, as the adage suggests, a picture is worth a thousand words. Still photography can document the technology of the culture (e.g., tools, weapons, machines, utensils), how these items are used (by whom, where, when, in what combinations, and so on), the sequences in a crafts process, and the sex roles associated with different items of technology. Third, photographs can be used as probes in the interview process. Since the photograph becomes the object of discussion, the informant feels less like a subject and more like an expert commentator. And finally, still photography can be used for "sociometric tracking." If a sufficient number of photos are taken of people interacting over a period of time, it is possible to quantify which members spend time with whom.

Like any data-gathering technique, still photography has certain methodological advantages and disadvantages. Among its special assets, the camera allows us to see without fatigue; the last exposure is as clear as the first. Unlike the human eye, the camera is not selective; it captures everything in any particular frame. Pho-

Photographs taken in the field can serve as probes during an interview as well as be useful sources of information.

tographs are a lasting record that can be used long after returning from the field. Photography also is often an easier and less time-consuming mode of data collection than written description.

The camera is not, however, without its liabilities. For example, some people object to being photographed, such as certain African peoples who believe that to be photographed is to have one's soul entrapped in the camera or the Amish whose religion forbids graven images. Moreover, photography can cause certain headaches for the fieldworker; for example, in some societies the person whose picture is taken may ask for multiple copies of the photo to give to friends and relatives.

Choosing a Technique. Which of the variety of techniques available for collecting cultural data will in fact be employed will depend largely on the nature of the problem being investigated. Kinship studies are likely to draw heavily upon the genealogical method, studies of child-rearing practices will rely on observation of parent-child relationships, while studies of values will most likely use the interview (a technique particularly well-suited to generating attitudinal data).

Another significant factor influencing the choice of techniques is the receptivity of the people being studied. It is important that the fieldworker carefully plan ahead of time which techniques will be appropriate to use and determine the types of data to collect as well as the segments of the population to study. If, after entering the field, the anthropologist finds that a technique is not working, he or she must be sufficiently flexible to revise the research design and sufficiently creative to come up with a workable alternative. In the final analysis, whatever technique is selected, it should be used in conjunction with other techniques. By using multiple techniques, the investigator can collect different types of data around the same set of issues which can be used to crosscheck one another.

The Pains and Gains of Fieldwork

It should be clear by now that the process of direct fieldwork is central to doing cultural anthropology. Unlike many other scientific endeavors, anthropological fieldwork inevitably has a powerful impact on the life of the practitioner. Spending a year or more at a time trying to live and work in an unfamiliar culture is bound to have life-altering consequences in some cases. The anthropologist is never quite the same after completing a fieldwork project (see DeVita 1992).

The anthropologist in the field is faced with a number of anxiety-producing situations that can be both stressful and growth inducing. In other words, both pains and gains are associated with doing anthropological fieldwork. For example, cultural anthropologists in the field rarely, if ever, follow their research design step-by-step in cookbook fashion. Despite the most meticulous research design and predeparture preparations, doing fieldwork is fraught with unanticipated difficulties. From day one in the field, the anthropologist can expect to be surprised. Napoleon Chagnon's initial encounter with the Yanomamo Indians of Venezuela and Brazil was hardly what he had anticipated:

My heart began to pound as we approached the village and heard the buzz of activity within the circular

As Napoleon Chagnon found out, gaining the confidence of the Yanomamo (known as the Fierce People) was not a simple matter.

compound . . . The entrance to the village was covered over with brush and dry palm leaves. We pushed them aside to expose the low opening to the village. The excitement of meeting my first Yanomamo was almost unbearable as I duck-waddled through the low passage into the village clearing.

I looked up and gasped when I saw a dozen burley, naked, sweaty, hideous men staring at us down the shafts of their drawn arrows! Immense wads of green tobacco were stuck between their lower teeth and lips making them look even more hideous, and strands of dark green slime dripped or hung from their nostrils—strands so long that they clung to their pectoral muscles or drizzled down their chins. We arrived at the village while the men were blowing a hallucinogenic drug up their noses. One of the side effects of the drug is a runny nose. The mucus is always saturated with the green powder and they usually let it run freely from their nostrils. My next discovery was that there were a dozen or so vicious, underfed dogs snapping at my legs, circling me as if I were to be their next meal. I just stood there holding my notebook, helpless and pathetic. Then the stench of the decaying vegetation and filth hit me and I almost got sick. I was horrified.

. . . I am not ashamed to admit that had there been a diplomatic way out, I would have ended my fieldwork then and there. I did not look forward to the next day—and months—when I would be left alone with the Indians; I did not speak a word of their language, and they were decidedly different from what I had imagined them to be. The whole situation was depressing, and I wondered why I ever decided to switch from physics and engineering in the first place. (1983:10–11, reprinted by permission)

Culture Shock

Not all introductions to fieldwork are as unsettling as this, of course. But even anthropologists whose fieldwork experience is less traumatic will undergo some level of stress caused by culture shock, the psychological disorientation caused by trying to adjust to major differences in lifestyles and living conditions. Culture shock, a term introduced by anthropologist Kalervo Oberg (1960), ranges from mild irritation to out-and-out panic. This general psychological stress occurs when the anthropologist tries to play the game of life with little or no understanding of the basic rules. The fieldworker, struggling to learn what is meaningful in the new culture, never really knows when she or he may be committing a serious social indiscretion that might severely jeopardize the entire fieldwork project.

When culture shock sets in, everything seems to go wrong. You frequently become irritated over minor inconveniences. The food is strange; people don't keep their appointments; no one seems to like you; everything seems so unhygienic; people don't look you in the eye; and on and on. Even though culture shock manifests itself in a number of symptoms, it is usually characterized by the following:

- A sense of confusion over how to behave.
- A sense of surprise, even disgust, after realizing some of the features of the new culture.
- A sense of loss of old familiar surroundings (e.g., friends, possessions, and ways of doing things).
- A sense of being rejected (or at least not accepted) by members of the new culture.
- A sense of loss of self-esteem because you don't seem to be functioning very effectively.
- A feeling of impotence at having so little control over the situation.
- A sense of doubt when your own cultural values are brought into question.

TABLE 5-2
Symptoms of Culture Shock

- Homesickness
- Boredom
- Withdrawal (e.g., spending excessive amounts of time reading; only seeing other Americans; avoiding contact with host nationals)
- Need for excessive amounts of sleep
- Compulsive eating
- Compulsive drinking
- Irritability
- Exaggerated cleanliness
- Marital stress
- Family tension and conflict
- Chauvinistic excesses
- Stereotyping of host nationals
- Hostility toward host nationals
- Loss of ability to work effectively
- Unexplainable fits of weeping
- Physical ailments (psychosomatic illnesses)

Source: L. Robert Kohls, *Survival Kit for Overseas Living* (Yarmouth, Maine: Intercultural Press Inc., 1984), p. 65.

Table 5-2 lists sixteen symptoms of culture shock. One would hope that the training to become an anthropologist and the specific preparations for entering the field would help to avoid extreme culture shock. Nevertheless, every anthropologist should expect to suffer, to some extent, from the discomfort of culture shock. Generally, the negative effects of culture shock subside as time passes, but it is likely that they will not go away completely. The very success or failure of an anthropological field project depends largely on how well the ethnographer can make the psychological adjustment to the new culture and go beyond the frequently debilitating effects of culture shock.

Biculturalism

Not all of the consequences of fieldwork, however, are negative. To be certain, culture shock is real and should not be taken lightly. Yet, despite the stress of culture shock—or perhaps because of it—the total immersion experience of fieldwork provides opportunities for personal growth and increased understanding. Spending weeks and months operating in a radically different culture can provide new insights into how the local people think, act, and feel. In the process of learning about another culture, however, we unavoidably learn a good deal about our own culture as well (see Gmelch 1994a:45–55). When we become *bicultural*—which is an inevitable consequence of successful fieldwork—we develop a much broader view of human behavior. Richard Barrett captures the essence of this bicultural perspective, which he claims enables cultural anthropologists

> . . . to view the world through two or more cultural lenses at once. They can thus think and perceive in the categories of their own cultures, but are able to shift gears, so to speak, and view the same reality as it might be perceived by members of the societies they have studied. This intellectual biculturalism is extremely important to anthropologists. It makes them continually aware of alternative ways of doing things and prevents them from taking the customs of our own society too seriously. (1991:20–21)

Recent Trends in Ethnographic Fieldwork

This chapter on ethnographic field research has taken an essentially scientific approach. We have explored the various stages of the ethnographic process as exemplified by the KKS. We have talked about generating hypotheses, dependent and independent variables, ways of maximizing the validity and reliability of the data, minimizing observer bias, and a fairly wide range of data-gathering techniques. The point of this chapter has been to demonstrate that cultural anthropology, like any scientific discipline, must strive toward objectivity by being sensitive to methodological issues.

Despite the quest for scientific objectivity, conducting ethnographic fieldwork is quite different from research in a chemistry or biology laboratory. To reflect the "native's point of view," the observer must interact with her or his subjects, thereby introducing a powerful element of subjectivity. Nowhere is the coexistence of subjectivity and objectivity more evident than in the widely used data-gathering technique of participant-observation. Participation implies a certain level of emotional involvement in the lives of the people being studied. Making systematic observations, on the other hand, requires emotional detachment. Participant-observers are expected to be emotionally engaged participants while at the same time being dispassionate observers. Participant-observation, by its very nature, carries with it an internal source of tension, for it is incompatible to sympathize with those people whom you are trying to describe with scientific objectivity. Traditionally, most cultural anthropologists have resolved this objectivity/subjectivity tension by reporting their findings in scientific terms. That is, they would describe customs, norms, and other cultural features in general terms without discussing specific informants or their own interactions with them.

Since the 1970s, however, a new type of ethnography has emerged that has become known as "narrative ethnography." Being less concerned with traditional notions of scientific objectivity, the narrative ethnographers are interested in co-producing ethnographic knowledge by focusing on the *interaction* between themselves and their informants. These narrative ethnographers are no longer interested in producing descriptive accounts of another culture written with scientific detachment. Rather, their ethnographies are conscious reflections on how their own personalities and cultural influences combine with the personal encounters with their informants to produce cultural data. According to Barbara Tedlock (1991:77–78):

> The world, in a narrative ethnography, is re-presented as perceived by a situated narrator, who is also present as a character in the story that reveals his own personality. This enables the reader to identify the consciousness which has selected and shaped the experiences within the text. . . . [N]arrative ethnographies focus . . . on the character and process of the ethnographic dialogue or encounter.

Thus, in the narrative ethnography the dialogue between ethnographer and informant becomes an integral part of the field experience as well as of the written ethnography.

The narrative approach to ethnography is most closely associated with the interpretative school of anthropology. To be certain, narrative ethnographies such as Ruth Behar's study of Esperanza (discussed in the previous chapter) are still the exception to the rule. Most ethnographers would agree that the narrative approach can be taken too far when we wind up learning more about the anthropologist than the culture. Nevertheless, this new approach to ethnographic research represents an important trend in recent years that raises a number of important questions for the fieldworker, including What is the best way to represent cultural reality?

As this chapter has demonstrated, cultural anthropology has developed a set of methods and data-gathering strategies that set it apart from other social science disciplines. Although anthropological fieldwork draws upon a wide number of techniques and strategies, its primary characteristic is its experiential nature— that is, cultural anthropologists conduct their research in a firsthand manner through participant-observation by interacting with the people being studied. According to Edgerton and Langness, the anthropologist in the field "shares in the people's day-to-day activities, watches as they eat, fight, and dance, listens to their commonplace and exciting conversations, and slowly begins to live and understand life as they do" (1974:3). This section examines how the research methods of cultural anthropology have been used to aid in the solution of pressing social problems. Specifically, the first case study discusses how anthropological data-gathering techniques can contribute to programs of agricultural reform in Ecuador; the second case study shows how ethnographic interviewing can be helpful in rehab programs for Skid Row alcoholics; and the final case study discusses how anthropological methods can contribute to a solution to our most serious health problem—the AIDS epidemic.

applied PERSPECTIVE

Anthropological Methods

Anthropological research on farming practices in Ecuador can contribute significantly to programs of agricultural reform.

As a technique for studying human behavior, participant-observation has relevance for and can be applied to a vast number of domains of human society. One such area is agricultural development in developing countries. National and international foreign assistance organizations spend hundreds of millions of dollars each year on programs designed to improve levels of agricultural productivity among the developing nations of the world. Before positive (i.e., more productive) changes in traditional farming technologies can be made, research needs to be conducted on (1) the nature of the traditional farming practices; (2) certain technical issues of farming, such as soil composition and climatic conditions; and (3) the psychological, political, and social obstacles to change. In recent years, however, the effectiveness of farming research in developing countries has been called into question.

It has been suggested (Tripp 1985) that cultural anthropologists—with their unique methods and perspective—can make significant contributions to strengthening farming research in developing countries that will eventually lead to more successful programs of agricultural reform. To be certain, this holistic approach to cultural analysis, which has been a hallmark of the anthropological perspective, can inform agricultural researchers by reminding them of "social context" and how farming is interrelated to other parts of the system. And, of course, many areas of anthropological expertise impact the decision-making process of farmers and, consequently, the likelihood of their accepting or rejecting certain agricultural reforms. These include the division of household labor, land allocation, food preferences, crop marketing strategies, and the allocation of food supplies within the household, among other things. But, in addition to these substantive contributions, we are interested here in the methodological contributions that cultural anthropology can make to the process of farm research in the developing world.

In a recent article, Tripp (1985) showed how a type of agricultural research called **on-farm research** (OFR) has drawn heavily upon the use of anthropological field methods. Although in past decades agricultural research was based largely on lengthy surveys and questionnaires, this approach has been criticized on the grounds that it is neither cost-effective nor particularly convenient for development planners to translate into practical terms. A new research strategy—designed to correct these two shortcomings—has recently emerged, called the **sondeo** (Hildebrand 1981). The *sondeo* involves the use of informal interviews and participant-observation by teams of agricultural and social scientists. Over the course of several weeks, the research team is able to develop a composite picture of the local farming system. This relatively rapid and effective approach to the diagnosis phase of research is a direct application of the experiential and interactive methodology of the cultural anthropologist.

Tripp illustrated how a program of farming research in northern Ecuador utilized a modified form of the *sondeo* for collecting diagnostic information. Owing to the scarcity of resources, the biological scientists (agronomists) were required to conduct all of the research themselves. The agronomists were schooled in a number of important analytical skills derived from anthropological field methods. Among the methods were participant-observation, informal interviewing, and systematic note taking.

As part of the research process, the agricultural researchers learned how to visit with local farmers in their fields and homes and participate in local community events. They became more skillful at recording the data they observed, which eventually led to unanticipated findings and, in the final analysis, improved the quality of the research. By using these personal, interactive research methods, the agronomists learned to assume an attitude common in anthropological fieldwork—that is, an attitude of honest curiosity rather than one of scientific or intellectual superiority. Thus, by using these anthropological methods, these agricultural researchers were able to overcome the costly survey methods of research and, in the process, derive data that were both relevant and ongoing throughout the duration of the project.

THOUGHT QUESTIONS

1. How would you define "on-farm research"? *Sondeo?*

2. One of the anthropological data-gathering techniques used to improve on-farm research in Ecuador was participant-observation. What are the advantages of using participant-observation? What are the disadvantages?

3. How would you describe the major anthropological contributions to on-farm research in Ecuador?

The collection of sociocultural data through the use of ethnographic interviewing has had important practical implications in the treatment of alcoholism among Skid Row men.

In the social science literature, the term *Skid Row men* refers to indigents who regularly consume inexpensive alcoholic beverages as a way of life, are

frequently picked up by the police for public drunkenness, and find themselves repeatedly in detox centers. According to most studies (Rooney 1961:444; Spradley 1970:225; Parsons 1951:289), Skid Row men have lost all significant involvement with their families. They are, in short, men without families and men who do not want families.

This general perception that Skid Row men do not maintain their family ties may be more the result of failing to investigate this aspect of their lives than a true measure of reality. Prompted by such a possibility, Singer (1985) decided to conduct ethnographic interviews with twenty-eight Skid Row men who had been admitted to an Alcoholic Detoxification Center in Washington, D.C. The interview schedule, comprising 100 open-ended questions, was designed to collect information on family background, drinking history, current lifestyles, and social networks. Singer reasoned that if, in fact, these Skid Row men do maintain kinship ties, it might be possible to use these kinship links as part of the strategy for therapeutic intervention.

Interestingly, the data revealed that this sample of Skid Row men maintained fairly regular contact with relatives. More specifically, 93 percent of the men both remained in regular contact with and felt emotionally close to at least one family member; 90 percent received nonmaterial aid from relatives; and 86 percent received material assistance from family. In spite of numerous disappointments caused by the alcoholics' inability to stay out of trouble, ties with certain kin (mostly female) were both persistent and emotionally laden. The Skid Row men were found to both respect and care for their supportive kin.

Based on these findings from the ethnographic interviews, Singer concluded that these female supportive kin may be an important link in the alcoholic rehabilitation programs for Skid Row men. Some of the men interviewed stated that some of their family had not given up on them and would be willing to participate in family therapy. Since there is general agreement among the therapeutic community that successful alcoholic rehabilitation requires the involvement of "significant others" who care, these findings can encourage the use of family therapy for the treatment of Skid Row alcoholics.

THOUGHT QUESTIONS

1. What popular myth about Skid Row men did Singer's research disprove?

2. What anthropological techniques did Singer use in his research? Are there other techniques that might have been more appropriate? Why or why not?

3. What practical implications could policymakers derive from Singer's research?

Anthropological research contributes to the ongoing search for a solution to the AIDS epidemic.

In the early 1980s, very few Americans had ever heard of acquired immune deficiency syndrome (AIDS). By the end of the decade, however, many public health officials regarded this sexually transmitted disease as the most

serious health epidemic of the twentieth century. Virtually unknown in the 1970s, AIDS has spread drastically from fewer than 200 reported cases in the United States in 1981 to about 31,000 cases in 1988 (U.S. Bureau of the Census 1990:116). Amazingly, the figures through 1993 of reported cases of AIDS in the United States is 244,939 cases (U.S. Bureau of Census 1993).

As Gorman (1986:157) has suggested, the AIDS epidemic is particularly difficult to get under control for a number of reasons. First, the disease attacks the human immune system, one of the most complex and inadequately understood systems of the body. Second, the group of viruses thought to cause the disease are so poorly understood that a chemical cure is not likely to be found in the immediate future. Thus, the biological factors in solving the AIDS threat are highly complex. Efforts to stem the epidemic are further complicated by cultural factors. That is, the high-risk populations (gay males and intravenous drug users) are not very visible subcultural groups. This creates additional problems for programs of AIDS prevention.

Until a vaccine for AIDS is developed, education remains the best strategy for reducing the spread of the disease. Since AIDS is sexually transmitted, the world's populations must learn as much as possible about how to avoid contracting the disease. Yet, before public health officials can design effective educational programs, they need a good deal of cultural/behavioral information on high-risk populations. Cultural anthropologists can make significant contributions to programs of preventive education by conducting ethnographic research on the cultural patterns of sexual behavior among such high-risk groups as gay males in the United States.

One such applied anthropological study was conducted by Douglas Feldman (1985) among gay males in New York City. Owing to the relatively sensitive nature of the gay community, such a study was fraught with methodological difficulties. Since there are no census data on gay males, Feldman could not draw a random sample of gays in New York. Instead he utilized the *Gayellow Pages* (a national directory of gay businesses and organizations) from which he drew a varied sample of organizations. After explaining the purpose of the study, Feldman solicited active participation in the study by having each organization distribute copies of a prepared (two-page) questionnaire to its employees or members. In all, some 1,600 questionnaires were distributed and 403 were returned, a response rate of 25 percent.

Feldman's study was designed to determine the concern about the AIDS epidemic of gay males in New York City and the extent to which that concern has affected gay men's sexual behavior. Respondents were asked the number of different sexual partners they had per month prior to learning about AIDS compared to after learning about it. The study revealed a dramatic decrease of 47 percent in the number of sexual partners before and after. Moreover, the nature of the sexual activity also changed substantially away from those activities that are most likely to transmit the disease.

To be certain, applied anthropological studies such as Feldman's have their limitations. The collection of behavioral data on sexual practices among any group of people will always be difficult because of its highly personal nature. When seeking such sensitive information from a subgroup often stigmatized by the wider society, problems of data validity are greatly magnified. Moreover, our knowledge about the AIDS epidemic is growing so rapidly that data become obsolete very quickly. Nevertheless, cultural anthropology has an important role to play in the monumental effort it will take to eradicate this dread disease. Anthropologists such as Feldman—who are interested in both anthropology and epidemiology—can contribute to the design of successful prevention programs by providing both attitudinal and behavioral data from the ethnographic study of gay communities in the United States. Gorman has effectively summarized the emerging role that applied anthropologists can play in the effort against AIDS:

> The public health crisis that attended the AIDS epidemic represents unique opportunities for the application of social scientific perspectives in epidemiology. Due to the combination of biological, technological, social and behavioral phenomena encompassed by AIDS, rarely has a health crisis represented such a unique nexus of disease and culture. AIDS as yet remains a puzzle whose pieces are only slowly being identified and pieced together. Anthropology has contributed and will continue to assist in the assembling of these pieces. (1986:169)

THOUGHT QUESTIONS

1. Why is the AIDS epidemic so difficult to control?

2. How could culture be a factor in the distribution of a disease such as AIDS?

3. Was a mailed questionnaire the most appropriate technique for this research? Why or why not?

4. What other areas concerning the AIDS epidemic need to be investigated by anthropologists?

Summary

1. Since the turn of the century, cultural anthropologists have conducted their research in a firsthand manner by means of direct fieldwork. Explicit discussion of how practicing cultural anthropologists actually do their fieldwork is a much more recent phenomenon, however.

2. A number of preparations must be made before any fieldwork experience is begun, including the securing of research funds, taking adequate health precautions such as immunizations, obtaining research clearance from the host government, gaining proficiency in the local language, and attending to a host of personal matters, such as making provisions for accompanying family members, securing passports and visas, purchasing equipment, and making sure that one's affairs at home are in order.

3. Although every fieldwork project in cultural anthro-

pology has its own unique character, all projects go through the same basic stages: (a) selecting a research problem, (b) formulating a research design, (c) collecting the data, (d) analyzing the data, and (e) interpreting the data.

4. Since no two fieldwork experiences are ever identical, it is important that cultural anthropologists match the appropriate data-gathering techniques to their own fieldwork situations. Among the tools at the fieldworker's disposal are participant-observation, interviewing, ethnographic mapping, census taking, document analysis, the collection of genealogies, and photography.

5. Some general guidelines are applicable to most fieldwork situations. First, when attempting to work one's way into a small community, it is advisable to work one's way down, rather than up, the political hierarchy. Second, when introducing oneself to the local population, it is important to select a single role for oneself and use it consistently. And third, as a way of firmly

establishing one's credibility with the local people, it is advisable to proceed slowly.

6. The use of the participant-observation technique has certain methodological advantages, including increasing rapport and being able to distinguish between real and normative behavior. Participant-observation is not, however, without its methodological shortcomings, such as (a) being time-consuming, (b) posing problems of data comparability, (c) presenting difficulties in recording data, and (d) interfering with the very thing that is being studied.

7. Ethnographic interviewing, which is particularly useful for collecting both attitudinal and behavioral data, is of two basic types: unstructured and structured interviews. In unstructured interviews, interviewers ask open-ended questions and permit interviewees to respond at their own pace. In contrast, in structured interviews, interviewers ask the same questions of all respondents, in the same order, and under the same set of social conditions.

8. Whenever cultural anthropologists conduct field research in cultures different from their own, they need to be personally flexible and should always expect the unexpected. Like anyone else trying to operate in an unfamiliar cultural setting, cultural anthropologists are susceptible to culture shock.

 Key Terms

analyzing data
census taking
collecting data
culture shock
dependent variable
document analysis
ethnographic mapping
event analysis
fieldwork
genealogizing
independent variable

informant
interpreting data
on-farm research
participant-observation
proxemic analysis
research clearance
research design
research proposal
sondeo
structured interview
unstructured interview

Suggested Readings

Bernard, H. Russell. *Research Methods in Cultural Anthropology*. Newbury Park, Calif.: Sage Publications, 1988. The most complete and up-to-date discussion of how to do cultural anthropological fieldwork. Drawing upon a wide variety of examples from actual fieldwork situations, Bernard takes the student step-by-step through the procedures for preparing for the field, collecting data, and analyzing the findings.

DeVita, Philip R., ed. *The Naked Anthropologist: Tales from around the World*. Belmont, Calif.: Wadsworth, 1992. A recent collection of very personal essays written by anthropologists about the agony and ecstasy of conducting fieldwork in many different parts of the world.

Fetterman, David M. *Ethnography: Step by Step*. Newbury Park, Calif.: Sage Publications, 1989. A practical guide for doing ethnographic field research, this volume deals with such topics as participant-observation, sampling, interviewing, the use of technical equipment, analyzing data, and actually writing an ethnography.

Jorgensen, Danny L. *Participant Observation: A Methodology for Human Studies*. Thousand Oaks, Calif.: Sage Publications, 1989. A practical handbook for the collection of anthropological data through the technique of participant-observation.

Messerschmidt, Donald A. *Anthropologists at Home in North America: Methods and Issues in the Study of One's Own Society*. Cambridge: Cambridge University Press, 1981. A collection of seventeen essays expressly written for this volume on theories, methods, and styles of doing research in contemporary North America.

Pelto, P. J., and G. H. Pelto. *Anthropological Research: The Structure of Inquiry*. 2d ed. New York: Cambridge University Press, 1978. An excellent introduction to the methods of collecting and analyzing cultural anthropological data.

Spradley, James P. *The Ethnographic Interview*. New York: Holt, Rinehart & Winston, 1979. A very readable discussion of the nature and value of ethnographic research. The author not only analyzes the uniqueness of the ethnographic interview process but also discusses it within the wider context of ethnographic fieldwork.

Stocking, George W. *Observers Observed: Essays on Ethnographic Fieldwork*. Madison, Wis.: University of Wisconsin Press, 1983. A volume comprising nine essays dealing with ethnographic fieldwork written by both anthropologists and historians. The essays by the historians offer a unique perspective on the participant-observation technique, which cultural anthropologists think of as distinctively their own.

Wengle, John. *Ethnographers in the Field: The Psychology of Research*. Tuscaloosa, Ala.: University of Alabama Press, 1988. A study of the psychological ramifications for cultural anthropologists of conducting participant-observation research in radically different cultures.

LANGUAGE

Like all humans, these West African women communicate both verbally (with language) and nonverbally (through gestures).

- How does human language differ from forms of communication in other animals?
- Are some languages superior to others?
- What is the relationship between language and culture?
- How do people communicate without using words?

The Nature of Language

Perhaps the most distinctive feature of being human is the capacity to create and use language and other symbolic forms of communication. It is hard to imagine how culture could even exist without language. Such fundamental aspects of any culture as religion, family relationships, and the management of technology would be virtually impossible without a symbolic form of communication. Our very capacity to adapt to the physical environment—which involves identifying usable resources, developing ways of acquiring them, and finally forming groups to exploit them—is made possible by language. It is generally held that language is the major vehicle for human thought, since our linguistic categories provide the basis for perception and concept formation. Moreover, it is largely through language that we pass on our cultural heritage from one generation to the next. In short, language is such an integral part of the human condition that it permeates everything we do. For excellent introductions to the anthropological study of language, see Fromkin and Rodman (1993) and Salzmann (1993).

The term *language*, like so many others that we think we understand, is far more complex than we might imagine. Language, which is found in all cultures of the world, is a symbolic system of sounds that, when put together according to a certain set of rules, conveys meanings to its speakers. The meanings attached to any given word in all languages are totally arbitrary. That is, the word *cow* has no particular connection to the large bovine animal that the English language refers to as a cow. The word *cow* is a no more or less reasonable word for that animal than would be *kaflumpha, sporge,* or *four-pronged squirter*. The word *cow* does not look like a cow, sound like a cow, or have any particular physical con-

nection to a cow. The only explanation for the use of the word is that somewhere during the evolution of the English language someone decided that the word *cow* would be used to refer to a large domesticated animal that gives an abundant quantity of milk. Other languages use totally different, and equally arbitrary, words to describe the very same animal.

Diversity of Language

Given the very arbitrary nature of languages, it should come as no surprise that there is enormous linguistic diversity among human populations. Even though linguists do not agree on precisely how many discrete languages exist, a reasonable estimate would be six thousand (Diamond 1993). The criterion used to establish such estimates is mutual unintelligibility. That is, linguists assume that if people can understand one another, they speak the same language; if they are unable to understand one another, they speak different languages. The application of this criterion is not as straightforward as it might appear, however, because there are always differing degrees of intelligibility. Nevertheless, despite our inability to establish the precise number of discrete languages found in the world today, the amount of linguistic diversity is vast. (Exhibit 6-1 illustrates the world's major language families.)

 looking ahead

For an example of how anthropological insights about language differences in the United States can contribute to the settling of a court dispute, see Applied Perspective 2 at the end of this chapter.

Communication—Human Versus Nonhuman

Communication is certainly not unique to humans, for most animals have ways of sending and receiving messages. Various bird species use certain calls to communicate a desire to mate; honeybees communicate the distance and direction of sources of food very accurately through a series of body movements; certain antelope species give off a cry that warns of impending danger; even amoebae seem to chemically send and receive crude messages by discharging small amounts of carbon dioxide.

Communication among primates, of course, is considerably more complex. Certain nonhuman primate species, such as gorillas and chimpanzees, draw on a relatively large number of modes of communication, including various calls as well as such nonverbal forms of communication as facial expressions, body movement, and gestures. Yet despite the relative complexity of communication patterns among nonhuman primates, these patterns differ from human patterns of communication in some significant ways. For example, since animal call systems are to a large extent genetically based, they are rigidly inflexible to the extent that each call always has the same form and conveys the same meaning.

Open and Closed Communication Systems. Chimpanzees make one sound when they have found a plentiful source of food, another when threatened, and a third when announcing their presence. Each of these three sounds is unique in both form and message. And each sound (call) is mutually exclusive. That is, the chimpanzee cannot combine elements of two or more calls in order to develop a new call. To this extent we speak of nonhuman forms of communication as being **closed systems of communication.** Humans, on the other hand, operate with languages that are **open systems of communication,** since they are capable of sending messages that have never been sent before.

Language enables humans to send literally an infinite array of messages, including abstract ideas, highly technical information, and subtle shades of meaning. Starting with a limited number of sounds, human languages are capable of producing an infinite number of meanings by combining sounds and words into meanings that may have never been sent before. To illustrate, by combining a series of words in a certain order, we can convey a unique message that has, in all likelihood, never been previously uttered: "I think that the woman named Clela with the bright orange hair left her leather handbag in the 1951 Studebaker that was involved in a hit-and-run accident later in the day." This productive capacity of human language illustrates how efficient and flexible human communication can be.

To suggest, as has been done in the past, that the communication system of such nonhuman primates as

chimps and gorillas is closed in contrast to the open system used by humans is perhaps an oversimplification. Some linguistic scholars (e.g., Noam Chomsky 1972) have posited that since human language is so radically different from other forms of animal communication, humans must be endowed with certain genetically based mental capacities found in no other species. As we have learned more about the communication systems of nonhuman primates, however, a growing number of scholars have questioned this theory by claiming that certain species like chimpanzees and gorillas have a latent capacity for language.

A major limitation to the development of language among gorillas and chimps is physical, for they do not possess the vocal equipment for speech. In an effort to circumvent this physical limitation, recent researchers have taught American Sign Language to chimpanzees and gorillas with some startling findings. In four years, Allen and Beatrice Gardner (1969) taught a chimp named Washoe to use 130 different signs. Of even greater significance is that Washoe was able to manipulate the signs in ways that previously had been thought possible only by humans. For example, Washoe was able to combine several signs to create a new word (having no sign for the word *duck,* she referred to it as *waterbird*), thereby "opening up" her system of communication.

In another important research effort in nonhuman communication, a gorilla named Koko by age four was able to use over 250 different signs within a single hour

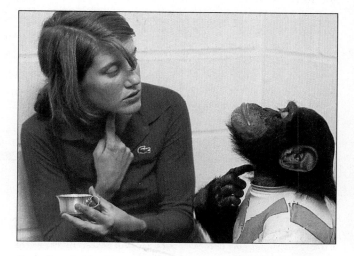

Even though this chimp has been trained to use American Sign Language, the differences between this form of communication and human language are vast.

EXHIBIT 6-1

Major Language Families of the World

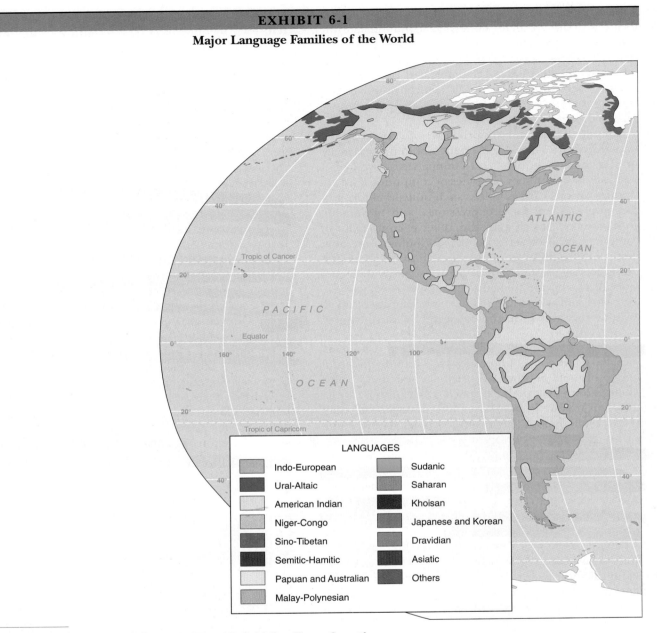

LANGUAGES

- Indo-European
- Ural-Altaic
- American Indian
- Niger-Congo
- Sino-Tibetan
- Semitic-Hamitic
- Papuan and Australian
- Malay-Polynesian
- Sudanic
- Saharan
- Khoisan
- Japanese and Korean
- Dravidian
- Asiatic
- Others

Source: Adapted with permission from H. J. deBlij and P. O. Muller, *Human Geography: Culture, Society, and Space* (New York: John Wiley & Sons, 1986) pp. 184–85.

and, like Washoe, was able to name new objects by combining several different signs. In addition, Koko was able to express her feelings and actually scored between 80 and 90 on a nonverbal IQ test.

These recent developments in communication studies among nonhuman primates would suggest that chimps and gorillas do in fact have more advanced powers of reasoning than had been believed earlier. Some researchers have used this evidence to support the notion that chimpanzee and gorilla linguistic abilities differ from those of humans only in degree, not in kind. In other words, we should not think in terms of

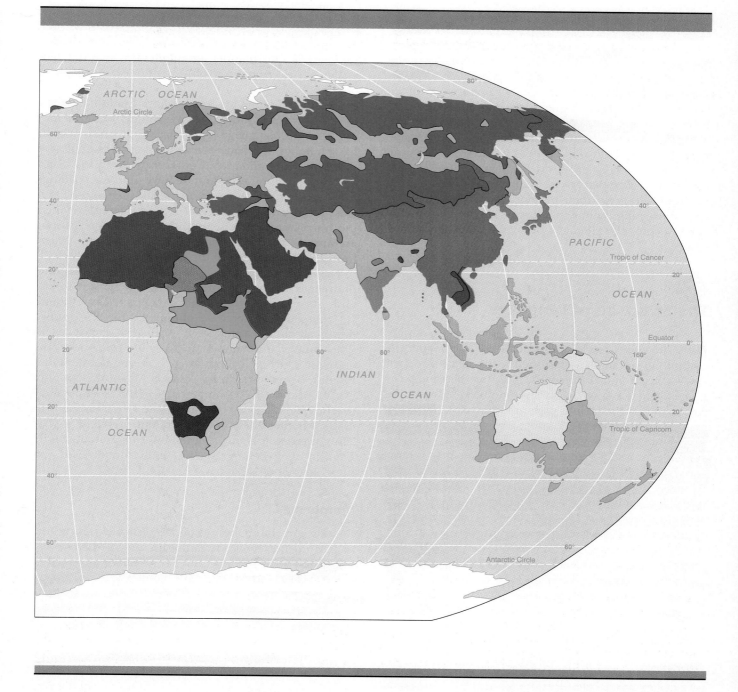

closed versus open systems of communication, but rather in terms of some systems being more open than others. Even if this is the case, however, it is important to remember that degree of the difference between human and nonhuman forms of communication remains immense.

Displacement. Human communication differs from other animal communication systems in at least two other important respects. One such feature of human language is its capacity to convey information about a thing or an event that is not present. This characteristic, known as **displacement,** enables humans to speak of purely hypothetical things, events that have happened in the past, and events that might happen in the future. In contrast to other animals, which communicate only about particular things that are in the present and in the immediate environment, humans are able through language to think abstractly. Another feature of human communication that distinguishes it from nonhuman forms of communication is that it is transmitted largely through tradition rather than through experience alone. Even though our propensity (and our physical equipment) for language is biologically based, the specific language that any given person speaks is passed on from one generation to another through the process of learning. Adults in a linguistic community who already know the language teach the language to the children.

The Structure of Language

Every language has a logical structure. When people encounter an unfamiliar language for the first time, they are confused and disoriented, but after becoming familiar with the language, they eventually discover its rules and how the various parts are interrelated. All languages have rules and principles governing what sounds are to be used and how those sounds are to be combined to convey meanings. Human languages have two aspects of structure: a sound (or phonological) structure and a grammatical structure. **Phonology** involves the study of the basic building blocks of a language, called phonemes, and how these phonemes are combined. The study of **grammar** involves identifying recurring sequences of phonemes, called **morphemes**, the smallest units of speech that convey a meaning. The descriptive linguist, whose job is to make explicit the structure of any given language, studies both the sound system and the grammatical system of as many different human languages as possible.

Phonology

The initial step in describing any language is to determine the sounds that are used. Even though humans have the vocal apparatus to make an extraordinarily large number of sounds, no single language uses all possible sounds. Instead, each language uses a finite number of sounds, called phonemes, which are the minimal units of sound that signal a difference in

meaning. The English language contains sounds for twenty-four consonants, nine vowels, three semivowels, and some other sound features for a total of forty-six phonemes. The number of phonemes in other languages varies from a low of about fifteen to a high of one hundred.

Clearly, the twenty-six letters of the English alphabet do not correspond to the total inventory of phonemes in the English language. This is largely because English has a number of inconsistent features. For example, we pronounce the same word differently (as in the noun and verb forms of *lead*), and we have different spellings for some words that sound identical, such as *meet* and *meat*. To address this difficulty, linguists have developed the International Phonetic Alphabet, which takes into account all of the possible sound units (phonemes) found in all languages of the world.

The manner in which sounds are grouped into phonemes varies from one language to another. In English, for example, the sounds represented by [b] and [v] comprise two separate phonemes. Such a distinction is absolutely necessary if an English speaker is to differentiate between such words as *ban* and *van* or *bent* and *vent*. The Spanish language, however, does not distinguish between these two sounds. When the Spanish word *ver* (to see) is pronounced, it would be impossible for the English speaker to determine with absolute precision whether the word begins with a [v] or a [b]. Thus, whereas [v] and [b] are two distinct phonemes in English, they belong to the same sound class (or phoneme) in the Spanish language.

Morphemes

Sounds and phonemes, while linguistically significant, usually do not convey meaning in and of themselves. The phonemes [r], [a], and [t] taken by themselves convey no meaning whatsoever. But when combined, they can form the word *rat*, *tar* or *art*, each of which conveys meaning. Thus, it is possible for two or more phonemes to be combined to form a morpheme.

Even though some words are made up of a single morpheme, we should not equate morphemes with words. In our example, the words *rat*, *tar*, and *art*, each made up of a single morpheme, cannot be subdivided into smaller units of meaning. In these cases, the words are in fact made up of a single morpheme. The majority of words, however, in any language are made up of two or more morphemes. The word *rats*, for example, contains two morphemes, the root word *rat* and the plural suffix [s], which conveys the meaning of more than one. Similarly, the word *artists* contains three morphemes: the root word *art;* the suffix *ist,* meaning one who engages in the process of doing art; and the plural suffix [s]. Some of these morphemes, like *art, tar,* and *rat,* can occur in a language unattached. Since they can stand alone, they are called **free morphemes.** Other morphemes, such as the suffix *ist,* cannot stand alone, for they have no meaning except when attached to other morphemes. These are called **bound morphemes** (see Exhibit 6-2).

Grammar

When people send linguistic messages by combining sounds into phonemes, phonemes into morphemes, and morphemes into words, they do so according to a highly complex set of rules. These rules, which are unique for each language, make up the grammar of the language and are well understood and followed by the speakers of that language. These grammatical systems, which constitute the formal structure of the language, consist of two parts: (1) the rules governing how morphemes are formed into words (**morphology**) and (2) the principles guiding how words are arranged into phrases and sentences (**syntax**). In some languages, meanings are determined primarily by the way morphemes are combined to form words (morphological features), while in other languages meanings are determined primarily by the order of words in a sentence (syntactical features).

The distinction between morphology and syntax can be illustrated by looking at an example from the English language. From a grammatical point of view, the statement "Tom fix Mary phone" does not make much sense. The order of the words in the statement (i.e., the syntax) is correct, but clearly some revision in the way that the words themselves are formed (i.e., morphology) is required for the statement to make grammatical sense. For example, since the English language requires information about verb tense, we must specify whether Tom fixed, is fixing, or will fix the phone. The English grammar system also requires information about the number of phones and the nature of the relationship between the phone and Mary. To make this statement grammatical, we can add an -ed to *fix,* an -s to *phone,* and an -'s to Mary. The revised statement ("Tom fixed Mary's phones"), which is now grammatically correct, tells us that Tom has already fixed two or more phones that belong to Mary.

Whereas the English grammar system requires that tense, number, and relationship be specified, other lan-

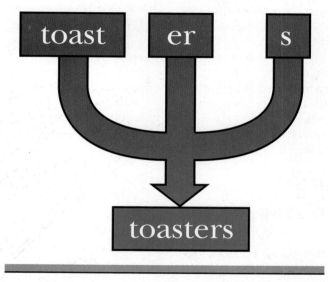

EXHIBIT 6-2
Morphemes Make Up Words

The word *toasters* is made up of the morphemes *toast, er,* and *s.* Which morphemes are free and which are bound?

guage systems require other types of information. For example, in Latin, a noun must have the proper case ending to indicate its role (i.e., subject, direct object, etc.) within the sentence. In some languages, such as Spanish, the ending on a noun determines the noun's gender (masculinity or femininity). In the Navajo language, certain verbs such as "to handle" will take different forms depending on the size and shape of the object being handled. Thus, every language has its own systematic way of ordering morphemes within a word to give linguistic meaning.

Syntax, on the other hand, refers to the aspect of grammar that governs the arrangement of words and phrases into sentences. In our original example ("Tom fix Mary phone"), the syntax is correct because the words are in proper sequence. The statement would be totally meaningless if the words were ordered "Fix Tom phone Mary," because the parts of speech are not in proper relationship to one another. Moreover, in English, adjectives generally precede the nouns they describe (such as "white horse"), whereas in Spanish adjectives generally follow the nouns they describe (such as "caballo blanco"). The order of the words, then, determines, at least in part, the meaning conveyed in any given language.

CROSS-CULTURAL MISCUE

Difficulties in communication can arise even between two people who ostensibly speak the same language. Although both New Yorkers and Londoners speak English, there are sufficient differences between American English and British English to cause communication miscues. Speakers of English on opposite sides of the Atlantic frequently use different words to refer to the same thing. To illustrate, Londoners put their trash in a dust bin, not a garbage can; they take a lift to the twentieth floor of a building, not an elevator; and they live in flats, not apartments. To further complicate matters, the same word used in England and the United States can convey very different meanings. For example, in England the word *homely* (as in the statement "I think your wife is very homely") means warm and friendly, not plain or ugly; for the British, the phrase "to table a motion" means to give an item a prominent place on the agenda rather than to postpone taking action on an item, as it means in the United States; and a rubber in British English is an eraser, not a condom. These are just a few of the linguistic pitfalls that North Americans and Britishers may encounter when they attempt to communicate using their own versions of the "same" language.

Are Some Languages Superior to Others?

Until the turn of the century, European linguists were convinced that Western languages were superior to all others in terms of elegance, efficiency, and beauty. It was generally assumed that small-scale, non-Western cultures characterized by simple technologies had equally simple languages. In short, preliterate people were thought to have primitive languages with a diminished capacity for expressing abstract ideas. Now, however, anthropological linguists, following the lead of Franz Boas, hold such a view to be untenable. Based on studies of American Indian languages, linguists have demonstrated time and again that people from technologically simple societies are no less capable of expressing a wide variety of abstract ideas than are people living in high-technology societies.

To illustrate this point, we can compare the English language with that of a traditionally technologically simple society—the Navajo people of the American Southwest. It is true that Navajo speakers are unable to make certain grammatical distinctions commonly made in English. For example, Navajo does not have separate noun forms for singular and plural (such as are found in English with the -s in *dogs* or the -ren in *children*); the third person pronoun is both singular and plural and gender nonspecific (it can be translated he, she, it, or they, depending on the context); and there are no adjectives, because the role of the adjective to describe nouns in English is played by the verb.

Although the Navajo language does not make the same grammatical distinctions as does the English language, in other areas it can express certain information with considerably more precision and efficiency than English. According to Peter Farb (1968:56), making a vague statement such as "I am going" is impossible in the Navajo language. Owing to the structure of this language, the verb stem would include additional information on whether the person is going on foot, by horseback, in a wagon, by boat, or in an airplane. If the selected verb form indicates that the person is going on horseback, it is necessary to further differentiate by verb form whether the horse is walking, trotting, galloping, or running. Thus, in the Navajo language a great deal of information is conveyed in the single verb form that is selected to express the concept of going. To be certain, the grammatical systems of the English and Navajo languages are very different. The English language can convey all of the same information, but it requires a far larger number of words. Nevertheless, it is hardly reasonable to conclude that one is more efficient at expressing abstract ideas than the other.

Language and Culture

For the cultural anthropologist, the study of language is important not only for the practical purpose of communicating while doing fieldwork but also because a close relationship exists between language and culture. It is widely accepted today that it would be difficult, if not impossible, to understand a culture without first understanding its language, and it would be equally impossible to understand a language outside its cultural context. It is for this reason that any effective language teacher will go beyond vocabulary and grammar by teaching students something about such topics as eating habits, values, and behavior patterns of native speakers. This important relationship between language and culture was recognized many decades ago by the father of modern American cultural anthropology, Franz Boas:

> . . . the study of language must be considered as one of the most important branches of ethnological study, because, on the one hand, a thorough insight into ethnology cannot be gained without a practical knowledge of the language, and, on the other hand, the fundamental concepts illustrated by human languages are not distinct in kind from ethnological phenomena; and because, furthermore, the peculiar characteristics of language are clearly reflected in the views and customs of the peoples of the world. (1911:73)

How Culture Influences Language

Although little research has been designed to explore how culture influences the grammatical system of a lan-

guage, there is considerable evidence to demonstrate how culture affects vocabulary. As a general rule, the vocabulary found in any language will tend to emphasize those words that are considered to be adaptively important in that culture. This notion, known as **cultural emphasis,** is reflected in the size and specialization of vocabulary.

In Standard American English, we find large numbers of words that refer to technological gadgetry (e.g., tractor, microchip, and intake valve) and occupational specialties (e.g., teacher, plumber, CPA, and pediatrician) for the simple reason that technology and occupation are points of cultural emphasis in our culture. Thus, the English language helps North Americans adapt effectively to their culture by providing a vocabulary well suited for that culture. Other cultures have other areas of emphasis. Based on field research conducted in the 1880s, Franz Boas noted that the Eskimos of Canada had large numbers of words for snow, ice, and seals, all three of which played a vital role in Eskimo adaptation to the environment and, indeed, in their survival. To illustrate, Boas reports that in addition to a general term for seal, the Eskimo language contains specific words referring to a seal basking in the sun and a seal floating on a piece of ice, as well as a number of terms for seals of different age and sex.

The Nuer. A particularly good example of how culture influences language through the elaboration of vocabularies is provided by the Nuer, a pastoral people of the Sudan, whose daily preoccupation with cattle is reflected in their language (Evans-Pritchard 1940). The Nuer have a vast vocabulary used to describe and identify their cattle according to certain physical features such as color, markings, and horn configuration. The Nuer have ten major color terms for describing cattle: white (bor), black (car), brown (lual), chestnut (dol), tawny (yan), mouse-gray (lou), bay (thiang), sandy-gray (lith), blue and strawberry roan (yil), and chocolate (gwir). When these color possibilities are merged with the many possible marking patterns, there are more than several hundred combinations. And when these several hundred possibilities are combined with terminology based on horn configuration, there are potentially thousands of ways of describing cattle with considerable precision in the Nuer language.

This highly complex system of terminology is directly related to the prominence of cattle in Nuer society. According to Evans-Pritchard (1940), cattle are used in a number of important ways. First, they serve a vital economic function in Nuer society (as they do in most

Although the Navajo and English languages have vastly different structures, these Navajo speakers can express abstract ideas every bit as effectively as native English speakers.

other pastoral societies) by providing the people with milk, blood, and meat on certain occasions. Second, cows are used to create and maintain social relationships between people. For a Nuer marriage to be legitimate, cows must be transferred from the lineage of the groom to the lineage of the bride. Third, cows not only influence the relationship between people but also serve as a link with the people's dead ancestors. Cows are used as sacrificial animals to get the attention of ancestor ghosts; in fact, it is impossible to communicate with the dead without frequent references to cattle. Fourth, every Nuer man takes as one of his names the name of an ox given to him at birth or at his initiation. Men are frequently called by names that refer to the physical features of these oxen, and most age-mates prefer to be addressed by this oxname. (For this reason, Evans-Pritchard [1940:18] notes that a Nuer genealogy sounds very much like an inventory of a family's cattle.) And fifth, the names and traits of cows as well as the oxnames of men are frequently the subject of songs,

poems, and stories. We could cite numerous other uses to which cattle are put, indicating their prominence within the Nuer culture. But suffice it to say that cattle are a dominant interest of the Nuer, or in Evans-Pritchard's own words:

> They are always talking about their beasts. I used sometimes to despair that I never discussed anything with the young men but livestock and girls, and even the subject of girls led inevitably to that of cattle. Start on whatever subject I would, and approach it from whatever angle, we would soon be speaking of cows and oxen, heifers and steers, rams and sheep, he-goats and she-goats, calves, and lambs, and kids. . . . Consequently he who lives among the Nuer and wishes to understand their social life must first master a vocabulary referring to cattle and to the life of the herd. (1940:18–19)

Cultural Emphasis in the United States—One Example.
In relatively small-scale cultures such as the Eskimos or

the Nuer, where most people's lives revolve around hunting or herding, areas of cultural emphasis are quite obvious. In middle-class American culture, however, which tends to be more complex occupationally, it is not always easy to identify a single area of cultural emphasis. Nevertheless, sports tends to be one area of life in U.S. culture that can be shared by people from a wide variety of occupational or class backgrounds. Consequently, as Hickerson points out, we have many colloquialisms in American English that stem from the game of baseball, our "national pastime":

- He made a grandstand play.
- She threw me a curve.
- She fielded my questions well.
- You're way off base.
- You're batting 1000 (500, zero) so far.
- What are the ground rules?
- I want to touch all the bases.
- He went to bat for me.
- He has two strikes against him.
- That's way out in left field.
- He drives me up the wall.
- He's a team player (a clutch player).
- She's an oddball (screwball, foul ball).
- It's just a ballpark estimate (1980:118).

How Language Influences Culture

A major concern of linguistic anthropology since the 1930s has been the question of whether language influences or perhaps even determines culture. There is no consensus among ethnolinguists, but some have suggested that language is more than a symbolic inventory of experience and the physical world and that it actually shapes our thoughts and perceptions. This notion was stated in its most explicit form by Edward Sapir:

> The fact of the matter is that the real world is to a large extent unconsciously built up on the language habits of the group. No two languages are ever sufficiently similar to be considered as representing the same social reality. The worlds in which different societies live are distinct worlds, not merely the same world with different labels attached. (1929:214)

The Sapir-Whorf Hypothesis. Drawing on Sapir's original formulation, Benjamin Lee Whorf, a student of Sapir's, conducted ethnolinguistic research among the Hopi Indians to determine if different linguistic structures produced different ways of viewing the world. Whorf's observations convinced him that linguistic structure was in fact the causal variable for different views of the world. This notion that different cultures see the world differently because of their different linguistic categories has come to be known as the **Sapir-Whorf hypothesis.**

Both Sapir and Whorf were positing the notion that language does influence the way people see the world. That is, language is more than a vehicle for communication; it actually establishes mental categories that predispose people to see things in a certain way. If, for example, my language has a single word—aunt—that refers to my mother's sister, my father's sister, my mother's brother's wife, and my father's brother's wife, it is likely that I will perceive all of these family members as genealogically equivalent and consequently will behave toward them in essentially the same way. Thus, Sapir and Whorf would suggest that both perception and the resulting behavior will be determined by the linguistic categories we use to group some things under one heading and other things under another heading.

Testing the Hypothesis. Since Sapir and Whorf's original formulation, a number of ethnolinguists have attempted to test the hypothesis. One study (Ervin-Tripp 1964) concluded that the very content of what is said by bilingual people will vary according to which language is being spoken. Working with bilingual Japanese-American women in San Francisco, Ervin-Tripp (1964:96) found that the responses to the same question given at different times by the same women varied significantly depending on the language used. To illustrate, when asked in English to finish the statement "Real friends should . . . ," the respondent answered, "be very frank"; when asked the same question in Japanese at a different time, she answered "help each other." Or, when asked, "When my wishes conflict with my family . . . ," the response in English was "I do what I want"; but in Japanese, the response was, "It is a time of great unhappiness." In other words, when the question was asked in Japanese, the bilingual respondent was more likely to give a "typical" Japanese response, and when questioned in English, she was more likely to give a "typical" American response. This is the type of evidence that has been presented to support the validity of the Sapir-Whorf hypothesis, since it strongly suggests that the language influences or channels perceptions as well as the content of verbal utterances.

One very creative attempt at testing the Sapir-Whorf hypothesis was conducted by Casagrande (1960), using a matched sample of Navajo-speaking children. Half of the sample, who spoke only Navajo, were matched on all significant sociocultural variables (such as religion, parental education, family income) with the other half, who spoke both Navajo and English. Since both groups were identical on all important variables except language, it would be logical to conclude that whatever perceptual differences emerged between the two groups could be attributed to language.

Having a thorough knowledge of the Navajo language, Casagrande understood that Navajo people, when speaking about an object, are required to choose among a number of different verb forms depending on the shape of the object. When asking a Navajo speaker to hand you an object, you use one verb form if the object is long and rigid like a stick and another verb form if it is long and flexible like a rope. Based on this Navajo linguistic feature, Casagrande hypothesized that children speaking only Navajo would be more likely to discriminate according to shape at an earlier age than the English-speaking children. English-speaking children would be more likely to discriminate according to other features such as size or color. This hypothesis was tested by having both groups of children participate in a number of tasks. The children were shown two objects (a yellow stick and a blue rope) and then asked to tell which of these two objects was most like a third object (a yellow rope). In other words, both groups of children were asked to categorize the yellow rope according to likeness with either the yellow stick or the blue rope. Casagrande found that the children who spoke only Navajo had a significantly greater tendency to categorize according to shape (yellow *rope* and blue *rope*) than the bilingual children who were more likely to categorize according to color.

According to the Sapir-Whorf hypothesis, then, language establishes in our minds categories that force us to distinguish those things we consider similar from those things we consider different. Language, in other words, is a coercive force that causes people to see the world in a certain way. If this is the case, the speakers of different languages will construct reality differently.

According to the Sapir-Whorf hypothesis, the power of language can also be seen in the way people use their native tongue by choosing one word over another when describing a concept. For example, language frequently can be used to make good things seem bad or, more frequently, to make bad things appear better than they really are. This is accomplished through the use of euphemisms, an indirect form of language used to conceal something inadequate, unpleasant, or embarrassing. For example, English speakers in the United States use certain euphemisms to lend an air of respectability

In certain bilingual populations, such as these Japanese-Americans, how a question is answered often will depend on the language in which it is asked.

to some fairly ordinary trades, for as Thomson (1994:83) reminds us:

> ... ratcatchers are fond of calling themselves "exterminating engineers" and hairdressers have long since showed a preference for "beautician." The -ician ending, in fact, has proved very popular, doubtless because it echoes "physician" and thus sounds both professional and scientific. In the late nineteenth century undertakers had already begun to call themselves "funeral directors," but starting in 1916 ennobled themselves even further by battening on the newer euphemistic coinage, "mortician." Meanwhile a tree trimmer became a "tree surgeon" (that love of medicine again) and a press agent became a "publicist" or, even more grandly, a "public relations counsel."

Drawbacks to the Hypothesis. The problem with the Sapir-Whorf hypothesis—and the reason that it remains a hypothesis rather than a widely accepted fact—is one of causation. Whorf and Sapir were linguistic de-

CROSS-CULTURAL MISCUE

For decades, a major focus of U.S. foreign policy has been on what we call the Middle East, an area that is largely Islamic in religion and Arabic in culture and language. In recent years, the U.S. government has sent Marines to Lebanon, had its embassy taken over in Tehran, engaged in retaliatory air strikes on Libya, and responded to the invasion of Kuwait by Iraq. Because of its close political, economic, and social ties to the state of Israel, the United States has been at loggerheads with most of the Arab world. All too often the American people—and far more seriously, our diplomatic community—seem to be reacting to events in the Middle East with only a minimal understanding of Arabic culture.

Linguistic style is one area where Americans often misinterpret Arabic cultures. Whereas some cultures (such as the Japanese) engage in linguistic understatement, Arabic speakers generally go to the opposite extreme through such linguistic conventions as exaggeration, overassertion, and repetition. For example, sometimes messages sent in Arabic are given more dramatic force by repeating certain pronouns; highly graphic metaphors and similes are commonly found in everyday speech; and to dramatize a point, Arabs frequently string together a long litany of adjectives modifying a single noun. Because of differences in communication styles, what we would consider to be a strongly worded statement might seem weak and unassertive to an Arab. Or, a very strongly worded statement in Arabic might seem absolutely fanatical to an American. It is important to bear in mind that in the Arabic world, very strongly worded statements—which have a psychologically cathartic function—are not taken literally as an accurate description of the speaker's real thoughts or intentions. Understanding such a linguistic style is particularly relevant in the diplomatic/political realm, where an overreaction to a strongly worded threat could lead to armed conflict and the loss of lives.

terminists who posited that language *determines* culture. In fact, Sapir suggested that people are virtual prisoners of their language when he stated that "human beings . . . are very much at the mercy of the particular language which has become the medium of expression for their society" (1929:209). Others, however, taking the opposite position, have suggested that language simply reflects, rather than determines, culture. To be certain, language and culture influence each other in a number of important ways. Yet problems arise when attempting to demonstrate that language determines culture, or vice versa, in any definitive way. What does seem obvious, however, is that all people, being constantly bombarded with sensory stimuli, have developed filtering systems to bring order to all of these incoming sensations. Sapir and Whorf have suggested that the filtering system is language, which provides a set of lenses that highlight some perceptions and deemphasize others.

Whatever may be the precise effect of language on culture, the Sapir-Whorf hypothesis has served to focus attention on this important relationship. For an interesting discussion of the Sapir-Whorf hypothesis and how it applies to language use in the United States, see Thompson (1994).

◉ Sociolinguistics

Anthropological linguistics has devoted much of its time and energy to the study of languages as logical systems of knowledge and communication. Recently, however, linguists have taken a keen interest in how people actually speak with one another in any given society. Whereas the earlier linguists tended to focus on uniform structures (morphology, phonology, and syntax), sociolinguists concentrate on variations in language use depending on the social situation or context in which the speaker may be operating.

In much the same way that entire speech communities adapt their language to changing situations, so too do the individuals in those speech communities. Bilingualism and multilingualism are obvious examples of the situational use of language. A Hispanic junior high school student in Miami, for example, may speak English in the classroom and Spanish at home. But frequently people who are monolingual will speak different forms of the same language depending on the social situation. To illustrate, the language that a college sophomore might use with a roommate would be appreciably different from that used when talking to his grandparents; or the choice of expressions heard in a football locker room would hardly be appropriate in a job interview. In short, what is said and how it is said are frequently influenced by such variables as the age, sex, and relative social status of the speakers.

The major focus of sociolinguistics is the relationship between language and social structure. What can we tell about the social relationships between two people from the language they use with each other? The analysis of terms of address can be particularly useful in this re-

The form of the English language that this U.S. teenager uses when speaking to her grand-mother is quite different from the form she would use when talking to her peers.

gard. Professor Green, for example, could be addressed as Dr. Green, Ma'am, Professor, Ms. Green, Elizabeth, Darling, Doc, Prof, or Beth, depending on who is doing the addressing. One would not expect that her mother or husband would refer to her as Ma'am or that her students would call her Beth. Instead we would expect that the term of address chosen would reflect appropriately the relative social status of the two parties. That is, in middle-class American society, the reciprocal use of first names indicates a friendly, informal relationship between equals; the reciprocal use of titles followed by last names indicates a more formal relationship between people of roughly the same status; and the nonreciprocal use of first names and titles is found among people of unequal social status. We would also expect that the same person might use different terms of address for Professor Green in different social situations. Her husband, for example, might call her Beth at a cocktail party, Darling when they are making love, and Elizabeth when engaged in an argument.

Diglossia

The situational use of language in complex speech communities has been studied by Charles Ferguson (1964) who coined the term **diglossia.** By this term, Ferguson was referring to a linguistic situation where two varieties of the same language (e.g., standard form, dialect, or pidgin) are spoken by the same person at different times and under different social circumstances.

Ferguson illustrates the concept of diglossia by citing examples from a number of linguistic communities throughout the world, including the use of classical or Koranic Arabic and local forms of Arabic in North Africa and the Middle East, the coexistence of standard German and Swiss German in Switzerland, and the use of both French and Haitian Creole in Haiti. In all of the speech communities where diglossia is found, there exists a long-standing connection between appreciably different linguistic varieties. Which form is used carries with it important cultural meanings. For example, in all cases of diglossia, one form of the language is considered to be "high" and the other "low" (see Table 6-1). High forms of the language are associated with literacy, education, and, to some degree, religion. The high forms are usually found as part of religious services, political speeches in legislative bodies, in university lectures, in news broadcasts, and in newspapers. Low forms are likely to be found in the marketplace; when giving instructions to subordinates; in conversations with friends and relatives; and in various forms of pop

TABLE 6-1	
Diglossia	
High Form	Low Form
Religious services	Marketplace
Political speeches	Instructions to subordinates
Legislative proceedings	Friendly conversations
University lectures	Folk literature
News broadcasts	Radio/TV programs
Newspapers	Cartoons
Poetry	Graffiti

Source: Charles A. Ferguson, "Diglossia," in *Language in Culture and Society: A Reader in Linguistics,* ed. Dell Hynes (New York: Harper & Row, 1964), pp. 429–439.

culture, such as folk literature, television and radio programs, cartoons, and graffiti.

It is generally agreed that high forms of the language are superior to low forms, and frequently the use of the high form is associated with the elite and the upwardly mobile. This general superiority of the high form is at least partially the result of its association with religion and the fact that much of the literature of the language is written in the high form.

Dialects. It is not at all uncommon for certain dialects in complex speech communities to be considered substandard or inferior to others. Such claims are made on social or political rather than linguistic grounds. That is, minority dialects are often assigned an inferior status by the majority for the purpose of maintaining the political, economic, and social subordination of the minority. People who are not from the South regard certain "Southernisms" such as "you'all" (as in the statement, "You'all come by and see us now") as quaint or colorful regional expressions at best or inferior and inappropriate incursions into Standard American English at worst. A more obvious example would be majority attitudes toward the nonstandard English dialect used by Black Americans in northern ghettos. Clearly, such usages as "You be going home" or "Don't nobody go nowhere" will never be used by major network newscasters. Although such expressions are considered to be inferior by the speakers of Standard English, the use of these forms demonstrate logically consistent grammatical patterns and in no way prevent the expression of complex or abstract ideas. Nonstandard English should not be viewed as simply a series of haphazard mistakes in Standard English. Rather it is a fully efficient language with its own unique set of grammatical rules that are consistently applied. Thus, in linguistic terms, the grammar and phonology of ghetto English are no less efficient than the language of the rich and powerful (see Hecht, Collier, and Ribeau [1993]).

looking ahead

Anthropological linguists can help resolve problems arising from minority dialects in the public schools. For an example, see Applied Perspective 1 at the end of this chapter.

Nonverbal Communication

To fully comprehend how people in any particular culture communicate, we must become familiar with their nonverbal forms of communication in addition to their language. **Nonverbal communication** is important because it both helps us interpret linguistic messages and frequently carries messages of its own. In fact, it has been suggested that as much as 70 percent of all messages sent and received by humans are nonverbal in nature.

Like language, nonverbal forms of communication are learned and, as such, vary from one culture to another. Even though some nonverbal cues have the same meaning in different cultures, an enormous range of variation in nonverbal communication exists between cultures. In some cases, a certain message can be sent in a number of different ways by different cultures. For example, whereas in the United States we signify affirmation by nodding the head, the very same message is sent by throwing the head back in Ethiopia, by sharply thrusting the head forward among the Semang of Malaya, and by raising the eyebrows among the Dyaks of Borneo. Moreover, cross-cultural misunderstandings can occur when the same nonverbal cue has different meanings in different cultures. To illustrate, the hand gesture of making a circle with the thumb and forefinger, which means OK in the United States, signifies "money" in Japan, indicates "worthlessness" or "zero" in France, and is a sexual insult in parts of South America.

Humans communicate without words in a number of important ways, including hand gestures, facial expressions, eye contact, touching, space usage, scents, gait, and posture. A thorough discussion of these and other aspects of nonverbal communication, based on the re-

The same gesture often carries different meanings in different languages. Beware! Don't do this in parts of South America. It doesn't mean "OK."

cent literature, would certainly take us beyond the scope of this textbook. A brief examination of three of the more salient types of nonverbal communication—hand gestures, eye contact, and touching—will help convey the importance of this form of human communication.

Hand Gestures

Consider how many hand gestures we use every day. We cup our hand behind the ear as a nonverbal way of communicating that we cannot hear. We thumb our noses at those we don't like. We can thumb a ride on the side of the highway. We can wave hello or goodbye. We tell people to be quiet by holding our forefinger vertically against our lips. We give the peace sign by holding up our forefinger and middle finger. And we send a very different message when we flash half of the peace sign. Some of the hand gestures used widely in the United States are also used and understood in Europe, which should come as no surprise, given our strong European heritage. Nevertheless, as Morris (1979) reminds us, a number of nonverbal hand gestures used in Western Europe have not been diffused across the Atlantic. For example, stroking the face between the cheek bones and the chin with the thumb and forefinger is a nonverbal way of saying "You look ill or thin" in the southern Mediterranean; pulling down on the lower eyelid with the forefinger means "Be alert" in parts of Spain, Italy, France, and Greece; and in Italy, pulling or flicking one's own ear lobe is a way of calling into question a man's masculinity ("You are so effeminate that you should be wearing an earring").

Eye Contact

The use of eye contact also varies widely from one culture to another. In the United States, a certain degree of eye contact is used to convey respect and attentiveness in normal conversation. In some cultures, however, people are taught from an early age that direct eye contact is threatening, disrespectful, or rude. According to Morsbach (1982:308), for example, Japanese avoid direct eye contact in normal conversation by focusing somewhat lower, around the region of the Adam's apple. Other cultures, on the other hand, insist on even more direct eye contact than might be expected in the United States. As Edward T. Hall reminds us, "Arabs look each other in the eye when talking with an intensity that makes most Americans highly uncomfortable" (1966:161). In such cultures, the somewhat lower level of eye contact typically found in the United States could be viewed as inattentive, impolite, and aloof.

Touching

Touching is perhaps the most personal and intimate form of nonverbal communication. Humans communicate through touch in a variety of ways or for a variety of purposes, including patting a person on the head or back, slapping, kissing, punching, stroking, embracing, tickling, shaking hands, and laying-on hands. Every culture has a well-defined set of meanings connected with touching. That is, each culture defines who can touch whom, on what parts of the body, and under what circumstances.

Some cultures have been described as high-touch cultures, while others are low-touch. Some studies (Montagu, 1972; Sheflen, 1972; and Mehrabian, 1981) have suggested that Eastern Europeans, Jews, and Arabs tend to be high-touch cultures, while such Northern European cultures as Germans and Scandinavians tend

Bowing is an important mode of nonverbal communication for these Japanese businessmen.

to be low-touch cultures. The difference between high- and low-touch cultures can be observed in public places, such as subways or elevators. For example, Londoners (from a low-touch culture) traveling in a crowded subway are likely to assume a rigid posture, studiously avoid eye contact, and refuse to even acknowledge the presence of other passengers. The French (from a high-touch culture), on the other hand, have no difficulty leaning and pressing against one another in a crowded Parisian subway.

Language and Communication Systems

Language is perhaps the most characteristic feature of Homo sapiens. Humans can send and receive a near infinite number of messages (both verbally and nonverbally) that convey meaning. Some of these meanings are abstract while others are concrete. To be certain, some other animal species have a limited capacity for symbolic communication. Humans, however, have developed this symbolizing capacity to such a degree that it serves as the single most distinctive hallmark of our humanity.

If, in fact, language is such a fundamental feature of our humanness, it should come as no surprise that it can have important implications for our everyday lives. This is particularly true when attempting to communicate across cultures. It is virtually impossible for anyone in the Western world today to avoid communicating—or attempting to communicate—with people from different cultural backgrounds. Whether we are Peace Corps volunteers in Nigeria, missionaries in Samoa, or machinery sales representatives from Toledo trying to make a sale in Singapore, it is absolutely imperative that we have an understanding of the communication patterns of the people with whom we are interacting. Even if we never leave our home communities, it is becoming increasingly unlikely that we could avoid interacting with linguistically different people even if we wanted to.

An anthropological linguist serves as an expert witness in a civil rights case heard by a federal district court.

When language may have a bearing on the outcome of a court case, anthropologists (or more precisely, sociocultural linguists) may be brought in to give expert testimony. In 1979, a federal court in Ann Arbor, Michigan concluded that black students from a public elementary school were being denied their civil rights because they were not being taught to read, write, and speak Standard English as an alternative to their dialect of Black English Vernacular (BEV). The presiding judge ruled that since the school system failed to recognize and use BEV as the basis for teaching Standard English, the black children were put at a disadvantage for succeeding in school and, consequently, in life as well (Chambers 1983).

To a very large degree, this precedent-setting court decision rested on establishing the basic premise that BEV actually exists as a bona fide language. It was popularly held—and indeed implicitly built into the reading curriculum in the Ann Arbor schools—that the language of black students was nothing more than slang, street talk, or a pathological form of Standard English. But as William Labov, a sociolinguist from the University of Pennsylvania, was able to establish to the satisfaction of the court, BEV is a full-fledged linguistic system with its own grammatical rules, phonology, and semantics. In other words, Labov's testimony demonstrated that

(1) the differences that exist between BEV and Standard English are governed by linguistic rules rather than being the result of errors in Standard English; (2) BEV is as capable of expressing a wide range of abstract and complex ideas as is Standard English; and (3) the BEV that is spoken by children in Ann Arbor is the same as the BEV spoken in New York, Washington, Chicago, and Los Angeles.

On the basis of Labov's testimony, the federal court concluded that language is a vital link between a child and the education the child receives. Children who speak the same language as the language of instruction learn more effectively than those who speak a nonstandard version of the language of instruction. It should be pointed out that the court did *not* rule that children had to be taught in BEV. Rather the court ordered that the local schools were to acknowledge the fact that language used at home and in the community can pose a barrier to student learning *when teachers fail to recognize it, understand it, and incorporate it into their instructional methods.*

Labov's contribution, however, went well beyond his testimony as an expert witness in federal court. Part of the judge's ruling ordered the Ann Arbor schools to develop strategies to inform the teachers how best to teach Standard English to children who enter the schools speaking BEV. After spelling out in considerable detail the linguistic features of BEV, Labov (1983:29–55) went on to show how this linguistic system interferes with learning Standard English and how this can be taken into account when developing new methods for teaching reading. Here is a situation, then, in which the data and insights from linguistic anthropology can make practical contributions to both civil rights litigation and instructional programming.

THOUGHT QUESTIONS

1. Why did the judge in this court case rule that black children were being placed at a disadvantage?
2. How was Labov able to argue that BEV was a bona fide language in its own right?
3. What practical contributions did Labov make to the area of language use in public education?
4. Of the various roles played by applied anthropologists that were discussed in chapter three, which best describes Labov's role(s) in this case study?

A cultural anthropologist's study of a linguistic misunderstanding between Native Americans and government bureaucrats serves as the basis for settling a court case.

Although we often describe the United States as a cultural and linguistic "melting pot," the country continues to be the home of a number of ethnically and linguistically diverse peoples. Even though most people living in the United States speak some English, that in itself does not ensure smooth cross-cultural communication. In fact, the literature in the field of

cross-cultural communications is filled with examples of cultural miscommunication. One well-described case in point is the misunderstanding that occurred between six Bannock-Shoshoni Native American women from the Fort Hall reservation and officials at the Social Service Agency in Pocatello, Idaho (Joans 1984).

This breakdown in communication involved the issue of social service payments. The six Native American women were accused in court of withholding information from the agency and failing to report money they had received. To be eligible for supplemental security income (SSI), the women were required to report all forms of income. Several of the women had received several thousand dollars of rent money from small landholdings. They rented the land in January of one year but were not paid until the following December, at which time they reported the income. The agency maintained that the money should have been reported as soon as the property was rented (January) rather than when the income was received. When agency officials learned of the unreported income, they stopped the SSI payments to the women and insisted that they return the money already paid to them. The women claimed that they did not understand the instructions, given in English, concerning the reporting of income. The agency claimed that the women knew full well about the regulations and simply chose to ignore them. When the case came to court, the central issue was whether or not the women understood what was expected of them.

Barbara Joans, an anthropologist at a local university, was brought in to try to resolve the issue. She reasoned that since the verbal exchanges between the six women and the agency officials had been conducted in English, she would design a study that would determine the extent to which the six Native American women understood the English language. To do this, she constructed a three-tiered English proficiency exam. Level one tested how well the women understood everyday questions such as Where is the gas station? Are you too hot? How much is the loaf of bread? Level two tested how well the women understood jokes, double entendres, mixed meanings, and puns. The third level consisted of government/bureaucratic language dealing with such subjects as police operations and the workings of the town council.

The findings of this study demonstrated that the women all understood level one English; only one of the women could follow the conversation using level two English; and none of the six Native American women understood level three English. Over the course of about three months, anthropologist Joans had frequent contact with the women in their homes, at the reservation trading post, in the lawyer's office, and in her own office. Based on this contact, Joans concluded that even though the women and the agency personnel all spoke English, they used the language very differently. On the basis of these findings, the judge ruled that, owing to the difference in language usage, the women did not understand what was expected of them and thus did not need to return any of the money. Since the women did not understand the SSI instructions, the judge ordered that they were not to be held responsible for their failure to report rent monies before they received them. The judge added that in the future the agency officials would have to use a Bannock-Shoshoni interpreter when they went to the reservation to describe program requirements. Thus, Joans used her knowledge of language usage, derived from anthropological research, to resolve a problem of miscommunication across cultures.

THOUGHT QUESTIONS

1. This case study revolves around a misunderstanding between Native Americans and government bureaucrats. Was this misunderstanding the result of cultural differences, class differences, or differences in power? Explain.

2. Is the United States more of a "melting pot" or a "salad bowl." Explain.

3. When such culturally distinct groups as Native Americans come up against mainstream institutions, miscommunication frequently occurs. With what other social institutions (other than welfare agencies) could miscommunications occur with Native American populations?

Summary

1. Language—and the capacity to use symbols—is perhaps the most distinctive hallmark of our humanity.

2. Though nonhumans also engage in communication, human communication systems are unique in several important respects. First, human communication systems are open—that is, they are capable of sending an infinite number of messages. Second, humans are the only animals not confined to the present, for they can speak of events that have happened in the past or might happen in the future. And third, human communication is transmitted largely through tradition rather than experience alone.

3. All human languages are structured in two ways. First, each language has a phonological structure comprising rules governing how sounds are combined to convey meanings. Second, each language has its own grammatical structure comprising those principles governing how morphemes are formed into words (morphology) and how words are arranged into phrases and sentences (syntax).

4. Despite considerable structural variations in the many languages of the world, there is no evidence to support the claim that some languages are less efficient at expressing abstract ideas than others.

5. Cultures can influence language to the extent that the vocabulary in any language tends to emphasize those words that are adaptively important in that culture. Thus, the highly specialized vocabulary in American English relating to the automobile is directly re-

lated to the cultural emphasis that North Americans give to that particular part of their technology.

6. According to the Sapir-Whorf hypothesis, language is thought to influence perception. Language, according to Sapir and Whorf, not only is a system of communicating but also establishes mental categories that affect the way in which people conceptualize the real world.

7. Sociolinguists are interested in studying how people use language depending on the social situation or context in which they might be operating.

8. As important as language is in human communication, the majority of human messages are sent and received without using words. Human nonverbal communication—which, like language, is learned and culturally variable—can be made in such ways as facial expressions, gestures, eye contact, touching, and posture.

Key Terms

bound morpheme
closed system
  of communication
cultural emphasis
  of a language
diglossia
displacement
free morpheme
grammar

morphology
nonverbal
  communication
open system
  of communication
phonology
Sapir-Whorf Hypothesis
syntax

Suggested Readings

Farb, Peter. *Word Play: What Happens When People Talk.* New York: Knopf, 1974. A highly readable account of linguistics for the nonspecialist.

Fromkin, Victoria, and Robert Rodman. *An Introduction to Language.* New York: CBS College Publishing, 1993. A spritely introduction to the field of anthropological linguistics.

Hecht, Michael L., Mary Jane Collier, and Sidney Ribeau. *African American Communication: Ethnic Identity and Cultural Interpretation.* Thousand Oaks, Calif.: Sage Publications, 1993. This volume explores African-American styles of communication, ethnic identity, language competence, and the relationship between African Americans and white Americans. The book is designed to help the reader better understand African-American communication patterns in their proper cultural context.

Hickerson, Nancy P. *Linguistic Anthropology.* New York: Holt, Rinehart & Winston, 1980. A readable, nontechnical introduction to the field of anthropological linguistics, with chapters on historical linguistics, the classification of languages, descriptive linguistics, psycholinguistics, sociolinguistics, and language and culture.

Hymes, Dell. *Language in Culture and Society: A Reader in Linguistics and Anthropology.* New York: Harper & Row, 1964. A classic collection of sixty-nine articles in the general area of language and culture compiled for both scholars and serious students of anthropological linguistics.

Lehmann, Winifred P. *Historical Linguistics, An Introduction* (2d ed.) New York: Holt, Rinehart & Winston, 1973. An introduction to the general principles of historical linguistics, this small volume analyzes the classification of languages, methods used in gathering and analyzing historical linguistic data, and how languages change.

Salzmann, Zdenek. *Language, Culture, and Society: An Introduction to Linguistic Anthropology.* Boulder, Colo.: Westview Press, 1993. A comprehensive, up-to-date introduction to anthropological linguistics, this text looks at phonology, the origins of language, the social context of language, nonverbal communication, and the ethnography of communications, among other topics.

Trudgill, Peter (Ed.). *Applied Sociolinguistics.* London: Academic Press, 1984. A collection of nine essays by sociolinguists designed to demonstrate the range of real-world activities to which sociolinguistic data can be of interest, including education, psychology, the law, and the media.

Wardhaugh, Ronald. *An Introduction to Sociolinguistics.* Oxford: Basil Blackwell, 1986. Designed as a beginning text in sociolinguistics, this volume deals with such topics as dialects and regional variations, speech communities, language change, gender differences, the relationship between language and culture, and language policy.

GETTING FOOD

CHAPTER SEVEN

A man fishing with a bow and arrow in Papua New Guinea.

- What are the different ways by which societies get their food?
- How do technology and environment influence food-getting strategies?
- How have humans adapted to their environments over the ages?

To survive, any culture needs to solve certain societal problems. As we pointed out in our discussion of cultural universals, all societies must develop systematic ways of controlling people's behavior, defending the group from outside forces, passing on the cultural traditions from generation to generation, mating, rearing children, and procuring food from the environment to meet their physical needs. Of all these basic societal needs, the need to secure food from one's surroundings is the most critical. The human body can survive for as long as a week or so without water and perhaps up to a month without food. Unless a society can develop a systematic and regular way of getting food for its members, the population will die off.

Like other aspects of culture, food-getting strategies vary widely from one society to another. Nevertheless, it is possible to identify five major food-procurement categories found among the world's populations:

Hunting and Gathering. The systematic collection of wild vegetation, the hunting of animals, and fishing.

Horticulture. A basic form of plant cultivation using simple tools and small plots of land and relying solely on human power.

Pastoralism. Keeping of domesticated animals (e.g., cows, goats, sheep) and using their products (e.g., milk, meat, blood) as a major food source.

Agriculture. A more productive form of cultivation than horticulture because of the use of animal power (e.g., horses, oxen) or mechanical power (tractors, reapers) and usually some form of irrigation.

Industrialization. The production of food through complex machinery.

Environment and Technology

Which food-getting strategy is actually developed by any given culture will depend, in large measure, on the culture's environment and technology. The relationship between physical environment and food-getting methods is not neat and tidy; that is, the earth cannot easily be divided into neat ecological zones, each with its own unique and mutually exclusive climate, soil composition, vegetation, and animal life. Nevertheless, geographers (e.g., James 1966) frequently divide the world's land surface into a number of categories, including grasslands, deserts, tropical forests, temperate forests, polar regions, and mountain habitats. Some of these environments are particularly hospitable to the extent that they support a number of modes of food acquisition. Others are more limiting in the types of adaptations they permit. Anthropologists generally agree that the environment does not determine food-getting patterns but rather sets broad limits on the possible alternatives. For example, subsisting on horticulture in the polar region is not an ecological possibility, but a number of other alternatives are possible.

It is technology—a part of culture—that helps people adapt to their specific environment. In fact, the human species enjoys a tremendous adaptive advantage over all other species precisely because it has developed technological solutions to the problems of survival. Since some cultures have more complex technologies than others, they have gained greater control over their environments and their food supplies. For example, the complex farming technology used in the American

Midwest produces more wheat than can be consumed domestically; at the other extreme, a small hunting-and-gathering society with a very simple level of technology has, at best, an imperfect and tenuous control over its environment and food supply. To suggest, however, that such variations in technological adaptations exist is not to imply that societies with simple technologies are either less intelligent or less able to cope with their environment. On the contrary, many societies with simple technologies adapt very ingeniously to their particular environment. As Collins reminds us:

> Among some Eskimo groups, wolves are a menace—a dangerous environmental feature that must be dealt with. They could perhaps be hunted down and killed, but this involves danger as well as considerable expenditure of time and energy. So a simple yet ingenious device is employed. A sharp sliver of bone is curled into a springlike shape, and seal blubber is molded around it and permitted to freeze. This is then placed where it can be discovered by a hungry wolf, which, living up to its reputation, "wolfs it down." Later, as this "time bomb" is digested and the blubber disappears, the bone uncurls and its sharp ends pierce the stomach of the wolf, causing internal bleeding and death. The job gets done! It is a simple yet fairly secure technique that involves an appreciation of the environment as well as wolf psychology and habits. (1975:235)

The specific mode of food getting, however, will be influenced by the interaction of a people's environment with its technology. To illustrate, the extent to which a foraging society is able to successfully procure food will depend on not only the sophistication of the society's tools but also the abundance of plant and animal life the environment provides. Similarly, the productivity of a society based on irrigation agriculture will vary according to the society's technology as well as such environmental factors as the availability of the water supply and the natural nutrients in the water. These environmental factors set an upper limit on the ultimate productivity of any given food-getting system and the size of the population it can support. Cultural ecologists refer to this limit as the environment's **carrying capacity** (Glossow 1978).

A natural consequence of exceeding the carrying capacity is damage to the environment, such as killing off too much game or depleting the soil. Because of this carrying capacity, societies cannot easily increase their food-getting productivity. Thus, if a society is to survive, it must meet the fundamental need of producing or procuring enough food and water to keep its population alive. But beyond satisfying this basic minimal need of survival, societies also satisfy their idiosyncratic and quite arbitrary *desires* for certain types of food. To a certain degree, people regularly consume those foods that are found naturally (or can be produced) in their immediate environment. But frequently people go out of their way to acquire some special foods while choosing not to use other foods that may be both plentiful and nutritious.

Although early anthropologists wrote off such behavior as irrational and arbitrary, cultural ecologists in recent years have examined these "peculiar" behaviors more carefully and have found that they often make sense in terms of the energy expended versus the caloric value of the foods consumed. This theory—known as the **optimal foraging theory**—suggests that foragers will pursue those animals and plant species that tend to maximize their caloric return for the time they spend searching, killing, collecting, and preparing (see Smith 1983). In other words, when specific foraging strategies are examined in ethnographic detail, decisions to seek out one food source and not others turn out to be quite rational, for they are based on a generally accurate assessment of whether or not the search will be worth the effort.

Major Food-Getting Strategies

The five forms of food procurement (**hunting and gathering, horticulture, pastoralism, agriculture,** and **industrialization**) are not mutually exclusive, for in most human societies we find more than one strategy. Where this is the case, however, one form will usually predominate. Moreover, within each category we can expect to find considerable variations largely because of differences in environment, technology, and historical experiences. These five categories of food getting are explored in more detail in the following sections.

Hunting and Gathering

Collecting food—as compared to producing food—involves the exploitation of wild plants and animals that already exist in the natural environment. People have been hunters and gatherers for the overwhelming majority of time that they have been on earth. It was not

Most anthropologists agree that the environment sets broad limits on the possible form that food-getting patterns may take. Cultures help people adapt to a number of generally inhospitable environments.

until the **Neolithic Revolution**—approximately 10,000 years ago—that humans for the first time produced their food by means of horticulture or animal husbandry. If we view the period of human prehistory as representing an hour in duration, then humans have been hunters and gatherers for all but the last ten seconds! With the rise of food production the incidence of hunting and gathering has steadily declined, as Murdock reminds us:

> Ten thousand years ago the entire population of the earth subsisted by hunting and gathering, as their ancestors had done since the dawn of culture. By the

time of Christ, eight thousand years later, tillers and herders had replaced them over at least half of the earth. At the time of the discovery of the New World, only perhaps 15 per cent of the earth's surface was still occupied by hunters and gatherers, and this area has continued to decline at a progressive rate until the present day, when only a few isolated pockets survive. (1968:13)

Even though most societies have become food producers, a handful of societies in the world today are still hunters and gatherers. These few hunting-and-gathering societies vary widely in other cultural features and are to be found in a wide variety of environments (semideserts, tropical forests, and polar region, among others). For example, some hunting-and-gathering societies such as the !Kung of the Kalahari Desert, live in temporary encampments, have small-scale populations, do not store food, and are essentially egalitarian. At the other end of the spectrum are groups like the Kwakiutl, American Indians from the northwest coast, who live in permanent settlements, have relatively high-density populations, live on food reserves, and recognize marked distinctions in rank. Despite these considerable variations among contemporary hunters and gatherers, however, it is possible to make the following generalizations about most of them:

1. *Hunting-and-gathering societies have relatively low densities of population.* The reason for this is that food collection has built-in checks that prevent it from becoming a particularly efficient method for procuring large amounts of food. In other words, increased efficiency in the collection methods of these societies ultimately destroy their source of food.

2. *Food-gathering societies are usually nomadic or seminomadic rather than sedentary.* As a direct result of this continual geographic mobility, hunting-and-gathering peoples usually do not recognize individual land rights. By and large, food collectors move periodically from place to place in search of wild animals and vegetation. Since game frequently migrates during the yearly cycle, hunters need to be sufficiently mobile to follow the game. Conversely, food producers such as cultivators tend to be more sedentary owing to the large investment that farmers usually have in their land. There are notable exceptions to both of these generalizations, however. Some food collectors, such as certain northwest coast American Indian groups, live in particularly abundant environments that permit permanent settlements; and some horticultural societies (such as the Bemba of Zambia) practice shifting cultivation and, for all practical purposes, are seminomadic.

3. *The basic social unit among hunting-and-gathering people is the family or the band, a loose federation of families.* Consequently, social control revolves around family institutions rather than more formal political institutions.

4. *Contemporary hunting-and-gathering peoples occupy the remote and marginally useful areas of the earth.* These areas include such out-of-the-way places as the Alaskan tundra, the Kalahari Desert, the Australian outback, and the Ituru Forest of central Africa. It is reasonable to suggest that these food-gathering societies, with their relatively simple levels of technology, have been forced into these marginal habitats by the food producers with their more dominating technologies.

The association of hunting and gathering with an absence of social, political, and economic complexity is an accurate portrayal of contemporary foraging societies. With several notable exceptions (such as the Ainu of northern Japan and certain northwest coast Indian groups), most contemporary foraging societies are relatively small scale, unspecialized, and uncentralized. In recent years, however, archaeologists have pointed out that foraging societies in prehistoric times in all likelihood had considerably greater social complexity (see, for example, Price and Brown 1985).

In most societies that rely on both hunting game and collecting wild vegetable matter, the latter activity provides the greatest amount of food. Although hunting wild animals is both spectacular and highly prized, it has been suggested that the bulk of the diets of most hunters and gatherers consists of foods other than meat. For example, Lee (1968:33) estimates that the !Kung of the Kalahari Desert derive between 60 percent and 80 percent of their diet by weight from vegetable sources. The near total absence of vegetable matter from the diet of the Eskimos is the notable exception to this generalization.

Early anthropological accounts tended to portray hunters and gatherers as living precariously in a life-or-death struggle with the environment. More recently, however, some anthropologists (Sahlins, Lee) have suggested that certain hunting-and-gathering groups are relatively well off despite inhabiting some very unproductive parts of the earth. The question of the relative abundance within hunting-and-gathering societies became a topic of heated debate at a conference on food collectors in 1966. Although this issue was not resolved in any definitive way, considerable evidence suggests that hunters and gatherers are capable of adapting to harsh environments with creativity and resourcefulness. Perhaps we can get a better idea of how hunters and gatherers procure their food by examining two very different contemporary groups—the !Kung of present-day Namibia and the Netsilik Eskimos of northern Canada—in greater detail.

 *looking ahead*

To see how anthropological information on hunters and gatherers in Indonesia has been used in planning government programs, see Applied Perspective 2 at the end of this chapter.

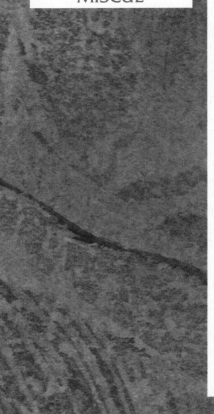

CROSS-CULTURAL MISCUE

In an attempt to locate an outlet for its products in Europe, a large U.S. manufacturer sent one of its promising young executives to Frankfurt to make a presentation to a reputable German distributor. The U.S. company had considerable confidence in the choice of this particular junior executive because the man not only spoke fluent German but also knew a good deal of German culture. When the American entered the conference room where he would be making his presentation, he did all the right things. He shook hands firmly, greeted everyone with a friendly *guten tag,* and bowed his head slightly as is customary in Germany. Drawing on his experience as a past president of the Toastmasters Club in his hometown, the U.S. executive prefaced his presentation with a few humorous anecdotes to set a relaxed mood. At the end of his presentation, however, he sensed that his talk had not gone well. In actual fact, the presentation was not well received, and the German company chose not to distribute the U.S. company's product line.

What went wrong? Despite careful preparation, the U.S. firm made two tactical miscues that conflicted with German business culture. First, despite the American executive's knowledge of his product line and his fluency in German, his age was one important factor working against him. Since executives in German corporations tend to be older than their U.S. counterparts, any young U.S. executive—no matter how competent—is not likely to be taken seriously because of his or her relative inexperience. The second factor contributing to the failure of the presentation was the American's attempt to set a relaxed tone by starting off with several jokes. Though an effective public-speaking technique for a luncheon talk at the Kiwanis Club, it was considered too frivolous and informal for a German business meeting.

The !Kung of the Kalahari Region. One of the best studied hunting-and-gathering societies, the !Kung inhabit the northwestern part of the Kalahari Desert, one of the least hospitable environments in the world. Inhabiting an area that is too dry to support either agriculture or the keeping of livestock, the !Kung are totally dependent upon hunting and gathering for their food. Food-procuring activities are fairly rigidly divided between men and women. Women collect roots, nuts, fruits, and other edible vegetables, while men hunt medium- and large-size animals. Although men and women spend roughly equivalent amounts of time on their food-procuring activities, women provide between two and three times as much food by weight as men.

Even though the term *affluence* or *abundance* tends to be relative, Lee (1968) presents convincing evidence to suggest that the !Kung are not teetering on the brink of starvation. In fact, there are reasons to believe that the !Kung food-gathering techniques are both productive and reliable. For example, the !Kung's most important single food item is the mongongo nut, which accounts for about half of their diet. Nutritionally, the mongongo, which is found in abundance all year long, contains five times more calories and ten times more protein per cooked unit than cereal crops. Thus, quite apart from hunting, the !Kung have a highly nutritional food supply that is more reliable than cultivated foods. It is little wonder that the !Kung do not have a strong urge to take up agriculture when there are so many mongongo nuts around.

Another measure of the relative affluence of the !Kung is their selectivity in taking foods from the environment. If they were indeed on the brink of starvation, we would expect them to exploit every conceivable source of food. But in actual fact, only about one-third of the edible plant foods are eaten, and only 17 of the 223 local species of animals known to the !Kung are hunted regularly (Lee 1968:35).

Moreover, if the !Kung were in a life-or-death struggle with the natural environment, their survival rate and life expectancy would be low. Infant mortality would be high, malnutrition would be rampant, and the elderly and infirm would be abandoned. This is hardly the demographic picture for the !Kung. Based on fieldwork conducted in the 1960s, Lee (1968:36) found that approximately 10 percent of his sample population was sixty years of age or older, a percentage that was not substantially different from industrialized societies.

And finally, the !Kung's relative abundance of resources can be judged from the amount of time they devote to procuring food. While food getting is the most important activity among the !Kung, the same is true for cultivators and pastoralists. Although the number of work hours varies from one hunting-and-gathering society to another, it appears that the !Kung, despite what might appear to be their harsh environment, are hardly overworked. Lee (1968:37) estimates that the average !Kung adult spends between twelve and nineteen hours per week in the pursuit of food. Usually, women can gather enough food in one day to feed their families for three days, leaving a good deal of time for such leisure activities as resting, visiting, entertaining visitors, and embroidering. Even though men tend to work more hours per week than women, they still have considerable leisure time for visiting, entertaining, and dancing.

The Netsilik Eskimos. Inhabiting one of the most inhospitable regions of the world, the Netsilik Eskimos—in stark contrast to the !Kung—stand out as a society that is living in a very delicate balance with the environment. Living in a barren region northwest of Hudson Bay in northern Canada, the Netsilik have had to adapt to an arctic climate of bitterly cold temperatures and short summers and a terrain almost totally devoid of edible plants. Under such conditions, the diet of these people is almost exclusively derived from animals (caribou, musk ox, and seals) and fish. To adapt to such a harsh environment, the Netsilik have developed a number of very creative strategies for maximizing their survival chances.

Since food collecting is virtually nonexistent, the Netsilik have a number of different hunting strategies at their disposal. During the harsh winter months after the caribou have migrated, the Eskimos rely almost exclusively on seal hunting. Since seals need to get air periodically through numerous breathing holes in the ice, the most efficient form of seal hunting involves large hunting parties. Thus, to maximize their chances for catching seals, the Netsilik Eskimos organize themselves during the winter months into large igloo communities of up to sixty people from several distantly related extended families. It is during this time that social life is most intense and various ceremonies are most likely to occur.

During the summer months as game becomes more accessible, the extended igloo communities disperse into smaller social units. Hunting takes on a number of new forms. Seal continue to be hunted at the breathing holes but are also hunted on top of the ice; caribou are hunted with bows and arrows; salmon and trout running upstream are caught with pronged spears; large-scale cooperative caribou hunts, using beaters and spearers, are conducted at certain caribou crossing places; and toward the end of the summer months, these smaller hunting groups engage in spear fishing for salmon through the thin river ice. During these summer months social activities are considerably less intense. Thus, the Netsilik Eskimos have adapted by organizing their economic and social lives around the availability of various types of game and the strategies required for hunting them. That is, large social and hunting groups that are most functional for winter seal hunting split up during the summer into smaller groups that tend to maximize food-getting possibilities from caribou hunting and salmon fishing.

Despite their resourcefulness in getting food, the Netsilik Eskimos are under continuous ecological pressure. Unlike the !Kung, they are constantly searching for food and consequently have precious little leisure time. Rasmussen (1931) reported that approximately 10 percent of the population died of starvation. Food getting in this extreme environment is highly stressful, as Balikci describes:

Traveling and moving camps was a very arduous task. Lack of dog feed severely limited the keeping of dogs to only one or two per family. The heavy sledges had

To survive in their harsh environment, the Netsilik Eskimos have had to develop a number of creative hunting strategies.

to be pulled or pushed by both men and women. Only very small children were allowed to sit on the sledge. Old people had to drag themselves behind, and were often left behind to sleep out on the ice if they had not caught up with the others. Seal hunting involved a motionless watch on the flat ice under intense cold maintained for many hours. . . . Beating the fast running caribou over great distances in the tundra was an exhausting task. Stalking the caribou with the bow and arrow also involved endless pursuits across the tundra, the hunters lying on the wet grass and trying to approach the game while hiding behind tufts of moss. . . . Hunting was a never-ceasing pursuit, the game had to be brought to camp at all cost, and the hunter had to stay out until a successful kill. (1968:81)

The two cases of hunting-and-gathering societies just cited—the !Kung and the Netsilik Eskimos—represent extremes in relative levels of abundance. The !Kung, with their year-round access to nutritional foods, are rarely in danger of starvation and appear to have considerable leisure time. The Eskimos, by contrast, must work long and arduously to acquire sufficient food to keep themselves alive. In terms of dietary abundance, the other hunting-and-gathering societies in the world are, no doubt, somewhere between these two extremes.

Food-Producing Societies

Approximately 10,000 years ago, humans made a revolutionary transition from hunting and gathering to food production (the domestication of plants and animals). For hundreds of thousands of years before this

time, humans had subsisted exclusively on hunting and gathering. Then, for reasons that are still not altogether clear, humans began to cultivate crops and keep herds of animals as sources of food. For the first time, humans gained a measure of control over their food supply. That is, through tilling of the soil and animal husbandry, humans were now able to produce food rather than have to rely solely on what nature produced for the environment. This shift from collecting to producing food, known as the Neolithic Revolution, occurred in several different areas of the world independently of one another. The earliest known plant and animal domestication occurred around 8000 B.C. in the so-called Fertile Crescent, including parts of Jordan, Israel, Syria, southern Turkey and northern Iraq, and western Iran. Other early centers of food production had emerged in China by around 6000 B.C., Thailand around 6800 B.C., and sub-Saharan African around 3000 B.C.

A number of theories have been suggested to explain why the Neolithic Revolution occurred. Although no definitive explanation has emerged, most archaeologists agree that the shift to food production was a response to certain environmental or demographic conditions, such as variations in rainfall or population pressures. Whatever the cause or causes may have been, there is little doubt of the monumental consequences of the Neolithic Revolution. What made the Neolithic Revolution so revolutionary was that it produced the world's first population explosion. Even though the early Neolithic communities were relatively small, they were far larger than any others in human prehistory. Throughout the Near East, Egypt, and Europe, thousands of skeletal remains have been unearthed from the Neolithic period (8000 B.C. to 3500 B.C.) compared to only a few hundred for the entire Paleolithic period, even though the Paleolithic lasted hundreds of times longer than the Neolithic.

Cultural Changes Resulting from Food Production. That food producing, as compared to hunting and gathering, should result in a dramatic increase in population is not difficult to understand. As pointed out earlier, hunters and gatherers are subject to natural dietary limitations, for increased efficiency can ultimately destroy their source of food. Cultivators, however, can increase the food supply (and thus support larger populations) simply by sowing more seeds. Moreover, children are more useful economically for farmers and herders than they are for hunters and gatherers. While children tend to be a burden for the hunter, for food producers they can be useful by weeding fields, scaring off birds or other small animals, and tending flocks at relatively young ages. Population studies (White 1973; and Kasarda 1971) have suggested that fertility rates tend to be higher in societies where children make an economic contribution.

Not only did populations become larger as a result of the Neolithic Revolution, they also became more sedentary. Whereas most hunters and gatherers must be sufficiently mobile to follow migrating game, cultivators are more likely to invest their time and energy in a piece of land, develop the notion of property rights, and establish permanent settlements. In other words, a gradual settling-in process occurred as a result of the Neolithic Revolution. This is not meant to imply, however, that all, or even most, people became tied to the land after the Neolithic Revolution. Many remained hunters and gatherers; some became nomadic or semi-nomadic pastoralists, and still others became shifting cultivators. Nevertheless, the Neolithic (or food-producing) Revolution initiated the gradual trend toward a more settled way of life.

The cultivation of crops also brought about other important, even revolutionary, cultural changes. For example, since farming is more efficient than food collecting, a single farmer can produce enough food to feed ten people. This, then, frees up nine people to engage in some activity other than food procurement. Thus, the Neolithic Revolution stimulated a greater division of labor. That is, people could for the first time become specialists, inventing and manufacturing the tools and machinery needed for a more complex social structure. Once some people were liberated from the food quest, they were able to develop new farm imple-

ments such as the plow, pottery storage containers, metallurgy, new and improved hunting and fishing technology, the wheel, and stone masonry, among other inventions. Without these and other inventions that resulted from an increase in labor specialization, it is unlikely that we would have ever reached the second revolution—the rise of civilization.

Horticulture. Horticulture refers to the simplest type of farming that uses basic hand tools such as the hoe or digging stick rather than plows or other machinery driven by animals or machines. Since horticulturalists produce relatively low yields, they generally do not have sufficient surpluses to allow them to develop extensive market systems. The land, which is usually cleared by hand, is neither irrigated nor enriched by the use of fertilizers. A major technique of horticulturalists is the **slash and burn method,** sometimes referred to as **swidden cultivation** or **shifting cultivation.** This technique involves clearing the land by manually cutting down the growth, burning it, and planting in the burned area. Even though the ash residue serves as a fertilizer, the land is usually depleted within a year or two. The land is then allowed to lie fallow to restore its fertility, or it may be abandoned altogether. This technique of slash and burn cultivating can eventually destroy the environment, for if fields are not given sufficient time to fallow, the forests will be permanently replaced by grasslands.

At first glance it would appear that slash and burn agriculture makes very poor use of the land. Since most land must be left fallow at any given time, the system of slash and burn cannot support the high densities of population that can be sustained by intensive agriculture. While it is true that there are inherent limitations to food production in the slash and burn technique, it does not necessarily follow that the mere application of intensive agricultural methods (i.e., clearing the forests, tractor plowing, and the use of chemical fertilizers) would automatically produce larger yields. In those areas where the slash and burn method is most often found (i.e., the tropics), conversion to intensive agriculture is not a viable alternative. For example, ecological studies of tropical areas have shown that most of the nutrients are located in the vegetation rather than in the soil itself. Clearing the land of existing vegetation would leave nutrient-poor soil. Moreover, the removal of the tree canopy would further deplete the nutrients from the soil through erosion and leaching from direct contact with the sun. Given these ecological conditions found in many tropical areas, the slash and burn method of cultivation remains a rational food-producing technique.

Swidden farming is a simple form of cultivation. Here the technique is practiced by a man in the Ivory Coast clearing the land to plant rice.

Slash and burn horticulturalists are frequently extremely adept at maximizing their resources. A number of slash and burn farmers produce quite abundant harvests of tropical forest products, and do so without destroying the land. To illustrate, McGee (1990:36) has shown that the Lacandon Maya of Chiapas, Mexico, disperse over forty different crops throughout their cleared fields (milpas). By spreading their many crops over a milpa, the Lacandon are imitating both the diversity and the dispersal patterns found in the natural primary forest. According to McGee:

> In contrast to monocrop agriculture as practiced in the United States, the milpa attempts to maintain rather than replace the structure of the tropical rainforest ecosystem. In effect, the milpa is a portion of jungle where a greater than normal population of food-producing crops has been concentrated. This concentration of food is aided by the fact that Lacandon farmers plant their milpas with crops that take advantage of different environmental niches within the same cleared area. For example, at ground level, hills of corn, beans, squash, and tomatoes are sown. A few meters above the surface grow tree crops such as bananas and oranges, and finally, subsurface root crops such as manioc and sweet potatoes are cultivated below the ground's surface. Thus, a Lacandon farmer achieves at least three levels of production from the same piece of land.

McGee points out that this form of slash and burn horticulture is quite efficient, for the typical Lacandon Mayan family can feed itself while working fewer than half the total number of days in a year.

Crops.   The crops grown by horticulturalists can be divided into three categories: tree crops, seed crops, and root crops. Tree crops include bananas or plantains, figs, dates, and coconuts; the major seed crops (which tend to be high in protein) are wheat, barley, corn, oats, sorghum, rice, and millet; the main root crops (which tend to be high in starch and carbohydrates) include yams, arrowroots, taro, manioc, and potatoes. Since seed crops require a greater quantity of nutrients than root crops, seed cultivators need longer periods of time to fallow their fields. In some cases, this can have consequences for settlement patterns. That is, if seed cultivators do in fact need a longer time to rejuvenate their fields, they may be less likely to live in permanent settlements than are root cultivators. However, even though swidden cultivation involves the shifting of fields, it does not necessarily follow that the cultivators also periodically shift their homes.

Many horticulturalists supplement their simple cultivation with other food-getting strategies. For example, some, such as the Yanomamo (Chagnon 1983:56–68), may engage in hunting and gathering; others, such as the Swazi (Kuper 1986:79–80), keep a variety of domesticated animals, including cows, goats, sheep, horses, donkeys, and pigs; while still others (e.g., the Samoans) supplement their crops with protein derived from fishing.

The Bemba.   A specific example will help illustrate the practice of horticulture. Audrey Richards (1960:96–109) provides a particularly good case study with her writings on the Bemba of present-day Zambia (formerly Northern Rhodesia). The Bemba, like a number of other peoples in South Central Africa, practice a type of shifting cultivation that involves clearing the land, burning the branches, and planting directly on the ash-fertilized soil without additional hoeing. Using the simplest technology (hoes and axes), the Bemba plant a fairly wide range of crops—including finger millet, bulrush millet, beans, cassava, and yams—but they rely most heavily on finger millet as their basic staple. Although predominantly horticultural, the Bemba do supplement their diet by some hunting, gathering, and fishing. The largest and most highly organized group politically in Zambia, the Bemba live in small, widely scattered, low-density communities comprising thirty to fifty huts.

Traditionally, Bemba society had a highly complex political system based on a set of chiefs whose authority rested on their alleged supernatural control over the land and the prosperity of the people. These supernatural powers were reinforced by the physical force that chiefs could exert over their subjects, whom they could kill, enslave, or sell. The power, status, and authority of the chiefs were based not on the accumulation of material wealth but rather on the amount of *service* they could extract from their subjects in terms of agricultural labor or military service. Interestingly, the marked status differences between chiefs (with their unchallenged authority) and commoners is not reflected in these people's diets. While chiefs and their families may have a somewhat more regular supply of food, both rich and poor people eat essentially the same types and quantities of food throughout the yearly cycle. Similarly, there are no appreciable differences in diet between Bemba men and Bemba women.

The use of draft animals involves a more complex form of crop production than slash and burn.

Since sparse rainfall at certain times of the year permits only one crop, a common feature of the Bemba diet is the alternation between scarcity and plenty. The harvest of finger millet, the mainstay of the Bemba diet, lasts only nine months (roughly from April through December). During the lean months of January through March, dramatic changes take place in village life. Owing to the low energy levels, most activity—both leisure and work-related—is reduced to a minimum. Given these alternating periods of feast and famine, it is not surprising that food and diet occupy a prominent place in Bemba culture. In much the same way that pastoralists frequently appear obsessed with their cattle, the Bemba tend to fixate on food. In fact, according to Richards, food and beer are the central topics of conversation among the Bemba:

> Any one who can follow the ordinary gossip of a Bemba village will be struck at once by the endless talk shouted from hut to hut as to what is about to be eaten, what has already been eaten, and what lies in store for the future, and this with an animation and a wealth of detail which would be thought quite unusual in this country. . . . The giving or receipt of food is a part of most economic transactions, and many come to represent a number of human relationships whether between different kinsmen or between subject and chief. . . . To speak of a chief is to mention before the end of the conversation his reputation for generosity or meanness in the giving of porridge and beer. To describe an attitude of any particular kinsman leads almost invariably to a comment, for instance, on the food in his granary, the numbers of relatives he supports, the share of meat he has asked for, or the amount of beer he contributed at the marriage of his daughter or the visit of an elder. In daily life the women, whether at work in the kitchen or sitting gossiping on their verandas at night, exchange interminable criticisms as to the way in which some particular dish of food has been divided, or the distribution of the four or five gourds of beer made at a brew. (1960:106)

Pastoralism.   Like horticulture, pastoralism first appeared in the Neolithic period. This form of food production involves the keeping of domesticated herd animals and is found in areas of the world that cannot support agriculture because of inadequate terrain, soils, or rainfall. These environments do, however, provide sufficient vegetation to support livestock, provided the animals are able to graze over a large enough area. Thus, pastoralism is associated with geographic mobility, for herds must be moved periodically to exploit seasonal pastures. (Barfield 1993).

Some anthropologists have differentiated between two types of movement patterns: **transhumance** and **nomadism.** With transhumance, some of the men in a pastoral society move their livestock seasonally to different pastures while the women, children, and the other men remain in permanent settlements. With nomadism, on the other hand, there are no permanent villages, and the whole social unit of men, women, and children

This terraced form of farming as practiced in Indonesia involves a considerable investment of labor.

Pastoralists such as these Tibetan sheepherders in the Himalayas must move their herds peri-odically to ensure adequate pasturage.

moves the livestock to new pastures. But as Rada and Neville Dyson-Hudson have pointed out (1980:18), the enormous variations even within societies render such a distinction somewhat sterile. For example, following seven Karamojong herds over a two-year period, the Dyson-Hudsons found that "each herd owner moved in a totally different orbit, with one remaining sedentary for a full year and one grazing his herd over 500 square miles."

Even though anthropologists tend to lump pastoralists into a single food-getting category, pastoralism is not a unified phenomenon. For example, there are wide variations in the ways animals are herded. The principal herd animals are cattle in eastern and southern Africa, camels in North Africa and the Arabian Peninsula, reindeer in the subarctic areas of Eastern Europe and Siberia, yaks in the Himalayan region, and various forms of mixed herding (goats, sheep, cattle, etc.) in a number of places in Europe and Asia. In addi-

tion to variations in the type of animals, a number of other social and environmental factors can influence the cultural patterns of pastoral people, including, among others, the availability of water and pasturage, the presence of diseases, the location and timing of markets, governmental restrictions, and the demands of other food-getting strategies (e.g., cultivation) that the pastoralists may practice.

The consensus among anthropologists is that pure pastoralists—that is, those who get all of their food from livestock—are either extremely rare or nonexistent. Since livestock alone cannot meet all of the nutritional needs of a population, most pastoralists need some grains to supplement their diets. Many pastoralists, therefore, either combine the keeping of livestock with some form of cultivation or maintain regular trade relations with neighboring agriculturalists.

It is clear that in pastoral societies livestock play a vital economic role not only as a food source but also as a resource for other uses to which their products can be put. In addition to the obvious economic importance of meat, milk, and blood as food sources, cattle provide dung (used for fertilizer, house building, and fuel), bone (used for tools and artifacts), skins (used for clothing), and urine (used as an antiseptic). But in addition to these important economic uses, livestock serve important noneconomic, or social, functions. Livestock frequently influence the social relationships among people in pastoral societies. To illustrate, an exchange of livestock between the families of the bride and the groom is required in many pastoral societies before a marriage can be legitimized. In the event of an assault or a homicide, in some societies livestock will be used to compensate the victim's family as a way of restoring normal social relations. The sacrifice of livestock at the grave site of ancestor gods is a way that people keep in touch with their gods. These and other **social uses of cattle** or other livestock should remind us that domesticated animals in pastoral societies not only serve as the major food source but also are intimately connected to other parts of the culture, such as the systems of marriage, social control, and religion.

 looking ahead

Anthropological insights into the nature of pastoral economies have been applied to economic development projects in developing countries. For a discussion of one such project in Tanzania, see Applied Perspective 1 at the end of this chapter.

Somali Pastoralism.   The pastoral Somali of the Horn of East Africa provide an excellent example of a pastoral society that engages in mixed herding. The Somali number over two million people in the Somali Republic itself, with an additional million currently living in southeastern Ethiopia and northern Kenya. As in other pastoral societies, not only do livestock supply the bulk of the Somali's subsistence, but, in fact, household composition and nomadic movements are dictated largely by environmental conditions and the seasonal needs of the herds.

Somali pastoralism is based on the keeping of sheep, goats, camels, cattle, donkeys, and horses. Sheep and goats contribute most to the Somali diet in the form of milk and meat. Camels provide some milk, but their main role in the Somali economy is to transport the collapsible huts during periods of migration. Zebu cattle, relatively rare among the Somali, are used as a source of milk for domestic use and ultimately as an export commodity. Donkeys are used exclusively as beasts of burden, and horses, while scarce, serve as a means of rapid transportation and as a status symbol.

The physical environment of the Somali is anything but hospitable. Much of the terrain is semidesert, with sparse rainfall and intermittent vegetation. The Somali recognize three fairly distinct ecological zones, which, depending on the season, provide differential quantities of the two resources absolutely essential to pastoralism—water and pasturage. Migration and temporary settlement take place in all three regions, depending on the four major seasons—two wet and two dry. Even under the best of conditions, these three ecological zones are so harsh that, as Lewis concluded, "the line between survival and disaster is precariously narrow" (1965:329).

To maximize their resources as well as their adaptation to an unforgiving environment, Somali herders divide into two distinct grazing units. One unit is the nomadic hamlet, based on sheep and goats, that engages in migratory patterns designed to meet the regular watering needs of these important food-producing animals. Socially, these herding units consist of small groups of nuclear families related through the male line. Nomadic hamlets are not stable units, however, for men periodically attach their nuclear or polygynous families to a number of different groups of kin during any given season. On the average, nomadic hamlets contain three nuclear families but can involve more, particularly during times of warfare, when larger groups can provide greater security.

In contrast to the nomadic hamlet, the camel camp, containing only grazing camels, serves essentially as the training grounds where boys learn the skills of camel husbandry. Life in the camel camp is austere, especially during the dry season. The boys and men of the camel camp live predominantly on camel's milk, have no means of cooking, sleep out in the open, and spend large amounts of time driving their animals between water and pasturage. Unlike the hamlets, which may include a number of types of kin, the camel camps include only kin related through the male line, a distinction that reflects how the different types of livestock are viewed. Whereas sheep and goats are owned by individuals, camels are viewed as representing the wealth of the larger kin group—the lineage. While goats and sheep are used primarily to meet individual dietary needs, camels are the principal currency in such important lineage transactions as bridewealth and blood

For the Masai of East Africa, cattle play both economic and social roles.

compensation. Owing to their different grazing requirements, the hamlets and the camel camps move independently of each other, being closer together during the wet seasons and more widely dispersed during the dry seasons.

Agriculture. Agriculture (intensive cultivation) differs from horticulture in that agriculture relies on animal power and technology rather than on human power alone. Agriculture, a more recent phenomenon than horticulture, is characterized by the use of the plow, draft animals to pull the plow, fertilizers, irrigation, and other technological innovations that make intensive cultivation much more efficient than horticulture. A single cultivator using a horse-drawn plow, for example, not only can put a larger area of land under cultivation but also, since the plow digs deeper than the hoe or digging stick, unleashes more nutrients from the soil, thereby increasing the yield per acre. Animal fertilizers (from the excrement of the draft animals) permit land

to be used year after year rather than having to remain fallow to restore its fertility naturally. Irrigation of fields that do not receive sufficient or consistent rainfall is another innovation contributing to the increased efficiency of intensive agriculture. Moreover, the invention of the wheel has been a boon to the intensive farmer in transportation, the water-raising wheel, and pottery making (storage vessels for surplus crops). Thus, through the application of technology, the intensive cultivator has access to a much greater supply of energy than is available to the horticulturalist.

This greater use of technology enables the agriculturalist to support many times more people per unit of land than the horticulturalist. There is a price for this greater productivity, however, since intensive agriculture requires a greater investment of both labor and capital. First, in terms of labor, agriculturalists must put in vast numbers of hours of hard work to prepare the land. In hilly areas, the land must be terraced and maintained, while irrigation systems may involve drilling wells, digging trenches, and building dikes. All of these activities—which admittedly increase the land's productivity enormously—are extremely labor intensive. Second, intensive agriculture, as compared to horticulture, requires a much higher investment of capital in terms of plows (which need to be maintained), mechanical pumps (which can break down), and draft animals (which can become sick and die).

Agriculture, a more recent phenomenon than horticulture, is closely associated with both higher levels of productivity and more settled communities. In fact, not until early horticultural societies had developed into more intensive forms of agriculture could humankind develop civilizations (i.e., urban societies). In other words, a fully efficient system of food production, brought about by intensive agriculture, is a necessary, if not sufficient, condition for the rise of civilization.

As farming became more intensive, the specialization of labor became more complex. Under a system of intensive agriculture, a single farmer could produce enough food for five people; this increase in productivity meant that four people could devote their time and energy to such activities as manufacturing, education, public administration, writing, or inventing rather than the pursuit of food. Thus, the intensification of agriculture did not cause, but rather enabled the development of a more complex division of labor. Societies became more stratified (i.e., marked by greater class differences); political and religious hierarchies were established to manage the economic surpluses and mediate between the different socioeconomic classes; and even-

tually, state systems of government (complete with bureaucracies, written records, taxation, a military, and public works projects) were established. Although the relationship is not necessarily a causal one, these structural changes could not have occurred without the development of an efficient system of food production that agriculture provided.

Peasantry.   With the intensification of agriculture and the rise of civilization came the development of the **peasantry.** Peasant farmers differ from American Indian horticulturalists, Polynesian fishing people, or East African herders in that they are not isolated or self-sufficient societies. Instead, peasants are tied to the larger unit (i.e., city or state) politically, religiously, and economically. More specifically, peasants are subject to the laws and controls of the state, are influenced by the urban-based religious hierarchies, and exchange their farm surpluses for goods produced in other parts of the state. Peasants usually make up a relatively large percentage of the total population and provide most of the dietary needs of the city dwellers.

The intimate relationship that peasants have with the cities and the state is succinctly stated by Foster, who refers to peasants as ". . . a peripheral but essential part of civilizations, producing the food that makes possible urban life, supporting the specialized classes of political and religious rulers and educated elite" (1967:7). Foster's statement is important because it reminds us that the relationship between the peasants and the state is hardly egalitarian. The peasants almost always occupy

Mechanized farming can support appreciably more people per unit of land than horticulture. Here a combine harvests soybeans in Illinois.

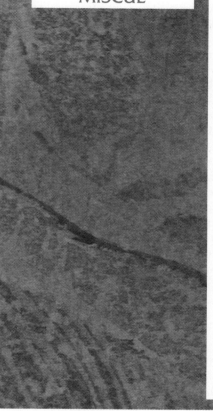

CROSS-CULTURAL MISCUE

The Masai are a group of pastoralists (cattle herders) living in Kenya and Tanzania. In fact, they have so many cows that the environment cannot support them very well. As a result, the land is overgrazed, and the cows are rather scrawny and give relatively little milk. With this in mind, the British colonial officials tried to get the Masai to reduce the size of their herds so that they would have healthier, fatter, and better milking cows. The British officials reasoned (correctly) that by reducing the number of cows, the Masai would actually have more milk and more beef in the long run. But the Masai strongly refused to reduce the size of their herds. The British concluded (this time incorrectly) that the Masai were simply too stupid to know any better.

The British officials, however, failed to understand the basic value system of the Masai—a value system that is very different from their own. Unlike dairy farmers in the West, the Masai are not interested in maximizing the total quantity of milk given by their cows since they already have far more milk than they can drink, and they are not in the business of selling milk. For the Masai, cows are far more than simply sources of milk. Rather, cows are significant for social reasons. For example, cows are used to legalize marriages, to bond friends together, and as a measure of one's prestige. In short, the more cows the Masai have, the better off they are. They are not interested in having fat cows that give large quantities of milk. Instead, they are interested in the sheer number of cows, even if they are scrawny and poor milkers. Given such a value system, it would be as unreasonable for the Masai to voluntarily thin out their herds as it would be for us to exchange five old wrinkled dollar bills for two new crisp dollar bills. From the Masai's perspective, it is the quantity, not the quality, of the cows that counts.

---

the lowest strata of society. Although they supply the rest of the society with its food, peasants have low social status, little political power, and scanty material wealth. The more powerful urbanites, through the use of force or military power, frequently extract both labor and products from the peasants in the form of taxation, rent, or tribute.

Industrialized Food Getting. As mentioned earlier, the domestication of plants and animals around 8000 B.C. expanded people's food-getting capacity geometrically from what it had been when they relied on hunting and gathering alone. Similarly, the intensification of agriculture brought about by the invention of the plow, irrigation, and fertilizing techniques had revolutionary consequences for food production. A third major revolution in our capacity to feed ourselves occurred several hundred years ago with the coming of the Industrial Revolution. Industrialized food production relies on technological sources of energy rather than human or animal energy. While water and wind power (in the forms of waterwheels and windmills) were used in the early stages of the industrial period, today industrialized agriculture employs motorized equipment such as tractors and combines. The science of chemistry has been applied to modern agriculture to produce fertilizers, pesticides, and herbicides, all of which increase agricultural productivity. In addition to the quantum leaps in agricultural productivity in the past two hundred years, technology has been applied with equally dramatic results to other areas of food production. For example, oceangoing fishing vessels literally harvest enormous quantities of fish from the seas, scientific breakthroughs in genetics and animal husbandry now produce increasingly larger supplies of meat and poultry, and a certain amount of food in the modern person's diet is actually manufactured or reconstituted.

Food getting—and agriculture in particular—in contemporary industrialized societies has experienced some very noticeable changes since the late eighteenth century. Before the Industrial Revolution, agriculture was carried out primarily for subsistence; farmers produced crops for their own consumption rather than for sale. Today, however, agriculture is largely commercialized in that the overwhelming majority of food today is sold by food producers to nonproducers for some form of currency. Moreover, industrialized agriculture requires relatively complex systems of market exchange because of its highly specialized nature.

Within the past several decades in the Western world, the trend toward commercialization of agriculture has seen its most dramatic expression in the rise of agribusiness—large-scale agricultural enterprises involving the latest technology and a sizable salaried workforce. The rise of agribusiness in recent years has been accompanied by the decline of mom-and-pop farms that drew mainly on family labor. As the number of family farms has declined and agriculture has become more highly mechanized, the developed world has witnessed a dramatic decrease in the percentage of the world's population that is engaged in food production.

Even though the industrialization of agriculture has produced farms of enormous size and productivity, these changes have not been without a very high cost. The machinery and technology needed to run modern-day agribusiness is expensive. Fuel costs to run the machinery are high. With the vast diversification of foods found in modern diets (oranges from Florida, cheese from Wisconsin, corn from Iowa, avocados from California, and coffee from Colombia), additional expenses are incurred for processing, transporting, and marketing food products. Moreover, large-scale agriculture has been responsible for considerable environmental destruction. For example, large-scale agriculture in various parts of the world has led to (1) lowering of water tables, (2) changes in the ecology of nearby bodies of surface water, (3) the destruction of water fauna by pesticides, (4) the pollution of aquifers by pesticides, (5) salinization of soil from overirrigation, and (6) air pollution from crop spraying.

Food Getting

In many developing countries, the process of national economic development almost always is interpreted as necessitating a change in traditional cultural patterns. Since development officials view these traditional cultural patterns as obstacles to necessary socioeconomic change, it is assumed that they need to be altered or obliterated as quickly as possible.

The process of economic development, however, involves more than the wholesale substitution of new ways of behaving for traditional ones. What is needed in the process of economic development in developing countries is not the elimination of traditional, long-standing cultural patterns but rather a thorough understanding of those patterns. If planners are to make rational decisions about what changes are even appropriate for achieving the goals of national economic development, they will need to know as much as possible about existing traditional economies. It may well be that in some situations, changing traditional economies will be contrary to the goals of economic development. Or, if it can be determined (and agreed upon) that certain changes in traditional economies would, in fact, contribute to national economic development, planners must have as much knowledge as possible about traditional cultures so that they can effect changes with the least amount of disruption possible. In either case, the process of economic development must begin with a comprehensive understand-

ing of traditional cultures—which cultural anthropologists are in the best position to provide.

Anthropological insights into traditional pastoral economies assist in the development of a beef ranching project in Tanzania.

The Tanzanian Livestock Project serves as an excellent example of how the participation of a cultural anthropologist contributed to an economic development program in East Africa. The project, aimed at developing commercial beef ranching in Tanzania, involved a socioeconomic restructuring of pastoral economies. The objective of the program was to modify the largely subsistence nature of cattle keeping so that it would be more market oriented and produce more income. This was to be accomplished by the creation of Ujamaa ("familyhood") ranches, whereby groups of local families from traditional pastoral societies would form cattle ranching partnerships under the skilled management of government husbandry experts. It was believed that if successful, such a commercialization of livestock would provide both needed capital to individual families and an increased food supply for domestic consumption and export.

Much to the credit of the project administrators, Priscilla Reining, a cultural anthropologist experienced with pastoral societies in northern Tanzania, was invited to participate in the appraisal of the project conducted by the World Bank. Reining was asked to assess a number of aspects of traditional culture that might have an impact on the formation of the proposed Ujamaa ranches, such as traditional sex roles, lines of authority, inheritance customs, value placed on age, and conceptions of property rights. Reining then had the difficult task of making recommendations on criteria for recruiting program participants, organizational features of the Ujamaa ranches, and incentives for participation.

Based on her understanding of the traditional cultures of these pastoral peoples, Reining made a number of recommendations designed to mesh the program goals with the traditional cultural features. In addition, Reining was able to point out to the program administrators the multiple uses of cattle for the local herding peoples. As mentioned earlier, cows have a different meaning for East African pastoralists than they do for Texas beef ranchers. To be certain, cattle are important economic commodities, but for the Tanzanian pastoralist, they are also important *socially* in terms of prestige, friendship bonds, and the legitimization of marriages. Armed with this understanding, the program administrators came to realize that commercial ranching would not be accepted overnight. The success of the program depended on how well the social organization of the Ujamaa ranches provided appropriate alternatives for the many social uses of cattle found in the traditional cultures. Speaking of the anthropological contribution to the project, one administrator concluded the following:

> It appears unlikely that the team, without an anthropologist, could have seen all of the ramifications of the changes the project was proposing. The anthropological input was significant; it added depth and understanding to our reasons for supporting ujamaa. (Husain 1976:78)

THOUGHT QUESTIONS

1. What was the major anthropological contribution to the Tanzanian live-stock project?

2. In what ways do cattle have different significance for pastoralists in Tanzania and Texas beef ranchers?

3. Anthropologist Reining's role in this project was to demonstrate the social (noneconomic) importance of cattle and suggest alternatives for taking these into consideration when planning a new livestock program. Should the job of anthropologists end with making suggestions or should they also become involved in selecting and implementing the alternatives? Why?

Knowledge of a traditional economy in Indonesia can be used to prevent counterproductive government decisions.

The Tanzanian Livestock Project illustrates how anthropological insights can be used to improve the design of an economic development project. Sometimes an understanding of the cultural realities of traditional peoples can lead to a decision to abandon a development scheme altogether because it is at odds with its own objectives. A case in point is a project involving the Punan society of Indonesia, a group of forest dwellers who collect, among other things, certain international trade items such as rattan and resins (see Hoffman 1988).

Unlike their settled agricultural neighbors, the Punan engage in no cultivation and have carved out for themselves a fairly specialized ecological niche as forest collectors. Although the Punan and their neighbors exploit different environments, they maintain extensive ties with each other. By exchanging forest products for food crops, the Punan and their neighbors are enriching each other's economies. Thus, the realities of Punan culture are that they contribute significantly to the modern export sector of the Indonesian economy and maintain very strong economic ties with their settled agricultural neighbors.

The Indonesian government holds a very different view of Punan culture. The official view is that as an isolated group of hunters and gatherers, the Punan have an economy that contributes nothing to the national economy. Proceeding on this faulty perception, the government has embarked on a "development" program designed to turn the Punan into productive agriculturalists. As Dove has commented:

> . . . it is clear that this policy, if successful, will severely reduce or even terminate the role of the Punan in the collection of forest products, with a similar impact upon the not unimportant contribution of forest products to Indonesia's export sector. Such an impact would run directly counter to the government's all-out effort to find exportable commodities to replace the country's dwindling supplies of oil and gas. (1988:11)

Here is an example, then, of an official development scheme that is based on erroneous cultural information. If completed, the program will reduce the appreciable contribution that the Punan are currently making to the export sector of the national economy. Thus, the Indonesian government may complete a project that will be less advantageous economically than to have done nothing at all. If the government does choose to "shoot itself in the foot," it will not be because it lacked an accurate description of the cultural realities of the Punan culture.

THOUGHT QUESTIONS

1. What are the major economic differences between the Punan and their agricultural neighbors?

2. Why does the Indonesian government think the Punan economy is a nonproductive part of the Indonesian national economy?

3. Can you think of examples from our own society where, in an attempt to improve things, the government has made conditions worse because it did not understand the culture of the people being affected?

Summary

1. If any culture is to survive, it must develop strategies and technologies for procuring or producing food from its environment. While not mutually exclusive, five major food procurement categories are recognized by cultural anthropologists: (a) hunting and gathering (foraging), (b) horticulture, (c) pastoralism, (d) agriculture, and (e) industrialization.

2. The relative success of various food-getting strategies will depend on the interaction between a society's technology and its environment. While different environments present different limitations and possibilities, it is generally recognized that environments influence rather than determine food-getting practices. The level of technology that any society has at its disposal is a critical factor in adapting to and utilizing the environment.

3. Carrying capacity is the limiting effect that an environment has on a culture's productivity. If a culture exceeds its carrying capacity, permanent damage to the environment usually results.

4. Hunting and gathering—the oldest form of food getting—relies on procuring foods that are naturally available in the environment. Approximately 10,000 years ago, people for the first time began to domesticate plants and animals. Since then the percentage of the world's population engaged in foraging has declined from 100 percent to a small fraction of 1 percent.

5. When compared to other food-getting practices, hunting-and-gathering societies, which tend to have low-density populations, are nomadic or seminomadic, live in small social groups, and occupy remote, marginally useful areas of the world.

6. Foraging societies tend to be selective in terms of the plant and animal species they exploit in their habitats. Which species are actually exploited for food can be explained by the optimal foraging theory, a theory developed by cultural ecologists that suggests that foragers do not select arbitrarily but rather on the basis of maximizing their caloric intake for the amount of time and energy expended.

7. Horticulture, a form of small-scale plant cultivation relying on simple technology, produces low yields with little or no surpluses. Horticulture most often utilizes the slash and burn technique, a form of cultivation that involves clearing the land by burning it and then planting in the relatively fertile ash residue.

8. Pastoralism, the keeping of domesticated livestock as a source of food, is usually practiced in those areas of the world that are unable to support any type of cultivation. This food-getting strategy most frequently involves a nomadic or seminomadic way of life, small family-based communities, and regular contact with cultivators as a way of supplementing their diets.

9. Agriculture, a more recent phenomenon than horticulture, utilizes such technology as irrigation, fertilizers, and mechanized equipment to produce high yields and support large populations. Unlike horticulture, agriculture is usually associated with permanent settlements, cities, and high levels of labor specialization.

10. Industrialized food getting, which began several centuries ago, uses vastly more powerful sources of energy than had ever been used previously. It relies on

high levels of technology (tractors, combines, etc.), a mobile labor force, and a complex system of markets.

Key Terms

agriculture
carrying capacity
horticulture
hunting and gathering
industrialization
Neolithic Revolution
nomadism
optimal foraging theory

pastoralism
peasantry
slash and burn method
  (shifting cultivation/
  swidden cultivation)
social uses of cattle
transhumance

Suggested Readings

Barfield, Thomas J. *The Nomadic Alternative*. Englewood Cliffs, N.J.: Prentice-Hall, 1993. A historical and ethnographic discussion of pastoral societies in East Africa, the Middle East, and Central Eurasia focusing on such topics as comparative social organization, relations with non-pastoral peoples, and the ecology of nomadic pastoralism.

Bicchieri, M. G. *Hunters and Gatherers Today*. New York: Holt, Rinehart & Winston, 1972. A collection of eleven socio-economic studies of hunting-and-gathering societies found throughout the world and the changes they have undergone during the present century.

Evans-Pritchard, E. E. *The Nuer*. Oxford: Oxford University Press, 1940. A classic ethnography about a pastoral society of the Sudan showing the central role that cattle play in the overall working of the society.

Harris, M., and E. B. Ross, eds. *Food and Evolution: Toward a Theory of Human Food Habits*. Philadelphia: Temple University Press, 1987. A compendium of twenty-four essays by scholars from a number of disciplines explore why people in different parts of the world and at different periods of history eat the things they do. Perspectives from a wide range of academic disciplines are represented, including physical anthropology, psychology, archaeology, nutrition, and primatology.

Lee, Richard B. *The Dobe !Kung*. New York: Holt, Rinehart & Winston, 1984. The basic ethnographic case study of the !Kung, foragers living in Botswana and Namibia, by one of the leading contemporary authorities on hunting-and-gathering societies.

Schrire, C., ed. *Past and Present in Hunter Gatherer Studies*. Orlando, Fla.: Academic Press, 1984. A collection of ten thoughtful essays on hunting-and-gathering societies by anthropologists who have worked with groups from southern Africa to Tasmania to the Philippines. The editor's aim in this work is to challenge the widely held notion that hunting-and-gathering societies have maintained their economic institutions through cultural isolation.

Service, Elman. *The Hunters*. 2d ed. Englewood Cliffs, N.J.: Prentice-Hall, 1979. A slim volume designed to describe primitive band societies to beginning students of anthropology. The author attempts to present a well-balanced, integrated view of hunting-and-gathering societies by analyzing technologies, the economies, ideologies, political systems, and social relationships.

ECONOMICS

CHAPTER EIGHT

A floating vegetable market in Bangkok, Thailand.

- How do anthropologists study economic systems cross-culturally?

- How are resources such as land and property allocated in different cultures?

- What are the different principles of distribution found in various parts of the world?

When we hear the word *economics,* a host of images comes to mind. We usually think of such things as money, supply and demand curves, lending and borrowing money at some agreed-upon interest rate, factories with production schedules, labor negotiations, buying stocks and bonds, foreign exchange, and gross domestic product. Although these are all topics that one might expect to find in an economics textbook, they are not integral parts of all economic systems. Many small-scale cultures exist in the world that have no standardized currencies, stock markets, or factories. Nevertheless, all societies (whether small scale or highly industrialized) face a common challenge—that is, they all have at their disposal a limited amount of vital resources, such as land, livestock, machines, food, and labor. This simple fact of life requires all societies to plan carefully how to (1) allocate scarce resources, (2) produce needed commodities, (3) distribute their products to all people, and (4) develop efficient consumption patterns for their products so as to help people maximize their adaptation to the environment. In other words, every society, if it is to survive, must develop systems of production, distribution, and consumption.

The science of economics focuses on the three major areas of production, distribution, and consumption as observed in the industrialized world. The subdiscipline of economic anthropology, on the other hand, studies production, distribution, and consumption *comparatively* in all societies of the world—industrialized and nonindustrialized alike. For current discussions of issues in economic anthropology, see Ortiz and Lees (1992) and Plattner (1989).

Economics and Economic Anthropology

The relationship between the formal science of economics and the subspecialty of economic anthropology has not always been a harmonious one.

Formal economics has its philosophical roots in the study of Western, industrialized economies. As a result, much of formal economic theory is based on assumptions derived from observing Western, industrialized societies. For example, economic theory is predicated on the assumption that the value of a particular commodity will increase as it becomes scarcer (i.e., the notion of supply and demand) or on the assumption that when exchanging goods and services, people naturally strive to maximize their material well-being and their profits.

Economists use their theories (based on these assumptions) to predict how people will make certain types of choices when either producing or consuming commodities. Owners of a manufacturing plant, for example, are constantly faced with choices. Do they continue to manufacture only men's jockey shorts, or do they expand their product line to include underwear for women? Do they move some or all of their manufacturing facilities to Mexico, or do they keep them in North Carolina? Should they give their workers more benefits? Should they spend more of their profits on advertising? Should they invest more capital on machinery or on additional labor? Western economists assume that all of these questions will be answered in a rational way so as to maximize the company's profits. Similarly, Western economists assume that individuals as well as corporations are motivated by the desire to maximize their material well-being.

Substantivists

A long-standing debate between different schools of economics and anthropology has centered on the question of whether these and other assumptions that Western economists make about human behavior are indeed universal. How applicable are these economic theories to the understanding of small-scale, nonindustrialized societies? Are the differences between industrial and nonindustrial economies a matter of degree or a matter of kind? Some anthropologists—representing the **substantive approach**— hold the position that classical economic theories cannot be applied to the study of nonindustrialized societies. This "school" has argued that tribal or peasant societies, based as they are on subsistence, are different in kind than market economies found in the industrialized societies.

Whereas in Western societies production and consumption choices are made on the basis of maximization of profits, in nonindustrialized societies they frequently are based on quite different principles, such as reciprocity or redistribution. The principle of reciprocity (as in the biblical injunction of "Do unto others as you would have them do unto you") emphasizes the fair exchange of equivalent values and as such is in direct contrast to the principle of maximizing one's profits. Likewise, the principle of redistribution, found in many subsistence economies, discourages the accumulation of personal wealth by moving or redistributing goods from those who have to those who do not. Such principles as reciprocity and redistribution, with their emphasis on cooperation and generosity, are in stark contrast to the principle of maximization, which encourages individual accumulation and competition and consequently can lead to jealousy, hostility, and antagonism.

Formalists

In direct opposition to the substantive school are the **formalists,** who contend that the concepts of Western economics are appropriate for the study of *any* economic system provided they are broadened. While admitting that Western economic theory (as currently conceived) is too narrow, the formalists hold that it should be possible to broaden that theory to include

non-Western economies. For example, even though many nonindustrialized societies may not operate on a "profit motive" in our monetary sense of the term, we should not conclude that the concept of maximization is totally irrelevant. The formalists would argue that people operating in small-scale economies may be motivated by the desire to maximize their standing in the community, their physical security, or the breadth of their social networks rather than their material well-being. If that is indeed the case, then the traditional economic concept of maximization can be broadened to include all economies.

Formalists suggest, moreover, that the substantivists have overly romanticized the nature of nonindustrialized economies to the extent that they lose sight of their economic significance. To illustrate, while admitting that certain pastoralists may use cows for a number of noneconomic reasons (such as legitimizing marriages, establishing social hierarchies, and making religious sacrifices), the formalists would remind us that these same cows have very definite economic uses as well as social uses. As Schneider (1957) and Gray (1960) have pointed out, cows among East African pastoralists represent (1) **capital goods** (they produce milk, blood, and manure), (2) **consumer goods** (they

Formal economic theory—based primarily on observations of Western society—assumes that all people naturally seek to maximize their economic well-being, as this couple in their elegant Mercedes convertible has done. Some economic anthropologists, however, would argue that such an assumption does not hold true for all cultures of the world.

produce meat for eating, hides for clothing, and bone for making artifacts), and (3) a form of *savings and investment* (they are a valuable reserve of economic resources on the hoof, which can be expanded through animal husbandry). The difficulty, of course, lies in the fact that since the economic behavior of certain nonindustrialized peoples is an integral part of the social structure, it is frequently difficult to separate the economic from the noneconomic.

Cross-Cultural Examination of Economic Systems

A good deal of debate has taken place over the past half century between the formalists and the substantivists. The formalists hold the view that the principles of classical economics can be useful for the study of all societies, while the substantivists hold that they cannot. Although these two "schools" start from two very different sets of philosophical assumptions, they may have more in common than each is willing to admit. In spite of the substantial differences of economic systems found throughout the world—as well as the different theories used to analyze them—it is possible to examine economic systems cross-culturally along certain key dimensions:

1. *The regulation of resources.* How land, water, and natural resources are controlled and allocated.
2. *Production.* How material resources are converted into usable commodities.
3. *Exchange.* How the commodities, once produced, are distributed among the people of the society.

The Allocation of Natural Resources

Every society has access to certain natural resources in its territorial environment, including land, animals, water, minerals, and plants. Even though the nature and amount of these resources vary widely from one group to another, every society has developed a set of rules governing the **allocation of resources** and how they can be used. For example, all groups have determined systematic ways for allocating land among their members. Hunters and gatherers must determine who can hunt animals and collect plants from which areas. Pastoralists need to have some orderly pattern for deciding access to pasturage and watering places. Agriculturalists must

work out ways of acquiring, maintaining, and passing on rights to their farmland.

In our own society, where things are bought and sold in markets, most of the natural resources are privately owned. Pieces of land are surveyed, precise maps are drawn, and title deeds are granted to those who purchase a piece of property. Individual property rights are so highly valued in the United States that under certain circumstances, a property owner is justified in killing someone who is attempting to violate those property rights. Relatively small pieces of land are usually held by individuals, while larger pieces of property are held collectively, either by governments (as in the case of roads, public buildings, parks, etc.) or by private corporations on behalf of their shareholders.

To be certain, there are limitations on private property ownership in the United States. To illustrate, certain vital resources such as public utilities are either strongly regulated or owned outright by some agency of government, rights of eminent domain enable the government to force owners to sell their land for essential public projects, and zoning laws set certain limits on how a property owner may use his or her land. Nevertheless, the system of resource allocation found in the United States is based on the general principle of private ownership, whereby an individual or a group of individuals have total or near total rights to a piece of property and consequently can dispose of it as they see fit.

Property rights are so strongly held in the United States (and other parts of the Western world) that some observers have suggested that humans have a genetically based territorial instinct that compels them to stake out and defend their turf (Ardrey 1968). However, the degree to which humans are territorial varies widely throughout the world. By and large, the notion of personal land ownership is absent in most societies that base their livelihood on hunting and gathering, pastoralism, or horticulture. Let us examine how each of these types of societies deals with the question of access to land.

Hunters and Gatherers

In most hunting-and-gathering societies, land is not owned, in the Western sense of the term, either individually or collectively. Hunters and gatherers have a number of compelling reasons to maintain flexible or open borders. First, since food collectors in most cases must follow the migratory patterns of animals, it makes little

Individual property rights are strongly valued and protected in the United States, but some other cultures of the world define property rights much more loosely.

sense for people to tie themselves exclusively to a single piece of land. Second, claiming and defending a particular territory requires time, energy, and technology that many hunting-and-gathering peoples either do not have or choose not to expend. Third, territoriality can lead to conflict and warfare between those claiming property rights and those who would violate those rights. Thus, for hunting-and-gathering societies, having flexible territorial boundaries (or none at all) is the most adaptive strategy.

Even though hunters and gatherers rarely engage in private ownership of land, there is some variation in the amount of communal control. At one extreme are the Eskimos and the Hadza of Tanzania, two groups that have no concept of trespassing whatsoever. Anyone in these societies can collect food wherever she or he pleases. The !Kung of the Kalahari area do recognize, to some degree, the association of certain territories with particular tribal bands, but it is not rigorously maintained. For example, members of one !Kung band are allowed to track a wounded animal into a neighbor's territory with impunity. Moreover, any !Kung can use the watering holes of any neighboring territory provided she or he seeks permission, which is always granted. This type of reciprocity, cooperation, and permissive use rights is adaptive in that it serves to increase the chances of survival of all !Kung peoples. In a small number of hunting-and-gathering societies—most no-

tably among certain native North American groups—local people live in permanent settlements and maintain strong control over land.

As a general rule, a hunting-and-gathering society will have open or flexible boundaries if animals are mobile and food and water supplies are relatively unpredictable. Conversely, food collectors are more likely to live in permanent settlements and maintain greater control over land in those areas where food and water supplies are more plentiful and predictable (Dyson-Hudson and Smith 1978:21–41).

Pastoralists

Like hunters and gatherers, nomadic or seminomadic pastoralists require extensive territory. For pastoralists to maintain their way of life, it is imperative that they have access to two vital resources for their livestock—water and pasturage. Depending on the local environment, the availability of these two resources may vary widely. In marginal environments where grass and water are at a premium, pastoralists will need to range over wide territories and consequently will require relatively free access to land. In more environmentally favorable regions of the world where grass and water are more abundant, one is likely to find greater control over land and its resources. In any event, pastoral groups must work out arrangements among themselves and with nonpastoralists to gain access to certain pasturage.

To avoid overgrazing and/or conflict, they may have to enter into agreements with other pastoralist families to share certain areas, or they may have to form contractual arrangements with sedentary cultivators to graze their animals on fallowing or recently harvested fields. The pastoral Fulani of northern Nigeria, for example, while remaining removed from village life on an everyday basis, nevertheless have had to maintain special contacts with sedentary horticulturalists for rights of access to water and pastures. According to Stenning, ". . . this has brought them into the orbit of the Muslim states of the western Sudan, in whose politics and wars they became involved principally to maintain or extend their pastoral opportunities" (1965:365).

Horticulturalists

In contrast to hunters and gatherers and most pastoralists, horticulturalists tend to live on land that is communally controlled, usually by an extended kinship group. Individual nuclear or polygynous families may be granted the *use* of land by the extended family for growing crops, but the rights are limited. For example, the small family units usually retain their rights for as long as they work the land and are in good standing with the larger family. Since they do not own the land, however, they cannot dispose of it by selling it. They simply use it at the will of the larger group. Such a method of land allocation makes sense, given their farming technology. Since horticulturalists frequently are shifting cultivators, there would be no advantage to having claims of ownership over land that cannot be used permanently.

This communal type of land tenure is well illustrated by the Samoans of Polynesia. Under their traditional system, any piece of land belongs to the extended family that clears and plants it. Individual members of the extended family work the land under the authority of a *matai*, an elected family member who holds the title to the land on behalf of the entire group. The *matai*'s authority over the land depends on his meeting his responsibility to care for his extended family. If he does not, the family can remove his title. Any individual of the extended family group has undisputed rights to use the land provided he or she (1) lives on the family land and (2) serves and pays allegiance to the *matai* (see O'Meara 1990:128–39).

Individual Property Rights

As we have demonstrated, all societies have rules for determining how resources are used, by whom, and under what conditions. In the United States and in most other parts of the Western world, resources such as land, capital, livestock, and minerals are allocated according to the principle of private individual ownership. Most English-speaking people have no difficulty understanding the concept of private ownership. When we say we "own" a piece of property, such as an automobile, such ownership carries with it the implication that we have absolute and exclusive rights to the automobile. We are able to sell it, give it away, rent it, trade it for another piece of property, or drive it off a cliff, if we so choose. We have, in other words, 100 percent rights to certain pieces of property.

This concept of individual **property rights** is so entrenched in our thinking and our culture that we sometimes fail to realize that many other cultures do not share that principle with us. This cultural myopia led some early anthropologists to ask the wrong types of questions when they first encountered certain non-Western peoples. To illustrate, when studying a small group of East African horticulturalists who also kept cattle, some early anthropologists—using their own set of linguistic categories—asked what to them seemed to be a perfectly logical question: Who owns that brown cow over there? In actual fact, no one owned the cow in our sense of the term, because no single individual had 100 percent rights to the cow. Instead, a number of people may have had limited rights and obligations to the brown cow. The man we see with the cow at the moment may have rights to milk the cow on Tuesdays and Thursdays, but someone else has rights to milk it on Mondays and Wednesdays. The cows are actually controlled by the larger kinship group (the lineage or extended family), while the individual merely has limited rights to use the cow. This fundamental difference in property allocation is reflected in the local East African language of Swahili, which contains no word that would be comparable to the English word *own*. The closest Swahili speakers can come linguistically to conveying the notion of ownership is to use the word *nina*, which means literally "I am with . . . ."

looking ahead

Anthropological insights into the motivation for accumulating personal property have enabled some anthropologists to shed light on such contemporary social problems as adolescent crack cocaine dealing in the United States. See, for example, Applied Perspective 2 at the end of this chapter.

Production

The initial step in meeting the material needs of any society is to establish a system of allocating the rights to resources to certain people. In very few situations, however, can resources be utilized by people in exactly the form they are found in nature. Animals must be butchered; grains must be ground and cooked; metal ores must be mined, smelted, combined with other chemical elements, and crafted before becoming tools; stones must be shaped before they can be put into the wall of a house. This process of obtaining goods from the natural environment and transforming them into usable objects is what economists refer to as **production.**

All humans must meet certain fundamental material needs (such as food, water, and shelter), but *how* these needs are satisfied varies enormously from society to society. Some groups, like the Pygmies of Central Africa and the Siriono of eastern Bolivia, meet most of their material needs with goods procured from hunting and gathering. Others, like the Masai and Samburu of East Africa, live essentially from the products of their livestock. Still others, like people of the United States and certain Western European nations, go well beyond meeting their basic physical needs through a complex system of technology and industrialization. How do we explain such diversity? Why is there such a vast range of systems of production? Why do two cultures inhabiting apparently similar environments develop substantially different systems of production?

Part of the answer to these questions can be explained in economic terms. For example, why any society produces the things it does will be determined, to some extent, by such economic factors as the accessibility of certain resources, the technology available for processing the resources, and the abundance of energy supplies. This is only part of the explanation, however, since cultural values also play a role in determining production. To illustrate, the Hadza of Tanzania, while aware of the horticultural practices of their neighbors, choose not to engage in horticulture themselves for the simple reason that it involves too much effort for the anticipated yield. Also, in one form or another, most societies fail to exploit all of the resources at their disposal. Some societies living alongside bodies of water have strong prohibitions against eating fish. The Hindus in India, despite an abundance of cows, refuse to eat beef on religious grounds. The Eskimos, even though they frequently experience food shortages, practice a number of taboos against eating certain types of food. And, of course, people in the United States would never dream of routinely eating the flesh of dogs, cats, or rats, although these animals are a rich source of protein.

The apparent failure by some societies to exploit all of the resources at their disposal may not stem from irrationality or arbitrariness. As some cultural ecologists have shown convincingly, often there are good reasons for certain types of economic behavior, which at first glance might appear irrational. The case of the sacred cow in Hindu India is a case in point. Even though the Indian population needs more protein in its diet, the Hindu religion prohibits the slaughter of cows and the eating of beef. This taboo has resulted in large numbers of half-starved cows cluttering the Indian landscape, disrupting traffic, and stealing food from marketplaces. But as Marvin Harris has demonstrated (1977:141–52;

In some parts of the world, such as Hindu India, there is not much demand for a U.S.-style hamburger. Each culture defines what is edible and what is not.

1979:479–82), the taboo makes good economic sense because it prevents the use of cows for less cost-effective purposes. To raise cows as a source of food would be an expensive proposition, given the economic/ecological conditions found in India. Instead, cows are used as draft animals and for the products they provide, such as milk, fertilizer, and fuel (dung). The religious taboo, according to Harris, rather than being irrational, serves to regulate the system of production in a very effective way by having a positive effect on the carrying capacity of the land.

Units of Production

Like other parts of culture, the way that people go about producing is not haphazard or random but rather is systematic, organized, and patterned. Every society breaks up its members into some type of productive unit comprising people with specific tasks to perform. In industrialized societies like our own, the productive unit is the private company that exists for the purpose of producing goods or services. These private firms range from small, individually owned retail operations on the one hand to gigantic multinational corporations on the other. Whatever the size and complexity, however, these private companies are made up of employees performing specific roles, all of which are needed to produce the goods and services, which are then sold for a profit. The employees do not consume the products of the firm, but instead receive salaries, which they use to purchase the goods and services they need.

Production in the Household.   In most nonindustrialized societies, the basic unit of production is the household. In these small-scale societies most, if not all, of the goods and services consumed are produced by the members of the household. The household may be made up of a nuclear family (husband, wife, and children) or a more elaborate family structure containing married siblings, multiple wives, and more than two generations. In a typical horticultural society, household members produce most of what they consume; their work includes planting, tending, and harvesting the crops; building houses; procuring firewood and other fuels from the environment; making their own tools; keeping some livestock; making their own clothes; and producing various containers for both storing and cooking foods. In the event that a particular task is too complex to be carried out by a single household, larger groups of family members or neighbors will likely join together to complete the task.

Even though both the business firm and the household serve as units of production, there are significant structural differences between them. Whereas the business firm is primarily—if not exclusively—just a unit of production, the household performs a number of overlapping functions. When two male kinsmen who are part of the same household work side by side threshing wheat, it is very likely that they play a number of other roles together. For example, one man, because of his advanced age, may be a religious specialist; the other man, owing to his leadership skills, may be called upon to play an important political role in the extended family; and both men may enjoy spending their leisure time together drinking beer and telling stories. Thus, this productive unit of the household is the very same group that shares certain religious, political, and social activities.

A second structural difference between the business firm and the household is that the household is far more self-sufficient. In most cases, the members of the household in small-scale societies can satisfy their own material needs without having to go outside the group. People employed in a business firm, on the other hand, rely on a large number of people for their material well-being, including the butcher, the television repairer, the barber, the schoolteacher, the auto mechanic, and all of those thousands of people who make all of the things with which people surround themselves.

A third difference is that a business firm concentrates exclusively on its economic function and is therefore a more productive unit than the household. Since the family household is more than just a productive unit and must also be concerned with the emotional, social, psychological, and spiritual needs of its members, it is likely to use some of its resources in nonproductive ways. Consequently, the family-based household is less likely to use highly productive, progressive, or innovative methods than the business firm.

Division of Labor

One very important aspect of the process of production is the allocation of tasks to be performed—that is, deciding which types of people will perform which categories of work. Every society, whether large or small, distinguishes, to some degree, between the work appropriate for men and women and for adults and children. Even though many societies have considerably more complex divisions of labor, all societies do, in fact, make distinctions on the basis of sex and age.

Sex or Gender Specialization.   Although a number of roles (jobs) found in the world are played by both women and men, many others are associated with one sex or the other. For example, women generally tend crops, gather wild foods, care for children, prepare food, clean house, fetch water, and collect cooking fuel. Men, on the other hand, hunt, build houses, clear land for cultivation, herd large animals, fish, trap small animals, and serve as political functionaries. It is important to note that in many parts of the developing world today, men are migrating to the cities in search of wage employment and leaving most agriculturally related tasks to be carried out by women.

A number of theories have been set forth to explain the very common, if not universal, division of labor by sex. One explanation is that since men have greater body mass and strength, they are better equipped physically to engage in hunting, warfare, and land clearing. A second argument is that women do the things they do because those tasks are compatible with child care. That is, unlike certain male tasks, such as hunting and warfare, women's tasks can be accomplished without jeopardizing the child's safety and without having to stray too far away from home. A third explanation is that, in terms of reproduction, men tend to be more expendable than women. In other words, because women have more limited (and therefore more valuable) reproductive capacities, they are less likely to be required to engage in dangerous activities. Although we can find exceptions to each of these explanations, all three theories, when taken together, go a long way toward helping

These women in Kashmir are engaging in activities that are compatible with looking after children.

us understand this very commonly found sexual division of labor.

Yet along with these apparently rational theories, we must also note that men and women are often assigned roles because of the various social, political, and historical forces operating in individual societies. When these forces are inadequately understood, they can appear to be quite arbitrary. For example, although sewing clothes is thought of as women's work in the United States (most North American men have neither operated a sewing machine nor made a purchase in a fabric store), among the traditional Hopi of Arizona, it is the men who are the spinners, weavers, and tailors. Moreover, in our own society, women have been virtually excluded from a number of occupations (such as jockey, U.S. senator, and major league baseball umpire), even though men have no particular physiological advantage over women in performing these jobs.

Sometimes the division of labor by sex is so rigid that both men and women remain ignorant of the occupational skills of the opposite sex. This point is well illustrated by the Mixe Indians of Mexico where men tradi-

tionally grew corn while women processed it for eating. According to Beals, Hoijer, and Beals:

> Men received no training in the processing of maize and were incapable of surviving unless a woman was available to process the maize that the man produced. Although man's work involving the planting and raising of maize constituted a complicated technological process, it only represented one half of the food producing revolution. The other half, the processing of the crop, was equally complicated and time consuming. The processing involved removing the maize from the cob; boiling it with the proper amount of lime for a sufficient time to remove the hard outer shell and soften the kernel; grinding it on a flat stone slab until it reached the proper texture; working water into the dough; and shaping it between the palms until a flat cake of uniform thickness was formed. The cake was then cooked at the correct heat on a flat griddle, properly treated to prevent sticking. A Mixe woman with a family of five would spend about six hours a day manufacturing tortillas. Under such circumstances it would be impossible for her to engage in the raising of the maize, just as it would be

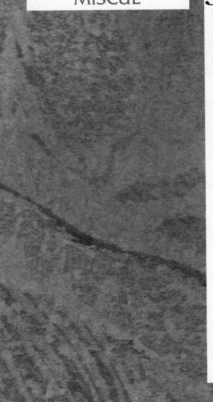

CROSS-CULTURAL MISCUE

John Blackwell, a mutual fund broker in Chicago, had a 6:00 P.M. appointment at the home of Hani Mahmoud, an Egyptian business-man, to discuss estate planning and the possible purchase of some mutual funds. After about an hour of drinking coffee and making small talk, Blackwell, who was anxious to get down to business, was surprised when Mahmoud suggested that he stay for dinner. Regretfully, Black-well declined the dinner invitation because of a previous engagement at 8:00 P.M. Before Blackwell left, the two men agreed to meet again, but when Blackwell called several days later to set up another meet-ing, he received a very cool reception. Although they eventually had another meeting, Mahmoud never did purchase any mutual funds from Blackwell.

Blackwell's failure to make the sale stemmed from his basic lack of un-derstanding of how business is conducted by Egyptians and others in the Middle East as well. Businesspersons in the United States want to get down to business right away without "wasting" time on "needless" social-izing. Getting to know one's business partner is not particularly critical in the United States because if any parts of a contract are broken, lawyers will be brought in to sue. Egyptians, however, are interested in getting to know their business partners as a prerequisite for doing busi-ness. They want to be sure that they can trust those with whom they do business and believe that the best way to build trust is to drink coffee, en-gage in small talk, inquire about family members, share food, or talk about current events. It is often considered insulting to start business too quickly, before first investing an appropriate amount of time in getting to know one another.

---

impossible for her husband to engage in the process-ing of the maize (1977:348–50).

Allocation of Tasks by Age. In much the same way that societies divide labor on the basis of sex, they allo-cate tasks according to age. Owing to their lack of knowledge and physical strength, children are fre-quently excluded from certain tasks. In our own society, where formal education routinely lasts through the late teens (and frequently beyond), young people generally do not engage in much productive work. By way of con-trast, children in less industrialized societies usually be-come involved in work activities at a considerably ear-lier age. At the other end of the age continuum, the el-derly, because of their waning physical strength, are fre-quently prohibited from engaging in certain tasks or are expected to engage in different activities from those performed when they were younger. For example, ac-cording to Hart and Pilling (1960:46), old men among the Tiwi of North Australia give up the strenuous work of hunting in favor of staying at home to make hunting tools, such as spears and throwing sticks, for the younger men. In the United States, the transition from being employed to being retired is considerably more abrupt. When most workers reach the age of 65, they usually receive a gold watch and cease their productive activity. Unlike the situation among the Tiwi, when workers in the United States retire, they usually suffer a noticeable loss of prestige.

Labor Specialization. Labor specialization—another term for **division of labor**—is an important descriptive characteristic of any society. At one extreme, subsistence societies with low population densities and simple technologies are likely to have a division of labor based on little more than sex and age. Most men in these societies engage in essentially the same activities, and the same holds true for most women. If specialists do exist, they are usually part-timers engaged in political leadership, ceremonial activities, or specialized toolmaking. At the other extreme are industrialized societies, where most people are engaged in very specialized occupations, such as stockbroker, TV repairer, kindergarten teacher, janitor, CPA, or thoracic surgeon. One need only consult the yellow pages of the phone directory for any major city in the United States to get an idea of the vast diversity of specialized occupations in our own society. These two extremes should be viewed as the poles on a continuum of division of labor, between which all of the societies of the world could be placed relative to one another.

One of the major consequences of the transition from hunting and gathering to plant and animal domestication (the Neolithic Revolution) has been the increasing amount of labor specialization in the world. Since agriculture is a far more efficient way of producing food than hunting and gathering, some people were freed up from the tasks of food production. Simple horticulture evolved into more complex forms of cultivation, which eventually led to the rise of civilizations (urban society).

With each advance in food-producing capacity came an increase in the complexity of labor specialization. This more complex division of labor is significant because the increase in specialized tasks provided a new basis for social solidarity. According to the nineteenth-century French social philosopher Emile Durkheim, in highly specialized societies where people engage in complementary roles, social solidarity arises from their mutual interdependence upon one another. That is, teachers need to be on good terms with a butcher, a carpenter, and an auto mechanic because teachers are so highly specialized that they cannot procure meat on their own, build a wood deck, or fix a faulty carburetor. Durkheim calls the social solidarity resulting from this labor specialization and mutual interdependence **organic solidarity.** By way of contrast, societies with mini-

mal division of labor also possess a form of solidarity, but of a different type. This type of solidarity, which Durkheim calls **mechanical solidarity,** is based on commonality of interests, social homogeneity, strict conformity, kinship, and mutual affection.

Distribution of Goods and Services

Once goods have been procured from the environment or produced, they need to get into people's hands. People frequently consume some of the commodities that they produce, but surpluses will enter the society's system of exchange. Systems of exchange are essential for every economy, for they allow people to dispose of their surpluses and, at the same time, maximize the diversity of the goods and services consumed. As Polanyi (1957) reminds us, goods and services are allocated in all societies according to three different modes of distribution: **reciprocity, redistribution,** and **market exchange.**

In the United States, most commodities are distributed according to a free market exchange system based on the principle of "each according to his or her capacity to pay." People receive money for their labor and then use that money to purchase the goods and services they need or want. In theory, at least, if people have the money, they can purchase a loaf of bread; if they don't, they can't. Even though this is the prevailing type, we can see examples of the other two modes operating in the United States as well. The principle of reciprocity operates, for example, when friends and relatives exchange gifts for birthdays, holidays, and other special occasions. We can see the principle of redistribution at work in the United States when people hand over a certain portion of their personal income to the government for taxes. Even though more than one mode of distribution can operate in any given society at a time, usually only one mode will predominate. Let us examine each of these three modes of distribution in greater detail.

Reciprocity

Reciprocity refers to the exchange of goods and services of relatively equal value between two parties without the use of money. Economic anthropologists generally recognize three types of reciprocity, depending upon the degree of closeness of the parties involved in the exchange: **generalized reciprocity,** balanced reciprocity, and **negative reciprocity** (Sahlins 1972:191–96).

Generalized Reciprocity. Generalized reciprocity, which is usually played out between family members or close friends, carries with it the highest level of moral obligation. It involves a form of gift giving without any expectation of immediate return. Generalized reciprocity is perhaps best illustrated by the type of giving that takes place between parents and children in our own society. Parents, by and large, give (or, at least, try to give) the children as much as they can while their children are growing up—food, toys, a set of encyclopedias, a room of their own, and the like. In fact, this providing of goods and services for children frequently continues after the children become adults. For example, parents may provide babysitting services, a down payment on a first home, or a subsidized vacation for their adult children.

In most cases, parents provide for their children materially without the expectation that their children will repay them at any time in the future. Because of the intimate bonds between parents and children, parents usually provide for their children out of a sense of love, obligation, and social responsibility. In reality, this sense of love and obligation usually becomes a two-way street, for children usually come to the assistance of their elderly parents when the parents become too old to care for themselves. Thus, even in this most generalized form of reciprocity, the exchange of goods and services frequently balances out over the long run.

Even though generalized reciprocity is found in our own society, it is not the predominating form of exchange as it is in smaller-scale societies, where the primary unit of economic organization is the nuclear or extended family and where material resources may be unpredictable and uncertain. An exchange system based primarily on generalized reciprocity is common among hunters and gatherers and indeed contributes to their very survival.

In most hunting societies, when a large animal such as a bushbuck is killed, the hunter will keep enough for his own immediate family and distribute the rest to his more distant relatives. With no refrigeration or other way of preserving meat, it would make little sense for the hunter to hoard all of the meat himself, for it would spoil before it could be eaten. Instead, sharing with others becomes the expected norm. And, of course, given the uncertainty of hunting, sharing your kill today would entitle you to share someone else's kill tomorrow. Such an economic strategy helps all family members sustain themselves by providing a fairly steady supply of meat despite the inconsistent success of most individual hunters. In such societies generosity is perhaps the highest ideal, while hoarding and stinginess are seen as being extremely antisocial.

We should not think of generalized reciprocity as being motivated totally by altruism. For all people who live at a subsistence level, maintaining reciprocal exchange relationships is vital to their economic self-interest. At subsistence levels, a person is more dependent on others for her or his material security. In the absence of

In hunting-and-gathering societies such as the !Kung of the Kalahari region, food is frequently distributed along kinship lines.

worker's compensation, unemployment insurance, and bank loans, people must rely on others in the event that their crops fail or they become too sick to hunt. Subsistence farmers, for example, might not survive without occasional help from their relatives, friends, and neighbors. A farmer may need extra seeds for planting, help with fixing a roof, or extra cash to pay for a child's school fees. The best way of ensuring that these needs will be met is to respond quickly and unselfishly to the requests of others for similar types of assistance.

Although we don't always recognize it, reciprocal gift giving in our own society takes a number of different forms. Either consciously or unconsciously, we often give gifts with the expectation of getting something in return. We may expect gratitude, acceptance, friendship, or obligation rather than a material item. Why, for example, do we give wedding invitations to our friends? Is it solely for the sake of sharing with them the joy of the ceremony? And when we give our brother a birthday present, would we not be hurt or disappointed if he did not reciprocate on our birthday? Thus, it would appear that in all societies, including our own, gifts almost always come with strings attached.

Balanced Reciprocity.   Balanced reciprocity is a form of exchange involving the expectation that goods and services of equivalent value will be returned within a specified period of time. In contrast to generalized reciprocity, balanced reciprocity involves more formal relationships, greater social distance, and a strong obligation to repay the original "gift." The repayment in balanced reciprocity does not have to be immediate, for, as Mauss (1954) has suggested, any attempt to repay the debt too quickly can be seen as an unwillingness to be obligated to one's trading partner.

A major economic motivation of balanced reciprocity is to exchange surplus goods and services for those that are in short supply. Shortfalls and surpluses can result from different levels of technology, environmental variations, or different production capacities. But whatever the cause, balanced reciprocity enables both parties in the exchange to maximize their consumption. The Indians of Oaxaca, Mexico, exemplify balanced reciprocity in the exchange of both goods and services. According to social custom, a man is expected to sponsor at least one fiesta celebrating a major saint's day. Such events, involving an elaborate amount of food, beverages, and entertainment, almost always were beyond the capacity of a man to provide by himself. Consequently, the man would solicit the help of his relatives, friends, and neighbors, thereby mortgaging his future surpluses. Those who helped out expected to be repaid in equivalent amounts when they were sponsoring a similar fiesta.

The Semang.   In some cases of balanced reciprocity, people will go to considerable lengths to maintain the relationship. For example, the Semang, a pygmoid people of the Malay Peninsula, engage in a form of "silent trade," whereby they studiously avoid any face-to-face contact with their trading partners. The Semang leave their products collected from the forest at an agreed-upon location near the village of their trading partners. They return at a later time to receive those commodities (usually salt, beads, and tools) left in exchange. By avoiding social contact, both the Semang and their exchange partners eliminate the risk of jeopardizing the relationship by haggling or arguing over equivalencies (Service 1966:17–18, 107).

The Kula Ring.   Perhaps the most widely analyzed case of balanced reciprocity is the **kula ring** found among the Trobriand Islanders off the coast of New Guinea. First described by Bronislav Malinowski (1922), the kula involves a highly ritualized exchange of shell bracelets and shell necklaces that pass (in opposite directions) between a ring of islands. The necklaces move in a clockwise direction while the bracelets move counterclockwise. Many of these shell objects have become well-known for their beauty, the noble deeds of their former owners, and the great distances they have traveled. Their main significance is as symbols of the reciprocal relationships between trading partners. These partnerships are frequently maintained for long periods of time.

The Trobriand Islanders and their neighbors have fairly diversified systems of production with considerable labor specialization. They produce garden crops such as yams and taro, are accomplished fishermen, build oceanworthy boats, raise pigs, and produce a wide range of crafts, including dishes, pots, baskets, and jewelry. When trading partners meet, they exchange shell necklaces for shell bracelets according to a set of ceremonial rituals. Then, for the next several days, they also exchange many of their everyday commodities, such as yams, boats, pigs, fish, and crafts items.

The shell necklaces and bracelets have no particular monetary value, yet are indispensable, for they symbolize each partner's good faith and willingness to maintain the longevity of the trading relationship. Trading partners must avoid at all costs any attempt to gain an advantage in the exchange. Generosity and honor are the order of the day. Whoever receives a generous gift is expected to reciprocate.

This very complex system of trade found among the Trobriand Islanders has been surrounded with ritual and ceremony. Individuals are under a strong obligation to pass on the shell objects they receive to other partners in the chain. After a number of years, these bracelets and necklaces will eventually return to their island of origin and from there continue on the cycle once again. Thus, the continual exchange of bracelets and necklaces ties together a number of islands, some of which are great distances from one another.

Since the ceremonial exchange of shell objects has always been accompanied by the exchange of everyday, practical commodities, the kula ring has clearly functioned as an effective, albeit complicated, system of exchange of goods. And yet, the kula ring has been more than just an economic institution. Since there were no all-encompassing political institutions to maintain peace among all of these islands, the maintenance of cordial relationships between trading partners no doubt served as a peacekeeping mechanism. Moreover, the kula ring has also played an important sociocultural role by creating and maintaining long-term social relationships and by fostering the traditional myths, folklore, and history associated with the circulating shell bracelets and necklaces.

Negative Reciprocity.　Negative reciprocity is a form of exchange between equals in which the parties attempt to take advantage of each other. It is based on the principle of trying to get something for nothing or to get the better of the deal. Involving the most impersonal (possibly even hostile) of social relations, negative reciprocity can take the form of hard bargaining, cheating, or out-and-out theft. In this form of reciprocity, the sense of altruism and social obligation is at its lowest, while the desire for personal gain is the greatest. Since negative reciprocity is incompatible with close, harmonious relations, it is most often practiced against strangers and enemies.

The concept of negative reciprocity is well illustrated by the relationship between the hunting-and-gathering Mbuti Pygmies of Central Africa and their horticultural neighbors. The Pygmies maintain a somewhat strained symbiotic relationship with their neighbors from whom they receive grains and metal in exchange for meat and their labor. Customarily, individual Pygmies will attach themselves for brief periods of time to certain villages. While there, the Pygmies will bring small gifts from the forest and will do some work while eating the food of the villagers. But, as Turnbull reports, this is an uneasy alliance:

In the village there is a constant battle between the villagers, who make every attempt to put the visiting Pygmies to work, and the Pygmies, who use all their guile to avoid being put to work. When their welcome is outstayed, and the villagers refuse to give any more handouts, the Pygmies simply return to the forest. (1965:294–95)

Redistribution

Another principle of exchange is redistribution, whereby goods are given to a central authority and then redistributed to the people in a new pattern. The process of redistribution involves two distinct stages: an inward flow of goods and services to a social center, followed by an outward dispersal of these goods and services back to society. Although redistribution is found in some form in all societies, it is most common in societies that have political hierarchies.

Redistribution can take a number of different forms. In its simplest form, we can see redistribution operating within large families, where family members give their agricultural surpluses to a family head, who in turn stores them and reallocates them back to the individual family members as needed. In complex societies with state systems of government, such as our own, taxation is a form of redistribution. That is, we give a certain percentage of our earnings to the government in exchange for certain goods and services, such as roads, education, and public health projects. The giving of gifts to charitable institutions (such as the Salvation Army or Goodwill) can also involve a form of redistribution, since the gifts are usually given to the poor or homeless.

food exchange

Tribute.　In some societies without standardized currency, tribal chiefs are given a portion of food and other material goods by their constituents. Some of these food items are then given back to the people in the form of a feast. Such a system of redistribution—known as tribute—serves several important social functions at once. In addition to serving as a mechanism for dispensing goods within a society, it is a way of affirming both the political power of the chief and the value of solidarity among the people.

A good illustration of tribute can be seen in traditional Nyoro, a society with a state system of government from Uganda (Taylor 1962:33). Even though most goods and services are dispersed within the family or local village, some redistribution followed feudal lines. The rank and file frequently gave gifts of beer, grain, labor, and livestock to the king and to various

In the United States, individuals and organizations help to redistribute goods and services from the "haves" to the "have-nots." Here volunteers contribute their labor to help fix the home of a low-income family.

levels of chiefs. The king and chiefs in return would give gifts to their trusted followers and servants. These gifts might involve livestock, slaves, or pieces of land. Among the Nyoro, the major criterion for redistribution was, by and large, loyalty to the political hierarchy. Consequently, the king and the chiefs had no particular incentive to make an equitable redistribution or to see that the commoners received in return something roughly equivalent to what they had donated.

Equitable distribution is rarely found in most situations where tribute is given. Instead, the chiefs, headmen, and other high-status people invariably come out ahead. For example, among the Fijian Islanders of Moala, somewhat larger quantities and higher-quality goods usually went to the chiefs and people of high status; leaders among the Hottentots in southern Africa frequently took the best portions of meat at the communal feasts; and according to Jesuit accounts, important Huron chiefs in North America always took the largest share of furs at ritual redistributions. As Betzig (1988:49) describes it, the redistributor "seems inclined to skin the fat off the top."

Big Men/Feast-Givers. In less-centralized societies that do not have formal chiefs, redistribution is carried out by economic entrepreneurs whom anthropologists call *big men*. Unlike chiefs, who usually inherit their leadership roles, big men are self-made leaders who are able to convince their relatives and neighbors to contribute surplus goods for the sake of community-wide feasting. Big men are found widely throughout Melane-

sia and New Guinea. By using verbal coercion and setting an example of diligence, they persuade their followers to contribute excess food to provide lavish feasts for the followers of other big men. The status of a local big man—as well as his followers—increases in direct proportion to the size of the feast, his generosity, and hospitality. Big men of the South Pacific distinguish themselves from ordinary men by their verbal persuasiveness, generosity, eloquence, diligence, and physical fitness. Unlike chiefs, who are usually not producers themselves, big men work hard to produce surpluses and encourage their followers to do so as well, all for the sake of giving it away. In fact, since generosity is the essence of being a big man, many big men often consume less food than ordinary people in order to save it for the feasts.

Bridewealth. In addition to tribute and big manship, several other social institutions also function to allocate material goods according to the principles of both redistribution and reciprocity. Since some of these social institutions perform functions other than economic ones, we often overlook their economic or distributive functions. One such social institution (discussed in considerable detail in Chapter 10) is bridewealth, which involves the transfer of valuable commodities (frequently livestock) from the groom's lineage to the bride's lineage as a precondition for marriage.

Even though bridewealth performs a number of non-economic or social functions—such as legalizing marriages, legitimizing children, creating bonds between

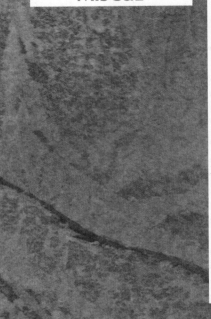

two groups of relatives, and reducing divorce—it also serves as a mechanism for maintaining the *relatively* equitable distribution of goods within a society. Since lineages are the giving and receiving groups and are made up of a relatively equal number of men and women, the practice of bridewealth ensures that all people will have access to the valued commodities. That is, no lineage is likely to get a monopoly on the goods, because each group must pay out a certain number of cows when marrying off a son while receiving a roughly equivalent number of cows when marrying off a daughter. Even though the amounts paid may differ depending on the social status of the bride's lineage, all lineages will have access to some of the material goods of the society.

Potlatch.   Still another customary practice that serves as a mechanism of redistribution is the **potlatch** found among certain Northwest Coast Indians of North America (Jonaitis 1991). Perhaps the best-known example of the potlatch was found among the Kwakiutl Indians of British Columbia, for whom social ranking was of great importance (see Rohner and Rohner 1970). Potlatches were ceremonies in which chiefs or prominent men publicly announced certain hereditary rights, privileges, and high social status within their communities. Such claims were always accompanied by elaborate feasting and gift giving provided by the person giving the potlatch. In fact, at a potlatch, the host would either give away or destroy all of his personal possessions, which could include such articles as food, boats, blankets, pots, fish oil, and various manufactured goods. The number of guests present and the magnitude of the personal property given away were a measure of the prestige of the host. The more the host could give away, the stronger would be his claim to high social status. In addition to serving as a way of allocating social status, the potlatch was an important mechanism for the dispersal of material goods, for each time a person was a guest at a potlatch, she or he would return home with varying degrees of material wealth.

Market Exchange

The third major form of distribution is based on the principle of market exchange, whereby goods and services are bought and sold frequently through the use of a standardized currency. In market exchange systems, the value of any particular good or service is determined by the market principle of supply and demand. Market exchange tends to be somewhat less personal than exchanges based on reciprocity or redistribution, which frequently involve ties of kinship, friendship, or political relationships. In this respect, market exchanges are predominantly economic in nature, since people are more interested in maximizing their profits than in maintaining a long-term relationship or demonstrating their political allegiance to a chief or leader.

Market exchange systems are most likely to be found in sedentary societies that produce appreciable surpluses and have a relatively complex division of labor. Societies with very simple technologies, such as hunters and gatherers, are likely to have no surpluses or such small ones that they can be disposed of quite simply by reciprocity or redistribution. The amount of labor specialization in a society also contributes to a market exchange system, for an increase in the division of labor brings with it a proliferation of specialized commodities and an increased dependency on market exchange.

Standardized Currency. A commonly found trait of market economies is the use of some type of standardized currency for the exchange of goods and services. Market economies do not always involve money, however. In some small-scale societies, for example, market exchanges may be based on barter—that is, the exchange of one good or service for another without using a standardized form of currency. In a bartering situation, a metal smith may exchange a plow blade for several bushels of wheat, or an artist and a migrant laborer may swap a piece of sculpture for three days of labor.

Some markets, such as this one in Bangkok, Thailand, serve social as well as economic functions.

Even in the highly complex market economy found in the United States, we find bartering institutions that facilitate the wholesale bartering of goods and services between large corporations. By turning over part of its surplus to a bartering corporation, a company that manufactures office furniture can exchange its surplus furniture for items it may need (such as air conditioners, automobile tires, or computers). More and more, individuals are using bartering (e.g., artists, therapists, typists, and other free-lance suppliers).

The major prerequisite of a market exchange is not whether the exchange is based on currency or barter, but rather that the relative value (or price) of any good or service is determined by the market principle of supply and demand. That is, we can consider an exchange to be based on the market principle when a pig can be exchanged for ten bushels of corn when pigs are scarce but will bring only four bushels of corn in exchange when pigs are plentiful.

Variety of Markets.   The extent to which markets are responsible for the distribution of goods and services in any given society varies widely throughout the world. The market economy of the United States, with its vast network of commercial interests and consumer products, represents one extreme. There is virtually nothing that cannot be bought or sold in our highly complex markets. In some of our markets (such as supermarkets, shops, and retail stores), buyers and sellers interact with one another in close proximity to the goods. But other types of markets in the United States are highly impersonal because the buyers and sellers have no personal interaction. For example, stock markets, bond markets, and commodities markets are all conducted electronically (through brokers), with buyers and sellers having no face-to-face contact with one another. Such markets, which exist for the sole purpose of buying and selling, serve an exclusively economic function and fulfill no social functions.

looking ahead

Anthropologists are now applying their studies of consumption to the area of market research. See, for example, Applied Perspective 1 at the end of this chapter.

At the opposite extreme are certain small-scale economies that have little labor specialization, small surpluses, and a limited range of goods and services exchanged in markets. Many of the material needs of a household are met by the productive activities of its members. Whatever surpluses exist will be brought to market for sale or exchange; the profits will be used to purchase other goods or to pay taxes. In such societies, the actual location of the market is important because many *social* functions are performed in addition to the economic exchange of goods and services. In traditional West Africa, for example, the market is the place where buyers and sellers meet to exchange their surplus goods. But it may also be the place where a man will go to meet his friend, settle a dispute, watch dancing, hear music, pay respects to an important chief, get caught up on the latest gossip, or see some distant relatives.

---

applied PERSPECTIVE

Economics

This chapter on economic systems from a cross-cultural perspective has examined how people control and allocate natural resources and produce and distribute essential commodities. The applied case studies that follow have been selected specifically for their relevance to economic issues. The first case illustrates how anthropologists' traditional interests in patterns of consumption are useful to contemporary businesses in their market research. The second case demonstrates how the ethnographic study of motivation among adolescent crack cocaine dealers can suggest possible ways of addressing this major social problem.

Traditional anthropological interests in consumption patterns are now being used by major corporations in their market research.

In this chapter we have pointed out that economies are comprised of systems of production, distribution, and consumption. In other words, all economies, wherever they may be found, involve organized and systematic ways of producing goods, distributing them to the members of the society, and then using those goods to satisfy basic human and societal needs. Anthropologists have traditionally studied consumption patterns as part of their analyses of economies. Recently, the business world has discovered that anthropologists' insights can be helpful, particularly in the area of market research.

In recent years, anthropologists have become increasingly important players in the market research industry. Marketing research is aimed at learning how and why people use certain products or fail to do so. Manufacturers need this information so they can modify their products in ways that will make them more attractive to consumers. During the 1980s, anthropologist Steve Barnett served as senior vice president of Planmetrics Cultural Analysis Group, a market research firm in New York that studied consumer behavior through direct observations (see Baba 1986). While many market researchers gather data by interviewing people randomly in shopping malls, Barnett and his associates used a number of innovative techniques designed to learn what people *actually* do rather than what they say they do. To illustrate, in order to learn more about dish-washing practices in the United States, Barnett put video cameras in people's kitchens for a period of three weeks. The information gathered by this direct observational research enabled Proctor and Gamble to alter its television commercials to bring them more into line with actual dish-washing behavior.

In addition to videotaping actual behavior, Barnett's anthropological approach to market research helped him develop another technique, which he refers to as the "unfocus group." This technique involves asking a target group of consumers to solve a problem related to the product. The purpose is to discover unconscious cultural codes and assumptions about the particular product.

One such exercise, conducted on behalf of a utility company, involved asking the unfocus group to build a nuclear power plant out of building blocks and other household items. Interestingly, all of the participants in this exercise enclosed their nuclear plant models in cake covers, suggesting that they believed enclosed plants were safer than those that are not enclosed. The unfocus group is a very subtle and unobtrusive way of getting at people's attitudes about various consumer products. This type of market research, which draws on traditional anthropological techniques and concerns with behavior patterns, attitudes, and cultural assumptions, provides us with an excellent example of how cultural anthropology is being applied to careers in the private sector.

THOUGHT QUESTIONS

1. Why have anthropologists become so important to the market research industry in recent years?

2. What is an "unfocus group" and how can such groups be useful in conducting marketing research?

3. How many different subcultural groups in the United States can you identify that should be researched before marketing a product such as Bud Light? What do you know about these groups that might affect how an advertising campaign might be structured?

An ethnographic study of adolescent crack cocaine dealers in Florida suggests some possible ways of alleviating the problem.

Because of cocaine's relatively high cost, cocaine addiction historically has been viewed as a rich person's problem. In the last several years, however, the introduction of a cheaper variety of cocaine—crack cocaine—has made this drug accessible to all segments of the population. By and large, the appearance of crack cocaine has been a destructive force for both individuals and society as a whole. The increased trafficking in crack cocaine has been responsible, at least in part, for the dramatic rise in crime, the growing incidence of AIDS (sex-for-crack exchanges), and the increasing number of children being born with drug addictions. One of the most disturbing aspects of the crack cocaine epidemic is the high rate of cocaine dealing among adolescents.

In an attempt to learn more about adolescent drug dealing, Richard Dembo and his associates (1993) conducted an ethnographic study of adolescent drug dealers in west central Florida. Working under a grant from the Juvenile Welfare Board of Pinellas County, Dembo and his colleagues conducted a pilot study of the motivations, perceptions, and experiences of adolescent crack cocaine dealers as well as other groups affected by the drug trafficking (e.g., police, clergy, educators, housing authority social workers, drug treatment workers, and adolescent aftercare officials). Thirty-four drug-dealing youth and sixteen non-drug-dealing youth were interviewed for about an hour each on such topics as (1) the extent to which income from drugs was used to help meet family expenses, (2) reasons for selling crack cocaine, (3) the perceived risks of dealing in cocaine, and (4) the negative effects of drug trafficking on the neighborhood.

Those adolescents who were dealing sold on average twenty-one weeks out of the year for an average weekly income of $672. The estimated mean financial worth of the adolescent dealers was $2,500. Most of the dealers said that they were not currently using cocaine. Two out of every three adolescent dealers said they had killed or hurt someone through their association with cocaine. The great majority of the dealers reported that they spent most of their income on personal luxury items (e.g., clothes, jewelry) or "business expenses" like guns or protection. It is estimated that they contributed less than 10 percent of their income to their families. Most of the dealers said that their main reason for selling cocaine was to earn a lot of money because legitimate jobs pay too little. Another reason they mentioned was that they believed the money they earned would make them more popular and give them higher status among their peers.

This ethnographic study of the culture of adolescent cocaine dealers has important policy implications, because it suggests certain strategies for dealing with this problem. For example, since wanting to make money is the major reason for selling cocaine, intervention strategies must include ways of improving the vocational and educational skills of adolescents so they will have more access to legitimate work. Since most of the adolescent dealers were not using cocaine, there is little reason to treat the problem as one of drug dependency. Adolescent dealing is motivated by economics, not drug addiction. Knowing this about the culture of adolescent dealers suggests that the following would be a rational strategy for addressing the problem: former dealers who have been successful in legitimate careers could serve as positive role models for adolescent dealers by encouraging and supporting those willing to enter legitimate career alternatives.

applied
PERSPECTIVE
continued

THOUGHT QUESTIONS

1. Why has crack cocaine dealing by adolescents increased so dramatically in the last several years?

2. What three major reasons for cocaine dealing among adolescents did this investigation reveal?

3. Considering that adolescent dealing is economically motivated, what do you think would be good strategies for influencing these youths to take up more legitimate careers? Does this involve simply motivating the youths in different ways or does it involve making some structural changes in our society?

Summary

1. The study of economic anthropology has involved a theoretical debate between the formalists and the substantivists. The formalists believe that the concepts of Western economics are appropriate for the study of all economic systems, while the substantivists do not.

2. Economic anthropology involves examining how resources are allocated, converted into usable commodities, and distributed.

3. While property rights to land are strongly held in the United States, in most hunting-and-gathering societies, land is not owned either individually or collectively. The extent to which people have free access to land in pastoral societies depends largely on local environmental conditions, with relatively free access to land found in environments where water and pasturage are scarce. Land rights are more rigidly controlled among horticulturalists and agriculturalists than among foragers and pastoralists.

4. People in some parts of the world do not share most North Americans' notion of property ownership. Instead of owning something in our sense of the word, people have limited rights and obligations to a particular object.

5. Every society—to one degree or another—allocates tasks according to gender. Since the same type of activity (e.g., weaving) may be associated with the opposite gender in different cultures, the division of labor by gender is sometimes seen as arbitrary.

6. The amount of specialization (division of labor) varies from society to society. Based on the extent of di-

vision of labor, the French sociologist Durkheim distinguished between two fundamentally different types of societies—those based on mechanical solidarity and those based on organic solidarity. According to Durkheim, societies with a minimum of labor specialization are held together by mechanical solidarity, which is based on a commonality of interests, while highly specialized societies are held together by organic solidarity, which is based on mutual interdependence.

7. Goods and services are distributed according to three different modes: reciprocity, redistribution, and market exchange. Reciprocity refers to the exchange of goods and services of roughly equal value between two trading partners; redistribution, found most commonly in societies with political bureaucracies, is a form of exchange whereby goods and services are given to a central authority and then reallocated to the people according to a new pattern; market exchange systems involve the use of standardized currencies to buy and sell goods and services.

8. Economic anthropologists generally recognize three types of reciprocity depending upon the degree of closeness of the parties: generalized reciprocity involves giving a gift without any expectation of immediate return; balanced reciprocity involves the exchange of goods and services with the expectation that equivalent value will be returned within a specific period of time; and negative reciprocity involves the exchange of goods and services between equals in which the parties try to gain an advantage.

9. Whereas reciprocity is essentially the exchange of goods and services between two partners, redistribution

involves a social center from which goods are distributed. The institutions of tribute paid to an African chief, bridewealth, and the potlatch found among the Northwest Coast American Indians are all examples of distribution.

10. Market exchange, based on standardized currencies, tends to be less personal than either reciprocity or redistribution because people in such an exchange are primarily interested in maximizing their profits. As a general rule, the more labor specialization in a society, the more complex the system of market exchange.

 ## Key Terms

allocation of resources	~~mechanical solidarity~~
balanced reciprocity	negative reciprocity
~~capital goods~~	~~organic solidarity~~
~~consumer goods~~	potlatch
division of labor	production
formalists	property rights
generalized reciprocity	reciprocity
~~kula ring~~	redistribution
market exchange	substantive approach

 ## Suggested Readings

Dalton, George, ed. *Tribal and Peasant Economies: Readings in Economic Anthropology.* Garden City, N.Y.: Natural History Press, 1967. An impressive collection of essays on economic systems from all over the world including Africa, Oceania, Asia, Europe, and the Americas.

Douglas, Mary, and Baron Isherwood. *The World of Goods: Toward an Anthropology of Consumption.* New York: W. W. Norton, 1979. A study of theories of consumption examined from a cross-cultural perspective.

Jonaitis, Alldona, ed. *Chiefly Feasts: The Enduring Kwakiutl Potlatch.* Seattle: University of Washington Press, 1991. A handsomely illustrated "coffee table" book that combines photography of the art and material culture of the Kwakuitl of southwestern Canada with five essays describing the meanings, history, and contemporary form of the potlatch.

Malinowski, Bronislav. *Argonauts of the Western Pacific.* New York: E. P. Dutton, 1922. A classic ethnography based on four years of uninterrupted fieldwork in which Malinowski describes in detail the kula exchange system found among the Trobriand Islanders.

Ortiz, Sutti, and Susan Lees, eds., *Understanding Economic Process.* Lanham, Md.: University Press of America, 1992. The essays in this volume, presented at the tenth annual meeting of the Society for Economic Anthropology, represent a ten-year review of the central issues in economic studies of market and nonmarket societies.

Plattner, Stuart, ed. *Economic Anthropology.* Stanford, Calif.: Stanford University Press, 1989. This recent compilation of articles in the field of economic anthropology covers the traditional topics of economic behavior in all of the different types of economic systems from foraging societies, through horticultural and agricultural societies, to industrialized societies. The collection also deals with more contemporary issues such as the informal economy, sex roles, and urban economic systems.

Pryor, F. L. *The Origins of the Economy: A Comparative Study of Distribution in Primitive and Peasant Economies.* New York: Academic Press, 1977. An empirical approach to the cross-cultural study of distribution systems in primitive and peasant economies.

Schneider, H. K. *Economic Man.* New York: Free Press, 1974. A study of the potential applications of formal economic theory to the noncommercial, nonindustrialized economies of the developing world.

KINSHIP AND DESCENT

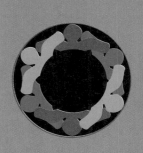

CHAPTER NINE

A Toraja family from Indonesia in front of their grain silo.

- Why have cultural anthropologists spent so much time studying kinship?
- What are the various functions of descent groups?
- What are the various ways by which cultures categorize kin?

It has been said on numerous occasions that humans are social animals. Even though other species display certain social features (such as baboons living in permanent troops), what sets humans apart from the rest of the animal world is the complexity of their social organization. People live in groups to a much greater degree than any other species. Individuals play specific social roles, have different statuses, and form patterned relationships with other group members.

Human social groups are formed on the basis of a number of factors, including occupation, kinship, social class, sex, age, ethnic affiliation, education, and religion. In most small-scale, nonindustrialized societies, social organization is based largely on kinship affiliation. That is, kinship is the basis for group membership, and most of an individual's social life is played out with other kin. By way of contrast, social relationships in industrialized societies are based on other factors, such as profession, neighborhood, or common interests, and to a lesser degree on kinship. Although different societies give different weights to these different factors, kinship is without question the single most important factor contributing to social structure. In other words, how people interact with one another in all societies is influenced by how they are related to one another. Even in the United States, where kinship ties are sometimes overshadowed by nonkinship ties, relations between kin are usually more long term, intense, and emotionally laden than are relations with nonkin.

Kinship Defined

The term *kinship* refers to those relationships—found in all societies—that are based on blood or, somewhat more loosely, on marriage. Those people to whom we

are related through birth or blood are our **consanguineal relatives;** those people to whom we are related through marriage are our **affinal relatives.** Each society has a well-understood system of defining relationships between these different types of relatives. Every society, in other words, defines the nature of kinship interaction by determining which kin are more socially important than others, the terms used to classify various types of kin, and the expected forms of behavior between them. Although the systems vary significantly from one society to another, one thing is certain—relationships based on blood and marriage are culturally recognized by all societies.

looking ahead

To see how an understanding of U.S. kinship systems can contribute to the success of a court-ordered custody mediation program, see Applied Perspective 2 at the end of this chapter.

In addition to being used between people who are related by either blood or marriage, kinship terms are applied to nonkin in some situations. This usage, known as **fictive kinship,** can take a number of different forms. For example, the process of adoption creates a set of relationships between the adoptive parents and child that have all of the expectations of relationships that are in fact based on either descent or marriage. Not infrequently, close friends of the family will be referred to as "aunt" or "uncle," even though they have no biological or marital relationship. College fraternities and sororities and some churches use kinship terminology (i.e., brothers and sisters) to refer to their members. Members of the Black community in the United States often refer to each other as "brother" or "sister." And, of course, the godparent-godchild relationship, which carries with it all sorts of kinship obliga-

Cultural anthropologists generally have studied societies in which kinship activities play a very important role. This farmer's family from Anhui, China, includes three generations.

tions, is frequently played out with nonkin. These examples should remind us that it is possible to have kinshiplike relationships (complete with well-understood rights and obligations) without having an actual biological or marital connection.

Since cultural anthropologists began conducting fieldwork, they appear to have spent a disproportionate amount of time and energy describing kinship systems. Not only have they devoted more time to studying kinship systems than any other single topic, but they have spent more time than other social scientists have on kinship systems. The reason that cultural anthropologists spend so much time on what Malinowski called kinship algebra is related to the type of societies that they have traditionally studied. Cultural anthropology, though interested in all societies of the world, has in actual practice tended to concentrate on small-scale societies where kinship relations tend to be all-encompassing. In highly urbanized, technological societies, such as those studied most often by sociologists, relatively few social relationships are based on kinship. In the United States, for example, social relationships that are essentially political, economic, recreational, or religious are usually not played out with our kin. In contrast, in small-scale, non-Western, preliterate, and technologically simple societies, kinship is at the heart of the social structure. Whom a person marries, where he or she lives, and from whom a person inherits property and status all depend on the person's place within the kinship system. In such societies, it might not be an exaggeration to say that kinship relations are tantamount to social relations.

Cultural Rules Regarding Kinship

To be certain, all kinship systems are founded on biological connections. Family and kinship groups would not exist if men and women did not mate and have children. However, kinship systems involve more than biological relationships. Rather, each society classifies its kin according to a set of *cultural* rules that may or may not account for biological factors. For example, according to our own kinship system, we refer to both our father's brother and our father's sister's husband as uncles even though the former is a blood relative and the latter is not. In many societies, a man will refer to his father's brother and his mother's brother (both blood relatives) by different terms and will be expected to behave very differently toward the two. This distinction between the biological and cultural dimensions of kinship can be seen in U.S. society when we refer to our adopted children as sons and daughters (with all of the rights and obligations that biological children have), even though they have no genetic connection. Thus, as we can see, the way that different societies sort and categorize kinship relationships is as much a matter of culture as it is a matter of biology.

Functions of Kinship Systems

All kinship systems, wherever they may be found, serve two important functions for the well-being of the total society. First, by its **vertical function,** a kinship system provides social continuity by binding together a number of successive generations. Kinship systems are most directly involved with the passing of education, tradition, property, and political office from one generation to the next. Second, kinship systems tend to solidify or tie together a society horizontally (that is, across a single generation) through the process of marriage. Since kinship systems define the local kin groups outside of which people must take a spouse, it forces groups to en-

ter into alliances with other kinship groups, thereby creating solidarity within a much larger society. This **horizontal function** of kinship was perhaps best illustrated by the case of the late King Sobhuza II of Swaziland who solidified his entire kingdom by taking a wife from virtually every nonroyal lineage in the country.

Using Kinship Diagrams

While kinship systems are found in every society, how any particular society defines the relationships between kin varies widely from one group to another. In different societies, people with the same biological connec-

One function of kinship systems is to bind together a number of successive generations, as with this child, mother, and grandmother in modern-day Japan.

CROSS-CULTURAL MISCUE

While the practice of exchanging gifts is found in most societies, the meanings attached to gift giving vary widely from society to society. In some societies gifts may be given in a fairly altruistic manner—that is, nothing is expected in return. More often, however, gift giving is used to create and strengthen social bonds between people, and consequently, some type of reciprocity is expected. Lee Cronk (1989) provides us with an interesting cross-cultural misunderstanding arising from different notions of gift giving between European settlers in America and Native Americans during the eighteenth century:

[The] Englishman newly arrived in America is welcomed to an Indian lodge with the present of a pipe. Thinking the pipe is a wonderful artifact, he takes it home and sets it on his mantelpiece. When he later learns that the Indians expect to have the pipe back, as a gesture of goodwill, he is shocked by what he views as their short-lived generosity. The newcomer did not realize that, to the natives, the point of the gift was not to provide an interesting trinket but to inaugurate a friendly relationship that would be maintained through a series of mutual exchanges. Thus, his failure to reciprocate appeared not only rude and thoughtless but downright hostile. "White man keeping" was as offensive to native Americans as "Indian giving" was to settlers.

tion may be defined differently, labeled differently, and expected to behave toward each other differently. And, as we shall see, societies can choose from a vast array of possibilities. Before trying to sort out the complexities of different kinship systems, it would be helpful to introduce a form of shorthand used by cultural anthropologists in analyzing kinship systems.

As a way of simplifying kinship systems, anthropologists use kinship diagrams rather than relying on verbal explanations alone. In this standardized notational system, all kinship diagrams are viewed from a central point of reference (called **EGO**), that person from whose point of view we are tracing the relationship. All kinship diagrams use the symbols found in Exhibit 9-1.

Starting with our point of reference (EGO) and using the five symbols, it is possible to construct a hypothetical family diagram as in Exhibit 9-2.

EXHIBIT 9-1
Kinship Diagram Symbols

Male △

Female ◯

Marriage =

Connect siblings ——

Connect parents and children |

EXHIBIT 9-2
Generic Kinship Diagram

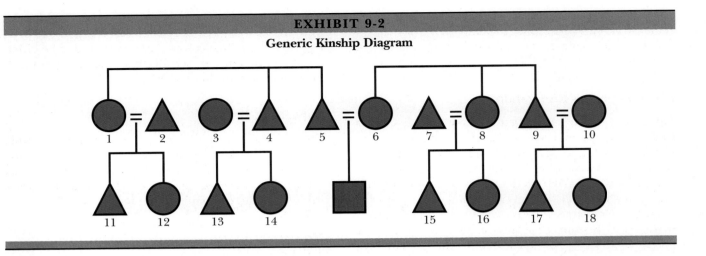

If we start with EGO (■) as our point of reference, we can refer to all of the people in the diagram (using our own U.S. terminology) in the following way:

1. Father's sister (aunt)
2. Father's sister's husband (uncle)
3. Father's brother's wife (aunt)
4. Father's brother (uncle)
5. Father
6. Mother
7. Mother's sister's husband (uncle)
8. Mother's sister (aunt)
9. Mother's brother (uncle)
10. Mother's brother's wife (aunt)
11. Father's sister's son (cousin)
12. Father's sister's daughter (cousin)
13. Father's brother's son (cousin)
14. Father's brother's daughter (cousin)
15. Mother's sister's son (cousin)
16. Mother's sister's daughter (cousin)
17. Mother's brother's son (cousin)
18. Mother's brother's daughter (cousin)

Principles of Kinship Classification

No kinship systems in the world use a different term of reference for every single relative. Instead, all kinship systems group relatives into certain categories, refer to them by the same term, and expect to behave toward them in a similar fashion. How a particular society cate-

gorizes relatives depends on which principles of classification are used. Various kinship systems use a number of principles to group certain relatives together while separating others, as discussed in the following subsections.

Generation

In some kinship systems—our own being a good example—distinctions between kin depend upon generation. Mothers, fathers, aunts, and uncles are always found in the generation immediately above EGO; sons, daughters, nieces, and nephews are always one generation below EGO; grandmothers and grandfathers are always two generations above EGO, and so forth. Although this seems like the natural thing to do, some societies have kinship systems that do not confine a kin category to a single generation. It is possible, for example, to find the same kin category in three or four different generations.

Sex or Gender

Some kinship systems group certain kin together because of common gender (Collier and Yanagisako 1987). In our English system, such kin categories as brother, father, uncle, nephew, son, and grandfather are always males, while sister, mother, aunt, niece, daughter, and grandmother are always females. The one area where we do not distinguish on the basis of gender is at the cousin level (but, then, the consistent application of a particular principle is not required). Even though this principle of gender operates at most levels of our own system, it is hardly universally applicable. In other words, some societies allow for the possibility of both males and females occupying a single kin category.

Lineality versus Collaterality

Lineality refers to kin related in a single line, such as son, father, grandfather. **Collaterality,** on the other hand, refers to kin related through a linking relative, such as the relationship between EGO and his or her parents' siblings. Whereas the principle of lineality distinguishes between father and father's brother, the principle of collaterality does not. That is, in some societies, EGO uses the term *father* to refer to both his or her father and his or her father's brother; similarly, EGO's mother and her sisters may be referred to by the single term *mother*.

Consanguineal versus Affinal Kin

Some societies make distinctions in kinship categories based on whether people are related by blood (*consanguineal kin*) or through marriage (*affinal kin*). Our own kinship system uses this principle of classification at some levels but not at others. To illustrate, we distinguish between sons and sons-in-law and between sisters and sisters-in-law. But in EGO's parents' generation, we fail to distinguish between mother's brother (a blood relative) and mother's sister's husband (an affinal relative), both of whom we call uncle.

Relative Age

In certain kinship systems, relative age serves as a criterion for separating different types of relatives. In such societies, a man will have one kinship term for younger brother and another term for older brother. These different terms based on relative age carry with them different behavioral expectations, for frequently a man will be expected to act toward his older brother with deference and respect while behaving much more informally toward his younger brother.

Sex of the Connecting Relative

Some societies distinguish between different categories of kin based on the sex of the connecting (or intervening) relative. To illustrate, a mother's brother's daughter and a mother's sister's daughter (who are both called cousins in our system) will be given two different kinship terms. One will be a cross cousin, while the other is called a parallel cousin. According to this principle, these two first cousins are considered to be different by virtue of the sex of their parents (mother's brother versus mother's sister).

Social Condition

Distinctions among kin categories can also be made based on a person's general life condition. According to this criterion, different kinship terms would be used for a married brother and a bachelor brother or for a living aunt and one who is deceased.

Side of the Family

A final principle has to do with using different kin terms for EGO's mother's side of the family and EGO's father's side of the family. The kinship system used in the United States makes no such distinction, for we have aunts, uncles, cousins, and grandparents on both sides of our family. In those societies that use this principle of classification, a mother's brother would be given a different term of reference than a father's brother.

The Formation of Descent Groups

As we have seen, kinship systems play an important role in helping people sort out how they should behave toward various relatives. In anthropological terms, **kinship systems** refer to all of the blood and marriage relationships that help people distinguish between different categories of kin, create rights and obligations between kin, and serve as the basis for the formation of certain types of kin groups.

Anthropologists also use the narrower term **descent** to refer to the rules a culture uses to establish affiliations with one's parents. These rules of descent often provide the basis for the formation of social groups. These social groups, which are called descent groups, are collections of relatives (usually lineal descendants of a common ancestor) who live out their lives in close proximity to one another.

In those societies that have descent groups, the group plays a central role in the lives of its members. Descent group members have a strong sense of identity, frequently share communally held property, provide mutual economic assistance to one another, and engage in mutual civic and religious ceremonies. In addition, descent groups function in other ways as well by serving as a mechanism for inheriting property and political office, controlling behavior, regulating marriages, and structuring primary political units.

Rules of descent can be divided into two distinct types. The first is **unilineal descent,** whereby people trace their ancestry through either the mother's line or the father's line, but not both. Unilineal groups that trace their descent through the mother's line are called **matrilineal descent** groups, while those tracing their descent through the father's line are called **patrilineal descent** groups. The second type of descent is known as **cognatic** (or nonunilineal) **descent,** which includes **double descent, ambilineal descent,** and **bilateral descent.** Since descent is traced in the United States according to the bilateral principle, many Westerners have difficulty understanding unilineal kinship systems.

Unilineal Descent Groups

Approximately 60 percent of all kinship systems found in the world are based on the unilineal principle. Unilineal descent groups are particularly adaptive because they are clear-cut and unambiguous social units. Since a person becomes a member of a unilineal descent group by birth, there is absolutely no confusion as to who is a group member and who is not. For those societies that rely on kinship groups to perform most of their social functions (e.g., marriage, dispute settlement, religious ceremonies), unilineal descent groups, with their clear-cut membership, can provide a social organization with unambiguous roles and statuses. Because it is clear to which group one belongs, a person has no questions about her or his rights of inheritance, prestige, and social roles.

Patrilineal Descent Groups.   Of the two types of unilineal descent groups, patrilineal descent is by far the most common. Patrilineal descent groups are found on all of the major continents and in a wide range of societies, including certain hunting-and-gathering American Indian groups, some East African farmers and pastoralists, the Nagas of India, the Kapauku Papuans of the New Guinea Highlands, and the traditional Chinese. In societies with patrilineal descent groups, a person is related through the father, father's father, and so forth. In other words, a man, his own children, his brother's children (but not his sister's children), and

This Kikuyu family of Kenya has a patrilineal descent system.

his son's children (but not his daughter's children) are all members of the same descent group. Females must marry outside their own patrilineages, and the children a woman bears belong to the husband's lineage rather than her own. The principle of patrilineal descent is illustrated in Exhibit 9-3.

Matrilineal Descent Groups.   In a matrilineal kinship system, a person belongs to the mother's group. A matrilineal descent group comprises a woman, her siblings, her own children, her sisters' children, and her daughters' children. Matrilineal descent groups make up about 15 percent of the unilineal descent groups found among contemporary societies. They are found in a number of areas of the world, including some Native Americans (e.g., Navajo, Cherokee, and Iroquois), the Truk and Trobrianders of the Pacific, and the Bemba, Ashanti, and Yao of Africa.

It is important not to confuse matrilineal descent with matriarchy, whereby women have greater authority and decision-making prerogatives than men. In most cases where matrilineal descent is practiced, men retain the lion's share of power and authority. Political offices are held by men, and it is men, not women, who control property. In matrilineal societies, both property and political office pass from one man to another but *through* a woman. To illustrate, whereas in a patrilineal society a man passes his property and hereditary political office to his own son, in a matrilineal society property and office pass from a man to his sister's son. In fact, in a matrilineal society, the most important male relation-

EXHIBIT 9-3

Patrilineal Descent

In a patrilineal descent system, a person is connected to relatives of both sexes related through men only. Sons and daughters belong to their father's descent group, as do the father's sons' children but not the father's daughters' children.

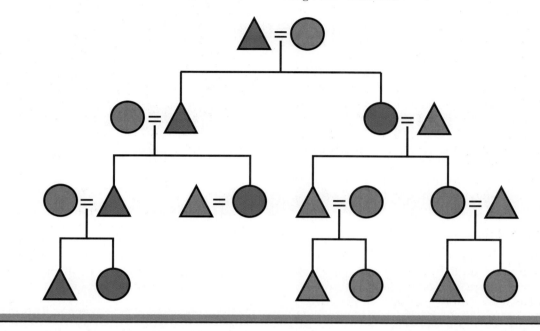

ship a man has is with his sister's son (or mother's brother). The principle of matrilineal descent is illustrated in Exhibit 9-4.

Types of Unilineal Descent Groups. Anthropologists recognize different types of kinship groups that are based on the unilineal principle. Categorized according to increasing levels of inclusiveness, the four major types of descent groups are (1) **lineages,** (2) **clans,** (3) **phratries,** and (4) **moieties.** These four types of unilineal descent groups can form an organizational hierarchy, with moieties comprising two or more phratries, phratries comprising two or more clans, and clans comprising two or more lineages. All societies may not have all four types of groups, but some can.

Lineages. A lineage is a unilineal descent group of up to approximately ten generations in depth; its members can trace their ancestry back (step-by-step) to a common founder. When descent is traced through the male line, the groups are known as patrilineages; when

traced through the female line, they are known as matrilineages.

Sometimes lineages undergo a process known as segmentation, a subdivision into smaller units depending on the social situation. This process can occur when antagonisms arise among lineage members. For example, a lineage can be divided into two secondary lineages, divided again into tertiary lineages, and further subdivided into minimal lineages. These minimal lineages may be only three or four generations in depth. Such a segmentation process is diagrammed in Exhibit 9-5.

At certain times and under certain social situations, different segments will be competing with one another, but at other times they will be allied. In Exhibit 9-5, since all of the minimal lineages are autonomous, normally (a) and (b) will not have a lot to do with each other. But, in the event that (d) should become involved in a dispute with (b), then (a) is likely to ally itself with (b) because of their common ancestry with (1). If, however, (d) would have a conflict with (f), it is likely that (a), (b), and (c) would all come to the

---

EXHIBIT 9-4

Matrilineal Descent

In a matrilineal descent system, a person is connected to kin of both sexes related through women only. Sons and daughters belong to their mother's descent group, as do the mother's daughters' children but not the mother's sons' children.

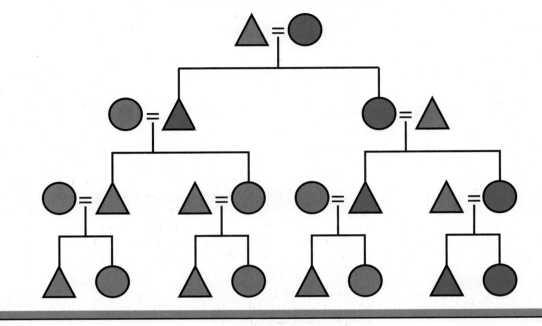

---

defense of (d), owing to their common genealogical connection to (A). It is also likely that (a) through (h) will all come together on certain ritual occasions to acknowledge their common relationship to (I). Thus, sublineages will be allied with one another at some times and in conflict with one another at other times.

Clans.   Another type of unilineal descent group is the clan, a group of kin usually comprising ten or more generations whose members believe they are all related to a common ancestor but are unable to trace that genealogical connection step-by-step. When clans and lineages are found together, the clan will most likely be made up of a number of different lineages. Depending on which line is emphasized, the clan can be either a matriclan or a patriclan.

In some societies, clans are close-knit groups, very much like lineages, whose members have a high degree of interaction with one another. More commonly, however, clan members are widely dispersed geographically and rarely get together for clanwide activities. Unlike

lineages, which serve as corporate, functioning *groups*, clans tend to be larger and more loosely structured *categories* with which people identify. Frequently, clans are associated with animals or plants (i.e., totems) that provide a focal point for group identity.

Phratries.   At the next order of magnitude are phratries, unilineal descent groups composed of two or more clans. In those societies in which phratries are found, the actual connections between the various clans usually are not recognized. Generally, phratries are rare and, when they are found, do not serve important social functions. Although phratries have been significant social, political, and religious groups in some cases, such as traditional Aztec society, this is the exception rather than the rule.

Moieties.   In some cases, societies are divided into two unilineal descent groups called moieties (a term derived from the French word for "half"). In those societies that have only two clans, the clans and the moieties are identical to each other. But when moieties are made up of more than two clans (as is usually the case), the moiety is the larger unit.

Moieties are an excellent example of social reciprocity. If, for example, a society is made up of two large exogamous moieties, each moiety provides the other group with its marriage partners. Moreover, moiety affiliation has been used for seating arrangements at ceremonial occasions or for sports competitions. And, among the Seneca Indians, one moiety performs mourning rituals for the other. Thus, although moieties can play important roles in the society, they are not a part of the political structure in the same way that lineages or clans are.

The Corporate Nature of Lineages.   One feature of all unilineal descent groups—whether we are talking about lineages, clans, phratries, or moieties—is that they clearly define who is a member and who is not. These collective kinship groups also endure over time. Even though individual members are born into the group and leave it by dying, the unilineal descent group continues on. Owing to both their unambiguous mem-

bership and continuity, unilineal descent groups are good examples of corporate entities that play a powerful role in the lives of the individual members.

We can cite a number of indicators of the corporate nature of unilineal descent groups. First, such unilineal groups as lineages frequently shape a person's identity in significant ways. When a stranger asks the simple question, "Who are you?" some lineage members will likely respond, "I am a member of such and such a lineage," rather than "I am John Smith." Lineage members, in other words, see themselves first and foremost as members of the kinship group rather than as individuals. Second, unilineal descent groups regulate marriage to the extent that relatively large numbers of kin on both the bride's and the groom's side of the family must give their approval before the marriage can take place. Third, property (such as land and livestock), rather than being controlled by the individual, is usually regulated by the descent group. The group allocates specific pieces of property to individual members for their use, but only because they are kin members in good standing. Fourth, even the criminal justice system in unilineal societies has a strong corporate focus. If,

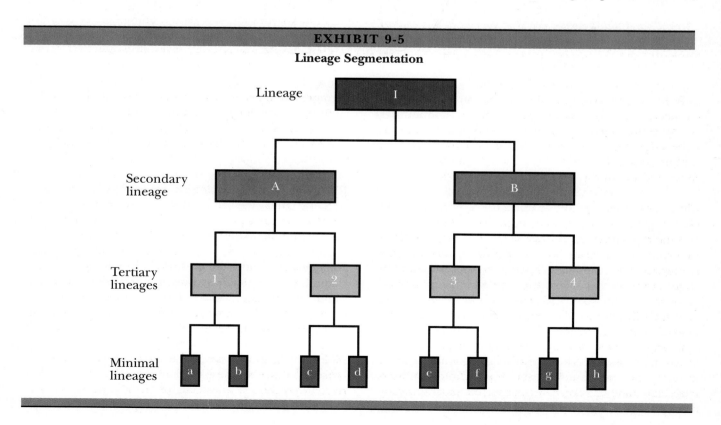

EXHIBIT 9-5

Lineage Segmentation

for example, a member of lineage (a) assaults a member of lineage (q), the entire lineage (q) will seek compensation from or revenge upon lineage (a). The assaulter would not be held solely accountable for her or his individual actions, but rather the group (i.e., lineage or clan) would in the final analysis be culpable.

The corporate nature of unilineal descent groups is no better illustrated than in the strong bonds of obligations that exist between members. The kinship group provides a firm base of security and protection for its individual members. If crops fail, an individual can always turn to her or his unilineal descent group members for assistance; in the event of any threat from outsiders, a person should expect support and protection from members of her or his own descent group. The strength of these bonds of obligation depends on the closeness of the ties. Mutual assistance is likely to be taken very seriously among lineage members, less so among clan members, and very little at the phratry or moiety level.

looking ahead

To see how an understanding of corporate lineages can assist in the development of agricultural programs in West Africa, see Applied Perspective 1 at the end of this chapter.

Cognatic (Nonunilineal) Descent Groups

Approximately 40 percent of the world's societies have kinship systems that are not based on the unilineal principle. Anthropologists refer to these nonunilineal kin groups as cognatic and classify them into three basic types: double descent, ambilineal descent, and bilateral descent.

Double Descent.   Some societies practice a form of double descent (or double unilineal descent), whereby kinship is traced both matrilineally and patrilineally. In such societies, an individual belongs to both the mother's and the father's lineage. Descent under such a system is matrilineal for some purposes and patrilineal for others. For example, movable property such as small livestock or agricultural produce may be inherited from the mother's side of the family, while nonmovable property such as land may be inherited from the father's side.

Double descent is relatively rare; only about 5 percent of the world's cultures practice it. One such culture, the Yako of Nigeria, has been particularly well described by Daryll Forde (1967). For the Yako, both matrilineality and patrilineality are important prin-

ciples of kinship. Among the traditional Yako, cooperation in everyday domestic life is strongest among members of the patriclan for the obvious reason that they live with or near one another. Resources such as land, forest products, and trees as well as membership in men's associations are inherited by patrilineal descent.

The mother's line is also important, even though matriclan members do not live in close proximity to one another. Since the Yako believe strongly that all life stems from the mother, a mother's children are honor bound to help each other and maintain peaceful and harmonious relations between themselves. Certain movable property, such as livestock and currency, passes from one matriclan member to another. Moreover, matriclans supervise funeral ceremonies and are responsible for providing part of the bridewealth payment. Thus, as the Yako well illustrate, in a double descent system the patrilineal groups and the matrilineal groups are active in different spheres of the culture.

Ambilineal Descent.   In societies that practice ambilineal descent, parents have a choice of affiliating their children with either kinship group. Unlike unilineal systems, which restrict one's membership to either the mother's *or* the father's group, ambilineal systems are considerably more flexible because they allow for individual choice concerning group affiliation. The range of choice varies from one ambilineal system to another. In some cases, the parents are expected to choose the group with which their children eventually affiliate. Other systems allow the individual to move continuously through life from one group to another, provided he or she affiliates with one descent group at a time. Still other systems permit the overlapping of membership with a number of groups at the same time. This flexibility does not come without a price, however. As a general rule, the greater the flexibility concerning membership, the weaker the group's loyalties, cohesiveness, and impact on the lives of its members.

Bilateral Descent.   In those societies that practice bilateral descent, such as our own, a person is related equally to both the mother's and the father's side of the family. A bilateral system tends to be symmetrical to the extent that what happens on one side of the kinship diagram also happens on the other side. In other words, the grandparents, aunts, uncles, and cousins are treated equally on both sides of the family. In unilineal systems, a person is affiliated with a large number of kin over many generations but only on one side of the family. By way of contrast, bilateral systems create links

CROSS-CULTURAL MISCUE

Understanding kinship systems in other cultures can have very practical repercussions on how effectively we do our jobs. Clyde Kluckhohn, who spent much of his anthropological career studying the Navajo Indians of the American Southwest, tells of an intelligent and successful Chicago public schoolteacher who was teaching in a Navajo reservation school. When he asked how her Navajo students compared to her Chicago students, she responded that she was puzzled by the apparent bizarre behavior of several of her Navajo students. She told Kluckhohn:

The other night we had a dance in the high school. I saw a boy who is one of the best students in my English class standing off by himself. So I took him over to a pretty girl and told them to dance. But they just stood there with their heads down. They wouldn't even say anything. (1949:19–20)

What appeared to the teacher to be strange behavior can make sense only if we first understand several features of Navajo culture—features that are radically different from the culture of a white middle-class schoolteacher from Chicago. First, the type of dancing that the teacher expected of these two Navajo teenagers is considered quite promiscuous by Navajo standards. Whereas middle-class North Americans attach little, if any, sexual meaning to the type of bodily contact involved in ballroom dancing, the Navajo think it highly inappropriate for adults of the opposite sex to move around the dance floor in a semi-embrace with the fronts of their bodies touching. Second, according to the Navajo kinship system, which is made up of exogamous clans, the incest taboo applies as strictly to all clan members as it does to members of one's own nuclear family. Unfortunately—and quite unbeknownst to the teacher—the Navajo boy and girl the teacher had chosen were members of the same clan and, as such, were strictly forbidden from engaging in the public display of intimacy implied in Western-style dancing. As Kluckhohn suggested, the humiliation that these two Navajo youngsters must have experienced would have been roughly equivalent to the embarrassment the teacher would have felt had the manager of a crowded hotel asked her to share a bed with her adult brother. Here, then, was a needlessly tragic miscommunication that was the direct result of the teacher's not understanding the nature of the marriage and family system found among her culturally different students.

from both sides of the family but usually include only relatively close kin from a small number of generations.

The kinship group recognized in a bilateral system is known as the **kindred**—a group of closely related relatives connected through both parents. Unlike unilineal descent, which forms discrete, mutually exclusive groups, bilateral systems give rise to the situation in which no two individuals (except siblings) have the same kindred. The kindred is not a group at all but rather a network of relatives.

Unlike the lineage or the clan, the kindred has no founding ancestor, precise boundaries, or continuity over time. In short, since kindreds are not corporate groups, they cannot perform the same types of functions—such as joint ownership of property, common economic activities, regulation of marriage, or mutual assistance—as unilineal groups. To be certain, an individual can mobilize some members of his or her kindred to perform some of these tasks, but the kindred does not function as a corporate entity. This type of loosely structured network of relatives works particularly well in a society like our own that highly values personal independence and geographic mobility.

Six Basic Systems of Classification

Every society has a coherent system of labeling various types of kin. In any given system, certain categories of kin are grouped together under a single category, while others are separated into distinct categories. In our own society, we group together under the general heading of "aunt" our mother's sisters, father's sisters, mother's brothers' wives, and father's brothers' wives. Similarly, we lump together under the heading of "uncle" our father's brothers, mother's brothers, father's sisters' husbands and mother's sisters' husbands. By way of contrast, other societies might have separate terms for all eight of these categories of kin. Whatever system of classification is used, however, cultural anthropologists have found them to be both internally logical and consistently applied. Even though individual societies may have their own variations, six basic classification systems have been identified: Eskimo, Hawaiian, Iroquois, Omaha, Crow, and Sudanese (see Exhibit 9-6).

Eskimo System

Found in approximately one-tenth of the world's societies, the **Eskimo system** of kinship classification (Ex-

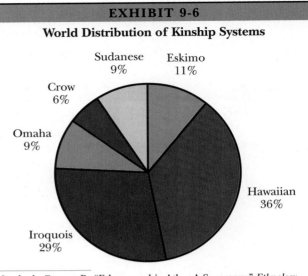

EXHIBIT 9-6

World Distribution of Kinship Systems

Sudanese 9%
Eskimo 11%
Crow 6%
Omaha 9%
Hawaiian 36%
Iroquois 29%

Murdock, George P., "Ethnographic Atlas: A Summary." *Ethnology* 6(2) (April 1967): 109–236.

hibit 9-7) is associated with bilateral descent. The major feature of this system is that it emphasizes the nuclear family by using separate terms (e.g., mother, father, sister, brother) that are not used outside the nuclear family. Beyond the nuclear family, many other relatives (such as aunts, uncles, and cousins) are lumped together. This emphasis on the nuclear family is related to the fact that societies using the Eskimo system lack large descent groups such as lineages and clans. Moreover, the Eskimo system is most likely to be found in societies (such as U.S. society and certain hunting-and-gathering societies) where economic conditions favor a relatively independent nuclear family.

Hawaiian System

Found in approximately a third of the societies in the world, the **Hawaiian system** (Exhibit 9-8) uses a single term for all relatives of the same sex and generation. To illustrate, a person's mother, mother's sister, and father's sister are all referred to by the single term *mother*. In EGO's own generation, the only distinction is one based on sex, so that male cousins are equated with brothers and female cousins are equated with sisters. The Hawaiian system, which uses the least number of terms, is frequently associated with ambilineal descent, which permits a person to affiliate with either the mother's or the father's kin. The Hawaiian system is found in those societies that submerge the nuclear fam-

EXHIBIT 9-7
Eskimo Kinship System

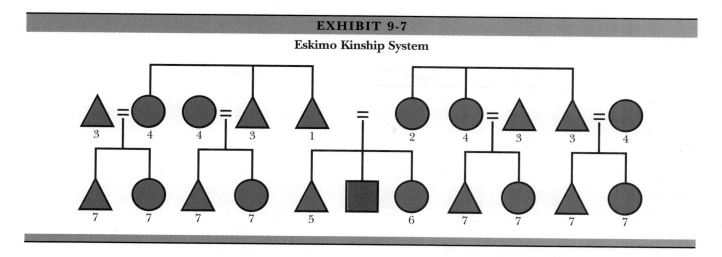

ily into a larger kin group to the extent that nuclear family members are roughly equivalent in importance to more distant kin.

Iroquois System

In the **Iroquois system** (Exhibit 9-9), EGO's father and father's brother are called by the same term, while EGO's father's sister is referred to by a different term. Likewise, EGO's mother and mother's sister are lumped together under one term, while a different term is used for EGO's mother's brother. Thus, a basic distinction of classification is made between the sex of one's parents' siblings (i.e., mother's brothers and sisters and father's brothers and sisters). At EGO's own generation, EGO's own siblings are given the same

term as the parallel cousins (children of one's mother's sister or father's brother), while different terms are used for cross cousins (children of one's mother's brother or father's sister). Thus, the terminological distinction made between cross and parallel cousins is logical, given the distinction made between the siblings of EGO's parents. The Iroquois system emphasizes the importance of unilineal descent groups by distinguishing between members of one's own lineage and those belonging to other lineages.

Omaha System

Whereas the Iroquois system reflects the importance of unilineal descent groups, the **Omaha system** (Exhibit 9-10) is more specific in that it emphasizes patrilineal

EXHIBIT 9-8
Hawaiian Kinship System

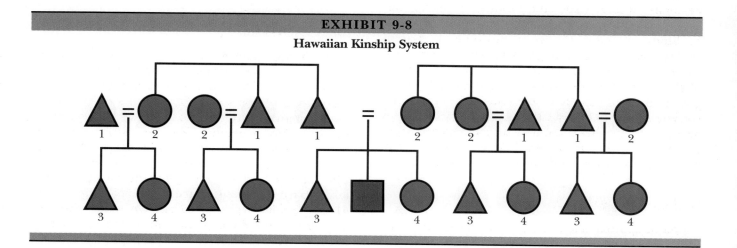

EXHIBIT 9-9

Iroquois Kinship System

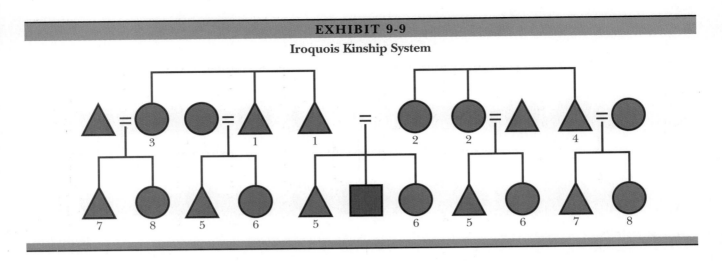

descent. Under this system, EGO's father and father's brother are referred to by the same term, and EGO's mother and mother's sister are also referred to by the same term. Equivalent terms are used for both parallel cousins and siblings, but separate terms are used for cross cousins. This pattern is internally consistent, because if EGO refers to some men and women as "father" and "mother," it follows logically that EGO should also refer to their children as "brothers" and "sisters."

On the mother's side of the family, there is a merging of generations. In other words, similar terms will be used for people in different generations. Since our own Eskimo system always uses separate terms for people in different generations, the type of generation merging found in the Omaha system seems somewhat strange to many Westerners. To illustrate this merging of generations, all men irrespective of age or generation who

are part of EGO's mother's patrilineage will be called mother's brother. This can be seen in Exhibit 9-10 with the cases of EGO's mother's brother (4) and EGO's mother's brother's son (4). In addition, similar kinship terms (2) are used for EGO's mother, mother's sister, and mother's brother's daughter.

That merging of generations does not occur on EGO's father's side of the family is a reflection of the greater importance of the father's patrilineage. That is, EGO's father and father's brothers are lumped together as a *separate* category from other males in the patrilineage because paternal uncles have the same level of authority over EGO as does EGO's biological father. This lumping together of several generations on the mother's side is indicative of the fact that EGO's connection to his or her mother's lineage is less important than to his or her father's lineage.

EXHIBIT 9-10

Omaha Kinship System

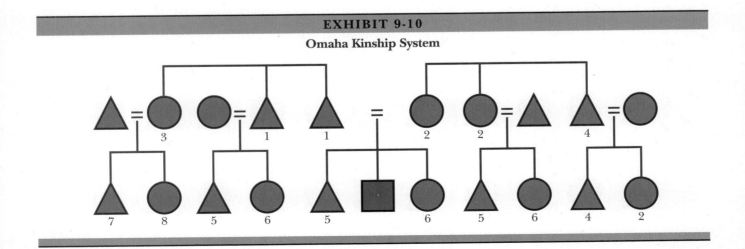

EXHIBIT 9-11
Crow Kinship System

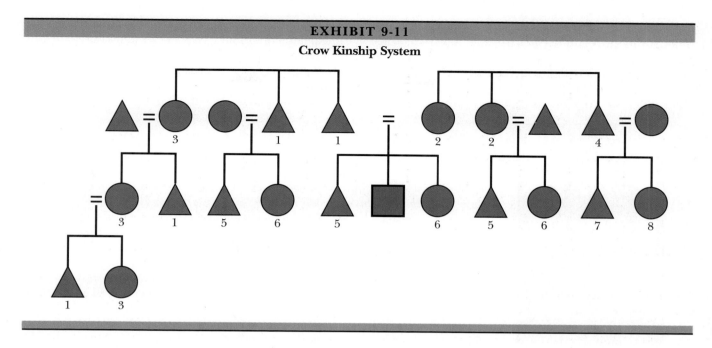

Crow System

By concentrating on matrilineal rather than patrilineal descent, the **Crow system** of kinship classification (Exhibit 9-11) is the mirror image of the Omaha system. The Crow and Omaha systems are similar in that both use similar terms for (a) EGO's father and father's brother, (b) EGO's mother and mother's sister, and (c) EGO's siblings and parallel cousins. But owing to its less important nature, the father's side of the family merges generations. That is, all males in the father's line, irrespective of generation, are combined under a single term (1), as are all women in that line (3). However, on EGO's mother's side of the family, which is the important descent group, generational distinctions are recognized.

Sudanese System

The **Sudanese system** (Exhibit 9-12), which is named after the region in Africa where it is found, is the most extremely descriptive (particularistic) system because it

EXHIBIT 9-12
Sudanese Kinship System (Descriptive)

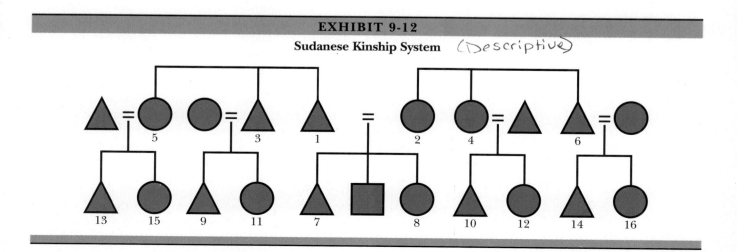

makes the largest number of terminological distinctions. For instance, under such a system, separate terms are used for mother's brother, mother's sister, father's brother, and father's sister as well as their male and female children. As shown in Exhibit 9-12, EGO has eight different types of first cousins. This highly precise system, which is generally associated with patrilineal descent, is found in some societies that have considerable differences in wealth, occupation, and social status. A possible explanation for this is that the Sudanese system permits the recognition of socioeconomic differences.

Kinship

Kinship relations, based on both blood and marriage, provide a principal means for dealing with basic human problems. In small-scale societies, people live out their lives almost exclusively within family and kinship groups. As societies become more complex and differentiated, some of the functions traditionally performed by kinship groups are taken over by other educational, political, religious, and social institutions. Irrespective of level of social complexity, people from all societies play out at least part of their lives within the context of kinship groups. In fact, kinship ties are so intense, intimate, and long-lasting that they constitute our most important level of social organization. Because kinship relations impact so strongly on our lives, it is vital to understand them when attempting to solve human problems. The case studies presented here were selected with this in mind. The first case shows how an agricultural development program in West Africa was improved by conducting research on family and kinship patterns among the local population. The second case reminds us that understanding our own kinship roles can help us make positive contributions to programs for mediating child custody disputes.

An applied anthropologist uses data on local family and kinship systems to help redesign an agricultural development program in the West African country of Guinea.

In much the same way that salvage archaeologists excavate sites (frequently in rapid fashion) that are endangered by the construction of dams, roads, or buildings, cultural anthropologists have been called upon in recent decades to help reformulate international development projects that are not working. When a development program is foundering because it hasn't adequately accounted for the sociocultural features of the target community, cultural anthropologists may be employed to salvage or correct the work of development specialists by analyzing the program and recommending changes that will enable it to meet its goals more effectively.

One such case of "salvage anthropology" was the redesign of an agricultural development project in the West African country of Guinea conducted by Robert Hecht (1986). Sponsored by USAID, the original project—called the Guinea Agricultural Capacity and Training Project—was a five-year, $4.9 million project designed to improve farm production by training agricultural researchers, extension workers, and administrators.

As originally conceived in the late 1970s, the project involved three main building activities: (1) an agricultural laboratory, (2) additional teaching facilities at the agricultural college, and (3) a research substation and demonstration farm. The project was directed at constructing these physical facilities and equipping them with American technology. The original program designers assumed that national agricultural productivity would be increased by improving the quality of research and the training of agricultural extension personnel. Since they assumed that modern technology from the United States would transform the rural areas, they did not think it necessary to be acquainted with the sociocultural realities of the rural farmers.

By 1981 it was apparent that the project had some serious problems. First, the construction of the three facilities was running nearly two years behind schedule, and the projected costs had escalated threefold to $15 million. Second, it became clear that plans for using these facilities were very inadequate. To address this problem of inadequate planning for using the facilities, USAID appointed a team made up of an anthropologist (Hecht), an economist, and an agronomist to study the program and make recommendations for change.

The salvage team concluded that the most glaring weakness of the project was that it totally ignored the cultural realities of most of the small farmers in Guinea. Since the original planners expected agricultural productivity to improve once U.S. technology was imported into Guinea, they saw no reason to focus on—or even understand—the rural cultural features. The original project planners neither consulted the farmers nor provided for their participation in the program. There were no mechanisms for obtaining feedback from the farmers or for enabling them to become auxiliary extension agents. In short, the original project did not include the peasant farmers (who produced the vast majority of crops) in designing, implementing, or evaluating the project.

To gain a better understanding of the problems facing the original project design, Hecht needed to gather data on the social and economic features of the Malinke peasants who made up the majority of the local population. On the basis of a number of village visits and ethnographic interviews, Hecht (1986:21–22) made some significant findings about the Malinke family and kinship system:

1. The average household is relatively large (approximately nine people), in part because of the high incidence of polygyny and in part because of the complex patrilineal kinship structure. These large kinship-based households have important implications for the project because of their potential for extended forms of economic cooperation among corporate lineage members (e.g., forming producer groups or building communal fertilizer storage facilities).

2. Since land in Malinke society is controlled by corporate lineages, a household had rights to land only by virtue of its membership in a patrilineal lineage. Rank among lineages in the village determined the allocation of land, with chiefly and higher-status lineages controlling more land than commoner lineages. Even within lineages, elders have more and better land than heads of more junior households. Given this hierarchy within the land tenure system, Hecht recommended that the revised project should ". . . be sensitive to the needs of those at the bottom of the distribution hierarchy, who possessed the smallest plots and least fertile land" (1986:22).

3. Most farm labor (which was not based on wages) among the Malinke was supplied largely by household members and supplemented by other kin outside the household.

The basic picture that emerged from Hecht's research among the Malinke was one of a kinship-based production system based on land that was controlled by corporate lineages and a workforce that was recruited along kinship lines. Only after this strong connection between the kinship and the agricultural systems had been revealed through anthropological research could adequate changes be made in this multimillion-dollar USAID project.

The traditional data-gathering techniques of household surveys, interviews, and participant-observation yielded the type of sociocultural data necessary for designing a workable program. As Hecht reminds us, ". . . the multidisciplinary or holistic approach usually associated with anthropology, and the emphasis placed by anthropologists on learning from the local population, may even make the anthropologist an appropriate person to serve as a team leader" (1986:25).

THOUGHT QUESTIONS

1. What basic assumptions had the original planners made that were erroneous and contributed to the near collapse of the project?

2. What data-gathering techniques did Hecht use in his applied anthropological research? Were these methods appropriate for the problem under investigation?

3. What is meant by the term "corporate lineage"? How was an understanding of this term instrumental in contributing to the success of the development project?

The collection of data on the U.S. kinship system, gender roles, and parenting helps one anthropologist develop a court-ordered custody mediation program for the state of Illinois.

It has been estimated (Tischler 1990:365) that approximately one of every two marriages contracted at the present time in the United States will eventually end in divorce. Frequently the breakup of a marriage can have devastating effects on the lives of children. This is particularly true when the divorce involves a bitter custody dispute. As a general rule, the more intransigent the disputants, the more harmful the effects on the children (as well as on the parents' own adjustment process of restructuring their lives). The prevalence of divorce in the United States in recent decades and the custody disputes that frequently follow led one anthropologist, Linda Girdner (1989), to focus her research efforts on the policies and practices relating to custody disputes between divorcing parents.

Girdner's original research examined the relationship between (1) legal customs in child custody cases and (2) the norms and symbols about gender and family in the United States. The research was designed to answer such questions as, What are the legal rules guiding decisions in custody cases? What does it mean to be a mother or a father in the United States? What codes of behavior are expected of "fit parents"? During the course of conducting this research, Girdner collected a good deal of descriptive data on the American kinship system, gender roles, and parenting as well as data on how this information relates to child custody policy and practices. The fieldwork took place during 1978–1979 in the circuit and family courts in a large suburban county in the eastern part of the United States. Data-gathering techniques involved informal interviews with judges, attorneys, parents, and witnesses, systematic observations of "court culture," and the examination of court records.

Utilizing the results from eighteen months of anthropological research, Girdner was trained as a family mediator, practiced family mediation for two years at a divorce clinic, and then participated in a number of ways in the development and implementation of a court-ordered custody mediation program in Illinois. Thus, over a several-year period, Girdner's initial role as a researcher became intertwined with the practitioner role. Based on her formal anthropological research and her experience as a custody mediator, Girdner put her knowledge and experience to use by helping to develop a custody mediation program with the local community and the state. Her utilization efforts, which lasted from 1981–1987, involved three phases: (1) an *education phase,* comprising classroom teaching, presentations and workshops for professionals, and presentations to the lay public; (2) a *developmental phase,* consisting of serving as an adviser to the Family Law Section of the Illinois State Bar Association, which eventually formulated a statewide set of standards for custody mediation; and (3) an *implementation phase,* which involved training, developing public awareness, and program evaluation. Girdner's critical involvement in research and practice relating to child custody issues illustrates quite dramatically how anthropological methods and insights into the U.S. kinship system can be useful for the amelioration of social problems.

THOUGHT QUESTIONS

1. In addition to researcher, what other applied anthropological role(s) did Girdner play?

2. Do you think that "custody mediation" programs are found in all societies? Why or why not?

3. What data-gathering methods did Girdner use in conducting her research? Are there other techniques that she didn't use that might have been appropriate and productive?

 **Summary**

1. Although kinship relations are more important in some societies than others, kinship is the single most important aspect of social structure for all societies. Kinship is based on both consanguineal (blood) relationships and affinal (marriage) relationships. Most societies recognize some type of fictive kinship, whereby kinship terms and obligations are applied to nonkin.

2. Kinship has both a biological and a cultural dimension. This is the reason some categories of relatives include some people who have biological connections and others who do not.

3. A fundamental feature of all kinship systems is that they group relatives into certain categories, refer to them by the same name, and expect to behave toward them in similar ways. How a particular culture categorizes its relatives varies according to different principles of classification. These principles are based on such criteria as generation, gender, lineality, consanguineality, relative age, sex of the connecting relative, social condition, and side of the family.

4. Many societies have sets of rules, called rules of descent, which affiliate people with different sets of kin. Patrilineal descent affiliates a person with the kin group of the father; matrilineal descent affiliates a

person with the kin group of the mother; and ambilineal descent permits an individual to affiliate with either the mother's or the father's kin group.

5. Patrilineal descent groups, which are more common than matrilineal, are found in most areas of the world. In a patrilineal system, a man's children belong to his lineage, as do the children of his son, but not the children of his daughter. Women marry outside their own lineage.

6. In matrilineal systems, a woman's children are affiliated with her lineage and not her husband's. Since the mother's brother is the social father of the woman's children, the relations between husband and wife in a matrilineal system tend to be more fragile than in patrilineal societies.

7. In those societies that trace their descent unilineally (through a single line), people recognize that they belong to a particular unilineal descent group or series of groups. These different levels of kinship organization include lineages (a set of kin who can trace their ancestry back through known links), clans (a unilineal group claiming descent but unable to trace all of the genealogical links), phratries (groups of related clans), and moieties (two halves of a society related by descent).

8. Bilateral descent, which is found predominantly among foraging and industrialized societies, traces one's important relatives on both the mother's and the father's side of the family. Bilateral systems, which are symmetrical, result in the formation of kindreds, which are more like loose kinship networks than permanent corporate functioning groups.

9. There are six primary types of kinship systems based on how the society distinguishes different categories of relatives: Eskimo, Hawaiian, Iroquois, Omaha, Crow, and Sudanese.

Key Terms

affinal relatives
ambilineal descent
bilateral descent
clan
cognatic descent
collaterality
consanguineal relatives
Crow system

descent
double descent
EGO
Eskimo system
fictive kinship
Hawaiian system
horizontal function
   of kinship

Iroquois system
kindred
kinship system
lineage
lineality
matrilineal descent
moieties

Omaha system
patrilineal descent
phratries
Sudanese system
unilineal descent
vertical function
   of kinship

Suggested Readings

Collier, Jane F., and J. Yanagisako, eds. *Gender and Kinship: Essays toward a Unified Analysis.* Stanford, Calif.: Stanford University Press, 1987. Starting from the assumption that intracultural kinship patterns can vary according to gender, this recent collection of articles makes a significant contribution to the analysis of the relationship between kinship and gender.

Fox, Robin. *Kinship and Marriage.* Baltimore: Penguin, 1967. An excellent introduction to a broad and complex field of cultural anthropology written for serious students and laypersons alike. Fox not only brings together a number of different theories to explain the workings of different types of systems but also suggests some interesting theories of his own on the question of incest.

Keesing, Roger M. *Kin Groups and Social Structure.* New York: Holt, Rinehart & Winston, 1975. A discussion of the theories of kinship suitable for advanced students of social structure.

Murdock, George P. *Social Structure.* New York: Macmillan, 1949. A classic cross-cultural study of variations in such aspects of social structure as family, marriage, the incest taboo, and the regulation of sexual behavior.

Pasternak, Burton. *Introduction to Kinship and Social Organization.* Englewood Cliffs, N.J.: Prentice-Hall, 1976. A brief introduction to the cross-cultural study of family and kinship written for the beginning student.

Radcliffe-Brown, A. R., and D. Forde, eds. *African Systems of Kinship and Marriage.* London: Oxford University Press, 1950. A collection of nine essays by British social anthropologists on kinship and marriage systems in sub-Saharan Africa. Radcliffe-Brown's 85-page introduction, although somewhat dated, remains one of the best summaries of the literature on kinship and marriage in the non-Western world.

Schusky, Ernest. *Manual for Kinship Analysis.* 2d ed. Lanham, Md.: University Press of America, 1982. A short text designed to give beginning anthropology students a clear statement of some of the essential features of kinship systems. By including a number of student activities, Schusky introduces the student to concepts of kinship logically and sequentially.

CHAPTER TEN

MARRIAGE AND THE FAMILY

A bride and groom in Lapland, Norway.

- Is the family found universally in all cultures?

- What functions do family and marriage systems perform?

- How do we explain the fact that all societies have some notion of incest?

- What different types of economic considerations are associated with marriage in the world's contemporary societies?

- In what ways do societies regulate whom a person can or cannot marry?

In all known societies, people recognize a certain number of relatives who make up that basic social group generally referred to as the family. This is not to imply, however, that all societies view the family in the same way. In fact, humans have developed a wide variety of types of families. To most middle-class North Americans, the family includes a husband and a wife and their children. To an East African herdsman, the family might include several hundred kin related through both blood and marriage. Among the Hopi Indians, the family would be made up of a woman and her husband and their unmarried sons and married daughters, along with *the* daughters' husbands and children. This chapter examines the variety of family types found throughout the world's population and the process of marriage that is responsible for the formation of families.

Marriage and the Family: Some Definitions

Even though we use the terms *family* and *marriage* every day, their meanings are ambiguous. Since social scientists and laypersons alike use these terms indiscriminately, it will be helpful to define them in more detail. A family is a social unit characterized by economic cooperation, the management of reproduction and child rearing, and common residence. It includes both male and female adults who maintain a socially approved sexual relationship. Family members, both adults and chil-

dren, recognize certain rights and obligations toward one another. The family is distinct from the institution of marriage, which is defined as a series of customs formalizing the relationship between male and female adults within the family. Marriage is a socially approved union between a man and a woman that regulates the sexual and economic rights and obligations between them. Marriage usually involves an explicit contract or understanding and is entered into with the assumption that it will be a permanent arrangement.

Sexual Union

As with any term, the definition of marriage frequently must be qualified. Marriage, according to our definition, is a socially legitimate sexual union. When a man and a woman are married, it is implied that they are having a sexual relationship—or that the society permits them to have one should they desire it. Although this is generally true, we should bear in mind that this social legitimacy is not absolute, for there may be specified periods during which sexual relations with one's spouse may be taboo. To illustrate, in many societies, sexual relations between spouses must be suspended during periods of menstruation and pregnancy. After a child is born, women in many societies are expected to observe a **postpartum sex taboo,** lasting in some cases until the child is weaned, which can be as long as several years. As Stephens has suggested, ". . . there may be other sex taboos in honor of special occasions: before a hunting trip, before and after a war expedition, when the crops are harvested, or during various times of religious significance" (1963:10).

Given this wide range of occasions where sex with one's spouse is illegitimate, it is possible that in some societies, husbands and wives will be prevented from having sexual relations for a significant segment of their married lives.

Permanence

A second qualification to our definition relates to the permanence of the marital union. Frequently, as part of the marriage vows recited in Western weddings, spouses pledge to live together in matrimony "until death do us part." Even though it is difficult to ascertain a person's precise intentions or expectations when entering a marriage, an abundance of data suggests that the permanence of marriage varies widely, and in no societies do all marriages last until death. Recent statistics, for example, indicate that more than one of every two marriages in the United States ends in divorce. Relatively impermanent marriages can also be found in smaller-scale societies. Leighton and Kluckhohn report that they frequently encountered Navajo men who had ". . . six or seven different wives in succession" (1948:83). In short, when dealing with the permanence of marriage, there will always be a discrepancy between ideal expectations and actual behavior.

Common Residence

A qualifying statement must also be added about the notion that family members share a common residence. Although, by and large, family members do live together, there are some obvious definitional problems. If we define "sharing a common residence" as living under the same roof, a long list of exceptions can be cited. In Western society, dependent children sometimes live away from home at boarding schools and colleges. Additionally, in this age of high-speed transportation and communication, it is possible for a husband and wife to live and work in two different cities and see each other only on weekends. On a more global scale, 94 of the 240 African societies listed in Murdock's *Ethnographic Atlas* (1967) are characterized by wives and their children living in separate houses from the husband. In some non-Western societies, adolescent boys live with their peers apart from their families; and in some cases, such as the Nyakyusa (Wilson 1960), adolescent boys have not only their own houses but indeed their own villages. In each of these examples, family membership and participation are not dependent upon living under the same roof.

Thus, as we are beginning to see, the terms *marriage* and *family* are not easy to define. For years, anthropologists have attempted to arrive at definitions of these terms that will cover all known societies. Frequently, anthropologists have debated whether or not families and the institution of marriage are universals. The Nayar of southern India are an interesting case, for, according to some (Gough 1959), they did not have marriage in the conventional sense of the term. Although pubescent Nayar girls took a ritual husband in a public ceremony, the husband took no responsibility for the woman after the ceremony, and frequently he never saw her again. Instead of cohabitating with her "husband," the Nayar bride continued to live with her parents while being visited over the years by other "husbands." The bride's family retained full responsibility for the woman and whatever children she might bear during her lifetime. Thus, it would appear that the Nayar do not have marriage according to our definition in that there is no economic cooperation, regulation of sexual activity, cohabitation, or expectation of permanency.

Marriage and the Family: Functions

Whether or not marriage is a cultural universal found in all societies depends, of course, on the level of abstraction in our definitions. Without entering into that debate here, suffice it to say that the formation of families through marriage serves several important functions for the societies in which the families operate. One social benefit that marriage provides is the creation of relatively stable relationships between men and women that regulate sexual mating and reproduction. Since humans are continually sexually receptive and (in the absence of contraceptives) sexual activity usually leads to reproduction, it is imperative that societies create and maintain relatively permanent unions that will regulate mating, reproduction, and child rearing in a socially approved manner.

A second social benefit of marriage is that it provides a mechanism for regulating the sexual division of labor that exists to some extent in all societies. For reasons that are both biological and cultural, men in all societies perform some tasks, while women perform others. To maximize the chances of survival, it is important for a society to arrange the exchange of goods and services between men and women. Marriage usually brings about domestic relationships that facilitate the exchange of these goods and services.

3. Third, marriage creates a set of family relationships that can provide for the material, educational, and emotional needs of children for a relatively long period of time. Unlike most other animal species, human children are dependent on adults for the first decade or more of their lives for their nourishment, shelter, and protection. Moreover, human children require adults to provide the many years of cultural learning needed to develop into fully functioning members of the society. Even though it is possible for children to be reared largely outside a family (as is done on the kibbutzim of Israel), in most societies marriage creates a set of family relationships that provide the material, educational, and emotional support children need for their eventual maturity.

looking ahead

Understanding family patterns of school students can be extremely useful in planning educational programs. To learn more about this type of applied anthropology, see Applied Perspective 1 at the end of this chapter.

The Universal Incest Taboo

Every society known to anthropology has established for itself some type of rules regulating mating (sexual intercourse). The most common form of prohibition is mating with certain types of kin who are defined by the society as being inappropriate sexual partners. These prohibitions on mating with certain categories of relatives are known as **incest taboos.** Following the lead of Fox (1967:54–55), it is important to distinguish between sexual relations and marriage. Incest taboos refer to prohibitions against having sexual relations with certain categories of kin. This is not exactly the same thing as rules prohibiting marrying certain kin. Although incest taboos and rules prohibiting marrying certain kin often coincide with each other (that is, those who are forbidden to have sex are also forbidden to marry), it cannot be assumed that they do in fact coincide.

The most universal form of incest taboo involves mating between members of the immediate (nuclear) family—that is, mothers-sons, fathers-daughters, and brothers-sisters, although there are several notable, yet limited, exceptions. For political, religious, or economic reasons, members of the royal families among the ancient Egyptians, Incas, and Hawaiians were permitted to mate with and marry their siblings, although this practice did not extend to the ordinary members of those societies. The incest taboo invariably extends beyond the scope of the immediate or nuclear family, however. In our own society, we are forbidden by law and custom from mating with the children of our parents' siblings (i.e., our first cousins). In some non-Western societies, the incest taboo may extend to large numbers of people on one side of the family but not on the other. And in still other societies, a man is permitted (even encouraged) to mate with and marry the

The family, such as this one in Ghana, West Africa, provides a structured environment that supports and meets the needs of children.

daughter of his mother's brother (first cousin) but is strictly prohibited from doing so with the daughter of his mother's sister (also a first cousin). Thus, while it seems clear that every society has incest taboos, the relatives that the incestuous group comprises vary from one society to another. Given that incest taboos are universally found throughout the world, anthropologists have long been interested in explaining their origins and persistence. A number of possible explanations have been set forth.

Natural Aversion Theory

One such theory, which was popular around the turn of this century, rests on the somewhat unsatisfying concept of human nature by suggesting that there is a natural aversion to sexual intercourse among those who have grown up together. Although any natural (or genetically produced) aversion to having sexual relations within the nuclear family is rejected today, there is some evidence to suggest that such an aversion may be developed. For example, according to Talmon (1964), sexual attraction between Israelis reared on the same **kibbutz** is extremely rare, a phenomenon attributed by the kibbutz members themselves to the fact that they had grown up together. Another study (Wolf 1968) of an unusual marital practice in Taiwan, whereby infant girls are given to families with sons to be their future brides, found that these marriages were characterized by higher rates of infidelity and sexual difficulties and fewer numbers of children. Thus, it would appear that in at least some situations, people who have grown up together and have naturally experienced high levels of familiarity have little sexual interest in each other. Nevertheless, this "familiarity theory" does not appear to be a particularly convincing explanation for the existence of the incest taboo.

If familiarity does lead to sexual aversion and avoidance, how do we explain why incest does in fact occur with considerable regularity throughout the world? Indeed, in our own society, it has been estimated that between 10 percent and 14 percent of children under eighteen years of age have been involved in incestuous relationships (Whelehan 1985:678). In short, the familiarity theory does not explain why we even need a strongly sanctioned incest taboo if people already have a natural aversion to incest.

Inbreeding Theory

Another theory that attempts to explain the existence of the incest taboo focuses on the potentially deleteri-

ous effects of inbreeding on the family. This inbreeding theory, proposed first in the late nineteenth century, holds that mating between close kin, who are likely to carry the same harmful recessive genes, tends to produce a higher incidence of genetic defects (which results in an increased susceptibility to disease and higher mortality rates). This theory was later discredited because it was argued that sharing the same recessive genes could produce adaptive advantages as well as disadvantages. Recent genetic studies, however, have given greater credence to the older theory that inbreeding does, in fact, lead to some harmful consequences for human populations. Conversely, outbreeding, which occurs in human populations with strong incest taboos, has a number of positive genetic consequences. According to Campbell (1979:74), these include (1) increases in genetic variation, (2) a reduction in lethal recessive traits, (3) improved health, and (4) lower rates of mortality.

Even though it is generally agreed today that inbreeding is genetically harmful to human populations, the question still remains whether or not prehistoric people understood this fact. After all, the science of Mendelian genetics did not become established until the turn of this century. It is not necessary, however, for early people to have recognized the adaptive advantages of avoiding inbreeding through an incest taboo. Rather, the incest taboo could have persisted through time for the simple reason that it was adaptively advantageous. That is, groups that practiced the incest taboo would have more surviving children than societies without the incest taboo. Thus, this greater reproductive success would explain, if not the origins of the incest taboo, at least why it has become a cultural universal.

Family Disruption Theory

While the inbreeding theory focuses on the biological consequences of incest, a third theory centers on its negative social consequences. This theory, which is most closely linked with Malinowski (1927), holds that mating between mother-son, father-daughter, or brother-sister would create such intense jealousies within the nuclear family that the family would not be able to function as a unit of economic cooperation and socialization. If, for example, adolescents were permitted to satisfy their sexual urges within the nuclear family unit, fathers and sons and mothers and daughters would be competing with one another, and consequently, normal family role relationships would be seriously disrupted. The incest taboo, according to this theory, originated as a mechanism to repress the desire to satisfy one's sexual urges within the family.

In addition to causing disruption among nuclear family members through sexual competition, incest creates the further problem of **role ambiguity.** If, for example, a child is born from the union of a mother and her son, the child's father will also be the child's half-brother, the child's mother will also be the child's grandmother, and the child's father will be married to the child's grandmother. These are just some of the bizarre roles created by such an incestuous union. Since different family roles, such as brother and father, carry with them vastly different rights, obligations, and behavioral expectations, the child will have great difficulty deciding how to behave toward his or her immediate family members. Does the child treat the male who biologically fathered him or her as a father or as a brother? How does the child deal with the woman from whose womb he or she sprung—as a mother or a grandmother? Thus, the incest taboo can be viewed as a mechanism that prevents this type of role ambiguity or confusion from occurring.

Theory of Expanding Social Alliances

Incest avoidance can also be explained in terms of positive social advantages for those societies that practice it. By forcing people to "marry out" of their immediate family, the incest taboo functions to create a wider network of interfamily alliances, thereby enhancing cooperation, social cohesion, and survival. Each time one of your close relatives mates with a person from another family, it creates a new set of relationships with whom your family is less likely to become hostile. This theory, first set forth by Edward Tylor (1889) and later developed by Levi-Strauss (1969), holds that it makes little sense to mate with someone from one's own group with whom one already has good relations. Instead, there is more to be gained—both biologically and socially—by expanding one's networks outward. Not only does mating outside one's own group create a more peaceful society by increasing the number of allies, but it also creates a larger gene pool, which has a greater survival advantage than a smaller gene pool.

The extent to which wider social alliances are created by requiring people to "mate and marry out" is illustrated by a study of Rani Khera, a village in northern India. In a survey of the village population, it was found (Lewis 1955:163) that the 226 married women residing in the village had come from approximately 200 separate villages and that roughly the same number of vil-

lage daughters married out. Thus, the village of Rani Khera was linked through marriage to hundreds of other northern Indian villages. In fact, this pattern of mating/marrying outside one's own group (created out of a desire to avoid incest) is an important factor integrating Indian society.

Mate Selection: Whom Should You Marry?

As we have seen, every society has the notion of incest that defines a set of kin with whom a person is to avoid marriage and sexual intimacy. In no society is it permissible to mate with one's parents or siblings (i.e., within the nuclear family), and in most cases the restricted group of kin is considerably wider. Beyond this notion of incest, people in all societies are faced with rules either restricting one's choice of marriage partners or strongly encouraging the selection of other people as highly desirable mates. These are known as rules of **exogamy** (marrying outside of a certain group) and **endogamy** (marrying within a certain group).

Rules of Exogamy

Owing to the universality of the incest taboo, all societies to one degree or another have rules for marrying outside a certain group of kin. These are known as rules of exogamy. In societies like the United States, which are not based on the principle of unilineal descent groups, the exogamous group extends only slightly beyond the nuclear family. It is considered either illegal or immoral to marry one's first cousin and, in some cases, one's second cousin, but beyond that one can marry other more distant relatives with only mild disapproval. In societies that are based on unilineal descent groups, however, the exogamous group is usually the lineage, which can include many hundreds of people, or even the clan, which can include thousands of people who are unmarriageable. Thus, when viewed cross-culturally, rules of exogamy based on kinship do not appear to be based on genealogical proximity.

Rules of Endogamy

In contrast to exogamy, which requires marriage *outside* one's own group, the rule of endogamy requires a person to select a mate from *within* one's own group.

The marriage of this man and woman in Eucador created a social alliance between their two extended families.

Hindu castes found in traditional India are strongly endogamous, believing that to marry below one's caste would result in serious ritual pollution. Caste endogamy is also found in a somewhat less rigid form among the Rwanda and Banyankole of eastern Central Africa. In addition to being applied to caste, endogamy can be applied to other social units, such as the village or local community, as was the case among the Incas of Peru, or to racial groups, as has been practiced in the Republic of South Africa for much of the present century.

Even though there are no strongly sanctioned rules of endogamy in the United States, there is a certain amount of marrying within one's own groups based on class, ethnicity, religion, and race. This general de facto endogamy found in the United States results from the fact that people do not have frequent social contacts with people from different backgrounds. Upper-middle-class children, for example, tend to grow up in the suburbs, take golf and tennis lessons at the country club, and attend schools designed to prepare students for college. By contrast, many lower-class children grow up in urban housing projects, play basketball in public playgrounds, and attend schools with low expectations for college attendance. This general social segregation by class, coupled with parental and peer pressure to "marry your own kind," results in a relatively high level of endogamy in many complex Western societies such as our own.

It should be noted that rules of exogamy and rules of endogamy are not opposites or mutually exclusive. Indeed, they can coexist in the same society provided the endogamous group is larger than the exogamous group. For example, it is quite possible to have an endogamous ethnic group (i.e., one must marry within one's ethnic group) while at the same time having exogamous lineages (i.e., one must marry outside one's own lineage).

Arranged Marriages

In Western societies, with their strong emphasis on individualism, mate selection is largely a decision made jointly by the prospective bride and groom. Aimed at satisfying the emotional and sexual needs of the individual, the choice of mates in Western society is based on such factors as physical attractiveness, emotional compatibility, and romantic love. Even though absolute freedom of choice is constrained by such factors as social class, ethnicity, religion and race, individuals in most contemporary Western societies are relatively free to marry whomever they please.

In many societies, however, the interests of the families are so strong that marriages are arranged. Negotiations are handled by family members of the prospective bride and groom, and for all practical purposes, the decision of whom one will marry is made by one's parents or other influential family members. In certain cultures, such as parts of traditional Japan, India, and China, future marriage partners are betrothed while they are still children. In one extreme example—the Tiwi of North Australia—females are betrothed or promised as future wives *before* they are born (Hart and

Pilling 1960:14). Since the Tiwi believe that females are liable to become impregnated by spirits at any time, the only sensible precaution against unmarried mothers is to betroth female babies before birth or as soon as they are born.

All such cases of **arranged marriages,** wherever they may be found, are based on the cultural assumption that since marriage is a union of two kin groups rather than merely two individuals, it is far too significant an institution to be based on something as frivolous as physical attractiveness or romantic love.

Arranged marriages are frequently found in societies with elaborate social hierarchies; perhaps the best example of which is Hindu India. Indeed, the maintenance of the caste system in India is dependent, by and large, upon a system of arranged marriages. As Goode reminds us:

> Maintenance of caste was too important a matter to be left to the young, who might well fall prey to the temptations of love and thus ignore caste requirements. To prevent any serious opposition, youngsters were married early enough to ensure that they could not acquire any resources with which to oppose adult decisions. The joint family, in turn, offered an organization which could absorb a young couple who could not yet make their own living. . . . This pattern of marriage has always been common among the nobility, but in India it developed not only among the wealthy, who could afford early marriages and whose unions might mark an alliance between two families, but also among the poor, who had nothing to share but their debts. (1963:208)

Arranged marriages in India are further reinforced by other traditional Indian values. Fathers, it was traditionally held, sinned by failing to marry off their daughters before puberty. Indeed, both parents in India shared the common belief that they were responsible for any sin the daughter might commit because of a late marriage. For centuries, Hindu civilization, with its heritage of eroticism expressed in the sexual cult of Tantricism, has viewed women as lustful beings who tempt men with their sexual favors. Thus, a girl had to be married at an early age to protect both herself and those men who might become sinners. And, if females were to become brides before reaching adolescence, they could hardly be trusted to select their own husbands.

Preferential Cousin Marriage

A somewhat less coercive influence on mate selection than arranged marriages is found in societies that specify a preference for choosing certain categories of rela-

For people in some parts of the world, as for this couple in Bombay, India, mate selection is often not a decision made by the bride and groom.

tives as marriage partners. A common form of preferred marriage is **preferential cousin marriage,** which is practiced in one form or another in most of the major regions of the world. Unlike our own kinship system, kinship systems based on lineages distinguish between two different types of first cousins—**cross cousins** and **parallel cousins.** This distinction rests on the gender of the parents of the cousin. Cross cousins are children of siblings of the opposite sex—that is, one's mother's brothers' children and one's father's sisters' children. Parallel cousins, on the other hand, are children of siblings of the same sex, namely, the children of one's mother's sister and one's father's brother. In those societies that make such a distinction, parallel cousins, who are considered family members, will be referred to as "brother" and "sister" and thus be excluded as potential marriage partners. However, since one's cross cousins are not thought of as family members, they are considered by some societies as not just permissible marriage partners but actually preferred ones.

The most common form of preferential cousin marriage is between cross cousins because it functions to strengthen and maintain ties between kin groups established by the marriages that took place in the preceding generation. That is, under such a system of cross cousin marriage, a man originally would marry a woman from an unrelated family, and then their son would marry his mother's brother's daughter (cross cousin) in the next generation. Thus, since a man's wife and his son's wife come from the same family, the ties between the two families tend to be solidified. In this respect, cross cousin marriage functions to maintain ties between groups in much the same way that exogamy does. The major difference is that exogamy encourages the formation of ties with a large number of kinship groups, while preferential cross cousin marriage solidifies the relationship between a more limited number of kin groups over a number of generations.

A much less common form of cousin marriage is between parallel cousins, the child of one's mother's sister or father's brother (Murphy and Kasdan 1959). Found among some Arabic-speaking societies of the Middle East and North Africa, it involves the marriage of a man to his father's brother's daughter. Since parallel cousins belong to the same family, such a practice can serve to prevent the fragmentation of family property.

The Levirate and Sororate

Individual choice also tends to be limited by another form of mate selection that requires a person to marry the husband or wife of deceased kin. The **levirate** is the custom whereby a widow is expected to marry the brother (or some close male relative) of her dead husband. Usually, any children fathered by the woman's new husband are considered to belong legally to the dead brother rather than to the actual genitor. Such a custom both serves as a form of social security for the widow and her children and preserves the rights of the husband's family to her sexuality and future children. The **sororate,** which comes into play when a wife dies, is the practice of a widower's marrying the sister (or some close female relative) of his deceased wife. In the event that the deceased spouse has no sibling, the family of the deceased is under a general obligation to supply some equivalent relative as a substitute. For example, in some societies that practice the sororate, a widower may be given as a substitute wife the daughter of his deceased wife's brother.

Number of Spouses

In much the same way that societies have rules regulating whom one may or may not marry, they have rules specifying how many mates a person may or should have. Cultural anthropologists have identified three major types of marriage based on the number of spouses permitted: **monogamy** (the marriage of one man to one woman at a time) and two forms of plural marriage—**polygyny** (the marriage of a man to two or more women at a time) and **polyandry** (the marriage of a woman to two or more men at a time).

Monogamy

The practice of having only one spouse at a time is so widespread and rigidly adhered to in the United States that most people would have great difficulty even imagining any other marital alternative. We are so accustomed to thinking of marriage as an exclusive relationship between husband and wife that for most North Americans, the notion of sharing a spouse is unthinkable. Any person who chooses to take more than one marriage partner at a time is in direct violation of conventional norms, religious standards, and the law and, if caught, will likely be fined or sent to jail.

So ingrained is this concept of monogamy in Western society that we frequently associate it with the highest standards of civilization, while associating plural marriage with social backwardness and depravity. Interestingly, many societies that practice monogamy manage to circumvent the notion of lifelong partnerships by either permitting extramarital affairs (provided they are discretely conducted) or practicing serial monogamy (taking a number of different spouses one after another rather than at the same time).

Polygyny

Even though monogamy is widely practiced in the United States and generally in the Western world, the overwhelming majority of world cultures do not share our values about the inherent virtue of monogamy. According to Murdock's *World Ethnographic Sample,* approximately seven out of every ten cultures of the world permit the practice of polygyny. In fact, in most of the major regions of the world, polygyny is the preferred form of marriage. It was practiced widely in traditional India and China and remains a preferred form of marriage throughout Asia, Africa, and the Middle East. There is even evidence to support the idea that polygyny played a significant role in our own Western background by virtue of the numerous references to polygyny in the Old Testament of the Bible.

looking ahead

Anthropological studies on polygyny have shed light on one of the world's most pressing human problems, overpopulation. For a discussion of the connections between polygyny and rates of fertility, see Applied Perspective 2 at the end of this chapter.

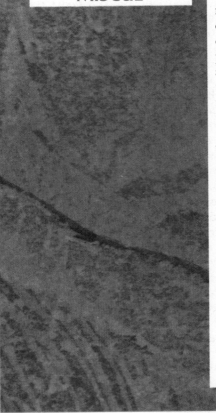

CROSS-CULTURAL MISCUE

Stearns (1986:21–22) provides us with a poignant example of how a Western-trained physician failed to communicate some important medical information to his patient in rural Yucatán because of their very different views of the world. A ninety-year-old Mayan woman from Yucatán visited a regional health clinic for the treatment of a digestive tract problem. After examining the woman, the physician gave her some pills and instructed her to take "one pill three times a day." Unfortunately, the woman never did take the pills because she had no cultural frame of reference to understand the directions. Although such directions are perfectly understandable to most Westerners, they had little meaning for the Mayan woman. What the doctor failed to understand was that the woman had never owned a wristwatch and could not tell time and that her culture had afforded her little practice in abstract visualization. Consequently, the somewhat abstract concept of "three times a day" made no sense to her. The outcome could have been quite different if the physician had been more culturally sensitive, for as Stearns (1986:22) reminds us:

Had the doctor observed routine activities of a wife in the Maya home, he would have seen women preparing tortillas three times a day for their families. After synthesizing this data collected while interacting in the village, the rural doctor might have employed a culturally appropriate solution: giving the woman instructions to take a pill each time she prepared tortillas for her husband.

Here, then, was a situation where the lack of cultural understanding resulted in the failure to accomplish a professional task—that is, cure the woman's digestive tract ailment.

To suggest that approximately 70 percent of the world's cultures practice polygyny is not tantamount to saying that 70 percent of the world's population practices polygyny. We must bear in mind that many of the cultures that practice polygyny are smaller-scale societies with relatively small populations. Moreover, even in polygynous societies, the majority of men at any given time still have only one wife. Even in those societies where polygyny is most intensively practiced, we would not expect to find more than 35 percent to 40 percent of the men actually having two or more wives. Polygyny in these societies is the preferred, not the usual, form of marriage. It is something for which men strive but only some attain. Just as the ideal of becoming a millionaire is more frequently not realized in the United States, so too in polygynous societies, only some men actually achieve the status of being polygynists.

There are a number of reasons why most men in polygynous societies never acquire more than one wife. First, marriage in many polygynous societies requires the approval (and financial support) of large numbers of kinsmen, and this support is not always easy to obtain. Second, in some polygynous societies it is considered inappropriate for men of low rank to seek additional wives, thereby restricting a certain segment of the males in the society to monogamy. And third, being the head of a polygynous household, which invariably carries with it high prestige, is hard work. The management of two or more wives and their children within a household requires strong administrative skills, particularly if the relations between the co-wives are not congenial. In short, most men in polygynous societies, for a variety of reasons, have neither the inclination, family power base, nor social skills needed to achieve the relatively high status of being a polygynist.

Economic Status of Women in Polygynous Societies.
The rate of polygyny varies quite widely from one part of the world to another. A critical factor influencing the incidence of polygyny is the extent to which women are seen as economic assets (where they do the majority of labor) or liabilities (where men do the majority of work). To illustrate, in such areas of the world as sub-Saharan Africa where women are assets, it has been estimated (Dorjahn 1959:102) that the mean rate of polygyny is approximately 35 percent, ranging from a low of 25 percent (Bushmen) to a high of 43 percent (Guinea Coast). Conversely, in those societies where women are an economic liability (such as among the Greenland Eskimos, where only about 5 percent of the men practice polygyny), few men can afford the luxury of additional wives (Linton 1936:183).

Sex Ratio in Polygynous Societies. For polygyny to work, a society must solve the very practical problem of the sex ratio. In most human populations, the number of men and women is roughly equal (in actual fact, there is a slight preponderance of male babies born in the world, with approximately 103 males born for every 100 females). The question therefore arises: Where do the excess women who are needed to support a system of polygyny come from? It is theoretically possible that the sex ratio could swing in favor of females if males were killed off in warfare, if women were captured from other societies, or if the society practiced male infanticide. All of these quite radical "solutions" may account for a small part of the excess of women needed for a polygynous marriage system in some societies.

More commonly, this numerical discrepancy is alleviated quite simply by postponing the age at which men can marry. That is, if females can marry from age fourteen on and males are prohibited from marrying until age twenty-six, a surplus of marriageable women always exists within the marriage pool. In some traditional societies, such as the Swazi of southern Africa, young adult men were required by their regimental organizations (i.e., age groups) to remain unmarried until the inauguration of the next regiment. Generally, this meant that men were not free to marry until their mid to late twenties. Since women were able to marry in their teens, the Swazi society had solved the numerical dilemma presented by polygyny by simply requiring men to marry considerably later in life than females.

Advantages of Polygyny. By and large, having two or more wives in a polygynous society is seen as a mark of prestige or high status. In highly stratified kingdoms, polygyny is one of the privileges of royalty and aristocrats, as was the case with the late King Sobhuza of Swaziland who, it was estimated, had well over a hundred wives. In societies that are stratified more on age than on political structure, such as the Azande of the Sudan and the Kikuyu of Kenya, polygyny is a symbol of prestige for older men. Whether aristocrat or commoner, however, having multiple wives means wealth, power, and high status for both the polygynous husband and the wives and children. That is, a man's status increases when he takes additional wives *and* a woman's status increases when her husband takes additional wives. For this reason, women in some African societies actually badger their husbands to take more wives. Clearly, these African women do not want to be married to a "nobody."

Sometimes multiple wives are taken because they are viewed by the society as economic and political assets. Each wife not only contributes to the household's goods and services but also produces more children, who are valuable future economic and political resources. The Siuai of the Solomon Islands provide an excellent example of how having multiple wives can be an economic advantage for the polygynous husband. Pigs are perhaps the most prized possession of Siuai adults. According to Oliver, "To shout at a person 'you have no pigs' is to offer him an insult . . ." (1955:348). Women are particularly valuable in the raising of pigs, for the more wives, the more hands to work in the garden, the more pig food, and, consequently, the more pigs. Oliver continues:

> It is by no mere accident that polygynous households average more pigs than monogamous ones. Informants stated explicitly that some men married second and third wives in order to enlarge their gardens and increase their herds. . . . Opisa of Turunom did not even trouble to move his second wife from her village to his own. She, a woman twenty years his senior, simply remained at her own home and tended two of his pigs. (1955:352–53)

A bedouin man from the Middle East is pictured here with his two wives and the wife of his brother.

Competition among Wives. Despite the advantages just discussed, living in a polygynous household is hardly without its drawbacks. Even though men desire multiple wives, they recognize the potential pitfalls. The major problem is jealousy among the co-wives, who frequently compete for the husband's attention, sexual favors, and household resources. In fact, in some African societies, the word *co-wife* is derived from the root word for jealousy. As LeVine relates, jealousy and dissension among co-wives is common among the Gusii of western Kenya:

> Each wife tends to be the husband's darling when she is the latest, and to maintain that position until he marries again. . . . This tendency in itself causes jealousy among the wives. In addition, any inequality in the distribution of gifts or money, or in the number of children born and died, or the amount of education received by the children, adds to the jealousy and hatred. A woman who becomes barren or whose children die almost always believes that her co-wife has achieved this through witchcraft or poisoning. She may then attempt retaliation. (quoted in Stephens, 1963:57)

Even though competition among wives in polygynous societies can be a threat to domestic tranquility, there are several ways to minimize the friction. First, some societies practice a form of polygyny called sororal polygyny, where a man marries two or more sisters. It is possible that sisters, who have had to resolve issues of jealousy revolving around their parents' attention, are less likely to be jealous of one another when they be-come co-wives. Second, co-wives in many polygynous societies are given their own separate living quarters. As Bohannan and Curtin (1988:114) remind us, since women may have more difficulty sharing their kitchens than their husbands, jealousy can be minimized by giving each co-wife her own personal space. Third, dissension will be lessened if the rights and obligations among the co-wives are clearly understood. Fourth, potential conflict among co-wives can be reduced by establishing a hierarchy among the wives. Since the senior wife often exerts considerable authority over more junior wives, she will be able to run a fairly smooth household by adjudicating the various complaints of the other co-wives.

Not only can the jealousies among co-wives be regulated, but some ethnographic reports from polygynous societies reveal considerable harmony and cooperation among the wives. Elenore Smith Bowen (1964:127–28) relates the story of Ava, a Tiv woman who was the senior of five wives:

> The women were fast friends. Indeed it was Ava who had picked out all the others. She saved up forty or fifty shillings every few years, searched out an industrious girl of congenial character, then brought her home and presented her to her husband: "Here is your new wife." Ava's husband always welcomed her additions to his household and he always set to work to pay the rest of the bridewealth, for he knew perfectly well that Ava always picked hard-working, healthy, handsome, steady women who wouldn't run away.

One way of reducing jealousy in polygynous households is to provide each co-wife her own physical space. Here, in a Kikuyu compound, each co-wife has her own hut and granary for storing her food supplies.

Polyandry

Polyandry involves the marriage of a woman to two or more men at a time. A much rarer form of plural marriage, polyandry is found in less than 1 percent of the societies of the world, most notably in Tibet, Nepal, and India. Polyandry can be fraternal (where the husbands are brothers) or nonfraternal.

Perhaps the best-known case of polyandry is found among the Toda of southern India, who practice the fraternal variety. When a woman marries a man, she also becomes the wife of all of his brothers, including even those that might not yet be born. Marriage privileges rotate among the brothers. Even though all of the brothers live together with the wife in a single household, there is little competition or sexual jealousy. Whenever a brother is with the wife, he places his cloak and staff at the door as a sign not to disturb him. When the wife becomes pregnant, paternity is not necessarily ascribed to the biological father (genitor) but is determined by a ceremony that establishes a social father (pater), usually the oldest brother. After the birth of two or three children, however, another brother is chosen as the social father for all children born to the woman thereafter.

Toda society is characterized by a shortage of females brought about by the traditional practice of female infanticide, and this shortage of women may be one of the reasons for the existence of polyandry among the Toda. Owing to the influence of both the Indian government and Christian missionaries, however, female infanticide has largely disappeared today, the male-female sex ratio has become essentially balanced, and polyandry among the Toda is, for all practical purposes, a thing of the past.

In addition to explaining the existence of polyandry by the shortage of women, there are certain economic factors to consider. According to Stephens (1963:44), senior husbands among the wealthier families in Marquesans society recruited junior husbands as a way of augmenting the manpower of the household. It has also been suggested (Goldstein 1987) that Tibetan serfs practice polyandry as a solution to the problem of land shortage. As a way of avoiding the division of small plots of land among their sons, brothers could keep the family land intact by marrying one woman. By marrying one woman, two or more brothers are able to preserve the family resources; that is, if a man took one (monogamy) or several (polygyny) wives, it would cost him his inheritance.

Economic Considerations of Marriage

Most societies view marriage as a binding contract between at least the husband and wife and, in many cases, between their respective families as well. Such a contract includes the transfer of certain rights between the parties involved—rights of sexual access, legal rights to children, and rights of the spouses to each other's

CROSS-CULTURAL MISCUE

Sometimes cross-cultural misunderstandings can have tragic consequences. In 1992 a Japanese exchange student studying in Louisiana was fatally shot by a homeowner who mistook him for a burglar. The Japanese student, Yoshi Hattori, and his American host had been invited to a Halloween party, but got lost and went to the wrong house. After ringing the doorbell, they came around to the garage where they encountered and startled the woman of the household who was in the garage. Frightened, she ran into the house and called her husband to get his gun. When her husband appeared at the door with his 44 Magnum, he told the Japanese student to "freeze," but the Japanese teenager kept on approaching toward him. Thinking that his life was in danger, the homeowner shot and killed the youth. It is thought that with his limited command of English, the Japanese exchange student mistook the word "freeze" for the word "please."

economic goods and services. Often the transfer of rights is accompanied by the transfer of some type of economic consideration. These transactions, which may take place either before or after the marriage, can be divided into five categories: **bride price, bride service, dowry, woman exchange,** and **reciprocal exchange.**

Bride Price

Also known as bridewealth, bride price is the compensation given upon marriage by the family of the groom to the family of the bride. According to Murdock's *World Ethnographic Sample* (reported in Stephens 1963: 211), approximately 46 percent of all societies give substantial bride price payment as a normal part of the marriage process. Although bride price is practiced in most regions of the world, it is perhaps most widely found in Africa, where it is estimated (Murdock 1967) that 82 percent of the societies require the payment of bride price, while most of the remaining 18 percent practice either token bride price or bride service (providing labor, rather than goods, to the bride's family).

Bride price is paid in a wide variety of currencies, but in almost all cases, the particular commodity used for payment is highly valued in the society. For example, reindeer are given as bride price by the reindeer-herding Chukchee; horses by the equestrian Cheyenne of the Central Plains; sheep by the sheep-herding Navajo; and cattle by the pastoral Masai, Samburu, and Nuer of eastern Africa. In other societies, marriage payments take the form of blankets (Kwakuitl), pigs (Alor), mats (Fiji), shell money (Kurtachi), spears (Somali), loin cloths (Toda), and even the plumes of the bird of paradise (Siane).

Just as the commodities used in bridewealth transactions vary considerably, so does the amount of the transaction. To illustrate, an indigent Nandi of Kenya, under certain circumstances, can obtain a bride with no more than a promise to transfer one animal to the bride's father. A suitor from the Jie tribe of Uganda, on the other hand, normally transfers fifty head of cattle and one hundred head of small stock (sheep and goats) to the bride's family before the marriage becomes official. Large amounts of bride price as found among the Jie are significant for several reasons. First, the economic stakes are so high that the bride and groom are under enormous pressure to make the marriage work. And second, large bride price payments tend to make the system of negotiations between the two families more flexible and, consequently, more cordial. When the bride price is low, the addition or subtraction of one item becomes highly critical and is likely to create hard feelings between the two families.

Not only do bridewealth payments vary between different cultures, but variations also exist within a single cultural group. In a recent study of bridewealth payments among the Kipsigis of western Kenya, Mulder (1988) found that intragroup variations depended upon several key factors. First, high bridewealth is given for brides who mature early and are plump because such women are thought to have greater reproductive success. Second, lower bridewealth is given for women who have given birth previously. And third, women whose natal homes are far away from their marital homes command higher bridewealth because they spend less time in their own mother's households and therefore are more available for domestic chores in their husband's household.

The meaning of bride price has been widely debated by scholars and nonscholars alike for much of the twentieth century. Early Christian missionaries, viewing bride price as a form of wife purchase, argued that such a practice was denigrating to women and repugnant to the Christian ideal of marriage. Many colonial administrators, taking a more legalistic perspective, saw bride price as a symbol of the inferior legal status of women in traditional societies. Both of these negative interpretations of bride price led to a number of vigorous, yet unsuccessful, attempts to stamp out the practice of bride price payments.

Less concerned with moral or legal issues, cultural anthropologists saw the institution of bride price as a rational and comprehensible part of traditional systems of marriage. Rejecting the interpretation that bride price was equivalent to wife purchase, anthropologists tended to concentrate on how the institution operated within the total cultural context of which it was a part. Given such a perspective, cultural anthropologists identified a number of important functions that the institution of bride price performed for the well-being of the society. For example, bride price was seen as security or insurance for the good treatment of the wife, as a mechanism to stabilize marriage by reducing the possibility of divorce, as a form of compensation to the bride's lineage for the loss of her economic potential and her childbearing capacity, as a symbol of the union between two large groups of kin, as a mechanism to legitimize traditional marriages in much the same way that a marriage license legitimizes Western marriages,

as the transference of rights over children from the mother's family to the father's family, and as the acquisition by the husband of uxorial (wifely) rights over the bride.

To avoid the economic implications of "wife purchase," Evans-Pritchard (1940) suggested that the term *bridewealth* be substituted for the term *bride price,* while Radcliffe-Brown (1950:47) used the word *prestation,* a term with even fewer economic connotations. Although a much needed corrective to the earlier interpretations of bride price as wife purchase, much of the anthropological literature has overlooked the very real economic significance of bride price. It was not until near the end of the colonial period that Gray (1960) reminded social scientists that it was legitimate to view bride price as an integral part of the local exchange system and that in many traditional societies, wives are dealt with in much the same way as other commodities. It is now generally held that a comprehensive understanding of the practice of bride price is impossible without recognizing its economic functions as well as its noneconomic functions.

Bride Service

In those societies with considerable material wealth, marriage considerations take the form of bride price and, as we have seen, are paid in various forms of commodities. But since many small-scale, particularly nomadic, societies, cannot accumulate capital goods, men will frequently give their labor to the bride's family instead of material goods in exchange for wives. This practice, known as bride service, is found in approximately 14 percent of the societies listed in Murdock's *World Ethnographic Sample.*

In some cases, bride service is practiced to the exclusion of property transfer; in other cases, it represents a temporary condition, and the transfer of some property is expected at a later date. When a man marries under a system of bride service, he often will move in with his bride's family, work or hunt for them, and serve a probationary period of several weeks to several years. This custom is similar to that practiced by Jacob of the Old Testament (Genesis, Chapter 29) who served his mother's brother (Laban) for his two wives Leah and her sister Rachel. In some cases where bride service is found, other members of the groom's family, in addition to the groom himself, may be expected to give service, and this work may be done not only for the bride's parents but also for her other close relatives, as is the case with the Taita of Kenya (Harris 1972:63).

Dowry

In contrast to bridewealth, a dowry involves a transfer of goods or money in the opposite direction, from the bride's family to the groom or to the groom's family. While the dowry is always provided by the bride's family, the recipient of the goods varies from one culture to another. In certain Western societies, the dowry was given to the groom, who then had varying rights to dispose of it. In rural Ireland, it was given to the father of the groom in compensation for land, which the groom's father subsequently bequeathed to the bride and groom. The dowry was then used, wholly or in part, by the groom's father to pay the dowry of the groom's sister.

The dowry is not very widely practiced throughout the world. Less than three percent of the societies in Murdock's sample actually practice it. It is confined to Eurasia, most notably in medieval and Renaissance Europe and among the Rajputs of Khalapur in India.

In certain European countries—where it is still practiced to some extent today—substantial dowry payments have been used as a means of upward mobility, that is, as a way to marry a daughter into a higher-status family. Around the turn of the century, a number of daughters of wealthy U.S. industrialists entered into mutually beneficial marriage alliances with European nobles who were falling upon hard economic times. The U.S. heiresses brought a substantial dowry to the marriage in exchange for a title.

Even though bridewealth is the usual form of marriage payment in Africa, there are several instances where the direction of payment is in the opposite direction. One such case is found among the Nilo-Hamitic Barabaig of Tanzania. Although a small number of goods are given to the bride's kin group, her family will confer upon her a dowry of from two to forty head of large stock depending on their means. These dowry cattle, which frequently outnumber the cattle held originally by the groom, are kept in trust as inheritance cattle for the bride's sons and as dowry cattle for the bride's daughters. Since the Barabaig are patrilocal, the wife and her dowry cattle reside at the husband's homestead. Even though the husband has nominal control over the herd, he still must ask his wife's permission to dispose of any of the cattle, for technically the herd belongs to his wife's father. Until the herd is finally redistributed among their own children, it will remain a source of friction between the husband and wife because the very existence of such a dowry gives the wife considerable economic leverage in her marital relations.

Woman Exchange

Another way of legitimizing marriage by means of economic considerations is the practice of woman exchange, whereby two men exchange sisters or daughters as wives for themselves, their sons, or their brothers. This practice, which is limited to a small number of societies in Africa and the Pacific, is found in less than 3 percent of the world's societies. According to Winter (1956:21), woman exchange was the primary means by which marriages were legitimized among the traditional Bwamba of Uganda. Such a system, however, suffers from a considerable disadvantage—that is, the exchange of one woman for another allows little room for individual variation. Bwamba women differ, as do women elsewhere, in terms of age, beauty, and procreative powers. Bwamba men prefer young, attractive, industrious, and fertile women. The exchange system, however, cannot cope with variations in these qualities.

In a system using conventional material objects such as bridewealth cattle, a man's preference may be reflected to a certain degree by the quality and quantity of his gifts. We should also bear in mind that the system of woman exchange has different implications for the distribution of women (especially in polygynous societies) than does a system using more conventional objects of exchange. Under the latter system, it is the wealthy man in the society who is able to obtain a large number of wives, whereas under the exchange system, the number of wives a man can obtain is limited to the number of sisters and/or daughters at his disposal.

Reciprocal Exchange

Reciprocal exchange is found in approximately 6 percent of the societies listed in Murdock's *Ethnographic Atlas*, most prominently in the Pacific region and among traditional Native Americans. It involves the relatively equal exchange of gifts between the families of both the bride and the groom. Such a custom was practiced by the traditional Vugusu people of western Kenya who exchanged a large variety of items between a sizable number of people from both families. According to Wagner, the gifts made and the expenses incurred were basically reciprocal, with only "a slight preponderance on the bride's side" (1949:423). The variety of the reciprocal gift giving and the number of people involved in Vugusu society tend to emphasize the generally valid tenet that marriages in many parts of the world are conceived not simply as a union between a man and a woman but rather as an alliance between two families.

Residence Patterns: Where Do Wives and Husbands Live?

In addition to establishing regulations for mate selection, the number of spouses one can have, and the types of economic considerations that must be attended to, societies set guidelines regarding where couples will live when they marry. When two people marry in our own society, it is customary for the couple to take up residence in a place of their own, apart from the relatives of either spouse. This residence pattern is known as *neolocal residence* (i.e., a new place). As natural as this may appear to us, it is, by global standards, a relatively rare type of residence pattern, practiced in only about 5 percent of the societies of the world. The remaining societies prescribe that newlyweds will live with or in close proximity to relatives of either the wife or the husband.

One question facing these societies is, Which children stay at home when they marry, and which ones leave? Also, of those who leave, with which relative are they expected to reside? Although these questions can be answered in a number of ways, most residence patterns fall into one of five patterns (percentages based on tabulations from Murdock's *Ethnographic Atlas* [1967]):

Patrilocal Residence. The married couple lives with or near the relatives of the husband's father (69 percent of the societies).

Matrilocal Residence. The married couple lives with or near the relatives of the wife (13 percent of the societies).

Avunculocal Residence. The married couple lives with or near the husband's mother's brother (4 percent of the societies).

Ambilocal (Bilocal) Residence. The married couple has a choice of living with either the relatives of the wife or the relatives of the husband (9 percent of the societies.)

Neolocal Residence. The married couple forms an independent place of residence away from the relatives of either spouse (5 percent of the societies).

When two people in the United States marry, they typically live in a home of their own apart from the relatives of either spouse.

To a significant degree, residence patterns have an effect on the types of kinship systems (discussed in the previous chapter) found in any society. There is, for example, a reasonably close correlation between patrilocal residence and patrilineal descent (tracing one's important relatives through the father's side) and between matrilocal residence and matrilineal descent (tracing one's important relatives through the mother's side). To be certain, residence patterns do not determine kinship ideology, but social interaction between certain categories of kin can be facilitated if those kin reside (and play out their lives) in close proximity to each other.

It should be kept in mind that these five residence patterns, like most other aspects of culture, are ideal types. Consequently, how people actually behave—that is, where they may reside—doesn't always conform precisely to these ideals. Sometimes, normative patterns of residence are altered or interrupted by events such as famines or epidemics that force newlyweds to reside in areas that will maximize their chances for survival or their economic security. To illustrate, during the Depression years of the 1930s, the normal neolocal pattern of residence in the United States was disrupted when many young married adults moved in with one set of parents to save money.

Family Structure

Cultural anthropologists have identified two fundamentally different types of family structure—the **nuclear family** and the **extended family.** The nuclear family is based on marital ties, while the extended family, a much larger social unit, is based on blood ties between three or more generations of kin.

The Nuclear Family

Consisting of husband and wife and their children, the nuclear family is a two-generation family formed around the conjugal or marital union. Even though the nuclear family to some degree is part of a larger family structure, it remains a relatively autonomous and independent unit. That is, the everyday needs of economic support, child care, and social interaction are met within the nuclear family itself rather than by a wider set of relatives. In societies based on the nuclear family, it is customary for married couples to live apart from both sets of parents (neolocal residence). The married couple is also not particularly obliged or expected to care for their aging parents in their own home. Generally, parents are not actively involved in mate selection for their children, in no way legitimize the marriages of their children, and have no control over whether or not their children remain married.

The nuclear family is most likely to be found in those societies with the greatest amount of geographic mobility. This certainly is the case in the United States, which currently has both considerable geographic mobility and the ideal of the nuclear family. During much of our nation's early history, the extended family—tied to the land and working on the family farm—was the rule rather than the exception. Today, however, the family farm housing parents, grandparents, aunts, uncles, cousins, and siblings is a thing of the past. Now, in response to the forces of industrialization, most adults move to wherever they can find suitable employment. Since one's profession largely determines where one will live, adults in the United States frequently live considerable distances from their parents or other non-nuclear family members.

In addition to being found in such highly industrialized societies as our own, the nuclear family is found in certain societies located at the other end of the techno-

logical spectrum. In certain foraging societies residing in environments where resources are meager (such as the Inuit of northern Canada and the Shoshone of Utah and Nevada), the nuclear family is the basic hunting-and-gathering unit. These nuclear families remain highly independent foraging groups that fend for themselves. Even though they cannot expect help from the outside in an emergency, they have developed a family structure that is well adapted to a highly mobile life. Thus, both U.S. society and some small-scale hunting-and-gathering societies have adopted the nuclear family pattern because of their need to maintain a high degree of geographic mobility.

Although the independent nuclear family has been the ideal in the United States for much of the present century, significant changes have occurred in recent years. According to the U.S. Census, only about one in three households consists of the nuclear family (parents and one or more children), a sharp decline from earlier decades. The other two-thirds of the U.S. households are made up of married couples without children, single adults, single parents, unmarried couples, roommates, extended family members, or adult siblings. As Kottak (1987:310–11) has suggested, these changing patterns of family life have been reflected in a number of television sitcoms. For example, during the 1950s the family was depicted by Ozzie and Harriet Nelson and their sons David and Ricky and by Ward and June Cleaver and their sons Wally and the Beaver. Within the last several years, however, an increasing number of TV shows have featured alternative living arrangements such as roommates, single adults, working mothers, and single parents. In fact, some of the most popular TV sitcoms in recent years feature characters who are neither related to nor living with one another (e.g., "Seinfeld", "Murphy" "Brown", and "Cheers").

There are several explanations for the decline of the nuclear family in the United States as we head into the twenty-first century. First, as more and more women complete higher education and enter the job market, they are more likely to delay marrying and having children. Second, the increasing cost of maintaining a middle-class household that includes the parents, children, a three- or four-bedroom house, a cocker spaniel, and a car or two has caused some couples to opt for remaining childless altogether. Third, the ever-increasing divorce rate in the United States has contributed to the increase in non-nuclear families in the recent decades.

The Extended Family

In societies based on extended families, blood ties are more important than ties of marriage. Extended families consist of two or more families that are linked by blood ties. Most commonly, this takes the form of a married couple living with one or more of their married children in a single household or homestead and under the authority of a family head. Such extended families, which are based on parent-child linkages, can be either patrilineal (comprising a man, his sons, and the sons' wives and children) or matrilineal (comprising a woman, her daughters, and her daughters' husbands and children). It is also possible for extended families to be linked though sibling ties rather than parent-child ties, such as those extended families consisting of two or more married brothers and their wives and children. According to Murdock's *Ethnographic Atlas* (1967), approximately 46 percent of the

Many of the societies studied by anthropologists are based on extended families. This multigenerational Yagua Indian family of the Amazon is held together by ties of both blood and marriage.

862 societies listed have some type of extended-family organization.

When a couple marries in a society with extended families, there is little sense that the newlyweds are establishing a separate and distinct family unit. In the case of a patrilineal extended family, the young couple takes up residence in the homestead of the husband's father, and the husband continues to work for his father, who also runs the household. Moreover, most of the personal property in the household is not owned by the newlyweds, but is controlled by the husband's father. In the event that the extended family is large, it may be headed by two or more powerful male elders who run the family in much the same way that a board of directors runs a corporation. Eventually, the father (or other male elders) will die or retire, allowing younger men to assume positions of leadership and power within the extended family. Unlike the nuclear family, which lasts only one generation, the extended family is a continuous unit that can last an indefinite number of generations. As old people die off, they are replaced through the birth of new members.

It is important to point out that in extended family systems, marriage is viewed more as bringing a daughter into the family than acquiring a wife. In other words, a man's obligations of obedience to his father and loyalty to his brothers are far more important than his relationship to his wife. When a woman marries into an extended family, she most often comes under the control of her mother-in-law, who allocates chores and supervises her domestic activities.

In some extended-family systems, the conjugal relationship is suppressed to such an extent that contact between husband and wife is kept to a minimum. Among the Rajputs of northern India, for example, spouses are not allowed to talk to each other in the presence of family elders. Public displays of affection between spouses are considered reprehensible, and in fact, a husband is not permitted to show open concern for his wife's welfare. Some societies take such severe measures to subordinate the husband-wife relationship because it is feared that a man's feelings for his wife could interfere with his obligations to his own blood relatives.

Why do so many societies in the world have extended families? There is some indication that extended families are more likely to be found in certain types of economies than others. As previously mentioned, economies based on either foraging or wage employment (which require considerable geographic mobility) are more likely to be associated with nuclear than with extended families. In addition, a rough correlation exists between extended-family systems and an agricultural way of life. Several logical explanations have been suggested for this correlation. First, extended families provide relatively large numbers of workers who are necessary for success in both farm production and the marketing of surpluses. Second, in farm economics where cultivated land is valuable, an extended family system prevents the land from being continually subdivided into smaller and less productive plots. As an alternative explanation, Pasternak, Ember, and Ember (1976) have suggested that extended-family systems develop in response to what they call "incompatible activity requirements." That is, extended families are likely to prevail in those societies where there is a lack of man and woman power to simultaneously carry out subsistence and domestic tasks.

Modern-Day Family Structure

Most Western social thinkers over the past century have been in general agreement concerning the long-term effects of urbanization and modernization on the family. In general, they see a progressive nuclearization of the family in the face of modernization. This position is perhaps most eloquently presented by William Goode, who has stated that industrialization and urbanization have brought about ". . . fewer kinship ties with distant relatives and a greater emphasis on the 'nuclear' family unit of couple and children" (1963:1). Although in many parts of the world we can observe the association

between modernization and fewer extended kinship ties, there are a number of exceptions, most notably in certain developing countries. To illustrate, in the Kenya Kinship Study (KKS) discussed in Chapter 5, no significant differences were found in the extended-family interaction between rural Kikuyu and Kikuyu living in Nairobi. This retention of extended-family ties in this urban/industrialized setting could be explained by several relevant economic factors. First, the combination of a fiercely competitive job market and few or no employment benefits (e.g., workers' compensation, retirement, unemployment insurance) means the average urban worker has little job security. Second, despite the creation of freehold land tenure in Kenya in recent years, land inheritance still takes place, by and large, within the extended family. Urban workers who sever ties with their rural-based extended kin relinquish their rights to inherit land, which for many remains the only haven from the insecurities of urban employment.

Interestingly, we do not need to focus on developing countries to find the retention of extended kin ties in urban, industrialized areas. For example, Carol Stack (1975) and J. W. Sharff (1981) have shown how urban Blacks in the United States use extended kinship ties as a strategy for coping with poverty. Moreover, at least one immigrant group in the United States—the Vietnamese—has used modern technology to help maintain and strengthen its traditional family values. Nash (1988) reports that immigrant Vietnamese families routinely rent Chinese-made films (dubbed in Vietnamese) for their VCRs. Whereas most films and TV program-

The strong support of Vietnamese families in the United States has enabled their children to excel in all levels of U.S. education.

ming in the United States tend to glorify the individual, Chinese films tend to emphasize the traditional Confucian value of family loyalty.

For at least the first half of the present century, popular opinion (buttressed by our Judeo-Christian tradition) held a fairly uniform notion of what form the typical family in the United States should take. The natural family, according to this view, was a nuclear family consisting of two monogamous heterosexual parents (the breadwinning male and the female homemaker) with their children. In the past four decades, however, this so-called typical family has become harder to find. In fact, there is no longer a "typical family" in the United States. According to census data for 1990, fewer than 27 percent of all families in the United States are comprised of married couples with children under eighteen years of age. Moreover, even fewer (approximately 20 percent) of all U.S. families fit the "typical" model with the breadwinning husband and the homemaking wife. As we approach the twenty-first century, nearly three out of every four families are atypical in that they are headed by (1) a female single parent, (2) a male single parent, (3) unmarried partners, or (4) childless or post-child-rearing couples. There are also step families, extended families, homosexual families, and communal families, all of which are acceptable alternative family forms.

Whether or not it is possible to determine definitively if marriage and family systems are universal, it is clear that both vary widely on a number of critical dimensions. This chapter has discussed many of these variations. Understanding differences in marriage and family patterns—like any other aspect of culture—can have important implications for contemporary social problems. This applied section considers two case studies: one examines how an anthropological understanding of traditional family patterns in Hawaii can help improve minority education, and the other illustrates how anthropological research on patterns of polygyny in the Peruvian Amazon can suggest possible solutions to the rapid population growth in that area.

Marriage and the Family

An educational anthropologist translates Hawaiian family cultural patterns into classroom practices to help improve minority education.

A basic premise of educational anthropology is that the cultural patterns that students bring with them into the classroom must be taken into account if these students are to be successfully integrated into the culture of the school. This is precisely the objective that educational anthropologist Cathie Jordan brought to her work with the Kamehameha Elementary Education Program (KEEP), a privately funded educational research effort designed to develop more effective methods for teaching Hawaiian children in the public schools.

For decades children of Hawaiian ancestry, particularly those from low-income families, have been chronic underachievers in the public school system. Classroom teachers often describe Hawaiian children as lazy, uncooperative, uninvolved, and disinterested in school. While differences do exist between their dialect, known as Hawaiian Creole English, and the Standard English used by teachers, the linguistic differences are minimal. Thus, Cathie Jordan and her colleagues at KEEP needed to look beyond linguistic differences to find an explanation for why Hawaiian children were not succeeding in school. Accordingly, KEEP focused on the wider Hawaiian culture—particularly interaction patterns within the family—in order to

discover learning skills the children had developed at home that could be used and built upon in the classroom.

When dealing with parents and siblings at home, Hawaiian children behave very differently than when interacting with teachers and classmates. From a very early age, Hawaiian children contribute significantly to the everyday work of the household. Tasks that all children are expected to perform regularly include cleaning, cooking, laundry, yard work, caring for younger siblings, and (for male siblings) earning cash from outside employment. Working together in cooperative sibling groups, brothers and sisters organize their own household work routines with only minimal supervision from parents. Young children learn to perform their household tasks by observing their older siblings and adults. And, according to Jordan and her colleagues (1992:6), these chores are performed willingly within a "context of strong values of helping, cooperation, and contributing to the family."

The paradox facing KEEP was, How could children be so cooperative and responsible in the family context yet so disengaged and lazy in school? A comparison of the home and school cultures revealed some major structural differences. When a mother wants her children to do a job around the house, she makes that known and then allows the children to organize how it will get done. In other words, she hands over the responsibility of the job to the children. In contrast, the classroom is almost totally teacher dominated. The teacher makes the assignments, sets the rules, and manages the resources of the classroom. Children are controlled by the classroom, rather than being responsible for it. Once these cultural differences between home and school were revealed by anthropological fieldwork, the educational anthropologist was able to suggest some changes for improving student involvement in school. The solution was fairly straightforward: that is, have teachers run their classrooms in much the same way as Hawaiian mothers run their households. Specifically, teachers should (1) minimize verbal instructions, (2) withdraw from direct supervision, and (3) allow students to take responsibility for organizing and assigning specific tasks. When these changes were made, Hawaiian students became more actively involved in their own education, and consequently, their achievement levels improved.

Here, then, is an example of how educational anthropologists can apply their findings to improve the learning environment for Hawaiian children. Interestingly, this case of applied anthropology did not follow the traditional solution to problems of minority education, which involves trying to change the child's family culture to make it conform to the culture of the classroom. Rather, Jordan and her colleagues at KEEP solved the problem by modifying the culture of the classroom to conform to those skills, abilities, and behaviors that the Hawaiian students brought with them from their family culture.

THOUGHT QUESTIONS

1. What is meant by educational anthropology?
2. Can you think of any subcultural groups living in the continental United States whose family patterns should be studied by the public school systems that are responsible for educating their children?

3. What other types of educational problems are applied anthropologists able to help solve?

An anthropological understanding of marital patterns among the Shipibo of the Peruvian Amazon sheds light on the serious problem of rapid population growth.

In this chapter we have examined a number of alternative forms of marriage found throughout the world. These include monogamy, as routinely practiced in the United States, and polygyny, in which a man has more than one wife at a time, which is a preferred form of marriage in many smaller (non-Western) cultures. Over the course of the past century, Western missionaries have put considerable pressure on these small-scale societies to give up the practice of polygyny in favor of monogamy. The Christian missionaries argue that polygyny is immoral, even though most would be hard-pressed to explain the widespread practice of polygyny in the Old Testament. In their well-intentioned, yet short-sighted, attempt to convert non-Western peoples to monogamy, missionaries have contributed to the serious worldwide problem of out-of-control population growth.

Warren Hern (1992), a medical anthropologist who has worked for decades with the Shipibo Indians in the Peruvian Amazon, has studied the relationship between polygyny and population growth. At first glance one might think that the practice of polygyny would contribute more to overall population growth than would the practice of monogamy. In actual fact, just the opposite is true. Although polygyny does permit some men to have more children than others, it permits women to have fewer children with longer intervals between births. Frequently associated with polygyny is postpartum sexual abstinence, in which a woman does not have sex with her husband for a certain period of time after giving birth. This postpartum sexual abstinence, which may last from several months to several years, functions to allow the child to breastfeed without competition, thereby improving his or her chances for survival. The overall effect of this abstinence is to lengthen the interval between pregnancies, thereby reducing the number of children born to wives in polygynous marriages.

Hern's research among the Shipibo Indians demonstrates that the practice of polygyny tends to keep overall birthrates down relative to monogamy. In 1983 and 1984, Hern studied six Shipibo villages in various stages of modernization. In the most traditional Shipibo village, as many as 45 percent of the women were in polygynous marriages; this figure dropped to 5 percent in the least traditional village. Hern found that among all women in polygynous marriages, the average interval between births was thirty-four months, four months longer than for women in monogamous unions. Moreover, women in polygynous marriages on average had 1.3 fewer children during their lifetime than monogamous women. Thus, for the Shipibo—and for many other traditionally polygynous peoples—the practices of polygyny and postpartum sexual abstinence tend to depress the overall birthrate. Consequently, when people convert from polygyny to monogamy (and are provided no alternative forms of birth control), the usual result is an increase in the overall number of births. According to Hern (1992:36):

many human societies that controlled their fertility in the past have lost the tradition of doing so in the frenzy of modern cultural change. The old methods that reduced births have not yet been replaced by the new technologies of fertility control. The result is chaos, suffering, more cultural change, and in some cases, even more rapid population growth.

The implications of Hern's study are clear: before Westerners insist on preaching against polygyny, they need to know what effects a change in marriage custom will have on such pressing human issues as rapid population growth.

THOUGHT QUESTIONS

1. How have missionaries viewed the practice of polygyny?

2. How can you explain the lower overall rates of fertility in societies practicing polygyny than in those that are strictly monogamous?

3. What advice would you give missionaries before they start trying to convince local polygynous societies to become monogamous?

Summary

1. Owing to the vast ethnographic variations found in the world, the terms *family* and *marriage* are not easy to define. Recognizing the difficulties inherent in such definitions, the family is a social unit, the members of which cooperate economically, manage reproduction and child rearing, and most often live together. Marriage—the process by which families are formed—refers to a socially approved union between male and female adults.

2. The formation of families through the process of marriage serves several important social functions by (a) reducing competition for spouses; (b) regulating the sexual division of labor; and (c) meeting the material, educational, and emotional needs of children.

3. Every culture has a set of rules (incest taboos) regulating which categories of kin are inappropriate partners for sexual intercourse. A number of explanations have been suggested for this universal incest taboo, including (a) the natural aversion theory, (b) the inbreeding theory, (c) the family disruption theory, and (d) the theory of expanding social alliances.

4. Cultures restrict the choice of marriage partners by such practices as exogamy, endogamy, arranged marriages, preferential cousin marriage, the levirate, and the sororate.

5. All societies have rules governing the number of spouses a person can have. Societies tend to emphasize either monogamy (one spouse at a time), polygyny (a man marrying more than one wife at a time), or polyandry (a woman marrying more than one husband at a time).

6. In many societies, marriages involve the transfer of some type of economic consideration in exchange for rights of sexual access, legal rights over children, and rights to each other's property. These economic considerations involve such practices as bride price, bride service, dowry, woman exchange, and reciprocal exchange.

7. All societies have guidelines regarding where a married couple should live after they marry. Residence patterns fall into five different categories. The couple can live with or near the relatives of the husband's father (patrilocal), the wife's relatives (matrilocal), or the husband's mother's brother (avunculocal) or the relatives of either the wife or the husband (ambilocal), or the husband and wife can form a completely new residence of their own.

8. Cultural anthropologists distinguish between two types of family structure: the nuclear family, comprising the wife, husband, and children; and the extended family, a much larger social unit, comprising relatives from three or more generations.

Key Terms

ambilocal (bilocal)
  residence
~~arranged marriage~~
avunculocal residence
bride price (bridewealth)
bride service
cross cousins
dowry
endogamy
exogamy
extended family
incest taboo
~~kibbutz~~
levirate
matrilocal residence

monogamy
neolocal residence
nuclear family
parallel cousins
patrilocal residence
polyandry
polygyny
~~postpartum sex taboo~~
preferential cousin
  marriage
reciprocal exchange
role ambiguity
sororate
woman exchange

Suggested Readings

Fernea, Elizabeth. *Guests of the Sheik: An Ethnography of an Iraqi Village.* Garden City, N.Y.: Doubleday, 1965. Fernea, who accompanied her anthropologist husband on a field trip to the Middle East, describes the sheltered world of women in a small desert town in southern Iraq. Her very personal account of the difficulties she encountered in adapting to the culture of Iraqi women should be required reading for anyone interested in understanding the institution of marriage in the Islamic world.

Fox, Robin. *Kinship and Marriage: An Anthropological Perspective.* Baltimore: Penguin, 1968. An excellent introduction to the cross-cultural study of marriage, particularly exogamous systems.

Friedl, Ernestine. *Women and Men: An Anthropologist's View.* New York: Holt, Rinehart & Winston, 1975. Gender roles, a topic closely associated with marriage, is the subject of this volume, which draws on ethnographic data from a number of different societies to suggest a series of hypotheses about the determinants and expressions of sex roles.

Goody, Jack, and S. J. Tambiah. *Bridewealth and Dowry.* Cambridge: Cambridge University Press, 1973. These two forms of marriage transactions are analyzed in the context of Africa, where bridewealth predominates, and Asia, where dowry is the most common practice.

Hart, C. W. M., Arnold Pilling, and Jane C. Goodale. *The Tiwi of North Australia.* 3d. ed. New York: Holt, Rinehart & Winston, 1988. A fascinating ethnographic account of the Tiwi of Melville Island (off the northern coast of Australia), who practice an extreme form of polygyny, whereby all females are always married and males spend much of their lives competing for the society's major status symbol—i.e., wives.

Mair, Lucy. *Marriage.* Baltimore: Penguin, 1971. Drawing on data from a wide variety of non-Western societies, the author examines the functions, regulations, symbolic rituals, and economic considerations of marriage.

Stephens, William N. *The Family in Cross Cultural Perspective.* New York: Holt, Rinehart & Winston, 1963. Citing literature from all over the world, this cross-cultural study of marriage and the family examines such topics as the universality of the family, plural marriage, mate selection, sexual restrictions, divorce, and conjugal roles.

Weston, Kath. *Families We Choose: Lesbians, Gays, Kinship.* New York: Columbia University Press, 1991. This award-winning book, based on participant-observation and in-depth interviews in the San Francisco area, examines gay and lesbian families in a historical perspective.

GENDER

What it means to be male or female in Tahiti is quite different from what it means in the United States.

- To what extent does biology influence maleness and femaleness?
- Are males dominant over females in all societies?
- How similar are gender roles throughout the world?
- Do women and men in the same culture speak differently?

One need not be a particularly keen observer of humanity to recognize that men and women differ physically in a number of important ways. Men on average are taller and have considerably greater body mass than women. There are noticeable differences between men and women in their sex organs, breast size, hormonal levels, body hair, and muscle/fat ratios. With their larger hearts and lungs and greater muscle mass, men have greater physical strength. Moreover, men and women differ genetically, with women having two X chromosomes and men having an X and a Y chromosome. Unlike humans, some animals (such as mice and pigeons) manifest no obvious sexual differences between males and females. But, because of these significant physiological differences, we say that humans are **sexually dimorphic.**

While most researchers can agree on the physiological (genetically based) differences between men and women, there is considerably less agreement on the extent to which these differences actually cause differences in behavior or in the way men and women are treated in society. As is the case with so many other aspects of behavior, the nature-nurture debate is operating in the area of behavioral differences between men and women. In other words, do men and women behave differently because of their genetic predisposition or because of their culture? During the twentieth century, ethnographers have shown that the definition of femaleness and maleness varies widely from society to society. Owing to this considerable cultural variability in behaviors and attitudes between the sexes, most anthropologists now prefer to speak of **gender** differences rather that sex differences. For purposes of this chapter, we can use Schlegel's (1990:23) definition of gender, which she defines as "the way members of the two sexes are perceived, evaluated, and expected to behave."

While the use of the term gender acknowledges the role that culture plays, it is not always possible to determine the extent to which culture or biology determines differences in behaviors or attitudes between the sexes. What we can say, however, is that biological differences influence (or set broad limits on) social definitions of maleness or femaleness to varying degrees. To illustrate, the fact that only women can give birth *can* provide a basis for developing a set of attitudes and behaviors for women that are maternal, supportive, and nurturing. Likewise, owing to their greater body mass, men *may* be defined as inherently strong, courageous, aggressive, and warlike. Nevertheless, many different social definitions of masculinity and femininity can be found throughout the world.

Margaret Mead's (1935) classic study of sex and temperament in three New Guinea cultures illustrates the range of gender variation found among the Arapesh, Mundugumor, and Tchambuli. Mead found that among the Arapesh both men and women were cooperative, nonaggressive, and responsive to the needs of others, all traits that Westerners would consider to be "feminine." By way of contrast, both sexes among the Mundugumor were expected to be fierce, ruthless, and aggressive. Among the Tchambuli, there was a complete reversal of the male-female temperaments found in our own society; that is, women were the dominant, impersonal partners who were aggressive food providers, while the males were less responsible, more emotionally dependent, and more preoccupied with art and spent more time on their hairdos and gossiping about the opposite sex. Mead argued that if those temperaments that we regard as feminine (i.e., nurturing, maternal, passive) can be held as a masculine ideal in one group and can be banned for both sexes in another, then we no longer have a basis for saying that **masculinity** and **femininity** are biologically based.

This husband and wife walking on Laguna Beach in California illustrate some of the more obvious physiological differences between men and women.

Though Mead's work has been criticized in recent years for its subjectivity, it nevertheless demonstrates the enormous variability in gender roles across cultures.

Cross-cultural studies further complicate our understanding of gender. In the United States, we generally envision only two sexes, male and female, leaving no room for other gender alternatives that are socially legitimate such as hermaphrodites or androgynous individuals. Westerners, uncomfortable with these ambiguous gender identities, tend to explain them away by categorizing them as pathological, illegitimate, and perhaps even criminal. Some cultures, however, not only accommodate the ambiguities of these gender alternatives, but actually see them as legitimate or, in some cases, as powerful. One stunning example is the male/female Hijra role found in Hindu India.

The notion of a combined male/female role is a major theme in Hindu art, religion, and mythology. For example, androgynous individuals and/or impersonators of the opposite sex are found widely in Hindu mythology among both humans and their deities. These same themes are played out in parts of contemporary India. For example, according to Serena Nanda (1990:20–21):

> In Tamil Nadu, in South India, an important festival takes place in which hijras, identifying with Krishna, become wives, and then widows, of the male deity Koothandavar. . . . For this festival, men who have made vows to Koothandavar dress as women and go through a marriage ceremony with him. The priest performs the marriage, tying on the traditional wedding necklace. After 1 day, the deity is carried to a burial ground. There, all of those who have "married" him remove their wedding necklaces, cry and beat their breasts, and remove the flowers from their hair, as a widow does in mourning for her husband. Hijras participate by the thousands in this festival, coming from all over India. They dress in their best clothes and jewelry and ritually reaffirm their identification with Krishna, who changes his form from male to female.

The Hijra of Hindu India are significant because they provide an example of a society that tolerates a wider definition of gender than is found in our own society. The Hijra, who undergo an emasculation rite, present themselves as being "like women," or female impersonators. Clearly, Hijra are neither male nor female in the conventional sense of the term. But rather than being viewed as social deviants who should be discouraged, the Hijra are seen as a special, even sacred, gender group.

Gender Roles

As mentioned in the chapter on economics, all societies make some distinctions between what men are expected to do and what women are expected to do. In some cases gender roles are rigidly defined while in others men's and women's roles overlap considerably. Yet despite the universality (and some variation) of division of labor by gender, the cultures of the world are noticeably uniform in the way they divide tasks between women and men. To illustrate, in most cases men engage in warfare, trap small animals, work with hard substances such as wood and stone, clear land, build houses, and fish. Women, on the other hand, tend

Pictured here is Tula, a man impersonating a woman. Although it is possible to find men dressing and behaving like women in the United States, this practice is not considered a legitimate lifestyle alternative by the wider society.

crops, gather wild fruits and plants, prepare food, care for children, collect firewood, clean house, launder clothing, and carry water. In addition, a number of tasks are performed by both men and women. These include tending small domesticated animals, making crafts (pottery, baskets, and the like), milking animals, planting and harvesting crops, and collecting shellfish.

looking ahead

To see how an understanding of women's roles in farming in Africa can contribute to agricultural reform programs, see Applied Perspective 2 at the end of this chapter.

Some of these gender-specific roles (such as hunting for men and child care for women) are very closely associated with one sex or the other. For example, Mur-

dock's *Ethnographic Atlas* (1967) classifies hunting as an exclusively male activity in over 99 percent of the societies listed; the remaining 1 percent are described as societies in which both males and females hunt, but "males do appreciably more than females." On the other side of the equation, child care is an overwhelmingly female activity, although in some cases men do make minor contributions. That such activities as hunting and child care are so thoroughly gender-specific requires some explanation.

A number of theories have been set forth to explain this very common division of labor by sex. One explanation is that since men have greater body mass and strength, they are better equipped to engage in such physical activities as hunting, warfare, and land clearing. To be certain, this explanation has a certain underlying logic, for men are better equipped physically than women to lift heavy loads, run fast, and fight ferociously. Proponents of this theory would argue that men are more likely than women to have the traits needed to be an efficient hunter—namely, strength, speed and endurance. As with any theory, however, this biological theory does not constitute a total explanation. There are some notable exceptions to the general rule that men engage in roles demanding maximum physical strength. To illustrate, in certain parts of East Africa, women routinely carry enormous loads of firewood on their backs for relatively long distances. Not only is this a normative practice, but among some groups a woman's femininity is directly related to the size of the load she is able to carry. Also, among the foraging Agta of the Philippines, hunting is not exclusively a male activity; women can and do hunt regularly. According to Dahlberg (1981:12):

> Hunting is not confined to the oldest daughters in families without sons, young widows, deserted wives, or unusually vigorous personalities. . . . Agta women do not hunt only in cooperation with men (as do Mbuti women in net hunting) nor do they hunt only in the absence of men (as do Chipewyan women). . . . The Agta do not restrict any type of food collecting to one sex. Hunters, both female and male, begin hunting when their stamina and ability make it worthwhile and cease when they lose strength. . . . Each hunter uses techniques that work for her or for him; hunting techniques are not sex typed.

While these exceptions do not invalidate the general rule, some have argued (Burton, Brudner, and White 1977:227) that the division of labor by gender is more the result of constraints stemming from childbirth and infant care than it is from differences in strength.

Do the greater size and weight of this Asmat male from Irian Jaya (Indonesia) provide an advantage in hunting?

This brings us to a second argument frequently used to explain this near universal type of sexual division of labor—that is, women do the things they do because those tasks are compatible with pregnancy, breastfeeding, and child care. Unlike certain male tasks, such as hunting and warfare, women's tasks can be accomplished without jeopardizing their own and their children's safety and without having to stray too far away from home. This theory suggests that pregnant women would be at a marked disadvantage in running after game; lactating mothers would need to interrupt their tracking/hunting activities several times a day to nurse their children; and given the relative danger involved in hunting, small children accompanying their mothers would not be safe. Judith Brown (1970) was the first to hypothesize that women tend to concentrate on tasks that are compatible with child care (i.e., nursing and looking after children). Such tasks tend to be monotonous and require little concentration, can be interrupted without reducing efficient performance, provide for the safety of small children, and can be performed in or near the home.

While this theory too is sensible and no doubt can account for some of the division of labor by sex, it doesn't tell the whole story. A number of ethnographic studies from around the world since the late 1970s have seriously questioned this connection between female reproductive/child care roles and the division of labor. To illustrate, Burton, Brudner, and White (1977) have argued that while pregnancy and breastfeeding do limit work roles for women, a woman's economic (work) obligations may take precedence over child care considerations. In other words, a woman may make alternative child care arrangements in order to engage in some type of work outside the home. This can be seen in parts of the preindustrial world, where women leave their small children in the care of older siblings or other adults, and in the United States, where working mothers leave their infants at professional day care centers. In addition, Raphael and Davis (1985) have shown how women purposefully choose supplemental feeding rather than breastfeeding for their children because of work considerations.

Sexual Stratification

It is generally recognized that the status of women varies from one society to another. In some societies, women tend to be in a clearly subordinate position in their social relationships with men. In other societies, the relationships between the genders are more egalitarian. While social scientists would generally agree that **sexual stratification** exists to some degree in all societies, there is considerably less agreement as to how one measures the status of men and women because sexual stratification involves a number of different components that may vary independently of one another. It is now recognized that there are a number of important indicators of women's status, including economic, power, prestige, autonomy, and ideological dimensions. To illustrate, when considering the relative status of women in any society, one needs to look at the roles played by women, the value that society places on their contributions, their legal rights, whether and to what degree they are expected to be deferential to men, their economic independence, and the degree to which they decide on the major events of their lives such as marriage, the professions, and conception. The multidimensional nature of women's status was illustrated by Whyte's (1978) comparative study of 93 societies, which identified 52 status dimensions found in the anthropological literature. Interestingly, all of these status dimensions varied independently of one another. In other words, no single cluster or complex of variables of women's status varied consistently from culture to culture. To illustrate, women in certain West African societies, owing to their influence in the marketplace, may have an appreciable amount of economic independence, but they nevertheless remain relatively

In some societies, women are not allowed in certain areas that are "for men only," such as this coffee house in Cairo, Egypt.

subordinate to their husbands in most other respects. Thus, determining the status of women is difficult because it is not a unidimensional phenomenon.

Another difficulty with ascertaining the status of women is that it is not static. In some societies, the relative status of men and women fluctuates along with political changes. To illustrate, during the reign of the Shah of Iran women's roles kept pace with modernization. During the 1960s and 1970s, increasingly large numbers of Iranian women abandoned the rules of **purdah** (domestic seclusion and veiling), obtained higher education, and gained entry to traditionally male professional roles. With the return of the religious and cultural fundamentalism under the Ayatollah Khomeini, however, women have returned to the veil and resumed more traditional female roles. Moreover, in a less dramatic fashion, the relative status of women in the United States has undergone some significant changes over the last several generations in terms of job opportunities and legal rights.

Yet another complicating factor in determining the status of women is the relative age of women in any given society. The Tiwi of North Australia are an interesting case in point. In this polygynous society, the accumulation of wives was a man's single most important measure of power and prestige. As Hart, Pilling, and Goodale (1988:58) describe it, women (i.e., daughters, sisters, and mothers) were for men "the main currency of the influence struggle, the main 'trumps' in the endless bridge game." Men would bestow their own daughters on other men in exchange for their daughters as future brides. An influential man could gain control of his sisters and his widowed mother as "chips" in his never-ending quest for additional wives for himself. Some observers have seen women in Tiwi society as nothing more than chattel—pieces of property with few rights of their own. This was, by and large, the case with younger women, because daughters were subordinate to the wishes of their fathers and wives were controlled by their husbands. But as widowed mothers or sisters, they could not be manipulated, or even coerced, by their sons or brothers. A son who wished to bestow his widowed mother or sister on a political ally needed her full consent and collaboration. Hart, Pilling, and Goodale (1988:59) go on to say:

> Young girls thus had no bargaining power but young widows had a good deal. . . . Thus, for women, as for men, age and political skill were the crucial factors in determining their position. . . . Not as independent operators, but as behind-the-scenes allies of their sons and brothers, Tiwi mothers and sisters enjoyed much more essential freedom in their own careers as oftenremarried widows than would appear at first sight in a culture that ostensibly treated all women as currency in the political careers of the men.

Muslim societies in the Middle East are among the most highly stratified along gender lines. As early as the seventeenth century B.C., the code of Hammurabi firmly established the legal subordination of women. While Muhammad in the seventh century A.D. set forth rules protecting the rights of women, they were never intended to be equal to the rights of men. Moreover, in recent centuries, these rules have come to be interpreted to mean that women should be confined to the domestic realm and almost totally isolated from the public sphere of power. Today, in many of the small towns in Iraq, Iran, and Syria, women have very low status. Many women, particularly those from upper-class families, adhere to the strict rules of purdah (domestic seclusion and veiling). If they must leave the seclusion of the family compound, as many poor and middle-class Arab women must do to help support the family by working, they must obtain their husband's permission and, then, must cover themselves from head to toe in black cloaklike garments. At mealtimes men are served first while the women eat the leftovers from the men's plates. Women have essentially no economic autonomy and legally are viewed as being under the authority of their husbands and fathers. Given the seclusion expected of Arab women and the strict insistence on virginity at marriage, women in the Muslim world have little or no control over their bodies or their sexuality, while no such restrictions apply to men.

In contrast to the marked status distinctions between the sexes found in traditional Middle Eastern cultures, the relationship between men and women in some foraging societies tends to be more egalitarian. For example, Turnbull (1981) reports a good deal of mutual respect between the sexes among the Mbuti Pygmies of Central Africa, particularly among elders of the group. Adult Mbuti refer to their parents as "tata" (elders) without distinguishing by gender. Mbuti men and women see themselves as equals in all respects but one—that women have the enormously important power of giving birth. This equation of womanhood with motherhood, which affords Mbuti women relatively high status, is played out through a number of rituals in their everyday lives. Even their natural habitat (the forest), which is considered to be both sacred and supreme, is often referred to as "mother." Moreover, Mbuti women choose their own mates, determine their own daily activities, and exercise considerable power as social critics.

In such hunting-and-gathering societies, the roles performed by men and women are very different, but their relative statuses are not. Such relative sexual equality is not surprising, however, for marked status differences of any type are rare in foraging societies. Some have suggested (e.g., Leacock 1978) that there is a direct relationship between unequal status and the ownership of private property. Since constant migration inhibits the accumulation of property, foraging societies tend to have very little private property, and sharp status distinctions are minimized for both men and women.

While it is possible to identify certain societies where gender distinctions are kept to a minimum, the overwhelming evidence suggests that in many critical areas of life women tend to be subordinate to men. To be certain, from time to time women in various cultures have wielded considerable power, but there is no evidence to

In many Islamic societies, women have relatively few rights and prerogatives.

support the notion that **matriarchy**—rule or domination of women over men—exists anywhere in the world or, for that matter, ever has existed (Bamberger 1974). Rather, what we find is that women, to one degree or another, are excluded from the major centers of economic and political power and control. Moreover, the roles that women play as mothers and wives invariably carry with them fewer prerogatives and lower prestige than male roles. Even in egalitarian societies, it is headmen, and not headwomen, who make such important decisions as how to allocate resources or whether to wage war against a neighboring group. Although we do find reigning queens in the world today, they are usually temporary holders of regal power. Less than 4 percent of the independent nations of the world have female heads of state (Information Please Almanac

1991), a clear indication of the worldwide subordination of women in terms of political power. Although to speak of **universal male dominance** is an oversimplification, the evidence does suggest a general gender asymmetry among most cultures of the world in the expression of power and influence.

This **sexual asymmetry** is often evident in the forms of language spoken by men and women. Sometimes the linguistic distinctions between men and women are reflected in vocabulary. Some languages have pairs of words (called doublets) that carry the same meaning, but men use one word and women the other. To illustrate, among the Island Carib of the West Indies, men use the word *kunobu* to mean "rain" while women use the word *kuyu* (Hickerson 1980:91). Among the Merina in Madagascar (Keenan 1974), for example, speech patterns associated with men, which are indirect, allusive, and formal, are considered both respectable and sophisticated. Merina women, on the other hand, are thought to be ignorant of the subtleties of sophisticated speech and, consequently, are considered to be inferior. Moreover, submissiveness and lack of social power can be observed in female speech patterns in the United States in terms of intonation, loudness, and assertiveness. To illustrate, women in the United States have a less forceful style of speaking than men in that they use a greater number of qualifiers (e.g., "It may be just my opinion but . . . "). Also, U.S. women frequently soften the impact of a declarative statement by ending it with a question such as ". . . wouldn't you agree?" (Kramer 1974).

These linguistic gender differences in the United States (referred to as "**genderlects**") have been the subject of a recent best-selling book by Deborah Tannen (1990), who claims that women and men in the United States have different linguistic styles and communication goals. Women engage in "rapport-talk" while men use "report-talk." The language of rapport-talk characteristic of women seeks to establish connections and negotiate relationships and reflects the tendency to seek agreement. Women's speech tends to be cooperative in character in that women acknowledge one another's contributions and engage in more active listening. Report-talk, by way of contrast, represents a male mode of discourse that emphasizes maintaining independence and establishing their place in a competitive social hierarchy. Men's conversations are less social and more individualistic and aim at controlling the flow of talk. In cross-sex conversations, men tend to dominate women by talking more, interrupting women more fre-

In what ways do men and women in the United States have different styles of communicating?

CROSS-CULTURAL MISCUE

When entering foreign markets, U.S. firms must understand and respect cultural differences if they are to be successful. Alecia Swasy (1993) relates how one U.S. corporate giant, Procter & Gamble, has not always been sensitive to cultural differences when attempting to sell its products abroad:

[In Japan] . . . some years ago a Camay television ad put Procter & Gamble in hot water with the Japanese. Pitching the soap as making women more attractive to men, the ad showed a man walking into the bathroom while his wife bathed. Women took great offense; in Japan it is the height of bad manners for a husband to impose on his wife's privacy in the bathtub.

---

quently, and focusing the conversation on the topics of their own choice.

Gender Ideology

This universal male dominance is buttressed by a **gender ideology,** which we can define as a system of thoughts and values that legitimize **sex roles,** statuses, and customary behavior. In religion, women are often excluded categorically by gender ideology from holding major leadership roles or participating in certain types of ceremonies. In some African societies, men's physical well-being is thought to be jeopardized by coming into contact with a woman's menstrual discharge. In Bangladesh, and in other Muslim cultures as well, men are associated with the right side while women are associated with the left side, a dichotomy that also denotes purity-pollution, good-bad, and authority-submission. Even in the area of food production, foods procured by men (such as meat from the hunt) are frequently more highly valued than those procured by women (such as roots or berries), even though the latter foods constitute the major source of nutrition. In many parts of the world, women are treated legally as minors in that they are unable to obtain a driver's license, bank account, passport, or even a birth control device without the consent of their husbands or fathers. One particularly effective ideological mechanism for keeping women in a subordinate position is found among the Luo of western Kenya whose creation myth (no doubt originated and perpetuated by men) blames women for committing the original sins that resulted in the curse of work for men.

These, then, are just some of the values reported in the ethnographic literature that legitimize the subordination of women. Nevertheless, we need to ask whether women in societies with such powerful gender ideologies actually buy into the ideologies. Do they, in other words, accept these ideological justifications for their subjugation? Because so many of these ethnographic reports were based on male testimony given to male ethnographers, it is likely that women, if their opinions were solicited, would describe themselves quite differently than they are portrayed in the ethnographic literature. Within the last several decades, a number of studies (Errington and Gewertz 1987; Kirsch 1985; and Strathern 1984) have been written from the perspective of female informants; they demonstrate how distorted our interpretations of gender ideology have been.

An example of this distortion is provided by Buckley (1993) who has shown how our own Western view of menstruation and pollution has led to a very one-sided view of the culture of the Yurok Indians of California. Early ethnographic accounts of the Yurok suggested that menstruating women had to seclude themselves as

a way of protecting men from the pollution of menstrual blood. Buckley's study of Yurok women, however,
gives a very different interpretation of female seclusion
during menstruation. Yurok women went into seclusion
for a ten-day period not because they saw themselves as
unclean or polluting, but because they were at the
height of their power. Since this was a time of medita-
tion, introspection, and personal growth, one should
not be distracted by mundane tasks or concerns of the
opposite sex. Rather, women were taught to be proud
of their menstrual cycle and were expected to accumulate spiritual energy by meditating about the mysteries of life. Thus, for Yurok women menstruation was a
highly positive part of their lives. As Buckley (1993:135)
describes it, "The blood that flows serves to 'purify' the
woman, preparing her for spiritual accomplishment."

In a more recent study, Gottlieb (1990) illustrates
how the correlation between menstrual fluids and pollution is an oversimplification of the ethnographic
facts. Based on research among the Beng of the Ivory
Coast, Gottlieb shows that the Beng do not hold the
classic analogy of equating men with purity and females
with pollution. Rather,

> in some contexts Beng women are indeed polluting,
> while in others they can prevent or even counteract
> pollution. In still other situations, men and women
> are equally, and mutually, polluting. In short, Beng
> women as a category are no more fully defined by pol-
> lution than are men as a category.

Thus, Gottlieb's research shows that simple equations
of women with pollution fail to take into account the
complexity of gender ideologies.

Still another study that illustrates the complexity of
gender ideology was conducted by Barnes (1990)
among Yoruba women in Lagos, Nigeria. Female subordination among the Yoruba can best be described as
contextual or situational. That is, women subordinate
themselves in some contexts by showing great deference to their husbands, male family elders, employers,
and public officials, while in other situations (such as
market activity) they are independent, assertive, and
powerful. Thus, we see a basic paradox in Yoruba society: that is, while female subordination is clearly the
norm, particularly in family affairs, it is widely held that
women can, and even should, strive for powerful positions in the world of economics and politics. Barnes explains the apparent paradox in terms of home ownership. Owing to their success in the markets, women are
able to attain high status through home ownership, and
once they become homeowners, they are able to cross

*While assuming a subordinate position in their family life, many
African women are able to maintain considerable power, authority,
and autonomy by virtue of their economic activities, as this petty
entrepreneur in Tananarivo, Madagascar, has managed to do.*

over into the realm of politics and public affairs. As
Barnes (1990:276–77) concludes, "[home] ownership
must be seen as a threshold for women in their desire
to gain economic independence and security, because
once they reach this point they automatically gain
the rights to move further into the domain of public
affairs."

These and many other studies in recent years have
raised interesting theoretical and methodological questions. For example, to what degree have our male-dom-
inated ethnographies of the past shaped our views of
those cultures? Indeed, much of this recent research
has challenged the prevailing views on the nature of
gender inequality and has called into question such
concepts as "universal male dominance." As we have
noted above, Buckley has shown that Yurok women, un-

like Yurok men, interpret their menstrual periods as times of great personal power, not as periods of ritual pollution. Gottlieb demonstrates that pollution is not associated exclusively with women among the Beng of West Africa, but that both genders can be polluting and that in some contexts women can counteract pollution. Barnes (1990) shows how women in Lagos, Nigeria, while depending on men for security, nevertheless seek and frequently gain power and authority through property ownership. All of these studies are important because they serve as a long overdue corrective to the male gender bias found in many of our ethnographies. They also serve as a reminder that gender issues are far more complex than one might think by looking at a society only from a male perspective. Nevertheless, these new studies, while providing a much richer and more accurate description of reality, should not obscure the fact that in most societies men still enjoy the majority of power, prestige, and influence.

Extreme Gender Ideology Can Lead to Exploitation

In some parts of the world, gender ideology is so extremely male biased that females can suffer dire consequences. For example, in rural North India, where gender preference for male sons is particularly strong, there has been a long-standing practice of **female infanticide and** daughter neglect. Sons are much more desirable than daughters because they are economic assets. They are needed for farming, are more likely to be wage employed, and are the recipients of marriage dowry, and since they don't leave home when they marry, they can support the parents in their later years.

By far the most malignant manifestation of **male gender bias** in North India is female infanticide, which involves outright killing of female children. Yet, there are also less direct and immediate forms of female child abuse, such as sustained **nutritional deprivation, which, if not fatal, can retard learning, physical development, or social adjustment.** Miller (1993) found considerable evidence of this less direct form of gender exploitation. For example, the sex ratio of children being admitted to hospitals is at least two to one in favor of boys, an imbalance due to the sex-selective child care practices of the parents. Cowan and Dhanoa (1983) examined a large sample of **infant mortality** cases in Ludhiana Dis-

trict in North India and found that 85 percent of all deaths between seven and thirty-six months were female. They also found that the prevalence of malnutrition for children between the ages of one and three was more than three times as high for females as it was for males. Moreover, Ramanamma and Bambawale (1980) provide evidence of sex-selective abortion. For 700 pregnant women applying for prenatal sex determination in a North Indian hospital, 250 fetuses were determined to be male, and 450 fetuses were female; all of the male fetuses were kept to term while 430 of the 450 female fetuses were aborted. All of these studies indicate how an extreme gender ideology can lead to a lethal form of gender exploitation.

Whereas some might dismiss female infanticide or abuse in India because it is occurring on the other side of the world, it is harder to ignore physical violence against women in our own society, a phenomenon that is the direct consequence of our gender ideology. While we often think of our own culture as the hallmark of civility, sexual violence against women, such as **rape** and **spouse abuse**, has been, and continues to be, a serious problem in the United States. Owing to

Due to gender ideology, this boy in Rajasthan, India, is more likely to receive medical attention than his sister.

underreporting, statistics on the prevalence of rape in the United States vary considerably. In the late 1980s, the National Crime Survey estimated that for the preceding six-month period, there were 1.3 per 1,000 completed or attempted rapes of females over twelve years of age (Lott 1994:164). In a survey of over 2,000 U.S. college women, Koss (1985) found that 12.7 percent reported having been forced to have anal, oral, or genital sex against their will and that an additional 24 percent had been forced to engage in other types of sexual activities. And the figures on physical abuse are equally appalling. According to Lott (1994:182–83), an estimated 3 to 4 million women in the United States are beaten in their own homes each year by their husbands, ex-husbands, or lovers; nearly 1,700 women die each year from spouse battering. We need not cite any additional statistics to make the point that male-biased gender ideologies can have negative, and often lethal, consequences for the subordinate gender.

Human Sexuality

Even though cultural anthropology has the reputation of concerning itself with documenting the exotic sexual practices of non-Western people, in actual fact the discipline of anthropology has not been interested in **human sexuality** until quite recently. Indeed, the subject of human sexuality was not formally recognized until 1961 when the AAA held a plenary session on the topic at its national meetings. To be certain, a number of anthropologists had documented exotic sexual practices, usually as part of general ethnographies, but prior to the 1960s, there had been relatively little research on comparative human sexuality. Within the last three decades, however, anthropologists have become more interested in the theoretical aspects of human sexuality. Perhaps the most fundamental generalization that has emerged in recent decades is that human sexuality varies widely from culture to culture. In other words, we find enormous variations throughout the world in terms of sexual behaviors permitted or encouraged before marriage, outside marriage, and within marriage.

While no societies fail to regulate sexual conduct, some societies are permissive while others are more restrictive. Some cultures have very serious sanctions against premarital sex while others treat it much more casually. Among the more sexually restricted cultures are the traditional Cheyenne Indians of the American Plains whose women were legendary for their chastity.

When adolescent Cheyenne girls began to attract the attention of suitors, they were constantly chaperoned by aunts to ensure a total abstinence of sexual behavior. The courting process was long and timid, frequently lasting five years before the couple could marry. Adolescent boys and girls had little or no contact, and young men were taught to suppress their sexual impulses, a Cheyenne value that they took with them into marriage. Premarital and extramarital sex were extremely rare among the Cheyenne, and in the event that they occurred, they were met with powerful social sanctions (Hoebel 1960:20–21).

Another example of a society with limited sexual expression is the Dani of New Guinea. Whereas the Cheyenne were socialized to avoid intimate sexual displays from early childhood and deviants were punished, the Dani simply appear to be disinterested in sexual behavior. According to Heider (1979:78–79), the Dani practice a five-year period of **postpartum sexual abstinence.** That is, husband and wife abstain from any sexual activity for five years after the birth of a child. Though all societies practice some form of abstinence after the birth of a child, usually it lasts for several weeks or several months; in some societies, however, it lasts until the child is weaned, which may take several years. Most North Americans—who feel that they must keep pace with the national average of 2.7 times per week— find Heider's claim hard to believe. Yet, after questioning his informants in a number of different ways, Heider found no contrary evidence. Not only do the Dani practice these long periods of abstinence, but they appear to have no other sexual outlets such as **extramarital activity** or homosexuality. Nor are Dani adults particularly "stressed out" by these five-year abstinences. Though Dani sexual restraint does not derive from awesome sanctions designed to punish the deviant, Dani people seem to learn in subtle ways that low sexual expressiveness is normal. As hard as it may be for Westerners to believe, the Dani simply have a low **sex drive.**

At the other extreme from such groups as the Cheyenne and the Dani are societies in which people are expected to have a great deal of sexual experience before marriage. Among such Oceanian societies as the Trobrianders, the Tikopia, and the Mangaians of Polynesia, premarital sex is not only permitted but encouraged; indeed, it is viewed as a necessary preparatory step for marriage. Young boys and girls in these societies receive sex education at an early age and are given permission to experiment during their adolescent years. Premarital lovers are encouraged, and in some societies in the Pacific, trial marriages are actually permitted.

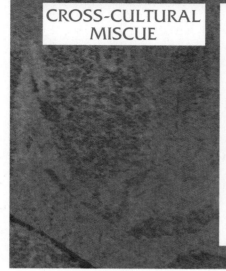

CROSS-CULTURAL MISCUE

Sometimes our culture can get us into trouble in spite of our best intentions. While conducting ethnographic fieldwork among the Kikuyu of Kenya in the 1970s, this author became involved in an embarrassing incident that he could not seem to prevent (Ferraro 1994:80):

Even before going to Kenya I had known through ethnographic readings that Kikuyu men routinely held hands with their close personal friends. After several months of living and working with Kikuyu, I was walking through a village in Kiambu District with a local headman who had become a key informant and a close personal acquaintance. As we walked side by side my friend took my hand in his. Within less than 30 seconds my palm was perspiring all over his. Despite the fact that I knew cognitively that this was a perfectly legitimate Kikuyu gesture of friendship, my own cultural values (that is, that "real men" don't hold hands) were so ingrained that it was impossible for me not to communicate to my friend that I was very uncomfortable.

The Mangaians of central Polynesia provide an interesting case of a society that draws a dichotomy between the public and private domains. This society is characterized by near total segregation of men and women in their public lives. Around the age of four to five, boys and girls separate into gender-defined groups that will identify them for the rest of their lives. Brothers and sisters, husbands and wives, old men and old women, and female and male lovers have very little social contact in their everyday lives. Nevertheless, in their private lives, away from the public eye, men and women engage in sexual behavior that is both frequent and intense. Sexual intercourse is a principal concern for both Mangaian men and women, a concern that is backed up by a detailed knowledge of the technical/biological aspects of sex. According to ethnographer Donald Marshall (1971:110), "the average Mangaian youth has fully as detailed a knowledge—perhaps more—of the gross anatomy of the penis and the vagina as does a European physician."

Like the Mangaians, the !Kung of southwestern Africa believe that sexual activity is a very natural, and indeed essential, part of life. !Kung adolescents are permitted to engage in both **heterosexual** and **homosexual** play, while extramarital sexual activity is condoned provided discretion is observed. Conversations between women about their sexual exploits are commonplace as is sexually explicit joking between men and women. According to Shostak (1983:31), sexual activity is considered essential for good mental and physical health, for as one female informant put it, "If a girl grows up without learning to enjoy sex, her mind doesn't develop normally . . . and if a woman doesn't have sex her thoughts get ruined and she is always angry."

Gender in the United States

When we think of traditional gender roles in the United States two words usually come to mind: **breadwinner** and **housewife.** According to this traditional view, males, who are frequently characterized as logical, competitive, goal-oriented, and unemotional, were responsible for the economic support and protection of the family. Females, on the other hand, with their warm, caring, and sensitive natures, were expected to restrict themselves to child rearing and domestic activities. This traditional view of gender roles in the United States, however, was only valid for a relatively brief period in our nation's history—from roughly

In the United States, some professions, such as nursing, are predominantly in the hands of women.

1860 through the 1950s. Sociologist Kingsley Davis (1988:73) has referred to the period between 1860 and 1920 as the "heyday of the breadwinner system"; he identifies 1890 as its peak because less than 3 percent of native-born married women in the United States worked outside the home at that time. Prior to industrialization, pioneer women were fully productive members of the rural homestead.

With the rise of industrialization in the late nineteenth century, the nation's economy shifted from agriculture to manufacturing. This rapid industrialization was indeed revolutionary because it tended to separate work life from family life. Unlike work on the family farm, factory work could not be easily combined with child rearing and domestic tasks. As women became more confined to the home, their direct contribution to economic production decreased. As men's and women's spheres were separated, the terms "breadwinner" and "housewife" became entrenched in our vocabulary. Interestingly, we have maintained this view of "separate spheres" for men and women well into the twentieth century even though forces for change that began to erode those separate spheres were well under way by the early 1900s.

While it is true that men entered the workforce in greater numbers than women during the present century, we must not assume that women did not also make significant contributions to factory production. This is particularly true of poor and working-class women, mi-

nority women, immigrant women, and single mothers. The entry of women into the workforce was facilitated by a number of factors during the twentieth century. First, as industrialization became more complex, more clerical workers were needed, and most of them were women. Second, as infant mortality rates fell, women bore fewer children, thereby increasing the number of years they could work outside the home. Third, many women gravitated toward the textile industry because they were thought to possess greater manual dexterity than men and therefore to be more adept at sewing clothes. Fourth, the rising rate of divorce has forced many women to support themselves and their children without the financial aid of a spouse. Fifth, the development of the baby bottle enabled many women to work outside the home without jeopardizing the nutritional needs of their infants. And, finally, recent economic downturns have driven an increasing number of women to join the workforce because two salaries are often needed to make ends meet.

Today, both men and women are in the paid labor force, with approximately 76 percent of men and 57 percent of women participating. One demographic feature that must be mentioned, however, is that the nature of the women working outside the home has changed dramatically over the past forty years. That is, the percentage of working women who have children under the age of six has increased appreciably. To illustrate, in 1950 only 12 percent of all women with children under

Gender

applied PERSPECTIVE

In this chapter we have explored gender differences in terms of sex roles, gender stratification, and expressions of human sexuality. A recurring theme in recent gender studies is that men and women in all societies have different culturally defined roles, statuses, personal identities, modes of communication, and, in some cases, ways of viewing the world. Until recently, the preponderance of male ethnographers has resulted in women's lives being underrepresented in the literature. But since women do, in fact, comprise approximately half of any society, their lives need to be described in as much detail as the lives of men. In the last several decades, however, with the training of a greater number of female cultural anthropologists, women have been the subject of ethnographic studies to a greater degree than in the past. The two case studies described here are good examples of how the culture of women is being studied and how that information is being used to address pressing societal problems. In the first case, medical anthropologist Margaret Boone uses ethnographic information on inner city women to shed new light on the problem of infant mortality in Washington, D.C. In the second case, anthropologist Anita Spring's study of women farmers in Africa demonstrates practical implications for increasing agricultural productivity in part of the world that has faced food shortages for decades.

the age of six were in the labor force; by 1990 the percentage had risen to over 57 percent. As Renzetti and Curran (1992:140–41) have pointed out, employed married women, particularly those with children, carry a **double work load** by being both wage employed and primarily responsible for housework and child care.

Another characteristic of the wage sector of the economy in the United States is that there is a relatively high rate of **occupational segregation** along gender lines. According to the U.S. Department of Labor, eight of the ten occupations with the most women were more than 75 percent female. These included such occupations as elementary schoolteachers, secretaries, registered nurses, and general office clerks. In certain other occupations, men predominate. For example, more than nineteen out of twenty truck drivers, carpenters, auto mechanics, and electricians in the United States are males. Men also tend to dominate the supervisory positions, even in areas where a majority of workers are women.

Not only are jobs segregated by gender in the United States, but men are better paid for their efforts. Wages for full-time female employees are only 70 percent of wages for full-time male employees. And although this is up from 61 percent three decades ago, the gap between male and female earnings remains wide. Irrespective of which data are used, women earn less than men. Many of the jobs that are predominantly female are low-paying jobs with relatively low upward mobility.

But even in professions that require high levels of training and education, such as teaching, library science, and nursing, women earn less than their male counterparts.

Although an increasing number of women are entering professions (such as law, medicine, and engineering) that require advanced education, occupations associated with low prestige and income still have high proportions of women. Moreover, a logical extension of this is the phenomenon known as the **feminization of poverty.** For example, more than half of all female-headed families with children are living below the poverty line—a poverty rate that is approximately four times higher than the poverty rate for male-centered families. The feminization of poverty is particularly acute when we look at minorities. Whereas 45 percent of the white female-headed families live in poverty, approximately 70 percent of African Americans and Hispanics are officially living in poverty.

Looking ahead

The anthropological study of the roles and behaviors of poor women in the United States has shed light on the serious social problem of infant mortality. See, for example, Applied Perspective 1 at the end of this chapter.

applied
PERSPECTIVE
continued

By redefining the problem of infant mortality, an applied anthropologist in Washington, D.C., offers the potential for new strategies for reducing the problem.

In the early 1980s Washington, D.C., had the highest infant death rate of any major city in the United States. Infant mortality is largely an African-American health problem in the United States because of the substantial number of Black women having babies with low birth weights. The number of babies with low birth weights and the accompanying high infant mortal-ity rate are higher for Blacks than for any other racial or ethnic minority in the United States and are approximately twice as high as among Whites.

This tragic problem of high infant mortality in the nation's capital was the subject of a unique applied anthropological study conducted by Margaret Boone (1982; 1985; 1987). Boone's research was funded by a National Science Foundation program designed to encourage various scientists to conduct research in organizations in which they were not usu-ally found. Even though the project was primarily research oriented, it also included an obligation to disseminate the results widely to politicians, policy makers, and others who could use the findings to help alleviate the problem. It was, in other words, a research grant with an applied component.

For eighteen months Boone worked at an inner city hospital in Washing-ton, D.C., gathering data on the sociocultural basis of poor health among Black mothers and their infants, and then brokering that information to people in Washington who were in a position to act on it. More specifically, she designed and carried out a controlled study of the health of African-American women and their infants comprised of in-depth interviews, the review of medical records, and daily participant-observation in the hospital. In her brokering role, she met periodically with members of the Mayor's Task Force on Infant Mortality, the Centers for Disease Control, medical personnel from other hospitals, city health officials, journalists, and repre-sentatives from various public and private health policy organizations.

The result of this applied anthropological study was to shift the defini-tion of the problem of infant mortality away from a purely medical expla-nation toward a broader definition that includes the sociocultural dimen-sion. To illustrate, Boone found a high correlation between women who bore low-birth weight babies and the following factors: absence of prenatal care, smoking, alcoholism, and previous poor pregnancy outcome, such as infant deaths, miscarriages, and previous abortions. Women with low–birth weight babies also had other characteristics in common, including psycho-logical stress during pregnancy, being the object of violence (e.g., beat-ings), and rapidly paced child bearing beginning in the teen years. Inter-estingly, Boone also found that mothers received most of their social and psychological support during pregnancy from girlfriends rather than from their own mothers.

By combining interview data and personal observations and reviewing both secondary sources and statistical data, Boone was able to construct portraits of the reproductive lives of inner city African-American women. According to Boone (1987:66), these sociomedical portraits had "an ethnographic quality of compelling realism that has been useful in policy-related work." The major significance of the anthropological perspective is that it allowed Boone to integrate the medical histories of these women with their behaviors, their interactions with others, and their values and attitudes. It is only after such studies, showing how social and cultural factors are related to poor Black health, that new solutions to problems of delivery services will emerge.

applied PERSPECTIVE *continued*

THOUGHT QUESTIONS

1. How do you explain the high infant mortality rates among African-Americans in the United States relative to other segments of the population?

2. What type of anthropological methods did Boone use to study the problem of infant mortality in Washington, D.C.? Why were they effective?

3. Can women's health be improved with new policies based on the type of research that Boone conducted?

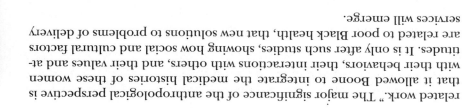

The study of the role of women in agriculture can help address the food crisis in sub-Saharan Africa.

Headlines about starving populations in Ethiopia, Somalia, and the Sahel have caught the attention of Westerners in recent years and have dramatized the food crisis that is plaguing many parts of Africa. Although billions of dollars in foreign aid from around the world have been spent on the problem, many of the programs aimed at increasing food production have not been as successful as they could have been because they have given insufficient attention to the role of women in agriculture. In recent years, however, with the assistance of applied anthropologists, the Food and Agricultural Organization (FAO) and other world organizations have recognized the need to better understand the role of women in agriculture and include them in research, extension, and development activities.

Anita Spring, an applied anthropologist from the University of Florida, has worked for a number of years on women's roles and contributions to agriculture in Africa. As chief of the Women in Agricultural Production and Rural Development Service of the FAO, she has conducted ethnographic research in Malawi as well as other sub-Saharan African countries. According to Spring and her colleagues, African women are, in fact, farmers, and as such, are extremely important in the food chain. They grow crops, care for livestock, distribute food products, and prepare food for consumption. Although significant variations exist, Spring estimated (1986:333) that women contribute between 60 and 80 percent of the labor and management of African food production. And with men leaving their families in rural areas to seek wage employment in cities, in mines, and on plantations, many African women are doing their usual farming work as well as that of their husbands. Unfortunately, since the 1960s, these ethnographic realities concerning the central role of women in food production have not been built into agricultural development programs. Since women have been seen as gardeners rather than farmers, their extension services have included classes on small-scale vegetable and poultry production

applied PERSPECTIVE *continued*

rather than major crop and livestock production. Programs developed for women usually involve classes on sewing, cooking, embroidery, and crafts. Men, on the other hand, are the targets of most of the important agricultural development efforts such as programs for the reallocation of land, new technologies for cash cropping, and credit acquisition.

Spring argues that if food production projects in Africa are to be made more effective, they must reach the right audiences. Many programs in Africa are addressed to men when, in fact, women have the major responsibility for agricultural production. Taking these ethnographic realities into account, Spring goes on to suggest a number of practical modifications to food production programs in Africa. These include the following:

1. Data on farm activities should be collected and analyzed by gender in order to demonstrate the very significant role that women play in food production, distribution, and processing.
2. Women should participate in farm systems research trials so planning can better understand the dynamics within farming households.
3. Once women's contributions to agriculture have been researched and understood, these data can be used to develop new agricultural technologies.
4. Agricultural extension workers must seek new ways of recruiting women farmers into their programs.
5. African women must be included in various programs that will enable them to take out loans to improve their agricultural productivity.
6. African women need to be involved in various private and government schemes of land reallocation.

Spring has suggested these modifications in food production programs in Africa in an attempt to increase overall food productivity on the continent. Development planners must consider local conditions and practices (by conducting direct ethnographic fieldwork, as Spring herself has done) and then target both *women and men* through their agricultural programs. Because of an inadequate knowledge of the role of women in African agriculture, women have been denied access to new technologies, land reform programs, and credit schemes. Tragically, most programs have not fully utilized women's agricultural capabilities and, consequently, have failed to do all they might to relieve the food crisis in Africa.

THOUGHT QUESTIONS

1. This case study demonstrates the need for taking the role of women into consideration when planning agricultural development programs. Why do you think women have been neglected in such programs in the past?
2. How has sexual stratification (i.e., power differences between men and women) contributed to the neglecting of women in agricultural planning in Africa?
3. Based on Spring's findings, what practical solutions would you suggest to the policy makers responsible for agricultural improvement programs in Africa?

 Summary

1. The term gender refers to the way members of the two sexes are perceived, evaluated, and expected to behave. Though biology sets broad limits on gender definitions, there exists a wide range of what it means to be feminine or masculine, as Margaret Mead demonstrated in her classic study of sex and temperament in New Guinea.

2. In very general terms, there is considerable uniformity in sex roles found throughout the world. For example, men engage in warfare, clear land, hunt and trap animals, build houses, fish, and work with hard substances; women tend crops, prepare food, collect firewood, clean house, launder clothes, and carry water.

3. The status of women is multidimensional, involving such aspects as the division of labor, the value placed on women's contributions, economic autonomy, social and political power, legal rights, levels of deference, and the extent to which women control the everyday events of their lives.

4. Muslim societies of the Middle East are among the most highly stratified along gender lines. At the other extreme, certain foraging societies, such as the Mbuti Pygmies of Central Africa, take the most egalitarian (or least stratified) approach to men and women. While these represent the two extremes of the status of women in the world, it is clear that in most critical areas women tend to be subordinate to men in just about all societies of the world.

5. Gender ideology is used in most societies to justify this universal male dominance. Deeply rooted values about the superiority of men, the ritual impurity of women, and the preeminence of men's work are frequently used to justify the subjugation of women. However, it has been demonstrated in recent years that women do not perceive themselves in the same ways that they are portrayed in these (largely male) gender ideologies.

6. In some societies, gender ideologies become so extreme that females suffer serious negative consequences such as female infanticide, child abuse, and nutritional deprivation among children and rape and spouse abuse among adults.

7. While recognizing considerable differences in degrees of permissiveness, all societies regulate the sexual conduct of their members. Some societies, such as the Cheyenne Indians of the American Plains, are very restrictive while others, such as the Mangaian of Polynesia, not only permit, but actually encourage, frequent and intense sexual activity between men and women.

8. While the terms "breadwinner" and "housewife" accurately described the middle-class American household around the turn of the century, the separate spheres implied by these two terms have been more myth than reality for much of the twentieth century. In fact, over the past four decades the number of women in the United States working outside the home has increased dramatically.

9. The economy of the United States is characterized by a high rate of occupational segregation along gender lines. Not only are occupations gender segregated, but women tend to earn considerably less than men. Moreover, there has been a trend in recent decades toward the feminization of poverty.

 Key Terms

breadwinner	masculinity
double work load	matriarchy
extramarital activity	nutritional deprivation
female infanticide	occupational segregation
femininity	postpartum sexual
feminization of poverty	abstinence
gender	purdah
gender ideology	rape
genderlects	sex drive
heterosexual	sex roles
homosexual	sexual asymmetry
housewife	sexual dimorphism
human sexuality	sexual stratification
infant mortality	spouse abuse
male gender bias	universal male dominance

Suggested Readings

Brettell, Caroline B., and Carolyn Sargent. *Gender in Cross Cultural Perspective.* Englewood Cliffs, N.J.: Prentice-Hall, 1993. A collection of forty-six articles written by anthropologists on such aspects of gender as inequity, sexuality, and division of labor. Each major section of the volume is prefaced by a substantive essay written by the editors.

Caplan, Pat, ed. *The Cultural Construction of Sexuality.* London: Tavistock, 1987. This collection of essays examines the relationship between sex, gender, and sexuality in a wide variety of cultures, ranging from Britain, the United States, and Italy in the West to Kenya, Jamaica, and Fiji in the developing world.

di Leonardo, Micaela, ed. *Gender at the Crossroads of Knowledge: Feminist Anthropology in the Postmodern Era.* Berkeley, Calif.: University of California Press, 1991. An up-to-date collection of essays that discusses the current thinking in feminist anthropology. In addition to a substantial introductory essay by the editor, the twelve articles deal with such topics as language and gender, feminism in primate studies, women in technological development, and the sexual division of labor.

Kahne, Hilda, and Janet Z. Giele, eds. *Women's Work and Women's Lives: The Continuing Struggle Worldwide.* Boulder, Colo.: Westview Press, 1992. A provocative set of essays examining women and paid employment in both developing and industrialized societies. The volume explores women's social status in different cultures and provides valuable data on pay equity, work schedules, and the informal economy.

Mencher, Joan P., and Anne Okongwu, eds. *Where Did All the Men Go?: Female Headed/Female Supported Households in Cross Cultural Perspective.* Boulder, Colo.: Westview Press, 1993. This recent collection of essays looks at the rising number of female-headed households and the increasing povertization of mothers and their children in different parts of the world. Specifically, the volume examines contributing factors to this worldwide phenomenon, coping strategies that women have developed, and policy recommendations for addressing the issue.

Mukhopadhyay, Carol C. "Anthropological Studies of Women's Status Revisited: 1977–87." In Bernard Siegel et al., eds., *Annual Reviews of Anthropology,* vol. 17, pp. 461–95. Palo Alto, Calif.: Annual Reviews, 1988. A comprehensive review of recent literature on the status of women in different cultures throughout the world with a 289-item bibliography.

Renzetti, Clair M., and Daniel Curran. *Women, Men, and Society.* 2d ed. Boston: Allyn and Bacon, 1992. A thorough and up-to-date examination of gender issues in the United States written by sociologists.

Sanday, Peggy Reeves, and Ruth G. Goodenough, eds. *Beyond the Second Sex: New Directions in the Anthropology of Gender.* Philadelphia: University of Pennsylvania Press, 1990. A recent volume of articles that reexamine traditional notions of gender by avoiding preconceived theories. Societies dealt with in this volume include the Mende of Sierra Leone, the Bedouins of Egypt, the Mendi of Papua New Guinea, and the United States.

Stockard, Jean, and Miriam M. Johnson. *Sex and Gender in Society.* 2d ed. Englewood Cliffs, N.J.: Prentice-Hall, 1992. An up-to-date discussion of gender issues from the perspective of contemporary American sociology—which is to say, that it deals largely with issues relating to Western society.

Suggs, David N., and Andrew Miracle, eds. *Culture and Human Sexuality: A Reader.* Pacific Grove, Calif.: Brooks Cole, 1993. A collection of articles on human sexuality, this recent volume contains case studies and more theoretical essays from a number of cultures in various parts of the world.

Tannen, Deborah. *You Just Don't Understand: Women and Men in Conversation.* New York: William Morrow, 1990. While drawing heavily on recent scholarly research, this highly readable discussion of the sociolinguistics of gender shows how men's and women's patterns and styles of speaking are substantially different.

POLITICAL ORGANIZATION
AND SOCIAL CONTROL

CHAPTER TWELVE

A West African chief of high status.

- What are the different types of political organization?
- What are the various theories concerning the origins of the state?
- In the absence of kings, presidents, legislatures, and bureaucracies, how is social order maintained in stateless societies?

As mentioned in the discussion of cultural universals in Chapter 2, all societies—if they are to remain viable over time—must maintain social order. Every society must develop a set of customs and procedures for making and enforcing decisions, resolving disputes, and regulating the behavior of its members. Every society must make collective decisions about its environment and its relations with other societies and about the eventuality of disruptive or destructive behavior on the part of its members. These topics generally are discussed under such headings as political organization, law, power, authority, war, social control, and conflict resolution. While exploring all of these subjects, this chapter deals with those cultural arrangements by which societies maintain social order, minimize the chances of disruption, and cope with whatever disruptions do occur (McGlynn and Tuden 1991; Vincent 1990).

When most North Americans think of politics or political structure, a number of familiar images come to mind, such as the following:

1. Political leaders such as presidents, governors, mayors, or commissioners.
2. Complex bureaucracies employing thousands of civil servants.
3. Legislative bodies ranging from the smallest town council to the U. S. Congress.
4. Formal judicial institutions that comprise municipal, state, and federal courts.
5. Such law enforcement bodies as police departments, national guard units, and the armed forces.
6. Political parties, nominating conventions, secret ballot voting, and the convening of the electoral college.

All of these are mechanisms that our own society uses for making and enforcing political decisions as well as coordinating and regulating people's behavior. Many societies in the world have none of these things—no elected officials, legislatures, formal elections, armies, or bureaucracies. We should not conclude from this, however, that such societies do not have some form of political organization, if by "political organization" we mean a set of customary procedures that accomplish decision making, conflict resolution, and social control.

Types of Political Organization

While political organization can be found in all societies, the degree of specialized and formal mechanisms varies considerably from one society to another. Societies differ in their political organization based on three important dimensions:

1. The extent to which political institutions are distinct from other aspects of the social structure; that is, in some societies, political structures are barely distinguishable from economic, kinship, or religious structures.
2. The extent to which **authority** is concentrated into specific political roles.
3. The level of **political integration** (i.e., the size of the territorial group that comes under the control of the political structure).

These three dimensions are the basis for the classification of societies (following Service 1978) into four fundamentally different types of political structure: **band societies, tribal societies, chiefdoms,** and **state societies.** Although societies do not all fit neatly into one or another of these categories, this fourfold scheme is useful to help us understand how different societies administer themselves and maintain social order.

CROSS-CULTURAL MISCUE

Even world leaders sometimes send unintentional nonverbal messages. As his motorcade passed a group of protesters in Canberra, Australia, in 1992, U.S. President George Bush held up his middle and forefingers with the back of his hand toward the protesters. He assumed that he was giving the "V for Victory" gesture, but failed to realize that in Australia that hand gesture is the same as holding up the middle finger in the United States.

Band Societies

The least complex form of political arrangement is the band, characterized by small and usually nomadic populations of hunters and gatherers. Although the size of a band can range anywhere from twenty to several hundred individuals, most bands number between thirty and fifty people. The actual size of particular bands is directly related to food-gathering methods; that is, the more food a band has at its disposal, the larger the number of people it can support. While bands may be loosely associated with a specific territory, they have little or no concept of individual property ownership and place a high value on sharing, cooperation, and reciprocity. Band societies have very little role specialization and are highly **egalitarian** in that few differences in status and wealth can be observed. Since this form of political organization is so closely associated with a hunting-and-gathering technology, it is generally thought to be the oldest form of political organization.

Band societies have a number of traits in common with each other. First, band societies have the least amount of political integration; that is, the various bands (each comprising fifty or so people) are independent of one another and are not part of a larger political structure. The integration that does exist is largely based on ties of kinship and marriage. All of the bands found in any particular culture are bound together by a common language and general cultural features. They do not, however, all pay political allegiance to any overall authority.

Second, in band societies political decisions are frequently embedded in the wider social structure. Since bands are composed of kin, it is difficult to distinguish between purely political decisions and those that we would recognize as family, economic, or religious decisions. Political life, in other words, is simply one part of social life.

Third, leadership roles in band societies tend to be very informal. In band societies, there are no specialized political roles or leaders with designated authority. Instead, leaders in foraging societies are frequently, but not always, older men respected for their experience, wisdom, good judgment, and knowledge of hunting. Most decisions are made through discussions by the adult men. The headman can persuade and give advice but has no power to impose his will on the group. The headman frequently gives advice on such matters as migratory movements, but he possesses no permanent authority. If his advice proves to be wrong or unpopular, the group members will look to another person to be headman. Band leadership, then, stems not so much from power but rather from the recognized personal traits admired by the others in the group.

The !Kung of the Kalahari exemplify a band society with a headman. Although the position of headman is hereditary, the actual authority of the headman is quite limited. The headman coordinates the movement of his people and usually walks at the head of the group. He chooses the sites of new encampments and has first pick of location for his own house site. But beyond these limited perks of office, the !Kung headman receives no other rewards. He is in no way responsible for organizing hunting parties, making artifacts, or negotiating marriage arrangements. These activities fall to the individual members of the band. The headman is not expected to be a judge of his people. Moreover, his material possessions are no greater than any other person's. As Marshall so aptly put it when referring to the !Kung headman, "He carries his own load and is as thin as the rest" (1965:267).

Tribal Societies

Whereas band societies are usually associated with hunting and gathering, tribal societies are found most often among food producers (horticulturalists and pastoralists). Since plant and animal domestication is far more productive than foraging, tribal societies tend to have populations that are larger, denser, and somewhat more sedentary in nature. Tribal societies are similar to band societies in several important respects. They are both egalitarian to the extent that there are no marked differences in status, rank, power, and wealth. In addition, tribal societies, like bands, have local leaders but do not have centralized leadership.

The major difference between tribes and bands is that tribal societies have certain **pan-tribal mechanisms** that cut across and integrate all of the local segments of the tribe into a larger whole. These mechanisms include such tribal associations as clans, age grades, or secret societies. Pan-tribal associations function to unite the tribe against external threats. These integrating forces are not permanent political fixtures, however. Most often the local units of a tribe operate autonomously, for the integrating mechanisms come into play only when an external threat arises. When the threat is eliminated, the local units return to their autonomous state. Even though these pan-tribal mechanisms may be transitory, they nevertheless provide wider political integration in certain situations than would ever be possible in band societies.

In many tribal societies, the kinship unit known as the clan serves as a pan-tribal mechanism of political integration. The clan is defined as a group of kin who consider themselves to be descended from a common ancestor, even though individual clan members cannot trace, step-by-step, their connection to the clan founder. Clan elders, while not holding formal political offices, usually manage the affairs of their clans (e.g., settle disputes between clan members) and represent their clans in dealings with other clans.

Another form of pan-tribal association based on kinship that is found in tribal societies is the **segmentary lineage system** (discussed in the chapter on kinship). While less common than tribal societies based on clans, those based on segmentary lineage systems are instructive because they demonstrate the shifting or ephemeral nature of the political structure in tribal societies. In a segmentary system, individuals belong to a series of different descent units (corresponding to different genealogical levels) that function in different social contexts.

The most basic or local unit is the minimal lineage, comprising three to five generations. Members of a minimal lineage usually live together, consider themselves to be the closest of kin, and generally engage in everyday activities together. Minimal lineages, which tend to be politically independent, form a hierarchy of genealogical units. For example, minimal lineages make up minor lineages; minor lineages coalesce into major lineages; and major lineages form maximal lineages. When a dispute occurs between individuals of different segments, people are expected to side with the disputant to whom they are most closely related. Thus, people who act as a unit in one context merge into larger aggregates in other social situations. This process of lineage segmentation means that segments will unite when confronted by a wider group. In the words of Middleton and Tait:

> . . . a segment that in one situation is independent finds that it and its former competitors are merged together as subordinate segments in the internal administrative organization of a wider overall segment that includes them both. This wider segment is in turn in external competitive relations with other similar segments, and there may be an entire series of such segments. (1958:6–7)

It is important to keep in mind that these various segments—minimal, minor, major, and maximal lineages—are not groups but rather alliance networks that are activated only under certain circumstances. This process tends to deflect hostilities away from competing kin and toward an outside, or more distant, enemy. Such a level of political organization is effective for the mobilization of a military force either to defend the entire tribe from outside forces or for expanding into the territories of weaker societies.

The pastoral Nuer of the southern Sudan serve as a good example of a tribal form of political organization (Evans-Pritchard 1940). The Nuer, who number ap-

Tribal societies such as the Masai of East Africa have certain pan-tribal mechanisms, such as clans and age organizations, that serve to integrate the tribe as a whole.

proximately 300,000 people, have no centralized government and no governmental functionaries with coercive authority. There are, of course, influential men, but their influence stems more from their personal traits than from the force of elected or inherited office. The Nuer, who are highly egalitarian, do not readily accept authority beyond the elders of the family. Social control among the Nuer is maintained by segmentary lineages in that close kin are expected to come to the assistance of one another against more distantly related people.

Chiefdoms

As we have seen, in band and tribal societies, local groups are economically and politically autonomous, authority is uncentralized, and populations tend to be generally egalitarian. Moreover, roles are unspecialized, populations are small in size, and economies are largely subsistent in nature. But as societies become more complex—with larger and more specialized populations, more sophisticated technology, and growing surpluses—their need for more formal and permanent political structures increases. In such societies, known as chiefdoms, political authority is likely to reside with a single individual, either acting alone or in conjunction with an advisory council.

The chiefdom differs from bands and tribes in that chiefdoms integrate a number of local communities in a more formal and permanent way. Unlike bands and tribes, chiefdoms are made up of local communities that are not equal, but rather differ from one another in terms of rank and status. Based on their genealogical proximity to the chiefs, nobles and commoners hold different levels of prestige and power. Chiefships are frequently hereditary, and the chief and his or her immediate kin constitute a social and political elite. Rarely are chiefdoms totally unified politically under a single chief; more frequently, they are composed of several political units, each headed by a chief.

Chiefdoms also differ from tribes and bands in that chiefs are centralized and permanent officials with higher rank, power, and authority than others in the society. Unlike bands or tribal headmen or headwomen, chiefs usually have considerable power, authority, and, in some cases, even wealth. Internal social disruptions are minimized in a chiefdom because the chief usually has authority to make judgments, punish wrongdoers, and settle disputes. Chiefs usually have the authority to distribute land to loyal subjects, recruit people into military service, and recruit laborers for public works projects. Chiefly authority is usually reinforced by certain alleged supernatural powers. Polynesian chiefs, for example, were believed to possess the supernatural power of *mana,* which lent a special type of credence to their authority.

Chiefs are also intimately related to the economic activities of their subjects through the redistributive system of economics (see the chapter on economics). Subjects give food surpluses to the chief (not uncommonly at the chief's insistence), which are then redistributed by the chief through communal feasts and doles. This system of redistribution through a chief serves the obvious economic function of ensuring that no people in the society go hungry. It also serves the important political function of providing the people with a mechanism for expressing their loyalty and support for the chief.

Within the past hundred and fifty years, a number of societies with no former tradition of chiefs have had chiefships imposed on them by some of the European colonial powers. As the European nations created their colonial empires during the nineteenth century, they created chiefs (or altered the nature of traditional chiefs) to facilitate administering local populations. For example, the British created chiefs for their own administrative convenience among chiefless societies in Nigeria, Kenya, and Australia. These new chiefs—who were given salaries and high-sounding titles such as paramount chief—were selected primarily on the basis of their willingness to work with the colonial administration rather than any particular popularity among their own people. In some cases, these new chiefs were held in contempt by their own people because they were collaborators with the colonial governments, which were often viewed as repressive and coercive.

The precolonial Hawaiian political system of the eighteenth century embodied the features of a typical chiefdom. According to Service (1975:152–54), Hawaiian society, covering eight islands, was layered into three basic social strata. At the apex of the threefold social hierarchy were the *ali'i*, major chiefs believed to be direct descendants of the gods; their close relatives often served as advisers or bureaucrats under them. The second echelon, known as the *konohiki*, were less important chiefs who were frequently distant relatives of the *ali'i*. And finally, the great majority of people were commoners, known as *maka'ainana*. Since there was little or no intermarriage between these three strata, the society was, by and large, castelike. But since the *ali'i* had certain priestly functions by virtue of their connection with the gods, Hawaiian society was a theocracy as well.

The Hawaiian economy during the precolonial period was based on intensive agriculture (taro, breadfruit, yams, and coconuts) with extensive irrigation. Owing to their control over the allocation of water, the major chiefs and their subordinates wielded considerable power and authority over the general population. In addition, chiefs were in control of communal labor, artisans, and gathering people for war. Hawaiian chiefs could also bring considerable coercive power to bear

on disputants to encourage them to settle their quarrel, although in actual practice most disputes were settled through collective action. In summary, the precolonial Hawaiian political system, according to Service,

> . . . was a theocracy, held together by an ideology that justified and sanctified the rule of the hereditary aristocracy, buttressed by age-old custom and etiquette. Such a system is in some contrast to a primitive state, which, although it attempts to rule ideologically and customarily, has had to erect the additional support of a monopoly of force with a legal structure that administers the force. (1975:154)

State Systems

The state system of government is the most formal and most complex form of political organization. A state can be defined as a hierarchical form of political organization that governs many communities within a relatively large geographic area. States possess the power to collect taxes, can recruit labor for armies and civilian public works projects, and have a monopoly on the right to use force. They are large bureaucratic organizations made up of permanent institutions with legislative, administrative, and judicial functions. Whereas bands and tribes have political structures based on kinship, state systems of government organize their power on a suprakinship basis. That is, a person's membership in a state is based on his or her place of residence and citizenship rather than on kinship affiliation. Over the past several thousand years, state systems of government have taken various forms, including Greek citystates; the far-reaching Roman Empire; certain traditional African states such as Bunyoro, Buganda, and the Swazi; theocratic states such as ancient Egypt; and such modern nation-states as Germany, Japan, and the United States.

 looking ahead

To see how tribal structures need to deal with state systems of government in the United States, look ahead to Applied Perspective 2 at the end of this chapter.

The authority of the state rests on two important foundations. *First,* the state holds the exclusive right to use force and physical coercion. Any act of violence not expressly permitted by the state is illegal and, consequently, punishable by the state. Thus, state governments make written laws, administer them through

State systems of government are characterized by a high degree of role specialization and a hierarchical organization. Many of these specialized political roles are played out in state capitol buildings such as this one in Montpelier, Vermont.

various levels of the bureaucracy, and enforce them through such mechanisms as police forces, armies, and national guards. The state needs to be continuously vigilant against threats both from within and from without to usurp its power through rebellions and revolutions. *Second,* the state maintains its authority by means of ideology. For the state to maintain its power over the long run, there must be a philosophical understanding among the citizenry that the state in fact has the legitimate right to govern. In the absence of such an ideology, it is frequently difficult for the state to maintain its authority by means of coercion alone.

State systems of government, which first appeared about 3500 B.C., are associated with civilizations. As such, they are found in societies with complex socioeconomic characteristics. For example, state systems of government are supported by intensive agriculture, which is required to support a large number of non-food-producing bureaucrats. This fully efficient food production system gives rise to cities, considerable labor specialization, and a complex system of both internal distribution and foreign trade. Since the considerable surpluses produced by intensive agriculture are not distributed equally among all segments of the population, state societies are stratified. That is, such forms of wealth as land and capital tend to be concentrated in the hands of an elite who often use their superior wealth and power to control the rest of the population. Moreover, the fairly complex set of laws and regulations needed to control a large and heterogeneous population give rise to the need for some type of writing, record keeping, and weights and measures.

State systems of government are characterized by a large number of **specialized political roles.** Many people are required to carry out very specific tasks such as law enforcement, tax collection, dispute settlement, recruitment of labor, and protection from outside invasions. These political/administrative functionaries are both highly specialized and full time to the extent that they do not engage in food-producing activities. These permanent political functionaries, like the society itself, are highly stratified or hierarchical. At the apex of the administrative pyramid are those with the greatest power—e.g., kings, presidents, prime ministers, governors, legislators—who enact laws and establish policies. Below them are descending echelons of bureaucrats responsible for the day-to-day administration of the state. As is the case in our own form of government, each level of the bureaucracy is responsible to the level immediately above it.

Variations in Political Structures: Some Generalizations

The preceding sections have looked at four fundamentally different types of political systems. Such a four-fold scheme, while recognized by other anthropologists, is not universally accepted. For example, in a classic study of political systems in Africa, Fortes and Evans-Pritchard (1940:5) distinguish between only two

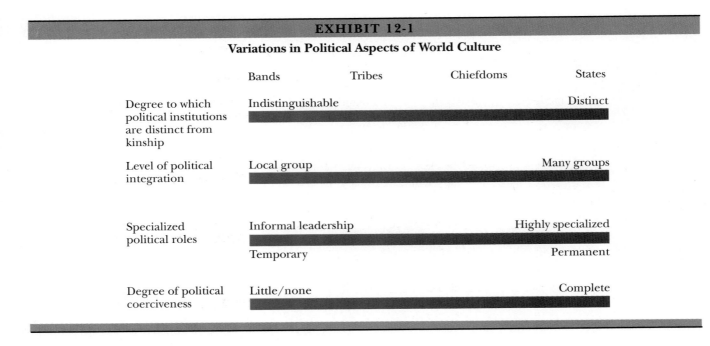

EXHIBIT 12-1

Variations in Political Aspects of World Culture

	Bands	Tribes	Chiefdoms	States

Degree to which political institutions are distinct from kinship: Indistinguishable — Distinct

Level of political integration: Local group — Many groups

Specialized political roles: Informal leadership — Highly specialized; Temporary — Permanent

Degree of political coerciveness: Little/none — Complete

types of structures: state systems and **acephalous** (headless) **societies.** Others (Cohen and Eames 1982:215) recognize three major forms of political structure: simple, intermediate, and complex. Such differences in the way that various ethnologists have conceptualized political structures should serve as a reminder that all of these schemes are ideal types. That is, all of the societies in the world cannot be fit neatly into one box or another. Instead of being discrete categories, in reality there is a continuum with bands (the simplest forms) at one extreme and states (the most complex forms) at the other. Thus, whether we use two, three, or four major categories of political organization, we should bear in mind that all political systems found in the world vary along a continuum on a number of important dimensions. To illustrate, as we move from bands through tribes and chiefdoms to states, gradations occur as in Exhibit 12-1.

These variations in political structures are accompanied by corresponding variations in other aspects of the cultures, as shown in Exhibit 12-2.

For the overwhelming majority of their existence, humans have lived in small hunting-and-gathering bands characterized by little or no political integration and few, if any, specialized political roles. Not until the Neolithic Revolution (domestication of plants and animals) occurred approximately 10,000 years ago were socioeconomic forces unleashed that permitted the forma-

tion of larger, more complex sociopolitical systems. With the new food-producing technologies brought in with the Neolithic Revolution, populations have become larger and more heterogeneous, and as a result, political organizations have become increasingly complex and centralized. Today, state systems of government predominate in the world, while small-scale band societies account for a very small (and decreasing) percentage of the world's societies.

Although the rise of state systems of government was clearly a significant development, there is relatively little consensus on why these complex forms of government emerged. By examining both ancient and contemporary societies, anthropologists and social philosophers have developed a number of explanations as to why some societies have developed state systems while others have not. Explanations for the rise of the state hinge on the question of what induces people to surrender at least a portion of their autonomy to the power and control of the state. Some theories suggest that people *purposefully* and *voluntarily* give up their sovereignty because of the perceived benefits. That is, these theorists reason that the limited loss of autonomy was outweighed by the benefits people derived from their integration into a wider political structure. These benefits included (1) greater protection from hostile, outside forces, (2) more effective means of conflict resolution, and (3) the opportunity for increased food production.

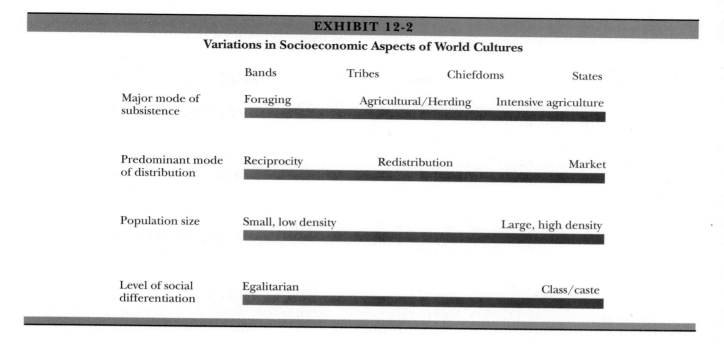

EXHIBIT 12-2

Variations in Socioeconomic Aspects of World Cultures

	Bands	Tribes	Chiefdoms	States
Major mode of subsistence	Foraging	Agricultural/Herding	Intensive agriculture	
Predominant mode of distribution	Reciprocity	Redistribution		Market
Population size	Small, low density		Large, high density	
Level of social differentiation	Egalitarian			Class/caste

A good example of this **voluntaristic theory of state formation** was put forth by the archaeologist V. Gordon Childe. According to Childe (1936:82–83), the introduction and development of intensive agriculture (stimulated by the introduction of the plow, irrigation, metallurgy, and draft animals) during the Neolithic Period created food surpluses. These food surpluses, in turn, freed up a certain segment of the population from tasks of food production, allowing them to engage in a wide variety of new occupational roles, such as weavers, traders, potters, and metal workers. This dramatic increase in occupational specialization created a need for some wider form of political integration in order to mediate between and protect all of the varied special interest groups and to provide the economic superstructure to enable all of them to work in an efficient and complementary fashion.

Another voluntaristic explanation of the emergence of the state is the **hydraulic theory of state formation,** suggested by Karl Wittfogel. According to this theory (Wittfogel 1957:18), small-scale irrigation farmers in arid or semiarid areas eventually came to see certain economic advantages to surrendering their autonomy and merging their small communities into a larger political entity capable of large-scale irrigation. Even though archaeological evidence indicates that certain states (e.g., China, Mexico, and Mesopotamia) developed prior to the development of large-scale irrigation,

centralized political governments do appear to be functional for those agricultural systems dependent on irrigation.

Still another theory of state origins, set forth by Robert Carneiro (1970), suggests that the existence of the state is the direct result of warfare. By offering a **coercive theory of state formation,** Carneiro holds that "force, and not enlightened self interest, is the mechanism by which political evolution has led, step by step, from autonomous villages to the state" (1970:217). Carneiro goes on to elaborate that while warfare is the mechanism of state formation, it operates only under certain environmental conditions—namely, in those areas that have limited agricultural land for expanding populations. To illustrate his theory, Carneiro uses the case of the Inca state that developed in the narrow valleys of the Peruvian coast, which were geographically circumscribed in that they faced the ocean, backed up to the mountains, and were flanked on either end by deserts. As populations grew in this region, there was no land into which to expand. Land pressure increased, resulting in intense land competition and eventually warfare. Increasingly more centralized political units developed to conduct the warfare and to administer subjugated peoples. Villages that lost wars became subjugated populations, while the victors headed up increasingly larger and more complex warring political units. Carneiro (1970:219) claims that similar political evolution occurred in other parts of the world characterized by circumscribed agricultural land such as the Nile Valley, Mesopotamia, and the Indus Valley.

Social Control

As the previous section explained, political structures vary from very informal structures such as bands at one extreme to highly complex state systems of government at the other extreme. Whatever form of political organization is found in a society, it must inevitably address the issue of **social control.** In other words, every society must ensure that most of the people behave themselves in appropriate ways most of the time. Statelike societies, such as our own, have a wide variety of formalized mechanisms that function to keep people's behavior in line, including written laws, judges, bureaucracies, prisons, electric chairs, and police forces. At the other extreme, small-scale band societies, such as the Eskimos or !Kung, while having no centralized political authority, nevertheless maintain social order among their members quite effectively through informal mechanisms of social control. In fact, people deviate from acceptable behavior considerably less in most band societies than in societies with more elaborate and complex forms of political organization.

Every society has defined what are normal, proper, or expected ways of behaving. These expectations, known as **social norms,** serve as behavioral guidelines and help the society work smoothly. To be certain, social norms are not adhered to perfectly, and, in fact, there is always a certain level of deviance from them (see, for example, Freilich, Raybeck, and Savishinsky 1990). But most people in any given society abide by them most of the time. Moreover, social norms take a number of different forms, ranging from etiquette to formal laws. Some norms are taken more seriously than others. On the one hand, all societies have certain social expectations of what is "proper," but such behavior is not rigidly enforced. To illustrate, although it is customary in the United States for people to shake hands when being introduced, a person's refusal to shake hands would not constitute a serious violation of social norms. The person who does not follow this rule of etiquette might be considered rude but would not be arrested or executed. At the other extreme, certain social norms (such as grand larceny or murder) are taken very seriously indeed because they are considered absolutely necessary for the survival of the society.

looking ahead

To see how an anthropologist contributed to the creation of a national legal system in Papua New Guinea, see Applied Perspective 1 at the end of this chapter.

All social norms, whether trivial or serious, are sanctioned. That is, societies develop patterned or institutionalized ways of encouraging people to conform to the norms. These sanctions are both positive and negative, for people are rewarded for behaving in socially acceptable ways and punished for violating the norms. **Positive sanctions** range from a smile of approval to being awarded the Congressional Medal of Honor. **Negative sanctions** include everything from a frown of disapproval to corporal punishment.

Social sanctions may also be formal or informal, depending on whether or not a formal law (legal statute) has been violated. To illustrate, if a woman in a restaurant is talking in a voice that can be easily overheard by people at nearby tables, she will probably receive stares from the other diners. But if she starts yelling at the top of her lungs in the restaurant, she will probably be arrested for disturbing the peace or disorderly conduct. The difference, of course, is that in the first case the woman wasn't breaking the law, while in the second case she was.

Exhibit 12-3 illustrates a continuum of the formal-informal dimension of social norms and sanctions in U.S. society.

Just as the types of social norms found in any society will vary, so will the mechanisms used to encourage people to adhere to those norms. For most North Americans, the most obvious forms of social control are the formal or institutionalized ones. When asked why we tend to "behave ourselves," we would probably think of formal laws, police forces, courts, and prisons. We don't rob the local convenience store, in other words, because if caught, we are likely to go to prison.

Most of our "proper" behavior is probably due to less formal, and perhaps less obvious, mechanisms of social control. In band and tribal societies that lack centralized authority, informal mechanisms of social control may be all that exists. The remainder of this chapter looks at those informal mechanisms of social control so characteristic of band and tribal societies and at more formal institutions aimed primarily at social control,

EXHIBIT 12-3

Continuum of Social Norms in the United States

Violation causes
weak emotional
reaction and mild
punishment

Type of Misconduct	Punishment
Wearing tuxedo to anthropology class	Raised eyebrows
Eating dinner with fingers rather than utensils	Ridicule
Illegal parking	Small fine
Shoplifting	Large fine or a short prison term
Grand larceny	Long jail term
Treason	Long jail term or death
Homicide	Long jail term or death

Violation causes
strong emotional
reaction and strong
punishment

ernmental in the Western sense of the term. They include very low levels of political integration, have few, if any, specialized political roles, and little **political coerciveness.** These small-scale political systems have been referred to as acephalous (i.e., headless) or as "tribes without rulers" (Middleton and Tait 1958). In the absence of formal governmental structures, how do these acephalous societies maintain some semblance of social order? The following subsections examine a number of informal mechanisms of social control that not only operate in acephalous societies but in many cases also operate in more complex societies.

Socialization.   Every society, if it is to survive, must pass on its social norms from one generation to another. It seems blatantly obvious that people will not be able to conform to the social norms unless they are taught them. Thus, all societies have some system of **socialization,** which involves teaching the young what the norms are as well as teaching that these norms—since they are inherently "proper"—should not be violated. People learn their social norms with a certain degree of moral compulsion. We learn, for example, that in the United States people wear clothes in public *and* that we should as well. Usually, we internalize our social norms so effectively that we would never consider violating them. Some social norms—like not appearing nude in public—are so thoroughly ingrained in us through socialization that the thought of violating them would be distasteful and embarrassing. Other social norms do not have the same level of moral intensity, such as driving within the speed limit or maintaining good oral hygiene. But as a general rule when people learn their norms, they are at the same time internalizing the moral necessity to obey them.

Public Opinion.   One of the most compelling reasons for not violating the social norms is **public opinion** or social pressure. In general, people from all parts of the world wish to be accepted by the other members of their society. Most people fear being rejected or talked about by their fellows. This strong desire to win the approval of other members of one's society is summed up in such comments as, "Don't do that! What will the neighbors think?" It is, of course, impossible to determine how many people are deterred from violating the social norms because of fear of negative public opinion. At the same time, we can cite many examples of how societies use social pressure very deliberately to keep people in line. Indeed, gossip, ostracism, rumor,

some of which involve laws and adjudicating bodies. It should be emphasized, however, that this distinction between formal and informal mechanisms should in no way imply that informal means of social control exist only in band and tribal societies. Although societies with complex political organizations (state societies in particular) are best known for written laws and courts, they also rely on an appreciable number of informal mechanisms of social control.

Informal Means of Social Control

Compared to complex state organizations, bands and tribes have little in the way that would appear to be gov-

Imprisonment serves as a negative sanction in societies with state systems of government.

The deliberate use of social pressure to maintain social control is particularly important and, in some cases, quite dramatic in acephalous societies. A case in point is the custom of the duel found in Tiwi society of North Australia (Hart and Pilling 1960). Men in traditional Tiwi society achieve power and status by amassing large numbers of wives. Under such conditions of intense polygyny, all females are married or betrothed before or at birth, while men do not take their first wives until their late thirties or early forties. Thus, at any given moment in time, all women are married to older men.

If a younger Tiwi male, say, one in his twenties, is to have any intimate relations with a Tiwi woman, it must, by definition, be with an older man's wife. When this occurs, the older man challenges the young adulterer to a duel, which, like the use of the stock and pillory, is always public. All the people in the community (men, women, and children) form a circle in an open field surrounding the older man and the accused adulterer. With the entire community watching, the older man throws spears at the younger man, along with a string of verbal insults. The younger man is expected to submit himself to this verbal harangue while sidestepping the spears. But before the event can end, the younger man must allow one of the spears to strike him, it is hoped in a nonvulnerable place.

The key to understanding the Tiwi duel is its public nature. Even though the alleged guilty party suffers some physical punishment (i.e., the superficial wound), the real punishment is the public disapproval of the younger man's behavior by all of the onlookers. The Tiwi duel, in other words, is an institutionalized form of public humiliation whereby public opinion is mobilized in an attempt to reform aberrant behavior. The Tiwi duel is a particularly effective mechanism of social control because it not only helps to reform the behavior of the accused but also serves as a reminder to all of the other members of the community who might be contemplating violating the social norms.

Corporate Lineages.   **Corporate lineages** play a dominant role in most small-scale (acephalous) societies. Members of corporate lineages (who can number in the hundreds) frequently live, work, play, and pray together. Property is controlled by the lineage, people derive their primary identity from the group, and even religion (in the form of ancestor worship) is a lineage matter. Acting like a small corporation, the lineage has a powerful impact on the everyday lives of its members and can exert considerable pressure on people to conform to the social norms.

sarcasm, and derision are all powerful corrective measures for reforming social behavior. For example, city and county governments in the United States print the names of tax delinquents in the local newspaper in an attempt to embarrass them into paying their taxes. In colonial America, the stock and pillory was an excellent example of how the society used public opinion to control people's behavior. Someone who was caught breaking the social norms (e.g., committing adultery or stealing) was confined to the stock and pillory, which, not coincidentally, was always located right in the center of town. Even though long confinements in the stock and pillory were very physically uncomfortable, the realization that all of your friends, relatives, and neighbors would see you and know of your crime was by far the greater punishment.

One means by which corporate lineages exert control over its members is economic. All important property, such as land and livestock, is controlled by the elders of the corporate lineage. Often property is allocated on the basis of conformity to societal norms. Those who behave as the society expects them to behave are likely to receive the best plots of land and use of the best livestock. Conversely, those who violate social norms are likely to be denied these valuable economic resources.

Corporate lineages, to some degree, also act as mechanisms of social control because of their scale. Corporate lineages serve as localized communities, numbering from several hundred to as many as several thousand relatives. Because members of the lineage have frequent and intense interaction with one another on a daily basis, it is virtually impossible for anyone to maintain her or his anonymity. People's lives are played out in such close proximity to one another that everyone knows what everyone else is doing. To illustrate, a man who wants to engage in socially inappropriate behavior (such as having an extramarital affair) would think twice because it would be difficult, if not impossible, to keep it a secret. By way of contrast, it is considerably easier to have an extramarital affair and remain undetected in a large city. Thus, the small-scale nature of corporate lineage communities tends to inhibit social deviance because it is much more difficult to "get away" with it.

The way roles are structured in corporate lineage societies also contributes to social control. In terms of role structure, corporate lineages have what Parsons and Shils (1952:83) refer to as diffuse roles. People play social roles in a number of different domains, such as kinship, economic, political, ritual/religious, and recreational roles. A role is diffuse when it ranges over two or more of these domains. For example, a diffuse role structure occurs when a man's grandfather (kinship role) is also his teacher (educational role), his priest (religious role), the local chief (political role), and his hunting partner (economic role). The man, in other words, has a number of overlapping roles; he is playing roles from a number of different domains with the same person. By way of contrast, roles in large-scale, complex societies such as our own tend to be segmented or narrowly defined so that single roles are played out with one person at a time. People in corporate lineage societies (with diffuse or overlapping roles) have a built-in incentive *not* to violate the social norms, for to do so would have very serious consequences. If the man in the preceding illustration offends his grandfather, he is not only negatively affecting his kinship domain but is also affecting the educational, economic, political, and religious domains.

Marriage in corporate lineage societies tends to be highly collective. That is, marriage in such societies is regarded primarily as an alliance between two lineages—that of the bride and that of the groom—and only secondarily as a union between individuals. In many cases, the marriage is legitimized by bridewealth (the transfer of property—frequently livestock—from the kin group of the groom to the kin group of the bride). When a man wants to get married, he cannot pay the bridewealth himself, since he does not have personal control over property. Like the rest of his relatives, he has limited rights and obligations to such pieces of property as cattle. If marriage cattle are to be transferred from one lineage to another, a group decision will need to be made. If, for example, eight cows must be given to the prospective bride's family before the marriage can be legitimate, the prospective groom must convince a number of his kin to give up their limited use of cows. In the event that the prospective groom has a reputation for violating the social norms, it is likely that the permission to transfer the cows will be withheld. Thus, the members of a corporate lineage, through their collective capacity to control marriage, possess considerable power to coerce people into appropriate behavior.

Supernatural Belief Systems. A powerful mechanism of social control in acephalous societies is the belief in supernatural forces such as gods, witches, and sorcerers. People will refrain from antisocial behavior if they believe that some supernatural (i.e., above-human) force will punish them for it. It is, of course, impossible to determine how many norms are *not* violated because people fear supernatural retribution, but we have to assume that the belief in supernatural sanctions acts as a deterrent to some degree. Nor is it necessary to prove that the gods, for example, will in fact punish the social deviants. If people believe that "god will get them" for doing something wrong, the belief itself is usually enough to discourage the deviant behavior.

Ancestor Worship. **Ancestor worship** is a form of supernatural belief that serves as an effective means of social control in some acephalous societies. In such societies, dead ancestors are considered fully functioning members of the descent group. In fact, the death of a respected elder marks that person's elevation in status to supernatural being rather than his or her departure

Many people, including these worshipers from Brunei, tend to con-form to the social norms out of a strong belief in supernatural forces.

from the group. Respect for the ancestor-gods is fre-quently demonstrated by sacrifices and proper behav-ior, for which the living members are believed to be re-warded or punished, depending on how well they meet these obligations.

The Lugbara society of Uganda provides a good example of ancestor worship. According to Middleton (1965:73–77), the well-being of the entire kinship group is ensured only if people behave in socially ap-propriate ways. The Lugbara believe personal and group tragedies are a direct result of the transgression of certain social norms, such as showing disrespect to both living and dead elders, adultery, incest, assault, or homicide.

The Lugbara generally believe that the ancestor-gods inflict with illness those living kin who endanger the well-being of the lineage by committing any of these of-fenses. Sickness of any type is explained in terms of an-

cestral displeasure with the conduct of the living. Thus, sickness (resulting from sin) is followed by either **ghost invocation** or **ghostly vengeance.** In ghost invocation, a living man—typically an elder—calls forth the wrath of the ancestor-gods against the alleged sinner. Ghostly vengeance is the belief that ancestor-gods inflict sick-ness on their own without having to be invoked.

Whether ancestral ghosts in traditional Lugbara soci-ety were directly responsible for sickness among the liv-ing is perhaps of greater interest to the theologian than to the anthropologist. What is of interest to the anthro-pologist, however, is the effects of the belief on the be-havior of the living, for it is the *belief* that has implica-tions for social control rather than its ability to undergo scientific verification. Such rites as ghostly invocation give regular expression to fears of supernatural retribu-tion, which in turn control, or at least influence, a per-son's conduct.

Witchcraft.   The belief in **witchcraft**, which is found of-ten in acephalous societies, also functions to control people's behavior by discouraging socially deviant be-havior. In societies that believe in witchcraft, a deviant runs the risk of being labeled a witch, and fear of being accused of witchcraft strongly encourages conformity. For example, in colonial America, nonconformists, free-thinkers, and others who didn't conform to expected behavioral norms were driven from their communities for allegedly being witches. Jean La Fontaine notes the way witchcraft serves as a mechanism of social control among the Bantu-speaking Gisu of East Africa:

> . . . witchcraft beliefs act as a form of social control in discouraging behavior that is socially unacceptable. In Bagisu the eccentric is branded a witch. . . . Children grow up with the realization that the stigma of non-conformity is dangerous; too great a departure from the norms of everyday conduct will attract the suspi-cion of others and lead to isolation and eventual de-struction. (1963:217)

Age Organizations.   In some acephalous societies, age organizations serve as effective means of social control. Those societies with age organizations have distinct groups of people passing periodically through distinct age categories. This involves the basic distinction that cultural anthropologists make between **age sets** and **age grades.** An age set is a group of people (usually men), initiated during a periodic ceremony and having a strong sense of group identity with one another. An age set lasts from its inception, usually when most members are late adolescents, until its last member has died. Age sets pass (as a group) through successive categories, called age grades, such as warriors, elders, or various subdivisions of these grades. Each age grade is associated with a well-understood set of social roles (i.e., they perform exclusive functions) and statuses (i.e., higher prestige is associated with increasing age). To illustrate this distinction further, an age set is analogous to a group of students who go through college together. The academic grades through which they pass—that is, freshman through senior—are comparable to the age grades. Thus, we can speak of a particular age set occupying the senior warrior grade at a particular moment in time.

Age organizations function to control behavior in a number of significant ways. *First,* since age organizations establish a clear set of roles and statuses, they are particularly effective as channels for the distribution of authority. Since men of every age grade have well-defined and well-understood roles, there is little room for infringing on the authority or domain of others. There is little incentive, in other words, to try to usurp the authority of those above you for the simple reason that provided you live long enough, you will eventually have that authority by virtue of your own advanced age.

Second, individuals enter the age set system at the lowest echelon through the process of initiation. These rites of passage are almost always preceded by intense periods of training in the norms and values of the society. These periods of intense socialization teach the soon-to-become adults not only the expected behaviors but also why the behaviors should be followed and the penalties for deviation.

Third, the bonds of camaraderie that exist between members of the same age set are usually so strong that age sets tend to take on the characteristics of a corporate group. Age set members who have experienced their initiation ceremonies together support one another throughout the remainder of their lives in much the same way as do members of the same lineage.

Unlike lineages, age sets are neither self-perpetuating nor property owning, but they exert the same type of pressure to conform on their members as lineages do on theirs.

Formal Means of Social Control

As previously noted, all societies use informal mechanisms of social control to some degree. Western cultures rely heavily on such mechanisms as socialization, public opinion, and supernatural sanctions to encourage people to maintain social order by behaving appropriately. Often these informal mechanisms of social control are not sufficient to maintain the desired level of conformity to the norms. Frequently, the violation of social norms results in disputes between people in the society. When such disputes become violent conflicts (such as theft, assault, or homicide), we refer to them as crimes. Since societies face the possibility of violent conflict erupting between their members, they need to develop explicit mechanisms to address and, it is hoped, resolve the conflicts.

Although no society in the world is immune from crime, the incidence of crime varies considerably from society to society. It appears that crime is more likely to

The age organizations into which these boys from Papua New Guinea are being initiated can serve as effective mechanisms of social control.

CROSS-CULTURAL MISCUE

Until recently, the importance of hand gestures has gone largely unnoticed. Hand gestures, however, can change the meaning of our words as well as carry meanings totally by themselves. We now know that unless we understand the meanings attached to certain hand gestures in different cultures, we are likely to send and receive unintended messages when dealing with people from different cultures. This was dramatically illustrated by the now famous clasped-hands-over-the-head gesture used by Soviet Premier Khrushchev when visiting the United States in the 1960s. This gesture, which for Russians is a sign of international brotherhood, was interpreted by most Americans as an arrogant gesture usually used by prizefighters after defeating an opponent. Needless to say, misreading this gesture did little to enhance U.S.-Soviet relations.

occur in large, heterogeneous, stratified societies than in small-scale societies. For example, the crime rate in U.S. cities is approximately ten times as high as in rural areas. Several logical arguments support these findings. First, as mentioned in the discussion of corporate lineages, people in small-scale societies have little or no anonymity, which makes getting away with a crime more difficult. Second, since people in small-scale societies know most of the other people, they are more likely to be concerned with negative public opinion. Third, the heterogeneous character of populations in large-scale, complex societies means that there will be a number of groups with different, and quite likely conflicting, interests. And finally, the fact that large-scale societies are almost always stratified into classes or castes means that certain segments (i.e., the lower strata) of the population may feel blocked from upward mobility and consequently may be more likely to want to violate the rights of those in the more privileged strata.

Song Duels.   Just as societies differ in terms of the incidence of crime, they also differ in the way they handle disputes and crimes. One example of a formal mechanism for resolving disputes was found among the Eskimos of Canada, Alaska, and Greenland. Since the Eskimos had relatively little property because of their nomadic way of life, conflicts rarely arose over violation of property rights. However, disputes did occur frequently between men over the issue of wife stealing. A man would attempt to steal the wife of a more prominent man as a way of elevating his own standing within the community.

A not uncommon way of resolving wife stealing among the Eskimos was to murder the wife stealer. In fact, Rasmussen (1927:250) found that all of the men he studied had been a party to a murder, either as the murderer or as an accessory, and invariably these murders stemmed from allegations of wife stealing. There were, however, alternative resolutions to disputes over wife stealing. One alternative was to challenge the alleged wife stealer to a derisive song contest, which was fought with song and lyrics rather than with weapons. The plaintiff and defendant, appearing in a public setting, would chide each other with abusive songs especially composed for the occasion. The contestant who received the loudest applause emerged the winner of this "curse by verse" **song duel.** Interestingly, the resolution of the conflict was not based on a determination of guilt or innocence, only on one's verbal dexterity.

Intermediaries.   Some societies use **intermediaries** to help resolve serious conflicts. The Nuer of the African Sudan are a case in point (Evans-Pritchard 1940:

163–64). Even though the Nuer political system is informal and uncentralized, one role in the society—the **Leopard-skin Chief**—is, to a degree, institutionalized. In the absence of any formal system of law courts to punish serious crimes such as murder, the Leopard-skin Chief serves as a mediator between the victim's family and the family of the murderer. When a homicide occurs, the murderer, fearing the vengeance of the victim's family, takes sanctuary in the home of the Leopard-skin Chief. In an attempt to prevent an all-out feud, the Leopard-skin Chief attempts to negotiate a settlement between the two families in order to avoid a feud. His role is to work out an equitable settlement between the two families whereby the murderer's family will compensate the victim's family with some form of property settlement (say, ten head of cattle) for the loss of one of its members.

If either side becomes too unyielding, the Leopard-skin Chief can threaten to curse the offending party. The Leopard-skin Chief does not decide the case, however. Rather, he is only an intermediary, with no authority to determine guilt or force a settlement between the parties. Intervening on behalf of the public interest, he uses his personal and supernatural influence to bring the disputing parties to some type of agreed-upon settlement of their dispute.

Council of Elders. A somewhat more structured mechanism for conflict resolution is a **council of elders** called a *kiama,* which is found among the Kikuyu of Kenya (Kenyatta 1962; Middleton and Kershaw 1965).

Traditionally, the *kiama* adjudicated disputes between individuals and groups of individuals on a wide range of matters, including theft, paternity cases, and homicide. Although Kikuyu *kiamas* continue to operate on the local community level, they deal only with relatively minor civil and criminal cases because serious crimes are handled by the official state-run court system.

The elders question the parties to the case and render judgment on guilt or innocence. If guilt is established, the *kiama* sets an amount of compensation to which the injured party is entitled. Frequently, the relationship between the guilty party and the victim determines the amount of compensation. Whatever amount is set, however, the emphasis is on compensating the injured party.

Unlike our own court system, which usually separates the guilty party from society by incarceration, the Kikuyu legal system stresses normalizing the relations in the community that have been disrupted by the conflict. Today the *kiamas* have no formal means of enforcing their decisions other than their own persuasiveness and stature within the local community. If the guilty party refuses to pay compensation, the case is referred to the official government court system, which usually accepts it.

Oaths and Ordeals. Another way of resolving conflicts—particularly when law enforcement agencies (such as governments) are not especially strong—is through religiously sanctioned methods such as oaths and ordeals. An **oath** is a formal declaration to some su-

This traditional Kikuyu kiama *(council of elders) still operates to settle disputes in Kenya.*

pernatural force that what you are saying is truthful or that you are innocent. Though they can take many different forms, oaths almost always are accompanied by a ritual act, such as smoking a peace pipe, signing a loyalty document, or swearing upon the Bible (as in our courts of law). Since some believe that to swear a false oath could lead to supernatural retribution, oaths can be effective in determining guilt or innocence.

An **ordeal** is a means of determining guilt by submitting the accused to a dangerous test. If the person passes the test, it is believed that a higher supernatural force has determined the party's innocence; if he or she fails, the gods have signaled the party's guilt. Ordeal by drinking poison was found among the Ashanti in West Africa. If, after drinking a poison concoction, the accused vomited, the person was considered innocent; if the accused didn't vomit, he or she died and was therefore considered guilty.

It has been suggested (Roberts, 1967; Meek, 1972) that oaths and ordeals are most likely to be found in relatively complex societies where the political leadership lacks the power to enforce judicial decisions; consequently, the leaders must rely on supernaturally sanctioned mechanisms such as oaths and ordeals to make certain that people will obey. Where political leaders wield greater power, oaths and ordeals are no longer needed.

Courts and Codified Law.   A characteristic of state systems of government is that they possess a monopoly on the use of force. Through a system of codified laws, the state both forbids individuals from using force and determines how it will use force to require citizens to do some things and forbid them from doing others. These laws, which are usually in written form, are established by legislative bodies, interpreted by judicial bodies, and enforced by administrators. When legal prescriptions are violated, the state has the authority, through its courts and law enforcement agencies, to fine, imprison, or even execute the wrongdoer. To suggest that the state has a monopoly on the use of force should not imply that only the government uses force. State systems of government are constantly having to deal with unauthorized uses of force, such as **crime** (violent disputes between individuals or groups), **rebellions** (attempts to displace the people in power), and **revolutions** (attempts to overthrow the entire system of government).

The system of codified laws used to resolve disputes and maintain social order in complex societies is distinct from other types of social norms. Legal anthro-

By means of codified laws, state systems of government maintain a monopoly on the use of force.

pologist E. Adamson Hoebel (1972:504–6) has identified three basic features of **law.** While his definition of law goes beyond the type of law found in Western societies, it certainly holds true for that type of law as well. First, law involves the legitimate use of physical coercion. Law without the force to punish or deprive is no law at all, although in most cases force is not necessary, because the very threat of force or compulsion acts as a sufficient deterrent to antisocial behavior. But when it is needed, a true legal system can draw upon the legitimate use of force. Second, legal systems allocate official authority to privileged people who are able to use coercion legitimately. Third, law is based on regularity and a certain amount of predictability. That is, since laws build on precedents, new laws are based upon old ones. This regularity and predictability eliminate much of the whim and capriciousness from the law.

Legal systems in complex societies such as our own have different objectives than systems of conflict resolution found in other societies. The objective of the Nuer Leopard-skin Chief and the Kikuyu council of elders, for example, was to compensate the victim and to reestablish harmony between the disputants and, consequently, peace within the community. Law enforcement and conflict resolution in complex societies, by way of contrast, tend to emphasize punishment of the wrongdoer, which frequently takes the form of incar-ceration or, in some cases, death. It is not, in other words, aimed at either compensation or reintegrating the offender back into the community. This emphasis on punishment in complex societies is understandable in that lawbreakers pose a particular threat to the authority of the government officials. Unless serious offenders are punished or separated from the rest of society, they are likely to threaten the very legitimacy of political and legal authority.

Political Organization

This chapter has examined political organization—how societies use legitimate power and authority to regulate behavior. In the process a number of different topics, including levels of political integration, specialization of political roles, degrees of political coerciveness, mechanisms of social control, concentrations of power and authority, and means of resolving conflicts, have been considered. As part of the political process, all of these topics are relevant to the applied anthropologist when working in programs of planned change. This final section looks at two specific examples of how an understanding of various aspects of political organization have contributed to the successful solution of societal problems. In the first case, the research of a legal anthropologist has helped the new government of Papua New Guinea to integrate its many traditional legal systems with the Western legal system that it inherited from the colonial period. The second case illustrates how the work of ethnohistorian Anthony Paredes was used to secure official recognition of the Poarch Creek Indians by the federal government, a measure that had far-reaching consequences for the group's economic revitalization.

An anthropologist's study of customary law in New Guinea leads to the creation of a new national legal system.

As a general rule, when Western governments administered their colonies during the nineteenth and twentieth centuries, they invariably superimposed on local populations their own Western legal systems, which were often at odds with the local customary laws. As the colonial period came to an end during the 1960s and 1970s, many newly independent governments were faced with the need to develop a new national legal system that would be based on the customs and traditions of their own people rather than on those of the former colonial powers. For many newly independent governments, this was a formidable task, owing to the vast cultural diversity that existed within their geographic borders.

One such former colony was the country of Papua New Guinea, which won its independence in 1975. Papua New Guinea had a population of three and a half million people who spoke approximately 750 mutually unintelligible languages and had at least as many customary legal systems (see Scaglion 1987:98). Thus, the Papuan New Guinea government was faced with the gargantuan twofold task of (1) identifying the legal principles of

these diverse customary legal systems and (2) reconciling them into a new statewide legal system. To accomplish these tasks, the parliament established a Law Reform Commission, which, shortly after its own creation, sponsored the Customary Law Project. Headed by legal anthropologist Richard Scaglion, this project was designed to conduct research on local customary law so as to determine how and to what extent it might serve as the basis for a national legal system (see Scaglion 1987).

As project director, Scaglion supervised a small cadre of local university students, who were fluent in the local languages and cultures. It was their job to collect original conflict case studies from which principles of customary law could be extracted. The primary data-gathering technique used in this project was the case method of legal anthropology first made popular by Llewellyn and Hoebel (1941) and later refined by Laura Nader (Nader and Todd 1978:5–8). The local student/researchers collected approximately 600 detailed case studies from all parts of the country; the case studies constituted a legal database that the Law Reform Commission could use for its unification of customary law.

The collection of these detailed case studies made two very important practical contributions to the emerging (postindependence) legal system in Papua New Guinea. First, this legal data bank on customary law and legal principles was immediately useful to lawyers. The computerized retrieval system of case studies was a great help to lawyers in searching out legal precedents for their ongoing court cases.

The second major contribution of the Customary Law Project was that it helped to identify, and subsequently alleviate, certain problems arising from a conflict between customary law and the existing national legal system. Family law was one such area. To be specific, under customary marriage practices, polygyny was a perfectly permissible alternative, but it was strictly forbidden under existing statutory law. Drawing upon the legal data bank of case studies, the Law Reform Commission, in conjunction with the legislative and judicial branches of the government, drafted a family bill that formally recognized the legality of customary marriages and provided for polygyny under certain conditions. Thus, new legislation was introduced into the parliament that incorporated elements of customary law into the national system.

Although the implementation phase of the Customary Law Project has been completed (i.e., the creation of the original data bank of case studies), the research on additional case studies is ongoing. With an ever increasing number of case studies from customary law, practicing lawyers will continue to have access to customary legal precedents relevant to the cases they are arguing in court. In addition, those responsible for the more long-term process of national legal reform will continue to draw upon the anthropological concepts, data, and methods established by the Customary Law Project under the direction of legal anthropologist Richard Scaglion.

THOUGHT QUESTIONS

1. Why was the government of Papua New Guinea faced with the particularly difficult dilemma of developing a national legal system?

2. What was the purpose of the Customary Law Project?

3. How would you describe the anthropological contribution that Scaglion made to the Customary Law Project?

Ethnohistorical research enabled the Poarch Creek Indians to establish their claim for official recognition by the federal government, which led to economic revitalization of the group.

In the early 1970s, cultural anthropologist Anthony Paredes began his studies of the Poarch Creek, an obscure cultural group of American Indians located in southern Alabama and numbering about 500 people (1992). As a student of ethnohistory and social change, Paredes was interested in studying how the Poarch Creek had managed to maintain their Indian identity in the face of considerable intermarriage with non-Indians and the virtual disappearance of their language and culture. During the course of his initial investigations, which used the ethnographic methods of interviewing and participant-observation, Paredes learned that since the 1940s the Poarch Creek community had actually been pursuing ways of overcoming such long-standing problems as poverty, underemployment, poor education, and poor health. One very effective way of addressing these problems was to petition the federal government to become an officially recognized Indian tribe. If the Poarch Creek community was successful in its petition, it would be eligible for economic support from a number of government agencies.

Although the Poarch Creek had begun petitioning for federal recognition before Paredes entered the community, the research (both ethnographic and archival) that Paredes conducted turned out to have a very practical use in addition to its scholarly value. The research was highly instrumental in the group's eventually successful petition for official recognition. To be successful in their claim, the Poarch Creek needed to demonstrate that they had maintained a continuous existence as a political unit with viable leadership that had authority over its members. A critical problem, however, was the conspicuous information gap in the late 1800s. There were sufficient historical records of government dealings with the Poarch Creek during the first half of the nineteenth century and ample evidence of more recent times gained through ethnographic interviewing with living tribal members. The challenge facing Paredes was to fill in the historical record of the late nineteenth and early twentieth centuries through a combination of archival research and ethnographic/ethnohistorical methods.

In the early 1980s, Paredes was hired by the tribal council to conduct research in the National Archives in Washington, D.C., and in the state archives in Montgomery, Alabama. Paredes helped reconstruct periods of tribal history by gathering bits and pieces of information from various government records including homestead files, obituaries, court cases, and various types of government correspondences. By locating historical materials, he was able to support, confirm, and amplify much of the data he had gained from interviewing his older tribal informants. In his own words, Paredes (1992:218) was "able to combine disparate bits of seemingly trivial information with data from ethnographic fieldwork to confirm informants'

recollections and cast new light on community organization and leadership in an earlier era."

Thus, what started out as a general scholarly inquiry into the recent history of the Poarch Creek Indians turned out to have important practical implications. The information collected by anthropologist Paredes was used to buttress the tribe's petition to the BIA (Bureau of Indian Affairs) for official recognition by the federal government. This petition for official recognition, which met with success in 1984, has had far-reaching benefits for the Poarch Creek community. Within the first two years of being officially recognized, the tribal community received approximately $2 million from the BIA, the Indian Health Service, and other federal agencies for the purpose of supporting tribal government operations, a health center, education, a housing project, and law enforcement. With the help of a federally secured loan, the tribe has purchased a motel on a nearby interstate highway. And, according to Paredes, the tribe has become one of the major employers in the county. Thus, the scholarly research of one anthropologist, initially aimed at reconstructing the history of the Poarch Creek Indians of Alabama, turned out to have a very significant impact on the revitalization of this group of Native Americans.

THOUGHT QUESTIONS

1. Why was it important for the Poarch Creek to receive official federal recognition?

2. Would recognition have been possible without the anthropological research conducted by Paredes?

3. How would you characterize the applied anthropological role that Paredes played in this case study?

Summary

1. All societies have political systems that function to manage public affairs, maintain social order, and resolve conflict. The study of political organization involves such topics as the allocation of political roles, levels of political integration, concentrations of power and authority, mechanisms of social control, and means for resolving conflict.

2. Political anthropologists generally recognize four fundamentally different levels of political organization based on levels of political integration and the degree of specialized political roles: bands, tribes, chiefdoms, and states.

3. Societies based on bands have the least amount of political integration and role specialization. They are most often found in foraging societies and are associated with low population densities, distribution systems based on reciprocity, and egalitarian social relations.

4. Tribal organizations are most commonly found among horticulturalists and pastoralists. With larger and more sedentary populations than are found in band societies, tribally based societies have certain pantribal mechanisms that cut across a number of local segments and integrate them into a larger whole.

5. At the next level of complexity are chiefdoms, which involve a more formal and permanent political structure than is found in tribal societies. Political authority in chiefdoms rests with a single individual, either acting alone or with the advice of a council. Most chiefdoms, which tend to have quite distinct social ranks, rely on feasting and tribute as a major way of distributing goods.

6. State systems—with the greatest amount of political

integration and role specialization—are associated with intensive agriculture, market economies, urbanization, and complex social stratification. States, which first appeared about 3500 B.C., have a monopoly on the use of force and can make and enforce laws, collect taxes, and recruit labor for military service and public works projects.

7. Theories put forth to explain the rise of state systems of government have centered on the question of why people have surrendered at least some of their autonomy to the power and authority of the state. Some theories (such as those of Childe and Wittfogel) suggest that people voluntarily gave up their autonomy in exchange for certain perceived benefits such as protection, more effective means of conflict resolution, and greater food productivity. Other explanations, such as that offered by Carneiro, hold that states developed as a result of warfare and coercion rather than voluntary self-interest.

8. In the absence of formal mechanisms of government, many band and tribal societies maintain social control by means of a number of informal mechanisms such as socialization, public opinion, corporate lineages, supernatural sanctions, and age organizations.

9. In addition to using informal means of social control, societies control behavior by more formal mechanisms whose major function is maintaining social order and resolving conflicts. These mechanisms include verbal competition, intermediaries, councils of elders, oaths, ordeals, and formal court systems.

Key Terms

acephalous society	hydraulic theory of state
age grade	formation
age set	intermediary
ancestor worship	law
authority	Leopard-skin Chief
band society	negative sanction
chiefdom	oath
coercive theory of state	ordeal
formation	pan-tribal mechanism
corporate lineage	political coerciveness
council of elders	political integration
crime	positive sanction
egalitarian	public opinion
ghost invocation	rebellion
ghostly vengeance	revolution

segmentary lineage system	state society
social control	tribal society
social norm	voluntaristic theory of
socialization	state formation
song duel	witchcraft
specialized political role	

Suggested Readings

Cohen, Ronald, and Elman R. Service, eds. *Origins of the State: The Anthropology of Political Evolution*. Philadelphia: Institute for the Study of Human Issues, 1978. A collection of essays on how and why state systems of government have evolved, written by such noted political anthropologists as Morton Fried, Elman Service, and Robert Carneiro. An excellent introductory essay is written by one of the editors, Ronald Cohen.

Ferguson, R. B., ed. *Warfare, Culture and Environment*. Orlando, Fla.: Academic Press, 1984. A compilation of eleven original essays on the anthropology of warfare, written from a materialist perspective. The editor's comprehensive introductory essay provides both a thorough discussion of many of the issues involved in the anthropology of warfare and a nineteen-page bibliography.

Fried, M. H. *The Evolution of Political Society: An Essay in Political Anthropology*. New York: Random House, 1967. A classic work in the field of political anthropology setting forth the fourfold typology of political organization—egalitarian societies, rank societies, stratified societies, and states—that has been widely used as a model for classifying different types of socio-political systems.

Kuper, Hilda. *The Swazi: A South African Kingdom*. 2d ed. New York: Holt, Rinehart & Winston, 1986. An excellent short monograph on the dual monarchy of the Swazis from traditional times up to the recent present.

McGlynn, Frank, and Arthur Tuden, eds. *Anthropological Approaches to Political Behavior*. Pittsburgh: University of Pittsburgh Press, 1991. A collection of sixteen essays that highlight the major theoretical concerns of political anthropology. These articles deal with such topics as conflict resolution, leadership, ideology, and authority among small-scale societies in Africa, Latin America, Europe, and Oceania.

Mair, Lucy. *Primitive Government*. Baltimore: Penguin, 1962. A regional study of traditional political systems in East Africa ranging from such minimal governments as the Nuer to the complex interlacustrine kingdoms, which include the Ganda, Soga, Nyoro, and Ankole.

Meggitt, Mervyn. *Blood Is Their Argument*. Palo Alto, Calif.: Mayfield, 1977. An ethnographic study of warfare among the Mae Enga tribesmen of New Guinea, which explores the modes of clan warfare, the reasons for fighting, the outcomes of the conflicts, and methods for establishing peace.

Vincent, Joan. *Anthropology and Politics: Vision, Traditions, and Trends.* Tucson, Az.: University of Arizona Press, 1990. This encyclopedic work traces the history of political anthropology from the 1870s through the present by examining the questions political anthropologists have asked, the ethnographies they wrote, and the conclusions they reached. The book contains a 76-page bibliography on political anthropology.

SOCIAL STRATIFICATION

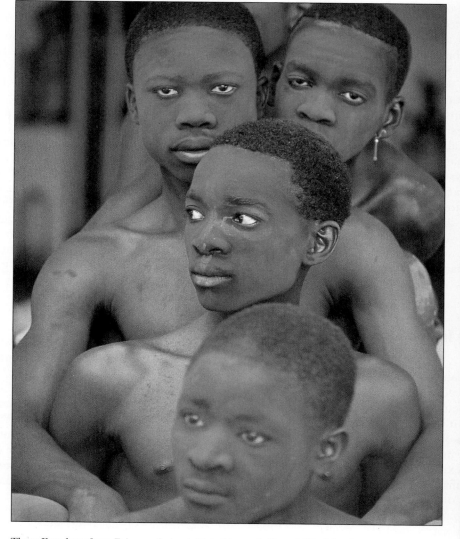

These Kota boys from Zaire are being initiated into adulthood. The blue faces symbolize the end of their childhood, blue being the color of death.

- To what extent do the societies of the world vary in terms of the equitable distribution of power, prestige, and wealth?
- How do class systems differ from caste systems?
- What are the different ways of interpreting systems of social stratification?

One important difference between the societies of the world is the degree to which individuals in any given society have equal access to wealth, power, and prestige. To one degree or another, all people are socially differentiated on the basis of such criteria as physical appearance, ethnicity, profession, family background, sex, ideology, age, or skill in performing certain kinds of economic or political roles. Societies confer a larger share of the rewards (i.e., wealth, power, and prestige) on those possessing the most admired characteristics. Scholars generally agree that all complex societies are stratified. That is, the societies make distinctions between certain groups or categories of people that are hierarchically ranked relative to one another. Many anthropologists, however, do not find systems of social stratification in the simpler societies of the world in the sense of a clear-cut division of the society into hierarchically ranked strata; even these societies, however, have role and status differences.

Dimensions of Social Inequality

Max Weber (1946) has delineated three basic criteria used for measuring levels of social inequality: wealth, power, and prestige. First, people are distinguished from one another by the extent to which they have accumulated economic resources or, in other words, their **wealth.** The forms that wealth may take vary from one society to the next. For the Mexican farmer, wealth resides in the land; for the Samburu of East Africa, a man's wealth is measured by the number of cows he has; and in the United States, most people equate their wealth with income earned in wages, property, stocks,

bonds, equity in a home, or other resources that have a cash value.

The extent of economic inequality found in any society varies from one society to the next. In some societies, such as the Pygmies, there are virtually no differences in wealth. By way of contrast, enormous differences in wealth exist in the United States. Economist Paul Samuelson has described the magnitude of the economic inequality in the United States in graphic terms: "If we made an income pyramid out of a child's blocks, with each layer portraying $1000 of income, the peak would be higher than the Eiffel Tower, but most of us would be within a yard of the ground" (1976:84).

A second dimension of social inequality, according to Weber, is **power,** which he defined as the ability to achieve one's goals and objectives even against the will of others. Power, to be certain, is often closely correlated with wealth, for economic success, particularly in Western societies, increases the chances of gaining power. Nevertheless, wealth and power do not always overlap. In certain parts of the world, power can be based on factors other than wealth, such as the possession of specialized knowledge or eloquence as a speaker. In such cases, the wealth or material possessions of the powerful and the not-so-powerful may not differ.

The third dimension of social stratification, according to Weber's formulation, is **prestige**—that is, the social esteem, respect, or admiration that a society confers on people. Since favorable social evaluation is based on the norms and values of a particular group, sources of prestige vary from one culture to another. For example, among certain North American Plains Indians, warriors on horseback held high prestige; in certain age-graded societies, such as the Samburu of Kenya, old men were accorded the highest prestige;

and in the United States, high prestige is closely associated with certain professions.

looking ahead

To see how the status of one profession (university professor) differs in two different cultures, see Applied Perspective 1 at the end of this chapter.

Research indicates that occupations in U.S. society carry different levels of prestige and that these rankings have remained remarkably stable throughout much of the present century (Counts, 1925; National Opinion Research Center, 1947; Hodge et al., 1964; and Coleman and Rainwater, 1978). Not surprisingly, physicians, corporation presidents, scientists, and top-ranking governmental officials have high levels of occupational prestige, while garbage collectors, shoe shiners, and street sweepers are at the low end of the prestige scale.

It should be kept in mind that although these three dimensions of social inequality (wealth, power, and prestige) are often interrelated, they can also operate independently of one another. To illustrate, it is possible to possess both power and wealth while having little prestige, as is the case with leaders of organized crime. Some people, such as classical pianists, may be highly esteemed for their musical virtuosity yet have modest wealth and little power or influence over people. And, odd as it may seem to Westerners, people in some societies (such as the Kwakiutl of British Columbia) acquire high prestige by actually destroying or giving away all of their personal possessions (refer to the discussion of the potlatch in the chapter on economics).

Types of Societies

Following the lead of Morton Fried (1967), most anthropologists distinguish three types of societies based on levels of social inequality: egalitarian, rank, and stratified societies. **Egalitarian societies** have few or no groups that have greater access to wealth, power, or prestige; they are usually found among hunters and gatherers, have economies based on reciprocity, and have little or no political role specialization. In **rank societies,** certain groups enjoy higher prestige, even though power and wealth are equally distributed; they are usually found among chiefdoms, have economies based on redistribution, and exhibit limited political role specialization. **Stratified societies** illustrate the greatest degree of social inequality in terms of all three forms of social rewards—that is, wealth, power, and prestige. They are found in industrialized societies, have market economies, and are associated with state systems of government. Rather than thinking of these three types of societies as discrete and mutually exclusive, it would be more accurate to view them as points on a continuum, ranging from egalitarian societies (the least amount of social inequality) to stratified societies (the greatest degree of social inequality).

Egalitarian Societies

In egalitarian societies, which are located at the low end of the inequality continuum, no individual or group has appreciably more wealth, power, or prestige than any other. Of course, even in the most egalitarian societies, personal differences in certain skills are acknowledged. Some people are more skilled than others at hunting, others may be recognized as particularly adept at crafts, while still others may be well known and respected for their skills at settling disputes. Even though certain individuals in an egalitarian society may be highly esteemed, they are not able to transform their special skills into wealth or power. No matter how much or how little respect an individual in an egalitarian society may have, he or she is neither denied the right to practice a certain profession nor subject to the control of others. Moreover, whatever esteem an individual manages to accrue is not transferable to his or her heirs.

In an egalitarian society, the number of high-status positions for which people must compete is not fixed. According to Fried, "there are as many positions of prestige in any given age-sex grade as there are persons capable of filling them" (1967:33). The esteem gained by being a highly skilled dancer will be given to as many individuals in the society as there are good dancers. If fifteen people are highly skilled dancers this year, all fifteen will receive high status. If next year there are twenty-four skilled dancers, all twenty-four will be so recognized. Thus, the number of high-status positions in an egalitarian society is constantly changing to reflect the number of qualified candidates. In other words, everyone, depending on her or his personal skill level, has equal access to positions of esteem and respect.

Band societies, such as the !Kung, tend to be highly egalitarian.

Egalitarian societies are found most readily among geographically mobile hunters and gatherers such as the !Kung of the Kalahari region, the Eskimos, and the Hadza of Tanzania. There are a number of logical reasons why unequal access to wealth, power, and prestige would be discouraged among nomadic foragers. First, the very nature of a nomadic existence inhibits the accumulation of large quantities of personal possessions. Second, since hunters and gatherers do not hold claims to territory, individuals can forage in whatever areas they please. In the event that someone might want to exercise control over others, they can choose to live in some other territory. Finally, hunters and gatherers tend to be egalitarian because sharing tends to maximize their chances for adaptation. When a hunter kills a large animal, he is unlikely to try to keep the entire carcass for himself, given the lack of refrigeration. Rather, it makes much more sense for the hunter to

share the meat with the expectation that others will share their kill with him. In fact, foraging societies, with economies based on the principle of generalized reciprocity, place a high value on sharing. Generosity in such societies is expected, while attempts to accumulate possessions, power, or prestige are ridiculed.

Frequently, egalitarian societies are transformed considerably when they come into contact with highly stratified (statelike) societies. Sometimes this transformation from egalitarian to nonegalitarian society is the result of normal cultural diffusion. Often it occurs because such a change meets the needs of colonial governments. For example, during the early part of the twentieth century, the British colonial government in Kenya created, for its own administrative convenience, local chiefs among the Kikuyu, a traditionally egalitarian people with no history of any type of chief. Although the colonial government thought it was creating new high-status positions, the Kikuyu people themselves adhered to their egalitarian ideals and failed to recognize the legitimacy of these new government-appointed chiefs.

Rank Societies

Rank societies have unequal access to prestige or status but not unequal access to wealth or power. In rank societies, there is usually a fixed number of high-status positions, which only certain individuals are able to occupy. The others are systematically excluded irrespective of their personal skills, wisdom, industriousness, or other personal traits. Such high-prestige positions as chief—which are largely hereditary in nature—establish a ranking system that distinguishes between various levels of prestige and esteem. In fact, kinship plays an important role in rank societies. Since some clans or lineages may be considered aristocratic, their members will qualify for certain titles or high-status positions. Other kin groups will be rank-ordered according to their genealogical proximity to the aristocratic kin groups. Thus, the number of high-status positions in ranked societies is limited, and the major criterion for allocating such positions is genealogical.

Even though the chiefs in a rank society possess great prestige and privilege, they generally do not accumulate great wealth, for their basic standard of living is not noticeably different from that of an ordinary person. Chiefs usually receive gifts of tribute from members of other kin groups, but they never keep them for their personal use. Instead, they give them all away through the process of redistribution (refer to the chapter on economics). In many ranked societies, chiefs are considered to "own" the land, but not in the Western sense of the term. The chief certainly has no power to keep anyone from using the land. The chief may control land to the extent that he encourages people not to neglect either the land or their obligation to contribute to the chief's tribute. But the chief has no real power or control over the land. He maintains his privileged position as chief not by virtue of his capacity to impose his will on others but rather by virtue of his generosity.

Examples of rank societies are found in most areas of the world, but most prominently in Oceania and among the Northwest Coast Indians of North America. In fact, for reasons that are not fully understood, some strikingly similar cultural traits are found in parts of Polynesia and among the Northwest Coast Indians residing in a narrow coastal region between northern California and southern Alaska. These cultural similarities are particularly noticeable in the area of status ranking. One such group that exemplifies a rank society is the Nootka of British Columbia (Service 1978). Like a number of ethnic groups in the American Northwest, the Nootka Indians, a hunting-and-fishing society, live in an area so abundant in food resources (e.g., big game, wild edible plants, waterfowl, and fish) that their standard of living is comparable to societies that practice horticulture and animal husbandry.

Social ranking among the Nootka Indians is closely related to the principle of kinship proximity. People are ranked within families according to the principle of primogeniture. Position, privileges, and titles pass from a man to his eldest son. All younger sons are of little social importance because they are not in direct line to inherit anything from the father. Furthermore, in much the same way that individuals are ranked within the family, lineages are graded according to the birth order (or genealogical proximity) of the founding ancestors of each lineage. Nootka society does not comprise clearly marked social strata but rather a large number of individual status positions ranked relative to one another. Thus, no two individuals have the exact same status.

Differential status takes a number of forms in Nootka society. First, the most visible symbol separating people of different rank is clothing. As a general rule, the higher the social position, the more ornate a person's dress. More specifically, wearing ornaments of teeth and shells or robes trimmed with the fur of sea otters is the exclusive privilege of chiefs. Second, an individual's status is directly linked to the bestowal of certain hereditary titles that are the names of important ancestors. Third, social position is expressed economically in terms of the amount of tribute (in surplus goods) a chief receives from the lower ranked individuals who acknowledge his higher status. The receipt of tribute in no way enhances the personal wealth of the chief, for he will redistribute the surplus goods back to the society in the form of elaborate feasts and ceremonies. Finally, social rank is determined by one's success in potlatch ceremonies, whereby prominent men compete with one another to see who can give away the largest quantities of material goods, such as food, blankets, and oil. Unlike Western societies, which equate high status with the accumulation of material wealth, the Nootka confer high status on those who can give away the greatest quantities of material goods. Even though potlatch ceremonies function to distribute needed material goods throughout the society, they also serve as a mechanism for validating rank.

Stratified Societies

Unlike rank societies, which are unequal only in terms of prestige, stratified societies are characterized by considerable inequality in all forms of social rewards—that is, power, wealth, and prestige. The political, economic, and social inequality in stratified societies is both permanent and formally recognized by the members of the society. Some people—and entire groups of people—have little or no access to the basic resources of the society, while others do. Various groups in stratified societies, then, are noticeably different in social position, wealth, lifestyle, access to power, and standard of living. The unequal access to rewards found in stratified societies is, by and large, inheritable from one generation to the next.

Although distinctions in wealth, power, and prestige began to appear in the early Neolithic Period (approximately 8000 B.C.), true stratified societies are closely associated with the rise of civilization in approximately 3500 B.C. A basic prerequisite for civilization is a population with a high degree of role specialization. As societies become more specialized, the system of social stratification also becomes more complex. Different occupations or economic interest groups will not have the same access to wealth, power, and prestige but rather will be ranked relative to one another. As a general rule, the greater the role specialization, the more complex the system of stratification.

Class versus Caste. Social scientists generally recognize two different types of stratified societies: those

In stratified societies different groups have different levels of power, prestige, and wealth, ranging from the homeless to the upper class.

based on **class** and those based on **caste.** The key to understanding this fundamental distinction is **social mobility.** In class systems, a certain amount of both upward and downward social mobility exists. In other words, an individual can change his or her social position dramatically within a lifetime. An individual, through diligence, intelligence, and good luck, could go from "rags to riches"; and conversely, a person born to millionaire parents could wind up as a homeless street person (Newman 1988). Caste societies, on the other hand, have no social mobility. Membership in a caste is determined by birth and lasts throughout one's lifetime. Whereas members of a class society are able to elevate their social position by marrying into a higher class, caste systems are strictly endogamous (allowing marriages only within one's own caste).

Another important distinction is how statuses (positions) within each type of society are allocated. Class systems are associated with an **achieved status** while caste systems are associated with an **ascribed status.** Achieved statuses are those that the individual chooses or at least has some control over. An achieved status is one that a person has as a result of her or his personal effort, such as graduating from college, marrying someone, or taking a particular job. By way of contrast, a person is born into an ascribed status and has no control over it. Statuses based on such criteria as sex, race, or age are examples of ascribed statuses, which are found mainly in caste societies.

It is important to bear in mind that stratified societies cannot all be divided neatly into either class or caste systems. In general, though class systems are open to the extent that they are based on achieved statuses and permit considerable social mobility, and caste systems tend to be closed in that they are based on ascribed statuses and allow little or no social mobility, either up or down. Having made these conceptual distinctions, however, we must also realize that in the real world, class and caste systems overlap. In other words, most stratified societies contain elements of both class and caste. Rather than think in either-or terms, we should think in terms of polarities on the ends of a continuum. There are no societies that have either absolute mobility (perfect class systems) or a total lack of mobility (perfect caste systems). Rather, all stratified societies found in the world fall somewhere between these two ideal polarities, depending on the relative amount of social mobility permitted in each.

Class Societies. Even though the boundaries between social strata in a class society are not rigidly drawn, social inequalities nevertheless exist. A social class is a segment of a population whose members share relatively similar lifestyles and levels of wealth, power, and prestige. The United States is a good example of a class society. In some areas of the United States, such as coal-mining towns in Appalachia, there may be only two classes—the haves and the have-nots. More fre-

CROSS-CULTURAL MISCUE

The scene is a classroom in an inner-city elementary school in Richmond, Virginia. Pedro, the nine-year-old son of a recent immigrant family from Puerto Rico, leaves his seat to sharpen his pencil. When the teacher, Ms. Harkins, asks Pedro where he is going, Pedro casts his eyes downward and tries to explain that he was going to the pencil sharpener. Ms. Harkins, thinking that Pedro has something to hide by not looking her in the eye, becomes so annoyed with him that she lifts up his chin and says, "Look at me when I'm talking to you!" Pedro cannot understand what he did wrong that made his teacher so angry.

This unfortunate scenario—played out all too often in our multicultural schools—is a classic example of how cross-cultural communication can be short-circuited. This needless escalation of ill will between student and teacher could have been avoided if Ms. Harkins had understood a fundamental feature of nonverbal communication in Pedro's Puerto Rican culture. In the teacher's mainstream U.S. culture, the student is expected to maintain a high level of eye contact with the teacher as a sign of respect. But in Puerto Rico, Pedro learned not only a different meaning of eye contact but also an opposite meaning. That is, in Puerto Rican culture, children are taught to *avoid* eye contact as a sign of respect for high-status people, such as teachers, priests, grandparents, and adults in general. Thus, while Pedro was trying to show the greatest respect for his teacher by avoiding eye contact, Ms. Harkins mistook his downcast eyes as a sign of disrespect or disinterest. This cross-cultural misunderstanding—stemming from a lack of knowledge about other cultures—hardly contributed to student-teacher rapport.

---

quently, however, social scientists have identified five (or more) social classes: upper, upper middle, lower middle, working, and lower classes (Bensman and Vidich 1987; Vanneman and Cannon 1987; and Sullivan and Thompson 1990).

looking ahead

To better comprehend how an understanding of different class groups in the United States can help redesign a public park, see Applied Perspective 2 at the end of this chapter.

The *upper class* in the United States, comprising approximately 4 percent of the population, consists of (1) old wealth (Carnegies, Rockefellers), (2) those who

have recently made fortunes (**nouveau riche**), and (3) top government and judicial officials who, despite modest wealth, wield considerable power.

The *upper middle class,* comprising about 12 percent to 15 percent of the U.S. population, is made up of business and professional people with relatively high incomes and modest amounts of overall wealth.

The *lower middle class,* constituting approximately one-third of our population, is made up of hard-working people of modest income, such as petty entrepreneurs, teachers, civil servants, and lower-level managers.

The largest segment of the U.S. population (approximately 45 percent) is the *working class,* comprised of such people as factory workers, construction workers, furniture movers, and appliance repairpersons.

Although we like to think that there is a good deal of upward social mobility in the United States, how likely is it that this youngster growing up in the South Bronx, New York, will gain entry into the upper class?

Although these blue-collar workers may earn more income than some members of the lower middle class, their class carries considerably less prestige.

At the bottom of the status hierarchy is the *lower class*, comprising migrant workers, the unemployed, and certain marginal groups that are barely surviving in society, such as the homeless, the noninstitutionalized mentally ill, and derelicts with severe substance abuse problems.

Our national mythology includes the belief that a good deal of social mobility exists in the United States. After all, there are no formal or legal barriers to equality, and we all grow up believing that it is possible for anyone (or at least, any white male) to become president of the United States. Although it is possible to cite a number of contemporary Americans who have attained great wealth, power, and prestige from modest beginnings, studies of social class in the United States have shown that most people remain in the class into which they are born and marry within that class as well.

In many cases, a child's physical and social environment will greatly influence her or his life's chances and identification with a particular class. To illustrate, the son of a school janitor in Philadelphia living in a lower-class neighborhood will spend his formative years playing in crowded public playgrounds, working at the grocery store after school, and generally hanging out with kids from the neighborhood. The son of a bank president, on the other hand, also living in Philadelphia, will attend a fashionable prep school, take tennis lessons at the country club, and drive his own car. When the two youths finish high school, the janitor's son will probably not continue his education, while the banker's son will go off to a good college, perhaps follow that with law school, and then land a high-paying job. Even though it is possible that the janitor's son could go to Harvard Law School and become very upwardly mobile, such a scenario is not very likely.

Members of the same social class share not only similar economic levels but also similar experiences, educational backgrounds, political views, memberships in organizations, occupations, and values. In addition, studies of social class have shown, not surprisingly, that members of a social class tend to associate more frequently with one another than with people in other classes. In other words, a person's life chances, while not determined, are very much influenced by that person's social class.

Caste Societies.   In contrast, societies based on caste rank their members according to birth. Membership in castes is unchangeable, people in different castes are segregated from one another, social mobility is virtually nonexistent, and marriage between castes is strictly prohibited. Castes, which are usually associated with specific occupations, are ranked hierarchically relative to one another.

Caste societies, wherever they may be found, have a number of characteristics in common. First, caste membership is directly related to such economic issues as occupation, workloads, and control of valuable resources. The higher castes have a monopoly on certain occupations, control the allocation of resources to favor themselves, and avoid engaging in difficult or low-status work. In short, the higher castes have more and do less. Second, members of the same caste share the same social status, owing in large part to their strong sense of caste identity, residential and social segregation from other castes, and uniformity of lifestyles. Third, caste exclusiveness is further enhanced since each caste has its own set of secret rituals, which tend to intensify group awareness. And fourth, the higher castes are generally most interested in maintaining the caste system for the obvious reason that they benefit from it the most.

Hindu Caste System.   While caste societies can be found in a number of regions of the world, such as among the Rwanda in Central Africa, the best known—and certainly the best described—example of the caste system is in Hindu India. Hinduism's sacred Sanskrit texts rank all people into one of four categories, called **varnas,** which are associated with certain occupations. Even though local villagers may not always agree as to who belongs to which *varna,* most people accept the *varna* categories as fundamentally essential elements of their society.

According to a Hindu myth of origin (see Mandelbaum 1970:22–23), the four major *varnas* originated from the body of primeval man. The highest caste Brahmins (priests and scholars) came from his mouth; the Kshatriyas (warriors) emanated from his arms; the Vaishyas (tradesmen) came from his thighs; and the Shudras (cultivators and servants) sprang from his feet. Each of these four castes is hierarchically ranked according to its ritual purity. Below these four castes—and technically outside the caste system—is still another category, called the Untouchables or, literally, outcastes. The Untouchables, who are confined to the lowest and most menial types of work, such as cleaning latrines or leatherworking, are considered so impure that members of the four legitimate castes must avoid all contact with them.

Ideally, all of Hindu India is hierarchically ranked according to these four basic castes. In actual practice, however, each of these four categories is further subdivided and stratified. To add to the complexity of the Indian caste system, the order in which these subcastes are ranked varies from one region to another. These local subgroups, known as **jati,** are local family groups that are strictly endogamous. All members of a *jati,* who share a common social status, are expected to behave in ways appropriate for that *jati.* A person's *jati* commands his or her strongest loyalties, serves as a source of social support, and provides the primary basis for personal identity. Thus, the *jati* serves as the important social entity in traditional Hindu society. The members of each *jati* maintain its corporateness in two ways: (1) through egalitarian socializing with members of their own jati and (2) by scrupulously avoiding any type of egalitarian socializing (e.g., marriage or sharing of food) with members of other *jati.* Though the *jati* were originally linked to traditional occupations, that is no longer the case. For instance, today most members of the traditional leather worker caste are landless laborers.

Even though the Indian government has attempted to discourage it legislatively, the caste system still plays an important role in the lives of most contemporary Indians. A major reason for the continued adherence to the principles of caste is that it is strongly sanctioned by

In India the untouchables, who must refrain from having social contact with members of the four major castes, are relegated to the most menial occupations.

the Hindu religion. According to Hindu religious teachings, members of higher castes must do everything possible to retain their ritual purity by avoiding any type of intimate interaction with members of lower castes; and correspondingly, members of lower castes must refrain from polluting higher castes.

An important tenet of Hindu religious teachings is reincarnation, the notion that at death a person's soul is reborn in an endless sequence of new forms. The caste into which a person is born is considered to be her or his duty and responsibility for that lifetime. Hindu scripture teaches that the good life involves living according to the prescriptions of the person's caste. It is taught that those who violate their caste prescription will come back in a lower caste or, if the transgression is sufficiently serious, in a nonhuman form. Hindu scripture is very explicit about the consequences of violating prescribed caste behaviors. For example, the Brahmin who steals the gold of another Brahmin will be reincarnated in the next thousand lives as a snake, a spider, or a lizard. That's a powerful sanction! In other words, it is believed that people's caste status is determined by how they behaved in former lives and that their present behavior determines their caste status in future lives.

Even though the prohibitions against social intercourse between castes are as rigidly defined as anywhere in the world, the amount of interdependence among local castes should not be overlooked. This interdependence is largely economic in nature rather than social. Like any society with a complex economy, India has an elaborate division of labor. In fact, one of the basic features of caste in India is that each *jati* is associated with its own traditional occupation that provides goods or services for the rest of the society. Certain lower-caste *jati* (such as barbers, potters, and leather workers) provide vital services for the upper echelon (landowning) castes from whom they receive food and animal products. For the economy to work, lower castes sell their services to the upper castes in exchange for goods. Thus, despite the very high level of social segregation between the castes in India, there is considerable economic interrelatedness, particularly at the village level.

Racial and Ethnic Stratification

The discipline of anthropology has as its primary goal to study the extraordinary physical and cultural diversity found among the world's population. This vast physical and cultural diversity is also of great interest to the peoples themselves because human relationships are often shaped by the differences, either real or imagined, between groups or subgroups of people. To one degree or another, all societies differentiate among their members, and these differences can become the basis for social inequalities. People are often characterized on the basis of their distinctive physical characteristics or their learned cultural traits. Those sharing similar physical traits are often defined as belonging to the same **race,** while those sharing similar cultural characteristics are said to belong to the same **ethnic group.**

Throughout history, in many parts of the world racial and ethnic differences have led to inequality, discrimination, antagonism, and, in some cases, violence. Each day we read in the newspaper about racial and/or ethnic conflict in various parts of the world—the Irish Republican Army bombing in England, the "ethnic cleansing" in Bosnia, terrorist attacks on Palestinians and Jews in Israel, and long-standing ethnic antagonisms between the Japanese and Koreans. And, of course, much closer to home we have racial rioting in Los Angeles, ethnic gang wars in our cities, and widespread resentment that recent immigrants from Southeast Asia are taking so many places in our best universities. So even in the United States—a country constitutionally and legally committed to social equality—physical (racial) or cultural (ethnic) differences still greatly affect relations between groups and their relative positions in the social hierarchy.

The terms "race" and "ethnicity" are sometimes used synonymously in everyday speech, but to anthropologists they have very different meanings. Technically, a race is *an interbreeding population whose members share a greater number of traits with one another than they do with people outside the group.* During the first half of the present century, physical anthropologists devoted considerable effort to dividing the world's populations into racial categories based on shared physical traits. They carefully measured such traits as hair color and texture, eye color and shape, thickness of lips, breadth of the nose, body stature, and skin color, among others. But when the measuring frenzy was over, what did we really have? Depending on who was doing the categorizing, some racial typologies had hundreds of categories (i.e., "races") while others had as few as three (Mongoloid, Caucasoid, and Negroid).

Race, then, is no more than a statistical statement about the occurrence of physical traits. When people who share a large number of biological traits intermarry, it is likely (but by no means certain) that they will have offspring who share those traits. When two blond-haired, blue-eyed Norwegians mate and have children, those children are statistically more likely to look like Scandinavians than like Nigerians. Similarly, when we cross two Chihuahuas, the offspring are more likely to look like Chihuahuas than Great Danes. Based on our knowledge of genetics, we know that there are no pure races, because recessive traits are not lost but can reappear in future generations. Since different populations have been interbreeding for thousands of years, a continuum of human physical types has resulted.

A major problem with racial classifications is that the schemes differ depending on the traits on which they are based. That is, it would be possible to put all of the world's people into a number of different categories based on skin color. But, if those same people were categorized according to body stature, many people would be assigned to different categories. Each physical trait is biologically determined by distinct genes that vary independently of one another. Therefore, having a particular color of hair in no way will determine what your eye color will be. All those physical anthropologists who have attempted to classify people according to race have arbitrarily selected the traits they have used. For example, instead of using skin color or blood type, we could classify people according to their earlobe structure (attached or detached earlobes), which is also a genetically determined physical trait. Although no one ever has, we could divide the world's population into two major races: those with attached earlobes and those with detached earlobes. Then, also quite arbitrarily, we could assert that people with attached earlobes (like your author) are clearly more intelligent than those with detached earlobes. Furthermore, they are of better character and are more likely to practice good personal hygiene. Moreover, we could then insist that we don't want people with detached earlobes living in our neighborhoods, going to our schools, or marrying our daughters. That stand would make as much scientific sense as basing such a position on any other physical characteristic, such as skin color.

As a scientific concept, then, race is not terribly significant, for it gives us very little insight into human behavior. Nevertheless, owing to the way people interpret physical differences, race is important socially. That is, it makes little difference that beliefs about race have no scientific basis. Race relations and stratification based on race are affected by people's beliefs, not necessarily by scientific facts. The consequences of people's beliefs can be very powerful. All too often in human history, groups have separated themselves according to

Though the concept of race has little scientific significance, it is extremely important socially.

physical differences. They soon decide that physically different people are inferior and then use that belief to exclude, exploit, or brutalize them.

Whereas race refers to physical traits, ethnicity refers to cultural traits that are passed on from generation to generation. These cultural traits may include religion, dietary practices, language, humor, clothing, cultural heritage, folklore, national origins, and a shared ancestry and social experience. Members of an ethnic group perceive themselves as sharing these (and perhaps other) cultural characteristics. Moreover, ethnic group members have a sense of ethnic identity whereby they define themselves and members of their group as "us" and everyone else as "them." Because of their cultural homogeneity, ethnic groups tend to cut across socioeconomic lines.

In some cases certain groups are both racially and ethnically distinct from their neighbors. For example, some Native Americans, such as the Zuni, have very distinctive physical features and also identify themselves strongly with their native language, political organizations, family networks, and cultural practices. Other groups such as Italian-Americans and Greek-Americans may look alike, but will form their own distinctive (and usually exclusive) social clubs and social networks.

For much of the present century, people in the United States have described the nation as a large "melting pot" in which people from many cultural backgrounds were fused into a homogeneous American nationality. However, this idea of mass cultural amalgamation has not been realized. Although significant numbers of individuals have broken out of their ethnic

Many ethnic groups, such as the Chinese in Los Angeles, maintain their own distinct neighborhood and sense of cultural identity even though they have lived in the United States for generations.

patterns, ethnic groups remain. In fact, the United States has experienced a revival of ethnic consciousness in recent decades, particularly in urban areas. We frequently hear about ethnic neighborhoods, ethnic foods, and various ethnic studies programs at universities. Thus, the notion of the "melting pot" appears to be more of a metaphor than a reality. Perhaps we should think of contemporary American society less as a melting pot and more as a "salad bowl," in which the individual ethnic groups are mixed together but retain their own distinctiveness and identity.

Some racial and ethnic groups are able to live together in relative peace and with a large degree of social equality. In most situations, however, racial and ethnic groups tend to engage in varying levels of conflict and inequality. How racial and ethnic groups relate to one another can be viewed as a continuum ranging from cooperation to outright hostility. Simpson and Yinger (1985) have identified six major forms of interracial and interethnic relations:

1. Assimilation. With **assimilation,** a racial or ethnic minority is assimilated or absorbed into the wider society. The many Asian and Pacific ethnic groups that have peacefully and voluntarily assimilated themselves into Hawaiian society over the past several centuries are an example.

2. Pluralism. With **pluralism,** two or more groups live in harmony with one another while retaining their own racial or ethnic heritage, pride, and identity. Swiss society, comprised of Germans, Swiss Germans, French, and Italians living together amicably, is a good example of a pluralistic society.

3. Legal Protection of Minorities. In societies where racial and ethnic groups are hostile toward one another, the government may step in to legally protect the minority group(s). In Great Britain the Race Relations Act makes it a criminal offense for anyone to publicly express any sentiments that might lead to racial or ethnic hostility.

4. Population Transfer. One "solution" to intergroup conflict is **population transfer,** which involves the physical removal of a minority group to another location. The forced relocation of 16,000 Cherokee Indians from North Carolina to Oklahoma in 1838 is a case in point.

5. Long-Term Subjugation. In some parts of the world, racial and ethnic minorities have been politically, economically, and socially repressed for indefinite periods of time. Until the recent changes, the repression of Blacks under the apartheid system in the Republic of South Africa was an example of the long-term institutionalized (legal) repression of one ethnic and racial group by another.

6. Extermination. This involves the actual physical annihilation of a racial or ethnic group. While Hitler attempted genocide on the largest scale in history, there are many other examples of extermination from around the world involving fewer deaths, such as the extinction of the Tasmanians by British settlers, the wholesale slaughter of Hutu ethnics by Tutsi ethnics in

Burundi, the equally wholesale slaughter of Tutsi by Hutu in Rwanda, and the "ethnic cleansing" occurring in Bosnia at the time of this writing.

It is important to note that these ways of classifying racial/ethnic relations are not mutually exclusive. More than one can exist in a society at the same time.

Theories of Stratification

The inequitable distribution of wealth, power, and prestige appears to be a fundamental characteristic of most societies, particularly those with complex, highly differentiated economies. Some modern societies—such as the former Soviet Union, the People's Republic of China, and Albania—have attempted to become classless by eliminating all vestiges of inequality. But even in these societies, high-ranking government officials have been far more generously rewarded than the rank and file.

The basic question is, Why is inequality a nearly universal trait of social life? The debate between social scientists, which at times has become heated, revolves around two conflicting positions, which are based on different philosophical assumptions and have distinct political implications. The more conservative position, the **functional theory,** holds that social inequality exists because it is necessary for the maintenance of society. The more liberal **conflict theory** explains social inequality as the result of benefits derived by the upper classes who use their power and privilege to exploit those below them.

The Functionalist Interpretation

By stressing the integrative nature of social systems, functional anthropologists argue that stratification exists because it contributes to the overall well-being of the society. According to Davis and Moore (1945), complex societies, if they are to survive, depend on the performance of a wide variety of jobs, some of which are more important than others because they require specialized education, talent, and hard work. If people are to make the sacrifices necessary to perform these vital jobs, they must be adequately rewarded. For example, since the skills of a physician are in greater demand by our society than are those of a garbage collector, the rewards (money and prestige) are much greater for the physician. Functionalists argue that these differential

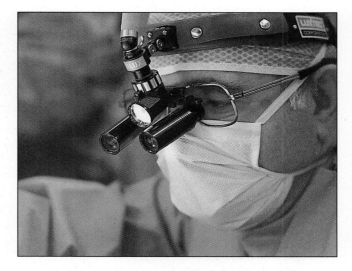

Functional theorists argue that stratification is necessary because it motivates the most highly skilled people to fill the important jobs in the society. They believe that if there were no status differences between physicians and garbage collectors, there would be no incentive to become a physician.

rewards are necessary if societies are to recruit the best trained and most highly skilled people for these highly valued positions. If physicians and garbage collectors received the same pay and social status, few people would opt to become physicians. Thus, according to the functionalist interpretation, social stratification is necessary or functional for the society because it serves as a mechanism for allocating rewards and motivating the best people to fill the key jobs in the society.

While the functionalist view seems quite plausible, it is not without its weaknesses. First, some critics of the functionalist position point out that stratified societies do not always give the greatest rewards to those filling the most vital positions. Rock singers, baseball players, and movie stars often make many times more money than teachers, pediatricians, or U.S. Supreme Court justices. Second, the functionalists do not recognize the barriers that stratification systems put in the way of certain segments of the society, namely, members of low prestige and powerless groups. Ethnic and racial minorities, women, and the poor don't always have equal opportunities to compete because they are too poor or have the wrong accent, skin color, or gender. Third, the functionalist position can be called into question because it tends to make a fundamentally ethnocentric assumption. That is, the functionalists assume that people in all societies are motivated by the desire to maximize their wealth, power, and prestige. In actual

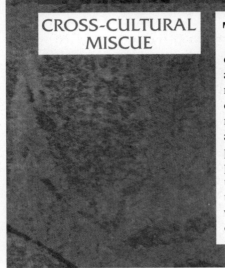

CROSS-CULTURAL MISCUE

The marketing manager of a U.S. knitwear firm was delighted with a multimillion-dollar order for men's underwear it received from a department store chain in Saudi Arabia. The jockey shorts were packaged in the usual way (three pair to a package, with a picture of a male modeling the briefs) and sent off to the customer in Saudi Arabia. However, Saudi customs officials were shocked to see an almost totally nude man on packages that would be displayed in plain sight of Saudi women and children. In a country with very strict cultural taboos on nudity, such packaging was considered a form of obscenity, hardly acceptable for public display in department stores. Consequently, to satisfy Saudi customs officials, the entire shipment of men's briefs had to be sent back to the United States for repackaging at a cost of thousands of dollars. This was certainly a high price to pay for not understanding the culture of one's customers.

fact, however, a number of societies tend to emphasize the relatively equitable distribution of social rewards rather than rewarding individuals for amassing as much as possible for themselves.

Conflict Theory Interpretation

Whereas the functionalist view starts with the assumption of social order, stability, and integration, conflict theorists assume that the natural tendency of all societies is toward change and conflict. According to this theory, stratification exists because those people occupying the upper levels of the hierarchy are willing and able to use their wealth, power, and prestige to exploit those below them. The upper strata maintain their dominance through the use of force or the threat of force and by convincing the oppressed of the value of continuing the system. Thus, those at the top use their wealth, power, and prestige to maintain—perhaps even increase—their privileged position.

This conflict theory of social stratification is derived largely from the late nineteenth-century writings of Karl Marx, who, unlike the functionalists, did not view stratification systems as either desirable or inevitable. Believing that economic forces are the main factors shaping a society, Marx (1909) viewed history as a con-

stant class struggle between the haves and the have-nots. Writing during the latter stages of the Industrial Revolution in Europe, Marx saw the classic struggle occurring between the **bourgeoisie** (those who owned the means of production) and the **proletariat** (the working class who exchanged their labor for wages).

Owing to their control of the means of production, the relatively small bourgeoisie exert significant influence over the larger working class. By controlling such institutions as schools, factories, government, and the media, the bourgeoisie can convince the workers that the existing distribution of power and wealth (i.e., the status quo) is preferable and that anyone can be successful if only he or she works hard enough. Thus, according to the classical Marxist view, the bourgeoisie create a "false consciousness" among the workers by leading them to believe that if they are not successful, it is because they have not worked hard enough rather than because their opportunities for advancement were blocked by the powerful upper class.

As long as the workers accept this ideology legitimizing the status quo, the inequities of the stratification system will continue to exist. Believing that class conflict is inevitable, Marx predicted that eventually the proletariat would recognize both the extent of their own exploitation and their collective power to change it.

When the workers develop a class consciousness, they will revolt against the existing social order, replace capitalism with communism, and eliminate scarcity, social classes, and inequality.

Functionalists versus Conflict Theorists

The functionalists and the conflict theorists—with their radically different interpretations of social inequality—have been locking horns for years. The functionalists hold that systems of stratification exist and are therefore necessary because they benefit the societies of which they are a part. The conflict theorists, on the other hand, claim that systems of stratification exist because they help the people at the top (i.e., the wealthy and powerful) maintain their privileged position. The functionalist position emphasizes the positive benefits of social stratification for the total society. The conflict theorists draw our attention to such negative aspects as the unjust nature of stratification systems and how that inherent unfairness can lead to rebellions, revolts, and high crime rates.

While there is truth in both of these interpretations, neither theory can be used exclusively to explain the existence of all types of stratification systems. The functionalists are correct to point out that open class systems, for example, are integrative to the extent that they promote constructive endeavor that is beneficial to the society as a whole. Yet, once established, these class systems often become self-perpetuating, with those at the top striving to maintain their superior positions at the expense of the lower classes. At the same time, the underclasses—through political mobilization, revitalization movements, and even violent revolutions—seek to free themselves from deprivation and exploitation. In short, functional integration is real, but then, so is conflict.

Not only do the functionalists and the conflict theorists represent two contrasting interpretations of social inequality, but they also have radically different policy implications for modern society. The functionalist view carries with it the implication that social stratification systems should be maintained because the best qualified people, through the competitive process, will be motivated to fill the top positions. In contrast, the view of the conflict theorists implies that social inequality should be minimized or eliminated altogether because many people in the lower strata never had a chance to develop their full potential. Thus, the functionalist position would want the government to take no action (e.g., welfare programs or a progressive income tax) that would redistribute wealth, power, or prestige. The conflict theorists would call for exactly the opposite governmental course of action, arguing that eliminating barriers to social mobility would unleash the hidden brilliance of those currently living in the underclasses.

A main objective of this chapter has been to show variations in the extent to which people have access to wealth, power, and prestige. At one extreme, egalitarian societies make relatively few distinctions between people on these three dimensions, while at the other extreme, stratified societies recognize marked distinctions. People occupying different social strata within a society often have different levels of affluence, ways of behaving, and values. Sometimes when operating in an unfamiliar cultural setting, we fail to fully appreciate the fact that people occupying different social strata have quite different views of the world. The first case study illustrates how an interpersonal problem was avoided by understanding the values attached to the role of university professor in two different cultures. The second case shows how architects used ethnographic field methods to study different socioeconomic class groups as part of a plan to revitalize an inner city park.

applied PERSPECTIVE

Social Stratification

A university mathematics professor draws upon knowledge of status systems in West Africa to avoid a potential misunderstanding between his students.

A mathematics professor from a large university in North Carolina was walking to class with an armload of books when he met a group of five students from his class. Four of the students were native North Carolinians,

while the fifth was an exchange student from Nigeria. When the professor and his students met, they greeted one another and proceeded to walk together to class. Almost immediately, the Nigerian student turned to the professor and asked if he could carry the professor's books. The professor declined the offer, but the Nigerian student insisted. As the professor finally relented and gave the books to the student, he noticed he was receiving some "funny looks" from his American students. It was immediately apparent to the professor that the American students thought that the Nigerian had offered to carry the books in an effort to curry favor and perhaps get a higher grade in the course than he might deserve. The American students were clearly put off by what they considered to be the Nigerian's blatant attempt to better his grade.

As the professor continued to walk to class with his students, he remembered a discussion he had had several weeks earlier with a colleague from the anthropology department. The anthropologist had mentioned that when he was a visiting professor at a Nigerian university, he was astounded at how much deference his students showed him. The recollection of the conversation raised an interesting question for the mathematics professor: Could this be a cross-cultural misunderstanding?

The professor decided to take the remaining minutes before class to discuss the apparent bad feelings the U.S. students were having toward their classmate from Nigeria. He presented the students with his perception of what had occurred. The U.S. students admitted that they were feeling a good deal of resentment because they felt the Nigerian student was not "playing fairly" in the competition for good grades. Hearing this, the Nigerian student was shocked that his gesture to carry the professor's books had been so utterly misunderstood. He went on to explain that he had offered to carry the books out of a deep sense of respect for the professor's high status. University professors in Nigeria have a much higher social status among the general population than they have in the United States. It would be considered demeaning for a professor in Nigeria to engage in any type of manual labor, including carrying a heavy load of books. The Nigerian student went on to explain that he had offered to carry the books so that the professor would not "lose face" by engaging in physical labor.

This all made perfectly good sense to the American students once their Nigerian classmate had explained it to them. The key, of course, to avoiding the potential cross-cultural conflict was understanding that the status system in Nigeria is appreciably different from that found in the United States. Much to his credit, the mathematics professor used his (albeit modest) knowledge of status systems in Nigeria to help diffuse some hard feelings among his students—and in the process taught them something about the need to understand cultural differences.

THOUGHT QUESTIONS

1. What is the difference between Nigerian and American students' perceptions of university professors?

2. In your dealings with foreign students on campus, have you noticed differences in the ways they treat their professors?

3. Do you think that a woman professor would have evoked the same response from the Nigerian student?

Applying anthropological data-gathering techniques, landscape architects use cultural data collected from different constituencies (i.e., strata) in an inner city to plan the rejuvenation of a public park.

applied **PERSPECTIVE** *continued*

A basic premise of this chapter is that, to one degree or another, all societies are segmented into groups that have different access to wealth, power, and prestige. In such societies as the United States, various groups differ appreciably in terms of their access to power, social position, lifestyles, and standards of living. These segments of U.S. society, which are referred to as classes, often display marked differences in life experiences, political positions, educational backgrounds, and values. Understanding the subcultural and class differences that exist in our own society is just as important as knowing something about the lifeways, values, and behavior patterns of culturally different people abroad.

Anthropologist Setha Low, a professor of landscape architecture at the University of Pennsylvania, put this basic principle into operation when planning the restoration of Farnham Park in Camden, New Jersey. A derelict park located along the Cooper River, Farnham Park was the subject of a rehabilitation project by a class of University of Pennsylvania architecture students during the 1980s. Located on a once ecologically rich tidal estuary, the park was drastically altered by decades of industrialization and was eventually abandoned because the surrounding area suffered from social and economic decline. At the time that the rehabilitation study was initiated, the site was surrounded by a highway, some schools, and several ethnic neighborhoods, all of which were suffering from urban decay. As one member of the study team described it:

> Certain areas of the park stand out in their unpleasantness—the large accumulation of trash at the west end of the pond is particularly unpleasant—tires, mattresses, appliances, plaster lie in piles along the drive and at the water's edge. A small pavilion near the school is littered with broken glass. . . . Large numbers of students stood around in groups on the corner and park edge opposite the high school during their lunch hours talking, smoking, buying food from the lunch trucks. . . . the major use of the park was abuse—drinking, dumping, breaking bottles. . . . (Low 1981:6–7)

Once the city expressed an interest in restoring the park, a number of important design questions emerged. What does the city, and particularly this neighborhood, need in the way of a park? What features should such a park have given the rapid rate of social and economic change? How does one answer these questions given the parameters, constraints, and opportunities of the site? The design team attempted to answer these questions by conducting a comprehensive research project using, among other techniques, anthropological data-gathering strategies, including participant-observation, ethnographic interviewing, and social mapping. Data were gathered on the values and behavior patterns of local residents, their current use of the space, their perception of problems, their past memories of the area, and their preferences for a park for the future.

A significant part of the data collection for this project involved the identification of the dominant values and cultural features of the major social constituencies. Who, in other words, were the major players who had

an interest in the rehabilitation of the park? The research team identified six interest groups:

1. The parkside residents who wanted a nice, quiet park for families to picnic.
2. The unemployed youth and teenagers who "hung out" on the basketball courts.
3. The teachers and administrators from nearby schools who wanted the park to be restored as a nature center for educational purposes.
4. The young children who wanted to use the gym equipment but were reluctant to do so because they were afraid of the older children.
5. Members of the city government who would finance the improvement to the park.
6. The county government officials who would finance the ongoing maintenance of the facility.

Each group was asked to prepare a sketch plan of the proposed park that reflected their own values, interests, and needs. These plans were then analyzed by the research team, which tried to identify points of commonality among the constituencies. Agreement was found on the following elements: (1) the restoration of the dike that would stabilize the size of the pond; (2) the creation of a large grassy area; (3) the maintenance of a wildlife area; (4) the provision of picnic tables; (5) the creation of sports fields; (6) the encouragement of fishing and other passive water sports; (7) the provision of special skills equipment; (8) the creation of a cultural activities center; and (9) the inclusion of biking, walking, and jogging trails. Once the team was able to identify elements that appealed to all constituencies, they were able to start the design phase of the park rehabilitation project.

Here, then, is another example of the utility of cultural knowledge. In this scenario illustrated by the work of Setha Low, we can see how an understanding of the norms, values, and behavior patterns of different subcultures in a community can inform the process that landscape architects use for designing public parks. The use of qualitative methods such as social mapping, participant-observation, and ethnographic interviewing can provide a solid social basis on which the aesthetic principles of architectural design can build. These techniques can also identify potential conflicts between the values of professional architects on the one hand and those of the user populations on the other. Then, in the event that such conflicts emerge, the anthropological approach serves to remind the architect that the perceptions, values, and interests of the user groups must be taken into account if the end product is to be functional.

THOUGHT QUESTIONS

1. In what ways can anthropologists be valuable employees of an architectural firm?
2. How can cultural knowledge contribute to the style and function of architectural design?
3. Would the restoration of the park have been successful (even possible) without the input of the major neighborhood groups? Why?

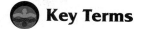

Summary

1. Social ranking is an important feature found to one degree or another in all societies. The degree to which societies distribute wealth, power, and prestige on an equitable basis can be used to distinguish between three different types of societies. Egalitarian societies are unstratified in that they allocate wealth, power, and prestige relatively equally. In rank societies, which are partially stratified, people have equal access to power and wealth but not to prestige. The most completely stratified societies are those based on classes or castes that have unequal access to wealth, power, and prestige.

2. Stratified societies, which are associated with the rise of civilization, range from open class societies, which permit high social mobility, to more rigid caste societies, which allow for no social mobility. Class societies are associated with achieved status, those positions that the individual can choose or at least have some control over. Caste societies, on the other hand, are based on ascribed statuses into which one is born and cannot change.

3. The United States is often cited as a prime example of a class society with maximum mobility. Although our national credo includes a belief in the possibility of going from rags to riches, most people in the United States remain in the class into which they are born, because social environment has an appreciable effect on a person's life chances.

4. Hindu India is often cited as the most extreme form of caste society found in the world. Social boundaries between castes are strictly maintained by caste endogamy and strongly held notions of ritual purity and pollution.

5. Race refers to a classification of people based on physical traits while ethnicity is a scheme based on cultural characteristics. Though the concept of race is not particularly meaningful from a scientific standpoint, it is important because people's ideas of racial differences have led to very powerful systems of stratification and discrimination.

6. There have been two conflicting interpretations of social stratification. The functionalist theory emphasizes the integrative nature of stratification systems by pointing out how class systems contribute to the overall well-being of a society by encouraging constructive endeavor. The conflict theorists believe that stratification systems exist because the upper classes strive to maintain their superior position at the expense of the lower classes.

Key Terms

achieved status
ascribed status
assimilation
bourgeoisie
caste
class
conflict theory
egalitarian societies
ethnic group
functional theory
jati
nouveau riche

pluralism
population transfer
power
prestige
proletariat
race
rank societies
social mobility
stratified societies
varnas
wealth

Suggested Reading

Bernardi, Bernardo. *Age Class Systems: Social Institutions and Policies Based on Age.* New York: Cambridge University Press, 1985. Drawing on ethnographic data largely from Africa, the author defines the characteristics of age class systems, their geographic distribution, and various anthropological approaches to their study.

Berreman, Gerald D., and Kathleen M. Zaretsky, eds. *Social Inequality: Comparative and Development Approaches.* New York: Academic Press, 1981. A collection of fifteen essays on the topic of social inequality that attempts to treat the subject (1) comparatively across a wide range of cultures, (2) comparatively over time, and (3) within the appropriate sociocultural context.

Fried, Morton. *The Evolution of Political Society.* New York: Random House, 1967. A widely quoted work that examines three fundamentally different types of societies (egalitarian, rank, and stratified) and how they relate to the political structure.

Jencks, Christopher. *Who Gets Ahead?: The Determinants of Economic Success in America.* New York: Basic Books, 1979. A descriptive study of individual success in the United States that looks at such variables as family background, cognitive skills, personality traits, years of schooling, and race.

Lenski, Gerhard E. *Power and Privilege: A Theory of Social Stratification.* New York: McGraw Hill, 1966. A wide-ranging analysis of human inequality that takes the reader through centuries and to all parts of the world. As the title of his first chapter indicates, Lenski asks the fundamental question of stratification studies: Who gets what and why? He then proceeds to answer the question by drawing liberally upon anthropological, historical, and sociological data.

Newman, Katherine S. *Falling from Grace: The Experience of Downward Mobility in the American Middle Class.* New York: Free Press, 1988. Based on 150 in-depth interviews, this study looks at downward mobility in the United States. Each year in the United States thousands of middle-class families find themselves on a plunge down the social ladder as they lose jobs, income, and the sense of power and well-being.

Schlegel, A., ed. *Sexual Stratification: A Cross Cultural View.* New York: Columbia University Press, 1977. A series of essays on the status of women in different societies.

RELIGION

CHAPTER FOURTEEN

A man prays at the Wailing Wall in Jerusalem.

- What is religion?
- What functions does religion play for both the individual and the society as a whole?
- What different forms does religion take among the societies of the world?

Defining Religion

Modern anthropologists have devoted considerable attention to the analysis of religion since they began to make direct field observations of peoples of the world. While twentieth-century anthropologists have not always agreed on how to interpret different religious systems, all would agree that the many religious practices found throughout the world vary widely from one another as well as from our own. These religious systems might involve sacrificing animals to ancestor gods, using a form of divination called ordeals to determine a person's guilt or innocence, or submitting oneself to extraordinary levels of pain as a way of communicating directly with the deities (Lehmann and Myers 1993).

While the forms of religion may vary enormously, they are all alike to the extent that they are founded on a belief in the supernatural. For our purposes in this chapter, we shall define religion as a set of beliefs and patterned behaviors concerned with supernatural beings and forces. Since human societies are faced with a series of important life problems that cannot all be resolved through the application of science and technology, they attempt to overcome these human limitations by manipulating certain supernatural forces.

Anthropologists have long observed that all societies have a recognizable set of beliefs and behaviors that can be called religious. According to George Peter Murdock's widely quoted list of cultural universals (1945: 124), all societies have religious rituals that propitiate supernatural forces, sets of beliefs concerning what we would call the soul, and notions about life after death. To be sure, certain nonreligious people can be found in all societies. But when we claim that religion (or a belief in the supernatural) is universal, we are referring to a cultural phenomenon rather than an individual one. For example, we can find individuals in the Western world who do not believe personally in such supernatural forces as deities, ghosts, demons, or spirits. Nevertheless, these people are part of a society that has a set of religious beliefs and practices to which many (perhaps a majority) of the population adhere.

Since religion, in whatever form it may be found, is often taken very seriously and passionately by its adherents, there is a natural tendency for people to see their own religion as the best while viewing all others as inferior. Westerners frequently use science, logic, and empirical evidence (for example, through the study of biblical texts) to bolster and justify their own religious practices. Nevertheless, science and logic are not adequate to either establish the inherent validity of Western religious beliefs or demonstrate that non-Western religions are false. In other words, no religion is able to demonstrate conclusively that its deities can work more miracles per unit of time than those of other religions, although some certainly try. The central issue for anthropologists is not to determine which religion is better or more correct, but rather to identify the various religious beliefs in the world as well as how they function, to what extent they are held, and the degree to which they affect human behavior.

Problems of Defining Religion

Despite this rather facile definition of religion, we should hasten to point out that there is no universal agreement among anthropologists as to how to distinguish between religious and nonreligious phenomena. The problem lies in the fact that religion in some societies is so thoroughly embedded in the total social structure that often it is difficult to distinguish the religious from economic, political, or kinship behavior. To illustrate, when a Kikuyu elder sacrifices a goat at the

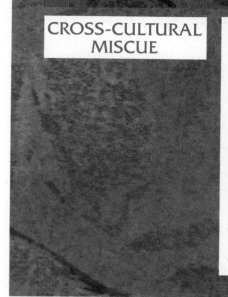

CROSS-CULTURAL MISCUE

Inattention to foreign cultures can result in some costly blunders when working in the international business arena. Alison Lanier, an international business consultant, tells of one U.S. executive who paid a very high price for ignoring the cultures of his international business partners:

A top-level, high-priced vice president had been in and out of Bahrain many times, where liquor is permitted. He finally was sent to neighboring Qatar (on the Arabian Gulf) to conclude a monumental negotiation that had taken endless months to work out. Confident of success, he slipped two miniatures of brandy in his briefcase, planning to celebrate quietly with his colleague after the ceremony. Result: not only was he deported immediately on arrival by a zealous customs man in that strictly Moslem country, but the firm was also "disinvited" and ordered never to return. The Qatari attitude was that this man had tried to flout a deeply held religious conviction; neither he nor his firm, therefore, was considered "suitable" for a major contract. (1979:160–61)

---

grave of an ancestor god, is he engaging in **religious behavior** (he is calling for the ancestor god to intervene in the affairs of the living), **economic behavior** (the meat of the sacrificed animal will be distributed to and eaten by members of the kinship group), or **kinship behavior** (kin will have a chance to express their group solidarity at the ceremonial event)?

Such a ritual sacrifice is all of these at the same time. In highly specialized societies, such as our own, people tend to divide human behavior into what, at least for them, are logical categories—e.g., social, economic, political, religious, educational, recreational. Since many small-scale, less specialized societies do not divide human behavior into categories used in Western society, it is frequently difficult for Westerners to recognize those aspects of human behavior that they think of as being religious.

Another difficulty in defining religion and the **supernatural** is that different societies have different ways of distinguishing between the natural world and the supernatural world. In our own society, we reserve the term *supernatural* for phenomena we cannot explain through reason or science. Other societies, however,

don't dichotomize the world into either natural or supernatural explanations. For example, the Nyoro of Uganda have a word for "**sorcery**" that means "to injure another person by the secret use of harmful medicines or techniques" (Beattie, 1960:73). Sorcery in Nyoro society can take a number of different forms. Placing a person's body substances (such as pieces of hair or fingernail clippings) in an animal horn and putting the horn on the roof of the person's house with the intention of causing that person harm is an act of sorcery in Nyoro society, but so is putting poison into an enemy's food or drink.

Given our own Western dichotomy between the natural and the supernatural, we would tend to interpret these two acts as substantially different in nature. We would interpret the first act as an attempt to harm another person by the use of magic. In the event that the intended victim should die, our own Western law courts would never hold the perpetrator culpable, for the simple reason that it could not be proven scientifically that placing the magical substances on the roof was, in fact, the cause of the death. Westerners, however, would view the poisoning as premeditated murder because it could be determined scientifically (i.e., through an au-topsy) that the poison did cause the person to die. This illustration should remind us that not all societies share our Western definition of *supernatural*. It is precisely because of this difference in viewing the natural and supernatural worlds that Westerners have so much difficulty understanding non-Western religions, which they usually label as irrational or contradictory.

Religion and Magic

Anthropologists studying supernatural beliefs cross-culturally have long been fascinated by the relationship between religion and **magic.** While some anthropologists have emphasized the differences between these two phenomena, others have concentrated on the similarities. In actual fact, it is important to examine both the similarities and the differences because even though religion and magic can be found operating separately, most often they are found in some combined or compound form.

Religion and magic share certain common features. Since both are systems of supernatural belief, they are nonrational; that is, they are not susceptible to scientific verification. In other words, whether religious or magical practices actually work or not cannot be empirically demonstrated. Rather, such practices must be accepted as a matter of faith. Moreover, both religion and magic are practiced—at least in part—as a way of coping with the anxieties, ambiguities, and frustrations of everyday life.

On the other hand, magic and religion differ in a number of important respects. First, religion deals with the major issues of human existence, such as the meaning of life, death, and one's spiritual relationship with deities. In contrast, magic is directed toward specific, immediate problems, such as curing an illness, bringing rain, or ensuring safety on a long journey. Second, religion uses prayer and sacrifices to appeal to or petition supernatural powers for assistance. Magical practitioners, on the other hand, believe they can control or manipulate nature or other people by their own efforts. Third, religion by and large tends to be a group activity while magic is more individually oriented. Fourth, whereas religion is usually practiced at a specified time, magic is practiced irregularly in response to specific and immediate problems. Fifth, religion usually involves officially recognized functionaries such as priests, while magic may be performed by a wide variety of practitioners who may or may not be recognized within the community as having supernatural powers.

This Nepalese healer engages in the supernatural practice of reading palms.

Despite these five differences, in actual practice elements of religion and magic are frequently found together. In any religion, for example, there is a fine line—some would argue, no line at all—between praying for god's help and coercing or manipulating a situation to bring about a desired outcome. Also, it is not at all unusual for a person to use elements of both religion and magic simultaneously. To illustrate, a soldier about to enter combat may ask the god(s) for protection through prayer while carrying a lucky rabbit's foot (a magical charm).

Magic involves the manipulation of supernatural forces for the purpose of intervening in a wide range of human activities and natural events. The ritualistic use of magic can be found in some societies to ensure the presence of game animals, to bring rain, to cure or prevent illness, or to protect oneself from misfortune. Magic, however, can also be (and frequently is) directed to cause evil. In some societies it is believed that certain people called witches or sorcerers use various supernatural powers to bring harm to people. Since these forms of "negative magic" hold such fascination for Westerners, it is instructive to examine them in greater detail.

Sorcery and Witchcraft

Although the terms **witchcraft** and **sorcery** are sometimes used synonymously, cultural anthropologists generally distinguish between them. As practiced in a wide variety of societies throughout the world, witchcraft is an inborn, involuntary, and often unconscious capacity to cause harm to other people. On the other hand, sorcery, which frequently involves the use of materials, potions, and medicines, is the deliberate use of supernatural powers to bring about harm. Some societies have specialized practitioners of sorcery, while in other societies sorcery can be practiced by anyone. Since sorcery involves the use of certain physical substances, the evidence for its existence is more easily found. Witchcraft, by contrast, is virtually impossible to prove or disprove, owing to the absence of any visible evidence of its existence.

Whereas sorcery involves the use of material substances to cause harm to people, witchcraft, it is thought, relies solely on psychic power (i.e., thoughts and emotions). In other words, witches can turn their anger and hatred into evil deeds simply by thinking evil thoughts. How witches are conceptualized varies widely from society to society, but in all cases, witches are viewed negatively. Witches, who are viewed universally as antisocial, are generally seen as being unable to control those human impulses that normal members of society are expected to keep in check. They have insatiable appetites for food, uncontrollable hatred, and perverted sexual desires. The Mandari believe that witches dance on their victims' graves. The Lugbara of Uganda speak of witches who dance naked, which for them is the ultimate social outrage. The Ganda and Nyoro of Uganda believe in witches who eat corpses. Among the Kaguru of Tanzania, witches are believed to walk upside-down, devour human flesh, commit incest, and in general fail to recognize the rules and constraints of normal society. In many parts of the world, witches are associated with the night, which separates them from normal people, who go about their business during the daytime. More-

over, witches are frequently associated with certain animals, such as bats, rats, snakes, lizards, or leopards, which may be black in color, dangerous, and nocturnal.

Sorcerers are generally believed to direct their malevolence purposefully against those they dislike, fear, or envy rather than acting randomly or capriciously. In any given society, hostile relations can occur between people who have some relationship to one another—e.g., an outsider who marries into a local village, rivals for a father's inheritance, co-wives in a polygynous household, men who are competing for a political office, or even rivals in competitive sports. People are therefore likely to attribute their own personal misfortune to the sorcery of some rival who might gain from harming them. Thus, accusations of sorcery are patterned to the extent that they reflect the conflicts, rivalries, and antagonisms that already exist among the people in any given society.

Though sorcery and evil forms of magic are usually associated with small-scale societies in the non-Western world, they are also practiced in the "civilized" world. Edward Moody (1974), for example, presents evidence of a group of Satanists in San Francisco who use sorcery-like techniques to curse their enemies. Members of the cult are taught to "hate your enemies with a whole heart, and if a man smite you on one cheek, SMASH him on the other . . . " (Moody 1974:334). If the group discovers that someone has harmed or hurt one of their members, the entire cult will ritually curse the perpetrator. In one case, which Moody personally witnessed, a man who allegedly slandered the name of the cult was given the most serious form of magical curse, the ritualistic casting of the death rune, the sole purpose of which is death and total destruction. When the death rune is cast, the victim's name is written in blood on a special parchment, and a lamb's-wool figurine is made to represent the victim. Then, according to Moody's account, in "an orgy of aggression . . . the lamb's-wool figure . . . was stabbed by all members of the congregation, hacked to pieces with a sword, shot with a small calibre pistol, and then burned."

After several weeks, the victim of the ritual entered the hospital with a bleeding ulcer and, when released, left the San Francisco area permanently. Did the curse result in the bleeding ulcer? To be certain, the Satanic cult claimed a resounding victory for black magic. Even though the victim was suffering from hypertension and had had problems with ulcers before, it is possible that his knowledge of the curse could have precipitated the bleeding ulcer and his hasty departure from the San Francisco area.

The anthropologist is not particularly interested in determining whether or not the Satanic curse actually had its intended outcome. What is important to the anthropologist is that this represents a dramatic example of how some people, even in industrialized societies, use sorcery or witchcraft to explain events in their lives.

Myths

Every society, from the smallest band society to the most complex industrial society, has a sacred literature called myth that states certain religious truths. Myths, embodying a specific worldview, contain stories of the gods, their origins, their activities, and the moral injunctions they teach. Unlike magic or witchcraft, myths serve to explain the large questions surrounding human existence such as why we are here. Myths not only have an explanatory function, but they also validate some of the essential beliefs, values, and behavior patterns of a culture. That is, a culture's mythology is closely connected to its moral and social order. It is important to point out that myths need not have any basis in historical fact. Although there may be elements of history in myth (and vice versa), the importance of myth from an anthropological perspective is that the narrative reflects, supports, and legitimizes patterns of thought and behavior.

A common form of myth is the myth of origin, which provides answers to questions about how things began. Frequently, these myths tell of the origins of the gods themselves, their adventures, and how they went about creating both humans and the natural environment. Some myths, which can be told in either sacred or profane settings, describe how various gods (or divinely inspired humans) brought about the existence of important cultural features such as government, fire, or agriculture. Another type of myth, known as a "trickster myth," is less serious in tone but carries important messages nevertheless. These often humorous myths serve at least two functions as Wallace (1966:57–58) reminds us:

> In trickster myths the successive triumphs and misadventures of an anthropomorphized animal—a raven, a rabbit, or a coyote, for instance—are told in such a way that not only the historical origins of certain features of the world are accounted for, but also a moral

is conveyed: the dangers of pride, the risk of gluttony, the perils of boastfulness.

Functions of Religion

Anthropological studies of religion are no longer dominated by the search for origins. More recent studies have focused on how religious systems function for both the individual and the society as a whole. Since religious systems are so universal, it is generally held that they must fill a number of important needs at both personal and societal levels.

Anthropologists have always been fascinated by the origins of religion, but until recently, the lack of written records and archaeological evidence has made the subject highly speculative. Within the last several decades, however, archaeological evidence has given us a more complete picture of the early origins of religion. Lehmann and Myers (1985:2) remind us that the tools, weapons, and artifacts found in Neanderthal graves (dating back about 100,000 years) have led anthropologists to conclude that these early people believed in an afterlife. Even more recently the study of paleolithic art by Lewis-Williams and Dowson (1988) has made a strong case for suggesting that symbolic representations that are religious in nature may have appeared as early as 200,000 to 300,000 years ago.

As anthropologists turned away from searching for the origins of religion, they became increasingly interested in a closely related question, How can we explain the universal existence of religion? This question has become all the more intriguing, particularly in light of the very elusive nature of religion. As far as we can tell, every society has some system of supernatural belief. Yet it is impossible to prove beyond a reasonable doubt that any supernatural powers (gods, witches, angels, devils, etc.) actually exist. Moreover, it should be obvious to most religious practitioners that supernatural powers don't always work as effectively as the practitioners think they should. For example, we pray to god for the recovery of a sick friend, but the friend dies nevertheless; a ritual specialist conducts a rain dance, but it still doesn't rain; or the living relatives sacrifice a goat at the grave site of the ancestor god, but still are not spared the ravages of the drought. Though supernatural beings and forces may not always perform their expected functions (i.e., bring about supernatural events), they do perform less obvious functions for both the individ-

Anthropologists generally agree that the tools and artifacts found in prehistoric grave sites provide evidence that these early people believed in an afterlife.

ual and the society as a whole. These latent functions, as they would be called by Robert Merton (1957), fall into two broad categories: (1) social and (2) psychological.

Social Functions of Religion

One of the most popular explanations for the universality of religion is that it performs a number of important functions for the overall well-being of the society of which it is a part. Let's consider three such **social functions** in which religion plays a role: (1) social control, (2) conflict resolution, and (3) intensifying group solidarity.

Social Control.   One very important social function of religion is that it serves as a mechanism of social con-

trol. Through a series of both positive and negative sanctions, religion tends to maintain the social order by encouraging socially acceptable behavior and discouraging socially inappropriate behavior. Every religion, irrespective of the form it takes, is an ethical system that prescribes proper ways of behaving. When social sanctions (rewards and punishments) are backed with supernatural authority, they are bound to become more compelling. Biblical texts, for example, are very explicit about the consequences of violating the Ten Commandments. Owing to a strong belief in ghostly vengeance, the Lugbara of Uganda scrupulously avoid engaging in any antisocial behavior that would provoke the wrath of the ancestral gods. As mentioned in the chapter on social stratification, Hindus in India believe that violating prescribed caste expectations will jeopardize their position in future reincarnations.

From an anthropological perspective, it is quite irrelevant whether these supernatural forces really do reward good behavior and punish bad behavior. Rather than concern themselves with whether and to what extent supernatural forces work the way they are thought to, anthropologists are interested in whether and to what extent people actually *believe* in the power of the supernatural forces. It is, after all, the *belief* in the power of the supernatural sanctions that will determine the level of conformity to socially prescribed behavior.

Conflict Resolution.   Another social function of religion is the role that it plays in reducing stress and frustrations that often lead to social conflict. In some societies, for example, natural calamities such as epidemics or famines are attributed to the evil deeds of people in other villages or regions. By concentrating on certain religious rituals designed to protect themselves against any more outside malevolence, people will avoid the potential disruptiveness to their own society that might occur should they take out their frustrations on the alleged evildoers. Moreover, disenfranchised or powerless people in stratified societies sometimes use religion as a way of diffusing their anger and hostility that might otherwise be directed against the total social system. To illustrate, in his study of **separatist Christian churches** in the Republic of South Africa, Sundkler (1961) showed how small groups of Black South Africans—who until recently were systematically excluded from the power structure by apartheid—created the illusion of power by manipulating their own set of religious symbols and forming their own unique churches. By providing an alternative power structure, these breakaway Christian churches served to reduce conflict in South Africa by diverting resentment away from the wider power structure.

Group Solidarity.   A third social function of religion is that in a number of important ways, it intensifies the group solidarity of those who practice it. Religion, for example, enables people to express their common identity in an emotionally charged environment. Powerful social bonds are often created between people who share the experiences of religious beliefs, practices, and rituals. Since every religion or supernatural belief system contains its own unique structural features, those who practice it will share in its mysteries, while those who do not will be excluded. In short, religion strengthens a person's sense of group identity and belonging. And, of course, as people come together for common religious experiences, they often engage in a number of other nonreligious activities as well, which further strengthens the sense of social solidarity.

looking ahead

The Amish are a good example of how religion influences a group's solidarity and identity. To see how an understanding of this religiously influenced group identity served as the basis for a Supreme Court ruling, see Applied Perspective 1 at the end of this chapter.

Psychological Functions of Religion

In addition to serving the well-being of the society, religion functions psychologically for the benefit of the individual. Anthropologists have identified two fundamentally different types of **psychological functions** of religion: (1) a cognitive function, whereby religion provides an intellectual framework for explaining those parts of our world that we don't understand, and (2) an emotional function, whereby religion helps to reduce anxiety by prescribing some straightforward ways of coping with stress.

Cognitive Function.   In terms of its cognitive/intellectual function, religion is psychologically comforting because it helps us explain the unexplainable. Every society faces a number of imponderable questions that have no definitive logical answers: When did life begin? Why do bad things happen to good people? What happens to us when we die? Even in societies like our own—where we have, or think we have, many scientific answers—many questions remain unanswered. A medical pathologist may be able to explain to the parents of a child who has died of malaria that the cause of death

Widespread participation in communal ceremonies, such as this funeral procession in Bali in Indonesia, serves to intensify the group solidarity of all those community members in attendance.

was a bite by an infected anopheles mosquito. But that same pathologist cannot explain to the grieving parents why the mosquito bit their child and not the child next door. Religion can provide satisfying answers to such questions because the answers are based on supernatural authority.

Unlike any other life-form, humans have a highly developed urge for understanding themselves and the world around them. But since human understanding of the universe is so imperfect, religion provides a framework for giving meaning to those events and experiences that cannot be explained in any other way. Religion assures its believers that the world is meaningful, that events happen for a reason, that there is order in the universe, and that apparent injustices will eventually be rectified. Humans have difficulty whenever unexplained phenomena contradict their cultural world-view. One of the functions of religion, then, is to enable people to maintain their worldview even when events occur that seem to contradict it.

Emotional Function. The emotional function of religion is to help individuals cope with the anxieties often accompanying illness, accidents, deaths, and other misfortunes. Since people never have complete control over the circumstances of their lives, they often turn to religious ritual in an attempt to maximize control through supernatural means. In fact, the less control people feel they have over their own lives, the more religion they are likely to practice. The fear of facing a frightening situation can be at least partially overcome by believing that supernatural beings will intervene on one's behalf; shame and guilt may be reduced by becoming pious in the face of the deities; and during times of bereavement, religion can provide a source of emotional strength.

People perform religious rituals as a way of invoking supernatural beings to control those forces over which they feel they have no control. This takes a number of different forms throughout the world. To illustrate, the Trobriand Islanders perform a series of magico-religious rituals for protection prior to a long voyage; to protect their gardens, men in parts of New Guinea put a series of leaves across their fences because they believe that the leaves will paralyze the arms and legs of any thief who raids the garden; and in Nairobi, Kenya, some professional football (i.e., soccer) teams reportedly hire their own ritual specialists to bewitch their opponents. In addition to providing greater peace of mind, such religious practices may actually have a positive indirect effect on the events they are intended to influence. For example, even if their witchcraft doesn't work, football players in Kenya are likely to play more confidently if they *believe* they have a supernatural advantage. This ability to act with confidence is a major psychological function of religion.

Although most North Americans think of themselves as highly scientific, on many occasions we too use supernatural forces to ensure that our activities will have a successful outcome. For example, anthropologist George Gmelch (1994) shows us how professional baseball players use ritual to try to control the uncertainty of a game:

> To control uncertainty Chicago White Sox shortstop Ozzie Guillen doesn't wash his underclothes after a good game. The Boston Red Sox's Wade Boggs eats chicken before every game (that's 162 meals of chicken per year). Ex-San Francisco Giant pitcher

Ron Bryant added a new stick of bubble gum to the collection in his bulging back pocket after each game he won. Jim Ohms, my teammate on the Daytona Beach Islanders in 1966, used to put another penny in the pouch of his supporter after each win. Clanging against the hard plastic genital cup, the pennies made an audible sound as the pitcher ran the bases toward the end of a winning season.

looking ahead

To see how the supernatural belief systems of patients can influence the work of medical caregivers, see Applied Perspective 2 at the end of this chapter.

Types of Religious Organization

Like other aspects of culture, religion takes a wide variety of forms throughout the world. To bring some measure of order to this vast diversity, it is helpful to develop a typology of religious systems based on certain elements of commonality. One useful and commonly used system of classification, suggested by Anthony Wallace, is based on the level of specialization of the religious personnel who conduct the rituals and ceremonies. Wallace (1966) identified four principal patterns of religious organization based on what he refers to as cults. Wallace uses the term "cult" in a general sense to refer to forms of religion that have their own set of beliefs, rituals, and goals. The four forms of religious organization he has identified are (1) **individualistic cults,** (2) **shamanistic cults,** (3) **communal cults,** and (4) **ecclesiastical cults.** According to Wallace's typology, these cults form a scale. Societies with ecclesiastical cults will also contain communal, shamanistic, and individualistic cults; those with a communalistic form will also contain shamanistic and individualistic cults; and those with shamanistic cults will also contain individualistic cults. Although it is possible that societies with only individualistic cults could have existed in earlier times, there are no contemporary examples of such religious systems.

Wallace's four types correspond roughly to different levels of socioeconomic organization. That is, in a very general way, individualistic and shamanistic cults are usually associated with hunting-and-gathering societies; communal cults are usually found in horticultural and pastoral societies; and ecclesiastical cults are characteristic of highly complex industrialized economies. We

TABLE 14-1

Characteristics of Different Religious Organizations

	Role Specialization	Subsistence Pattern	Example
Individualistic	No role specialization	Hunter/gatherer	Crow vision quest
Shamanistic	Part-time specialization	Hunter/gatherer/ pastoralism/horticulture	Tungus shamanism
Communal	Groups perform rites for community	Horticulture/pastoralism	Totemistic rituals
Ecclesiastical	Full-time specialization in hierarchy	Industrialism	Christianity and Buddhism

Source: Adapted from Anthony F. C. Wallace, *Religion: An Anthropological View* (New York: Random House, 1966).

should bear in mind, however, that this association between forms of religious organization and socioeconomic types is only approximate at best, for there are some notable exceptions. For example, certain American Plains Indians and some aboriginal Australians had communal forms of religion even though they were hunters and gatherers and lived in bands. (See Table 14-1 for a summary of the characteristics of the different religious organizations.)

Individualistic Cults

Individualistic cults have no religious specialists and represent the most basic level of religious structure according to Wallace's typology. Each person has a relationship with one or more supernatural beings whenever he or she has a need for control or protection. Since individualistic cults do not make distinctions between specialists and laypersons, all people are their own specialists; or as Marvin Harris (1991:290) has put it, these cults represent a type of do-it-yourself religion. Even though no known societies rely exclusively on the individualistic form of religion, some small-scale band societies do, in fact, practice it as a predominant mode.

The **vision quest,** a ritual found among a number of traditional Plains Indian cultures, provides an excellent example of an individualistic cult. During traditional times, it was expected that through visions, people would establish a special relationship with a spirit that would provide them with knowledge, power, and protection. Sometimes these visions came to people through dreams or when they were by themselves. More often, however, the individual had to purposefully seek out the visions through such means as fasting, bodily mutilation, smoking hallucinogenic substances, and spending time alone in an isolated place.

A person would go on a vision quest if he or she wanted special power (e.g., to excel as a warrior) or knowledge (e.g., to gain insight into a future course of action). A Crow warrior, for example, would go to a place that was thought to be frequented by supernatural spirits. Here he would strip off his clothes, smoke, and abstain from drinking and eating. He might even chop off part of a finger or engage in other types of self-inflicted torture for the sake of getting the spirits' attention. In some cases the vision seekers never did receive a vision, but frequently, Crow vision seekers were successful.

Crow visions took a variety of forms, but usually had several elements in common. First, the visions usually came in the form of a spirit animal, such as a bison, eagle, or snake. Second, the vision seeker gained some special knowledge or power. Third, the vision often appeared on the fourth day of the quest, four being a sacred number for the Crow. Finally, the animal spirit would adopt the quester by functioning as his or her own protector spirit.

It is important to bear in mind that for the Crow the vision quest was a normal way of dealing with the stresses and strains of everyday life. Robert Lowie reminds us of the wide range of problems that were addressed in Crow vision quests:

... the young man who has been jilted goes off at once to fast in loneliness, praying for supernatural succor. An elk spirit may come and teach him a tune on a flute, as a means of luring the maiden back. The young man plays his tune, ensnares the haughty girl, and turns her away in disgrace, thus regaining his self-respect. Similarly, a wretched orphan who has been mocked by a young man of family hastens to the mountains to be blessed by some being, through whose favor he gains glory and loot on a raid, and can then turn the tables on his tormentor. A woman big with child fasts and in a vision sees a weed which she subsequently harvests and through which she ensures a painless delivery. A gambler who has lost all his property retrieves his fortune through a revelation; and by the same technique a sorrowing kinsman identifies the slayers of his beloved relative and kills them. These are all typical instances, amply documented in personal recollections of informants and in traditional lore, showing the intrusion of religion into the frustrations of everyday living. (1963:537)

Shamanistic Cults

In addition to having individualistic cults, all contemporary societies also operate at the shamanistic level. Shamans are part-time religious specialists who are thought to have supernatural powers by virtue of birth, training, or inspiration. These powers are used for healing, divining, and telling fortunes during times of stress, usually in exchange for gifts or fees. Shamanistic cults represent the simplest form of religious division of labor, for as Wallace reminds us, "the shaman in his religious role is a specialist; and his clients in their relation to him are laymen" (1966:86). The term **shaman,** derived from the Tungus-speaking peoples of Siberia (Service 1978:127), encompasses a number of different types of specialists found throughout the world, including medicine men and women, diviners, spiritualists, palm readers, and magicians.

Shamans are generally believed to have access to supernatural spirits that they contact on behalf of their clients. The reputation of a particular shaman often rests on the power of the shaman's "spirit helpers" and her or his ability to contact them at will. Shamans contact their spirits while in an altered state of consciousness brought on by smoking, taking drugs, rhythmic drumming, chanting, or monotonous dancing. Once in a trance, the shaman, possessed with a spirit helper, becomes a medium or spokesperson for that spirit. While possessed, the shaman may perspire, breathe heavily, take on a different voice, and generally lose control over his or her own body. In this respect, traditional shamans found in non-Western societies are not appreciably different from professional channelers in the United States who speak on behalf of spirits for their paid clients.

How an individual actually becomes a shaman varies from society to society. In some societies, it is possible to become a shaman by having a particularly vivid or powerful vision in which spirits enter the body. In other societies, one can become a shaman by serving as an apprentice under a practicing shaman. Among the Tungus of Siberia, mentally unstable people who often experience bouts of hysteria are the most likely candidates for shamanism because hysterical people are thought to be the closest to the spirit world (Service 1978:127). In societies that regularly use hallucinogenic

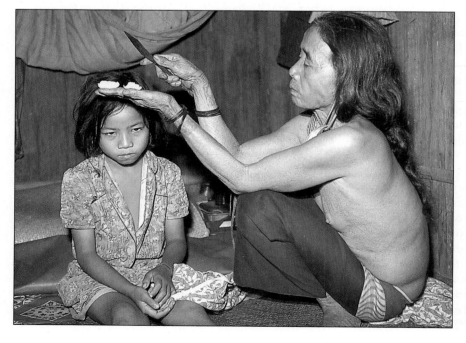

A shaman cures a girl in East Borneo in Indonesia.

drugs, almost any person can achieve the altered state of consciousness needed for the practice of shamanism. For example, Michael Harner (1973:17) reports that among the Jivaro Indians of the Ecuadorian Amazon who use hallucinogenics widely and have a strong desire to contact the supernatural world, about one in four men is a shaman.

As practiced by the Reindeer Tungus of Siberia, shamans are individuals who have the power to control various spirits, can prevent those spirits from causing harm, and, on occasions, can serve as a medium for those spirits (Service 1978:127–28). Tungus shamans—who can be either men or women—use special paraphernalia, such as elaborate costumes, a brass mirror, and a tambourine. The rhythmic beating of the tambourine is used to induce a trance in the shaman and to produce a receptive state of consciousness on the part of the onlookers. The shaman, possessed by the rhythmic drumming, proceeds to journey into the spirit world to perform certain functions for individual clients or the group as a whole. These functions may include determining the cause of a person's illness, finding a lost object, conferring special powers in a conflict, or predicting future events. Shamanism among the Tungus does not involve the power to cure a particular illness, but rather only determines the cause of the malady. In this respect, the Tungusic shaman is a medical diagnostician rather than a healer or medicine man or woman.

Communal Cults

Communal cults—which involve a more elaborate set of beliefs and rituals—operate at a still higher level of organizational complexity. Groups of ordinary people (organized around clans, lineages, age groups, or secret societies) conduct religious rites and ceremonies for the larger community. These rites, which are performed only occasionally or periodically by nonspecialists, are considered to be absolutely vital to the well-being of both individuals and the society as a whole. Even though these ceremonies may include such specialists as shamans, orators, or magicians, the primary responsibility for the success of the ceremonies lies primarily with the nonspecialists, who at the conclusion of the ceremony, return to their everyday activities. Examples of communal cults are the ancestral ceremonies among the traditional Chinese, puberty rites found in certain sub-Saharan African societies, and totemic rituals practiced by some aboriginal peoples of Australia.

Communal rituals fall into two broad categories: (1) **rites of passage** that celebrate the transition of a person from one social status to another; and (2) **rites of solidarity,** which are public rituals serving to foster group identity and group goals and having very explicit and immediate objectives, such as calling upon the supernatural beings/forces to increase fertility or prevent misfortune. Let us look at these two types of communal cults in greater detail.

Rites of Passage.   Rites of passage are ceremonies that mark a change in a person's social position. These ritualistic ceremonies, which have religious significance, help both individuals and the society deal with important life changes, such as birth, reaching puberty, marriage, and death. Rites of passage are more than ways of merely recognizing certain transitions in a person's life, however. When a person marries, for example, he or she not only takes on a new status but also creates an entire complex of new relationships. Rites of passage, then, are important public rituals that recognize a wider set of altered social relationships.

According to Van Gennep (1960), all rites of passage, in whatever culture they may be found, tend to have three distinct ritual phases: separation, transition, and incorporation. The first phase—separation—is characterized by the stripping away of the old status. In cases of puberty rites, for example, childhood is ritually or symbolically "killed" by pricking the initiate's navel with a spear. In the second phase, the individual is in an in-between stage, cut off from the old status but not yet integrated into the new status. Since this transition stage is associated with danger and ambiguity, it frequently involves the endurance of certain unpleasant ordeals as well as the removal of the individual from normal, everyday life for a certain period of time. The third and final phase involves the ritual incorporation of the individual into the new status. Ethnographic data from all over the world have supported Van Gennep's claim that all rites of passage involve these three discrete phases.

These three ritual phases are well demonstrated in the rites of adulthood practiced by the Kikuyu of Kenya, who initiate both girls and boys (Middleton and Kershaw 1965). The Kikuyu, like other traditional East African societies, practice initiation ceremonies as a way of ensuring that children will be converted into moral and socially responsible adults. Despite some regional variations, the Kikuyu initiation rite includes certain rituals that conform to Van Gennep's threefold scheme.

Kikuyu initiation into adulthood involves a physical operation—circumcision for males and clitoridectomy for women. Days before the physical operation, the initiates go through a number of rituals designed to separate them from society and their old status as well as place them in close relationship to god. First, the initiates are adopted by an elder man and his wife; this event symbolically separates them from their own parents. Second, the initiates spend the night before the circumcision singing and dancing in an effort to solicit the guidance and protection of the ancestral gods. Third, the initiates have their heads shaved and anointed, symbolizing the loss of the old status. And finally, they are sprayed with a mixture of honey, milk, and medicine by their adoptive "parents" in another separation ritual, which Middleton and Kershaw (1965: 58) refer to as "the ceremony of parting."

As Van Gennep's theory suggests, the second (transition) phase of the Kikuyu initiation ceremony is a marginal phase filled with danger and ambiguity. The initiates undergo the dramatic and traumatic circumcision or clitoridectomy as a vivid symbolization of their soon-to-be assumed responsibility as adults. Both male and female initiates are physically and emotionally supported during the operation by their sponsors, who cover them with cloaks as soon as the operation is completed. Afterwards, the initiates spend between four and nine days in seclusion in temporary huts (*kiganda*), where they are expected to recover from the operation and reflect upon their impending status as adults.

The third and final phase of Kikuyu initiation rituals involves the incorporation of the initiate (with his or her new status) back into the society as a whole. At the end of the seclusion period, the new male adults have certain ceremonial plants put into the large loops in their earlobes (a form of body mutilation practiced during childhood) symbolizing their newly acquired status as adult men. This phase of incorporation (or reintegration) involves other rituals as well. The men symbolically put an end to their transition stage by burning their *kiganda*; their heads are again shaved; they return home to be anointed by their parents, who soon thereafter engage in ritual intercourse; they ritually discard their initiation clothing; and they are given warrior paraphernalia. Once these incorporation rituals have been completed, the young men become full adults with all of the rights and responsibilities that go along with their new status.

Rites of Solidarity.   The other type of communal cult is directed toward the welfare of the community rather than the individual. These rites of solidarity permit a wider social participation in the shared concerns of the community than is found in societies with predominantly shamanistic cults. A good example of a cult that fosters group solidarity is the ancestral cult, found widely throughout the world. Ancestral cults are based on the assumption that after death, a person's soul continues to interact with and affect the lives of her or his living descendants. In other words, when people die, they are not buried and forgotten, but rather are elevated to the status of ancestor ghost or god. Since these ghosts, who are viewed as the official guardians of the social and moral order, have supernatural powers, the living descendants practice certain communal rituals designed to induce the ancestor ghosts to protect them, favor them, or at least not harm them.

Like many of their neighboring cultures in northern Ghana, the Sisala believe that the ancestor ghosts are the guardians of the moral order. All members of Sisala lineages are subject to the authority of the lineage elders. Since the elders are the most important living members of the group, they are responsible for overseeing the interests and harmony of the entire group. Though responsible for group morality, the elders have no direct authority to punish violators. The Sisala believe that the primary activity of the ancestor ghosts is to punish those living lineage members who violate behavioral norms. To be specific, ancestor ghosts are thought to take vengeance on any living members who steal from their lineage mates, fight with their kin, or generally fail to live up to their family duties and responsibilities. Mendonsa (1985:218–19) describes a specific case, which graphically illustrates the power of ancestral cults among the Sisala:

> At Tuorojang in Tumu there was a young man named Cedu. He caught a goat that was for the ancestor of his house (*dia*), and killed it to sell the meat. When the day came for the sacrifice, the elders searched for the goat so they could kill it at the *lele* shrine. They could not find it, and asked to know who might have caught the goat. They could not decide who had taken the goat, so they caught another and used it for the sacrifice instead. During the sacrifice, the elders begged the ancestors to forgive them for not sacrificing the proper goat. The elders asked the ancestors to find and punish the thief. After the sacrifice, when all the elders had gone to their various houses, they heard that Cedu had died. They summoned a diviner to determine the cause of death, and found that Cedu had been the thief. He had been killed by the ancestors because he was the person who stole the goat which belonged to the ancestors.

This case illustrates the Sisala's belief in the power of the ancestor ghosts to protect the moral order. When a breach of the normative order occurs, the elders conduct a communal ritual petitioning the ghost to punish the wrongdoer. As with other aspects of religion, the anthropologist is not concerned with whether the diviner was correct in determining that Cedu died because he stole the goat. Instead, the anthropologist is interested in the communal ritual and its immediate social effects: namely, that it (1) served to restore social harmony within the lineage and (2) served as a warning to others who might be contemplating stealing from their lineage members.

Ecclesiastical Cults

The most complex form of religious organization according to Wallace is the ecclesiastical cult, which is found in societies with state systems of government. Examples of ecclesiastical cults can be found in societies with a pantheon of several high gods (e.g., tra-

---

EXHIBIT 14-1

Major Religions of the World

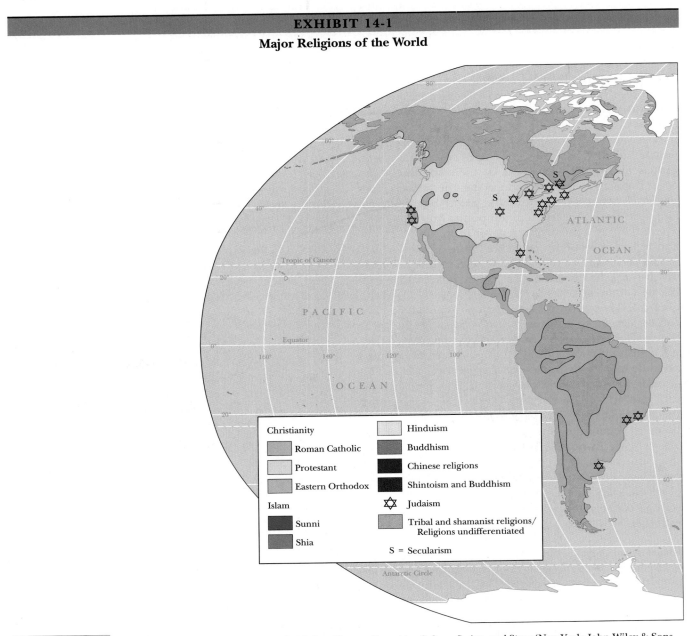

Christianity		Hinduism
Roman Catholic		Buddhism
Protestant		Chinese religions
Eastern Orthodox		Shintoism and Buddhism
Islam	✡	Judaism
Sunni		Tribal and shamanist religions/ Religions undifferentiated
Shia		S = Secularism

Source: Adapted with permission from H. J. deBlij and P. O. Muller, *Human Geography: Culture, Society, and Space* (New York: John Wiley & Sons, 1986) pp. 200–201.

ditional Aztec, Incas, Greeks, or Egyptians) or in those with essentially monotheistic religions, such as Hinduism, Buddhism, Christianity, Judaism, or Islam (see Exhibit 14-1). Ecclesiastical cults are characterized by fulltime professional clergy, who are formally elected or appointed and devote all or most of their time performing priestly functions. Unlike shamans who con-

duct rituals during times of crisis or when their services are needed, these full-time priests conduct rituals that are calendrical (that is, occurring at regular intervals).

In addition, these priests are organized into a hierarchical or bureaucratic organization under the control of a centralized church or temple. Frequently, but not always, these clerical bureaucracies are either controlled

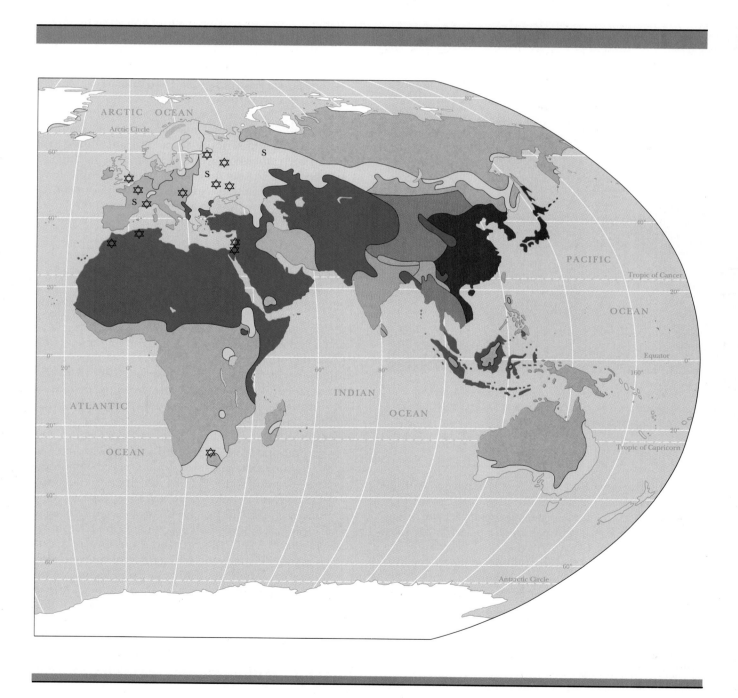

This Asmat man from Irian Jaya is wearing around his neck the skull of a dead ancestor, which is believed to have the supernatural power to protect the wearer.

by the central government or closely associated with it. In many ecclesiastical cults, the prevailing myths and beliefs are used to support the supremacy of the ruling class. In fact, it is not unusual for the priests to be part of that ruling class. Because of this close association between the priesthood and the politicoeconomic institutions, women have not traditionally played very active roles as priests. This is another important difference between priests and shamans, for at least as many women as men are practicing shamanism throughout the world. Even in modern complex societies, women are particularly active as mystics, channelers, palm readers, astrologers, and clairvoyants.

In societies with ecclesiastical cults, a clearly understood distinction exists between laypersons and priests. Laypersons are primarily responsible for supporting the church through their labor and their financial contributions. The priests are responsible for conducting the religious rituals on behalf of the lay population, either individually or in groups. While the priests serve as active ritual managers, the lay population participates in ritual in a generally passive fashion. Since the members of the lay population have little control over religion, they become spiritually dependent on the priests for their ritual/supernatural well-being.

Although ecclesiastical cults have enormous control over people's lives, they certainly have not wiped out other forms of religion. Eskimos who have converted to Christianity, for example, may continue to consult a shaman when ill; Africans from Tanzania often still worship their ancestors while being practicing Roman Catholics; and in our own society, many people have no difficulty consulting a palmist, a psychic, or an astrologer even though they adhere to one of the large, worldwide, monotheistic religions.

Religion and Change: Revitalization Movements

Reading about the functions of religion might lead one to conclude that religion is a highly conservative force within a society. After all, religion contributes to the maintenance of the status quo by keeping people in line through supernatural sanctions, relieving social conflict, and providing explanations for unfortunate events. But under certain circumstances, religion can play an important role in transforming a society. At times, certain societies have experienced such high levels of stress and strain that the conservative functions of religion cannot hold them together. Instead, new religions or sects spring up to create a totally new social order. A number of different terms have been used in the literature to describe these new religious forces of social change, including **nativistic movements,** found among American Indians; **cargo cults,** found in Melanesia; the **separatist churches** of southern Africa; **mahdist movements** in the Muslim world; and **millenarian movements** found in Christian areas of the world.

All of these religious movements, with their aim of breathing new life and purpose into the society, are called **revitalization movements** by Anthony Wallace (1966:30–34). The common thread running through them all is that they tend to occur during times of cultural stress brought about by rapid change, foreign domination, and perceived deprivation. Since these three conditions are frequently, but not always, associated with colonialism, many revitalization movements have appeared in societies that have been under colonial domination.

While recognizing considerable differences in the details surrounding various revitalization movements, Wallace (1966:158–63) suggests that most follow a fairly uniform process. Starting from the state of equilibrium (in which change occurs, although slowly, and individual stress levels are tolerable), a society is pushed out of equilibrium by such forces as conquest and social domination. These conditions lower the self-esteem of an increasing number of individuals and place them under intolerable stress. People become disillusioned, and the culture becomes disorganized (e.g., higher crime rates and a general increase in antisocial behavior). When the social fabric deteriorates sufficiently, revitalization movements are likely to appear in an effort to bring about a more satisfying society. Some movements call for a return to the better days of the past; others seek to establish a completely new social order.

Native American Revitalization Movements

While revitalization movements have been found in many parts of the world, nowhere have they been more widespread and better documented than among Native American groups. The tragic suffering of American Indians since their earliest contact with Europeans has resulted in a number of revitalization movements, including the movement among the Seneca Indians headed by Handsome Lake, several versions of the Ghost Dance, and the Peyote cults found among the Plains Indians. In recent decades, these religious revitalization movements have been replaced by more secular/political efforts to reclaim Indian land, resources, and dignity through the courts, political activism, and civil disobedience.

One of the earliest Native American revitalization movements was started by Handsome Lake (Deardorff 1951; and Parker 1913). By the year 1800, the Seneca Indians of New York State had fallen upon hard times. They had lost much of their land to the whites, who held them in contempt because they were on the losing side of the French and Indian War. The Seneca were confined to reservations, and their numbers had been severely reduced by such European diseases as measles and smallpox. Once a proud nation of warriors, hunters, and traders, the Seneca by the start of the nineteenth

A Roman Catholic priest is a full-time religious specialist who works within a hierarchical organization.

CROSS-CULTURAL MISCUE

While on a one-year assignment to Malaysia, Barbara Hoffman, an accountant from a large firm in Atlanta, was invited to the home of one of her local Malay colleagues. Upon her arrival, Barbara was introduced to her host's wife and four-year-old daughter. Barbara was so taken by the little girl's beauty that she patted the child on the head and commented to the parents that she thought the child was absolutely gorgeous. Much to Barbara's surprise, the mother responded by saying that the child was really not very pretty at all. Although the rest of the evening was cordial, Barbara sensed that she had somehow upset her colleague's wife.

In actual fact, Barbara had inadvertently committed two cross-cultural gaffes. First, in this part of the world, the head is considered to be the most sacred part of the body; it is the place where one's spiritual power resides. Although patting a child on the head in our own culture is a gesture of endearment, in Malayasia it is viewed as a violation of the most sacred part of the body. Second, complimenting a child's attractiveness or health is regarded as possibly inviting bad fortune for the child. If evil people or evil spirits believe that a child is particularly healthy or beautiful, they might become jealous and want to harm the child. So, unlike parents in the United States who frequently boast of their children's attractiveness, health, and intelligence, parents in Malaysia are likely to play down those traits to protect their children from harm.

---

century were defeated, dehumanized, and demoralized. Alcoholism became rampant, while conflicts and accusations of witchcraft increased.

From this state of cultural disorganization came a prophet—Handsome Lake—who was visited by god in a vision and told to stop drinking and start a new revitalizing religion. The deity warned that the Seneca would suffer a great catastrophe (e.g., fire, destruction, and death) if they did not mend their ways. Most of the prescriptions set down by Handsome Lake constituted a new set of moral principles and rules of behavior. Followers of the new religious movement were expected to stay sober, be peaceful, and lead pure and upright lives.

Handsome Lake instituted a number of other important cultural changes as well. For example, he urged his followers to adopt European agricultural practices involving both men and women working in the fields. In terms of the Seneca family, he emphasized the priority of the conjugal unit of man and wife over the matrilineage. Divorce, which had always been high in traditional Seneca society, was no longer permitted. Thus, Handsome Lake's revitalization movement led to far-reaching cultural changes. The Seneca became models of sobriety, their family structure was altered, they initiated new farming practices, and they changed the traditional division of labor between men and women.

Since so many revitalization movements arise in opposition to powerful social, economic, and political forces, they frequently do not accomplish their avowed goals. Many of the Native American revitalization movements over the past several centuries have not ended the white domination. The People's Temple movement, led by the Reverend Jim Jones, ended catastrophically when Jones and hundreds of his followers committed mass suicide.

At other times in recent history, certain revitalization movements have met with considerable, if not total, success. Examples of successful revitalization efforts include the Protestant Reformation of sixteenth-century Europe, the creation of Mormonism in Utah, and the Black Muslim movement in contemporary America. But even when revitalization movements do not succeed in their objectives, such movements can serve useful purposes by providing a renewed sense of individual and group identity during times of suppression, frustration, and alienation. Equally important, they can stimulate changes in the existing social order in a more gradual fashion.

This chapter has looked at the variety of forms that religion takes throughout the world. As with other aspects of culture, religious values, beliefs, and practices can impact peoples' behavior in a number of areas of their lives. This Applied Perspective section illustrates how an understanding of specific religions and/or supernatural belief systems can be useful in the solution of societal problems. In the first case, anthropologist John Hostetler served as an expert witness in a U.S. Supreme Court case involving the issue of religious freedom among the Amish of Wisconsin. The second case demonstrates how medical caregivers in the United States need to take into account the supernatural belief systems of their culturally different patients if they are to provide them with the best possible health care.

Religion

Anthropological testimony serves as the basis for a Supreme Court ruling.

Anyone traveling through rural Pennsylvania, Indiana, or Ohio is likely to see bearded men in black hats driving horse-drawn buggies and women wearing long dresses reminiscent of the nineteenth century. These people, seemingly so out of place in today's modern world, are the Old Order Amish, one of the oldest and most visible minorities in the United States. Amish society is characterized by several cultural themes to which they strongly adhere. First, they strive to separate themselves from the world to the extent that they avoid worldly goods, practice strict endogamy, and even refrain from entering into business partnerships with non-Amish. Second, they place high value on adult baptism and the acceptance of many social obligations that baptism symbolizes. Third, the Amish maintain a highly disciplined church-community. Fourth, they maintain the purity of their church-community by excommunicating and/or shunning any erring members. Fifth, the Amish live their lives in harmony with the soil and nature.

In the early 1970s, the Amish were involved in a legal battle with the state of Wisconsin that went all the way to the U.S. Supreme Court. The central issue revolved around whether the state's compulsory education law violated the free exercise of religion of the Amish. Holding the religious belief that their church-communities should be separate from the world, the Amish raise their children to be members of a self-sufficient community that rejects many of the values and physical trappings of mainstream U.S. society. The Amish argue that if they are required to send their children to

public high schools, their self-sufficient church-communities would be destroyed in a generation or two.

In its landmark decision in *Wisconsin v. Yoder,* the U.S. Supreme Court ruled that for the state to require Amish parents to send their children to public school beyond the eighth grade was a violation of their constitutional rights. By agreeing with the Amish argument, the Court exempted the Amish from compliance with the state's compulsory education law on the grounds of their religious beliefs. In rendering its decision, the Court drew heavily upon the testimony of John Hostetler, an anthropologist who served as an expert witness at the lower-level court proceedings. In fact, as one observer (Rosen) commented:

> . . . a close reading of the Supreme Court opinion clearly demonstrates that the anthropological testimony in this case may well have been indispensable to the Court's assertion that enforcement of the school attendance law would have had an unusually harsh effect on the entire community of Amish people. (nd:20)

Hostetler argued that to require Amish teenagers to attend high schools that fostered such radically different social and religious values would subject them to great psychological harm. The conflicting values between mainstream schools and Amish church-communities would cause considerable alienation between Amish parents and their children. Central to Hostetler's argument is the anthropological theory of the integrated nature of a culture. Hostetler was able to convince the Court that Amish culture is an organic whole, the parts of which are intimately interconnected. More specifically, he pointed out the close interconnection between Amish religion and the Amish people's daily communal life.

Basing much of its decision on Hostetler's anthropological testimony, the Court concluded:

> Aided by a history of three centuries as an identifiable religious sect and a long history as a successful and self-sufficient segment of American society, the Amish in this case have convincingly demonstrated the sincerity of their religious beliefs, the interrelationship of belief with their mode of life, the vital role that belief and daily conduct play in the continued survival of Old Order Amish communities and their religious organization, and the hazards presented by the State's enforcement of a statute generally valid to others.

Owing to the closeness of fit between Hostetler's testimony and the Court's decision, it seems safe to conclude that this landmark case might well have had a different outcome had John Hostetler not used his anthropological insights as an expert witness.

THOUGHT QUESTIONS

1. In what ways is Amish society different from mainstream U.S. society?
2. What is the anthropological theory concerning the "integrated nature of a culture" and how does it apply to this case study?

3. What social function of religion (discussed earlier in this chapter) would have been disrupted had this case been decided differently?

Medical caregivers in the United States need to be sensitive to the supernatural belief systems of their culturally different patients.

Today, medical anthropologists generally are aware that religion or supernatural beliefs play an important role in the delivery of health care services. In many cultures, the causes of certain illnesses are explained in supernatural terms rather than natural or scientific terms. These supernatural explanations can take a number of different forms, including attributing illness to witches, evil spirits, the wrath of god, voodooism, dead ancestors, and bad magic. How these folk beliefs and explanations are dealt with by members of the Western, scientifically based medical community will influence the effectiveness of the health systems they design for culturally distinct populations. It is the applied anthropologist who is in the best position to serve as a liaison between Western medical personnel and their traditional non-Western patients.

The collaborative work of Joan McKenzie, a nursing consultant, and Noel Chrisman, a medical anthropologist, illustrates how an understanding of religious explanations among Filipino Americans can be helpful to the healing process. Filipino Americans generally believe that illness is caused by such supernatural factors as sorcerers, witches, and ancestral spirits. They also believe that these dangerous supernatural forces can be neutralized through the use of talismans, prayers, and folk healers. Although Filipino Americans also use Western medicine, they frequently turn to folk healers when Western health practitioners fail to provide a cure.

Western medical personnel tend to dismiss, out of hand, such explanations of illness and folk cures as mere superstition. But McKenzie and Chrisman argue that it is important for health practitioners to know about these folk beliefs in order to develop effective therapeutic relationships with their patients. As has been demonstrated repeatedly by medical anthropology, some folk remedies can be clinically therapeutic, others can be therapeutically neutral, and still others can be clinically harmful.

McKenzie and Chrisman (1977:329) cite several cases of how folk remedies can be clinically beneficial. For example, the Filipino-American folk cure for colic involving the mother's rubbing her hands together and placing them on the infant's abdomen is not substantially different from the remedy suggested by the public health nurse—that is, giving the infant warm water and placing the baby on its abdomen to create slight pressure. Other folk remedies—such as giving a patient with a cold a glass of vinegar to drink to flush impurities from the system—are therapeutically neutral, for they are neither beneficial nor harmful. It is advisable, according to McKenzie and Chrisman, for Western medical people to integrate these beneficial or neutral folk practices into their health care strategies in order to build rapport with their culturally distinct patients, thereby

increasing the chances that other health measures will be followed. Moreover, as McKenzie and Chrisman have suggested:

> The blending of folk remedies with scientific cures can help bridge the communication gap between nurse, client, and family, thereby increasing trust. Once trust is established, the individual and his family will be much more open to the replacement of a potentially harmful folk practice by a medically validated one. (1977:329)

The role of applied anthropologists in this process of working with culturally different patients should be obvious. By studying the folk medical practices of different subcultural groups in the United States, applied anthropologists will be able to identify the nature of these practices and how and to what extent they are based on supernatural beliefs and, in cooperation with health professionals, indicate how they might be integrated into the overall health care systems.

THOUGHT QUESTIONS

1. Why are some folk remedies just as successful as scientifically developed remedies?

2. What are the benefits to the patient when health professionals combine traditional/folk practices with scientific medicine?

3. What role(s) would a medical anthropologist play as a full-time employee of a modern hospital in the United States?

Summary

1. While all cultures have supernatural beliefs, the forms the beliefs take vary widely from society to society. It is often difficult to define supernatural belief systems cross-culturally because different societies have different ways of distinguishing between the natural and the supernatural.

2. The anthropological study of religion does not attempt to determine which religions are better than others or which gods are able to work the most miracles per unit of time. Rather, cultural anthropologists concentrate on describing the various systems of religious belief, how they function, and the degree to which they influence human behavior.

3. Religion differs from magic in that religion deals with big issues such as life, death, and god, while magic deals with more immediate and specific problems. Whereas religion asks for help through prayer, magic is a direct attempt to control and manipulate supernatural forces.

4. Witchcraft and sorcery are two types of supernatural belief systems that cause harm to people. Whereas sorcery involves the deliberate attempt to cause people misfortune through the use of certain material substances, witchcraft is an inborn and generally involuntary capacity to work evil.

5. Religion performs certain social functions. It enhances the overall well-being of the society by (a) serving as a mechanism of social control, (b) helping to reduce the stress and frustrations that often lead to social conflict, and (c) intensifying group solidarity.

6. Religion also performs certain psychological functions by (a) providing emotional comfort by helping to

explain the unexplainable and (b) helping a person cope with the stress and anxiety often accompanying illness or misfortune.

7. Following the scheme suggested by Wallace, there are four distinctive patterns of religious organization: (a) individualistic cults, (b) shamanistic cults, (c) communal cults, and (d) ecclesiastical cults. These four types of religion vary roughly with increasing levels of socioeconomic complexity; individualistic cults are associated with hunting-and-gathering societies while ecclesiastical cults are found in highly industrialized societies.

8. The most basic level of religious organization is the individualistic cult characterized by an absence of religious specialists. The vision quest practiced by certain North American Indian cultures is an example of an individualistic cult.

9. Shamanistic cults involve the least complex form of religious division of labor. Shamans are part-time religious specialists who, it is believed, help or cure their clients by intervening with the supernatural powers while in an altered state of consciousness.

10. Communal cults involve groups of ordinary people who conduct religious ceremonies for the well-being of the community. Examples of communal cults are the rites of passage (e.g., circumcision ceremonies) found widely throughout sub-Saharan Africa and the ancestral cults that function to foster group solidarity among members of a kinship group.

11. Ecclesiastical cults, which are found in societies with state systems of government, are characterized by full-time professional clergy who are usually organized into a hierarchy.

12. Revitalization movements—religious movements aimed at bringing new life and energy into a society—usually occur when societies are experiencing rapid culture change, foreign domination, or perceived deprivation. Revitalization movements have taken a number of different forms, including nativistic movements, cargo cults, and millenarian movements.

 **Key Terms**

cargo cults	economic behavior
communal cults	individualistic cults
ecclesiastical cults	kinship behavior

magic	separatist Christian church
mahdist movement	shaman
millenarian movement	shamanistic cults
nativistic movement	social functions
psychological functions	of religion
of religion	sorcery
religious behavior	supernatural beliefs
revitalization movement	vision quest
rite of passage	witchcraft
rite of solidarity	

 Suggested Readings

Douglas, Mary. *Purity and Danger*. Baltimore: Penguin, 1966. This provocative book is a systematic study of the rules of purity and pollution found in various societies, which, the author claims, can be understood only within the context of a society's total set of values and ideas.

Lehmann, Arthur C., and James E. Myers, eds. *Magic, Witchcraft, and Religion*, 3d ed. Palo Alto, Calif.: Mayfield, 1993. Now in its third edition, this reader is an excellent collection of essays on supernatural belief systems. The essays are scholarly, representative of the field of religious anthropology, and understandable by university undergraduates.

Lewis, I. M. *Ecstatic Religion: A Study of Shamanism and Spirit Possession*. 2d ed. London: Routledge, 1989. Discussing the sociocultural aspects of shamanism in Africa, Asia, and South America, Haitian voodooism, and Christian mysticism, Lewis argues that spiritual possession is nearly a universal phenomenon.

Mair, Lucy. *Witchcraft*. New York: McGraw Hill, 1969. A summary of the major anthropological thinking on the subject of witchcraft. The author looks at the nature of witchcraft, how witches are detected, the treatment of witches, and various theories on why witchcraft exists.

Norbeck, Edward. *Religion in Human Life: Anthropological Views*. New York: Holt, Rinehart & Winston, 1974. A slim but informative volume that covers the anthropology of religion by focusing on two main themes: (1) the description of religious events, functions, and rituals and (2) the nature of the anthropological study of religions worldwide.

Pandian, Jacob. *Culture, Religion, and the Sacred Self: A Critical Introduction to the Anthropological Study of Religion*. Englewood Cliffs, N.J.: Prentice-Hall, 1991. A relatively small but comprehensive discussion of the scope and objectives of the anthropological study of religion. Through the cross-cultural analysis of shamanism, myth, religious movements, and ritual, Pandian offers the reader an interpretation of the relationship between supernatural beliefs and the cultural formation of the self.

Swanson, Guy. *The Birth of the Gods: The Origin of Primitive Beliefs*. Ann Arbor: University of Michigan Press, 1960. Following the lead of Durkheim, Swanson discusses how the form of a number of non-Western religious practices is influenced by other parts of the social structure.

Wallace, Anthony F. C. *Religion: An Anthropological View*. New York: Random House, 1966. An old yet still valuable analysis of the anthropology of religion that discusses some general theories, the structure, goals, functions, and ritual processes of religion from a cross-cultural perspective.

ART

CHAPTER FIFTEEN

A starlike fabric design made by Kuna artisans from Panama.

- How do anthropologists define the arts?
- What are the various functions of art in society?
- How do music and dance reflect other aspects of a culture?

Artistic expression is one of the most distinctive human characteristics. No group of people known to cultural anthropologists spend all of their time in the utilitarian pursuit of meeting their basic survival needs. In other words, people do not hunt, grow crops, make tools, and build houses purely for the sake of sustaining themselves and others. After their survival needs are met, all cultures, even technologically simple ones, decorate their storage containers, paint their houses, embroider their clothing, and add aesthetically pleasing designs to their tools. They compose songs, tell riddles, dance creatively, paint pictures, make films, and carve masks. All of these endeavors reflect the human urge to express oneself and take pleasure from aesthetics. It would be hard to imagine a society without art, music, dance, and poetry. As the study of cultural anthropology reminds us, artistic expression is found in every society, and aesthetic pleasure is felt by all members of humankind (see Coote and Shelton 1992).

What Is Art?

For centuries, people from a wide range of perspectives—including philosophers, anthropologists, politicians, art historians, and professional artists themselves—have proposed definitions of art. As Mills has suggested, "definitions (of art) vary with the purposes of the definers . . ." (1957:77). To illustrate, the artist might define art in terms of the creative process; the politician's definition would emphasize the communicative aspects of art that could mobilize public opinion; the art historian or knowledgeable collector would focus on the emotional response that art produces; and the cultural anthropologist might define art in terms of the role or function it plays in religious ceremonies. Nevertheless, despite these diverse definitions, any definition of art, if it is to have any cross-cultural applicability, must include certain basic elements:

1. The artistic process should be creative, playful, and enjoyable and need not be concerned with the practicality or usefulness of the object being produced.
2. From the perspective of the consumer, art should produce some type of emotional response—either positive or negative.
3. Art should be **transformational.** An image from nature, such as a cheetah running at full speed, may be aesthetically pleasing in that it evokes a strong emotional response, but it is not art. It becomes art only when someone transforms the image into a painting, dance, song, or poem.
4. Art should communicate information by being representational. In other words, once the object of art is transformed, it should make a symbolic statement about what is being portrayed.
5. Art implies that the artist has developed a certain level of technical skill not shared equally by all people in a society. Some people have more highly developed skills than others owing to the interplay of individual interests and opportunities with genetically based acuities.

Centuries of continual debate by reasonable people have failed to produce a universally agreed-upon definition of art. While not presuming to propose a universal definition, it will be useful, for purposes of this chapter, to suggest a working definition of art based on the five elements just listed. Art, then, refers to both *the process and the products of applying certain skills to any activity that transforms matter, sound, or motion into a form that is deemed aesthetically pleasing to people in a society.*

By using these five features, we can include a wide variety of types of artistic activities in our definition of art. In all societies people apply imagination, creativity, and technical skills to transform matter, sound, and movement into works of art. The various types of artistic expression include (1) the graphic or plastic arts, such as painting, carving, weaving, sculpture, and basket making; (2) the creative manipulation of sounds and words in such artistic forms as music, poetry, and folklore; and

Navajo sand painting is a somewhat unusual form of graphic art.

satisfying aesthetic experiences. In some societies, such as our own, what constitutes good art is determined largely by a professional art establishment comprising art critics, museum and conservatory personnel, professors of art, and others who generally make their living in the arts. Although other societies may not have professional art establishments, their artistic standards tend to be more democratic in that they are maintained by the general public. Thus, the decoration on a vase, the rhythm of a song, the communicative power of a dance, or the imagery of a painting will be subject to the evaluation of artists and nonartists alike.

looking ahead

To see how an anthropologist used historical art motifs to stimulate a new craft industry, see Applied Perspective 2 at the end of this chapter.

Differences in Art Forms

As Chapter 2 pointed out, the term **primitive** has fallen out of fashion when referring to societies that are radically different from our own. When associated with **art,** however, the term has had greater staying power. Despite numerous attempts by art historians and some anthropologists to disassociate themselves from the term, it still retains some legitimacy. This reluctance to eliminate the use of primitive was expressed in the newest edition of Janson's *History of Art*:

> Primitive is a somewhat unfortunate word. . . . Still, no other single term will serve us better. Let us continue, then, to use primitive as a convenient label for a way of life that has passed through the Neolithic Revolution but shows no signs of evolving in the direction of "historic" civilizations. (1986:35)

Despite such attempts by art historians to perpetuate the use of primitive, the term will not be used in this text because of its misleading connotations of both inferiority and evolutionary sequencing. Instead, the term *small-scale* will be used to describe those relatively egalitarian societies with small populations, simple technologies, and little labor specialization.

Having disposed of the term *primitive,* we can now proceed to look at some of the major differences in art forms between small-scale and complex societies (this

(3) the application of skill and creativity to body movement that gives rise to dance. It should be pointed out that these three neatly defined categories of artistic expression will sometimes include forms that are not familiar to Westerners. Westerners usually think of graphic and plastic arts as including such media as painting, sculpture, and ceramics, but in the non-Western world people may also include the Nubians' elaborate body decoration (Faris 1972), Navajo sand painting (Witherspoon 1977), and the Eskimos' body tattooing (Birket-Smith 1959). Moreover, sometimes activities that in our own society have no particular artistic content will be elevated to an art form in other societies. The Japanese tea ceremony is an excellent case in point.

Every society has a set of standards that distinguish between good art and bad art or between more and less

In complex societies, artistic standards are defined by full-time specialists such as philosophers, curators, professors of art, and art critics, many of whom are associated with such institutions as the Metropolitan Museum of Art in New York City.

discussion is developed in much fuller detail by Anderson 1990:224–30). One difference stems from the general lifestyles and settlement patterns found in these logically opposite types of societies. Since small-scale societies tend to be foragers, pastoralists, or shifting cultivators with nomadic or semi-nomadic residence patterns, the art found in these societies must be highly portable. It is not reasonable to expect people who are frequently on the move to develop an art tradition comprising large works of art such as larger-than-life sculptures or large painted canvases. Instead, art in small-scale societies is limited to forms that people can take with them relatively easily, such as (1) performing arts (song, dance, and story telling); (2) body decoration, such as jewelry, body painting, tattooing, and scarification; and (3) artistic decorations on practical artifacts such as weapons, clothing, and food containers.

Another significant difference between the art of small-scale societies and complex societies stems from their different levels of social differentiation (i.e., labor specialization). As societies began to develop increasingly more specialized roles following the Neolithic Revolution (c. 8000 B.C.), some segments of the population were freed from the everyday pursuits of food getting. The subsequent rise of civilizations was accompanied by the emergence of full-time specialists, such as philosophers, intellectuals, literati, and aesthetic critics, whose energies were directed, among other things, at distinguishing between good art and bad art. The standards of aesthetic judgment have become much more

explicit and elaborately defined by specialists in more complex societies. To be certain, aesthetic standards exist in small-scale societies, but they are less elaborate, more implicit, and more widely diffused throughout the entire population.

A third major contrast arises from differences in the division of labor. As a general rule, as societies become more specialized, they also become more highly stratified into classes with differential levels of power, prestige, and wealth. Those aesthetic critics responsible for establishing artistic standards in complex societies are invariably members of the upper classes or are employed by them. Thus, art in complex societies becomes associated with the elite. Not only are the standard setters often members of the elite, but art in complex societies frequently is owned and controlled by the upper classes. Moreover, in some complex societies, art both glorifies and serves the interests of the upper classes. In contrast, since small-scale societies are egalitarian, art tends to be more democratic in that all people have relatively equal access to it.

The Functions of Art

To gain a fuller understanding of art, we must move beyond our working definition to an examination of the roles art plays for both people and societies. The very fact that artistic expression is found in every known society would suggest that it functions in some important ways in human life. The two different approaches to functionalism taken by Malinowski and Radcliffe-Brown can be instructive for our analysis of the functions of art. As mentioned in Chapter 4, Malinowski tended to emphasize how various cultural elements function for the psychological well-being of the individual. Radcliffe-Brown, by way of contrast, stressed how a cultural element functions to contribute to the well-being or continuity of the society. While we will examine the various functions of art for both the individual and society, it should be pointed out that in terms of the analysis of art, Radcliffe-Brown's more structural approach has been the more fruitful.

Emotional Gratification for the Individual

Quite apart from whatever positive benefits art may have for the total society, it is generally agreed that art is a source of personal gratification for both the artist and the viewer. It would be hard to imagine a world in which people engaged only in pursuits that contributed to their basic survival needs. Although most people devote the lion's share of their time and energy to meeting those needs, it is equally true that all people derive some level of enjoyment from art because it provides at least a temporary break from those practical (and often stressful) pursuits. After the crops have been harvested, the African horticulturalist has time to dance, tell stories, and derive pleasure from making or viewing pieces

of art. Likewise, as a diversion from their workaday lives, many Westerners seek gratification by attending a play, a concert, or a museum. It was, no doubt, this personal gratification one derives from art that prompted Selzer to comment that "art . . . is necessary only in that without it life would be unbearable" (1979:196).

The psychologically beneficial functions of art can be examined from two perspectives: that of the artist and that of the beholder. For the artist, the expression of art permits the release of emotional energy in a very concrete or visible way—that is, by painting, sculpting, writing a play, or performing an interpretive dance. Artists, at least in the Western world, are viewed as living with a creative tension, which, when released, results in a work of art. This release of creative energy also brings pleasure to the artist to the extent that she or he derives satisfaction from both the mastery of techniques and the product itself.

From the perspective of the viewer, art can evoke pleasurable emotional responses in several important ways. For example, works of art can portray events, people, or deities that conjure up positive emotions. The symbols used in a work of art can arouse a positive emotional response. The viewer can receive pleasure by being dazzled by the artist's virtuosity. These pleasurable responses can contribute to the mental well-being of art viewers by providing a necessary balance with the stresses in their everyday lives.

It is possible, however, for art to also have the opposite effect by eliciting negative emotions. The artistic process, if not successful from the artist's point of view,

This monumental piece of art—the Sphinx— was designed to evoke positive feelings about the ancient Egyptian government and the pharaohs responsible for its creation.

can result in increased frustrations and tension. More-over, any art form is capable of eliciting disturbing or even painful emotions that can lead to psychological discomfort for the viewer.

Art as a Contribution to Social Integration

In addition to whatever positive roles it may play for the individual, art functions to help sustain the longevity of the society in which it is found. Again, as the function-alist anthropologists remind us, art is intimately con-nected to other parts of the social system. One need only walk into a church, a synagogue, or a temple (or any other place of worship) to see the interrelationship between art and religion. Moreover, art has been used in many societies to evoke positive sentiments for sys-tems of government and individual political leaders. This section explores some of the ways that art func-tions to contribute to the maintenance and longevity of a society.

looking ahead

To see how an art form was used for propaganda purposes during the Gulf War in 1991, see Applied Perspective 1 at the end of this chapter.

Through various symbols, art, in whatever form it may take, communicates a good deal about the values, beliefs, and ideologies of the culture of which it is a part. The art forms found in any given society reflect the major cultural themes and concerns of the society. To illustrate, prominent breasts on female figures are a major theme in much of the wood sculpture from West Africa. This dominant theme reflects a very impor-tant social value in those West African societies—that is, the social importance of having children. Somewhat closer to our own cultural traditions, much of the art in Renaissance Europe reflected many of the religious themes central to Christianity. Thus, certain forms of graphic arts function to help integrate the society by making the dominant cultural themes, values, and be-liefs more visible. By expressing these cultural themes in a very tangible way, art ultimately functions to strengthen the existing culture by reinforcing those cul-tural themes.

Other forms of art, such as music, also help to strengthen and reinforce both social bonds and cul-tural themes. For example, cultural values are passed

Much of the art found in Western churches—such as this one in Bayren, Germany—reflects the basic themes of Christianity.

on from generation to generation using the media of song and dance. As part of the intense education in African bush schools, various forms of dance are used to teach proper adult attitudes and behaviors to those preparing for initiation. The role of music as a mecha-nism of education is well illustrated by Bert, Ernie, Ker-mit, and the other characters of "Sesame Street" who sing about such values as cooperation, acceptable forms of conflict resolution, the fun of learning, and race re-lations. Music also can be used to solidify a group of people. Any history of warfare would be woefully in-complete without some mention of the role that martial music played to rally the people together against the common enemy.

Graphic and Plastic Arts

The **graphic** and **plastic arts** include a number of forms of expression and a wide variety of skills. Though the Western notion of graphic and plastic arts usually refers to painting, sculpture, printmaking, and architecture, the anthropological definition also includes such art forms as weaving, embroidery, tailoring, jewelry making, and tattooing and other forms of body decoration. In some societies one form of art, such as wood carving, may be highly developed, while others, such as painting or metalworking, may be nonexistent. The analysis of these art forms is further complicated because different cultures use different materials and technologies depending, in part, on what materials are available locally. Whereas Native Americans of the Northwest Coast are well-known for their carvings of wood, other cultures may use horn, bone, ivory, or soapstone. In some small-scale societies, the nature of people's ceramic art will be determined by the availability of locally found clays. Often the level of technology will influence whether a culture uses metals such as gold, silver, and bronze in its art traditions.

Cross-Cultural Variations

Not only do different art traditions draw upon different materials, techniques, and media, but the nature of the creative process can also vary cross-culturally. To illustrate, in the Western tradition, the practice of commissioning a piece of art is quite common. For a fee, portrait artists use their creative talents to paint realistic (and usually flattering) likenesses of their prominent clients. However, it is not likely that a client could commission an Eskimo artist to carve a walrus from a piece of ivory. According to the Eskimo notion of the creative process, that would be much too willful, even heavy-handed. Whereas the Western artist is solely responsible for painting the canvas or molding the clay in a total act of will, the Eskimo carver will never force the ivory into any uncharacteristic shapes. The Eskimo artist does not create, but rather helps to liberate what is already in the piece of ivory. Carpenter describes the Eskimo's notion of the role of the artist:

As the carver holds the unworked ivory lightly in his hand, turning it this way and that, he whispers, "Who are you! Who hides there!" And then: "Ah, Seal!" He rarely sets out to carve, say, a seal, but picks up the ivory, examines it to find its hidden form and, if that's not immediately apparent, carves aimlessly until he sees it, humming or chanting as he works. Then he brings it out: Seal, hidden, emerges. It was always there: he did not create it, he released it; he helped it step forth. (1973:59)

Of all of the various forms of art found in the world, the graphic and plastic arts have received the greatest amount of attention from cultural anthropologists. This is understandable because until recently the analysis of the plastic and graphic arts was the most manageable. Until the recent development of such data-gathering technology as sound recorders, motion pictures, and videotape recorders, for example, the analysis of music

Art comes in many forms, some utilitarian, and others not. Here a man from Srinagar, Kashmir, weaves a rug.

and dance was difficult. The graphic and plastic arts, however, are very physical and can be removed from their cultural contexts, displayed in museums, and compared with relative ease. Moreover, a painting or a sculpture has a permanence of form not found in music, dance, or drama.

⬤ Art and the Status Quo

A popular perception of artists and their works in the Western world is that they are visionary, nonconformist, and often antiestablishment. While this is often the case in contemporary Western societies, much of the graphic and plastic arts found in other societies (and indeed in our own Western tradition in past centuries) functions to reinforce the existing sociocultural system. Art, for example, can help instill important cultural values in the younger generations, coerce people to behave in socially appropriate ways, and buttress the inequalities of the stratification system within a society. We will briefly examine several ways that the graphic and plastic arts can contribute to the *status quo*.

Social Control

First, art can serve as a mechanism of social control. While art historians generally recognize that art has a strong religious base, they have been less cognizant of the role art plays in other cultural domains. A notable exception has been Roy Sieber (1962), an art historian who has demonstrated how wooden masks serve as agents of social control in several tribal groups in northeastern Liberia. It was generally believed by the Mano, for example, that the "god-spirit" mask embodied the spiritual forces that actually control human behavior. The death of a high-status man was marked by carving a wooden death mask in his honor. A crude portrait of the deceased, the death mask was thought to be the ultimate resting place of the man's spirit.

Through the medium of these pieces of art, the spirits were thought to be able to intervene in the affairs of the living. Specifically, the masks played an important role in the administration of justice. When a dispute arose or a crime was committed, the case was brought before a council of wise and influential men who reviewed the facts and arrived at a tentative decision. This decision was then confirmed (and given supernatural force) by one of the judges who wore the death mask while concealing his own identity. Thus, in addition to whatever other functions these artistically carved masks may play among the Mano, they definitely serve as mechanisms of social control and conflict resolution.

Art also plays an important role in controlling behavior in more complex societies. In highly stratified societies, state governments sponsor art for the sake of instilling obedience and maintaining the status quo. In some of the early civilizations, for example, state-sponsored monumental architecture, such as pyramids, ziggurats, and cathedrals, was a visual representation of

Art auction at Christie's in London. Since many pieces of Western art bring high prices, they can serve as very visible symbols of social status for the upper classes.

CROSS-CULTURAL MISCUE

Matt Erskine, an associate with an international consulting firm in Washington, D.C., was on a four-month assignment at the firm's office in Singapore. Excited about living and working in a new country, Matt was interested in making new friends and learning as much as possible about Singapore. He was delighted when shortly after his arrival he was invited for dinner at the home of one of his Malay colleagues. As a sign of his appreciation, Matt brought as a gift for his hosts a handsome "coffee table" book on his hometown of Washington, D.C. Matt's hosts thanked him for the gift, but then set it aside without unwrapping it. Even though Matt had an enjoyable evening, he found it quite odd—and was somewhat disappointed—that he wasn't able to share with his hosts their reaction to the book that he had picked out for them. The hurt feelings, however, could have been avoided had Matt understood that Malays—and indeed many Asian peoples—think it rude to open a gift in the presence of the giver.

the astonishing power of both the gods and the rulers. Most people living in these state societies would think twice before breaking either secular or religious rules when faced with the awesome power and authority represented in these magnificent works of art.

Preservation of the Status Quo

By serving as a symbol for social status, art also contributes to the preservation of the status quo. To one degree or another, all societies make distinctions between different levels of power and prestige. As societies become more highly specialized, systems of stratification become more complex, and the gap between the haves and the have-nots becomes wider. Power is expressed in a number of different ways throughout the world, including the use of physical force, the control over political decisions, and the accumulation of valuable resources. One particularly convincing way to display one's power is symbolically through the control of valuable items in the society. The accumulation of practical objects such as tools would not be a particularly good symbol of high prestige because (1) everyone has some and (2) one hardly needs an overabundance of

everyday practical objects to meet one's own needs. The accumulation of art objects, however, is much more likely to serve as a symbol of high prestige because art objects are unique, not commonly found throughout the society, and frequently priceless. This association of art with status symbols is seen in many societies with ranked populations. For example, virtually all of the art in ancient Egyptian civilizations was the personal property of the pharaohs. The high status of the hereditary king of the Ashanti of present-day Ghana is symbolized by a wide variety of artistic objects, the most important of which is the Golden Stool. In the Western world, many public art galleries are filled with impressive personal collections donated by powerful, high-status members of society (Getty, Hirschorn, and Rockefeller, among others).

Music

We often hear the expression "music is the universal language." By this people mean that even if two people do not speak one another's language, they can at least appreciate **music** together. But like so many popular sayings, this one is only partially true. Although all people do have the same physiological mechanisms for hearing, what a person actually hears is influenced by his or her culture. Westerners tend to miss much of the richness of Javanese or Sri Lankan music because they have not been conditioned to hear it. Whenever we encounter a piece of non-Western music, we hear it (process it) in terms of our own culturally influenced set of musical categories involving scale, melody, pitch, harmony, and rhythm. And since those categories are defined differently from culture to culture, the appreciation of music across cultures is not always assured. To illustrate this point, Slobin and Titon tell a story about a famous Asian musician who attended a symphony concert in Europe during the mid-nineteenth century:

> Although he was a virtuoso musician in his own country, he had never heard a performance of western music. The story goes that after the concert he was asked how he liked it. "Very well," he replied. Not satisfied with this answer, his host asked (through an interpreter) what part he liked best. "The first part," he said. "Oh, you enjoyed the first movement?" "No, before that!" To the stranger, the best part of the performance was the tuning-up period. (1984:1)

Ethnomusicology

The cross-cultural study of music is known as **ethnomusicology,** a relatively recent field involving the cooperative efforts of both anthropologists and musicologists (Nettl 1991). Though still not a well-defined field of study, ethnomusicology has made rapid progress lately owing to the recent developments in high-quality recording equipment needed for basic data gathering. Slobin and Titon (1984:2–8) have identified four major concerns of ethnomusicology:

1. Ideas about Music. How does a culture distinguish between music and nonmusic? What functions does music play for the society? Is music viewed as beneficial or harmful to the society? What constitutes beautiful music? On what occasions should music be played?

2. Social Structure of Music. What are the social relationships between musicians? How does a society distinguish between various musicians on the basis of such criteria as age, gender, race, ethnicity, or education?

3. Characteristics of the Music Itself. How does the style of music in different cultures vary (scale, melody, har-

Ethnomusicologists would be interested in studying both the music of this Ukrainian andura player and how that music reflects the wider culture of which it is a part.

mony, timing)? What different musical genres are found in a society (lullaby, sea chantey, hard rock, and so on)? What is the nature of musical texts (words)? How is music composed? How is music learned and transmitted?

4. Material Culture of Music. What is the nature of the musical instruments found in a culture? Who makes musical instruments and how are they distributed? How are the musical tastes reflected in the instruments used?

As these areas of interest indicate, ethnomusicology is concerned with both the structure and techniques of music and the interconnections between music and other parts of the culture. Yet, during the course of cross-cultural studies of music, ethnomusicologists have been torn between two approaches. At one extreme, they have searched for musical universals—elements found in all musical traditions. At the opposite extreme, they have been interested in demonstrating the considerable diversity found throughout the world. Nettl describes this tension:

> . . . in the heart of the ethnomusicologist there are two strings: one that attests to the universal character of music, to the fact that music is indeed something that all cultures have or appear to have . . . and one responsive to the enormous variety of existing cultures. (1980:3)

All ethnomusicologists—whether their background is in music or cultural anthropology—are interested in the study of music in its cultural context. One of the most extensive studies of the relationship between music and other parts of culture was conducted by Alan Lomax and his colleagues (1968). Specifically, Lomax found some broad correlations between various aspects of music and a culture's level of subsistence. Foraging societies were found to have fundamentally different types of music, song, and dance than more complex producers. By dividing a worldwide sample of cultures into five different levels of subsistence complexity, Lomax found some significant correlations. For example, differences emerged between egalitarian, small-scale societies with simple subsistence economies and large-scale, stratified societies with complex systems of production (see Table 15-1).

These are just some of the dimensions of music that Lomax was able to relate to different types of subsistence. This monumental study, which required large samples and extensive coding of cultural material, was open to criticism on methodological grounds. The difficulties involved in such an approach help explain why ethnomusicology has made considerably greater gains in the analysis of musical sound than in the study of the cultural context of music. Nevertheless, the efforts of Lomax and his associates represent an important attempt to show how music is related to other parts of culture.

Dance

Dance has been defined as purposeful and intentionally rhythmical nonverbal body movements that are culturally patterned and have aesthetic value (Hanna 1979:19). While dance is found in all known societies, the forms it takes and the meanings attached to it vary widely from society to society. In some societies, dance involves enormous energy and body movement, while in other societies, it is much more restrained and subtle. Since the variety of postures and movements the human body can make is vast, which body parts are active and which postures are assumed will differ from one dance tradition to another. In some African societies (e.g., Ubakala of Nigeria), drums are a necessary part of dance, while in others (e.g., Zulu) they are not. Dancing alone is the expected form in some societies, while in others it is customary for groups to dance in circles, lines, or other formations.

Functions of Dance

As with other forms of artistic expression, the functions of dance are culturally variable. Dance is likely to function in a number of different ways both between and

TABLE 15-1

Comparison of Music from Egalitarian Societies and Stratified Societies

Egalitarian Societies with Simple Economies	Stratified Societies with Complex Production Systems
Repetitious texts	Nonrepetitious texts
Slurred articulation	Precise articulation
Little solo singing	Solo singing
Wide melodic intervals	Narrow melodic intervals
Nonelaborate songs (no embellishments)	Elaborate songs (embellishments)
Relatively few instruments	Relatively large number of instruments
Singing in unison	Singing in simultaneously produced intervals

Classical dancing in Thailand.

within societies. While dance often performs several functions simultaneously within a society, some functions will be more prominent than others. To illustrate, dance can function *psychologically* by helping people cope more effectively with tensions and aggressive feelings; *politically* by expressing political values and attitudes, showing allegiance to political leaders, and controlling behavior; *religiously* by various methods of communicating with supernatural forces; *socially* by articulating and reinforcing relationships between members of the society; and *educationally* by passing on the cultural traditions, values, and beliefs from one generation to the next.

Dance and Other Aspects of a Culture

Lomax and his colleagues (1968:224–26) have demonstrated quite graphically how dance is connected to other aspects of a culture. Specifically, their research showed how dance tends to reflect and reinforce work patterns. By examining over 200 films, they were able to find a number of similarities between work styles and dance styles. The Netsilik Eskimos provide an interesting—and not atypical—example. For the Netsilik, dancing consists of solo performances which take place during the winter months in a large communal igloo. Lomax describes the dance in considerable detail:

One after another, the greatest hunters stand up before the group, a large flat drum covered with sealskin in the left hand, a short, club-like drumstick in the other. Over to the side sit a cluster of women chanting away as the hunter drums, sings, and dances. The performer remains in place holding the wide stance used by these Eskimos when they walk through ice and snow or stand in the icy waters fishing. Each stroke of the short drumstick goes diagonally down and across to hit the lower edge of the drum and turn the drumhead. On the backstroke it strikes the other edge, reversing the motion which is then carried through by a twist of the left forearm. The power and solidity of the action is emphasized by the downward drive of the body into slightly bent knees on the downstroke and the force of trunk rising as the knees straighten to give full support to the arm on the upstroke. The dance consists largely of these repeated swift and strong diagonal right arm movements down across the body.... (1968:226–27 Copyright by AAAS. Reprinted with permission of the publisher.)

Many of the motions found in Netsilik dance are the very ones that are necessary for successful hunting in an Arctic environment as Lomax describes:

A look at Eskimo seal hunting or salmon fishing shows this same posture and pattern of movement in use—a harpooning, hooking movement. The salmon-fisher stands hip deep in the clear waters of the weir, thrusting his spear down and across, lifting the speared fish clear of the water, twisting it off the barb, and threading it on the cord at his waist in a series of swift, strong, straight, angular movements tied together by powerful rotations of the forearm. At the seal hole on the ice pack, where the hunter may wait in complete stillness during the five frozen hours before the nose of the seal appears, there is time for only one thrust of the spear: a miss spoils a day's hunting in subarctic temperature. His harpoon, then, flies in a lightning stroke, diagonally down across the chest. (1968:226–27 Copyright by AAAS. Reprinted with permission of the publisher.)

We can see thus that the stylistic movements found in Netsilik dance are essentially identical to those found in their everyday hunting activities. The qualities of a good Eskimo hunter—speed, strength, accuracy, and endurance—are portrayed and glorified in dance. In other words, as part of their leisure activity, Eskimo hunters, through the medium of dance, redramatize the essentials of the everyday subsistence activities that are so crucial for their survival.

Verbal Arts

Creative forms of expression using words are found in all societies of the world. In Western societies—which place a great deal of emphasis on the written form—one might immediately think of the common literary genres of the novel, the short story, and poetry. Western societies also have a strong tradition of unwritten verbal arts, which are frequently subsumed under the general heading of **folklore.** In preliterate societies these unwritten forms are the only type of verbal art. Although the term *folklore* is a part of everyday vocabulary, it has eluded a precise definition. Alan Dundes has attempted to define folklore by listing a considerable number of forms that it might take. While recognizing that this is only a partial listing, Dundes includes the following:

Myths, legends, folktales, jokes, proverbs, riddles, chants, charms, teases, toasts, tongue-twisters, and greeting and leave-taking formulas (e.g., see you later alligator). It also includes folk custom, folk dance, folk drama (and mime), folk art, folk belief (or superstition), folk medicine, folk instrumental music (e.g., fiddle tunes), folksongs (lullabies, ballads), folk speech (e.g., slang), folk similes (e.g., blind as a bat), folk metaphors (e.g., to paint the town red), and

names (e.g., nicknames and place names). Folk poetry ranges from oral epics to autograph-book verse, epitaphs, latrinalia (writing on the walls of public bathrooms), limericks, ball-bouncing rhymes, finger and toe rhymes, dandling rhymes (to bounce the children on the knee), counting-out rhymes (to determine who will be "it" in games), and nursery rhymes. The list of folklore forms also contains games; gestures; symbols; prayers (e.g., graces); practical jokes; folk etymologies; food recipes; quilt and embroidery designs; . . . street vendors cries; and even the traditional conventional sounds used to summon animals or to give them commands. . . . (1965:2)

While this list is neither comprehensive nor exhaustive, it does give us some idea of the wide range of verbal arts that have been, or could be, studied by cultural anthropologists. Even though we could focus on any of these forms of verbal art, our discussion concentrates on those forms that have received the greatest amount of attention—namely, myths and folktales.

Myths

As mentioned in the previous chapter, **myths** are specific types of narratives that involve supernatural beings and are designed to explain some of the really big issues of human existence, such as where we came from, why we are here, and how we account for the things in our world. They are, in other words, stories of our search for significance, meaning, and truth.

The relationship between the artistic expressions of myth and other aspects of a culture is well illustrated by the myths of creation found among the Yanomamo of Venezuela and Brazil. According to Chagnon (1983: 95), the Yanomamo have two separate creation myths, one for men and one for women. Both myths illustrate two fundamental themes of Yanomamo culture: fierceness and sexuality. According to the myth of male creation, one of the early ancestors shot the god of the Moon in the stomach with an arrow. The blood that dripped from the wound onto the ground turned into fierce men. The blood that was the thickest on the ground turned into the most ferocious men, while the blood that was more spread out turned into men who engaged in more controlled violence. Nevertheless, the fierceness of the Yanomamo people today is seen as a direct result of the early violence described in the male creation myth.

According to the other creation myth—which attempts to account for the beginning of Yanomamo

CROSS-CULTURAL MISCUE

In recent decades, an increasing number of U.S. major league baseball players have signed contracts to play in Japan. Many unsuspecting American ballplayers think that if they can pitch, field, or hit a baseball effectively at home, they will be equally successful playing in the Japanese league. Although America's pastime is played according to the same rules in Japan, the values, attitudes, and behaviors surrounding the game are worlds apart.

At the heart of the cultural differences between baseball in Japan and the United States is the concept of *wa*, translated as "group harmony" (Whiting 1979). Baseball players in the United States—not unlike people in other sectors of American life—emphasize individual achievement. American ballplayers are constantly vying with one another for the most impressive set of statistics. Those with the best stats can demand the highest salaries. If management fails to meet their demands, the better players are likely to refuse to show up for spring training.

In contrast, Japanese ballplayers are expected to put the interest of their team above their own personal interests. Since it is assumed that the Japanese manager is always right, any disagreement with a manager's decision is a serious disruption of the team's *wa*. In the Japanese view, *wa* is the most important factor in having a winning team. As Whiting reminds us, "If you ask (a Japanese manager) how to know a team's *wa* is awry, he'd probably say, 'Hire an American'" (1979:61).

Whiting goes on to document a number of cases of U.S. ballplayers who had considerable difficulty adjusting to the radically different behavior expected on Japanese teams. Many American ballplayers—despite their own personal success on the field—frequently found themselves being traded because their very individualistic (and typically American) behavior was seen as damaging the team's *wa*. The American players who have been successful in Japan have understood the importance of *wa*. Thus, even in the high-priced world of professional sports, it is imperative for athletes who want to be successful to understand cultural differences.

women—the men created from the blood of the Moon god were without female mates. While collecting vines, one of the men noticed that the vine had a wabu fruit attached to it. Thinking that the fruit looked like what a woman should look like, he threw it to the ground, and it immediately turned into a woman. The other men in the group, struck with intense feelings of lust, began copulating frantically with the woman. Afterward the men brought the woman to the village, where she copulated with all of the other men of the village. Eventually, she gave birth to a series of daughters, from whom descended all other Yanomamo women. This highly sexual account of the creation of women is certainly consistent with everyday Yanomamo life, for as Chagnon reminds us, ". . . much of their humor, insulting, fighting, storytelling, and conceptions about humans revolve around sexual themes" (1983:94).

It is generally thought in the Western world that myths, such as those of the Yanomamo, are symptomatic of small-scale, non-Western, preliterate peoples. The entire history of Western civilization, particularly since the Enlightenment, has witnessed what Lane (1989) has described as a "demythologization"—a steady rejection of myth and illusion as we "progress" toward science, rationality, and critical insight.

Yet even the highly reason-oriented West is not without its mythology. How else can we account for the enormous popularity in recent years of the works of Joseph Campbell on mythology, the proliferation of seminars and books based on Jungian psychology, and such futuristic mythological figures as Luke Skywalker and Obi-Wan Kenobi? We continue to learn a great deal about living from myths, and indeed much of our scientific Western culture has been molded by the power of myth, an art form that continues to have relevance for both Western and non-Western societies alike.

Folktales

In contrast to myths, **folktales** (or **legends**) are more secular in nature, have no particular basis in history, and exist largely for the purposes of entertainment. Like myths, folktales are instructive, although they lack the largely sacred content of myths. Since most folktales have a moral, they play an important role in socialization. Particularly in those societies without writing, folktales can be significant in revealing socially appropriate behavior. The heroes and heroines who triumph in folktales do so because of their admirable behavior and character traits. Conversely, those people who behave in socially inappropriate ways almost always get their comeuppance. To illustrate, tales with very strong social messages are told to Dahomean children in West Africa around a fire (Herskovits 1967:275–76). Usually held at the compound of an elder, these storytelling sessions are designed to (1) entertain, (2) provide moral instruction for children, and (3) develop the children's storytelling skills by encouraging them to tell tales of their own. Despite the very different settings, a storytelling session among traditional Dahomeans is quite similar to parents reading "Jack and the Beanstalk" or "Cinderella" to their children in front of the fireplace.

Folktales can be seen as an art form from two perspectives. Like written works of literature, folktales are creative expressions that can be analyzed in terms of plot, character development, and structure, even though the original author or authors may have been long forgotten. In much the same way that literary critics have analyzed the structure and meaning of Western literature (poetry, prose, etc.), the literary and artistic structure of folklore in both complex and small-scale societies can be analyzed. For example, Hymes (1977) has demonstrated how the folklore narratives of the Native American Chinooka people of Oregon and Washington was highly organized in terms of lines, verses, stanzas, scenes, and acts. According to Hymes:

> A set of discourse features differentiates narratives into verses. Within these verses, lines are differentiated, commonly by distinct verbs. . . . The verses themselves are grouped, commonly in threes and fives. These groupings constitute "stanzas" and, where elaboration of stanzas is such as to require a distinction, "scenes." In extended narratives, scenes themselves are organized in terms of a series of "acts." (1977:431)

The elaborative structures of these folk narratives allow us to regard them and similar texts as legitimate works of art.

In addition to the artistic structure, artistry is present in the telling and retelling of folktales. Even though the basic elements of the original tale cannot be changed, the tale teller retains the right to embellish and dramatize the story as he or she sees fit. The rhythm of the storyteller's utterances, the dramatic emotions expressed, and the use of nonverbal gestures all possess an artistic content of their own. Chagnon reminds us that in Yanomamo folklore a certain amount of artistry is in the telling:

> Some of the characters in Yanomamo myths are downright hilarious, and some of the things they did are funny, ribald, and extremely entertaining to the Yanomamo, who listen to men telling mythical stories or chanting episodes of mythical sagas as they prance around the village, tripping out on hallucinogens, adding comical twists and nuances to the sidesplitting delight of their audiences. Everybody knows what Iwariwa did, and that part cannot be changed. But *how* he did it, what minor gestures and comments he made, or how much it hurt or pleased him as he did it is subject to some considerable poetic license, and it is this that is entertaining and amusing to the listener. (1983:93 Copyright, reprinted by permission of the publisher.)

Art

Because art entertains and provides pleasure, it is often seen as an aspect of culture that has little or no practical relevance. Such a view, however, is short-sighted and reveals a basic misunderstanding of the concept of culture. If we take seriously the idea that cultures are integrated wholes—with the various elements interrelated to one another—it would be unreasonable to consider any part of a culture irrelevant, because it is, at least potentially, connected to all other parts of the system. This segment of the chapter discusses two cases in which an understanding of artistic styles was useful for solving problems or meeting needs in other parts of the culture.

An understanding of an artistic form of Arabic rhetoric can be useful for interpreting diplomatic and political relations between contemporary Arab states.

The Persian Gulf conflict, precipitated by the Iraqi invasion of Kuwait in August 1990, resulted in the most massive mobilization of military personnel and conventional weapons in history. High casualty rates and massive destruction of property were suffered by both Kuwait and Iraq. Moreover, massive divisions and realignments were made among the various states in the Arab world. While the Western press concentrated on the military and diplomatic maneuverings in the conflict, there was actually another war being waged—a propaganda war—between the principal Arabic players in the conflict: Iraq, Kuwait, and Saudi Arabia.

According to Ya'ari and Friedman (1991), for the months before the Allied bombing, the two sides in the conflict used an archaic rhetorical art form to trade insults over the airwaves. This traditional genre, known as **hija,** has biblical precedents in the episodes where warriors (e.g., Goliath) would loudly ridicule their adversaries while boasting of their own power. This ancient Semitic tradition was based on the assumption that warriors could acquire supernatural power by insulting their opponents in rhyme or, as Ya'ari and Friedman (1991:22) have put it, "cursing in verse." For centuries, the most highly esteemed poets in the Arabic literary tradition have been those with a flair for offensive and vitriolic insults. This *hija* rhetorical art form has its own format, meters, and rhyming patterns. Classical *hija* starts with boastful self-praise and then moves into a series of abusive insults.

Unbeknownst to most Westerners, there was a revival of *hija* rhetoric immediately after the Iraqi invasion of Kuwait in August of 1990. Without commercial interruption, Saudi, Iraqi, and Kuwaiti (in exile) television broadcast hours of *hija* poetry, praising the justness of their own cause and lambasting the opposition. Interestingly, many of the subtleties of this ancient artistic form of rhyming put-down are not widely understood by the viewing public. The poems are highly ambiguous—even to those well educated in classical Arabic—because conventionally *hija* poets choose words, phrases, and metaphors that have been out of general use for centuries. Even though the use of such an archaic and esoteric art form would seem to dilute its effectiveness as a propaganda device, the messages were not lost on the general public. Although many of the subtleties escaped the average citizen, the general messages came through on a gut level. The verses, intoned with dramatic cadence, conjured up heroic images of one's own leaders and satanic images of the opposition's leaders.

The content of the *hija* poetry flowing over the airwaves was often vicious. With the buildup of Allied troops—some of whom were women—in Saudi Arabia prior to the outbreak of hostilities, the Iraqi *hija* poets took the Saudis to task for "hiding behind the skirts of women," a scathing insult to Arab masculinity. Not to be outdone, Saudi *hija* poets constructed their own vitriolic verse berating Iraqi leader Saddam Hussein for attacking his enemies at night and for being a contemptible neighbor. Specifically, Hussein was portrayed as an ungrateful neighbor who repudiated the help he had received in his earlier struggles with Iran. Moreover, the Saudi *hija* poets delivered the ultimate put-down to Hussein by denouncing him as a Jew.

The significance of the recent revival of *hija* rhetoric goes beyond its role as a patriotic mechanism or as a popular form of entertainment. As Ya'ari and Friedman have suggested, these *hija* recitations "provide channels for a kind of offbeat diplomacy by which more messages are transmitted across the lines than through conventional diplomatic means" (1991:24). In other words, the ebb and flow of the conflict can be assessed by analyzing the strength of the verbal venom coming from each camp. Provided one understands the art form, these quasi news programs may be an even more accurate barometer of contemporary political and diplomatic relations than official newscasts or press releases. Even though U.S. intelligence may not have drawn upon this artistic form of poetry as a source of information, reportedly both Saddam Hussein and King Fahd of Saudi Arabia received daily intelligence summaries of what the opposition poets were saying.

THOUGHT QUESTIONS

1. How would you define *hija* and how was it used by Iraq, Kuwait, and Saudi Arabia during the Gulf War?

2. Does the United States have art forms that can give people from other countries a better understanding of our political climate?

3. Has the United States or other Western nations ever used art in the media as a propaganda device? To what ends?

The findings of anthropologists have served as the basis for a renaissance in traditional pottery making among the Tewa of New Mexico.

A basic theme running through this textbook is that cultural anthropology is not just a discipline for those interested in curious and esoteric facts, but rather is eminently practical. When perusing museums exhibiting Native American arts and crafts, we frequently concentrate on one of two things: (1) certain artistic issues (e.g., design features, skills of the artist, use of colors) or (2) the cultural/historical significance of the objects. That such objects should be aesthetically appealing or educational is a good enough reason for anthropologists to collect them and display them in museums. Sometimes these traditional forms of art, such as pottery, can have far-reaching impacts on the lives of contemporary peoples. Such was the case at the Tewa pueblo of San Ildefonso in northern New Mexico.

According to Whitman (1963), in 1907 the School of American Research, under the direction of E. L. Hewett, initiated a series of archaeological excavations of the ancient ruins of the Pajarito Plateau. The workers employed for this archaeological dig were all local Tewa Indians from San Ildefonso. The Tewa laborers—and particularly the women who periodically visited the site—took a keen interest in the pottery vessels that were being unearthed from the ruins. Some of the women, who were themselves local potters, held lively discussions of the ancient pottery styles and designs that had died out during the first century after the Spanish conquest. Within several years, it had become apparent that the contemporary potters were attempting to emulate the excellent quality of the ancient ceramic vessels. Gradually, the local pottery makers began to improve the quality of their wares. Realizing the importance of this process, the staff at the School of American Research became directly involved by encouraging the women to incorporate the ancient artistic features into their own work. Pieces of ancient pottery (as well as photographs of other pieces in museums) were brought to the attention of the local Tewa potters by staff from the school.

In 1915, Hewett was put in charge of the displays of Indian culture at the Panama-California Exposition. As part of that exhibit, several women potters from San Ildefonso demonstrated their techniques before large audiences. Because of that experience and exposure, these local potters came to realize that their work—which by now had incorporated a number of traditional features and styles—could bring infinitely higher prices from tourists than they had ever imagined.

Over the course of the next several decades, as the pottery industry at San Ildefonso was infused with the styles of the ancient pottery unearthed by the archaeologists, its quality improved. Equally as important, this revitalization of ancient ceramics had profound economic and social consequences for the Tewa pueblo as well. To illustrate, by the late 1930s, pottery had become the major source of income in the pueblo. Not only did it provide many people with a means of livelihood, but it also enabled people to purchase such commodities as radios and furniture and send their children to college. In other words, this craft renaissance provided the people of San Ildefonso with a dramatic increase in economic independence. Moreover, this craft revitalization enabled the Tewa to rediscover and reassert their past cultural identity. Thus, in this case, the effort to reconstruct a past culture through archaeology has had the additional consequences of breathing new life into the work of native artists, reviving native artistic styles, providing desirable economic development, and creating a resurgence of ethnic pride in the process.

THOUGHT QUESTIONS

1. What role did anthropology play in positively affecting a local group of people?

2. What were some of the beneficial consequences for the people of San Ildefonso?

3. Are there examples from other cultures where the findings of anthropologists have been used to rejuvenate a local craft industry?

 Summary

1. Although there is no universal definition of art, for purposes of this chapter we have defined art as *the process and products of applying certain skills to any activity that transforms matter, sound, or motion into a form that is deemed aesthetically pleasing to people in a society.* The creative process of making art should be enjoyable, produce an emotional response, be transformational, convey a message, and involve a certain level of skill on the part of the artist.

2. The forms of artistic expression discussed in this chapter include (a) the graphic/plastic arts (painting, carving, weaving, etc.), (b) music, (c) dance, and (d) verbal art (myth, folklore, etc.).

3. Rather than using the term *primitive* to refer to certain types of art, we use the term *small-scale,* which refers to those essentially egalitarian societies with small populations, simple technology, no written language, and little labor specialization. In contrast to the art found in small-scale societies, the art of more complex societies is more permanent, has more elaborate and explicit standards of evaluation, and is associated with the elite.

4. Art contributes to the well-being of both the individual and the society. For the individual, art provides emotional gratification to both the artist and the beholder. From the social perspective, various forms of art strengthen and reinforce both social bonds and cultural themes, act as a mechanism of social control, and serve as a symbol of high status particularly in complex societies.

5. The study of ethnomusicologist Alan Lomax suggests that the music traditions found in small-scale societies differ from more complex societies in that the former are characterized by more repetitive texts, slurred articulation, little solo singing, nonembellished songs, relatively few instruments, and singing in unison.

6. Verbal art includes, among other forms, myths and folktales. Myths tend to involve supernatural beings while folktales are more secular in nature. Like other forms of art, the verbal arts are intimately connected to other aspects of a culture, as illustrated by the Yanomamo myth of creation.

 Key Terms

dance	folktales
ethnomusicology	graphic arts
folklore	*hija*
legends	plastic arts
music	primitive art
myths	transformational

Suggested Readings

Anderson, Richard L. *Calliope's Sisters: A Comparative Study of Philosophies of Art.* Englewood Cliffs, N.J.: Prentice-Hall, Inc., 1990. This jargon-free study provides a unique look at the aesthetics in ten major culture areas of the world, including the San, the Eskimos, the Aztecs, the Japanese, and the Western world. The philosophies of art from the ten culture areas are used to make comparative statements about the nature of art, its origins, and its role in human affairs.

Coote, Jeremy, and Anthony Shelton, eds. *Anthropology, Art, and Aesthetics.* Oxford: Clarendon Press, 1992. A scholarly collection of writings on how anthropologists treat art and aesthetics, this recent volume contains articles on a wide range of topics from a number of different parts of the world, including Oceania, Mexico, the southern Sudan, and Australia. Prefacing these substantive (culture-specific) articles is a more general piece by Raymond Firth that discusses the changing relationship between art and anthropology over the past sixty years.

Dundes, Alan. *Folklore Matters.* Knoxville: University of Tennessee Press, 1989. A collection of essays written by one of the leading figures in the study of folklore. Of particular relevance are the essays on folklore and identity and how anthropologists use the comparative method in the study of folklore.

Hanna, Judith L. *To Dance Is Human: A Theory of Nonverbal Communication.* Austin: University of Texas Press, 1979. A comprehensive ethnological treatment of dance as a significant part of culture. It is particularly strong in drawing upon various forms of dance throughout the world to illustrate how this artistic form functions within religious, political, and social institutions.

Layton, Robert. *The Anthropology of Art.* New York: Columbia University Press, 1981. A scholarly introduction to the field of the anthropology of art with special attention given to art and social life, art and visual communication, stylistic variations, and the creative process.

Lomax, Alan. *Folk Song Style and Culture.* Washington, D.C.: American Association for the Advancement of Science, 1968. A classic study of musical styles around the world and how they relate to other aspects of culture.

Marriott, Alice. *Maria: The Potter of San Ildefonso.* Norman: University of Oklahoma Press, 1948. A very personal account of the life of one of the leading potters in the Tewa pueblo of New Mexico. The book, based on first-person observations, provides insights into the process of Tewa craft revitalization discussed in the applied perspective section of this chapter.

Nettl, Bruno, and Philip V. Bohlman, eds. *Comparative Musicology and Anthropology of Music*. Chicago: University of Chicago Press, 1991. A collection of writings discussing a wide range of issues in the study of the anthropology of music by some of the leading scholars in the field.

Titon, Jeff Todd, et al. *Worlds of Music: An Introduction to the Music of the World's Peoples*. New York: Schirmer Books, 1984. An introductory survey of music in various parts of the world including Native North American, African, Black North America, Europe, and India.

Waterman, Christopher Alan. *Juju: A Social History and Ethnography of an African Popular Music*. Chicago: University of Chicago Press, 1990. An excellent study of popular music in present-day Nigeria in terms of aesthetics, social relationships, and historical context.

CULTURE CHANGE

A traditional geisha in Kyoto, Japan, makes the point that some things change while others remain the same.

- How do cultures change?
- What are some obstacles to culture change?
- What does it mean to be modern?

In a very real sense, any ethnographic description of a specific group of people is like a snapshot at one particular time. Should the ethnographer conduct a restudy of the same group five years later, it is likely that a number of cultural features will have changed. Some cultures (usually small-scale, preliterate, and technologically simple societies) tend to change slowly. Modern, complex, highly industrialized societies tend to change much more rapidly. Whatever the rate of change, however, we can bank on one thing when dealing with cultures: nothing is as constant as change.

If we require proof of this basic maxim, we need only turn to the republished (1969) 1902 edition of the Sears, Roebuck catalog. Glancing through the pages, one is struck by the enormity of the changes that have taken place in our material culture since the turn of the century. Because of its comprehensiveness, the catalog, in the words of Cleveland Amory, ". . . mirrors the dreams and needs of Americans at a time when life was less complex than it is today" (1969: Introduction). In other words, it provides a near total inventory of our material culture at the turn of the century. Today many items in the 1902 catalog—such as horse-drawn plows, patent medicines, and hightop leather shoes—can be found only in museums. Other items in the 1902 edition still exist as part of our material culture, but in drastically altered form, such as sewing machines, windmills, men's toupees, lawn mowers, and typewriters.

We can learn much about the attitudes and values of our turn-of-the-century ancestors from the material goods these people surrounded themselves with. For example, the catalog advertised a substantial number of books on palmistry, astrology, and hypnotism. Many were "self-help" books that came in very handy in rural areas. Nearly a quarter of the book section was devoted to family Bibles. Another dramatic measure of the magnitude of changes that have occurred in U.S. culture is the three-page section devoted to the advertisement of corsets and bustles, designed to rearrange or accentuate certain features of the female anatomy. On nearly every page of the catalog, we are reminded of the vast cultural changes—both material and nonmaterial—that have occurred in U.S. society since the early 1900s.

As mentioned in Chapter 2, it is generally recognized that cultures change as a result of both internal and external forces. Internal mechanisms of change are known as inventions or innovations, while cultures change by external sources through the process of cultural diffusion or borrowing. Although diffusion is responsible for the greatest amount of culture change, it is important to examine both processes of change in greater detail.

Inventions/Innovations

An **invention** is any new thing, idea, or behavior pattern that emerges from within the society. Some inventions are very deliberate and purposeful while others are unconscious and unintentional. Ralph Linton (1936:311), one of the most prominent scholars of culture change in the twentieth century, has suggested that over the long run, the unconscious inventor has had a greater impact on culture change than has the conscious inventor. The unconscious or accidental inventor contributes to culture change without being driven by an unmet societal need or even realizing that she or he is making a contribution. As Linton put it, "their inventions are, as a rule, of little individual importance, but they loom large in the aggregate" (1936:311).

These numerous unintentional inventors frequently go unnoticed and unrewarded, even though they may be making a very significant cumulative contribution to their culture. Yet, it is the deliberate, intentional inventor who tends to receive the greatest rewards and recognition. From our own recent history, Eli Whitney was sufficiently motivated to invent the cotton gin by the need to produce more cotton; Jonas Salk discovered the polio vaccine to eradicate a crippling disease; and hundreds of other inventors have come up with new

An examination of a turn-of-the-century Sears catalog reveals the vast changes that have occurred in U.S. culture during the present century.

gadgets and ideas because they wanted to do something better or more efficiently.

There is a good deal of truth in the adage "Necessity is the mother of invention." Frequently, an invention will develop because there is a pressing need for it. Linton (1936:313–15) relates a case of an invention that occurred around the turn of the century on the island of Hiva Oa. A man from the neighboring Gilbert Islands took up residence on Hiva Oa, married a local woman, and became a fisherman. It soon became apparent to him, however, that theft of outrigger canoes was rampant on the island. Motivated by the desire to avoid having his own boat stolen, he invented a new type of outrigger canoe with a detachable outrigger. By removing the outrigger assemblage, he could leave the canoe on the beach unattended. Within a short time, this new detachable outrigger almost totally replaced

the previous model because there was a felt need for this particular invention.

For years, social scientists have tried to discover which people tend to become inventors or innovators. (It should be pointed out that **innovation** and *invention* are not synonymous, for it is possible to be an innovator without being an inventor. Innovators are the first people to adopt or use a new thing or idea.) Why do some people invent new things, ideas, and behavior patterns, while most do not? And once something is invented, which people are most likely to adopt the invention? A number of interesting theories have been set forth. Some (Rogers 1983; Tarde 1903; Smith 1976) have suggested that both inventors and innovators tend to be **marginal people** living on the fringes of society. Not bound by tradition or convention, these marginal people can see problems and their solutions with a fresh perspective. Spindler summed up this position when she noted that "Innovators are often 'marginal men,' who are, for a variety of reasons, somewhat divorced from the core of their culture and thus more free to create" (1984:15).

Rogers's (1983:263–65) research suggests that innovators and early adopters are most likely to come from upper-class, wealthy, and well-educated segments of society. He goes on to speak of a basic paradox whereby those people who most need the benefits of an innovation are generally the least likely to adopt it. Rogers illustrates this paradox by looking at the adoption of contraception in developing countries. Citing his own research, Rogers (1973:408) notes that elite families, which already had small numbers of children, were the most receptive to adopting contraceptives, while lower-status (poorer) families, which averaged between five and six children, were the most resistant.

Others theorists tend to take a more psychological approach by looking at the effects of child rearing on innovative personalities. Hagen (1962:201), for example, holds that innovators are most likely to come from families with excessively demanding fathers or from families with weak fathers and nurturing mothers. In his classic studies on achievement, McClelland (1960) found that early training in the mastery of certain skills often leads to entrepreneurial success. As interesting as many of these theories are, we still do not have a very definitive understanding as to why some people are innovators and others are not. An idea may appear to be sound, a technological invention may appear to be efficient, or a new behavior may appear to make sense, and yet it will not be adopted by a particular group of people. The problem, of course, is that there are a multitude of variables—some social, some cultural, and others psychological—and some are operating in some situations but not in others.

Diffusion

In addition to changing through inventions and discoveries, cultures change through the process of cultural diffusion—the spreading of a thing, an idea, or a behavior pattern from one culture to another. As important as inventions and discoveries are to culture change, the total number of inventions in any given society is generally quite small. In fact, Linton (1936:325) estimates that no more than 10 percent of all of the cultural items found in any culture—including our own—originated in that culture. If every culture had to rely solely on its own inventions, human progress over the centuries would indeed be slow. Cultures have developed as rapidly as they have precisely because the process of diffusion has enabled humans to pool their creative/inventive resources.

General Patterns of Diffusion

Since diffusion plays such a prominent role in culture change it is appropriate to examine this process in some detail. Even though cultural diffusion varies from situation to situation, a number of generalizations about the process are worth mentioning.

Selectivity.   The process of diffusion is selective in nature. When two cultures come into contact, not every cultural item is exchanged with another. If that were the case, there would be no cultural differences in the world today. Rather, only a small number of cultural elements are ever diffused from one culture to another. Which cultural item will be accepted will depend largely on the item's utility and compatibility with already existing cultural traits. For example, it is not very likely that men's hair dyes designed to "get out the gray" will diffuse into parts of rural Africa where a person's status is elevated with advancing years. Similarly, most people in the United States have resisted adopting the metric system because they see no particular advantage to taking the time and effort to learn it. According to Rogers (1983:14–16), the speed with which an innovation is adopted—or whether it will be adopted at all—usually is affected by whether or not (1) it is seen to be superior to what already exists, (2) it is consistent with existing cultural patterns, (3) it is easily understood, (4) it is able to be tested on a trial basis, and (5) its benefits are clearly visible.

Reciprocity.   Diffusion is a two-way process. We should not assume that cultural items diffuse only from technologically complex societies to simpler societies. The anthropological record from many parts of the world clearly shows that cultural traits are diffused in both directions. European contact with Native Americans is a case in point. Even though Europeans introduced much of their culture to Native Americans, they nevertheless received a number of cultural features in return, including articles of clothing such as ponchos, parkas, and moccasins; medicines such as quinine, anesthetics, and laxatives; and food items such as corn, beans, squash, yams, and even the so-called Irish potato.

Modification.   Once a cultural element is accepted into a new culture, it may undergo changes in form or function. The pizza is a good example of how a cultural item can change form as it diffuses. The pizza, which diffused from Italy to the United States in the late nineteenth century, has been modified in a number of significant ways to conform to American tastes. It is likely that its Italian originators would hardly recognize a pizza made on French bread, English muffins, or pita bread and topped with pineapple, tuna fish, or jalapeno peppers.

Sometimes the reinterpretation process involves a change in the way an item is used. While living in Kenya, this writer observed a stunning example of functional reinterpretation. The Masai of Kenya and Tanzania practice the custom of piercing their earlobes and enlarging the hole by inserting increasingly larger round pieces of wood until a loop of skin is formed. Rather than using pieces of round wood for this purpose, one group of Masai were observed using Eveready flashlight batteries obtained from the United States. In this case, the form of the batteries was the same, but the function was definitely reinterpreted.

Likelihood.   Some parts of culture are more likely to be diffused than others. As a general rule, items of material culture are more likely candidates for diffusion than are ideas or behavior patterns. A traditional farmer in Senegal, for example, is more likely to be convinced of the advantages of a bulldozer over a shovel for moving dirt than he is of substituting Buddhism for his form of ancestor worship.

Variables.   There is reason to believe that diffusion is also affected by a number of important variables: the duration and intensity of contact, the degree of cultural integration, and the similarities between the donor and recipient cultures. Although we know a good deal about the process of diffusion, social scientists still are not able to predict with certainty when and where diffusion will take place.

Acculturation

The concepts of diffusion and acculturation have some things in common; in fact, **acculturation** is a special type of diffusion that takes place as a result of sustained contact between two societies, one of which is subordinate to the other. Thus, both diffusion and acculturation involve culture change as a result of contact with another group. But whereas diffusion involves a single trait or a complex of traits, acculturation involves the widespread reorganization of one or both cultures over a short period of time. While both the dominant and subordinate culture may experience changes, the subordinate culture always changes most dramatically. Acculturation can have a variety of consequences. The subordinate culture could become extinct, it could be incorporated as a distinct subculture of the dominant group, or it could be assimilated (blended) into the dominant group. But whatever form it may take, acculturation refers to the forced borrowing under conditions of external pressure.

The extent of the external pressure put upon a subordinate culture varies considerably from one acculturation situation to another. Some cultural anthropologists (e.g., Mead 1956) have described situations of acculturation in which the less dominant culture "freely chooses" to emulate the culture of the more dominant society. At the other extreme we find examples of excessive coercion, such as the Spanish conquest of Mexico, which involved the brutal exploitation of the local population by both the Spanish government and the Spanish church (see Beals, Hoijer, and Beals 1977: 624–27 for more details).

We should bear in mind that not all anthropologists agree on how to interpret the levels of coercion that subordinate peoples are subjected to. Some anthropologists (Bodley 1982; Diamond 1960) feel strongly that there is no such thing as voluntary acculturation. They hold that there are simply different degrees of

Items of material culture are more likely to be diffused than are ideas or behavior patterns. Here one aspect of U.S. culture—the golden arches of McDonald's—has been diffused to Tokyo, Japan.

force and coercion. As Diamond has stated, ". . . acculturation has always been a matter of conquest . . . refugees from the foundering groups may adopt the standards of the more potent society in order to survive as individuals. But these are conscripts of civilization, not volunteers" (1960:vi).

At the "free choice" end of the spectrum are the Manus of the South Pacific as described by Margaret Mead (1956). When Mead first studied the Manus in the late 1920s, the people lived in stilt houses over the lagoons, had no writing, wore simple grass skirts, and lived in extended-family groups. When she returned to restudy the Manus in the 1950s, Mead found a culture that was actively and intentionally seeking education and a place in the modern world. During that intervening quarter of a century, the Manus had been exposed to hundreds of thousands of American soldiers who

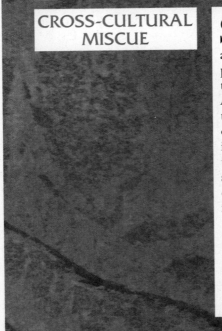

CROSS-CULTURAL MISCUE

Sometimes well-intentioned but short-sighted environmental sanitation programs can go awry when the planners are not sufficiently aware of local cultural realities. Through various types of foreign aid programs, U.S. technicians have made major efforts to introduce sanitary latrines into many developing countries. Although most North Americans do not regard latrines, or outhouses, as the height of sanitation, they do represent a significant advance over some traditional ways of disposing of human waste. Latrines built by U.S. technicians are fashioned after outhouses found in some rural areas of the United States; they are inexpensive wooden structures with a raised seat perforated by several holes. This latrine design, however, is not particularly well received in other parts of the world. George Foster relates an incident from El Salvador:

Several years ago a coffee planter, interested in the welfare of his employees, built a latrine for each house according to the standard American model. He was upset when his employees refused to use them. Finally an old man offered a suggestion. "Patron, don't you realize that here we are squatters?" . . . Latrines with raised seats seem to cause constipation among people who customarily defecate in a squatting position. (1973:103)

passed through the Admiralty Islands during World War II. They had been exposed to large doses of American technology as well. The American armed forces built roads, houses, and runways with the help of Manus labor. Mead claims that the Manus emulated the Americans not only because the Americans had an impressive array of technology but also because they treated the Manus with greater respect than had earlier contacts. So complete was the transformation in a mere quarter of a century that Mead spoke of the Manus as having given up their old lives for new ones.

Whereas most previous studies of rapid culture change were quick to point up the deleterious effects on the affected culture, Mead's restudy of the Manus suggests that rapid culture change doesn't have to be disruptive. Mead claimed that if the local people are willful participants in the change, the disruptive effects of change will be minimal, however rapidly the change may come. Even though Mead may have overestimated

the Manus' willful participation in the acculturation process and underestimated the disruptive effects on their lives, this nevertheless serves as an excellent example of acculturation without much coercion.

Sometimes people will voluntarily become acculturated because they believe that the adoption of certain technologies or behaviors will increase their adaptation to the environment. A case in point is the extensive culture change that resulted from the rapid adoption of snowmobiles by the reindeer-herding Skolt Lapps of Finland. According to Pelto (1973:67–75), the first snowmobile was introduced into Finland in 1962, and nine years later fifty-eight of the seventy families under study owned at least one snowmobile.

Traditional Lapp culture had always placed considerable emphasis on transportation systems and mobility. The seminomadic Skolt Lapps had adapted to their environment by maintaining two separate households— their nucleated villages inhabited during the winter months and their calving and fishing ground, which they inhabited during the spring. From these seasonal homesteads, the Lapp herders would travel intensively rounding up their herds. The concern with transportation as a key to successful adaptation was expressed in songs and folklore, their recreational activities (i.e., reindeer races), and even their courting and marriage rituals. As Pelto reports, "personal mobility, it was told to me again and again, is a main characteristic of the successful reindeer man: 'You have to be able to get around'" (1973:55). Thus, it is not difficult to understand the fascination that the Skolt Lapps had with the snowmobile: it provided them with a technological quantum leap in efficient mobility. In the process of adopting the snowmobile to reindeer herding, however, the Skolt Lapps experienced far-reaching changes in both their technology and their sociocultural patterns.

Linked Changes

Chapter 2 introduced the concept that cultures are more than the sum of their parts. Rather, cultures are systematic wholes, the parts of which are interconnected. If, in fact, cultures are integrated wholes, it would follow that a change in one part of the culture is likely to bring about changes in other parts. In other words, most changes that occur in cultures are **linked changes.** The introduction of a single technological innovation, for example, may well set off a series of changes in other parts of the culture. This proposition can be illustrated by looking at one such innovation—television—which was introduced into U.S. society during the 1950s. When the TV set, as part of our technological system, replaced the radio as the major form of electronic communication in U.S. households, it had far-reaching consequences for other nontechnological parts of the culture, such as the family system, the political process, and our religious institutions.

looking ahead

To better understand how a change (the building of a highway) can have negative consequences for local residents, see Applied Perspective 1 at the end of this chapter.

The advent of television has, without question, altered the nature of the American family. Before televi-

sion became widespread, dinnertime provided an occasion for family members to have face-to-face interaction with one another. With the coming of television and the so-called TV dinner, however, parents and children began spending dinnertime interacting with the "electronic Cyclops" rather than with one another. Campaign politics has never been the same since the arrival of television. Whereas Truman and Dewey conducted their presidential campaigns largely from the back of a railroad car in 1948, subsequent candidates were brought into our homes via television advertisements and televised debates. Today's candidates for public office need to be as attentive to such variables as lighting, clothing, and makeup as they are to the substantive issues in the campaign. In the area of organized religion, evangelicalism has been greatly enhanced by television. One can legitimately question whether Billy Graham would have such a lucrative ministry, Oral Roberts would have a university named after him, or Jim Bakker would have served time in federal prison if television did not exist.

Obstacles to Culture Change

In every culture there are always two opposing sets of forces—those promoting the status quo and those promoting culture change. At certain times, the forces of conservatism are in control, while at other times, the forces of change are in ascendancy. These two sets of forces are really two sides of the same coin. People are motivated to change their culture by a host of factors, including the desire for prestige, economic gain, or a new, more efficient way of solving a problem. There are also certain barriers to culture change that are important to understand, particularly if one works as a change agent. Some of the more prominent change-retarding factors are discussed in the following subsections.

Cultural Boundary Maintenance

A very important mechanism for preventing culture change is the creation and **maintenance** of **cultural boundaries** that keep people separate from other groups. Sometimes these boundaries are physical to the extent that most or all of the people live in one geographic area while excluding those who are not in the group. The more physically isolated a group is, the less susceptible it is to cultural diffusion. A culture does not need to be physically remote from other cultures, however, to avoid, or at least retard, culture change. Rather a culture can maintain its distinctiveness by imposing certain *cultural* boundaries that strengthen and glorify its own cultural traditions and discourage cultural borrowing from other groups. Such aspects of culture as language, eating habits, clothing, folklore, and humor are all used by cultures in one way or another to both emphasize their uniqueness and exclude outsiders.

Language.   Perhaps no other part of culture is more unique to a group than its language. As discussed in Chapter 6, language is more than merely a system for sending and receiving messages. It is also highly reflective of a people's ethos or worldview. In other words, language is an embodiment of the people's values. If a group of people want to remain culturally separate, the way to do it is to (1) use their own language exclusively, (2) forbid the use of other languages, and (3) discourage outsiders from speaking their language. Perhaps the most dramatic expression of linguistic exclusiveness takes the form of battles revolving around national language policy. The selection of Hindi in India or Swahili in Tanzania as a national language can be seen as an attempt to assert a particular cultural tradition while excluding others.

Clothing.   In large part because of its high visibility, clothing is another important symbol of group identity used to distinguish "us" from "them." To maintain their own unique cultural identity, people (particularly when away from home) are likely to wear their own ethnic or national dress. Africans wearing brightly colored kenti cloth, Chinese wearing Mao jackets, or American bikers wearing black leather jackets are all examples of expressions of cultural uniqueness. Sometimes feelings run high about the meanings conveyed by ethnic dress. For example, a man from the Swiss-German section of Switzerland who was married to a German woman refused to allow his seven-year-old son (who was half German) to wear *lederhosen,* a distinctive type of leather pants from southern Germany, because he wanted to make sure that everyone knew his son was Swiss and not German (personal communication).

Eating Styles.   Eating customs are another critical dimension of ethnicity that can serve as a cultural barrier to contact with other groups. In most, if not all cultures, eating is a highly social activity. What foods are eaten, in what manner, how often, and particularly with whom are all factors that vary from one culture to another.

Every culture uses the sharing of food in one way or another to maintain social ties and group solidarity. A good illustration is Hindu India, where people are strictly forbidden from eating with members of other castes. In some societies, the communal aspects of eating are emphasized to a far greater degree than they are in the United States. For example, Amharic speakers from Ethiopia not only eat food from a common basket but on special social occasions will actually put the food into each other's mouths rather than in their own. Moreover, by creating and maintaining certain food taboos, cultures set themselves apart from other cultures that do not recognize such prohibitions.

Relative Values

Sometimes people resist changes in their culture because the proposed change is not compatible with the existing value system. Change agents (such as overseas development workers, Peace Corps volunteers, or missionaries) often fail to understand why some people are so resistant to certain changes and don't seem to comprehend the advantages of the change. People from a particular culture may refuse to participate in an agricultural improvement project not because they do not understand the likely outcome of the project, but because the change would bring about a situation that would be less desirable (according to their values) than the *status quo.*

An illustration of resistance to change due to relative values occurred in Kenya in the early 1970s. Because of shortfalls in the maize production for several years running, the government, which controlled the sale of all maize meal in the country, decided to alleviate the shortage by mixing 10 percent wheat flour with 90 percent maize meal. Government officials reasoned that the ground wheat (obtained free from foreign assistance programs abroad) would make their dwindling maize supply last longer and avoid shortages in the retail stores. But the population reacted strongly against the government's attempt to "dilute" their basic staple (maize meal), which is used to make *ugali,* a porridge eaten at most meals. It seems that the maize meal mixed with 10 percent wheat had a somewhat different taste and consistency than 100 percent maize meal. As it turned out, according to the local value system, the *quality* of their maize meal was more important than the *quantity.* In other words, the people in Kenya were willing to put up with some degree of food shortages, provided the usual quality of their primary food source was not sacrificed.

The sharing of food and eating habits serve as a cultural barrier to contact with other cultural groups.

Another example of relative values serving as a barrier to culture change comes from South America (Ferraro 1994:129). A U.S. timber company harvesting wood in a remote area of the rain forest was experiencing difficulties recruiting labor from among the local Indian communities. In an attempt to attract laborers away from its main competitor (a German company), the U.S. firm invested heavily in housing for its employees, offered considerably higher wages than its competitor, and guaranteed the workers a forty-hour workweek (the Germans paid their workers by the hour). Yet despite these economic advantages, the majority of workers continued to work for the German firm. The explanation for this apparent "irrational" behavior on the part of the Indian work force is that what might be of value to workers in Detroit is not what appeals to Indian workers in the South American rain forest. For the Indian workers, flexibility of their time was more important than housing or high wages. Under the system used by the German firm—which paid an hourly wage rather than a forty-hour/week salary—the workers were able to take time off for their festivals and ceremonies without fear of losing their jobs.

Cultures as Organic Wholes

The functional interrelatedness of the parts of culture—particularly among small-scale, technologically simple cultures—can serve as a conservative force discouraging people from culture change. After a number of generations of adapting to their environments, many small-scale societies are in a state of relative equilibrium. That is, solutions to most societal problems have been worked out (albeit imperfectly), and a balance of social relationships have been established between various members of the group. To change one part of such a culture is likely to threaten existing social and economic relationships. To illustrate, Alan Beals (1962) cites the case of Gopalpur, a village in South India, which for centuries has utilized farming techniques that do not produce great yields. The use of modern technology, pesticides, chemical fertilizers, and more modern irrigation systems would, in all likelihood, result in increased agricultural productivity. But by adopting new farming techniques, the local farmer would jeopardize some significant social and economic relationships. As Beals put it:

> At every step, the farmer wishing to improve his agricultural practices must weigh the claims of the new method against the known economic and social benefits of the traditional method. To purchase improved agricultural equipment, the farmer must sever his traditional relationship with the Blacksmith and Carpenter. This is more than an economic relationship. Not only are the Carpenter and Blacksmith neighbors and friends, but they have religious functions that make their presence essential on such occasions as births, marriage, and death. (1962:79)

As Beals demonstrates, accepting changes in one part of a culture (e.g., agricultural technology) is likely to bring about undesirable changes in other parts of the culture (e.g., social and religious relationships). By refusing to adopt new farming technology, the rural farmer is not necessarily reacting in an ultra-conservative way, but rather is responding very sensibly.

Modernization

In everyday usage, **modernization** has many connotations, but in anthropological terms, it refers to the process by which traditional societies take on some of the sociocultural characteristics of industrialized societies. Most social scientists generally can agree on what have been the major sociocultural changes over the past several centuries. On most people's list would be such trends as advances in machine technology, industrialization, the growth of centralized political bureaucracies, urbanization, and the proliferation of nonkinship-based social groups, to mention just a few. There is considerably less consensus, however, on how to explain these major sociocultural trends.

A number of scholars have attempted to explain the process of modernization by proposing grand theories that frequently identify a single primary variable. Marx (orig. 1859) tended to focus on the centrality of modes of production and the resulting class structures. Max

Weber (1930) singled out certain key values associated with the Protestant Reformation (hard work, diligence, thrift, and upward mobility) as the prime movers behind modernization. Everett Hagen (1962) has suggested that modernization has its roots in certain sociopsychological processes revolving around personality development during childhood. While the debate over the causes of modernization has continued over the decades, the very processes of modernization that these grand theorists are attempting to explain not only have persisted but have actually accelerated and intensified.

Main Focuses of Modernization

The study of modernization has essentially followed two broad approaches. The first, and by far the most common focus over the past century, has been on the *institutional* level. It focuses on how entire societies gain control over their environments by applying more and more technology to increasingly more complex levels of social organization. Social scientists studying the modernization of *political* institutions focus on increasing trends toward political centralization, the rise of bureaucracies, the broadening of political functions, and the proliferation of new social groups (i.e., interest groups) that participate in the political process. The study of the modernization of *economic* institutions has examined such trends as increased labor specialization, the intensification of technology and inanimate sources of energy, increasing interdependence of markets, and rising standards of living. Students of the modernization of *social* institutions have concentrated on the rise of voluntary social organizations, the shift from the extended to the nuclear family, and the increased complexity of systems of social stratification.

The other major approach to the study of modernization—which tends to be more psychological than sociocultural—focuses on the *individual's* change from traditional to modern. Rather than concentrating on institutional changes, this second approach concerns itself with the role of the individual in the process of modernization. Whereas the first approach stresses changing social and cultural structures, the second emphasizes ways of thinking, feeling, and valuing. Following the lead of Inkeles (1983), Kluckhohn and Strodtbeck (1961), and Berry (1980), the subsequent discussion of modernization essentially defines modernity as a state of mind.

In recent years, the study of modernization has come under attack by a number of anthropologists. They claim that focusing on the differences between traditional

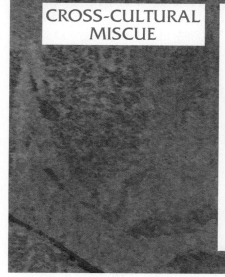

CROSS-CULTURAL MISCUE

Sometimes a lack of knowledge about other cultures can have catastrophic consequences. During the 1970s, the Nestle Food Company marketed its powdered infant formula in parts of the world that did not have uncontaminated water supplies. When mothers in these developing countries purchased the powdered formula, they had no choice but to mix it with contaminated water. This inevitably caused diarrhea, dehydration, and, in many cases, death among their infant children. The company's initial decision to market the powdered formula was a tragic error that could have been avoided had the company been willing to act upon some fundamental insights of cultural anthropology. After living with local populations and gaining insights into their life ways, cultural anthropologists are familiar with the cause and effect relationship between diarrhea and contaminated drinking water. If Nestle's had heeded this basic information, perhaps hundreds of thousands of babies would not have died needlessly.

(i.e., developing) and modern (i.e., industrialized) societies has led to two unfounded assumptions: first, that modern traits are superior to traditional ones; and second, that traditional people *should* adopt more modern ways of thinking and acting as quickly as possible if they know what is good for them. It is certainly true that many (indeed most) economic development programs sponsored by Western governments are founded on both of these assumptions. Economic assistance programs such as those sponsored by USAID and the World Bank are structured in ways that encourage the change from traditional to modern. While the findings of modernization studies have certainly been used by policymakers to achieve certain political ends, our purpose here is simply to get a clearer picture of some of the major dimensions of culture change. By contrasting modern and traditional traits, we are in no way implying that modern is better than traditional. Rather, we see "traditional traits" and "modern traits" as being logical end points on a continuum ranging from most traditional to most modern. These contrasts should be viewed as simply different responses to the world that may shed some light on the process of change. In other words, modern traits have no moral or ethical priority

over traditional ones, nor is there any prescriptive implication that traditional peoples *should* move toward more modern attitudes and behaviors.

By looking at the individual in the process of modernization, we have identified a number of dimensions of individual modernity—traits that make a person modern. While not suggesting that such a list is exhaustive, these traits include those discussed in the following subsections.

Receptivity to New Experiences

The modern person is more willing to accept new ways of thinking and behaving than is the traditional person. The traditional person tends to view novelty and change with skepticism and mistrust. Anything that disrupts traditional patterns is seen as potentially dangerous and should be avoided. This conservative orientation is embodied in a Spanish proverb heard widely throughout Latin America: "What is old and known is worth more than something new yet to be understood" (Foster 1973:84). The modern person, on the other hand, welcomes change, or at least is willing to take the risks that often accompany change. For example, a modern family that is getting along reasonably well in their present situation would nevertheless choose to relocate if they thought there was a good chance of improving its quality of life.

Even though not all people in the United States are open to change, the U.S. advertising industry certainly draws heavily upon this "love affair" with the new. We are told that since our toothpaste is "new and improved," it must be better than what existed before. Furthermore, in the United States, one effective way of criticizing something—be it a camera, a dress, or an idea—is to call it old-fashioned.

Expanding Opinions

A person is more modern if she or he shows a disposition to form and express opinions on a wide range of issues, both within and outside the immediate environment. Modern people are able to visualize themselves in positions of authority offering advice on how they might solve pressing societal problems. Inkeles and his colleagues (1983:37) have identified an additional dimension of this particular trait of modernity. Not only do modern people hold more opinions than their traditional counterparts, but they also have a greater awareness of and appreciation for the diversity of opinion.

This trait of expressing opinions is very closely associated with levels of education. That is, the more information a person gains through formal education on a wide range of contemporary topics, the more likely he or she will be to both develop an interest in a particular topic and form a personal opinion about it. In fact, this trait of modernity presupposes the acquisition of information. Being modern, in other words, involves more than having opinions; it also involves possessing the factual data to support those opinions. It is one thing for a person to hold the opinion that one political party is more interested in the average worker than is another party. It is something else to be able to cite specific pieces of legislation supported by each political party to buttress that opinion.

The Precise Reckoning of Time

A major component of being modern revolves around the definition of time. The modern person takes time very seriously and frequently makes minute distinctions between very small units of time such as seconds and minutes. The modern person treats time as a commod-

In modern societies, time is considered a valuable commodity and is taken very seriously.

ity, which, like money, can be spent, saved, or wasted. To ensure that she uses her time prudently, the modern woman schedules appointments in advance, establishes timetables, and sets deadlines for herself. Since modern people are so conscious of dividing time into precise units, promptness, or being "on time," is highly valued.

This modern definition of time is perhaps nowhere more developed than in the United States, where time plays a central role in people's lives. To illustrate, we punch timeclocks to measure our work; we measure in hundredths of a second how long it takes to swim fifty meters; even our eating is usually done in response to the clock, for we often eat not because we are hungry but because it is lunchtime or dinnertime; and most adults in the United States have strapped to their wrists a small device that divides minutes into sixty equal parts so that they will never be caught without knowing, quite precisely, what time it is.

Controlling One's Destiny

The modern person believes that he or she has control over his or her own destiny. In highly traditional societies, people tend to be fatalistic—that is, they see their lives as being in the hands of other (external) forces such as gods, governmental officials, the church, wealthy landlords, or nature. In modern societies, however, people believe that they not only can but should control their own destinies, their social and physical environments, and nature itself. If a river overflows its banks and destroys his house, the modern man will want to dam up the river and change its course. If the modern married couple wants to wait five years before having children, they will control the process of conception by using various contraceptive devices at their disposal. If gravity is a barrier to walking on the moon, the modern person will want to build a larger rocket engine to blast through the earth's gravitational pull. In other words, modern people believe that given sufficient time, energy, and money, there is little or nothing that can escape their control or few situations that cannot be changed.

Planning for the Future

The modern person is oriented toward long-term planning, both in public affairs as well as in his or her own private life. The modern person supports the notion that government should engage in long-term planning efforts. He or she agrees, for example, that the municipal government should be purchasing land today that will be used for new road construction two decades from now when automobile traffic will be greatly increased. Modern people are always focused on the future. They pay life insurance premiums today to protect their families in the event that they should die prematurely some time in the future. They invest in stocks, IRAs, and long-term CDs to put away a nest egg for their retirement years. They are fascinated with futuristic books such as *Megatrends* (Naisbitt 1982) and *The Third Wave* (Toffler 1981), which make predictions about where the society, indeed the world, is heading. In short, the modern person places a high value on planning for the future and working in the here and now to make the future a better time in which to live.

The Application of Universally Applicable Standards

Another important characteristic of modernity is the belief that rewards in the society should be based on a universally applicable set of standards, not on whim or any other type of irrational basis. The modern person would choose to hire employees based on some objective assessment of their skills and ability to handle the job (grades in school, standardized tests, outside references) rather than because they are related to the boss. Under a modern way of thinking, a worker would receive a promotion because of the efficiency of her or

Modern people—who believe in controlling the forces of nature—were responsible for building Biosphere II in the Catalina Mountains of Arizona.

his performance on the job, not because the manager happens to like the worker's hairstyle. This notion of rewarding people on the basis of some universally applied set of rules has been referred to as **universalism** (Parsons and Shils 1952:81) and **distributive justice** (Inkeles 1983:38–39). Whatever term we choose to use, we can recognize it as an ideal in the modern factory, office, or government bureaucracy.

Formal Education for Science, Technology, and New Learning

All societies, however traditional or modern, have systems of education, that is, ways of passing on the basics of the culture to the next generation. In traditional societies, education has as its main objective the preservation of traditional values. Koranic schools in Islamic cultures, for example, rely heavily on a rote method of learning to inculcate traditional religious wisdom. By way of contrast, modern people want to learn not only the three R's but also science, technology, and new ways of thinking and creating. Whereas traditional people think that science and modern learning are dangerous intrusions into the mysterious realm of religion, the modern person sees science and formal education as the best way of improving the quality of life. Modern people want to increase the rationality of their lives through education, while traditional people want to preserve the mystery of the sacred realm.

looking ahead

To see how a desire for formal education can contribute to the success of programs of population control in developing countries, see Applied Perspective 2 at the end of this chapter.

The Complexity of Studying Modernization

This discussion of modernization—and particularly our neat list of differences between the traditional and the modern—may appear overly simplistic. By drawing such contrasts, we are running the risk of suggesting that there is a clear-cut dichotomy between the traditional and the modern. In actual fact, there is no simple progression of change from traditional to modern. All peoples of the world are constantly choosing which traditional features they will retain and which modern ones they will embrace. Owing to local variations in cultural, economic, and political environments, different peoples have been making very creative adaptations to forces of modernization for decades. Thus, responses to modernization and other forces of change have varied widely from one part of the world to another.

Nevertheless, people all over the world are, to one degree or another, feeling the effects of the process of modernization. The impact on people—which can be traumatic—is most intense in developing countries. People in parts of Africa, Asia, and Latin America are experiencing massive changes in their cultures within a single generation or two. Simple, yet familiar, technologies have given way to the mysteries of the factory. The security of extended-family patterns are giving way to more nuclear families or single-parent families. Traditional religions are being undermined by the proselytizing of outside religions. Parents and children are separated from one another owing to the demands of migrant labor. Traditional systems of authority are breaking down. An enormous generation gap is developing between adjacent generations that have had radically different life experiences.

Adjustments to these rapidly changing sociocultural environments are exceedingly difficult if not impossible for most people. We must remember that in the United States and Europe, modernization occurred gradually over a number of generations. People of the developing world, however, are faced with monumental changes within the course of a single generation. This type of exposure to the forces of rapid modernization does not come without a high psychological cost. Many people find themselves caught between two different—and in some cases, diametrically opposed—systems of values. Sometimes people give up their traditional life without fully embracing any new alternative. At other times, an individual may be expected to behave according to different sets of cultural norms depending on the social situation. For example, a woman living in Mexico City is expected to behave according to one set of principles at the office but according to another set of principles when visiting her grandmother. The effort to live in two different worlds can be extremely anxiety producing.

To add to the confusion of trying to function in the midst of rapid change, many peoples in developing countries have in recent decades come to the sobering realization that much of the modern world that was so appealing initially is unattainable, at least in their lifetimes. In some developing countries, the population is growing more rapidly than GDP, which means that each year the country's material/economic well-being is worse than it was the year before. The gap between the haves and the have-nots is widening each year. People make enormous sacrifices to pay for their children's ed-ucation only to find there are no jobs to absorb these well-educated young people into the economy. In short, many people who have moved to cities in search of a more modern way of life, have been frustrated by the lack of opportunities to fulfill their dreams.

A major theme running through this chapter has been the concept of the interconnectedness of the parts of culture. That is, a change in one part of a cultural system causes changes in other parts. This notion is not just an interesting theory but has very practical implications for applied anthropologists who work in programs of planned change. When working to introduce change into another culture, either at home or abroad, it is imperative that applied anthropologists know how the part that is being changed is interconnected to other parts so as to avoid causing potentially harmful changes from taking place in other parts of the culture. The first case discusses how a cultural impact study conducted by an anthropologist revealed how a change in one part of the people's cultural environment was having harmful effects on other parts. The second case demonstrates how an anthropological study of changing attitudes and behaviors concerning marriage and family issues had important implications for a multimillion-dollar USAID project on family planning in Swaziland.

Culture Change

Short-term anthropological research on the environmental impact of an interstate highway helps resolve a class action suit in federal district court.

In the early 1970s, a group of urban residents in Charlotte, North Carolina, brought a class action suit against all those parties involved in building a highway through their neighborhood. Since the highway in question was part of the U.S. interstate highway system, the defendants in the case were the municipal government of Charlotte, the North Carolina Department of Transportation, and the U.S. Department of Transportation. Since much of the highway construction had already been completed at the time the lawsuit was filed, the plaintiffs were not asking the court to stop the remainder of the construction permanently. They did claim, however, that the construction of a major six-lane interstate highway through their neighborhood was having serious negative consequences. In particular, the suit charged that all three levels of government, in violation of federal law, had failed to conduct an environmental impact study on the neighborhood. On these grounds, the presiding judge ordered that all further construction on the highway be halted until an environmental impact study was conducted to (1) determine the negative effects the highway was having on the lives of local residents and (2) make recommendations for helping to alleviate some of the more serious consequences.

At the request of the attorneys for the plaintiffs and with the approval of the court, an urban anthropologist was hired to conduct a short-term environmental impact study on the project's effects on the community. Since

work was totally halted (and people were temporarily out of work) until the study was completed, the court impressed upon this newly recruited applied anthropologist that time was of the essence. Unlike more conventional anthropological field studies, which can take a year or longer, this study was expected to take no longer than several weeks to complete.

Despite the very real time constraints, some traditional anthropological data-gathering methods were employed. Using maps from the planning commission, it was possible to reconstruct the transportation flow between different parts of the neighborhood before the highway construction and determine how that flow had been disrupted. Extensive interviews were conducted with members of the community association, local entrepreneurs, and randomly selected neighborhood residents. And finally, the old anthropological standby—participant-observation—was used to actually observe the movement of people at certain key times, such as early-morning rush hour, late-afternoon rush hour, and Sunday mornings when people went to church.

Based on people's comments and personal observations, it became clear that the construction of a multilane highway through the center of the neighborhood had significantly disrupted the lives of the residents. A change in the people's physical environment had affected other parts of their culture and lifestyles.

The most damaging impact on the neighborhood had to do with the way people got around to take care of their everyday affairs, such as going to school, doing their grocery shopping, and attending their neighborhood churches. Since this was a low-income neighborhood (somehow planners never seem to build highways through the high-rent districts!), the majority of people did not own cars. They relied on public bus transportation to travel to other parts of the city, but since much of their lives was played out in the neighborhood itself, they had used a number of well-traveled pedestrian routes. The highway had cut off most of these routes. Now a person who lived on one side of the highway had no way of walking to the other side to shop or attend church. For those with automobiles, the construction of the highway made car travel within the neighborhood somewhat less convenient. But for the majority of people who relied on walking, the transportation patterns were disrupted almost completely.

Based on these findings, two recommendations were made to the court. First, since the only vehicular bridge spanning the highway had no provisions for pedestrian traffic, it was recommended that the builders add sidewalks, curb ramps for bicycles and baby carriages, traffic lights, and other amenities that would enable pedestrians to walk in safety. The second recommendation was to construct a separate pedestrian bridge over another part of the highway that would link part of the residential area with the neighborhood elementary school. This would add a second avenue for pedestrians to link up with both halves of the community as well as provide a traffic-free passageway for elementary schoolchildren. The court accepted both recommendations and required the defendants to carry them out as a precondition for the resumption of construction.

Here, then, is yet another example of how anthropological data and insights can be used to solve a particular societal problem. This short-term anthropological research project started with a fundamental idea about culture change. That is, a change in one part of the system is likely to bring about changes in other parts of the system. Through conventional field techniques (albeit for a short period of time), it was possible to document the degree to which a change in the people's material culture (i.e., system of roads and pathways) had affected their everyday patterns of transportation and social interaction. Once the sociocultural problems were identified, it was possible to make recommendations that, while not eliminating, would at least soften the negative impact of the highway construction on the lives of the local residents.

THOUGHT QUESTIONS

1. What negative consequences could the building of a six-lane highway have on the inhabitants of the neighborhood through which it runs?

2. Why do you think that most development projects in the United States are planned in low-income neighborhoods?

3. What other types of societal problems can be solved by the research findings of urban anthropologist?

A study of changing marriage patterns in Swaziland leads to policy recommendations for a program in population control.

Throughout much of the non-Western world, the issue of population control continues to be a major problem facing development planners. Even though population policy remains a sensitive issue in some developing countries, most development strategists agree on the critical role that fertility plays in national development. High birthrates lead to a host of deleterious effects, including high levels of internal and external migration, unemployment and underemployment, a decline in standards of living, and stagnation or a decline in socioeconomic development. If development agencies are to make progress in improving health conditions, agricultural productivity, employment opportunities, and educational facilities, they need to make the issue of population control their top priority.

In the early 1980s, USAID, the foreign aid branch of the U.S. government, was keenly aware of how closely the question of fertility was connected to some of the other programs they were administering in Swaziland, a southern African country with one of the highest birthrates in the world. To shed light on their population control efforts in Swaziland, USAID officials funded an anthropological research project designed to examine the implications of changing patterns of marriage on fertility (Ferraro 1980). By drawing on a wide variety of both historical and contemporary research strategies, the study documented a number of changes in marital practices in Swaziland over this century. Major trends were examined in such areas as type of marriage contracted, the amounts of bridewealth transferred, age at marriage for men and women, the incidence of polygyny, divorce rates, and conjugal roles.

Trends that emerged from this study on the changing average age of marriage were particularly relevant to USAID's efforts at population

control. Based on information dating back to the 1920s, it was found that the average age at which women married in the early 1980s had increased by between six and seven years. Whereas Swazi women formerly married in their mid- to late teens, the evidence from several different sources indicated the average age at the time of the research was early to mid-twenties. Much of the change in the average age of women at marriage can be explained by the greater educational opportunities for women. This more advanced age at which women were marrying tended to suppress the overall number of births, since it substantially reduced the number of child-bearing years for the average married woman in Swaziland.

This 1980 study of changing patterns of marriage in Swaziland looked at attitudes toward marriage as well as actual behavior. The study found a generally strong inverse relationship between levels of education and traditional attitudes about marriage, conjugal relationships, and family size. That is, the greater the exposure to formal education, the less likely an individual will support such traditional practices as arranged marriages, polygyny, and unlimited family size.

These findings on the relationship between education and family size were supported by other studies as well. For example, Vilakazi's (1979: 11–12) sample of educated women from urban Swaziland showed both a strong rejection of traditional family values and an equally strong affirmation of birth control values. Moreover, the 1976 census data (Blacker and Forsyth-Thompson, et al. 1979:166) revealed a reduction in family size among women with secondary or higher education. Thus, the findings from all three studies—along with the data on changing age at marriage—all tended to justify a fairly straightforward policy recommendation that was given to USAID for its program in population control. That is, one way of contributing to a decline in the birthrate in Swaziland is to support programs of secondary and higher education for women. Such a recommendation (which can contribute to the solution of the very serious social problem of runaway population rates) could have been made only after first studying the changing cultural patterns of the Swazis during the twentieth century.

THOUGHT QUESTIONS

1. Why is it so important for a developing country like Swaziland to reduce its birthrates?

2. What is the relationship between reducing birthrates and programs of higher education for women?

3. What is USAID and how does it function?

Summary

1. Although the rate of change varies from culture to culture, no cultures remain unchanged. The two principal ways that cultures change are internally through the processes of invention/innovation and externally through the process of diffusion.

2. Inventions can be either deliberate or unintentional. Although intentional inventors usually receive the most recognition, over the long run, unintentional inventors

have probably had the greatest impact on culture change. Because they are not bound by conventional standards, many inventors and innovators tend to be marginal people living on the fringes of society.

3. It is generally recognized that the majority of cultural features (things, ideas, and behavior patterns) found in any society got there by diffusion rather than invention. The following generalizations can be made about the process of diffusion: (a) cultural diffusion is selective in nature, (b) it is a two-way process, (c) it is likely to involve changes in form and/or function, (d) some cultural items are more likely candidates for diffusion than are others, and (e) it is affected by a number of important variables.

4. Acculturation is a specialized form of cultural diffusion that refers to forced borrowing under conditions of external pressure. While some anthropologists have described situations of acculturation in which the non-dominant culture has voluntarily chosen the changes, others claim that acculturation always involves some measure of coercion and force.

5. Since the parts of a culture are to some degree interrelated, a change in one part is likely to bring about changes in other parts. This insight from cultural anthropology should be of paramount importance to applied anthropologists, who are frequently involved directly or indirectly with planned programs of culture change.

6. Among the barriers to culture change are the following: (a) some societies can maintain their cultural boundaries through the exclusive use of language, food, and clothing; (b) some societies can resist change in their culture because the proposed change is not compatible with their existing value systems; and (c) sometimes people will resist change because they are unwilling to disrupt existing social and economic relationships.

7. Modernization refers to the process of traditional societies taking on some of the characteristics of industrialized societies. At the institutional level, this involves trends toward political centralization, increased labor specialization, the nuclearization of the family, and the rise of voluntary social organizations.

8. When viewed from the perspective of the individual, modernization involves, among other things, an increase in one's receptivity to new experiences, a more precise reckoning of time, a greater sense of controlling one's destiny, and an orientation toward the future.

 Key Terms

acculturation
cultural boundary
   maintenance
diffusion
distributive justice
innovation

invention
linked change
marginal people
modernization
universalism

Suggested Readings

Arensberg, Conrad M., and A. H. Niehoff. *Introducing Social Change: A Manual for Americans Overseas.* Chicago: Aldine, 1964. An old, yet important, book demonstrating the need for understanding other cultures when involved in programs of planned change abroad.

Bernard, H. R., and P. J. Pelto, eds. *Technology and Social Change.* 2d ed. Prospect Heights, Ill.: Waveland Press, 1987. A collection of thirteen essays discussing the effects of modern technology on non-Western cultures.

Bodley, John H. *Victims of Progress.* 3d ed. Mountain View, Calif.: Mayfield, 1990. An important book that examines the sometimes disastrous effects of Westernization and industrialization on tribal societies. Bodley discusses the high price small-scale societies pay for "progress" and the role that Western institutions play in this cultural devastation.

Inkeles, Alex. *Exploring Individual Modernity.* New York: Columbia University Press, 1983. A sequel to his earlier volume entitled *Becoming Modern* (1974), this long-term study examines the characteristics of the modern person and the forces of modernity in developing countries.

Kottak, Conrad P. *Assault on Paradise: Social Change in a Brazilian Village.* New York: Random House, 1983. A readable and highly personal account of changes occurring in Arembepe, a village in Brazil. An excellent book for introductory students because it not only documents important sociocultural trends but also highlights the changes that have taken place in the ethnographer over the span of two decades.

Pelto, P. J. *The Snowmobile Revolution: Technology and Social Change in the Arctic.* Menlo Park, Calif.: Benjamin Cummings, 1973. A study of sociocultural change documenting how a single technological device, the snowmobile, brought about vast economic and social changes among the reindeer-herding Skolt Lapps of Finland.

Rogers, Everett M. *Diffusion of Innovations* 3d ed. New York: Free Press, 1983. A quantitative, up-to-date, and richly documented study of the mechanism of cultural diffusion that discusses, among other topics, the history of diffusion research, how innovations are generated, rates of adoption of innovations, diffusion networks, and change agents.

Tonkinson, Robert. *The Jigalong Mob: Aboriginal Victors of the Desert Crusade*. Menlo Park, Calif.: Benjamin Cummings, 1974. In this study of sociocultural change among a group of Australian aborigines, the author provides a wealth of data on how one group was able to maintain its ethnic pride and traditional values in the face of Western colonialism.

Spindler, Louise S. *Culture Change and Modernization: Mini-Models and Case Studies*. Prospect Heights, Ill.: Waveland, 1984. A discussion of the process of culture change for introductory students, drawing liberally from many ethnographic studies for examples.

THE FUTURE OF ANTHROPOLOGY

One need not be a scholar of culture change to notice that the pace at which cultures are changing is accelerating with every decade. By comparison, the everyday lives of our grandparents seems simple and slow-moving. Today many people, at least in the industrialized world, are overwhelmed by how quickly their culture is changing. In fact, in 1971 Toffler wrote about future shock, which he defines as the psychological disorientation resulting from living in a cultural environment that is changing so rapidly that people feel they are constantly living in the future.

Culture change is occurring at such an accelerated pace today that it is frequently difficult to keep up with all of the changes. Moreover, because of the recent revolution in transportation and electronic communications, the world is getting smaller. Today it is possible to travel to the other side of the earth on an SST in about the same time it took our great-grandparents to travel fifty miles in a horse and carriage. Via satellite we can see instant transmissions of live newscasts from anywhere in the world. Owing to this vastly improved capacity to communicate with and travel to other parts of the world, cultural diffusion has increased dramatically in recent decades. Consequently, the differences between cultures have been diminishing.

If the cultural world is, in fact, shrinking, it has led some people to wonder whether the discipline of cultural anthropology is losing its subject matter. Such people argue that it will be just a matter of years before all of the cultures of the world are homogenized into a single culture, leaving the discipline of anthropology without a field of study. If one takes a very traditional view of anthropology—the aim of which is to document the cultural and biological features of isolated indigenous peoples—then the future of the discipline is indeed bleak. It is certainly true that exotic cultures (relatively untouched by the modern world) are few and far between today.

As we approach the twenty-first century, however, only a handful of cultural anthropologists are studying the quickly diminishing number of pristine cultures that were being studied at the beginning of the century. The research interests and activities of the discipline have adapted to the realities of the changing world. The fact that formerly hunting-and-gathering societies are now involved in market economies and consumerism should not lead us to conclude that all cultural differences are disappearing. Even though some of the obvious differences between cultures may be decreasing, there is little evidence to suggest that the world is becoming a cultural melting pot. Thus, despite rapid culture change, there will, no doubt, be sufficient cultural diversity to keep anthropologists occupied well into the future.

If cultural anthropologists are no longer seeking out and describing the "uncontaminated" cultures of the world, what kind of future does the discipline have? Without making any wild prognostications, we can predict that the discipline of cultural anthropology will, in all likelihood, continue to move in the direction it has set for itself in the past several decades. Among the recent concerns and trends that are likely to continue well into the future are a concern for the cultural survival of indigenous peoples, a greater emphasis on the study of complex societies such as our own, and greater interest in developing strategies for using anthropological data to solve societal problems. Although we will discuss these concerns separately, all three are closely interrelated and, no doubt, affect one another.

Cultural Survival of Indigenous Peoples

In recent years, cultural anthropologists have become increasingly concerned about the rapid disappearance of indigenous populations of the world. According to the World Council on Indigenous Peoples (quoted in Bodley 1982), an indigenous population is any ". . . people living in countries which have populations composed of different ethnic or racial groups who are descendants of the earliest populations which survive in the area, and who do not, as a group, control the national government of the countries within which they live" (166–167). Classic examples of "indigenous peoples" are those small-scale cultures in Asia, Africa, and the Americas that came under the influence of the colonial powers during the past several centuries.

Many anthropologists are concerned about the survival of these indigenous peoples not because they form the subject matter of much anthropological research, but because their disappearance raises some basic human rights issues. A growing number of cultural anthropologists feel strongly that indigenous populations over the past several centuries have been negatively affected by the onslaught of civilization. Cultural patterns—and in some cases the people themselves—have been eradicated as a direct result of civilization's pursuit of "progress" and economic development.

The Industrial Revolution in nineteenth-century Europe was "revolutionary" to the extent that it led to explosions in both population and consumerism, which in turn had drastically negative effects on indigenous peoples. The technological efficiency of the Industrial Revolution resulted in a quantum leap in population growth. To illustrate, prior to the Industrial Revolution, it took 250 years for the world's population to double, whereas by the 1970s it took only thirty-three years (Bodley 1982:3). At the same time that populations were exploding in the industrializing world, there was a concomitant growth in the notion of consumerism. If economies were to grow and prosper, production needed to be kept high, which could be accomplished only if people purchased and consumed the products of industry. In order to meet the needs of a growing population with ever-increasing desires to consume, people needed to control and exploit natural resources wherever they might be found.

A major motivation for the colonization of the non-Western world was economic in that the natural resources found in Asia and Africa were needed to fuel European factories. The so-called scramble for Africa, which was initiated when the leaders of Europe set national boundaries in Africa at the Conference of Berlin in 1884, was a very "civilized" and "gentlemanly" way of dividing up the continent's natural resources for the industrializing nations of Europe. Unfortunately, the rights of indigenous populations were hardly protected. In many cases, land and resources needed by the indigenous peoples were simply appropriated for use by the colonial powers. Landless populations were forced to become laborers, dependent on whatever wages the colonial governments and businesses wished to pay. Native resistance to this systematic exploitation was usually met with force. In some cases, large segments of the population were killed or died from European diseases. In other less severe situations, indigenous peoples were economically exploited, systematically kept at the lowest echelons of the society, and forced to give up their traditional identities.

Specific examples of the demise of indigenous populations are all too commonly found in the literature (see, for example, Bodley 1982, and Burger 1987). The tragic annihilation of the population of Tasmania in the nineteenth century is one of the more dramatic examples. Through the use of military force and heavy-handed missionary efforts, not only was the aboriginal culture of Tasmania eliminated, but the people themselves were literally exterminated, many by deliberate killings, because the white settlers wanted the land for sheepherding. Around the turn of the last century the Germans administered their "protectorate" in southwest Africa (currently Namibia) upon the principle that native populations should give up their land for European use. When the indigenous Herero people refused, the Germans made good on their threats to wage a war of extermination, justifying their military actions on the basis of social Darwinism and white supremacy. But we need not go to the far corners of the earth to find tragic examples of the exploitation of native peoples. The litany of atrocities committed against Native Americans in the name of progress and Manifest Destiny date back to the earliest European settlements. The massacre of the Pequot in Connecticut in 1637 and the massacre of the Sioux at Wounded Knee in 1890 are just two examples from our own history.

In recent years, the most dramatic examples of the degradation of indigenous peoples has come from Brazil, where Indians are being swept away by the relentless frontier of colonialism and economic development. To illustrate, during the 1960s, an Indian village in Brazil was attacked by a gang of gunslingers allegedly hired by a large Brazilian corporation that wanted the Indians off the land. Davis (1977:79–80) described the "Massacre at Parallel Eleven" in which the hired "hit men" attempted to wipe out the village and its inhabitants by throwing dynamite from a low-flying airplane. During the 1970s, the threats to indigenous peoples, while not quite so blatantly directed toward genocide, were no less devastating. By building roads through the Amazonian frontier, the Brazilian government has introduced such diseases as influenza and measles to the indigenous peoples of the region. By the 1990s, tens of thousands of gold prospectors had invaded the territory of the Yanomamo, extracted millions of dollars worth of gold from the land, and left the Yanomamo ravaged by disease. In a feeble attempt to protect the indigenous Yanomamo, the Brazilian government ordered the destruction of 110 airstrips built by the gold miners on Yanomamo land. But the miners circumvented the government efforts to destroy their airstrips by using helicopters, which do not require landing strips—an indication of just how difficult it is to protect indigenous peoples from the onslaught of the industrial world (Brooke 1990).

Cultural anthropologists have not only been documenting the demise of indigenous peoples, but many have also been using their specialized knowledge to help these endangered cultures survive. In one of the most urgent forms of applied anthropology, a number of cultural anthropologists in recent years have contributed to the efforts of Cultural Survival, Inc., a nonprofit organization that supports projects on five continents designed to help indigenous peoples survive the changes brought about by contact with industrial societies. Founded in 1972, Cultural Survival works to guarantee the land and resource rights of tribal peoples while at the same time supporting economic development projects run by the people themselves. As part of their work with Cultural Survival, cultural anthropologists have conducted research on vital cultural issues, served as cultural brokers between the indigenous people and government officials, and published literature informing the public about the urgency of these survival issues. Given the ever increasing number of indigenous populations that are facing cultural extinction—including the San of southern Africa, the Sherpas of Nepal, and the Kurds in the Middle East—it is likely that cultural anthropologists will continue to apply their expertise to help these people avoid cultural genocide.

The Study of Complex Societies

When most people think of cultural anthropology they envision an anthropologist, notebook in hand, interviewing a scantily clad native inside a mud hut. Although cultural anthropologists from the United States have traditionally tended to concentrate their research efforts on small-scale, non-Western societies, an increasing number in recent years have turned their attention to studying their own complex societies. A number of factors converged to set this trend in motion. First, a handful of anthropologists after World War II conducted some of the first urban anthropological studies in such places as Timbuktu, Mexico City, and Kamala because the so-called tribal peoples were migrating to cities in ever increasing numbers during the postwar period. Second, the trend toward the study of complex urban societies by anthropologists was stimulated, at least in the United States, by the growing interest in applied anthropology. After the affluent decade of the 1950s, the 1960s witnessed the rediscovery of ethnicity and poverty, both of which were defined as urban problems. Consequently, U.S. policymakers have been more willing in recent decades to use the findings of cultural anthropologists to help solve some of these pressing social problems at home. Third, anthropologists have turned to the study of various aspects of our own complex society because research opportunities in more traditional societies have diminished. Since gaining independence, many developing countries have been increasingly reluctant to grant research permission to Western anthropologists. Moreover, shortages in research funding have prevented many Western scholars from conducting anthropological studies abroad.

When anthropologists study their own complex societies, however, they encounter some unique problems. One such problem is that cultural anthropologists run the risk of prejudice or distortion because they lack the outsider perspective. Another difficulty—and one that has not been adequately resolved—concerns just how well anthropologists studying complex societies are able to live up to their own tradition of holism. A holistic approach—i.e., examining a culture within its total context—is much more manageable when studying a small-scale society comprising several thousand people than it is when studying a social system comprising eight million people, such as New York City. Rather than writing holistic ethnographies of cities, anthropologists operating in urban or complex societies have adopted a more limited focus by studying small ethnic neighborhoods, specialized occupational groups, or other subcultural groups that operate within the more complex whole. Nevertheless, as a field of study, cultural anthropology has a good deal to offer the study of complex societies. For example, cultural anthropologists bring to the study of cities and complex societies a sensitivity to ethnic diversity; a tradition of framing their research problems in broad, holistic terms; and the research method of participant-observation, which provides an important supplement to the more quantitative methods of urban sociologists.

The anthropological study of U.S. society has explored a wide variety of topics. To illustrate, cultural anthropologists in recent years have studied hippie lifestyles, street gangs, retirement communities, adaptive strategies of urban tramps, and Black urban families. Within a more institutional framework, retirement communities, hospitals, classrooms, and volunteer fire departments have all been subjects of anthropological analysis. Certain occupations, such as construction workers and railroad engineers, have been treated as occupational subcultures by some anthropologists. And even certain aspects of popular culture in the United States—football, films, soap operas, and food—have all been studied by cultural anthropologists as symbols of our cultural values. Since cultural anthropology involves the comparative study of culture in whatever form it may take—and since the United States provides many interesting cultural variations—this trend toward greater anthropological analysis of our own culture is likely to continue into the future.

The Greater Utilization of Anthropological Knowledge

This introductory text in cultural anthropology has been written with an applied perspective. Since introductory students will follow a variety of career patterns, this text has been designed to demonstrate how the insights from anthropology can be used by people from a number of professions. The text has illustrated how anthropological knowledge can be used to solve problems by architects, law enforcement officials, businesspersons, medical personnel, educators, foreign aid personnel, court officials, family planners, and others. While this applied perspective has demonstrated how anthropology has contributed to the solution of societal problems, much still needs to be done to increase the extent to which anthropological knowledge can *actually* be utilized by policy and decision makers. It is one thing to point out the potential uses of anthropological information, but it is quite another to actually use that information to make a difference in the quality of our lives.

As applied anthropology continues to become more prominent into the twenty-first century, more and more anthropologists with an eye toward practical concerns are seeking new strategies to ensure that anthropological insights will have an impact on the policy process. It is no longer enough for applied anthropologists to simply conduct their research and report their findings. According to Rylko-Bauer, Van Willigen, and McElroy (1989), applied anthropologists also need to develop a comprehensive utilization strategy that will maximize the likelihood that the findings will be used by policy-makers and decision makers. Such a strategy, they suggest, should include the following elements:

1. Collaboration in the research process between applied anthropologists and potential users will increase the chances that findings will be used, because it "demystifies" the research, provides opportunities for valuable feedback, and increases the commitment to the research.
2. Applied anthropologists must become familiar with the organizations sponsoring their research. Speci-

fically, they need to be clear about the organization's goals and philosophy, who are the relevant people in the decision-making chain of command, and what is the normal decision-making process.
3. Applied anthropologists must be sufficiently knowledgeable about the community under study to be able to identify possible sources of resistance to using the findings.
4. Since policy makers frequently need cultural information quickly, applied anthropologists need to develop more time-efficient methods if their findings are to be utilized.

Thus, applied anthropologists are becoming more astute in structuring their research with an eye toward utilization, a trend that will, no doubt, continue into the future.

In addition to developing strategies for the utilization of applied research findings, there is an enormous potential for the use of already existing anthropological data. As we continue to experience a revolution in communication and transportation, all peoples of the world are being thrown together with increasing frequency. Businesspersons, diplomats, educators, technical assistance personnel, missionaries, scholars, and citizen-tourists are traveling throughout the world in greater numbers than ever before. Unhappily, advances in our understanding of other cultures have not kept pace with the advances in communications and transportation technology. Thus, a growing number of people are expected to perform their professional activities in an unfamiliar cultural environment, but this need not be the case.

For years cultural anthropologists have collected enormous quantities of data on the various cultures of the world. While cultural data exist on most peoples of the world, it is not always accessible or understandable by nonanthropologists. The great bulk of cultural data are hidden away in obscure anthropological journals and written in language that would require a Ph.D. in anthropology to comprehend. Perhaps one of the greatest challenges facing anthropology as it approaches the twenty-first century is to become involved in a process that will make anthropologists' already existing data available and usable to nonanthropologists. In short, anthropologists must themselves become (or train others to become) cultural brokers who translate anthropological findings into terms that nonanthropologists can use to cope more effectively with the cultural environments in which they find themselves.

APPENDIX
ANTHROPOLOGY AND JOBS

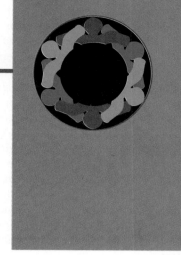

With the costs of college education continuing to sky-rocket, more and more parents are asking their college-aged children some very practical questions. For example, parents want to know why their children are majoring in anthropology. Behind such a question is, of course, the more pragmatic question: What kind of job can you get with a B.A. in anthropology?

It is important to bear in mind that a B.A. in cultural anthropology—like most other undergraduate fields of study—is a liberal arts degree and not some type of professional certification. In other words, an undergraduate degree in anthropology does not prepare a person to become a professional research anthropologist any more than an undergraduate degree in political science equips a person to achieve high political office. The B.A. in anthropology does provide excellent background for graduate study in anthropology at the Ph.D. level, which is the normal route to becoming a professional anthropologist.

For those not interested in pursuing a career as an anthropologist, the B.A. in anthropology provides valuable skills and insights that can be relevant for a wide variety of other professions. Since cultural anthropology involves the study of human behavior in whatever form it may take, a B.A. in anthropology can be useful for any job that requires an understanding of human cultural behavior. Such a general statement, however, is of little use to the recent college graduate who is pounding the pavement in search of employment. The term *anthropologist* or *cross-cultural expert* is not a stan-dard job classification in the employment section of a newspaper's classified ads. In recent decades, however, a number of jobs in both government and industry have developed that focus on certain cross-cultural issues and involve working with people from different cultural and subcultural backgrounds. Many of the case studies appearing in the "Applied Perspective" sections of this text illustrate how anthropological skills have been applied to a number of different professional areas. For example, case studies showed how anthropological skills and insights have been used to help architects design relevant housing for subcultural groups, develop a highly successful reforestation program in Haiti, shed light on the public health aspects of the AIDS epidemic, and provide courts with culturally relevant information for the resolution of legal cases, to mention but a few applications.

As mentioned in Chapter 3, the prevalence of applied anthropology within the discipline has increased in recent decades, most notably during the 1970s and 1980s. Due in large part to a shrinking academic job market—coupled with federal legislation requiring environmental impact studies and historical preservation—more professionally trained anthropologists are now employed in nonacademic positions than are in colleges and universities. As more and more Ph.D.-level anthropologists are making their way into nonacademic jobs, employment opportunities for those with less than Ph.D. training in anthropology are also increasing. Today people with training in cultural anthropology are putting their observational and analytical skills to work in a variety of ways in both the public (governmental) and private (business) sectors of the economy.

Opportunities for employment with the U.S. federal government are wide ranging. In the area of international development, an increasing number of jobs are opening up for people who understand cross-cultural behavior. Such organizations as the U.S. Agency for International Development (USAID)—the organization that administers U.S. foreign aid—hire people trained in anthropology to provide the background needed to successfully implement certain programs of planned change, such as programs for family planning, agricultural development, educational reform, and disease prevention. As many development agencies throughout the world have learned the hard way, the most well-intentioned programs of planned change can have disastrous results unless something is known about the cultures of the target populations. Before spending (in some cases) millions of dollars on development programs for developing countries, such organizations as USAID want to have as much relevant information as possible about the local cultures.

While anthropological skills are valuable for various types of government work abroad, at least as many cultural anthropologists are working for various branches of government (federal, state, and municipal) at home. Since the United States, contrary to popular myth, is not a perfect melting pot, a good deal of ethnicity can be found in the fifty states. Thus, as long as substantial cultural differences exist in the United States, there will be a need for anthropological skills and insights to help bureaucrats work effectively with all cultural subgroups.

Since anthropology deals with understanding cultural differences, and since governments are in the business of providing services for all people, there should be a considerable overlap of interests between cultural anthropologists and government bureaucrats. To illustrate, people with anthropological training have worked in government positions at home in the following areas: aging, criminal justice, cultural resources management, education, family planning, human and civil rights, information systems, medical care, museums, nutrition, program evaluation, public housing, public relations and communications, refugee settlement, research grant writing, social impact analysis, substance abuse, urban planning, and welfare policy. While this list is hardly definitive, it does give a general idea of the scope of jobs related to training in anthropology.

Today a growing number of students of anthropology are finding their way into new and exciting areas of employment, particularly in the private sector of the economy. The following is a sample of recent employment experiences in the world of business by those with training in anthropology:

Steven Barnett was hired by an advertising agency in charge of creating an ad campaign for the Sylvester Stallone movie *Rambo III*. Barnett conducted ethnographic research on how a cross section of U.S. theater goers viewed Rambo. Barnett's findings that Rambo was viewed almost as a comic book hero resulted in an ad campaign that played down ". . . the cold war politics and played up Rambo as a larger-than-life cultural icon" (Heller 1988: A-24).

Some U.S. companies are interested in hiring those trained in cultural anthropology to collect relevant information on their culturally diverse workforces as a way of minimizing conflicts between the corporate culture and the culture(s) of their workers.

Lucy Suchman, working as a researcher for Xerox, makes anthropological observations of airport workers to learn how they keep track of people, airplanes, luggage, and air freight. Xerox hopes to use these findings to help improve its handling of documents, design more user friendly equipment, and improve its instruction manuals (Deutsch 1991: C-11).

Companies that are manufacturing, marketing, or negotiating abroad need help from anthropologically trained people when working in culturally unfamiliar waters.

Allison Cohen, described as a marketing ethnographer, conducts firsthand research into people's kitchen cabinets, refrigerators, and medicine cabinets to determine their buying patterns. Rather than using mailed questionnaires, as has been the case in more traditional marketing research, people like Cohen are hired by marketing firms to observe U.S. consumer behavior in its natural context. Advertising agencies are willing to hire these "Margaret Meads of marketing" because they feel they will be able to develop more effective ad campaigns if they first know something about what is being bought and why (Miller, Shenitz, and Rosado 1990: 59–60).

Lorna McDougall, an employee at Arthur Andersen's Center for Professional Education, uses anthropological data-gathering techniques to study why some people learn more effectively through the lecture method and others learn better through more interactive methods. The findings from this research will enable the instructors at the center to use the most effective teaching techniques in their corporate training (Deutsch 1991: C-11).

The preceding discussion has attempted to provide some idea as to how those with training in anthropology can fit into the world of work. As Van Willigen reminds us, "the (job) market is not very much aware of anthropologists as such . . ." (1986: 209). In the final analysis, each student is responsible for carving out a spot in the job market for herself or himself. In other words, since no jobs in the nonacademic world are exclusively for cultural anthropologists, it is important for the graduate in cultural anthropology to prepare for the job search by gaining an understanding of the organization offering the job as well as a clear appreciation of what he or she brings to the job situation. In reference to the latter, anthropology graduates are better equipped in certain areas than are those graduating with any other liberal arts degree. First, anthropology graduates are well acquainted with cross-cultural differences and similarities, an area of expertise of particular importance in a multicultural society such as our own. Second, training in anthropology instills an understanding of such information-gathering skills as interviewing and participant-observation. And third, a general understanding of cultural phenomena, along with certain research techniques, can be extremely valuable to any organization that deals with people from different cultural or subcultural backgrounds.

GLOSSARY

Acculturation a specific form of cultural diffusion in which a subordinate culture adopts many of the cultural traits of a more powerful culture.

Acephalous society a society without a political head such as a president, chief, or king.

Achieved status the status an individual acquires during the course of her or his lifetime.

Adaptive nature of culture implies that culture is the major way human populations adapt or relate to their specific habitat in order to survive and reproduce.

Affinal relatives kinship ties formed through marriage (i.e., in-laws).

Age grade permanent age categories in a society through which people pass during the course of a lifetime.

Age set a group of people roughly the same age who pass through various age grades together.

Agriculture a form of food production that requires intensive working of the land with plows and draft animals and the use of techniques of soil and water control.

Allocation of resources rules adopted by all societies that govern the regulation and control of such resources as land, water, and their by-products.

Ambilineal descent a form of descent that affiliates a person to a kin group through either the male or the female line.

Ambilocal residence the practice of a newly married couple taking up residence with either the husband's or the wife's parents.

Analyzing data one of five stages of fieldwork in which the cultural anthropologist determines the meaning of data collected in the field.

Ancestor worship the worshiping of deceased relatives. These souls are considered supernatural beings and fully functioning members of a descent group.

Anthropological linguistics the scientific study of human communication within its sociocultural context.

Applied anthropology the application of anthropological knowledge, theory, and methods to the solution of specific societal problems.

Archaeology the subfield of anthropology that focuses on the study of prehistoric and historic cultures through the excavation of material remains.

Arranged marriage any marriage in which the selection of the spouse is outside the control of the bride and groom.

Ascribed status the status a person has by virtue of birth.

Assimilation the process of absorbing a racial or ethnic group into the wider society.

Authority legitimate power exercised with the consent of the members of a society.

Avunculocal residence the practice of a newly married couple taking up residence with or near the husband's mother's brother.

Balanced reciprocity the practice of giving with the expectation that a similar gift will be given in the opposite direction either immediately or after a limited period of time.

Band society the basic social unit found in many hunting-and-gathering societies, characterized by being kinship based and having no permanent political structure.

Barbarism the middle of three basic stages of a nineteenth-century theory developed by Lewis Henry Morgan that all cultures evolve from simple to complex systems: savagery, barbarism, and civilization.

Bilateral descent a type of kinship system whereby individuals emphasize both their mother's kin and their father's kin relatively equally.

Bound morpheme a combination of two or more phonemes.

Bourgeoisie a Marxian term referring to the middle class.

Breadwinner a traditional gender role found in the United States that views males as being responsible for the economic support and protection of the family.

Bride service work or service performed for the bride's family by the groom for a specified period of time either before or after the marriage.

Bridewealth (bride price) the transfer of goods from the groom's lineage to the bride's lineage to legitimize marriage.

Capital goods goods or wealth used to purchase or produce other goods.

Cargo cults revitalization movements in Melanesia intended to bring new life and purpose into a society.

Carrying capacity the maximum number of people a given society can support given the available resources.

Caste a rigid form of social stratification in which membership is determined by birth and social mobility is nonexistent.

Census taking the collection of demographic data about the culture being studied.

Chiefdom an intermediate form of political organization in which integration is achieved through the office of chiefs.

Civilization a term used by anthropologists to describe any society that has cities.

Clan a unilineal descent group comprised usually of more than ten generations consisting of members who claim a common ancestry even though they cannot trace step-by-step their exact connection to a common ancestor.

Class a ranked group within a stratified society characterized by achieved status and considerable social mobility.

Coercive theory of state formation argues that the state came into existence as a direct result of warfare.

Collaterality refers to kin related through a linking relative.

Collecting data stage of fieldwork involving selection of data-gathering techniques and the gathering of information pertinent to the hypothesis being studied.

Communal cults societies where groups of ordinary people conduct religious ceremonies for the well-being of the total community.

Conflict theory a theory of social stratification that argues that society is always changing and in conflict because individuals in the upper stratum use their wealth, power, and prestige to exploit those below them.

Consanguineal relatives one's biological or blood relatives.

Corporate lineage a kinship group whose members engage in daily activities together.

Council of elders a formal control mechanism composed of a group of elders who settle disputes between individuals within a community.

Crime harm to a person or property that is considered illegitimate by a society.

Cross cousins children of one's mother's brother or father's sister.

Crow system a kinship system, associated with matrilineal descent, in which similar terms are used for (1) one's father and father's brother, (2) one's mother and mother's sister, and (3) one's siblings and parallel cousins.

Cultural anthropology the scientific study of cultural similarities and differences wherever and in whatever form they may be found.

Cultural boundary maintenance the practice of cultural groups keeping themselves separate from other cultural groups.

Cultural diffusion the spreading of a cultural trait (i.e., material object, idea, or behavior pattern) from one society to another.

Cultural emphasis of a language the idea that the vocabulary in any language tends to emphasize words that are adaptively important in that culture.

Cultural materialism a contemporary orientation in anthropology which holds that cultural systems are most influenced by such material things as natural resources and technology.

Cultural relativism the idea that cultural traits are best understood when viewed within the cultural context of which they are a part.

Cultural universal those general cultural traits found in all societies of the world.

Culture shock a psychological disorientation experienced when attempting to operate in a radically different cultural environment.

Dance intentional rhythmic nonverbal body movements that are culturally patterned and have aesthetic value.

Dependent variable a variable that is affected by the independent variable.

Descent tracing one's kinship connections back through a number of generations.

Descriptive linguistics the branch of anthropological linguistics that studies how languages are structured.

Diffusion *see* cultural diffusion.

Diglossia the situation in which two forms of the same language are spoken by people in the same language community depending on the social situation.

Displacement the ability that humans have to talk about things that are remote in time and space.

Distributive justice *see* universalism.

Division of labor the set of rules found in all societies dictating how the day-to-day tasks are assigned to the various members of a society.

Document analysis examination of data such as personal diaries, newspapers, colonial records, etc., to supplement information collected through interviewing and participant-observation.

Double descent a system of descent in which individuals receive some rights and obligations from the father's side of the family and others from the mother's side.

Double work load where employed married women, particularly those with children, are both wage employed and primarily responsible for housework and child care.

Dowry the transfer of goods or money from the bride's family to the groom or groom's family in order to legalize or legitimize a marriage.

Dysfunction the notion that some cultural traits can cause stress or imbalance within a cultural system.

Ecclesiastical cults highly complex religious systems consisting of full time priests.

Egalitarian society a society that recognizes few differences in status, wealth or power.

EGO the person in kinship diagrams from whose point of view we are tracing the relationship.

Emic a perspective in ethnography that uses the concepts and categories that are relevant and meaningful to the culture under analysis.

Enculturation the process by which human infants learn their culture.

Endogamy a rule requiring marriage within a specified social or kinship group.

Epidemiology the study of the occurrence, distribution, and control of disease in populations.

Eskimo system the kinship system most commonly found in the United States; it is associated with bilateral descent. Usually, a mother, father, brother, and sister are found in a nuclear family.

Ethnic group a group of people sharing many of the same cultural features.

Ethnocentrism the practice of viewing the customs of other societies in terms of one's own; the opposite of cultural relativism.

Ethnographic mapping a data-gathering tool that locates where the people being studied live, where they keep their livestock, where public buildings are located, etc., in order to determine how that culture interacts with its environment.

Ethnography the anthropological description of a particular contemporary culture by means of direct fieldwork.

Ethnolinguistics the study of the relationship between language and culture.

Ethnology the comparative study of cultural differences and similarities.

Ethnomusicology the study of the relationship between music and other aspects of culture.

Ethnoscience a theoretical school popular in the 1950s and 1960s that tries to understand a culture from the point of view of the people being studied.

Etic a perspective in ethnography that uses the concepts and categories of the anthropologist's culture to describe another culture.

Event analysis photographic documentation of such events as weddings, funerals, and festivals in the culture under investigation.

Exogamy a rule requiring marriage outside of one's own social/kinship group.

Extended family a family form that includes two or more related nuclear families.

Extramarital activity sexual activity outside marriage.

Female infanticide the killing of female children.

Femininity the social definition of femaleness, which varies from society to society.

Feminization of poverty refers to the high proportion of female-headed families below the poverty line, which may result from the high proportion of women found in occupations with low prestige and income.

Fictive kinship relationships between individuals who recognize kinship obligations although the relationships are not based on either consanguineal or affinal ties.

Fieldwork the practice in which an anthropologist is immersed in the daily life of a culture in order to collect data and test cultural hypotheses.

Folklore unwritten verbal arts that can take a variety of forms such as myths, legends, and folktales.

Formalists school of economic anthropologists that suggests that the ideas of Western economics can be applied to any economic situation.

Fox project an early attempt at action anthropology, this program involved both research and intervention in the culture of the Fox Indians.

Free morpheme morphemes that appear in a language without being attached to any other morphemes.

French structuralism a theoretical orientation that holds that cultures are the product of unconscious processes of the human mind.

Function the contribution that a particular cultural trait makes to the longevity of the total culture.

Functionalism/functional theory a theory of social stratification holding that social stratification exists because it contributes to the overall well-being of a society.

Functional unity a principle of functionalism that states that a culture is an integrated whole consisting of a number of interrelated parts.

Gender the way members of the two sexes are perceived, evaluated, and expected to behave.

Gender ideology a system of thoughts and values that legitimizes sex roles, statuses, and customary behavior.

Genderlects linguistic gender differences.

Genealogizing a technique of collecting data in which the anthropologist writes down all the kin relationships of informants in order to study the kinship system.

Generalized reciprocity the practice of giving a gift with an expected return.

Genetics the study of inherited physical traits.

Ghost invocation the practice of a living person (typically an elder) calling forth the wrath of ancestor gods against an alleged sinner.

Ghostly vengeance the belief that ancestor gods (ghosts) will punish sinners.

Grammar the systematic ways that sounds are combined in any given language to send and receive meaningful utterances.

Hawaiian system associated with ambilineal descent, this kinship system uses a single term for all relatives of the same sex and generation.

Heterosexual sexual desire toward members of the opposite sex.

Hija an archaic rhetorical art form found in some Arabic cultures involving boastful self-praise and abusive insults.

Historical linguistics the study of how languages change over time.

Holism a perspective in anthropology that attempts to study a culture by looking at all parts of the system and how those parts are interrelated.

Homosexual sexual desire toward members of one's own sex.

Horticulture a form of small-scale crop cultivation characterized by the use of simple technology and the absence of irrigation.

Housewife a traditional gender role found in the United States that views females as responsible for child rearing and domestic activities.

Human paleontology *see* paleoanthropology and paleontology.

Human Relations Area Files (HRAF) the world's largest anthropological data retrieval system used to test cross cultural hypotheses.

Human sexuality the sexual practices of humans, usually varying from culture to culture.

Hunting and gathering a food-getting strategy involving the collection of naturally occurring plants and animals.

Incest taboo the prohibition of sexual intimacy between people defined as close relatives.

Independent variable the variable that can cause change in other variables.

Individualistic cults the least complex form of religious organization in which each person is his or her own religious specialist.

Industrialization a process resulting in the economic change from home production of goods to large-scale mechanized factory production.

Infant mortality infant death rate.

Informant a person who provides information about his or her culture to the ethnographic fieldworker.

Innovation changes brought about by the recombination of already existing items within a culture.

Intermediary a mediator of disputes between individuals or families within a society.

Interpreting the data the stage of fieldwork, often the most difficult, in which the anthropologist searches for meaning in the data collected while in the field.

Interpretive anthropology a contemporary theoretical orientation which holds that the critical aspects of cultural systems are such subjective factors as values, ideas, and world views.

Iroquois system a system associated with unilineal descent in which the father and father's brother are called by the same term, as are the mother and mother's sister.

Jati local subcastes found in Hindu India.

Kibbutz a communal farm or settlement in Israel.

Kindred all of the relatives a person recognizes in a bilateral kinship system.

Kinship system those relationships found in all societies that are based on blood or marriage.

Kula ring a form of reciprocal trading found among the Trobriand Islanders involving the use of white shell armbands and red shell bracelets.

Kulturkreise a concept of German-Austrian anthropologists that suggested there were a number of different cultural complexes (culture circles) that served as sources of cultural diffusion.

Law cultural rules that regulate human behavior and maintain order.

Leopard-skin chief an example of an intermediary found among the Nuer of the African Sudan.

Levirate the practice of a man marrying the widow of a deceased brother.

Lineage a unilineal descent group whose members can trace their line of descent to a common ancestor.

Lineality kin related in a single line such as son, father, and grandfather.

Linked changes changes in one part of a culture brought about by changes in other parts of the culture.

Magic a system of supernatural beliefs that involves the manipulation of supernatural forces for the purpose of intervening in a wide range of human activities and natural events.

Mahdist movement a term used to describe revitalization movements in the Muslim world.

Market exchange a form of distribution where goods and services are bought and sold and their value determined by the principle of supply and demand.

Masculinity the social definition of maleness, which varies from society to society.

Matriarchy the rule of domination of women over men.

Matrilineal descent a form of descent whereby people trace their primary kin connections through their mothers.

Matrilocal residence the practice of a newly married couple living with the wife's family.

Mechanical solidarity a type of social integration based on mutuality of interests found in societies with little division of labor.

Moiety one of two complementary descent groups in a society.

Monogamy the marital practice of having only one wife at a time.

Morphology the study of the rules governing how morphemes are turned into words.

Multilinear evolution mid-twentieth century anthropological theory of Julian Steward who suggested that specific cultures can evolve independently of all others even if they follow the same evolutionary process.

Negative reciprocity a form of economic exchange between individuals who try to take advantage of each other.

Negative sanction punishment for violating the norms of a society.

Neolithic Revolution a stage in human cultural evolution (around 10,000 years ago) characterized by the transition from hunting and gathering to the domestication of plants and animals.

Neolocal residence the practice of a newly wedded couple taking up their residence in a place independent from both the husband's and the wife's family.

New applied anthropology arose during the 1970s and 1980s, and is characterized by contract work in public agencies away from academia.

Nomadism a lifestyle involving the periodic movement of human populations in search of food or pasture for livestock.

Nonverbal communication the various means by which humans send and receive messages without using words (e.g., gestures, facial expressions, touching, etc.).

Nouveau riche people with newly acquired wealth.

Nuclear family the most basic family unit composed of wife, husband, and children.

Nutritional deprivation a form of child abuse involving withholding food; can retard learning, physical development, or social adjustment.

Oath the practice of having a god bear witness to the truth of what a person says.

Occupational segregation the predominance of one gender in certain occupations.

Omaha system a kinship system that emphasizes patrilineal descent. In this system the mother's patrilineal descent is distinct only by sex and not by one's generation.

On-farm research a type of applied agricultural research based on anthropological field methods.

Optimal foraging strategy a theory that foragers look for those species of plants and animals that will maximize their caloric intake for the time spent hunting and gathering foods.

Ordeal a painful, and possibly life-threatening, test inflicted on someone suspected of wrongdoing.

Organic analogy early functionalist idea that holds that cultural systems are integrated into a whole cultural unit in much the same way that the various parts of a biological organism (e.g., respiratory system, circulatory system) function to maintain the health of the organism.

Organic solidarity a type of social integration based on mutual interdependence; found in societies with a relatively elaborate division of labor.

Paleoanthropology the study of human evolution through fossil remains.

Paleontology the specialized branch of physical anthropology that analyzes the emergence and subsequent evolution of human physiology.

Pan-tribal mechanism mechanisms such as clans, age grades, and secret societies found in tribal societies that cut across kinship lines and serve to integrate all of the local segments of the tribe into a larger whole.

Parallel cousins children of one's mother's sister or father's brother.

Participant-observation a fieldwork method in which the cultural anthropologist lives with the people under study and observes their everyday activities.

Pastoralism a food-getting strategy based on animal husbandry found in regions of the world that are generally unsuited for agriculture.

Patrilineal descent a form of descent whereby people trace their primary kin relationships through their fathers.

Patrilocal residence the practice of a newly married couple living with the husband's family.

Peasantry rural peoples, usually on the lowest rung of society's ladder, who provide urban inhabitants with farm products but have little access to wealth or political power.

Phonology the study of a language's sound system.

Phratry a unilineal descent group comprised of a number of related clans.

Physical anthropology (biological anthropology) the subfield of anthropology that studies both human biological evolution and contemporary racial variations among peoples of the world.

Polyandry the marriage of a woman to two or more men at the same time.

Polygyny the marriage of a man to two or more women at the same time.

Population biology the study of the interrelationship between population characteristics and environments.

Postpartum sexual abstinence a husband and wife abstaining from any sexual activity for a length of time after the birth of a child.

Potlatch a form of competitive giveaway found among the Northwest Coast American Indians that serves as a mechanism for both achieving social status and distributing goods.

Power the capacity to produce intended effects on oneself, other people, social situations, or the environment.

Preferential cousin marriage a preferred form of marriage between either parallel or cross cousins.

Prestige social honor or respect within a society.

Primatology the study of nonhuman primates in their natural environments for the purpose of gaining insights into the human evolutionary process.

Primitive art art belonging to relatively egalitarian societies with small populations, simple technologies, and little labor specialization.

Production a process whereby goods are obtained from the natural environment and altered to become consumable goods for society.

Project Camelot an aborted U.S. Army research project designed to study the cause of civil unrest and violence in developing countries; created a controversy among anthropologists as to whether the U.S. government was using them as spies.

Proletariat the term used in conflict theories of social stratification to describe the working class who exchange their labor for wages.

Property rights Western concept of individual ownership, an idea unknown to non-Western cultures where a large kinship group, instead of the individual, determines limited rights to property.

Proxemic analysis the study of how people in different cultures use space.

Psychic unity a concept popular among some nineteenth-century anthropologists who assumed that all people when operating under similar circumstances will think and behave in similar ways.

Purdah rules involving domestic seclusion and veiling for women in small towns in Iraq, Iran, and Syria.

Race a subgroup of the human population whose members share a greater number of physical traits with one another than they do with those of other subgroups.

Ranked society a society in which people have unequal access to prestige and status but not unequal access to wealth and power.

Rape a type of sexual violence usually targeted at women; forced sexual activity without one's consent.

Rebellion an attempt within a society to disrupt the status quo and redistribute the power and resources.

Reciprocal exchange the equal exchange of gifts between the families of both the bride and groom to legitimize marriage.

Reciprocity a mode of distribution characterized by the exchange of goods and services that have approximately equal value between parties.

Redistribution a form of economic exchange in which goods (and services) are given by members of a group to a central authority (such as a chief) and then distributed back to the donors, usually in the form of a feast.

Research clearance permission of the host country in which fieldwork is to be conducted.

Research design overall strategy for conducting research.

Revitalization movement a religious movement designed to bring about a new way of life within a society.

Revolution an attempt to overthrow the existing form of political organization, the principles of economic production and distribution, and the allocation of social status.

Rite of passage any ceremony celebrating the transition of a person from one social status to another.

Rite of solidarity any ceremony performed for the sake of enhancing the level of social integration among a group of people.

Role ambiguity confusion as to how one is expected to behave.

Sanction any means used to enforce compliance with the rules and norms of a society.

Sapir-Whorf hypothesis the notion that a person's language shapes her or his perceptions and view of the world.

Savagery the first of three basic stages of cultural evolution in the theory of Lewis Henry Morgan; based on hunting and gathering.

Segmentary lineage system a lineage system where individuals belong to a series of different descent units that function in different social contexts.

Sex drive desire for sexual activity.

Sex roles society's expectations about how men and women should behave.

Sexual asymmetry the universal tendency of women to be in a subordinate position in their social relationships with men.

Sexual dimorphism refers to the physiological differences between men and women.

Sexual stratification a division in society where all members are hierarchically ranked according to gender.

Shaman a part-time religious specialist who is thought to have supernatural powers by virtue of birth, training, or inspiration.

Shamanistic cult a form of religion in which part-time religious specialists called shamans intervene with the deities on behalf of the clients.

Shifting cultivation (swidden, slash and burn) a form of plant cultivation in which seeds are planted in the fertile soil prepared by cutting and burning the natural growth; relatively short periods of cultivation are followed by longer periods of fallow.

Social control mechanisms found in all societies that function to encourage people not to violate the social norms.

Social mobility the ability of people to change their social position within the society.

Social norm an expected form of behavior.

Social stratification the ranking of subgroups in a society according to wealth, power, and prestige.

Social uses of cattle the use of livestock by pastoralists not only for food and its by-products but also for purposes such as marriage, religion, and social relationships.

Socialization teaching the young the norms in a society.

Sociolinguistics a branch of anthropological linguistics that studies how language and culture are related and how language is used in different social contexts.

Sondeo a research strategy of on-farm research involving the use of informal interviews and participant-observation by teams of agricultural and social scientists.

Song duel a means of settling disputes over wife stealing among the Eskimos involving the use of song and lyrics to determine one's guilt or innocence.

Sorcery the performance of certain magical rites for the purpose of harming other people.

Sororate the practice of a woman marrying the husband of her deceased sister.

Specialized political roles when large numbers of people are required to carry out very specific tasks such as law enforcement, tax collection, dispute settlement, recruitment of labor, and protection from outside invasion.

Spouse abuse a form of violence usually targeted at women.

State system of government a bureaucratic, hierarchical form of government comprised of various echelons of political specialists.

Stratified societies societies characterized by considerable inequality in all forms of social rewards, that is, power, wealth, and prestige.

Structured interview an ethnographic data-gathering technique in which large numbers of respondents are asked a set of specific questions.

Substantive approach school of economic anthropologists who hold that the classical Western approach to economic principles cannot be applied to nonindustrialized cultures.

Sudanese system an extremely particularistic and descriptive kinship system found in North Africa that is associated with patrilineal descent.

Supernatural beliefs a set of beliefs found in all societies that transcend the natural, observable world.

Tabula rasa the idea that humans at birth have little or no predetermined behavior and, in order to survive, must learn coping skills from others into whose culture they are born.

Transhumance movement pattern of pastoralists in which some of the men move livestock seasonally while the other members of their group, including women and children, stay in permanent settlements.

Tribal society a type of small-scale society comprised of a number of autonomous political units sharing common linguistic and cultural features.

Unilineal descent tracing descent through a single line (e.g., matrilineal, patrilineal) as compared to both sides (bilateral descent).

Unilinear evolutionists anthropologists such as Tylor and Morgan who attempted to place particular cultures into specific evolutionary phases.

Universal evolution White's approach to cultural evolution, which developed laws that apply to culture as a whole and argued that all human societies pass through similar stages of development.

Universal functions a functionalist idea that holds that every part of a culture has a particular function.

Universal male dominance the notion that men are dominant over women in all societies.

Universalism the notion of rewarding people on the basis of some universally applied set of rules.

Unstructured interview an ethnographic data-gathering technique—usually used in early stages of one's fieldwork—in which interviewees are asked to respond to broad, open-ended questions.

Value-free philosophy the attitude of most anthropologists before 1950 that they should avoid their own personal values when it comes to their work.

Varnas caste groups in Hindu India that are associated with certain occupations.

Vicos project a successful anthropological intervention in the 1950s that focused on transforming nonproductive haciendas (farms) into economically productive and autonomous communities.

Vision quest a ritual found among a number of Plains Indian cultures where through visions people establish special relationships with spirits who provide them with knowledge, power, and protection.

Wealth the accumulation of material objects that have value within a society.

Witchcraft an inborn, involuntary, and often unconscious capacity to cause harm to other people.

BIBLIOGRAPHY

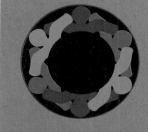

Amory, Cleveland
1969 Introduction: The 1902 Edition of the Sears, Roebuck Catalogue. New York: Bounty Books.
Anderson, Richard L.
1990 Calliope's Sisters: A Comparative Study of Philosophies of Art. Englewood Cliffs, N.J.: Prentice-Hall.
Angrosino, Michael V.
1976 The Evolution of the New Applied Anthropology. In Do Applied Anthropologists Apply Anthropology? Michael V. Angrosino, ed. Pp. 1–9. Athens, Ga.: Southern Anthropological Society.
Appell, G. N.
1978 Ethical Dilemmas in Anthropological Inquiry: A Case Book. Waltham, Mass.: Crossroads Press.
Applebaum, Herbert, ed.
1987 Perspectives in Cultural Anthropology. Albany, N.Y.: State University of New York Press.
Ardrey, Robert
1968 The Territorial Imperative. New York: Atheneum.
Axtell, Roger E.
1991 Gestures: The Do's and Taboos of Body Language Around the World. New York: John Wiley and Sons.
Baba, Marietta L.
1986 Business and Industrial Anthropology: An Overview. NAPA Bulletin 2, National Association for the Practice of Anthropology (a unit of the American Anthropological Association).

Balikci, Asen
1968 The Netsilik Eskimos: Adaptive Processes. In Man the Hunter. Richard B. Lee and Irven DeVore, eds. Pp. 78–82. Chicago: Aldine-Atherton.
Bamberger, Joan
1974 The Myth of Matriarchy: Why Men Rule in Primitive Society. In Women, Culture and Society. Michelle Zimbalist Rosaldo and Louise Lamphere, eds. Pp. 263–80. Stanford, Calif.: Stanford University Press.
Barfield, Thomas
1993 The Nomadic Alternative. Englewood Cliffs, N.J.: Prentice-Hall.
Barnes, Sandra T.
1990 Women, Property, and Power. In Beyond the Second Sex: New Directions in the Anthropology of Gender. Peggy Reeves Sanday and Ruth G. Goodenough, eds. Pp. 253–80. Philadelphia: University of Pennsylvania Press.
Barrett, Richard A.
1991 Culture and Conduct: An Excursion in Anthropology. Belmont, Calif.: Wadsworth.
Beals, Alan
1962 Gopalpur: A South Indian Village. New York: Holt, Rinehart and Winston.
Beals, Ralph L., Harry Hoijer, and Alan R. Beals
1977 An Introduction to Anthropology. 5th edition. New York: Macmillan.
Beattie, John
1960 Bunyoro: An African Kingdom. New York: Holt, Rinehart and Winston.

1964 Other Cultures: Aims, Methods, and Achievements in Social Anthropology. New York: Free Press.

Behar, Ruth
1993 Translated Woman: Crossing the Border with Esperanza's Story. Boston: Beacon Press.

Benedict, Ruth
1934 Patterns of Culture. New York: Houghton Mifflin.
1943 Obituary of Franz Boas. Science 97:60–62.
1946 The Chrysanthemum and the Sword. Boston: Houghton Mifflin.

Bensman, Joseph, and Arthur Vidich
1987 American Society: The Welfare State and Beyond. Rev. edition. South Hadley, Mass.: Bergin and Garvey.

Bernard, H. Russell
1988 Research Methods in Cultural Anthropology. Newbury Park, Calif.: Sage Publications.

Berry, J. W.
1980 Social and Cultural Change. In Social Psychology. Handbook of Cross Cultural Psychology. Volume 5. H. C. Triandis and W. W. Lambert, eds. Boston: Allyn and Bacon.

Betzig, Laura
1988 Redistribution: Equity or Exploitation? In Human Reproductive Behavior: A Darwinian Perspective. Laura Betzig, M. B. Mulder, and Paul Turke, eds. Pp. 49–63. Cambridge: Cambridge University Press.

Birket-Smith, K.
1959 The Eskimos. 2d edition. London: Methuen.

Blacker, J. G. C., and P. R. Forsyth-Thompson et al.
1979 Report on the 1976 Swaziland Population Census. Volume 1. Unpublished manuscript.

Boas, Franz
1911 Handbook of American Indian Languages. Bureau of American Ethnology. Bulletin 40.
1911 The Mind of Primitive Man. New York: Macmillan.
1919 Correspondence: Scientists as Spies. The Nation. December 20:797.

Bodley, John
1982 Victims of Progress. 2d edition. Palo Alto, Calif.: Mayfield.

Bohannan, Paul, and Philip Curtin
1988 Africa and Africans. Prospect Heights, Ill.: Waveland Press.

Boone, Margaret S.
1982 A Socio-Medical Study of Infant Mortality among Disadvantaged Blacks. Human Organization 41(3):227–36.

1985 Social and Cultural Factors in the Etiology of Low Birthweight among Disadvantaged Blacks. Social Science and Medicine 20(10): 1001–11.
1987 Practicing Sociomedicine: Redefining the Problem of Infant Mortality in Washington, D.C. In Anthropological Praxis: Translating Knowledge into Action. Robert M. Wulff and Shirley J. Fiske, eds. Pp. 56–71. Boulder, Colo.: Westview Press.

Bowen, Elenore Smith
1964 Return to Laughter. Garden City, N.Y.: Doubleday.

Brady, Ivan, ed.
1983 Speaking in the Name of the Real: Freeman and Mead on Samoa (special section). American Anthropologist 85(4):908–47.

Brooke, James
1990 Brazil Blows Up Miners' Airstrip, Pressing Its Drive to Save Indians. New York Times, May 23.

Brown, Donald E.
1991 Human Universals. New York: McGraw-Hill.

Brown, Judith
1970 A Note on the Division of Labor by Sex. American Anthropologist 72:1073–78.

Buckley, T.
1993 Menstruation and the Power of Yurok Women. In Gender in Cross Cultural Perspective. Caroline B. Brettell and Carolyn F. Sargent, eds. Pp. 133–48. Englewood Cliffs, N.J.: Prentice-Hall.

Burger, Julian
1987 Report from the Frontier: The State of the World's Indigenous Peoples. Zed Books/Cultural Survival Report 28.

Burton, M. L., L. A. Brudner, and D. R. White.
1977 A Model of the Sexual Division of Labor. American Ethnologist, 4:227–51.

Campbell, Bernard G.
1979 Mankind Emerging. 2d edition. Boston: Little, Brown.

Carneiro, Robert
1970 A Theory of the Origin of the State. Science. Pp. 733–38. August 21.

Carpenter, Edmund
1973 Eskimo Realities. New York: Holt, Rinehart and Winston.

Casagrande, Joseph B.
1960 The Southwest Project in Comparative Psycholinguistics: A Preliminary Report. In Men and Cultures: Selected Papers of the Fifth International Congress of Anthropological and Ethnological Sciences. Anthony F. C. Wallace, ed.

Pp. 777–82. Philadelphia: University of Pennsylvania Press.

Chagnon, Napoleon A.
1983 Yanomamo: The Fierce People. 3d edition. New York: Holt, Rinehart and Winston.

Chambers, John, ed.
1983 Black English: Educational Equity and the Law. Ann Arbor, Mich.: Karoma Publishers.

Childe, V. Gordon
1936 Man Makes Himself. London: Watts.
1950 The Urban Revolution. Town Planning Review 21:3–17.

Chomsky, Noam
1972 Language and Mind. New York: Harcourt Brace Jovanovich.

Cohen, Eugene N., and Edwin Eames
1982 Cultural Anthropology. Boston: Little, Brown.

Coleman, Richard P., and Lee Rainwater
1978 Social Standing in America. New York: Basic Books.

Collier, Jane F., and J. Yanagisako, eds.
1987 Gender and Kinship: Essays toward a Unified Analysis. Stanford, Calif.: Stanford University Press.

Collins, John J.
1975 Anthropology: Culture, Society and Evolution. Englewood Cliffs, N.J.: Prentice-Hall.

Condon, John, and Fathi Yousef
1975 An Introduction to Intercultural Communication. Indianapolis: Bobbs-Merrill.

Coote, Jeremy, and Anthony Shelton, eds.
1992 Anthropology, Art, and Aesthetics. Oxford: Clarendon Press.

Council of the American Anthropological Association.
1971 Statement on Ethics: Principles of Professional Responsibility. May (as amended through November 1976).

Counts, G. S.
1925 The Social Status of Occupations: A Problem in Vocational Guidance. School Review 33:16–27. January.

Cowan, Betty, and Jasbir Dhanoa
1983 The Prevention of Toddler Malnutrition by Home-based Nutrition Education. In Nutrition in the Community: A Critical Look at Nutrition Policy, Planning, and Programmes. D. S. McLaren, ed. Pp. 339–56. New York: John Wiley and Sons.

Cowan, J. Milton
1979 Linguistics at War. In The Uses of Anthropology. Walter Goldschmidt, ed. Pp. 158–68.

Washington, D.C.: American Anthropological Association.

Cronk, Lee
1989 Strings Attached. The Sciences. Pp. 2–4. May/June.

Dahlberg, Frances
1981 Introduction. In Woman the Gatherer. New Haven: Yale University Press.

Davis, Kingsley, and Wilbert Moore
1945 Some Principles of Stratification. American Sociological Review 10:242–49. April.
1988 Wives and Work: A Theory of the Sex-Role Revolution and Its Consequences. In Feminism, Children, and the New Families. Sanford Dornbusch and Myra Strober, eds. Pp. 67–86. New York: Guilford Press.

Davis, Shelton H.
1977 Victims of the Miracle: Development and the Indians of Brazil. Cambridge: Cambridge University Press.

Deardorff, Merle
1951 The Religion of Handsome Lake. In Symposium on Local Diversity in Iroquois Culture, W. N. Fenton, ed. Washington D.C.: Bureau of American Ethnology, Bulletin 149.

Dembo, Richard, Patrick Hughes, Lisa Jackson, and Thomas Mieczkowski.
1993 Crack Cocaine Dealing by Adolescents in Two Public Housing Projects: A Pilot Study. Human Organization 52(1):89–96.

Deutsch, Claudia H.
1991 Anthropologists Probe Company Cultures, The Charlotte Observer, February 24, P. 11-C.

DeVita, Philip R., ed.
1992 The Naked Anthropologist: Tales from around the World. Belmont, Calif.: Wadsworth.

DeVita, Philip R., and James D. Armstrong
1993 Distant Mirrors: America as a Foreign Culture. Belmont, Calif.: Wadsworth.

Diamond, Jared
1993 Speaking with a Single Tongue. Discover. February.

Diamond, Stanley
1960 Introduction: The Uses of the Primitive. In Primitive Views of the World. Stanley Diamond, ed. Pp. v–xxix. New York: Columbia University Press.

Dorjahn, Vernon
1959 The Factor of Polygyny in African Demography. In Continuity and Change in African Cultures. William R. Bascom and M. J. Herskovits, eds. Chicago: University of Chicago Press.

Dove, Michael R.
1988 The Real and Imagined Role of Culture in
Development: Case Studies from Indonesia.
Honolulu: University of Hawaii Press.

Downs, James F.
1971 Cultures in Crisis. Beverly Hills, Calif.: Glenco
Press.

Dundes, Alan
1965 What Is Folklore? *In* The Study of Folklore. Alan
Dundes, ed. Englewood Cliffs, N.J.: Prentice-Hall.

Durkheim, Emile
1933 Division of Labor in Society (G. Simpson, trans.).
New York: Macmillan.

Dyson-Hudson, Rada, and Neville Dyson-Hudson
1980 Nomadic Pastoralism. Annual Review of
Anthropology 9:15–61.

Dyson-Hudson, Rada, and Eric A. Smith
1978 Human Territoriality: An Ecological
Reassessment. American Anthropologist
80:21–41.

Eastman, Carol
1983 Language Planning: An Introduction. San
Francisco: Chandler and Sharp.

Edgerton, Robert B., and L. L. Langness
1974 Methods and Styles in the Study of Culture. San
Francisco: Chandler.

Errington, Frederick, and Deborah Gewertz
1987 Cultural Alternatives and a Feminist
Anthropology: An Analysis of Culturally
Constructed Gender Interests in Papua New
Guinea. Cambridge: Cambridge University Press.

Ervin-Tripp, Susan
1964 An Analysis of the Interaction of Language,
Topic, and Listener. American Anthropologist
(special publication) 66:86–102.

Esber, George S.
1977 The Study of Space in Advocacy Planning with
the Tonto Apaches in Payson, Arizona. Doctoral
Dissertation, University of Arizona.
1987 Designing Apache Homes with Apaches. *In*
Anthropological Praxis: Translating Knowledge
into Action. Robert M. Wulff and Shirley J. Fiske.
Pp. 187–96. Boulder, Colo.: Westview Press.

Evans-Pritchard, E. E.
1940 The Nuer. Oxford: Oxford University Press.

Farb, Peter
1968 How Do I Know You Mean What You Mean?
Horizon 10(4):52–57.

Faris, James C.
1972 Nuba Personal Art. Toronto: University of
Toronto Press.

Feldman, Douglas A.
1985 AIDS and Social Change. Human Organization
44(4):343–47.

Ferguson, Charles A.
1964 Diglossia. *In* Language in Culture and Society:
A Reader in Linguistics and Anthropology.
Dell Hymes, ed. Pp. 429–39. New York: Harper &
Row.

Ferraro, Gary
1973 Tradition or Transition?: Rural and Urban
Kinsman in East Africa. Urban Anthropology
2(2):214–31.
1980 Swazi Marital Patterns and Conjugal Roles: An
Analysis and Policy Implications. Unpublished
report submitted to USAID, Mbabane, Swaziland.
May.
1994 The Cultural Dimension of International
Business. Englewood Cliffs, N.J.: Prentice-Hall.

Fetterman, David M.
1987 A National Ethnographic Evaluation of the
Career Intern Program. *In* Anthropological
Praxis: Translating Knowledge into Action.
Robert M. Wulff and Shirley J. Fiske, eds. Pp.
243–52. Boulder, Colo.: Westview Press.
1988 A National Ethnographic Evaluation: An
Executive Summary of the Ethnographic
Component of the Career Intern Program Study.
In Qualitative Approaches to Evaluation in
Education: The Silent Scientific Revolution,
David Fetterman, ed. Pp. 262–73. New York:
Praeger.
1989 Ethnography: Step by Step. Newbury Park, Calif.:
Sage Publications.

Fitchen, Janet F.
1988 Anthropology and Environmental Problems in
the United States: The Case of Groundwater
Contamination. Practicing Anthropology
10(3–4): 5+.

Forde, Daryll
1967 Double Descent among the Yako. *In* African
Systems of Kinship and Marriage. A. R. Radcliffe-
Brown and Daryll Forde, eds. Pp. 285–332.
London: Oxford University Press (orig. 1950).

Fortes, M. and E. E. Evans-Pritchard
1940 African Political Systems. London: Oxford
University Press.

Foster, George M.
1967 Tzintzuntzan: Mexican Peasants in a Changing
World. Boston: Little, Brown.
1973 Traditional Societies and Technological Change.
2d edition. New York: Harper & Row.

Fox, Robin
1967 Kinship and Marriage. Baltimore: Penguin.
Frazer, James
1958 The Golden Bough. New York: Macmillan.
Freeman, Derek
1983 Margaret Mead and Samoa: The Making and Unmaking of an Anthropological Myth. Cambridge, Mass.: Harvard University Press.
Freilich, Morris, Douglas Raybeck, and Joel Savishinsky, eds.
1990 Deviance: Anthropological Perspectives. South Hadley, Mass.: Bergin and Garvey.
Fried, Morton H.
1967 The Evolution of Political Society: An Essay in Political Anthropology. New York: Random House.
Friedl, John, and John E. Pfeiffer
1977 Anthropology: The Study of People. New York: Harper & Row.
Fromkin, Victoria, and Robert Rodman
1993 An Introduction to Language. New York: CBS College Publishing.
Garbarino, Merwyn S.
1977 Sociocultural Theory in Anthropology: A Short History. New York: Holt, Rinehart and Winston.
Gardner, R. Allen, and Beatrice T. Gardner
1969 Teaching Sign Language to a Chimpanzee. Science. Pp. 664–72. August 15.
Gearing, Frederick O., Robert McNetting, and Lisa R. Peattie, eds.
1960 Documentary History of the Fox Project. Chicago: University of Chicago Department of Anthropology.
Geertz, Clifford
1973 The Interpretation of Cultures. New York: Basic Books.
1983 Local Knowledge: Further Essays in Interpretive Anthropology. New York: Basic Books.
1984 Distinguished Lecture: Anti Anti-Relativism. American Anthropologist 86:263–78. June.
Girdner, Linda
1989 Custody Mediation: Taking the Knowledge Act on the Policy Road. *In* Making Our Research Useful: Case Studies in the Utilization of Anthropological Knowledge. John Van Willigen, Barbara Rylko-Bauer, and Ann McElroy, eds. Pp. 55–70. Boulder, Colo.: Westview.
Glasser, Irene
1989 Social Policy Implications of Soup Kitchen Research. Practicing Anthropology 11(1):17–18.
Gmelch, George

1994a Lessons from the Field. *In* Conformity and Conflict. 8th edition. James P. Spradley and David McCurdy, eds. Pp. 45–55. New York: Harper Collins.
1994b Ritual and Magic in American Baseball. *In* Conformity and Conflict. 8th edition. James P. Spradley and David McCurdy, eds. Pp. 351–61. New York: Harper Collins.
Goldschmidt, Walter
1979 Introduction: On the Interdependence between Utility and Theory. *In* The Uses of Anthropology. Walter Goldschmidt, ed. Washington, D.C.: American Anthropological Association.
Goldstein, Melvyn C.
1987 When Brothers Share a Wife. Natural History 96(3):39–48.
Goode, William J.
1963 World Revolution and Family Patterns. New York: Free Press of Glencoe.
Goodenough, Ward H.
1956 Componential Analysis and the Study of Meaning. Language 32:195–216.
Gorman, E. Michael
1986 The AIDS Epidemic in San Francisco: Epidemiological and Anthropological Perspectives. *In* Anthropology and Epidemiology. Craig R. Janes et al., eds. Pp. 157–72. Dordrecht, Holland: D. Reidel Publishing.
Gottlieb, Alma
1990 Rethinking Female Pollution: The Beng Case (Cote d'Ivoire). *In* Beyond the Second Sex: New Directions in the Anthropology of Gender. Peggy Reeves Sanday and Ruth G. Goodenough, eds. Pp. 113–38. Philadelphia: University of Pennsylvania Press.
Gough, Kathleen
1959 The Nayars and the Definition of Marriage. Journal of the Royal Anthropological Institute 89:23–34.
Gouldner, Alvin
1960 The Norm of Reciprocity: A Preliminary Statement. American Sociological Review 25:161–78.
Gray, Robert F.
1960 Sonjo Brideprice and the Question of African "Wife Purchase." American Anthropologist 62:34–57.
Gronseth, Evangeline
1988 Anthropology in Clinical Nursing on the San Carlos Reservation. Practicing Anthropology 10(2):10–12.

Hagan, E.
1962 On the Theory of Social Change. Homewood,
      Ill.: Dorsey Press.
Hall, Edward T.
1966 The Hidden Dimension. Garden City, N.Y.:
      Doubleday.
Hamada, Tomoko
1988 Working with Japanese: U.S.-Japanese Joint
      Venture Contract. Practicing Anthropology
      10(1):4–5.
Hanna, Judith Lynne
1979 To Dance Is Human: A Theory of Nonverbal
      Communication. Austin: University of Texas
      Press.
Harner, Michael J.
1973 "The Sound of Rushing Water." In
      Hallucinogens and Shamanism, Michael J.
      Harner, ed. Pp. 15–27. New York: Oxford
      University Press.
Harris, Grace
1972 Taita Bridewealth and Affinal Relations. In
      Marriage in Tribal Society. Meyer Fortes, ed. Pp.
      55–87. Cambridge: Cambridge University Press.
Harris, Marvin
1968 The Rise of Anthropological Theory. New York:
      Thomas Y. Crowell.
1977 Cannibals and Kings: The Origins of Culture.
      New York: Random House.
1979 Comments on Simoons' Questions in the Sacred
      Cow Controversy. Current Anthropology
      20:479–82.
1979 Cultural Materialism: The Struggle for a Science
      of Culture. New York: Random House.
1991 Cultural Anthropology. 3d edition. New York:
      Harper-Collins.
Hart, C. W. M., and Arnold R. Pilling
1960 The Tiwi of North Australia. New York: Holt,
      Rinehart and Winston.
Hart, C. W. M., Arnold Pilling, and Jane Goodale
1988 The Tiwi of North Australia. 3d edition. New
      York: Holt, Rinehart and Winston.
Hatch, Elvin
1985 Culture. In The Social Science Encyclopedia.
      Adam Kuper and Jessica Kuper, eds. P. 178.
      London: Routledge and Kegan Paul.
Hecht, Michael L., Mary Jane Collier, and Sidney
      Ribeau
1993 African American Communication: Ethnic
      Identity and Cultural Interpretation. Thousand
      Oaks, Calif.: Sage Publications.
Hecht, Robert M.

1986 Salvage Anthropology: The Redesign of a Rural
      Development Project in Guinea. In Anthropology
      and Rural Development in West Africa. Michael
      M. Horowitz and Thomas M. Painter, eds. Pp.
      13–26. Boulder, Colo.: Westview Press.
Heider, Karl
1979 Grand Valley Dani: Peaceful Warriors. New York:
      Holt, Rinehart and Winston.
Heller, Scott
1988 From Selling Rambo to Supermarket Studies,
      Anthropologists Are Finding More Non-
      Academic Jobs. The Chronicle of Higher
      Education, June 1, 1988, P. A-24.
Hern, Warren M.
1992 Family Planning, Amazon Style. Natural History
      101(12): 30–37. December.
Herskovits, Melville
1967 Dahomey: An Ancient West African Kingdom.
      Volume 1. Evanston: Northwestern University
      Press (orig. 1938).
1972 Cultural Relativism: Perspectives in Cultural
      Pluralism. New York: Vintage Books.
Hickerson, Nancy P.
1980 Linguistic Anthropology. New York: Holt,
      Rinehart and Winston.
Hildebrand, P.
1981 Combining Disciplines in Rapid Appraisal: The
      Sondeo Approach. Agricultural Administration
      8:423–32.
Hill, Carole, and Roy S. Dickens
1978 Cultural Resources: Planning and Management.
      Boulder, Colo.: Westview Press.
Hoben, Alan
1986 Assessing the Social Feasibility of a Settlement
      Project in North Cameroon. In Anthropology
      and Rural Development in West Africa. Michael
      M. Horowitz and Thomas M. Painter, eds. Pp.
      167–94. Boulder, Colo.: Westview Press.
Hockett, C. F.
1973 Man's Place in Nature. New York: McGraw-Hill.
Hodge, Robert W., Paul M. Siegel, and Peter H. Rossi
1964 Occupational Prestige in the United States,
      1925–1963. American Journal of Sociology
      70:286–302. November.
Hoebel, E. A.
1960 The Cheyennes: Indians of the Great Plains. New
      York: Holt, Rinehart and Winston.
1972 Anthropology: The Study of Man. 4th edition.
      New York: McGraw-Hill.
Hoffman, Carl L.
1988 The "Wild Punan" of Borneo: A Matter of

Economics. *In* The Real and Imagined Role of Culture in Development. Michael R. Dove, ed. Pp. 89–118. Honolulu: University of Hawaii Press.

Holmberg, Alan R.
1971 The Role of Power in Changing Values and Institutions of Vicos. *In* Peasants, Power, and Applied Social Change: Vicos as a Model. Henry F. Dobyns, Paul Doughty, and Harold D. Lasswell, eds. Beverly Hills, Calif.: Sage Publications.

Horowitz, Michael M.
1986 Ideology, Policy, and Praxis in Pastoral Livestock Development. *In* Anthropology and Rural Development in West Africa. Michael M. Horowitz and Thomas M. Painter, eds. Pp. 249–72. Boulder, Colo.: Westview Press.

Husain, Tariq
1976 Use of Anthropologists in Project Appraisal by the World Bank. *In* Development from Below: Anthropologists and Development Situations. David C. Pitt, ed. Pp. 71–81. The Hague: Mouton.

Hymes, Dell
1977 Discovering Oral Performance and Measured Verse in American Indian Narrative, New Literary History 8(3):431–57.

Information Please Almanac
1991 44th edition. Boston: Houghton Mifflin.

Inkeles, Alex
1983 Exploring Individual Modernity. New York: Columbia University Press.

James, Preston E.
1966 A Geography of Man. 3d edition. Waltham, Mass.: Blaisdell.

Janson, H. W.
1986 History of Art. New York and Englewood Cliffs, N.J.: Harry Abrams and Prentice-Hall. (Revised by Anthony F. Janson.)

Joans, Barbara
1984 Problems in Pocatello: A Study in Linguistic Understanding. Practicing Anthropology. 6(3/4).

Jonaitis, Alldona, ed.
1991 Chiefly Feasts: The Enduring Kwakiutl Potlatch. Seattle: University of Washington Press.

Jordan, Cathie, Roland Tharp, and Lynn Baird-Vogt
1992 "Just Open the Door": Cultural Compatibility and Classroom Rapport. *In* Cross Cultural Literacy: Ethnographies of Communication in Multiethnic Classrooms. Marietta Saravia-Shore and Steven F. Arvizu, eds. Pp. 3–18. New York: Garland.

Jorgensen, Danny L.
1989 Participant Observation: A Methodology for Human Studies. Thousand Oaks, Calif.: Sage Publications.

Kaplan, David, and Robert Manners
1986 Culture Theory. Englewood Cliffs, N.J.: Prentice-Hall.

Kasarda, John D.
1971 Economic Structure and Fertility: A Comparative Analysis. Demography 8(3):307–18.

Keefe, Susan E.
1988 The Myth of the Declining Family: Extended Family Ties among Urban Mexican-Americans and Anglo-Americans. *In* Urban Life: Readings in Urban Anthropology. 2d edition. George Gmelch and Walter Zenner, eds. Pp. 229–39. Prospect Heights, Ill.: Waveland Press.

Keenan, Elinor
1974 Norm-makers, Norm-breakers: Uses of Speech by Men and Women in a Malagasy Community. *In* Explorations in the Ethnography of Speaking. Richard Bauman and Joel Sherzer, eds. Pp. 125–43 London: Cambridge University Press.

Kenyatta, Jomo
1962 Facing Mount Kenya. New York: Vintage Books.

Kirsch, A. T.
1985 Text and Context: Buddhist Sex Roles/Culture of Gender Revisited. American Ethnologist 12:302–20.

Kluckhohn, Clyde
1949 Mirror for Man: Anthropology and Modern Life. New York: Wittlesey House (McGraw-Hill).

Kluckhohn, Florence, and Fred L. Strodtbeck
1961 Variations in Value Orientations. Evanston: Row, Peterson.

Kohls, L. Robert
1984 Survival Kit for Overseas Living. Yarmouth, Maine: Intercultural Press.

Koss, Mary P.
1985 The Hidden Rape Victim: Personality, Attitudinal, and Situational Characteristics. Psychology of Women Quarterly 9:192–212.

Kottak, Conrad P.
1987 Anthropology: The Exploration of Human Diversity. 4th edition. New York: Random House.

Kramer, Cheris
1974 Folk Linguistics: Wishy-Washy Mommy Talk. Psychology Today 8(1):82–85.

Kroeber, A. L.
1917 The Superorganic. American Anthropologist 19(2):163–213.

Kroeber, A. L., and C. Kluckhohn
1952 Culture: A Critical Review of Concepts and Definitions. Papers of the Peabody Museum of American Archaeology and Ethnology 47(1).

Kuper, Hilda
1986 The Swazi: A South African Kindom. 2d edition. New York: Holt, Rinehart and Winston.

Labov, William
1983 Recognizing Black English in the Classroom. *In* Black English: Educational Equity and the Law. John Chambers, ed. Pp. 29–55. Ann Arbor, Mich.: Karoma Publishers.

La Fontaine, Jean
1963 Witchcraft in Bagisu. *In* Witchcraft and Sorcery in East Africa. J. Middleton and E. Winter, eds. Pp. 187–220. New York: Praeger.

Lane, Belden C.
1989 The Power of Myth: Lessons from Joseph Campbell. The Christian Century 106:652–54. July 5.

Lanier, Alison
1979 Selecting and Preparing Personnel for Overseas Transfers. Personnel Journal: 160–63. March.

Lee, Richard B.
1968 What Hunters Do for a Living, or How to Make Out on Scarce Resources. *In* Man the Hunter. Richard B. Lee and Irven DeVore, eds. Pp. 30–48. Chicago: Aldine-Atherton.

Lehman, Arthur C., and James E. Myers, eds.
1993 Magic, Witchcraft, and Religion. 3d edition. Palo Alto, Calif.: Mayfield.

Lehmann, Arthur C., and James E. Myers, eds.
1985 Magic, Witchcraft, and Religion: An Anthropological Study of the Supernatural. Palo Alto, Calif.: Mayfield.

Leighton, Dorothea, and Clyde Kluckhohn
1948 Children of the People. Cambridge: Cambridge University Press.

Levi-Strauss, Claude
1969 The Elementary Structures of Kinship. Boston: Beacon Press.

Lewis, I. M.
1965 The Northern Pastoral Somali of the Horn. *In* Peoples of Africa. James Gibbs, ed. Pp. 319–60. New York: Holt, Rinehart and Winston.

Lewis, Oscar
1952 Urbanization without Breakdown. Scientific Monthly 75:31–41. July.
1955 Peasant Culture in India and Mexico: A Comparative Analysis. *In* Village India: Studies in the Little Community. McKim Marriott, ed. Pp. 145–70. Chicago: University of Chicago Press.

Lewis-Williams, J. D., and T. A. Dowson
1988 The Signs of All Times: Entoptic Phenomena in Upper Palaeolithic Art. Current Anthropology 29(2): 201–45. April.

Linton, Ralph
1936 The Study of Man. New York: Appleton-Century-Crofts.

Llewellyn, K., and E. Adamson Hoebel
1941 The Cheyenne Way: Conflict and Case Law in Primitive Jurisprudence. Norman: University of Oklahoma Press.

Lomax, Alan, et al.
1968 Folk Song Style and Culture. Washington, D.C.: American Association for the Advancement of Science.

Lott, Bernice
1994 Women's Lives: Themes and Variations in Gender Learning. 2d edition. Pacific Grove, Calif.: Brooks/Cole.

Low, Setha M.
1981 Anthropology as a New Technology in Landscape Planning. Unpublished paper presented at the meetings of the American Society of Landscape Architects.

Lowie, Robert
1963 Religion in Human Life. American Anthropologist 65:532–42.

McClelland, D. C.
1960 The Achieving Society. New York: Van Nostrand.

McGee, R. J.
1990 Life, Ritual and Religion among the Lacandon Maya. Belmont, Calif.: Wadsworth.

McGee, W. J.
1895 Some Principles of Nomenclature, American Anthropologist 8:279–86.

McGlynn, Frank, and Arthur Tuden, eds.
1991 Anthropological Approaches to Political Behavior. Pittsburgh: University of Pittsburgh Press.

McKenzie, Joan L., and Noel J. Chrisman
1977 Healing Herbs, Gods, and Magic: Folk Health Beliefs among Filipino-Americans. American Journal of Nursing 77(5):326–29.

Malinowski, Bronislaw
1922 Argonauts of the Western Pacific. New York: Dutton.
1926 Crime and Custom in Savage Society. London: Kegan Paul.
1927 Sex and Repression in Savage Society. London: Kegan Paul, Trench, Trubner and Company.

Mandelbaum, David G.
1970 Society in India, Volume 1. Berkeley: University of California Press.

Marshall, Donald S.
1971 Sexual Behavior on Mangaia. *In* Sexual Behavior: Variations in the Ethnographic Spectrum. Donald S. Marshall and Robert Suggs, eds. Pp. 103–62. New York: Basic Books.

Marshall, Lorna
1965 The !Kung Bushmen of the Kalahari Desert. *In* Peoples of Africa. James Gibbs, ed. Pp. 243–78. New York: Holt, Rinehart and Winston.

Marx, Karl
1904 The Critique of Political Economy. (I. N. Stone, trans.) Chicago: International Library Publication Company (orig. 1859).
1909 Capital. (E. Unterman, trans.). Chicago: C. H. Kerr (orig. 1867).

Mauss, M.
1954 The Gift. (I Cunnison, trans.) New York: Free Press.

Mead, Margaret
1928 Coming of Age in Samoa. New York: Morrow.
1950 Sex and Temperament in Three Primitive Societies. New York: Mentor (orig. 1935).
1956 New Lives for Old. New York: Morrow.

Meek, Charles K.
1972 Ibo Law. *In* Readings in Anthropology. J. D. Jennings and E. A. Hoebel, eds. New York: McGraw-Hill.

Mehrabian, Albert
1981 Silent Messages. 2d edition. Belmont, Calif.: Wadsworth.

Mendonsa, Eugene
1985 Characteristics of Sisala Diviners. *In* Magic, Witchcraft, and Religion: An Anthropological Study of the Supernatural. Arthur C. Lehmann and James E. Myers, eds. Pp. 214–24. Palo Alto, Calif.: Mayfield.

Merton, Robert K.
1957 Social Theory and Social Structure. Glencoe, Ill.: Free Press.

Middleton, John
1965 The Lugbara of Uganda. New York: Holt, Rinehart and Winston.

Middleton, John, and Greet Kershaw
1965 The Kikuyu and Kamba of Kenya. London: International African Institute.

Middleton, John, and David Tait, eds.
1958 Tribes without Rulers: Studies in African Segmentary Systems. London: Routledge and Kegan Paul.

Miller, Annetta, Bruce Shenitz, and Lourdes Rosado
1990 You Are What You Buy, Newsweek, June 4, 1990. Pp. 59–60.

Miller, Barbara D.
1993 Female Infanticide and Child Neglect in Rural North India. *In* Gender in Cross Cultural Perspective. Caroline Brettell and Carolyn Sargent, eds. Pp. 423–35. Englewood Cliffs, N.J.: Prentice-Hall.

Mills, George
1957 Art: An Introduction to Qualitative Anthropology. Journal of Aesthetics and Art Criticism 16(1):1–17.

Miner, Horace
1953 The Primitive City of Timbuctoo. Philadelphia: American Philosophical Society.

Montagu, Ashley
1972 Touching: The Human Significance of the Skin. New York: Harper & Row.

Moock, Joyce L.
1978–1979 The Content and Maintenance of Social Ties between Urban Migrants and Their Home-Based Support Groups: The Maragoli Case. African Urban Studies, No. 3 (Winter):15–32.

Moody, Edward J.
1974 Urban Witches *In* Conformity and Conflict: Readings in Cultural Anthropology. James Spradley and David McCurdy, eds. Pp. 326–36. Boston: Little, Brown.

Morgan, L. H.
1871 Systems of Consanguinity and Affinity of the Human Family. Washington, D.C.: Smithsonian Institution.
1963 Ancient Society. New York: World (orig. 1877).

Morris, Desmond
1988 Watch Your Body Language. The Charlotte Observer, P. 5. October 23.

Morris, Desmond, Peter Collett, Peter Marsh, and Marie O'Shaughnessy
1979 Gestures: Their Origins and Distribution. New York: Stein and Day.

Morsbach, Helmut
1982 Aspects of Nonverbal Communication in Japan. *In* Intercultural Communication: A Reader. 3d edition. Larry Samovar and R. E. Porter, eds. Pp. 300–16. Belmont, Calif.: Wadsworth.

Mulder, Monique B.
1988 Kipsigis Bridewealth Payments. *In* Human Reproductive Behavior: A Darwinian Perspective. Laura Betzig, M. B. Mulder, and Paul Turke, eds. Pp. 65–82. Cambridge: Cambridge University Press.

Murdock, George
1945 The Common Denominator of Cultures. *In* The Science of Man in the World Crisis. Ralph

Linton, ed. P. 123. New York: Columbia University Press.

1949 Social Structure. New York: Macmillan.

1967 Ethnographic Atlas: A Summary. Ethnology 6(2):109–236.

1968 The Current Status of the World's Hunting and Gathering Peoples. *In* Man the Hunter. Richard B. Lee and Irven DeVore, eds. Pp. 13–20. Chicago: Aldine-Atherton.

Murphy, R. F., and L. Kasdan

1959 The Structure of Parallel Cousin Marriage. American Anthropologist 61:17–29.

Murray, Gerald F.

1984 The Wood Tree as a Peasant Cash-Crop: An Anthropological Strategy for the Domestication of Energy. *In* Haiti—Today and Tomorrow: An Interdisciplinary Study. Charles R. Foster and Albert Valdman, eds. Pp. 141–60. Latham, N.Y.: University Press of America.

1986 Seeing the Forest While Planting the Trees: An Anthropological Approach to Agroforestry in Rural Haiti. *In* Politics, Projects, and People: Institutional Development in Haiti, Derick W. Brinkerhoff and J. Garcia-Zamor, eds. Pp. 193–226. New York: Praeger.

1987 The Domestication of Wood in Haiti: A Case Study in Applied Evolution. *In* Anthropological Praxis. Robert Wulff and Shirley Fiske, eds. Pp. 223–40. Boulder, Colo.: Westview Press.

Nader, Laura, and H. F. Todd, Jr.

1978 The Disputing Process: Law in Ten Societies. New York: Columbia University Press.

Naisbitt, John

1982 Megatrends: Ten New Directions Transforming Our Lives. New York: Warner Books.

Nanda, Serena

1990 Neither Man nor Woman: The Hijras of India. Belmont, Calif.: Wadsworth.

Nash, Jesse W.

1988 Confucius and the VCR. Natural History. Pp. 28–31. May.

National Opinion Research Center

1947 Jobs and Occupations: A Popular Evaluation. Opinion News 9:3–13. September.

Nettl, Bruno

1980 Ethnomusicology: Definitions, Directions, and Problems. *In* Music of Many Cultures, Elizabeth May, ed. Pp. 1–9. Berkeley: University of California Press.

Nettl, Bruno, and Philip V. Bohlman, eds.

1991 Comparative Musicology and Anthropology of Music. Chicago: University of Chicago Press.

Newman, Katherine S.

1988 Falling from Grace: The Experience of Downward Mobility in the American Middle Class. New York: Free Press.

Nolan, Riall W.

1986 Anthropology and the Peace Corps: Notes from a Training Program. *In* Anthropology and Rural Development in West Africa. Michael M. Horowitz and Thomas M. Painter, eds. Pp. 93–116. Boulder, Colo.: Westview Press.

Oberg, Kalervo

1960 Culture Shock: Adjustments to New Cultural Environments. Practical Anthropology. Pp. 177–82. July/August.

Oliver, Douglas

1955 A Solomon Island Society. Cambridge, Mass.: Harvard University Press.

O'Meara, Tim

1990 Samoan Planters: Tradition and Economic Development in Polynesia. Fort Worth: Holt, Rinehart and Winston.

Ortiz, Sutti, and Susan Lees, eds.

1992 Understanding Economic Process. Lanham, Md.: University Press of America.

Paige, K. E., and J. M. Paige

1981 The Politics of Reproductive Ritual. Berkeley/Los Angeles: University of California Press.

Paredes, J. Anthony

1992 "Practical History" and the Poarch Creeks: A Meeting Ground for Anthropologist and Tribal Leaders. *In* Anthropological Research: Process and Application. Pp. 209–26. John Poggie, Billie R. DeWalt, and William W. Dressler, Albany: State University of New York Press.

Parker, Arthur C.

1913 The Code of Handsome Lake, The Seneca Prophet. Albany: New York State Museum Bulletin, No. 163.

Parker, Patricia L., and Thomas F. King

1987 Intercultural Mediation at Truk International Airport. *In* Anthropological Praxis. Robert Wulff and Shirley Fiske, eds. Pp. 160–73. Boulder, Colo.: Westview Press.

Parsons, Talcott

1951 The Social System. New York: Free Press.

Parsons, Talcott, and E. Shils

1952 Toward a General Theory of Action. Cambridge, Mass.: Harvard University Press.

Partridge, William L., and Elizabeth M. Eddy

1978 The Development of Applied Anthropology in America. *In* Applied Anthropology in America.

Elizabeth M. Eddy and William L. Partridge, eds. Pp. 3–45. New York: Columbia University Press.

Pasternak, Burton, Carol Ember, and Melvin Ember
1976 On the Conditions Favoring Extended Family Households. Journal of Anthropological Research 32(2):109–23.

Peacock, James L.
1986 The Anthropological Lens. Cambridge: Cambridge University Press.

Pelto, Pertti J.
1973 The Snowmobile Revolution: Technology and Social Change in the Arctic. Menlo Park, Calif.: Benjamin Cummings.

Plattner, Stuart, ed.
1989 Economic Anthropology. Stanford, Calif.: Stanford University Press.

Polanyi, Karl
1957 The Economy as Instituted Process. *In* Trade and Market in the Early Empires. Karl Polanyi, Conrad Arensberg, and Harry Pearson, eds. Pp. 243–70. New York: Free Press.

Pospisil, L.
1958 Kapauku Papuans and their Law. New Haven: Yale University Press.

Price, T. Douglas and James A. Brown
1985 Prehistoric Hunter Gatherers: The Emergence of Cultural Complexity. Orlando, Fla.: Academic Press.

Pryor, F. L.
1986 The Adoption of Agriculture. American Anthropologist 88:879–97.

Radcliffe-Brown, A. R.
1950 Introduction. *In* African Systems of Kinship and Marriage. A. R. Radcliffe-Brown and D. Forde, eds. Pp. 1–85. London: Oxford University Press.

Ramanamma, A., and U. Bambawale.
1980 The Mania for Sons: An Analysis of Social Values in South Asia. Social Science and Medicine 14:107–10.

Raphael, D., and F. Davis
1985 Only Mothers Know: Patterns of Infant Feeding in Traditional Cultures. Westport, Conn.: Greenwood Press.

Rasmussen, Knud
1927 Across Arctic America. New York: G. P. Putnam's sons.
1931 The Netsilik Eskimos: Social Life and Spiritual Culture. Report of the Fifth Thule Expedition, 1921–24, 8(1,2). Copenhagen: Glydendalske Boghandel.

Renzetti, Claire M., and Daniel J. Curran
1992 Women, Men, and Society. Boston: Allyn and Bacon.

Richards, Audrey I.
1960 The Bemba—Their Country and Diet. *In* Cultures and Societies of Africa. Simon and Phoebe Ottenburg, eds. Pp. 96–109. New York: Random House.

Roberts, John M.
1967 Oaths, Autonomic Ordeals, and Power. *In* Cross Cultural Approaches: Readings in Comparative Research. Clellan S. Ford, ed. New Haven: HRAF Press.

Rogers, Everett M.
1973 Communication Strategies for Family Planning. New York: Free Press.
1983 Diffusion of Innovations. 3d edition. New York: Free Press.

Rohner, Ronald P., and Evelyn C. Rohner
1970 The Kwakiutl: Indians of British Columbia. New York: Holt, Rinehart and Winston.

Rooney, James F.
1961 Group Processes Among Skid Row Winos. Quarterly Journal of Studies on Alcohol 22:444–60.

Rosen, Lawrence
no date The Anthropologist as Expert Witness. Mimeographed paper on file with the Applied Anthropology Documentation Project at the University of Kentucky.

Ross, M. H.
1986 Female Political Participation. American Anthropologist 88:843–58.

Rylko-Bauer, Barbara, John Van Willigen, and Ann McElroy
1989 Strategies for Increasing the Use of Anthropological Research in the Policy Process: A Cross-Disciplinary Analysis. *In* Making Our Research Useful. John Van Willigen, Barbara Rylko-Bauer, and Ann McElroy, eds. Boulder, Colo.: Westview Press.

Sahlins, Marshall
1972 Stone Age Economics. Chicago: Aldine-Atherton.

Salisbury, Richard F.
1976 The Anthropologist as Societal Ombudsman. *In* Development from Below: Anthropologists and Development Situations. David C. Pitt, ed. Pp. 255–65. The Hague: Mouton.

Salzmann, Zdenek
1993 Language, Culture, and Society: An Introduction to Linguistic Anthropology. Boulder, Colo.: Westview Press.

Samovar, Larry A., and Richard E. Porter, eds.
1994 Intercultural Communication: A Reader. Belmont, Calif.: Wadsworth.

Samuelson, Paul A.
1976 Economics. 10th edition. New York: McGraw-Hill.

Sapir, Edward
1929 The Status of Linguistics as a Science. Language 5:207–14.

Scaglion, Richard
1987 Customary Law Development in Papua New Guinea. *In* Anthropological Praxis. Robert Wulff and Shirley Fiske, eds. Pp. 98–107. Boulder, Colo.: Westview Press.

Schlegel, Alice
1990 Gender Meanings: General and Specific. *In* Beyond the Second Sex: New Directions in the Anthropology of Gender. Peggy R. Sanday and R. G. Goodenough, eds. Pp. 21–41. Philadelphia: University of Pennsylvania Press.

Schneider, Harold K.
1957 The Subsistence Role of Cattle among the Pokot in East Africa. American Anthropologist 59:278–300.

Scrimshaw, Susan C. M.
1976 Women's Modesty: One Barrier to the Use of Family Planning Clinics in Ecuador. Monographs of the Carolina Population Center. Pp. 167–83.

Selzer, Richard
1979 Confessions of a Knife. New York: Simon and Schuster.

Serrie, Hendrick
1986 Anthropological Contributions to Business in Multicultural Contexts. *In* Anthropology and International Business. Henrick Serrie, ed. Pp. ix–xxx. Williamsburg, Va.: Dept. of Anthropology at William and Mary.

Service, Elman R.
1966 The Hunters. Englewood Cliffs, N.J.: Prentice-Hall.
1975 Origins of the State and Civilization. New York: Norton.
1978 Profiles in Ethnology. 3d edition. New York: Harper & Row.

Sharff, Jagna W.
1981 Free Enterprise and the Ghetto Family. Psychology Today. March.

Sheflen, Albert E.
1972 Body Language and the Social Order. Englewood Cliffs, N.J.: Prentice-Hall.

Shostak, Marjorie
1983 Nisa: The Life and Words of a !Kung Woman. New York: Vintage Books (Random House).

Sieber, Roy
1962 Masks as Agents of Social Control. African Studies Bulletin 5(11):8–13.

Simon, Paul
1980 The Tongue Tied American. New York: Continuum Press.

Simpson, George E., and J. Milton Yinger
1985 Racial and Cultural Minorities: An Analysis of Prejudice and Discrimination. 5th edition. New York: Plenum.

Singer, Merrill
1985 Family Comes First: An Examination of the Social Networks of Skid Row Men. Human Organization 44(2):137–42.

Slobin, Mark, and Jeff T. Titon
1984 The Music Culture as a World of Music. *In* Worlds of Music: An Introduction to the Music of the World's Peoples. Jeff T. Titon et al, eds. Pp. 1–11. London: Collier Macmillan Publishers.

Smith, Anthony D.
1976 Social Change: Social Theory and Historical Processes. London: Longman.

Smith, E. A.
1983 Anthropological Applications of Optimal Foraging Theory: A Critical Review. Current Anthropology 24:625–51.

Spindler, Louise S.
1984 Culture Change and Modernization. Prospect Heights, Ill.: Waveland Press.

Spradley, James
1970 You Owe Yourself a Drunk. Boston: Little, Brown.

Spring, Anita.
1986 Women Farmers and Food in Africa: Some Considerations and Suggested Solutions. *In* Food in Sub-Saharan Africa. Art Hansen and Della E. McMillan, eds. Boulder, Colo.: Lynne Rienner Publishers.
1988 Using Male Research and Extension Personnel to Target Women Farmers. *In* Gender Issues in Farming Systems Research and Extension. S. Poats, M. Schmink, and A. Spring, eds. Pp. 407–26. Boulder, Colo.: Westview Press.
1994 Agricultural Development and Gender in Malawi. Landham, Md.: University Press of America.

Stack, Carol
1975 All Our Kin: Strategies for Survival in a Black Community. New York: Harper & Row.

Stearns, Robert D.
1986 Using Ethnography to Link School and Community in Rural Yucatan. Anthropology and Education Quarterly 17(1):6–24.

Stenning, Derrick J.
1965 The Pastoral Fulani of Northern Nigeria. *In* Peoples of Africa. James Gibbs, ed. Pp. 363–401. New York: Holt, Rinehart and Winston.

Stephens, William N.
1963 The Family in Cross Cultural Perspective. New York: Holt, Rinehart and Winston.

Stewart, T. D.
1979 Forensic Anthropology. *In* The Uses of Anthropology. Walter Goldschmidt, ed. Pp. 169–83. Washington, D.C.: American Anthropological Association.

Strathern, Marilyn
1984 Domesticity and the Denigration of Women. *In* Rethinking Women's Roles: Perspectives from the Pacific. Denise O'Brien and Sharon Tiffany, eds. Pp. 13–31. Berkeley: University of California Press.

Sturtevant, William
1964 "Studies in Ethnoscience." American Anthropologist, 66(3) Part 2:99–131.

Sullivan, Thomas J., and Kenrick Thompson
1990 Sociology: Concepts, Issues, and Applications. New York: Macmillan.

Sundkler, Bengt
1961 Bantu Prophets of South Africa. 2d edition. London: Oxford University Press.

Swasy, Alecia
1993 Don't Sell Thick Diapers in Tokyo. New York Times. October 3.

Talmon, Yohina
1964 Mate Selection in Collective Settlements. American Sociological Review 29:491–508.

Tannen, Deborah
1990 You Just Don't Understand: Women and Men in Conversation. New York: Morrow.

Tarde, Gabriel
1903 The Laws of Imitation (trans. by Elsie Clews Parsons). New York: Holt.

Taylor, Brian K.
1962 The Western Lacustrine Bantu. London: International African Institute.

Tedlock, Barbara
1991 From Participant Observation to the Observation of Participation: The Emergence of Narrative Ethnography. Journal of Anthropological Research 47(1):69–94. Spring.

Thomson, David S.
1994 Worlds Shaped by Words. *In* Conformity and Conflict. 8th edition. James P. Spradley and David McCurdy, eds. Pp. 73–86. New York: Harper Collins.

Tiger, Lionel, and Robin Fox
1971 The Imperial Animal. New York: Holt, Rinehart and Winston.

Tischler, Henry L.
1990 Introduction to Sociology. 3d edition. Fort Worth: Holt, Rinehart and Winston.

Toffler, Alvin
1971 Future Shock. New York: Bantam Books.
1981 The Third Wave. Toronto: Bantam Books.

Tripp, Robert
1985 Anthropology and On-Farm Research. Human Organization 44(2):114–24.

Turnbull, Colin
1965 The Mbuti Pygmies of the Congo. *In* Peoples of Africa. James Gibbs, ed. Pp. 281–317. New York: Holt, Rinehart and Winston.
1981 Mbuti Womanhood. *In* Woman the Gatherer. Frances Dahlberg, ed. Pp. 205–19. New Haven: Yale University Press.
1982 The Ritualization of Potential Conflict between the Sexes among the Mbuti. *In* Politics and History in Band Societies. Eleanor Leacock and Richard Lee, eds. Cambridge: Cambridge University Press.

Tylor, Edward B.
1871 Origins of Culture. New York: Harper & Row.
1889 On a Method of Investigating the Development of Institutions: Applied to Laws of Marriage and Descent. Journal of Royal Anthropological Institute 18:245–69.

U.S. Bureau of the Census
1993 Statistical Abstract of the United States, 1993. 113th edition. Washington, D.C.: U.S. Government Printing Office.

U.S. National Commission on the Causes and Prevention of Violence
1969 Justice: To Establish Justice, To Ensure Domestic Tranquility. Washington, D.C.: U.S. Government Printing Office.

Van Gennep, Arnold
1960 The Rites of Passage. Chicago: University of Chicago Press (orig. 1908).

Vanneman, Reeve, and L. W. Cannon
1987 The American Perception of Class. Philadelphia: Temple University Press.

Van Willigen, John
1993 Applied Anthropology: An Introduction. South Hadley, Mass.: Bergin and Garvey.

Van Willigen, John, Barbara Rylko-Bauer, and Ann McElroy
1989 Making Our Research Useful. Boulder, Colo.: Westview Press.

Vilakazi, Absolon L.
1979 A Study of Population and Development. Mbabane: Ministry of Agriculture and Cooperatives.

Vincent, Joan
1990 Anthropology and Politics: Vision, Traditions, and Trends. Tucson: University of Arizona Press.

Wagner, Gunter
1949 The Bantu of North Kavirondo. London: Published for the International African Institute by Oxford University Press.

Wallace, Anthony F. C.
1966 Religion: An Anthropological View. New York: Random House.

Weber, Max
1930 The Protestant Ethic and the Spirit of Capitalism. London: Unwin University Books.
1946 From Max Weber: Essays in Sociology. (Hans Gerth and C. Wright Mills, trans. and eds.) New York: Oxford University Press.
1947 The Theory of Social and Economic Organization (translated by Talcott Parsons). New York: Oxford University Press.

Whelehan, Patricia
1985 Review of Incest: A Biosocial View by Joseph Shepher (New York: Academic Press, 1983). American Anthropologist 87:677.

White, Benjamin
1973 Demand for Labor and Population Growth in Colonial Java. Human Ecology 1(3):217–36.

White, D. R., M. L. Burton, and M. M. Dow
1981 Sexual Division of Labor in African Agriculture. American Anthropologist 83:824–49.

White, Leslie
1959 The Evolution of Culture. New York: McGraw-Hill.

Whiting, John W., and Irvin L. Child
1953 Child Training and Personality: A Cross Cultural Study. New Haven: Yale University Press.

Whiting, Robert
1979 You've Gotta Have "Wa." Sports Illustrated. Pp. 60–71. September 24.

Whitman, William
1963 The San Ildefonso of New Mexico. *In* Acculturation in Seven American Indian Tribes.

Ralph Linton, ed. Gloucester, Mass.: Peter Smith (orig. 1940).

Whyte, M. K.
1978 The Status of Women in Preindustrial Societies. Princeton: Princeton University Press.

Williams, Thomas R.
1967 Field Methods in the Study of Culture. New York: Holt, Rinehart and Winston.

Wilson, Monica
1960 Nyakyusa Age Villages. *In* Cultures and Societies of Africa. Simon and Phoebe Ottenberg, eds. Pp. 227–36. New York: Random House.

Winkelman, M. J.
1987 Magico-Religious Practitioner Types and Socioeconomic Conditions. Behavioral Science Research 22.

Winter, Edward H.
1956 Bwamba: A Structural Functional Analysis of a Patrilineal Society. Cambridge: Published for the East African Institute of Social Research by W. Heffer.

Wissler, Clark
1917 The American Indian: An Introduction to the Anthropology of the New World. New York: D. C. McMurtie.

Witherspoon, Gary
1977 Language and Art in the Navajo Universe. Ann Arbor, Mich.: University of Michigan Press.

Wittfogel, Karl
1957 Oriental Despotism: A Comparative Study of Total Power. New Haven: Yale University Press.

Wolf, Arthur
1968 Adopt a Daughter-in-Law, Marry a Sister: A Chinese Solution to the Incest Taboo. American Anthropologist 70:864–74.

Wolf, E.
1964 Anthropology. Englewood Cliffs, N.J.: Prentice-Hall.

Ya'ari, Ehud, and Ina Friedman
1991 Curses in Verses. Atlantic 267(2):22–26.

INDEX

PHOTO CREDITS